RASCALLY SIGNS IN SACRED PLACES

RASCALLY SIGNS

THE UNIVERSITY OF NORTH CAROLINA PRESS *Chapel Hill & London*

IN SACRED PLACES

THE POLITICS OF CULTURE IN NICARAGUA

DAVID E. WHISNANT

© 1995

The University of North Carolina Press

All rights reserved

Manufactured in the United States of America

The paper in this book meets the guidelines for
permanence and durability of the Committee on
Production Guidelines for Book Longevity of
the Council on Library Resources.

Library of Congress Cataloging-in-Publication Data

Whisnant, David E., 1938–

    Rascally signs in sacred places: the politics of culture
in Nicaragua / David E. Whisnant.

    p.   cm.

    Includes bibliographical references and index.

    ISBN 0-8078-2209-4 (alk. paper). —

    ISBN 0-8078-4523-X (pbk.: alk. paper)

    1. Nicaragua — Civilization.   2. Politics and culture —
Nicaragua — History.   3. Nicaragua — Cultural policy.   I. Title.

F1523.8.W45   1995

306.2'097285 — dc20   94-41811

CIP

99 98 97 96 95   5 4 3 2 1

This book was
published with the
assistance of the
H. Eugene and
Lillian Youngs
Lehman Fund of
the University of
North Carolina
Press. A complete
list of books
published with
the assistance of
the Lehman Fund
appears at the
end of the book.

TO ARCHIE

As he said of his own father, a veteran of the Russian Revolution of 1905, Archie Green is one for whom the skills of head and hand are one. Since his student days at Berkeley in the 1930s, Archie has commanded his energies, kept the faith, kept himself clear, and kept going.

As a skilled shipwright on the San Francisco waterfront, Archie worked to democratize the maritime union and began his lifelong quest to comprehend the complex culture of working people. For twenty years as a carpenter and keen ethnographic and political observer by day and a scholar by night, and as an activist in the union and engaged public citizen, he listened to workers' speech, studied their work habits, collected their pranks, jokes, and rituals, and listened to their songs. In the process, he became a pioneer collector of occupational songs and country music. After taking a degree in library science when he was already in his mid-forties, Archie spent some years as a labor librarian before going on to his Ph.D. in folklore and a new career as a professor of English and labor studies. Especially since the mid-1960s, Archie has been a constant and crucial source of guidance and encouragement to several generations of students. Countless books and articles on labor lore, old-time music, country music, vernacular culture, and cultural work in the public sector acknowledge his help explicitly and show many a mark of his counsel. And now in a retirement that has been more productive than most people's active working lives, he continues his lifelong political-cultural work.

Meeting Archie twenty-five years ago was one of the most fortunate events of my life. In his inimitable way, he praised my own fledgling work far beyond its merits, and introduced me to more people than I could keep straight, commending me to their attention by assuring them I knew all sorts of things about culture and the politics of culture that I emphatically did not know. During all the years since, I have been buoyed up constantly by his generosity of spirit, his political insight, his confidence in the intelligence and dignity of working people and the worth of their expressive culture, his commitment to forging equitable public policy and building humane public institutions, and his determination never to give up trying to understand, never to lose faith in the project.

For more than fifty years, Archie has kept at it—for ballad singers in the mountains and *corrido* singers on the border, for hillbilly pickers and gospel singers, for lintheads and coal miners, for honky-tonkers and midnight cowboys, for John Henry and Mother Jones, Joe Hill and Jimmie Rodgers, Ella Mae Wiggins and Sarah Ogan Gunning, Merle Travis and Merle Haggard, indeed for all of us. To him this one stone in the wall that continues to be built by many hands is respectfully and gratefully dedicated.

War and plantation bitters men, and all such people, who invade all

sacred places with their rascally signs, and mar every landscape one

might gaze upon in worship.

Mark Twain, passing through the Nicaraguan transit route,

December 1866

Creo que la misión de la América Latina . . . es educar a los Estados Unidos.

Es enseñarle cúales son los límites de su política.

Carlos Fuentes, upon receiving the *Orden de la Independencia*

Cultural Rubén Darío, January 1988

CONTENTS

ACKNOWLEDGMENTS

The writing of this book has been a longer process than I anticipated, and my indebtedness to the helpfulness, advice, and encouragement I received from others has mounted correspondingly. From our first meeting in the mid-1970s, my colleague Willie Lamouse Smith at the University of Maryland–Baltimore County has been a constant source of encouragement. At a rather advanced age I began to study Spanish with my colleagues Jack Sinnegen, Germán Westphal, and Robert Stone; their enthusiasm for and support of my project were of incalculable benefit.

This work began in a faculty research seminar at Tulane University, generously funded by the National Endowment for the Humanities and under the able direction of Ralph Lee Woodward Jr., who has continued to offer crucial advice and support. The Roger Thayer Stone Center of Tulane University provided several travel grants. The staff of Tulane's Latin American Library was unfailingly patient and helpful; I am especially grateful to Cecilia Montenegro Teague.

The Council on the International Exchange of Scholars provided a generous Central American Republics research grant that enabled me to undertake five months of research and field work in Nicaragua. During part of that time I enjoyed the hospitality of Martín and Ana Salgado, and the friendship of Leo Salgado. Amelia Barahona of Patrimonio Cultural facilitated my work in many ways, as did Leonora Martínez DeRocha of the Museo Nacional. Jorge Eduardo Arellano generously allowed me to make use of his personal library. Kathy McBride was a source of many valuable insights into the subtleties of life and politics in Sandinista Nicaragua. The staff of the Biblioteca Nacional were unfailingly helpful; I am especially grateful to María Antonieta Ruíz Sirias, Sixto Galo, Vilma Aráuz, and Will Flores. Both before and after my stay in Nicaragua, I benefitted from many conversations about Nicaragua with René Salgado and Xiomara Vasquez, and was supported and encouraged by their warm friendship.

Subsequently at the University of North Carolina at Chapel Hill, my new colleagues in Latin American Studies supported me in countless important ways. I am especially grateful to John Chasteen, Kenneth Coleman, Gil Joseph, Alicia Rivero-Potter, María Salgado, Rosa Perelmutter, and Adam Versenyi. I owe particular gratitude to Lars Schoultz, Director of the Institute of Latin American Studies, who has supported and encouraged me at every turn. Institute staff members Josie McNeil, Sharon Mújica, and Ines Morcombe have been unfailingly helpful. Among especially valued colleagues in other disciplines were Rafael Lara-Martínez, David Moltke-Hansen, James Peacock, Daniel Patterson, Della Pollock, and Charles Zug. The Institute for the Arts and Humanities made available a summer research grant that proved invaluable. The University Research Council generously provided funds for a one-semester leave that was vital to moving the writing process to a conclusion, and also offered funds for a research assistant and a publication subvention. The Department of English provided vital flexibility in my teaching assignments, repeatedly offered funds for research assistants, and supported my applications for research funds both inside and outside the University of North Carolina.

I have followed the threads of my analysis through the collections of many institutions and have received unstinting help from their dedicated staffs. I am grateful to Deborah Jakubs of the Duke University Library, to Dorrie Reents Budet of the Duke University Museum of Art, to the Latin American Library of the Library of Congress, the University of Maryland–Baltimore County Library, the University of North Carolina Library (especially to William Ilgen, who took a personal interest in my work and helped me immeasurably at many points), the Yale University Library (especially César Rodríguez), the Folkens Museum Etnografiska in Stockholm (especially Staffan Brunius), the Smithsonian's Museum of Natural History (Hope Connors, Molly Coxson, and Felicia Pickering), the Peabody Museum of Ethnology and Archaeology at Harvard University (especially Barbara L. Narendra), and the Franklin D. Roosevelt Library in Hyde Park, New York.

Throughout my work on this book, other colleagues and personal friends have offered steady encouragement. Among the most valued of them are Olivia Cadaval, Robert Cantwell and Lydia Wegman, Archie Green, Charles Stansifer, Willie Lamousé-Smith, and Peter Kuznick. Patricia E. Sawin read the entire manuscript and offered many useful suggestions.

I am also grateful to the editorial, design, production, and marketing staffs of the University of North Carolina Press, with whom I have worked with such pleasure not only on this project, but on many others stretching back now more than a dozen years. I am especially grateful to Lewis Bateman, Barbara Hanrahan, Rich Hendel, and Pamela Upton.

Finally, as always I am deeply mindful of the sustaining threads of pride and delight my daughters Beverly and Rebecca have woven through my life during my more than twenty-five years of writing books. They are the reason above all other reasons. The latter stages of my work on this book have also been immeasurably enriched by the presence of Anne Virginia Mitchell, who came to share her life with me; her stability, her confidence and generosity, and her irrepressible spirit have been critically important upon countless occasions.

The errors of fact and interpretation that undoubtedly remain in this book I must of course take unique responsibility for myself. Fortunately there are other books against which my facts and interpretations may be compared, and there will be yet others. I hope that my book, whatever its faults, may function as a useful resource for those who are yet to labor on others.

RASCALLY SIGNS IN SACRED PLACES

INTRODUCTION

Scholarly books, like books of any sort, are written for many reasons, take shape through many different processes, and are directed to audiences more diverse than just scholarly ones. Each of my own books has been (as I said on the first page of the first one) an artifact of my own need to understand something I knew little about when I undertook to learn and to write. I have tried, moreover, to make each a book that would be not only helpful to other scholars and specialists, but also accessible and engaging to a wide array of readers who (for an even wider array of reasons) share, or might come to share, my need to know. I hope this will prove to be such a book.

If this were a film instead of a book, it might appropriately open with a series of vignettes cut together rapidly to suggest the kaleidoscopic array of moments, epochs, events, processes, people, and institutions that must figure in any treatment of such an encompassing subject as the politics of culture. But since it is a book instead of a film, and it does indeed take a thousand words to convey such an image or moment, I must content myself with only a few vignettes, which may at least begin to suggest both where this book came from and what it will be about.

VIGNETTE #1. Some years ago, after having spent a dozen years writing about the politics of culture in the southern Appalachian region of the United States, I read the moving testimony of Rigoberta Menchú, a young woman from the ancient Quiché culture of the Guatemalan highlands — its communities the focus of brutal repression by the military government installed by the United States after the CIA-backed coup of 1954. In one particularly poignant moment, Menchú describes the annual folkloric celebration mounted by the president for urban elites, military commanders, members of the legislature, foreign ambassadors and dignitaries, and tourists. The Quiché-speaking "queens" of each indigenous community (previously chosen through a degrading "nickel-a-vote" process) are dressed in picturesque native costumes, forced to learn formal greetings to say to the dignitaries in Spanish, and photographed *ad infinitum* (cf. Urban and Hendrickson in Urban and Sherzer 1991, 10–11 and 286–306). But when the festival ends, the "queens" are rudely shunted from the scene into tawdry rooming houses normally frequented by drunks and prostitutes. Rigoberta reflects that *la person que lleva [el traje indígena] es algo como si fuera nada* (it is as if the person who wears [the native dress] were nothing) (Burgos 1985, 233–34; cf. Whisnant 1989).

VIGNETTE #2. Standing on a Managua street in 1987, photographing a revolutionary mural painted on a long fence around some ruins from the

1

earthquake, I suddenly realized that a group of women were shouting at me from across the street that that art was not *their* art, that it most emphatically did not represent *their* views, and that above all I should not use the photograph later to show folks at home that all Nicaraguans were united in Sandinista solidarity.

VIGNETTE #3. Driving me through the traffic-choked streets of Managua, my opinionated taxi driver kept assuring me that, Sandinista revolutionary fervor notwithstanding, the country had no problems *another* invasion by the U.S. Marines couldn't cure. And to make doubly sure I would not draw too many facile conclusions about what I (thought I) was seeing and learning, he cautioned me again and again on our many subsequent rides that *Nosotros nicaragüenses somos mentirosos* (We Nicaraguans are liars).

VIGNETTE #4. Sitting in her garden outside Managua one late evening, a bright, thirty-five-year-old married woman doctor in Managua tells me she drives her husband to the bus stop each evening so he can go to visit his young mistress, and returns to pick him up when he calls her in the wee hours of the morning. She cannot leave him and find another husband, she says, because most Nicaraguan men consider thirty-five-year-old women with children too old and unattractive. And besides, she patiently explains, her dilemma is not different from that of any other professional woman she knows.

These vignettes suggest but a few of the themes and issues that I engage in this book: the use of indigenous or traditional culture to serve a variety of convoluted cultural-political purposes — to mask internal cultural repression and destruction, to throw a sacralizing folk-cultural mantel over political business-as-usual, to boost tourism, to modulate the cultural alienation of local elites, to reinforce existing boundaries of legitimacy and power; the mobilization of culture for state legitimation; the multitudinous forms of cultural hegemony; the collusion of victims in their own oppression; the durability of cultural formations such as gender definitions and gendered behaviors.

During my nearly twenty-five years or so of writing about culture, I have learned to expect to be asked — frequently with a mixture of puzzlement and challenge — "what do you *mean* by 'culture'?" The edge of challenge in the question is particularly acute if one declines to claim a neatly nameable (e.g., Marxist, Freudian, post-structuralist, postmodern, Derridian, Foucauldian) theoretical perspective. It is almost equally likely that, once one has written about culture, some reviewer will note that "the concept of culture being employed is unfortunately never given *precise definition*." But what one has available, as innumerable commentators have observed, is a nearly limitless array of definitions, many of them useful in some way(s) under certain circumstances and for certain purposes, each of them inadequate or misleading in some respect(s), no one of them completely unproblematically applicable even in a given circumstance.[1]

The definitions (plural) of culture I employ here necessarily vary as the focus of analysis changes from historical period to historical period and from one cultural form or process of cultural change to another. It is necessary, for example, to speak of the *indigenous* culture of the people first encountered by the Spanish when they came to Nicaragua in 1523, of the later *traditional* or *campesino* culture of the mestizo survivors of those groups, of the *popular* or *mass* or *consumer* culture brought by nineteenth- or twentieth-century great-power economic and political intervention into Nicaragua (everything from patent medicines to phonographs, from baseball to Boy Scouts), of *elite* culture (from the Europeanized tastes of the nineteenth-century coffee growers to the Miami boutique clothing of the twentieth-century cotton growers), and of the culture of yet other sectors and subsystems as well. In every case, it will be clear that I use the term *culture* to mean not merely esthetic expression or a limited set of authenticated, canonical forms or practices, but an entire way of life, including beliefs, habits of mind, expressive and other practices of daily life, ritual behavior, values, and worldview—culture, that is, as it might be defined collaboratively by a cultural historian, an anthropologist, a folklorist, an ethnographer, and a sociolinguist, rather than by a curator in an elite museum, a connoisseur of painting or china, or even a jazz critic.

What guides my analysis here is less a closed definition or a single unified theory than a (I hope coherent) set of concerns selected and sharpened slowly over the years through—as Raymond Williams once explained when asked how he had done certain parts of his work—"reading from one book to another." Repeatedly I have found myself trying to comprehend hegemonic patterns of cultural domination, particularly those linked synergistically to still other modes of domination, such as colonial occupation and subjugation; processes (whether formal or informal, institutionalized or not) of cultural legitimation and delegitimation; the cultural preferences and styles of regional, economically marginalized, enclaved, or politically disempowered cultural groups, and the efforts such groups make toward cultural recovery and revitalization; the role of traditional or vernacular culture in broader opposition movements (political or otherwise); the exquisitely complex process of conceptualizing and implementing official cultural policy, and its relationship in turn to the de facto cultural policy that is always embedded in economic, social, and foreign policy; elite control of cultural policy and institutions; the use of culture to justify a variety of policies in supposedly "non-cultural" areas (such as economic development) and to rationalize various forms of exploitation; and the complex interchanges between elite or popular or consumer or mass-mediated culture on the one hand, and traditional or vernacular or marginalized culture on the other. Finally, in sum, I am fascinated by the links between culture and power, in their innumerable forms and manifestations. These are, at any rate, the concerns about culture that inform this book.

The shorthand phrase I use here to refer to those forms and manifestations is *the politics of culture*. With reference to the conquest, for example, the politics of culture means (among other things) cultural genocide and forced acculturation. During the nineteenth century it embraces the expropriation of communally held lands from traditional communities by the coffee oligarchy and the rationalization and mobilization of labor, the importation of European models of "modernization," and the smug Americanizing cultural agenda of William Walker's filibusters. During the late 1920s the struggle over the meaning of General Sandino's guerrilla war to oust the U.S. Marines was a particularly dramatic example of the operation of an intensely conflicted politics of culture. The same must be said of the Somoza regime's efforts to prohibit certain forms of cultural production and expression while fostering others and turning them to its own political uses, and of the Sandinistas' projection of a "new man" and a new gender politics for a new revolutionary culture.

The two narrative chapters of Part 1 focus on the period between the aboriginal settlement of Nicaragua and the end of the nineteenth century. Since those chapters cover such long historical periods, they are necessarily quite schematic. Others have told parts of the story of this period in great detail, of course; my chapters attempt to present a specifically *cultural* narrative in a unified way. Part 2 presents four additional narrative chapters focusing on the Somoza and Sandinista periods. The first of each pair focuses on each government's conception of culture, its political instrumentalization and mobilization of culture, its implementation of cultural policy, and its design and operation of cultural programs and institutions. The second of each pair concentrates on patterns and processes of opposition to each government's cultural agenda and activities. My aim in these chapters is not to provide a full and continuous historical-cultural narrative (the record of both governments is too bulky and complicated for that), but to foreground and place within a conceptual-analytical frame some of the most important elements of the politics of culture within those periods. The four case studies of Part 3 offer a more detailed treatment of several processes and pivotal figures that were important at certain junctures in Nicaraguan cultural history. The case studies also cut across historical periods to explore some perennially contested issues and themes.

More specifically, within Part 1, Chapter 1 treats the years between the earliest settlement of Nicaragua and independence. It opens with a brief synoptic consideration of the strongly regionalized pre-conquest "bridge culture" system of lower Central America and Nicaragua, which contrasted strongly with the more developed "high culture" areas to the north and south. A brief examination of the impact of new biota brought by the conquistadores (plants, animals, diseases), of slavery, of forced labor, and of pressures to acculturate suggests that the conquest left virtually no feature of pre-conquest culture untouched. In the years following initial contact and subjugation, Spanish colonial institutions brought profound and irreversible social and cultural transformations, and led to sporadic and mostly ineffective but nevertheless dramatic episodes of native resistance. I conclude by suggesting that over the long term (that is, the three hundred years of the colonial period), certain interrelated aspects of ideology and social-political organization achieved a stability that carried them forward as primary structural determinants of most of Nicaragua's subsequent history.

Chapter 2 treats the years between independence and the close of the Zelaya administration in 1909 (a better marker than the end of the century), paying particular attention to some salient mid-century events and processes. I examine the perennial conflict between León- and Granada-based elites to define the country's identity and control its natural resources, labor force, and developmental agenda—a conflict that continued until mid-century, when it became for a short time overshadowed by the early phases of intervention by the United States. Overtly motivated by economic and political considerations tied to the transit route but profoundly cultural in many of their bases and effects, the cultural politics of that intervention emerged most dramatically in the William Walker filibuster war of the late 1850s. After the filibusters departed, however, the hereditarily antagonistic León-Granada elites converged around a nationalist, agroexport-based, modernizing development agenda that in turn led to the further disorientation and destruction of much traditional, community-based culture. Despite sporadic resistance from non-elite sectors, elite cultural dominance continued to be consolidated during the Zelaya administration (1894–1909).

From the U.S.-aided fall of the Zelaya government in 1909 until the advent of the Somoza regime in 1936, Nicaraguan history is more interesting economically and politically than culturally, with the exception of the career of Nicaragua's premier poet Rubén Darío (1867–1916) and of Augusto C. Sandino's guerrilla struggle against the U.S. Marines (1927–33), to both of which I turn later in Chapters 8 and 9. Hence from my synoptic chapter on the politics of culture in the nineteenth century I move directly to culture during the Somoza period (1936–79).

Chapter 3, which opens Part 2, examines a half-dozen constitutive elements of the cultural politics of the Somoza period: the regime's general neglect of public cultural policy and institutions, its manipulation of culture for political purposes, and its controlling, censoring, and repressing of cultural institutions and activities; the post–World War II transformation of traditional cultural systems as a result of agroexport development schemes; the increasing penetration of Nicaragua by the commercial culture of the United States (consumer products, Hollywood film, and comic strips, for example), linked in turn to systematic U.S. cultural intervention; the use of culture (through binational programs of "cultural exchange") as an instrument of larger policy objectives; and the private cultural initiatives that arose in response to the Somoza regime's neglect, manipulation, and repression.

Chapter 4 argues that for all its skill and effectiveness in manipulating, appropriating, and controlling culture, the Somoza regime was beset with cultural resistance—both organized and unorganized, and from many quarters—throughout its more than four decades in power. Important generative centers of that resistance were the politically ambivalent *vanguardia* movement of the early 1930s, the Generation of 1940 writers, the political-cultural movement among students from the mid-1940s onward, and the insurgency of the indigenous *barrios* in the middle to late 1970s. The chapter concludes with a brief account of Ernesto Cardenal's oppositional cultural-political community in the Solentiname archipelago, where he experimented with ideas and models subsequently incorporated into Sandinista cultural policy.

Chapter 5 schematizes the ideas about culture that the Sandinistas made central to their cultural project, and evaluates the practical cultural work they undertook. Some impressive cultural accomplishments came quickly, but with virtually every policy sector demanding attention immediately and on a massive scale, budgetary, psychic, and political capacities for response were stretched to the limit. To complicate matters further, the cultural formation of most of the Sandinista leadership had prepared them but poorly to deal with some of the most problematic features of the country's complex cultural system. Many aspects of Nicaragua's historical cultural formation also presented formidable obstacles to rapid or substantial change. The bulk of the chapter chronicles—against the ground of these complexities—the creation of the Ministry of Culture and the elaboration of its constituent agencies and programs.

Although the Ministry of Culture demonstrated considerable imaginative flair in conceiving cultural institutions and designing cultural programs, its inability to bring conceptions and designs to fruition and to deal straightforwardly with communities and cultural groups became increasingly evident as the months and years passed. Meanwhile, the country's artists quarreled increasingly about the proper role of culture in the larger process of reconstruction, a quarrel that lay at the root of the rising structural competition and ideological disagreement between the two principal cultural institutions: the Ministry of Culture and the *Asociación Sandinista de Trabajadores Culturales* (Sandinista Association of Cultural Workers; ASTC). Foregrounding the cultural politics that lay within such conflicts, Chapter 6 attempts both to sketch their larger outlines and to detail their operation through several brief case studies.

Chapter 7 (the first of the four case study chapters constituting Part 3) examines the unauthorized removal of archaeological treasures from Nicaragua by collectors, dealers, and major museums during the nineteenth century—an intensely competitive process that highlighted some aspects of the politics of culture with special clarity: the expropriation by colonial powers of the cultural property of subject peoples; the mixed agendas of supposedly disinterested scientific archaeologists; the racist and nationalistic components of competition among ethnological museums; and emerging questions concerning the ethics of collecting, museum display, and the return of cultural artifacts from modern museums to their countries of origin.

Chapters 8 and 9 offer analyses of the cultural politics surrounding Nicaragua's two most venerated cultural figures: the internationally acclaimed modernist poet Rubén Darío (1867–1916) and General Augusto C. Sandino (1895–1934). Both are key figures in a long-running and intensely conflicted negotiation over political ideology and national cultural identity. With regard to Darío, I focus especially upon the struggle to define and appropriate the "cultural capital" (Pierre Bourdieu's term) he embodied, his ambivalent relationship to Nicaragua during his lifetime, his culturally and politically significant social aspirations, his political formation, and the several sharply distinguished cultural-political constructions placed upon his life and work.

The chapter on Sandino excavates and examines some of the cultural strata from which his political-military campaign and self-projection arose, as well as the cultural processes through which the Sandino legend and the myth were at length constructed. As in the chapter on Darío, I focus comparatively upon the Somoza and Sandinista constructions, but because Sandino became (as Darío never did) a pawn in U.S.-Nicaraguan relations, I also engage briefly with the cultural politics within that larger framework. The chapter concludes with a consideration of the role of gender paradigms and ideals in the construction of such cultural-political figures.

The final case study of Part 3 (Chapter 10) provides a broader account of gender relations in Nicaragua. It centers on the tension between the essential durability and continuity of those relations on the one hand, and Nicaraguan women's persistent quest for liberation and equity on the other, and on the nodes and structures of resistance to that quest. As an analytical tool I employ the notion of cultural recalcitrance, by which I mean the synergistic operation of all culturally based or culture-linked forms of opposition (intentional or not, organized or not, from whatever quarter) to modifying the established gender order.[2] My principal objectives in the chapter are to explore some basic aspects of gender definitions and power relations within the gender order; to sketch the pre-Sandinista history of the women's movement in Nicaragua; to chronicle some dramatic moments of "cultural recalcitrance"; to show the relative inability of formal ideology, official policy, or women's organized opposition to modify or overcome that recalcitrance; and to examine the cultural politics of resulting conflicts over the nature of social policy and the directions of social change with respect to gender. The chapter concludes by examining the decade between the Sandinista triumph of 1979 and the advent of the U.S.-backed Chamorro government.

I have no illusion that this book "covers" completely all of the periods, subjects, actors, processes, and issues with which it engages. No book can do that, and certainly not one that takes as long a historical view as this one does. My hope is that what I do present will be encountered by readers as provocative, illuminating in some ways, and suggestive of promising lines of inquiry for others to follow. It blends original research with what I hope will be a helpful synthesis of the excellent work of others. In following such a procedure I have been mindful of the paradox that current methodological standards demand grounded and detailed analyses on the one hand, but that at the same time, *using* such analyses done by others as a platform for one's own synthesizing inquiry is likely to evoke criticism as "relying too heavily on secondary sources." Readers will have to decide for themselves whether I have made appropriate use of others' work as a platform for original research and fresh analysis. My own sense is that historical scholarship at its best is a cooperative and collaborative enterprise: primary source-based work at one level permits synthesizing work at another. I have tried to do some of both here, as anyone must who engages with such a broad topic. As the pagan harpooner Queequeg tells the philosophical Ishmael in *Moby Dick*, "The world is a joint-stock company; we cannibals have to help those Christians."

A word about this book's intended audience(s): I hope that both Latin Americanists and non–Latin Americanists will profit from it. To make it intelligible to the latter, I have defined key terms whose customary use will already be completely familiar to the former. I have also taken care to provide sufficient bibliographical references in my notes to allow non–Latin Americanists to push further in areas that especially interest them, and (equally importantly) to remind all readers repeatedly that mine is a schematic treatment, and that there is much more to be said on these matters. I have also translated all Spanish words and brief phrases that have no obvious English cognates. I hope that these accommodations will make what I have written accessible to any serious student of the politics of culture, whatever the nature or site of her or his usual work. In particular, I hope that this book may prove useful to students of the politics of culture in non–Latin American contexts. Much of what interests me here is peculiar to Nicaragua and to Latin America, but much of it is encountered whenever and wherever people try to hold (on) to what they have and know when things are changing around them, to define and maintain boundaries of value and practice between Self and Other, to use culture to defend or extend their power. That is to say, always and everywhere.

Finally, I am acutely aware of the dangers of writing about a culture not one's own. There is something inescapably audacious about it, because no matter how diligently and conscientiously one studies and observes, no matter how rigorous one's methodology, pure one's motives, or correct one's politics, one will inevitably in some respects misconstrue, at some points fail to understand, in some moments reveal one's ignorance. On the other hand, as I have repeatedly been reminded by reading about the Appalachian region where I myself grew up, "outsiders" frequently have much to contribute that is valuable and that is unlikely to be contributed by "insiders" — partly because "outsiders" are less invested in how the story comes out, partly because their very lack of intimate familiarity with the subject allows them to see and comment insightfully on things "insiders" are either unaware of or too familiar with to consider important.

At the beginning of each book I have written before, I have said in one way or another that it is a report on my process of learning, in its present (and necessarily permanent and permanently frustrating) state of incompleteness. This one is as well. I offer it for whatever help it might be to colleagues known and unknown who struggle to understand related matters, and to all those—in Nicaragua and wherever else—whose loving efforts on behalf of humankind rest partly upon a conviction that culture, as both impediment and promise, is central to the enterprise.

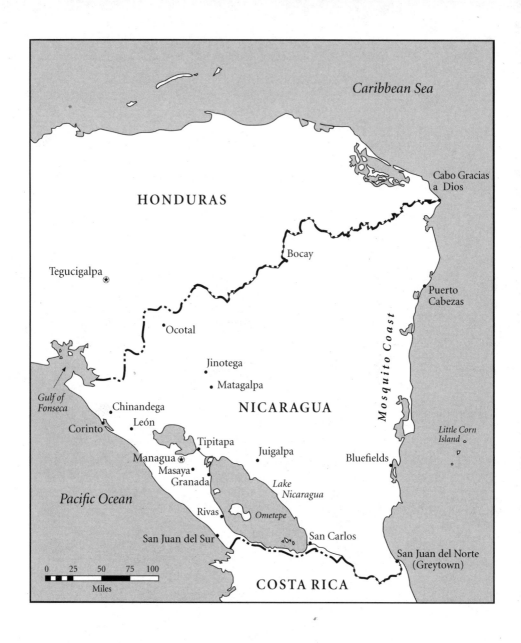

Caribbean Sea

HONDURAS

Cabo Gracias
a Dios

Bocay

Tegucigalpa ⊛

Puerto
Cabezas

Ocotal

Jinotega

Matagalpa

NICARAGUA

Mosquito Coast

Gulf of
Fonseca

Chinandega

León

Corinto

Tipitapa

Managua ⊛

Masaya
Granada

Pacific Ocean

Rivas

*Lake
Nicaragua*

Ometepe

San Juan del Sur

Juigalpa

Bluefields

*Little Corn
Island*

San Carlos

San Juan del Norte
(Greytown)

0   25   50   75   100

Miles

COSTA RICA

CHAPTER 1 BEAUTIFUL AND PLEASANT LAND CULTURE AND CULTURAL CHANGE BEFORE INDEPENDENCE

More ceremonies and rites and customs and notable things remain to be told . . . of this province . . . and to recount them all would be impossible . . . because war and contact with Christians and the passage of time have consumed and put an end to the lives of the old people . . . and because of the greed of the judges, governors, and others who were in such haste to remove Indians from their land as slaves. — Oviedo, *Historia general y natural de las Indias* (1547)

The politics of culture in Nicaragua following independence from Spain (the primary focus of this study) owed some of both their most stubborn structural features and their evolving character to developments during the colonial period, and indeed to the pre-conquest cultural systems that colonial development transformed so radically.[1] At least the following factors are important in this regard: (1) the marginal relationship of pre-conquest Nicaragua to the "high culture" areas located to the north and south of it; (2) the culture that the conquistadores found when they arrived in Nicaragua, some features of which proved remarkably durable during (and even following) the colonial period; (3) the character of the conquest itself, which came to Nicaragua later than it did elsewhere in Latin America, and had a somewhat different character; (4) post-conquest development under Spanish institutions, which shaped the politics of culture in permanent ways; (5) the entrenchment of certain interrelated aspects of ideology and social-political organization, each of which had permanent cultural implications: the development of the León-Granada axis, the dominance of the Catholic church, *mestizaje* and the emergence of a race-linked class system, the establishment of an agroexport economy, and the establishment of gender relations highly resistant to change; (6) native resistance to conquest; and (7) the separate historical development of the Atlantic and Pacific regions of the country.[2]

PRE-CONQUEST CULTURE IN LOWER CENTRAL AMERICA AND NICARAGUA

Little is known of lower Central American history before 8000 B.C., when percussion tools and some woodworking implements began to appear.[3] Successive migration streams proceeding from Mesoamerica into Nicaragua—bringing a maize-based agriculture—settled mostly on the Pacific coast, and those from South America—bringing one based on manioc—on the Atlantic. While manioc produced abundant food on small plots with little labor, thrived on wetlands, and required neither scheduled harvesting nor special storage facilities, maize required large raised or terraced fields, was more labor intensive, had to be planted and harvested on a regular schedule, produced relatively low yields, and was difficult to store. Thus the manioc-based societies of the east tended to be smaller and simpler than the expansionist, maize-based ones of the west.[4] In the five hundred years prior to the conquest, the ranked, agriculturally based societies of lower Central America underwent considerable change and upheaval as the population grew, chiefdoms developed, civil replaced shamanistic control, and regional variations began to mark ceramics and other products (Lange and Stone 1984, 363).

In some respects, Nicaragua represented a special case within lower Central American pre-conquest development—a "cultural periphery" lying south of the more developed societies of El Salvador and western Honduras (Lange and Stone 1984, 3, 85-114; Lange et al. 1992, 265-72). Immigrants who arrived in Nicaragua after the dawn of the Christian era—the Chorotega, Maribio, Nicarao, Nahuat-Pipil, and Nahuatl—were divided into two linguistic groups, the OtoMangue and the Uto-Azteca. Among OtoMangue speakers, the Chorotega settled around the later sites of León and Granada, and as far south as the Nicoya peninsula, while the Nicarao settled near the later site of Rivas, and the Maribio chose the coastal area east of Realejo, between Subtiava and Chinandega. Uto-Aztecan speakers followed in three major migrations, around the ninth to tenth centuries (Lange et al. 1992, 268; Newson 1987, 23-30).

West coast immigrants settled for the most part in relatively small groups on fertile volcanic soils near Lake Managua and Lake Nicaragua, and (although grouped into somewhat larger, more hierarchically organized communities than their east coast neighbors) appear not to have been affiliated through larger political structures like those found to the north and south (Lange et al. 1992, 260; Lange and Stone 1984, 56–57). Thus instead of being a "single cultural unit," Lange concludes, pre-conquest Nicaragua seems to have been "a fragmented and regionalized political, economic, and religious landscape" made up of "a series of functioning multi-ethnic communities," speaking different languages (which did not necessarily correlate with other cultural patterns), occupying contiguous territories, and having different types of government (Lange et al. 1992, 13, 268–75).

Thus was constituted what has come to be called the "bridge culture" of pre-conquest Nicaragua: one that bridged between the more advanced ones to the north and south, and that was itself still very much in a state of flux at the time of conquest. The focal points of development were neither as large, highly elaborated, nor densely settled as they were elsewhere in lower Central America, probably because the relative scarcity of "ecological niches" tended to hold down population growth, and the relative redundance of natural resources reduced struggles for resource control and hence the formation of trading monopolies and states associated with them (Lange and Stone 1984, 56, 375–76). Among the Chorotega, Maribio, and Nicarao, however, there were chiefdoms supported by "socially stratified populations" organized around "intensive agricultural production." The Nicarao chiefdoms were ruled by a single chief whose power rested on income from cacao groves and tribute from commoners, but Chorotegan chiefdoms were ruled by an elected council. Major towns had temple complexes (*orchilobos* or *teobas*) containing both idols and armories. In general, land was communally owned, and the most important crops were maize (which reportedly grew higher than a man's head), beans, manioc, and sweet potatoes. But cacao, cotton, tobacco, coca (used to cure thirst, fatigue, and headaches), calabashes, and peppers were also grown, as well as several varieties of fruit trees. Domesticated animals were limited to turkeys and mute dogs (used both for hunting and for food) (Newson 1987, 48–57; Stanislawski 1983, 4–6).

A few of the rich, varied, and vital cultural forms and modes of expression that the Spanish encountered in Nicaragua were destined to survive the conquest, and some were transformed, but the majority perished quickly and forever. A few pre-conquest structural features (east/west cultural and demographic differences, higher population density in the west, and the country's relatively low overall population) endured far beyond the conquest, and helped shape Nicaraguan cultural, economic, and political life for centuries.

The more highly developed civilizations of Mesoamerica had not taken over lower Central America prior to the Spanish conquest, Willey notes, both because they were not sufficiently organized to extend their empires so far south, and because the potential rewards of doing so were not sufficiently enticing (Lange and Stone 1984, 376). Even the avaricious Spanish waited three decades after Columbus's first voyage before committing themselves to the task. The process began in earnest in 1524, when Hernández de Córdoba founded Bruselas, León, and Granada (Newson 1987, 91–92; Stanislawski 1983, 1–2; Radell and Parsons 1971, 298–99).

The chronicler Gonzalo Fernández de Oviedo y Valdés, who arrived in Nicaragua toward the end of 1527, found it *[una] de las más hermosas é aplaçibles tierras* (one of the most beautiful and pleasant lands) in the New World.[5] The natural world Oviedo encountered was beautiful and full of grace, and the social and cultural world of its inhabitants left him stunned in admiration: "What human mind can comprehend such diversity of language, of customs . . . of these Indians? Such variety of animals. . . ? Such a multitude of trees, laden with . . . fruit. . . ? How many plants and herbs, useful and advantageous to man? . . . So many high and fertile mountains. . . ?" (quoted in Rodríguez 1984, 118–19).[6] The mamey tree, Oviedo said, was "one of the most beautiful trees there could be in the world, because they are great trees with many branches and beautiful and fresh leaves, and of lovely verdure . . . and graceful." Oviedo was amazed by the *ceibas*, under the branches of three or four of which several thousand people could shade themselves on market days (Oviedo [1547] 1855, 83; cf. Incer 1990, 161–78).

Social and intellectual life flourished, Oviedo reported; records of it were kept in parchment books made from deerhide, written and decorated with red and black ink. As late as 1540, Italian Giralmo Benzoni watched several thousand Indians ornamented with feathers, plumes, and strings of shells sing and dance to the music of drums, reed and earthenware flutes, trumpets (*excoletes*), whistles, and small bells (*chilchil*) (Brinton [1883] 1969, xxvii–xl). Native artisans worked in stone, gold, and silver; others produced rush and palm mats, leather, and wax items (Lange and Stone 1984, 350–73; Newson 1987, 181).[7]

Pre-conquest Nicaragua was indeed in many ways a "beautiful and pleasant land," but it was not one the Spanish were content to enjoy and leave alone. Virtually no aspect of pre-conquest culture was left untouched in the post-conquest transformation, beginning with the "biological imperialism" that forever altered even the natural world itself.

BIOLOGICAL IMPERIALISM: NEW SPECIES, NEW DISEASES. When Columbus and his successors stepped onshore, they brought not only the Spanish language, Catholicism, firearms, and alien ideas and institutions, but also horses, cattle, pigs, rabbits, rats, vermin, weeds, and pathogens in profusion.[8] Such organisms flourished in what Crosby calls "virgin soil epidemics," as the *conquistadores* and their minions Europeanized the natural environments of colonial Spanish America: plowed their fields, razed their forests, overgrazed their pastures, and burned their prairies (Crosby 1986, 94, 101, 291–92).

Although data for the transformation of specific elements of the natural environment in Nicaragua are scarce, there is no reason to suppose that non-native biota that migrated throughout Latin America would have left Nicaragua untouched. New cultivated plants (and worse, weeds) multiplied profusely: clover came early, as did orange trees (which soon constituted a virtual plague). In Peru the worst offenders were trébol (clover), turnips, mustard, mint, and camomile. Within a decade or two, some species reached grotesque sizes and densities in their new environment: endive and spinach grew more than head-high; wild artichokes stretched to the horizon. Fully half the European species introduced would eventually establish themselves from Patagonia through North America (Crosby 1986, 147–60, 164).

The transformation of animal species was equally dramatic. Offspring of the eight pigs (the "weediest" of the new species, Crosby calls them) that Columbus brought to Hispañola in 1493 were soon roaming throughout Spanish America. Cattle and horses had spread into Mexico by the 1520s and as far north as Florida by 1565. Rats and mice were even worse; Garcilaso de la Vega reported vast numbers of them in Peru by 1572 (Crosby 1986, 173–77, 182–90).

The cultural impacts of such biological transformation were profound: diets changed as new plants and animals appeared; agricultural systems changed, together with their associated social, labor, and ritual patterns; reproductive patterns changed as demographic and social patterns changed; health conditions changed as diets changed and new diseases appeared.

The transformation also extended to the human population itself, through both diseases (another dimension of the larger ecological imperialism) and slavery. Pathogens, Crosby notes, were "among the 'weediest' of organisms" brought to the New World by Europeans, and their effect was devastating. Indigenous peoples were by no means free of disease before the conquest; Crosby concludes that they contended with pinta, yaws, venereal syphilis, hepatitis, encephalitis, polio, intestinal parasites, and some strains of tuberculosis.[9] But they had never suffered measles, cholera, diphtheria, trachoma, whooping cough, chicken pox, bubonic plague, malaria, yellow fever, scarlet fever, amebic dysentery, influenza, or smallpox. Smallpox was the deadliest, most easily transmissible, and quickest-spreading of them all; Crosby calls it "the disease with seven-league boots." It had arrived in Mesoamerica by early 1519, and by the 1520s or 1530s had spread all the way to the pampas. Death rates from such diseases were enormous, and the resulting cultural changes were profound (Crosby 1986, 196–201).[10]

Miraculously, no epidemics of European diseases were reported in Mesoamerica until smallpox broke out in Guatemala in 1520 and spread south through Nicaragua and into Panama. Further epidemics spread in rapid succession. It is difficult to say how many people died from them in Nicaragua, partly because the country's pre-conquest population itself is difficult to ascertain. Estimates based on Spanish colonial tax records, baptismal records, and calculations of the capacity of various types of soil to support a given population density with available technology suggest a population for Nicaragua of between 825,000 and perhaps twice that many. Of that number, some 70 percent were on the west coast where the Spanish conquest was concentrated (Newson 1982, 254–57; Newson 1987, 84–88, 335).

That the diseases came to Nicaragua there is no doubt. In 1529, mine workers at San Andrés and Gracias a Dios were decimated by *figo y enfermedades* (probably bubonic plague), which also killed many Indians around León two years later. In May of 1530, Governor Castañeda reported that "many Indians have died from pestilences, stomach pain and fevers," and a letter three years later referred to a great outbreak of measles that killed more than six thousand (perhaps one-third of the total remaining indigenous population). An epidemic in 1573 in Nicoya killed three hundred Indians in twenty days.[11] Large numbers of others died in battle and from food shortages and famines (such as a major one in 1528 that induced Indians to kill each other for food). Other famines followed in 1586 and 1610 (Stanislawski 1983, 11; Newson 1987, 119, 247–48), taking a further toll on the already decimated indigenous population.

SLAVERY. As with disease and intestinal parasites, slavery was not unknown among indigenous people in Nicaragua prior to the conquest. Oviedo and other chroniclers reported that the Nicarao sold slaves obtained through war and other means (such as buying children from poor families) for one hundred cacao beans or almonds (ten times the cost of a rabbit in the market) (Oviedo [1547] 1855, 67; Newson 1987, 58; cf. Sherman 1979, 15–19).

Although eventually *encomienda*-based agroexport production and tribute payment would be the major profit-extracting mechanisms for the Spanish in Nicaragua, during the second quarter of the sixteenth century slaves and minerals promised the quickest return and required the least investment. Although technically prohibited by the crown except for certain offenses (cannibalism, rebellion, refusal to submit to royal authority), slavery developed so quickly and on such a wide scale as to be effectively beyond control for many decades.[12] Slaves were used for every conceivable kind of labor, and by masters in virtually all social sectors above them—even by priests and bishops of the Catholic church (Zúñiga 1981, 31).

Nicaragua became a major source of slaves because it had large aggregations of conveniently located sedentary populations. Along with Honduras, it developed into a center of very active trading and (as Sherman notes) a scene of "notorious abuses." Slaves were caught on slaving expeditions, obtained by trade, or extorted from *caciques*. Branded on the face or arm, most were exported from Realejo through Panama to Peru for work in the mines (Sherman 1979, 15, 30, 41, 77–78).[13]

Shipments may have departed as early as 1524; certainly the trade was established by 1526, when Pedrarias Dávila became governor. It quickly became, Radell concluded, "the most profitable economic activity in Nicaragua," in which five ships were employed full-time. After the death of Pedrarias Dávila in 1531, Governor Castañeda expressed some concern for Indians in general and took modest steps to curb the slave trade, but had little actual restraining impact. As a slave-trader and promoter of slavery, Rodrigo de Contreras, who followed Castañeda as governor, proved as avaricious and brutal as his father-in-law Pedrarias Dávila before him.[14]

By 1533–34, Radell estimates, some fifteen to twenty Realejo-based caravels were "exclusively engaged in the Nicaraguan slave trade." On some voyages death rates were as high as 85 percent. Estimates of the number of slaves captured, branded, and exported from Nicaragua vary from fifty thousand to ten times that number. From the size of the ships, the length of trips, and the like, Radell estimates that between 1527 and 1548 approximately a half-million slaves were shipped—the majority of them in the single decade 1527–36. The impact of the trade was quite uneven; those populations near León and the port of Realejo appear to have suffered most (Newson 1987, 85, 103–5; Radell in Deneven 1976, 67–76; Radell and Parsons 1971, 300).[15]

The slave trade was eventually ended not primarily for humanitarian or ethical reasons, but because supplies of slaves ran low and the labor power of remaining Indians was needed for other profit-making endeavors. The most eloquent ethical and humanitarian arguments of them all were those of Fray Bartolomé de las Casas, who spent relatively brief periods in the 1530s in Nicaragua, which he described as a "very happy" province where a "very gentle and pacific" people lived in "happiness, health, amenity and prosperity" (quoted in Mejía Sanchez 1986, 151–61).[16]

Into such an ambience, Las Casas says, came "the tyrannies and servitude of the Christians," who brought to indigenous people "so many hurts, so much killing, so much cruelty, so much captivity and injustice." Las Casas described the depredations of the Spanish graphically: "They sent fifty men on horseback to put the lance to a whole province . . . which left neither man nor woman nor old person nor child alive, for some very trivial reason, like for not having come quickly enough at their call, or not having brought them enough corn . . . or enough Indians to serve them. . . . And since the land was flat, no one could flee from the horses, nor from the infernal ire of the Spanish." But the "most horrible pestilence," Las Casas said, was enslavement. To fill their requirements for slaves, the Spanish would demand that the *caciques* supply them. If they did not, they would be burned alive or thrown to hungry dogs (Sherman 1979, 287–88). From families with two children, one would be taken; from those with three, two were taken.[17]

Formally outlawed by the New Laws of 1542, the trade lingered in Nicaragua until 1550 (Newson 1987, 11–15, 106; cf. Woodward 1988, 43–45). During the nearly thirty years that it lasted, it wreaked nearly unimaginable havoc upon the "gentle and pacific" population of Nicaragua.

FORCED LABOR. Those native people of Nicaragua who escaped disease and slavery stood a good chance of being worked to death in the mines, forests, and shipyards, and on the indigo plantations. Death rates were particularly high among miners. Gold mining began in Nicaragua as early as 1531; two years later, two hundred Indians died in a single mining accident. Those who survived at all worked in wet, cold, dangerous conditions, and many became deathly ill and tried to walk back to their villages. Newson notes that contemporary accounts say that "it was possible to tell the way to the mines by the skeletons of Indians along the roadside." Revolts among miners and attacks by Indians on the mines led to a ban on their further employment in mines in 1546 (Newson 1982, 276; Sherman 1979, 98–99).

Indian workers in the ship-building industry had to carry wood on their backs from the central highlands to the coast, frequently working away from home for three to four years at a time. Others manufactured tar and pitch, prepared fish for the ships' crews, and served as menials on the ships. Many highland Indians sickened and died in the sweltering heat of the ports (Sherman 1979, 237–39).

Conditions were also deadly for indigo workers. The process of extracting the dye involved steeping the plants in warm water, which gave off a noxious vapor, drew swarms of disease-bearing insects, and produced a process liquid that burned the skin. The abuses continued until the early seventeenth century, long after the crown had banned such practices (Newson 1982, 27–82; Sherman 1979, 252).

The overall decline in the indigenous population of Nicaragua from all causes (though considerably greater on the west than on the east coast) was no less than catastrophic. As early as 1527, the Crown—informed that Nicaragua was being depopulated rapidly—appointed the priest Diego Alvarez

Indigo works in Nicaragua in the mid-nineteenth century. (From Squier, *The States of Central America*, 1858)

Osorio as Protector and Defender of the Indians in Nicaragua, but Alvarez's combat against the *encomenderos* and others who were exploiting Indians availed little (Zúñiga 1981, 29–31). Within twenty-five years of the arrival of the Spanish, the Pacific coast population had dropped by more than 92 percent. Managua, where perhaps forty thousand people had lived, could count only 265 tributary Indians in 1548; Jalteva (Granada) had dropped from eight thousand to a few hundred (Newson 1987, 110, 337). By 1578, Bishop Antonio de Zayas was estimating a remaining population of about eight thousand, which for the Pacific lowlands area represented a decline of about 97.5 percent (Radell 1969, 77–80; Newson 1982, 260–69; cf. Newson 1987, 239).

SOCIAL AND CULTURAL IMPACTS. The impacts of such a decimation and redistribution of the population upon indigenous life were both immediately catastrophic and structurally long-lasting—genetically, socially, and culturally (Newson 1987, 110–16). Genetically, whole populations were wiped out, and the remainder altered through *mestizaje*. The will to survive and reproduce was diminished, and birth rates fell.[18] Diets changed as crops requiring high labor inputs had to be abandoned, livestock were introduced, and time available for hunting and gathering wild foods diminished.[19]

Social and political transformations paralleled genetic ones. The best agri-

SACRAMEИTODELMA

Properly married Christian Indians. (From Guamán Poma de Ayala, *Nueva crónica y buen gobierno*, 1987)

cultural lands were allocated to Spaniards. Community organization changed after the 1540s as native populations were concentrated into *reducciones* in order to thwart rebellions, collect tribute payments and supervise agricultural production (Stanislawski 1983, 47–48). At every level, Spanish administrative structures replaced traditional ones, as when the "good custom" of elected councils of elders who ruled some Indian towns was terminated (Oviedo 1547 [1855], 304). Native *caciques* were incorporated into the colonial administrative system, and their hereditary status and privileges altered. To separate *caciques* from their people and identify them with the Spanish, they (and only they among the Indians) were permitted to ride horses. But to dramatize their subordination to the Spanish, their hereditary privileges (such as ownership of slaves) were curtailed, and some were forced to perform humiliating tasks (Newson 1987, 180–82).

Changes in the ecology, economy, and social and political systems all in turn had profound impacts on the culture, but other changes were more directly cultural. Indigenous languages were subordinated to Spanish.[20] The cultural landscape changed as native buildings and towns were destroyed or abandoned, and Spanish town organization and architecture replaced them. Traditional ceremonies were suppressed and time-honored traditions were erased. Bigamy and polygamy were discouraged and patrilocal rather than matrilocal residence was encouraged. To establish nuclear families as the cultural norm, newly married couples were required to build their own houses (Newson 1987, 185–89).

Thus the conquest changed the cultural system of Nicaragua permanently: many features of indigenous culture disappeared completely and others were transformed; alien cultural patterns were imposed and new syncretisms emerged. From 1524 onward, indigenous cultural survivals, alien importations, and emerging syncretisms alike developed principally under the influence of Spanish rather than indigenous institutions.

CULTURE AND NATIVE LABOR: THE ENCOMIENDA, THE REPARTIMIENTO, AND TRIBUTE

Not many years after the conquest began in Nicaragua, Spanish colonists realized that it scarcely made sense to ship Indians as slaves to Peru when their labor was essential to the colonial project within Nicaragua itself. The principal mechanisms used to organize and exploit that labor power were the *encomienda*, the *repartimiento* (which replaced it formally but continued its essential functions), and the tribute system, which was a central feature of (and outlasted) both.

THE ENCOMIENDA. Nicaragua's indigenous people were not unfamiliar with forced labor drafts or tribute payments; native *caciques* had employed both prior to the conquest (Newson 1987, 12). Indeed that already-established pattern facilitated the imposition of the *encomienda*, since *caciques* accustomed to receiving labor and tribute payments could be mobilized to receive them for their new colonial masters.

First used against the Moors in Spain, the *encomienda* system of allocating native labor to Spanish colonists was established by the Laws of Burgos in 1503 (cf. Simpson [1960] 1978, 5–6).[21] Although certain of its provisions offered protection to the Indians, the laws were directed mainly toward extracting labor and tribute payments from them. In practice, the *encomienda* wreaked havoc among Nicaragua's indigenous people, and lasted far longer than the less than twenty years during which it was legal (from the conquest in 1524 to the New Laws of 1542). The earliest grants in Nicaragua date from about five years after the conquest; by 1548 most of the indigenous population had been grouped into a few dozen *encomiendas* (Newson 1987, 97, 151; Romero Vargas 1988, 108). *Encomienda* Indians planted, tended, and harvested crops; worked in the mines and shipyards; made pitch and tar; worked as household servants; and spun and wove cloth. Particularly onerous and deadly work was that of the *tamemes* (human beasts of burden). Since—as Sherman notes wryly—"no one in Central America suggested seriously that Spaniards carry their own loads," Indians were greatly in demand as *tamemes*, and some-

COMEИDERO
CRISTIAИOCOMEИ
DERO·DE   IИSDESTER

comen deco   comen deros

Encomendero. (From Guamán Poma de Ayala, *Nueva crónica y buen gobierno*, 1987)

times carried their loads six hundred miles or more (Newson 1987, 99–100; Sherman 1979, 111–28). Vast numbers died in the process.[22]

Although some *encomenderos* were, as Stanislawski observes, "men of conscience who remained immune to the fever of acquisition," the majority had few scruples. Relations among *encomenderos* were characterized by acrimony and antagonism, competition and constant litigation, and mutual recrimination; in the scarce labor market created by the earlier slave trade and continuing epidemics, they fought each other viciously (Stanislawski 1983, 126).

Culturally, the *encomienda* system reinforced and extended the effects of the earlier years of the conquest as it transformed native communities, economies, and associated cultural features such as diet, agricultural systems, land tenure, family structure, and the rhythms of daily life. Concurrently, it built the foundations of landholding and wealth distribution upon which the post-conquest, non-indigenous cultural order eventually was erected.

Although *encomiendas* in Nicaragua tended to be smaller than those elsewhere in Latin America, the larger ones produced substantial (in some cases fabulous) wealth.[23] The largest *encomiendas* were those of Governor Francisco de Castañeda; the "scandalously predatory" Rodrigo de Contreras (governor after 1535), who seized for himself and his family vast amounts of the best land in the country; the "fabulously wealthy" Pedro de los Ríos, who owned various pig farms, numerous slaves, and a house in León; and the litigious and unprincipled Benito Díaz, who arrived as an "illiterate teenaged adventurer," became an official of the city of Granada, and married the daughter of Governor Contreras. At least one *encomienda* (the eighth largest in the country) came to be held by a woman, the greedy and vicious Yseo de Santiago, widow of original León settler Mateo de Lezcano (Newson 1987, 98).[24]

Although the *encomienda* was declared illegal by the New Laws of 1542, the *encomenderos* quickly found ways to circumvent the ban. The most effective mechanism proved to be the *repartimiento*.[25]

THE REPARTIMIENTO. Formally the *repartimiento* required each village to offer a certain percentage (usually 20 percent) of its tributary Indians to work for stipulated periods at fixed wages. But exactions increased as time passed, gradually converting the Indian population into wage laborers.

Repartimiento tasks varied greatly. Indians worked in the indigo and sugar cane *haciendas*, in the mines, in the homes of officials or the clergy, in defense against hostile Indian or pirate attacks, and in various public works projects. As with the *encomienda*, regulation of the *repartimiento* was lax, and opportunities to abuse Indians caught within the system were abundant. Public officials and the clergy forced the Indians to sell marketable goods at low prices, and to buy other essential ones at high prices. They had to cultivate fields, tend cattle, and provide food for priests. Beginning in the seventeenth century, *corregidores* began to augment their meager salaries through the *repartimiento de hilados*, which forced women to spin yarn and weave cloth for long hours at low pay. *Repartimiento* workers were supposed to be paid in cash, but most often were paid in cacao or other goods; many were never paid at all (Newson 1987, 161–66, 278–79; Romero Vargas 1988, 129–56; Woodward [1976] 1985, 43–44; Sherman 1979, 85–128).[26] As more and more Indians were required for *repartimiento* labor, some fled to avoid it, and others drifted into free wage labor; those remaining in the villages couldn't provide for their own needs. Direct resistance generally availed little. The *repartimiento* remained in effect in Nicaragua until 1812, much later than elsewhere in Latin America (Newson 1987, 277).

TRIBUTE. A consistent feature of both the *encomienda* and the *repartimiento* system was the payment of tribute in goods or (later) money. In the mid-sixteenth century, maize was the most important item of tribute, but beans, cotton, woven mantles, salt, honey, rush mats, sandals, harnesses for horses, henequen cordage, and other items also were used (Stanislawski 1983, 26–45). The cultural and social costs of the system were high. Tribute payments redirected labor away from the production of traditional commodities for use or trade within the community, and toward production of marketable commodities. Tribute requirements also reduced available quantities of essen-

Native woman being forced to weave.
(From Guamán Poma de Ayala, *Nueva crónica y buen gobierno*, 1987)

tial goods and foodstuffs, disrupted the normal values, social structures, and daily and seasonal rhythms of native life, and hence both implicitly devalued and explicitly menaced Indian culture.

Onerous and exploitative at best, the tribute system was rife with abuse. Legally, the *encomienda* system out of which it originally arose required colonial officials (*oidores*; literally, "listeners") to visit *encomiendas* every three years, count the tributary Indians (generally adult males, except for *caciques* and those physically unable to work), look at crops, specify levels of tribute (*tasaciones*), and redress any abuses of the Indians. In practice, however, abuses and irregularities abounded. Visits were infrequent, so that villages had to pay tributes on Indians who had died or fled since the last *tasación*; desertions to avoid tribute payments were high, and harsh measures (such as burning homes) were taken to try to force them to return; excessive tributes were collected; and failure to pay (even if the result of poor harvests) brought brutal punishments such as whipping or jailing (Newson 1987, 153–60, 273, 284; Romero Vargas 1988, 112–21).

The social and cultural costs of the tribute system were evident to John Cockburn as he traveled through Nicaragua in the early 1730s: "There was not a Man to be seen in the Town," Cockburn reported, and what poor Women we found there, look'd like Pictures of Famine; and well they might, for they had nothing but a few green Suppotoes . . . to subsist on, Things scarcely eatable for any Creature. . . . Every single Man of [Pueblo Nuevo] is obliged to pay the King of Spain six Pieces of Eight yearly, and every married Man twelve, or in Case of Non-payment to be sent to the Mines without Redemption. This heavy Imposition, with what they are bound to allow the Clergy, they account an insupportable Grievance, and were they not very industrious, as well as ingenious, they could not perform such hard Tasks. These People make a Sort of fine Matts, and Hammocks of Cane, and likewise curious Baskets of the same; all of which they paint very beautifully, and carry to Panama, where they sell them at a low Rate to discharge their Tribute. (Cockburn 1735, 113–14, 242)

NATIVE RESISTANCE

In dramatic detail, the chronicler Oviedo preserved accounts of the encounter between the *conquistadores* and Nicaragua's indigenous people, including an episode in which Gil González Dávila met resistance from the *cacique* Diriangén. Diriangén arrived at the encounter with five hundred men, musicians playing, flags flying, women adorned with gold. Pausing to serenade González, who asked them who they were and why they came, they explained that they had heard of armed men who went about on four-footed animals, that they wanted to be baptized as Christians, and would return in three days. It was a ruse, however; Diriangén proved himself a fierce opponent of the conquest. At least according to the Nicaraguan *conquistador* Gil González Dávila's narrative, however, the two *caciques* Nicoya and Nicaragua peaceably converted to Christianity, although the latter also joined Diriangén's resistance (Oviedo [1547] 1855, 170ff.; Rodríguez 1984, 50–63). Thus emerged the array of political-cultural postures of unyielding resistance, accommodation, collaboration, and ambivalent vacillation that were to characterize Nicaragua's entire future experience with a perennial series of invaders, adventurers, and entrepreneurs from beyond its borders.

Those Indians who chose to resist colonial exploitation (by no means a unanimous choice) invented a variety of means for doing so. Colonial era confessional manuals reveal, for example, that Indians forced to attend Catholic confession contrived not to be purely passive victims of the process, but instead routinely deflected and distorted it. "They take what is bad for good, and vice versa," complained one confessor, and "they examine their conscience very superficially or not at all." "They tell stories," complained another. "To confess a sin they first give a thousand excuses to lessen and mask it to make it look less bad, and for that purpose they use fastidious words so as not to be understood" (Gruzinski in Lavrin 1989, 105).

The more direct resistance tactics of native groups sometimes extended to open rebellion. Such resistance began even with the first exploration by Gil González in 1523 and continued sporadically thereafter. Governor Pedrarias initiated brutal repressive measures as early as 1527, including—according to Oviedo—allowing savage dogs to tear apart eighteen Indians in the plaza at León (Oviedo in Wheelock Román [1974] 1981, 31; cf. 52, 63; Incer 1990, 115). In 1582, Fray Juan Piçarro's public whipping of the brother of a Nicaraguan *cacique* incited the *cacique* to seize the friar and rise in rebellion (Sherman 1979, 295). Serious armed resistance continued throughout much of the colonial period: in Subtiava in 1681 and 1725, Sébaco in 1693, El Viejo in 1759, and many other places (Wheelock Román [1974] 1981, 49–55; Romero Vargas 1988, 146).

More often than it emerged directly and violently, however, resistance took indirect, sublimated, covert, and witty forms. Some of the most durable proved to be the broad array of satiric dramatic pieces performed (frequently in connection with church festivals) throughout most of the colonial period as a counter to a parallel series of such pieces intended by colonial authorities to induce native peoples to submit to the new colonial order (Arellano 1991b, 278–80). By far the best known and most influential of the satiric pieces in Nicaragua was *El Güegüence*.

El Güegüence, whose authorship and date of composition have been extensively debated, appears to have begun being performed sometime during the middle to late colonial period.[27] Rejecting previous suggestions concerning authorship (an Indian, a creole merchant, group composition), Arellano argues that it may have been written by a priest, or at least by someone "of superior mentality familiar with the life and beliefs, conduct and customs" of the indigenous people of central Nicaragua (Arellano 1991b, 283). The *dramatis personae* of the elaborately costumed performance include the royal governor (Tastuanes) and his daughter (Lady Suchi-Malinche), the local Indian chief (Alguacil), Güegüence and his children (Don Forcico and Don Ambrosio), the royal secretary and the registrar.[28]

As the play opens, the governor halts the songs and dances the Indians are performing for the Royal Council because they are beneath the dignity of the Council, and orders that no one be permitted in the province without his permission.[29] The chief says his people have no fit clothing, and blames Güegüence, whom the governor summons before him. When the governor challenges Güegüence for his lack of a permit, Güegüence diverts him by claiming to have great riches. Doubting the claim, however, the governor questions both of Güegüence's sons. The older tells him it is the truth; the younger says it is all a lie. To prove his honesty, Güegüence offers to show the governor what he has in his tent-shop. The impossible things he shows irritate the governor, and Güegüence changes the subject by bragging on his older son. The governor is intrigued, and asks the three to dance for him. As they perform a masquerade called *el macho ratón* (the mule), Güegüence asks for the hand of the governor's daughter. The governor sends for her and other young women, but his secretary cautions that the prospective son-in-law must be dressed elegantly. Güegüence hastily explains that he asked for his older son, who then begins to inspect the young women, each of whom he disparagingly rejects. He is so charmed by the governor's daughter that he marries her, however. The mules are then brought in, and Güegüence examines them one by one, seizing the opportunity to make a series of vulgar jokes. The sons then mount the mules and leave, and the royal party tells Güegüence to begone.

The colonial officials are repeatedly burlesqued and satirized through intentional misunderstanding, feigned deafness, double entendres, obscene jokes, and slapstick action. Those dramaturgical stratagems mask (intentionally poorly, of course) behavior that would otherwise be intolerable in a social inferior: lack of respect, avoidance of established forms of deference, impudence, defiance, vulgarity, rowdiness, and insults. ("What fine nails has my friend, the Captain Chief Alguacil," Güegüence exclaims. "They are like those of a scratching monkey!") In turn, many of the stratagems arise from the multicultural status of the partly acculturated Indian population, and draw upon their skillful code switching and frame manipulation. Spanish words are "misheard" because of their similarity to Nahuatl words that mean something entirely different (and usually insulting to the authorities); masculine and feminine endings for Spanish words are switched with comic result (*criada* [servant-girl or washerwoman] for *criado* [official servant to the governor]).

The cumulative result, as in all such genres, is a complex set of social, political, and cultural inversions: powerlessness becomes power, weakness becomes strength, ignorance becomes knowledge, the conquered becomes conqueror, the devalued becomes valued.[30] The wit and delegitimizing power of those inversions has caused successive generations of Nicaraguan scholars to view *El Güegüence* as "the first and most durable literary expression of the popular Nicaraguan spirit": "disputative words and deeds, disrespect for authority, defensive malice and contempt for sophistication, mordacity in the face of injustice and condemnation of servility, crafty and tricky verbal resources, fantasizing irony . . . and imagination without limit" (Arellano 1991b, 282).

As burdensome and culturally destructive as the *encomienda*, the *repartimiento*, and the tribute system were, and as relatively ineffective as Indian resistance to them (and to other burdens of the conquest) was, those systems eventually did disappear—at least as formal arrangements—with the coming of independence, even if substantial traces of them remained in land tenure patterns, the social status of certain families, attitudes toward work, and the agricultural and labor systems. But other features of the post-conquest transformation carried on beyond independence not as traces, but as permanent structural features of cultural life in Nicaragua.

ENDURING FOUNDATIONS FOR CULTURAL DEVELOPMENT

At least six aspects of the transformation of Nicaragua during the colonial period remained beyond independence as lasting determinants of cultural development: the bipolar León-Granada axis, the hegemony of the Catholic church, *mestizaje* and the race-linked class system, an agroexport economy, a gender system built upon male dominance, and the politically and culturally separate development of the Atlantic coast.

THE LEÓN-GRANADA AXIS. One of the paradoxes of the conquest was that for all their destructiveness, the Spanish incorporated certain aspects of indigenous social and political organization into the colonial project. In general, for example, they located their towns in the midst of substantial concentrations of Indian population—in order to control them, use their labor, extract tribute, and symbolize Spanish power to dominate them (Newson 1987, 48). The two most important new cities superimposed upon older ones were León, established at Imabite in the middle of the dense Indian population of the province of Nagarando between Subtiava and the coast, and Granada, situated in the province of Nequecherí next to the Indian town of Jalteva and in the midst of a large group of other Chorotegan towns (Incer 1990, 211). By the end of the sixteenth century, the majority of the perhaps five hundred Spaniards in Nicaragua lived in either León or Granada, which between them were destined to form "the axis of domination" of the country (Romero Vargas 1988, 211). Despite their rivalry, these two towns determined the direction of Nicaragua's cultural as well as economic and political development from the early colonial period onward.

The rivalry was grounded in the very conditions of their founding (Newson 1987, 48; Romero Vargas 1988, 178, 281; Incer 1990, 74–75). Granada, the first colonial capital, was founded by upper-class Spaniards, but the first residents of León were mostly low-ranking Spanish footsoldiers. Chosen later by Pedrarias Dávila as a seat of operations oriented toward controlling Honduras, León soon became the capital (Radell 1969, 62). That oscillation continued until the mid-nineteenth century, and the conflicted cultural politics that surrounded it has continued even to the present day. Both cities fought for economic and political dominance as well as cultural preeminence.

In effect, León and Granada divided most of the country's wealth between them. In the original post-conquest partitioning of lands and tributary Indians, about half the Indian towns (separated by a boundary line passing through Managua) were given to Granada, and the other half to León. Each ended up with about the same number of tributary Indians, but León had more large *encomiendas* and better volcanic soil than did Granada, as well as more *encomenderos* who were powerful because they were close to the center of government (Stanislawski 1983, 17, 22, 133–36).

As the seventeenth century opened, Granada—which had the advantage of Atlantic-bound shipping across Lake Nicaragua and down the San Juan River—was booming (Incer 1990, 214–15). Granada merchants were shipping indigo from Managua, cochineal and tobacco from Chontales, cloth from Masaya and Nindirí (site of one of the largest *encomiendas* in the country), as well as corn and leather. The city drew further wealth from its satellite area around Rivas, to which it was connected commercially and through the family networks that established and maintained the norms and values of the culture (Stanislawski 1983, 176–78, 259, 269).

Granada suffered greatly from pirate attacks during the seventeenth century, but by the eighteenth its major commercial families were prospering again. One of the largest was headed by Don Narciso José de Argüelles. By buying fifty thousand acres over a twenty-five-year period, he became Nicaragua's biggest landholder of the colonial period and a major merchant of imported goods. When he went out, one gathers from his will, he dressed in leather boots with silver buttons, silk stockings, lace shirts, and gold-embroidered vests. For riding he wore a blue velvet suit trimmed with gold and slipped his boots into silver-mounted stirrups. A few other Granada families—the Vegas, Lacayos, Montiels, and Chamorros—were also able to indulge in such elegance. Progenitor Don Diego Chamorro married four times and had twenty children. His wealth came from raising cattle and cacao (partly with slave labor), and his splendid house boasted a library, tables decorated with Chinese porcelains, and crystal (Romero Vargas 1988, 248, 271–75).[31]

After it became the capital of the province in 1527, León functioned as the seat of military, civil, and (after 1531) ecclesiastical authority (Romero Vargas 1988, 173–76; Newson 1981, 93; Incer 1990, 63–73, 82–85, 93–97). Although it came quickly to be a city of some opulence, León was moved to the northwest in 1610, the official reason being to escape threats of renewed eruptions from the volcano Momotombo, although Romero Vargas argues that the move was

Volcano El Viejo as seen from León in mid-nineteenth century. (From *Harper's New Monthly Magazine*, 1857)

actually undertaken to be nearer a better supply of Indian labor (Incer 1990, 143–45; Romero Vargas 1988, 173–76).[32] Shortly after the removal, León had only eighty Spanish inhabitants, but a new cathedral was under construction by 1620. By the time the Dominican friar Thomas Gage visited the new city some two decades later, León was solidly reestablished, partly due to its proximity to the Pacific port of Realejo (hence to traffic bound for Panama and Peru) (Incer 1990, 214–15). The "chief delight of the inhabitants," Gage observed, "is in their houses, in the pleasure of the country adjoining, and in the abundance of all things for the life of man's extraordinary riches are not so much enjoyed there as in other parts of America. They are contented with fine gardens . . . [and] gay houses, and so lead a delicious, lazy, and idle life, not aspiring much to trade and traffic" (Gage [1648] 1958, 307).

After León was attacked by pirates in 1681 and burned by them in 1685, it was rebuilt with forced Indian labor. While economic conditions and pirate attacks induced many Spanish to live principally in rural areas rather than in the city, by 1776 some twelve hundred Spanish had houses near the central plaza. Nearly equal number of mestizos and more than five thousand mulattoes lived in the San Felipe area between them and the forty-two hundred Indians of Subtiava (Newson 1987, 149; Romero Vargas 1988, 173–76; Incer 1990, 235, 339–42).

Throughout the seventeenth and eighteenth centuries, the balance of political power and cultural dominance oscillated between León and Granada as economic conditions changed, markets shifted, pirate attacks came and went, and families mingled or remained separate. León's essential shipping port of Realejo began to decline after the pirate attacks of the late 1680s and the waning of the shipbuilding industry (tied in turn to falling trade with Peru); its wealthiest citizens moved to El Viejo, and its two convents were allowed to decay. One contemporary account characterized it as "a collection of misery and a vent of despair." Meanwhile, Granada's new satellite town of Nicaragua (later renamed Rivas) grew quickly in importance; by 1778 it had more than half again as many Spanish inhabitants as León. Granada leaders— resentful ever since León was chosen as the capital of the new *intendencia* of Nicaragua in 1786—mounted an open rebellion against León in 1811, put down when forces from León besieged Granada and imprisoned its leading citizens (Newson 1987, 257–59, table 18; Woodward [1976] 1985, 67).[33]

Whatever the relative prominence of León or Granada at any particular historical moment, however, the axis of political, economic, social, and cultural development for Nicaragua invariably ran between the two cities. That structural fact remained stable throughout the pre-independence period, and indeed far beyond it. Struggle as they might between themselves, they never had reason to doubt that the two together would continue to define the cultural substance and orientation of Nicaraguan life.

THE CATHOLIC CHURCH. The first missionaries sailed with Columbus on his second voyage (1493), and the evangelization of the New World began in Santo Domingo in 1500. Between 1509 and 1518, some 125 priests (about 60 percent Dominican and 20 percent Franciscan) followed. The systematic evangelization of Mexico began in 1524, at the very moment of the conquest of Nicaragua (Dussel 1981, 38–39, 47–49, 74–75, 344; Tormo 1962, 66, 115).

The first priest to go to Nicaragua, it appears, was Diego de Aguero, who arrived with the *conquistador* Gil González Dávila in 1523 (Comisión de Estudios de Historia de la Iglesia en América Latina 1985, 50; Foroohar 1989, 1; Zúñiga 1981, 23).[34] The religious orders—more messianic than the secular priests—followed soon thereafter. By 1539 there were four Mercedarians and six Jerónimos, and the Dominicans sent thirty-four between 1543 and 1561. During the century after 1575, the Franciscans sent a few more than a hundred, outnumbering the Dominicans after 1600. Both the Mercedarians and the Franciscans established convents in León soon after their arrival; probably the first was a Mercedarian convent founded in 1526 (Borges Morán 1960, 478–536; Zúñiga 1981, 26, 46; Newson 1987, 167; Romero Vargas 1988, 216). Last to arrive were the Jesuits in 1616. Conducting their work under the direct authority of the pope, and with an exclusively missionary purpose, the Jesuits were more inclined to try to understand Indian religion (Dussel 1981, 45,

Native religious sculptures discovered by E. George Squire on Zapatero Island in mid-nineteenth century. (From Squier, *Nicaragua: Its People, Scenery, Monuments, and the Proposed Canal*, 1852)

58). By the time they arrived, however, it was for the most part too late; the conquest and aggressive Christianization had been underway for more than ninety years, and much irreversible damage to Indian culture had long since been done.

With regard to the conflict between Catholicism and native religious beliefs and practices, the church alternated between a relatively tolerant syncretism and a *tabula rasa* approach that denied all validity to Indian religion and culture (Dussel 1981, 64). Whatever the evolving internal disagreements and temporal or regional differences within the missionary enterprise, its core practices were those spelled out in the Laws of Burgos (1513): churches were to be built and provided with "images of Our Lady" and bells to call Indians to worship; Indians were to "cross themselves and bless themselves, and together recite the Ave María, the Pater Noster, the Credo and the Salve Regina"; they were to be taught "the Ten Commandments and the Seven Deadly Sins and the Articles of the Faith"; they were to confess once a year (Simpson [1960] 1978, 17, 21).

The culture and religion of Nicaraguan Indians were anathema to all but a precious few of the Spanish. The people of Nicoya, reported Oviedo, "are idolaters who have many idols of earth and wood" in their houses of prayer (*orchilobos*), and priests who oversee diabolical sacrifices. Oviedo told of personally destroying an Indian temple near León, and of using the wooden posts to build a stable for his horses. Accompanying Fray Bobadilla on a missionary tour among the Indians in 1538, Oviedo reported that "an infinite number of idols" were burned, images of Mary raised in their stead, and the Indians forced to sweep and clean the Christian churches (Oviedo [1547] 1855, 69, 186, 305, 353; Rodríguez 1984, 116–17, 125).[35] During the very year that

Forced confession. Priest has a rosary in one hand and a whip in the other. (From Guamán Poma de Ayala, *Nueva crónica y buen gobierno*, 1987)

the Spanish arrived, Bobadilla himself had burned the Indians' books, maps, pictures, and other documents in the plaza in Managua (Rodríguez 1984, 23).

Missionary efforts to communicate with and convert the Indians varied greatly in method, but few respected Indian culture or tolerated its survival.[36] Gruzinski's analysis of the Catholic system of confession from the sixteenth to the eighteenth century, and especially of the Indians' reactions to it, affords insight into the rationale and power of the conversion enterprise.[37] Whereas traditional habits of thought among indigenous peoples appear to have been highly social, fluid, and (as Gruzinski characterizes them) "constructed upon a broad range of oppositions, distinctions, and parallelisms," the European Catholic system upon which the confession was based emphasized "fixed categories . . . [which] claim[ed] to be universal and [left] no margin for . . . improvisation."

Confession itself—as revealed in contemporary confession manuals—demanded fixed processes of introspection, memorization and formulation of sins, and disclosure of transgressions. It imposed alien norms and structures upon Indian personality and social interaction, such as high degrees of individualization and guilt, Christian forms of matrimony, and the nuclear family. Its impact was especially severe in the area of sexuality, in which confession was structured in terms of a soul-heaven / body-hell dyad that Indians found culturally and morally incoherent. Such concepts and practices, Gruzinski observes, "erod[ed] the traditional ties and interpersonal relations" that held indigenous communities together, and broke down "the ancient solidarity and social networks," "physical and supernatural ties," and "the concept of the marital union as part of a cosmic vision dominated by the play of fate." The list of sins Indians confessed and for which they were punished (frequently by whipping or confinement) included idolatry, witchcraft, cannibalism, incest, sodomy, concubinage, drunkenness, truancy, and numerous other transgressions (Borges 1960, 119–21, 205–6; cf. Newson 1987, 191).

The missionaries' broader program of acculturation required Indians to respect Spanish law, fear and obey the clergy, learn European hygenic practices, wear clothes ("go about clad," as the 1513 amendments to the Laws of Burgos phrased it), adopt monogamy, and forsake their round houses for square ones that could more easily be divided up into rooms, thereby curtailing what the Spanish saw as deviant sexual practices. Indians who converted had their hair cut as a public symbol of compliance (Borges 1960, 179, 205–6, 240). The result of such forced acculturation was the virtual eradication of the "ethico-mythical nucleus" of Indian culture, as well as the radical transformation of many related aspects of Indian life (Dussel 1981, 43).

Attempts to defend Indians against the various forms of abuse, cultural debasement, and exploitation to which they were subjected by the colonial project arose simultaneously with the conquest itself (especially among Dominican friars), but availed relatively little (Gutiérrez in Richard 1980, 141–45; Dussel 1981, 47–52, 405–6; Prien 1985, 140, 159–96). The great champion of Nicaragua's Indians was of course Bartolomé de las Casas (Prien 1985, 168–71; Llorente in Las Casas [1552] 1987, 123–200; Wagner and Parish 1967; Zúñiga 1981, 36). During his relatively brief stays in Nicaragua in the 1530s, Las Casas's denunciations of the treatment of Indians brought him into conflict with Nicaragua's brutal governor Rodrigo de Contreras, whose expeditions into the interior to enslave Indians Las Casas denounced publicly (Wagner and Parish 1967, 83; Ayón 1882, 1:377–400; Sherman 1979, 10). Bishop Valdivieso, who arrived in 1544, continued Las Casas's crusade (Gámez 1889, 177–81; Dussel 1981, 52; Ayón 1882, 1:232–39; Wagner and Parish 1967, 143–53). *Encomenderos* in Nicaragua, already angry because the New Laws of 1542 had terminated the *encomienda* system, were so infuriated by Valdivieso's opposition to their treatment of Indians that they rose in armed revolt and murdered him (Woodward [1976] 1985, 43; Stanislawski 1983, 72; Foroohar 1989, 3). In 1551 Valdivieso was succeeded by Bishop Carrasco, who held the post for only two years, and lacked Valdivieso's courage and ardor (Ayón 1882, 1:269).[38]

Whether it is true in any general sense that, as Dussel has argued, the Indians accepted Christianity "for reasons which were essentially pagan," it is incontrovertible that vast numbers of Indians in Nicaragua were "converted" by means of mass baptisms whose efficacy and durability there were many reasons to doubt, and whose character reveals salient aspects of the politics of culture in colonial Nicaragua (Dussel 1981, 67). Such baptisms were especially common during the first fifteen years after the conquest (1524–39). The conquistador Gil González claimed to have baptized more than thirty-two thousand in 1522, and Oviedo estimated that more than one hundred thousand had been baptized by 1530 (Dussel 1981, 66–67; Prien 1985, 232–33; Borges 1960, 495; Newson 1987, 86).

Oviedo was skeptical not only about such baptisms, but also about the whole Christianizing process. "Very rare and few," he reported, "are the Indians who can be said to be Christians among those baptized in adolescence or beyond" (Oviedo [1547] 1855, 311). Oviedo's report of his journey with friar Francisco Bobadilla through Nicaragua to assess the efficacy of Indian conversions and baptize new converts highlights the lack of congruence between Spanish and Indian culture—and hence the impact of the former on the latter.[39]

The interviews presented a classic drama of confused and failed communication across cultural differences, with questions "conditioned by a Christian view of the world and of western culture," Rodríguez observes, and thus "inadequate for obtaining the information desired" (Rodríguez 1984, 139). Asked by Bobadilla if he knew there was a god who created earth, men, and other things, the *cacique* Chicoyatonal of Teoca responded candidly that he knew nothing of such matters. An inquiry about his knowledge of heaven and hell left him startled (*se espantaba de lo que le fué preguntado*). Another elder of the village was confident (because his parents had told him, he said) that it was the Indian deities (*teotes*) Tamagostat (male) and Çipattoval (female) who created the earth.[40] Still another *cacique*, asked who told him he was a Christian and poured water over his head, said he didn't remember. Sixty-year-old Indian priest Taçoteyda, asked whether he was or wanted to be a Christian, said that he wasn't and had no desire to be. "I am old," he said, "and am not a *cacique* [anyway]," suggesting that he was not oblivious to the class bias of the missionary effort (Oviedo [1547] 1855, 311–27).

The cultural disparity became more and more evident as Bobadilla plied the Indians with a host of related questions: Who created the gods? Do they eat anything? Was the world destroyed after it was created? How did anyone (including the gods themselves) escape such a destruction? Where do the dead go? Does the whole body go there? Can the Indian gods bring dead people back to life? To whom do you pray, and how, and why? Who takes care of the temples, and who may enter them? Why do you go naked when cotton is so plentiful? (Oviedo [1547] 1855, 317–50).

The Indians' answers repeatedly dramatized cultural differences. Asked what their gods were made of, flesh or wood, an Indian responded that they were of flesh and (even more pointedly) that they were the same color (*moreno*—brown or dark-skinned) as the Indians, and that they ate the same things and dressed the same way as the Indians. Other answers highlighted differences between the two cultures' ways of preserving theological beliefs and cultural memory. Asked how they preserved such beliefs and memories without the Bible that he showed them, the *cacique* Avagoaltegoan assured his inquisitor that "our ancestors said it," and that the information "flows from one to another so that we remember it." In the presence of other priests and conquistadors, Bobadilla asked thirteen *caciques* and native priests ("of those infernal temples," Oviedo noted) where the Indians of Nicaragua had come from. The Indians replied that they didn't know exactly, but it was from the west, and they came because they were held in vassalage by other Indians, "as we now serve the Christians" (Oviedo [1547] 1855, 316–28).

A few of the Indians' responses were tolerable to the Spanish (such as that brides found not to be virgins might be returned to their families and that they practiced a type of confession), but other cultural practices seemed especially to justify forcible acculturation. The Indians admitted that they celebrated festivals in which people were at liberty to "be idle, get drunk, and sing and dance around the plaza"; that they practiced human sacrifice and cannibalism; and that they mutilated their sexual organs (Oviedo [1547] 1855, 332–38, 345–51).

To gain greater control over the transformative process and to make it more durable, the church designed a variety of mechanisms. As early as 1533, Governor Castañeda ordered all *encomenderos* to send Indian boys to the convent San Francisco in León to be educated in the faith (Comisión de Estudios 1985, 52–53). Later there were repeated efforts to gather large numbers of Indians together into closely controlled *reducciones*. First developed in the Antilles as early as 1503 and on the mainland after 1530, religious *reducciones* brought the missionaries into conflict with the *encomenderos* because they removed Indians from the already scarce labor supply (Incer 1990, 255; Prien 1985, 208–10).[41] Nevertheless, by 1684 at least three *reducciones* had been established (Lóvago, Lovigüisca, and Camoapa). Such activities continued through the end of the seventeenth century, and intensified from the 1740s onward (Romero Vargas 1988, 64–65; Comisión de Estudios 1985, 55–56; Newson 1987, 280).

Religious *reducciones* were not notably successful in Nicaragua. The Recol-

iħs
DVRMILONPERESOSO-PV

Indian couple absenting themselves from work in the Reducción. (From Guamán Poma de Ayala, *Nueva crónica y buen gobierno*, 1987)

lect Order, established by the Franciscans in 1682 specifically to convert Indians on the frontier, founded a number of towns during the early eighteenth century, but by 1751 only two remained (Newson 1987, 281–82). Thrown together with other linguistic and cultural groups, and lacking a tolerance for sedentary life, the Indians disliked life in the *reducciones*. Disease also decimated some *reducciones*, its deadly effects exacerbated by the relatively dense populations. The increase of hostile activity by the British on the east coast during the early eighteenth century also made Indians there especially unwilling to settle in *reducciones*, which therefore tended to be unstable and short-lived (Newson 1987, 281–82, 305). Some Indians shirked their assigned work, and others simply abandoned the *reducciones*. Frequently they fled into the mountains, and the disheartened friars "went elsewhere in search of new and more persevering converts" (Incer 1990, 270). Other Indians were more direct in their opposition: they attacked the *reducciones* and killed the priests before fleeing.

How resistant certain elements of Indian culture were to Christianization is evident in reports by the British traveler John Cockburn from the early 1730s. After two hundred years of missionary activity, the complex tensions between effective conversion, syncretism, and retention of native ways were still dramatically in evidence. Headed for the towns of St. Michael's and Cauwattick, Cockburn met a "mallata" (mulatto?) man unacquainted with the most familiar of Christian symbols. Asked what the "painting" on his arm signified, Cockburn said, "I told him, I thank'd God, we were Christians, and *Englishmen*, and that one of the Marks on my Arms represented our Saviour on the Cross" (Cockburn 1735, 79).

Elsewhere, syncretism was evident. "When . . . publick Festivals are kept here," Cockburn reported, "they will carry their Musick into the Churches, and dance in their Masquerade Habits, before the image of the Virgin." His account of one funeral (at which a Catholic priest officiated and the body was buried) included details obviously drawn from both Christianity and native tradition. But at another funeral "performed after the Heathen Manner of these People . . . they cover'd the Body with Leaves, and then placed a large Quantity of Wood about it, which when they had fired, the Company . . . join'd Hands and surrounded the Pile, and never ceased singing and dancing till the Wood and Body were both consumed; after which, they dug a Hole in the Earth, and bury'd the Ashes" (Cockburn 1735, 166, 183).

Cockburn also witnessed the fury the Indians sometimes still rained upon their missionary guests to signify both their determination to hold on to their own ways and their identification of the Catholic church with Spanish colonial oppression. "During my residence [in *Chiriqui*]," he reported, "came a Company of roving Indians into the Town and plunder'd it of much Riches." After they had "ravaged the Town," they seized the Franciscan priest, scalped him, stuck his body (still alive) on a pole, lit a fire around him, and danced until his body was consumed. Such retribution, they said, "was but a small Revenge for that Torrent of Indian Blood heretofore spilt by the Spaniards" (Cockburn 1735, 236ff.).[42]

If the fate of the hapless Franciscan priest witnessed by Cockburn defined one end of a complex cultural-political spectrum, the more general pattern was the development of a syncretistic popular or folk Catholicism that incorporated more or fewer native elements, depending upon an area's proximity to important centers of colonial control (Prien 1985, 283–84; Barnadas in Bethell 1984, 1:528).[43] Such a Catholicism tended to slight the finer points of theology in favor of the sacraments, ritual, and other fanfare that allowed "converts" to appear Catholic while preserving as much as possible of native religion and dramatizing their own sense of oppression. Thus images of the suffering Christ, Christian martyrs, and of the Virgin Mary proved especially compelling, for example. Although some priests created "paraliturgies" to accommodate the Indians, in the main native worshipers simply took what made sense or was useful to them, what was most easily incorporated into pre-Columbian religious systems, and worried little about the rest. Native dances were incorporated into Christian festivals, native festivals were transformed into Christian ones, native deities were given Christian names, and native idols were presented with offerings on Christian holidays (Dussel 1981, 63; Prien 1985, 283–312). Thus for Nicaraguan Indians living near the volcano of Masaya, the feast of San Jerónimo de Masaya was not fully distinct from earlier rituals honoring the god of the volcano (Comisión de Estudios 1985, 193–96).

If what happened at the level of belief and practice was ambivalent and rather murkily syncretistic, formally and institutionally the process was much clearer: throughout the colonial period the church continued to increase its wealth and solidify its institutional base within Nicaraguan life as a central determinant of subsequent cultural development. By the seventeenth century, both the religious orders and the secular church had amassed substantial money and property — from tithes, bequests, interest on loans, investments, and even from their own *haciendas*. Nunneries also became major economic institutions as they gathered in their converts' dowries and inheritances, bought property, and lent money. Indian labor was also used extensively to build and maintain churches and monasteries (Barnadas in Bethell 1984, 1:531–32; Haring and Lavrin in Greenleaf 1971, 177–81 and 182–94, respectively).

The growth of the church's wealth and power was not unopposed, however. After 1754 members of religious orders were forbidden to interfere in the drawing up of wills, and after 1775 confessors could not receive inheritances (Haring in Greenleaf 1971, 177–81). Although the post-independence United Provinces of Central America constitution of 1824 declared Catholicism the official religion and outlawed other churches, Liberal president Francisco Morazán (who took office six years later) abolished the monasteries of the Franciscan, Mercedarian, and Recollect orders and confiscated their property. Whatever constraints the state placed upon the church, however, Barnadas concludes, the "whole clerical estate intuitively identified its destiny with that of the white minority and allowed itself to be used by the oppressive civil power as an instrument for the 'pacification' of non-whites." Thus "the church was there to serve the colonial state rather than the Indians," for whom the net result was an increase in state-church hegemony and a consequent decline in respect or tolerance for indigenous culture (Dussel 1981, 87; Barnadas in Bethel 1984, 1:39). The Indians had already lost their strongest advocate with the expulsion of the Jesuits in 1767, and by the end of the colonial period the church had lost much of its remaining moral reluctance to decimate Indian culture.

MESTIZAJE AND THE RACE-CLASS SYSTEM. As the conquest receded into the past, survival of indigenous culture (against the church or whatever other antagonists) was less and less an issue, since indigenous people constituted an ever-smaller percentage of the increasingly mixed-blood population.

Although the Indian population slowly recovered from the genocidal conquest itself (it more than doubled between 1684 and 1778), the non-Indian population multiplied by nearly twenty-two times during the same period (from 1,663 to 35,726), and more than 90 percent of the total were *ladinos* (Newson 1987, 329; Romero Vargas 1988, 46–49).[44]

Despite the dramatic rise in the non-Indian and non-Spanish population, not until the seventeenth century was any attempt made to segregate mestizos, mulattoes, and blacks within distinct *barrios*. By the early eighteenth century, what Romero Vargas has called a "pigmentocracy" was well established in Nicaragua. Those non-natives who considered themselves racially pure were careful to mark their power and prestige with one or more of the many honorifics Spaniards had employed since the early days of the conquest.[45] Blázquez de Avila, named canon of the cathedral of León in 1723, was described as the son of parents "nobles and principals, old Christians free of all bad race, both of whose lines have served since the Moors took the plaza of Orán" (Romero Vargas 1988, 182–86). Of Don Francisco de la Vega y Troyano, progenitor of Nicaragua's eminent Vega family, it was said that "parents and grandparents both maternal and paternal and other ancestors have been, were and are old Christians, clean and of clean and pure blood, without any stain of Indians, Moors, *sambenitados* or other reputed sect."[46]

But words could not stay the process of *mestizaje*. From the sixteenth century onward, the *ladinos*, paradoxically protected from forced labor or tribute payment by their forced marginalization, had multiplied rapidly. Nicaraguan Indian villages became more and more *ladino*; by the mid-eighteenth century, only El Viejo, Subtiava, and Masaya were still recognizably Indian (Newson 1987, 131, 284). In Nueva Segovia, the formerly Indian villages of Jelapa, El Jícaro, and Condega were converted into *ladino* villages (Romero Vargas 1988, 299). By the end of the eighteenth century, *ladinos* were the largest population group in Nicaragua. The 1776 census showed a Spanish population of less than 5 percent (3,143 out of 65,509). Only a few more than half of those lived in the old strongholds of León and Granada; most of the rest had dispersed into Rivas, Matagalpa-Chontales, and Las Segovias (Romero Vargas 1988, 188, 285–86).

Rising *ladino* population led quite naturally to the founding of new *barrios ladinos*. San Felipe in León and Santa María de Haro in Granada were founded as early as 1651; Esquivel de San Juan in Nueva Segovia and fifteen others appeared by 1800. By 1685, Metapa — founded as a *ladino* village in the late 1660s — consisted of 40 percent Spanish, 10 percent Indians, and the other half mestizos, mulattoes, and negroes; in 1776, Spanish and Indians each constituted 10 percent, and the other 80 percent were mestizos, mulattoes, and negroes. Similar patterns obtained in Rivas and El Realejo, as well as in León and Granada. Only one out of seven people in León was Spanish, and one out of fourteen in Granada. Vast numbers of the *ladinos* lived in small agricultural communities (called *valles, rancherías, poblaciones,* or even *hatos* [herds or gangs]), frequently outside both civil law and the ministrations of the church (Romero Vargas 1988, 288, 296, 299, 303 [table], 305).[47]

Inevitably, the emerging racial-class-cultural system became laden with ambiguities. Any marriages outside the original Spanish and Indian groups were problematic for the Spanish because they clouded legal and social structures as well as cultural norms and categories, but many occurred nevertheless. Indians complained when they had to work for *ladinos*. Mestizos, who considered themselves superior to the Indians, borrowed terminology from the Spanish to try to stabilize the ever-shifting boundaries, referring to themselves as "clean mestizos" (*mestizos limpios*). One especially fastidious mestizo family proclaimed itself to be "of clean birth, descended on both sides from very honorable Spanish and mestizo parents and grandparents, and linked by legitimate marriages with the principal families" (Romero Vargas 1988, 348–50).

Whatever the social and cultural ambiguities, however, the emerging *ladino* majority proved itself versatile, and fared well, working as small producers or agricultural workers in the countryside, and in the cities as servants, small businessmen, or artisans. In Realejo in 1740, eleven out of thirteen shipwrights were *ladinos*, as were seventeen out of twenty-eight carpenters. Elsewhere, others worked as sculptors, painters, silver workers, musicians, teachers, and tailors.

Social and economic opportunities for *ladinos* increased following the eighteenth-century attacks from pirates and hostile Indians. The Spanish were not disposed to expend the effort to defend the cities themselves, and using Indians as troops cut into tribute payments. But *ladinos* paid no tribute anyway, and there were plenty of them available. Formed into poorly armed and poorly paid infantry who cleared the way for the elite Spanish cavalry, *ladino* units secured the frontier against Indians and the San Juan River against pirates. But the Spanish, fearful of insubordination and rebellious plots among *ladino* troops, confined *ladino* officers to the lower ranks. To make an example of the insubordinate mulatto captain Antonio Padilla of León in 1741, Padilla was taken out of jail, tied to a post, and flogged to death, and his cadaver was hung in the main plaza. One hand was later nailed to the door of his house, and his head put on a post at the main crossroads. The governor then petitioned the Crown not to name any more non-Spaniards as captains (Romero Vargas 1988, 324–29). Neither petitions nor hands nailed to doorposts could stay the tide, however; Nicaragua was already, and would ever afterward be, overwhelmingly *ladino*.

AGROEXPORT ECONOMY. Among the most basic determinants of Nicaragua's cultural development from the conquest onward was the elaboration of an agroexport economy built around a few crops. Some ancient indigenous crops such as indigo, tobacco, cacao, and cotton were converted into export crops after the conquest; other export crops such as sugar and coffee were introduced by Europeans. Export-scale production of some crops (such as indigo) lasted a relatively short time; others (such as coffee), once established, became permanent fixtures on the physical and cultural landscape.

Although agroexport production was important throughout Central America, local conditions shaped it in special ways in Nicaragua. Because the population at contact was relatively sparse and minable minerals were not abundant, profits from the slave trade, mining, and Indian tribute were both modest and soon exploited to their fullest extent. The remaining alternative was agroexport production—an option made doubly attractive by the fact that, even before the conquest and the massive reductions in population, the capacity of the land to produce crops had always been greater than the demands made upon it (Lange et al. 1992, 15).

The Spanish tried first to develop cacao as an agroexport crop, turning the valley of Nicaragua into one of two major cacao-producing areas in Central America. Although profitability proved erratic and labor requirements were high, Rivas had nearly three hundred cacao *haciendas* by the 1750s, and some seven hundred were operating throughout the country as late as 1817. Cacao was still used by farmers to pay for goods in the cities into the 1840s (Newson 1987, 264; Burns 1991, 57; Romero Vargas 1988, 226ff.; Sherman 1979, 240–49).

In some respects indigo proved superior to cacao for profit-making purposes, since it required little capital investment and lower labor inputs and was compatible with raising cattle, which ate surrounding weeds but not indigo plants (Sherman 1979, 251–55).[48] Indigo was being grown near Granada by 1583, when it was named Nicaragua's major product, and near Realejo by 1599. León had twenty-five major producing centers by 1723. Indigo created many fortunes before gradually declining as a result of the Crown's restrictions upon the use of native labor in its production, the advent of crop-destroying locusts, conflicts between growers and merchants, competition from producers in Venezuela and elsewhere, and eventual replacement by much cheaper artificial dyes (Newson 1987, 132–43, 261–63; Woodward [1976] 1985, 45–46, 70–71; Romero Vargas 1988, 224, 233).

Some of the impacts of agroexport production upon indigenous people were mitigated by the passing of time. Population rose again after its initial genocidal decline, for example. Some indigenous cultural practices were maintained despite the social transformations incident upon the move to agroexport production, and others survived in creatively syncretistic forms.

But the expropriation of Indian lands and the myriad associated cultural losses and dislocations—a central feature of agroexport conversion—were permanent.

Within the land tenure system that developed after the conquest, indigenous lands consisted of both the municipal lands (*ejidos*) and the common lands (*tierras del común*)—the former contiguous with the community and the latter scattered around it. According to indigenous custom and practice, both were absolutely inalienable: no one could give, sell, or mortgage them to anyone for any purpose. Some portions were used by individuals for subsistence, some were kept in a forest reserve, and others were grazed by the cattle of the *cofradías*. By careful management of such resources, Indian communities were able to accumulate considerable wealth they could use to perpetuate aspects of their culture—even while conveying the impression of passive acculturation. Mainly through the systematic contribution of community labor channeled principally into cattle raising, indigenous communities sometimes were able to build substantial treasuries (*cajas de comunidad*).[49] They were administered by the Indians under Spanish supervision, accounts were carefully kept, and the *cofradías* prospered. By 1782, the five *cofradía* herds of Lóvago totaled about three thousand head.

Although the *cofradías* and their funds were putatively placed in the service of Spanish-Catholic institutions and ideology, at a deeper level they could be and often were evidence of the survival of aspects of indigenous culture—a survival, as Romero Vargas puts it, of "ancient practices in the shadow of the Catholic saints." In 1662, for example, a colonial *visitador* complained that the Indians were using such funds to prepare huge meals, get drunk, dance, and "recall the memory of their antiquity."

Cofradía funds generated from indigenous common lands were supposed to be used only to pay salaries of public officials and for specified liturgical purposes, but as time passed both church and civil officials found ways to tap them for other purposes, and plausible rationales for doing so. For eighty years (1719–99), Indians of Chinandega fought the Briceño family, which had established a sugar plantation on Indian lands; León's Indians had to fight local cattle-raising elites who usurped theirs. The Spanish saw the Indians' manner of managing and using their lands as lax and unproductive; by their logic, such lands could and should be expropriated and put to "more productive use" by growing money crops.

The Spanish took possession of Indian lands in many ways, the most common of which was simple usurpation. Less often, they purchased them from the Indians, but a legal device more frequently employed than outright purchase was to make a *denuncia* that declared them uninhabited and uncultivated, and then pay a fee (*composición*) to take them over (Newson 1987,

133). Plot after plot (many of them very large) passed into non-Indian hands; between 1700 and 1767 alone, 202 titles were granted. The Managua area had nearly 290 cattle *haciendas*, and some in the Acoyapa area had as many as 5,000 head of cattle (Romero Vargas 1988, 224–36).

In their varying ways, all of the agroexport industries and economies had profound impacts upon culture. They reorganized native land, labor, and community, and hence virtually every element of indigenous, local, or vernacular culture, both within and beyond the production areas themselves. As Newson observes, the process resulted in the "increasing control of Indian lands and labor by non-Indians," the transformation of Indians into wage laborers, the disintegration of Indian communities and culture, and the lack of sufficient lands to support a (paradoxically) increasing Indian population (Newson 1987, 284–88, 325).[50] To the agroexport-based elite, agroexport provided the wherewithal to model themselves upon more esteemed foreign cultural paradigms, and to enforce their demand that their lower-class and back-country subordinates follow suit. Until independence, those paradigms came principally from Spain; from then until the end of the nineteenth century, they were borrowed from western Europe (especially France for the west coast and England for the east); thereafter, the United States was the primary supplier (as we shall see in later chapters).

WOMEN AND THE GENDER ORDER

Pre-conquest Nicaragua was by no means a paradise for women. Oviedo reported the local indigenous custom of sending virgin girls to the coast to earn their dowries for marriage by working for a time in public houses of prostitution watched over by older women (Oviedo [1547] 1855, 37, 67, 306, 447). On the other hand, the cynicism and abuse of such commercial arrangements was to some degree balanced by certain rituals that acknowledged the power and freedom of women. During one particular festival among the Nicarao, a woman was free to have sexual relations with whomever she chose, for pay or not (*con quien se lo paga ó á ellas les plaçen*), without jealousy or retribution from her husband, thus giving evidence of her freedom as both commercial and moral agent. There were also some customary restraints on male sexual behavior: adultery or bigamy could cause a man to lose his inheritance or be exiled. Adulterers could also be flogged and required to pay compensation to the woman's husband (Oviedo [1547] 1855, 448; Newson 1987, 59–60).

With respect to the larger gender order, there were marked variations among the several pre-conquest cultural groups.[51] In some (such as the

Chorotega), women were dominant; in others (such as the Nicarao), men were. Marital paradigms included monogamy, polygamy, and polyandry, and the allocation of domestic, agricultural, and artisanal tasks between men and women varied greatly. In much of Pacific Nicaragua, it appears, local trading was under the control of women; only certain men (some officials, virgin boys, men from allied villages, slaves held for sale) were allowed even to enter the markets (Newson 1987, 56–60; Rodríguez 1984, 131–34).[52]

Thus with regard to gender, the most important change that attended the conquest was not the importation of specific rules and practices that had never before existed among the indigenous population, but the establishment of exclusively male-dominant social, economic, political, and cultural paradigms, and the consequent double exploitation of women, who shared with men the pervasive domination by the Spanish, but also suffered a more specific subordination within the post-conquest gender order.

"The arrival of the Spaniards in Central America," Sherman concluded, "had a more varied effect on Indian women than on any other group in native society" (Sherman 1979, 304–27).[53] In some instances, women immediately became commodities as local rulers traded them for favors from the Spanish. The conquerors' subsequent demands for both women's labor and their bodies devastated indigenous families, although women who were especially attractive—or who themselves were of the nobility—sometimes suffered less. Thus life for most women during the early years of Spanish rule was ridden with hardship: high infant mortality, prostitution, venereal disease, and concubinage (which was widespread—especially, Sherman concludes, among the clergy). Vast numbers of women were sold into slavery. The relatively few defenses available to women were themselves pathological: lowered rates of reproduction, neglect and abandonment of children, infanticide, and suicide.

Conditions for indigenous women in Nicaragua were similar to those throughout colonial Central America. For one to three pesos a month, depending upon how attractive they were, women were rented to sailors journeying to Peru. Enraged because a Nicaraguan Indian woman had tried to defend herself when he tried to rape her, one Spaniard set fire to her hut and burned her alive—an offense for which he was fined five pesos.[54]

Direct physical and sexual abuse of women by Spaniards was paralleled by their instrumental use. Spanish women took young Indian mothers into their homes as wet nurses. Other Indian women had to bake bread or spin and weave. Encomenderos urged indigenous women to marry young in order to raise birth rates (hence the labor force). Many were used as porters (*tamemes*), carrying large loads of maize or other goods on their backs, in addition to their young children. While it was extremely rare for an Indian to marry

su hija su f y suma
de los pobres y ñs

soberbia y la sncia   q los

Indian parents defending their daughter
from sexual abuse at the hands of Spanish
officials. (From Guamán Poma de Ayala,
Nueva crónica y buen gobierno, 1987)

a Spanish woman, lower-class Spaniards sought to enhance their social and economic position by marrying the dowried daughters of *caciques* (Sherman 1979, 317).

Although the Laws of Burgos (1512–13) extended some minor protections to women (requiring rest for pregnant women, for example), and some colonial officials were disciplined for mistreating them (such as the governor of Nicaragua, who in 1541 was scolded for renting out women for sexual purposes), the pervasive paradigm of subjugation put in place by the conquest proved remarkably durable. It persisted and elaborated itself throughout the colonial period and remained as a key determinant of Nicaragua's cultural development thereafter.[55]

SEPARATE DEVELOPMENT OF THE ATLANTIC COAST

What is known about Nicaragua's Atlantic coast area prior to the conquest is quite scanty, but the little that is known suggests that the cultural-political problems the twentieth-century Sandinista government encountered in dealing with the area have very deep roots indeed. Although the area appears to have had a noticeable population increase between about 300 B.C.

and A.D. 500, perhaps resulting from the late adoption of maize agriculture, and to have developed a "ranked, hierarchical social structure," it apparently traded little with other regions except for northwest Costa Rica. At least up to about A.D. 1200, there was little trade between eastern and western Nicaragua (Lange and Stone 1984, 179, 195–232).

During the half-millennium prior to conquest, the history of the east coast was marked by warfare among a half-dozen more or less distinct groups (Newson 1982, 33). The Sumu, one of the largest groups, were split into perhaps five linguistic subgroups and may have extended as far as the western shore of Lake Nicaragua. The Rama were centered in the vicinity of Bluefields and Punta Gorda. East coast settlements were probably smaller than those in the west, more strung out along the river valleys, lacking comparable temples and marketplaces, and more egalitarian socially and economically than settlements on the Pacific coast (Newson 1982, 34–37, 64; Lange et al. 1992, 266).

The Spanish conquest hardly touched the Atlantic coast of Nicaragua. Columbus passed by (and named) Cape Gracias a Dios (near the northeastern boundary of present-day Nicaragua) on his fourth and last voyage in 1502, but not until 1539 did a Spanish expedition succeed in navigating the San Juan river (then called the *desaguadero*, or drain) from Lake Nicaragua to its mouth. By the end of the century, the river was regularly used as a passage between the lake and Panama (although perilous rapids slowed traffic), and Granada's inland position protected it from coastal buccaneering raids and allowed it to grow into a thriving port (Dozier 1985, 6–10).

Details of the post-conquest cultural transformation of Atlantic coast Indians are scarce until the early seventeenth century. The tributary system created demands for new crops and livestock production, but bringing a few of the semi-nomadic Indians into religious *reducciones* had little widespread or durable effect, and the mining industry to the east of the lakes — which wanted no more colonists — acted as a barrier against further Spanish pressure from the west (Newson 1982, 64, 193–98). Although the Spanish endeavored to control and protect the river passage into Lake Nicaragua, they confined their serious colonization efforts to the opposite coast. Bit by bit, therefore, dominance on the Atlantic coast passed to the British.

Following an early landing at Cape Gracias a Dios in 1633, the British moved slowly south to the Río Escondido, where the Dutch buccaneer Abraham Blauvelt had established a foothold (later named Bluefields by the British). Early buccaneer accounts describe small groups of "waterside people" in villages of open thatched huts scattered along the coast, fishing for the abundant green turtles and practicing swidden agriculture (bananas, cas-

Shelling turtles on Atlantic Coast. (From a review of Samuel A. Bard [pseud. for E. George Squier], *Waikna: Adventures on the Mosquito Shore*, in *Harper's New Monthly Magazine*, 1855)

sava, coconuts, sugar cane, and other crops), living in relative social equality and without formal political structure (Nietschmann 1973, 26–34; Vilas 1989, 17; Helms 1971, 15).

The British proved less interested in Spanish-style conquering and colonizing than in gaining the acquiescence of the indigenous inhabitants to the removal of immensely valuable natural resources and establishing a lucrative trade with them.

Proceeding to cut mahogany and dye woods, to trade for skins, turtle meat, gums, roots, and rubber, and to grow sugar cane with slave labor, the British established friendly relations with the Indians, trading rum, firearms, and other valued goods for their services as guides and soldiers. Even after the British presence increased dramatically, cultural change came more slowly than on the Spanish-controlled west coast. Because proportionally less Indian land was alienated, and black slaves rather than Indians were used as workers on the plantations, the British made no systematic attempt to convert Indians to Christianity; local customs therefore had a better chance of surviving (Newson 1982, 201–6).

British trading activities with indigenous coastal groups led to military alliances, and by 1645 the British and their Indian allies were able to mount an assault up the Escondido against Matagalpa. Twenty years later, British pirates attacked Granada, ending its heyday of development as a protected port. By the end of the seventeenth century, the British had formalized their alliances with coastal groups by installing a Miskito "king." Decked out in silk hats, red coats, shirts, and broadswords, later Miskito kings were attended by British-appointed "governors," "generals," and "admirals." By 1739 Great Britain was confident enough of its control to appoint its first superintendent of the Mosquito coast (Dozier 1985, 15–17; Incer 1990, 363–64). Having never before been united, either socially or politically, the Atlantic coast Indians (principally the Miskitos) were thus at least formally welded into a "nation."

Bolstered by the "crafted regalia of kingship," the Miskitos "acquired symbols of ethnic identification and of cultural and political superiority" in comparison both to other coastal groups and to those living in the interior (Helms 1989, 3).

Supplied with British firearms, the Miskitos expanded their territorial control rapidly, drove other coastal Indian groups inland, and came to dominate most of the coastal region as well as to support raids on the interior. Spain's construction of a fort at the rapids on the San Juan River made attacks from the east more difficult, but the British continued to incite the Indians against Spain's inland settlements (Dozier 1985, 12–16; Nietschmann 1973, 30; Vilas 1989, 18, 31–32). East coast Indians under British command repeatedly attacked inland towns during the late eighteenth century. Attacking Boaco with both bows and arrows and firearms, Indians sacked the church, stole sacred vessels, tore vestments from sacred images and hurled the images to the floor, and shot the priest at point-blank range (Incer 1990, 364–75). Further to the south, British attacks up the San Juan River were complicated both by Spanish fortifications and by malaria, dysentery, and other tropical maladies. Even after the British managed to take Spain's Fort Inmaculada Concepción on the river in 1780, they had to abandon the effort to control the river after Indian troops deserted and their own were decimated by dysentery (Incer 1990, 367; Dozier 1985, 18–25; cf. Kemble 1884–85, 203–36).

Thus despite its nearly total control of western Nicaragua, Spain proved able to exercise little influence over the Atlantic coast. The waning years of the eighteenth century saw Catholic Spain embroiled in a series of shifting alliances and conflicts with Protestant northern European countries, and hence less able to oversee and protect its Latin American colonies. A brief crackdown following Ferdinand VII's return to the Spanish throne at the conclusion of the Napoleonic wars availed little in Central America, even with the assistance of the authoritarian captain general of Guatemala, José Bustamente. The Treaty of Versailles (1783) ended English-Spanish hostility, and the Mosquito Convention of 1786 required the British to evacuate the Mosquito coast. Following the removal of British colonists (mostly to Belize), the Spanish tried to take over the evacuated garrisons and colonies, but their efforts were ineffectual, and by the end of the century they had ceased (Dozier 1985, 27–29; Newson 1982, 256; cf. Naylor 1989, 39–73).

CULTURAL REMNANTS

The three hundred years of intense pressure and change that followed the Spanish conquest of Nicaragua and the later British domination of its Atlantic coast entailed nearly unimaginable cultural destruction and transformation as well as adaptive syncretism. Through the entire saga, however, some elements of indigenous culture hung on stubbornly. In the mid-seventeenth century English traveler Thomas Gage witnessed Indian musicians in a church procession playing instruments they had played long before the Spanish came: conch shell trumpets, wooden and pottery drums, rattles, and ceramic flutes (Gage [1648] 1958, 131, 242–46). A six-week stay in Nicoya nearly a century later left traveler John Cockburn marveling at the vitality and health of Indian culture. "No Place affords a more delightful Prospect," he said,

> or is kept in greater Order and Neatness. The Indians suffer nothing to grow near it, except Fruit-Trees, for fear of harboring Vermine. . . . As to the People, they are of so quiet and peaceable a Disposition, and so free from Noise and Tumult. . . . I never heard any of them quarrel, or so much as dispute with one another, but every one seemed calm and easy, and much inclined to adhere to each other's Advice. They would often come out on Moon-light Nights, and divert themselves by singing and dancing to their Wind Musick, which is soft, and not unpleasant. They would frequently ask us to sing and dance with them, which we sometimes did after our Manner, to humour them, and they would laugh heartily at us, and seem very desirous to know the Words as they were uttered in the Songs. (Cockburn 1735, 122, 159–64)

On another occasion Cockburn heard Indians still playing some of their ancient instruments at a festival part of whose "Revelling and Merriment" consisted of riding rapidly on horseback beneath a chicken suspended head-down between two trees, and trying to snatch off the chicken's head. Since horses were introduced by the Spanish, it seems safe to assume that the game was not an indigenous one. At the same time, however, Cockburn found the Indians still sleeping in the grass hammocks they had always slept in and still making pottery that Cockburn said was "finer than any China I ever saw" (Cockburn 1735, 71–82; cf. Newson 1987, 295). Later Cockburn met Indians who he said "still retain their ancient freedom, and continue at mortal Enmity with the Spaniards" (Cockburn 1735, 179).[56]

Hence in a variety of configurations and to many different degrees, elements of Indian culture survived despite the cataclysmic losses of the conquest and the colonial period. In masked and acculturated forms, in complex syncretisms, in islands of calm and uncompromising defiance, Nicaragua's remaining indigenous people had held onto at least some of what was theirs, and had worked to solidify their position in the larger social and cultural order. By the time the Spanish finally lost power in the 1820s, however, it was clear that the future of Nicaragua belonged not to the few remnants of its indigenous people, but to the *ladinos* and the modernizing elites. As we shall see in the next chapter, the entrepreneurial adventurers who flocked to Nicaragua in the days just prior to and just after independence found that future tantalizing indeed.

CHAPTER 2 RASCALLY SIGNS IN SACRED PLACES

THE POLITICS OF CULTURAL CHANGE IN THE NINE-
TEENTH CENTURY

It is decided as clearly as fate that the Americans, or the white race are to govern the destiny of this Central American country. . . . In fact, were it populated with a different race, [Nicaragua] would be *one of the garden-spots of the world.* — Flavel Belcher to Joseph Belcher, 30 June 1856 from San Juan del Sur, Nicaragua (Flavel Belcher Letters [C-B 524], The Bancroft Library, University of California, Berkeley)

People who are from big countries, like children from rich families, believe that the collective superiority of their country or the riches acquired by their fathers is a merit intrinsic to those nationals or to those children, and look disapprovingly at those who belong to small countries or poor families. — Salvador Mendieta (1934)

Orlando Roberts, who came to Bluefields on the Mosquito coast in 1817, found a relatively tranquil scene. The only planter on the coast was a Frenchman who was growing cotton, coffee, and sugar cane. The articles most in demand in the three small stores (two run by Jamaicans and one by a North American) hinted at the turmoil to come, however: machetes and cutlasses, axes and saws, locks, hinges and nails, rum, gunpowder and muskets. Still-sleepy Bluefields, Roberts thought, would sooner or later "become a place of very considerable importance." Granada seemed to "afford great facilities for making it the depot for the greatest commerce in South America, or perhaps in the world" (Roberts 1827, 33, 104–9, 233, 300; cf. Incer 1990, 513–41).

Nearly ten years later, John Hale—another traveler who came to establish a colony of Englishmen and North Americans—predicted that although Lake Nicaragua was still navigated regularly only by one schooner, Nicaragua

Meeting of travelers in Nicaragua in the mid-nineteenth century. (From Boyle, *A Ride across a Continent*, 1868)

would "shortly become the emporium of vast and extensive commerce. . . . Nothing more is requisite, than for good and industrious colonists, to bring [its] immense resources into active operation." Nicaragua's "simple and courteous people," he said, "[look] towards the United States as a glorious example" (Hale 1826, 29–32).

But such expectations of unproblematic and beneficial growth and change were too sanguine. As the foregoing chapter explained, Nicaragua was in the first place saddled with a set of essentially regressive colonial structures. It was also, mainly because of its strategic location, poised for renewed interventions by major powers. Thus early post-independence surmises about how attractive to entrepreneurs Nicaragua would soon become were prescient, but the results for Nicaraguan people themselves were not as salutary as many early observers predicted they would be.

Nicaragua's cultural history from independence to the end of the Zelaya administration in 1909 (a better marker than the end of the century) exhibited a number of salient patterns: (1) the gradual convergence of León and Granada's historically opposed elites around a Liberal-Positivist developmental agenda that spelled disaster for Indian people and their culture; (2) the early phases of economic, political, and cultural intervention by the United States, most dramatically evident in the transit-route turmoil and the William Walker filibuster war of the 1850s; (3) resistance by non-elite groups to elite programs for change; (4) a dialectic between the consolidation of elite cultural dominance and a drive for national cultural (as well as economic and political) independence during the Zelaya administration (1893–1909); and (5) a continuation of the post-conquest separate development of the Atlantic coast. This chapter offers both a schematic discussion of these patterns and processes, and more detailed analysis of some personalities and episodes that highlight their specifically cultural features and implications.

ELITE CONVERGENCE AND COLLABORATION

Although the historic rivalry between the elites of León and Granada continued through the early post-independence years (and in some respects far beyond), the two groups gradually converged around a Liberal-Positivist agenda for national development that served their own economic, political, and cultural interests far better than those of any of the non-elites.

During the years just before and after independence, the León-Granada rivalry was still intense. As innovative producers and exporters were encouraged by eighteenth-century prosperity, León Liberals had grown in power and influence, and the rivalry was not attenuated by the struggle for independence (Booth 1985, 11–14; Burns 1991, 7, 15–17, 104).[1] These rivalries were further complicated by the class-race stratification (outlined in the foregoing chapter) that was fundamental to Nicaragua's cultural organization. Thus the principal trade in Granada, Orlando Roberts reported shortly after independence, "was entirely in the hands of a few old Spaniards, . . . and their transactions were managed with such secrecy, as to preclude all chance of competition—the native Creoles seldom or never receiving any notice of an arrival, until they saw the goods going into the warehouses, which, in appearance, almost resemble prisons, but are well stocked with the most valuable productions of the country" (Roberts 1827, 233–35).

The stresses and contradictions notwithstanding, life was comfortable for the elites of both cities. León's elite lived in large whitewashed houses entered through ornamental gates that opened on porticoed courtyards ornamented with trees, shrubs, and flowers, and frequently graced by a fountain. Rooms were lofty and appointed with the work of skilled local cabinetmakers. A large cathedral dominated the central plaza, and clean pebbled footpaths covered by overhanging roofs bordered the streets (Roberts 1827, 224–25). Thirty years later, the same contradictions were in evidence in Granada. "The Spanish Creoles," Carl Scherzer reported when he passed through in 1857, "still retain all the advantages of wealth and political influence, and they exhibit a decided mental superiority over the other races, however corrupt and degraded in other respects. . . . Almost all official persons, are Creoles . . . or, at least, endeavour to pass for such, and carefully conceal the smallest mixture

Street view of León, ca. 1850. (From Squier, *Nicaragua: Its People, Scenery, Monuments, and the Proposed Canal*, 1852)

of Indian blood that may have polluted the pure Castilian fluid" (Scherzer 1857, 61).

Although the historic Liberal-Conservative struggle between León and Granada was a real conflict with high stakes and with its own internal race-linked factions, the two groups were in fact merely two factions of a relatively homogeneous landholding and bureaucratic elite—Roman Catholic, readers of Enlightenment authors, mostly university-educated, mostly residents of León or Granada and married into each others' families. A major feature of their formal agenda was to transform Nicaragua into a modern European-style state; the motivating subtext of that agenda was to continue to enjoy the benefits they both had always enjoyed, even through decades of internecine warfare (Burns 1991, 231).

Unfortunately, the elites' shared Positivist agenda (of order, progress, reason, modernization) proved culturally devastating for the majority of the country's remaining indigenous people.[2] Nicaraguan Liberals and Conservatives alike "thought they heard the roar of barbarism from the country-side before the gates of their cities," and therefore "assumed the duty to introduce

Granada from the West, 1854. (From Squier, *The States of Central America*, 1858)

civilization" to their compatriots. Liberal tactics for doing so differed somewhat from Conservative ones, but the overall strategy was shared (Burns 1991,
21–27, 101–6).[3] The mid-century choice of Managua as a compromise capital
midway between León and Granada was thus a fitting symbol of the elites'
consensual agreement to move beyond the old Liberal-Conservative conflict
in pursuit of their shared interests.

The Positivist, modernizing ideology which guided that movement led the
elites to depreciate local (especially indigenous) culture in favor of the culture
of more materially advanced nations: by promoting immigration, by emu-
lating European architecture and urban design, by affecting European styles
of dress and domestic decoration (Parisian fashions, English textiles), and by
sending sons to Europe to be educated. Traveling through Nicaragua in the
late 1850s, Carl Scherzer reported, "Among the opulent inhabitants of Granada the French fashions have also of late years replaced the simple national
costume, though not so entirely with the women as with the men" (Scherzer
1857, 61). By 1867 there were two small schools of music in Masaya, and
touring *zarzuela* companies were performing in cities and towns (Cardenal
Argüello 1962).

The elites' reformist cultural paradigm made special targets of indigenous ("barbarous") people whose own cultural preferences were ignored and
whose passive resistance to economic exploitation was read as "laziness" issuing from a lack of "the respect for wealth that characterizes civilization . . .

[or] noble aspiration to improve their lot." The preferred remedy was to Europeanize the Indians by educating them. Thus Nicaragua's first public education law (1836) required instruction in the "three Rs" and Christian doctrine—designed principally to produce patriotic citizens and docile workers unlikely to challenge elite prerogatives or control (Burns 1980, 35–49, 95; Burns 1991, 139–42).

Measures designed to acculturate and pacify indigenous people gained new force from the constitution of 1858 and from president (1859–67) Tomás Martínez's drive to stimulate agroexport production—including coffee, the major boom in which was still a few years away. If agroexport production was to increase, Nicaragua's perennial labor shortage had to be remedied by increasing the supply of Indian labor, and desirable land—much of which remained under Indian control despite massive expropriations during the colonial era—had to be made available to coffee growers.

The Nicaraguan constitutions of 1826 and 1832 had guaranteed the right of indigenous people to hold lands in common, but after the passage of the first law to encourage coffee growing in 1832, those guarantees came under increasing attack. The first land expropriations began as early as 1838, and the first coffee plantations began to appear in the mid-1840s. Two laws of 1852 required all lands to be surveyed, and the next year the government announced its intention to sell "vacant" land and adjust communal holdings. Sales of Indian lands reached their height during the presidencies of Pedro Joaquín Chamorro in the mid-1870s (following the agrarian law of 1877) and of Roberto Sacasa in the early 1890s.[4] Debt peonage, vagrancy laws, and prohibitions against growing basic subsistence crops also helped force indigenous people into wage labor on the plantations (Wheelock [1975] 1980, 17–20, 28–31, 88–89; Wheelock [1974] 1981, 109–18; Burns 1991, 138). Such measures also had the secondary effect of further dispersing the native population as campesinos fled to the mountains, to the Atlantic coast, and to the cities.

The elites' reorganization of land and labor was bolstered by other provisions of the constitution of 1858 (which did not even mention communal lands). It provided for a stronger national president, further restricted rights to vote and hold office, and gave the national government greater powers to put down civil disturbances—all measures detrimental to the interests of the indigenous population (Burns 1991, 132–33, 222–32).

Clearly, the elites had much to gain both from such direct measures and from other putatively progressive policies of the Martínez government (such as direct elections and increased public education): they could displace the Indian populations and force them into the labor market, take over their lands, remove Indian communities as an alternative focus of loyalty, and push the Indians into schools designed to acculturate them. Thus in exchange for a few abstract "freedoms" that were functionally useless or irrelevant, Indians saw their entire economic, social, and cultural organization dismantled and decimated. At least symbolically, the "coffee road to riches" along which President Martínez guided Nicaragua was lined with the corpses of both individual Indians and of their communities, just as corpses had lined the roads to the mines in the post-conquest era (Burns 1991, 233–35).

The impact upon the Indian population of the alienation of their land and wealth was starkly evident to travelers in the gold-bearing lands of the Chontales area (in the central highlands east of Lake Nicaragua). The lands had passed into the hands of English capitalists from down-on-his-luck creole owner Luis Quiroz, who—unable to find promising veins or development capital—was running a bar to survive. Hearing of his woes, as Royal Navy Captain Bedford Pim later told the story, a local Indian promised (in exchange for three cows) to take Quiroz to a place where he could find "enough [gold] to last . . . a lifetime." The area to which the Indian led him was the site of what later became the fabulous Javali mine, developed aggressively by English investors. "You still see pure Indians in the Chontales Mountains," Captain Pim reported in the late 1860s, "but they are not numerous, and are retiring into the solitude of the forest as fast as the white men . . . approach." Among the "several pure Indians" who came to a "nocturnal fête" at one mining town, Pim said, was "the son of the one who had shown the Javali for three cows, and who was then working in the mine" (Pim 1869, 84, 107, 125, 203–4).

Some of the costs and contradictions of the social, economic, and cultural transformation were starkly evident to British naturalist and mining engineer Thomas Belt, who came ashore at Greytown on Nicaragua's Atlantic coast in 1868 and worked for four years as an engineer for a Chontales gold mine. Belt found Nicaragua's Indians "industrious by nature . . . taciturn, stolid, dignified, [and] moderate." Signs that their culture was still alive were abundant: cock-fighting at Acoyapo; the weaving of palm-leaf hats, the making of music with whistle and drum, and the drinking of *chiche* in Tatagalpa; the grinding of maize in Jinotega (Belt [1874] 1985, 49, 278, 293).

But the traumatic impact of elite development strategies was also evident during a night Belt spent with three "miserably poor" Indian families in a twenty-foot-square hut near Ocotal. There was no furniture except cots made of hides stretched over poles, the dirt floor was littered with corn husks, a clay stove served for cooking, and the residents were dull and listless. Belt asked the man of the house why anyone would prefer to live in the mountains under such conditions, rather than on the more cultivable slopes near Jinotega, and seemed persuaded by his reply that the air was fresher and there was less fever.

Buttoning his coat against the wind that was whistling through the house,

Chontales gold mine, ca. 1870. (From Belt, *The Naturalist in Nicaragua*, 1874)

Belt then lay down in his hammock to puzzle through the tension between striving for physical comfort and economic advancement on the one hand, and honoring the claims of custom and tradition on the other. "[They] have been born and bred where they live," he mused, "and knowing how strong is the force of custom and how attached the Indians are to their homes, I do not wonder that they stay from generation to generation in this bleak range. I can imagine that if removed to the low lands they would sigh for their mountain home, to smell the fragrance of the pine trees, and to hear once more the wind whistling through their branches" (Belt [1874] 1985, 244).

The "rude portions of stone statues" near Acoyapo and Juigalpa, the Indian burial places near Esquipula on the River Mico, and the pottery shards everywhere spoke to Belt of the destruction of a vital culture. Indians of the pre-Columbian era, he said, "bestowed equal pains and labour on their work, undeterred by the hardness of the materials or the rudeness of their tools. When we turn from these works and remains of a great and united tribe to the miserable huts of the present natives, we feel how great a curse the Spanish invasion has in some respects been to Central America. . . . [The] fashioners of these statues . . . stood by each other . . . tilled the ground and lived on the fruits of it." To Belt, the Indians' stubborn preference for their ancient town names over Spanish ones suggested that they had survived by conscious choice and persistent effort. "Those communities are the happiest and best governed," Belt judged, "who retain most of their old customs and habits. The civilisation that Cortez overthrew was more suitable for the Indians than that which has replaced it. . . . [The] conquest . . . was a deplorable calamity. [Pre-Columbian] civilisation . . . was unique . . . [and] its learning, magnificence, and glory have gone forever" ([1874] 1985, 52, 165–71, 282, 293–94).

As an agent of contemporary modernizing forces, Belt ascribed guilt for such lamentable and irremediable destruction to the *conquistadores* and their colonial era successors, rather than to those actors whose impact was in fact greatest at mid-century: Nicaragua's converging elites and a new set of post-independence foreign intervenors confident that their moral and cultural superiority qualified them to direct Nicaragua's affairs. Chief among the latter was the United States.

NORTH AMERICAN DECADE: 1849–1858

During the twenty years between Nicaragua's final independence as a completely separate state in 1838 and the constitution of 1858, Burns has noted, governing elites were "heavily influenced by the North Atlantic experience and quite divorced from the local experience of the folk majority" (Burns 1991, 25).[5] That orientation played directly into the hands of North American politicians and entrepreneurs (two complexly and increasingly overlapping groups). It took twenty years of turbulent transit-route traffic and the William Walker filibuster war for local elites to reevaluate their expectations of wholly beneficent outcomes from welcoming entrepreneurial northern emissaries into their midst.

In April 1847, the U.S. Congress let the first contract to transport mail to the Atlantic coast of Nicaragua by steamship, and a few months later the first steamship actually reached Nicaraguan waters (Burns 1991, 165). The discovery of gold in California in 1848 galvanized entrepreneurs who saw quick profits to be gained from transporting fortune-hunters up the San Juan River and across Lake Nicaragua rather than around Cape Horn. The torrent of transit passengers who crossed Nicaragua (and the storekeepers and others who flocked in to minister to their needs) brought their money (not much of which ended up in the hands of local working people) as well as their culture (food, styles of dress, commercial products, music, religion, political ideas, virtues, and vices), much of which had a lasting impact upon local ways. Thus whatever else it was, the transit traffic functioned as a powerful cultural intervention.

In March 1849, the first organized group of Americans passed through the Nicaraguan transit route on the way to California (Burns 1991, 170). William G. Doolittle, who had left New York on the brig *Mary Ann* in February, had to help fellow passengers bolt a small two-section boat together for getting beyond the rapids in the river. Thirty years later, Doolittle still recalled that he and his fellow travelers were "nearly on the brink of starvation" when provisions ran out, and had to scavenge in the sand for turtle eggs and make chowder from a shark they caught.[6] As much as three years later, passengers still had to pack their own provisions, tolerate long delays during bad weather, and risk catching tropical diseases. Eri Hulbert and William Walker (no relation to the filibuster) set out together to make the crossing in the spring of 1852, but only Walker made it. After paying fourteen dollars a night to sleep on the floor at the American Hotel in Virgin Bay, and eating "rice, oranges, poor bread, and slop for coffee" while they were delayed for thirty-two days by rain, Hulbert died of a tropical fever. "The amount of suffering and death was horrable [sic]," Walker told Hulbert's wife when he wrote to her that her husband had been buried in "the American burying ground" in Nicaragua.[7]

The transit route was mainly a private entrepreneurial venture that the United States facilitated and supported diplomatically, but the U.S. government was also interested in building and controlling a permanent canal, and in order to do so had to study possible routes.[8] In mid-1849, President Zachary Taylor dispatched twenty-eight-year-old engineer E. George Squier as U.S. chargé d'affaires to Central America, with instructions to negotiate another canal treaty with Nicaragua better than the one recently negotiated by the previous Polk administration. The record Squier left of his reconnoitering highlighted many aspects of the coming cultural interaction between Nicaragua and those who came adventuring—whether individual entrepreneurs or powerful nation-states.[9]

Traditional lifeways were still much in evidence in the mid-century Nicaragua Squier passed through. Women were still spinning cotton on small wheels in Granada, and on a more primitive spinning apparatus in the indigenous community of Subtiava. The people of Masaya made mats, palm-leaf hats, and hammocks "celebrated throughout all Central America." The artist who traveled with Squier sketched calabash drinking vessels and carved *jícaro* shells, and Squier reported cock-fighting, bull-baiting, and rope-dancers at a circus (Squier 1852, 1:138, 212, 285–88, 330–36). He was charmed by the "evening chaunt" of the bowman on a San Juan River flatboat. The chorus, he said, "was taken up by the entire crew, with a precision . . . which could only result from long practice." But if the boatmen's song may have been a surviving indigenous cultural form, Nicaraguan culture was also already strongly marked by the syncretistic processes of a history of which the mid-century turmoil was but the latest phase. Clarinets and Spanish guitars, German polkas and waltzes, and soldiers playing violins vied with the native music of an Indian dance Squier saw in León (Squier 1852, 1:96, 123, 178, 270–71, 334).

Within the mixture, the North American cultural presence was already

The American Hotel on the Nicaraguan transit route. (From *Frank Leslie's Illustrated Newspaper*, 16 August 1856)

strong. Gordon's Passenger Line of New York had already been operating on the San Juan for a year by the time Squier arrived, and North Americans had built hotels in Granada and Realejo (Bermann 1986, 25–26; Folkman 1972, 8–9). Passing up the river just after he entered the country at San Juan del Norte (still a small village of reed huts except for the large board custom house at the center where British officials lived), Squier glanced into a hut on the bank and saw a "very pretty yellow girl" in a hammock ("with one naked leg hanging indolently over the side," he observed somewhat leeringly). Throwing aside her long black curls, she called to him "*Adios, California.*" Days earlier, Squier explained as if rushing to exempt himself from suspicion, a party of Californians had passed, and "had evidently been on familiar terms with the *señora.*"[10]

For the most part, Squier approved of the advent of North American culture. In Granada (which he said boasted of "several American hotels and mercantile houses") he enjoyed an evening in the home of *señorita* Teresa — trained in music in the U.S. It was "worth something," he said, to hear the *señorita* skillfully render "passages from familiar operas." And on an estate near Chichigalpa he was pleased to find a parlor furnished in the latest New York style.[11]

But like many other apostles of progress, Squier also had his moments of doubt, of regret, of nostalgia for an arcadian culture he saw changing before his eyes. Passing through the indigenous community of Nindirí near Masaya, he waxed lyrical: "Nindirí! How shall I describe thee, beautiful Nindirí, nestling beneath thy fragrant, evergreen roof of tropical trees, entwining their branches above thy smooth avenues, and weaving green domes over the simple dwellings of thy peaceful inhabitants! . . . This little Indian village . . . far surpassed, in point of picturesque beauty, anything we had yet seen." Returning to what proved to be one of his most frequent preoccupations (Nicaraguan women), Squier's eyes fixed upon

> Indian women, naked to the waist, [sitting] beneath the trees spinning snow-white cotton . . . while their noisy, naked little ones tumbled joyously about on the smoothly-beaten ground, where the sunlight fell in flickering, shifting mazes. . . . Quiet primitive Nindirí! seat of the ancient caziques and their barbaric courts, even now, amidst the din of the crowded city, and the crush and conflict of struggling thousands, amidst grasping avarice and importunate penury, bold-fronted hypocrisy and heartless fashion . . . how turns the memory to thee, as to some sweet vision of the night, some dreamy Arcadia, fancy-born, and half unreal! (Squier 1852, 1:214–15)

To the young, patriotic, idealistic Squier, Nicaragua presented a confusing cultural panorama: well-turned operatic phrases in a Granada salon, singing boatmen and flirtatious native maidens, a modish New York–style parlor, half-naked and fecund brown-skinned women spinning virgin cotton in a dreamy tropical Arcadia of lavish fruit trees and gamboling naked children.[12] Arching over all was his image of himself and his compatriots as carriers of cultural and material salvation to a backward country.

Following the Squier expedition, the Nicaraguan transit traffic rose dramatically. Most of the 26,000 transit passengers between 1848 and 1851 went by way of Panama, but by the end of 1851 some 5,000 had opted for the Nicaragua route. Their numbers peaked at about 24,000 per year in 1853–54. By 1858 the turmoil of the William Walker filibuster war effectively closed the route, and after it reopened in 1862 it never attracted more than about 13,000 travelers per year. Although the Panama route was always more popular, more than 150,000 North Americans passed through the Nicaragua route in eighteen years, and their cultural impact upon life along the route was great (Folkman 1972, 163).

Arriving in San Juan del Norte in March 1849, New Yorker Samuel Smith

Wood found wretched accommodations, terrible food, "halfnaked women and naked babies" in the streets, and the river full of sharks. Returning two years later, after finding a rather meager living peddling spittoons and whiskey glasses to California saloons, Wood set himself up as a storekeeper for other Americans passing up the river.[13]

Wood's letters and ledger sheets for the next four years index the flow of foreign manufactured goods into Nicaragua, revealing the efforts of foreigners to take what they considered their cultural necessities with them into the interior of the country, and suggesting the cultural impact of those goods (and habits associated with them) upon the way local people lived and understood themselves. Wood's letters to his wife and his suppliers ask for construction tools to open up the countryside and exploit its resources (steel wedges, axes, iron shovels, monkey wrenches, percussion caps); carpenter's tools to build hotels—or houses for those who meant to stay and stake a claim (hammers and nails, saws and sandpaper, hinges, paint and brushes, steel latches, and stovepipe); food for the trip up the river or for boarding house tables (canned vegetables and meats, sugar and sardines, tea and ground coffee, bread and crackers, jelly and jam); "fancy goods" useful for keeping respectable, striking a pose, or scrambling for position (razors and "sad irons," patent leather boots, linen pants and shirts, fancy combs and silk shoes for ladies); and plenty of ale, wine, and "good Claret" (the last of which Wood ordered fifty boxes at a time).[14]

Wood's fellow storekeepers did a brisk business selling U.S. patent medicines to anxious and dyspeptic city-bred adventurers bound upriver. They regularly hawked Mustang Liniment ("most popular liniment now used in the United States; travelers who are bound for the interior would do well to furnish themselves with a supply") and Dr. John Bull's Sarsaparilla ("for all diseases arising from impure blood"). Jacob's Cordial was a godsend for those suffering simultaneously their first encounter with the tropics and the dementia of gold fever; besides curing "all bowel diseases," it was guaranteed to "dispel gloomy and hysterical feelings" and "counteract nervousness and despondency." Inadvertently baring the secret of the psychic cures promised by its competitors, an ad for Balsam of Wild Cherry and Iceland Moss guaranteed it to be free of opium and morphine.[15]

The impact of such economic-cultural intervention was most dramatic in the Atlantic coast harbor towns, whence it drove up the rivers into the interior as relentlessly as one of Samuel Wood's steel wedges. By 1852, Folkman reports,

> At Point Arenas, across the bay from San Juan del Norte, [Accessory] Transit Company workshops and houses had replaced the rude huts of the

Mosquito Indians. . . . Across the bay the thatched huts which constituted the old village of San Juan del Norte had disappeared and new and more imposing structures had sprung up. The forest had receded on all sides, and streets, regularly laid out, replaced the old narrow paths. Several two-story edifices of pine boards, framed in the United States and brought out in sections, served as hotels for the weary travelers.

Further up the river at Castillo Viejo, "a small city of about two hundred inhabitants and several hotels had sprung up out of the forest. The Castillo Hotel . . . supported a gaudy bar well stocked with fancy decanters of liquor" (Folkman 1972, 50–51).

On the west coast, the social and cultural effects of the transformation were hardly less in evidence. Dr. Jacob D. B. Stillman, who left California late in 1850 in company with a hundred or so burned-out and disappointed miners, found the port of Realejo "filthy and ruinous." Pieces of pavement, foundations of large masonry walls, and the broken arches and dome of a former convent testified to the city's colonial importance, but the best Realejo had to offer was the American Hotel, at which a San Franciscan dished out terrible food at extortionary prices and provided grass hammocks for beds (Stillman 1967, 11–30).[16]

Traveling by horseback from Realejo to Granada, Stillman noted the social, economic, and cultural costs of the transformation through which Nicaragua was passing at mid-century. León he found "ruinous and desolate," its cathedral's walls still pocked by civil war gunshots. At Nagarote, another American-owned guest house offered bad food, worse beds, and outrageous prices. The "brutal conduct of many of my countrymen" in Central America, Stillman lamented, "perpetuates the most indecent outrages upon a people whom they call unenlightened, but who are greatly their superiors in every virtue that gives value to civilization" (Stillman 1967, 31). The contrast that native culture offered to the venality of U.S. enterprise in Nicaragua was most evident to Stillman (as earlier to Squier) in Nindirí, which the foreign merchants whose shops already ringed the square in nearby Masaya had not yet discovered. "Never had my eyes rested upon a more captivating scene," he recalled.

The town was laid out in squares separated by avenues, and subdivided by hedge rows into smaller squares, in the center of each of which was a neat thatched cottage, and around the sides were groves of [fruit] trees. . . . These inclosures are perfectly neat, not a dead leaf is allowed to remain on the ground, and the whole town resembled a neatly kept botanical garden more than the abode of thousands of human beings. . . . [Here] they had

Northward and southward views of King Street, San Juan del Norte, 1854. (From Squier, *The States of Central America*, 1858)

retained all their primitive customs. A stone church, and an inclosure for a bull fight . . . are all that could remind us that the Spaniard had been there. . . . Their domestic utensils are all such as were used before the discovery of the continent. . . . Some of them were wrought with great labor, were highly ornamented, and very ancient, having been handed down from generation to generation. (Stillman 1967, 51–52) [17]

As the century progressed, however, such idyllic islands grew scarcer. The money to be made from hauling passengers across Nicaragua was too enticing for the pressure to let up.

Nearly ten years after the transit route opened, the tension between cultural continuity and disruptive change were starkly evident to traveler Daniel Cleveland, who listened for hours as black workers extemporized verse after verse of their work songs while they pulled on ropes attached to his steamer at Greytown. But the frame houses of foreigners and the transit company along the shore ill-concealed the "rude huts of the natives" behind.[18] On a small steamer going up river at night, Cleveland caught a dramatic stroboscopic image of traditional life as the furnace door opened momentarily: "The sides of the hut were open, and we saw the Indian occupants swinging in hammocks or crouched about the floor making cigarros; a few sticks burning at one end of the room, and a bunch of plantains and a few rude cooking utensils near by; without, rows of bananas hung on the palm roof and behind them the great trees of the forest. . . . An alligator upon the bank lazily turned his head toward us and then plunged into the water. A few birds awakened by the light twittered and screamed among the branches" (17–18).

On up river was Castillo, which consisted of "about thirty huts . . . built of long slender poles or canes held and woven together by vines, with palm leaf roof" and "some more aristocratic buildings" — stores, restaurants, and lodging houses. Traditional cockfights were still being held every Sunday, Cleveland observed, and "everyone from the poorest peon to the president must have his cock, and stake his money . . . upon his wonderful courage and strength" (35, 43). By night, one could almost believe that nothing was changing. "The scene . . . was picturesque," Cleveland reported,

Each hut was illuminated within [and had?] a candle burning in front. The darkness of the night threw their interiors into stronger relief. Without, we saw a long line of glittering points of light, with the shadowy outlines of the buildings, and of the natives moving to and fro. Within, the natives disrobed of all clothing not rendered absolutely necessary by the demands of decency, and even of some of that, were swinging in a hammock, sometimes two together, and smoking, or huddled in groups upon the floor, looking listless and good-for-nothing. . . . A monkey was seated on one

Indian hut at Masaya, ca. 1848. (From Stillman, *An 1850 Voyage*, 1967)

side of the table, and a parrot on the other. Some doors were filled by señoritas in their white garments, smoking *cigarros* and watching the passing "Californias." (48)

But in the light of day it was evident that things were changing rapidly. "Upon the arrival of the steamboat," Cleveland said,

the town shakes off something of its accustomed apathy and every preparation is made to trade with the Americans. Every house then blossoms out into a store and restaurant, and almost anything else that will bring in money, and displays to the most tempting advantage its little stock of abominable liquors, Nicaraguan *cigarros*, hammocks and eatables. . . . Every hut, however poor, has something for sale. . . . Everything in Castillo is for sale. The inhabitants must all make enough now to support themselves until the arrival of the next steamboat. (36, 38)

The situation was the same all along the route. At Virgin Bay on the west bank of the lake, five hundred passengers slid down a plank from the steamer in "pandemonium"; each engaged a *carretero* and his ox-cart for the overland leg of the journey. "Native booths" were strung all along the road to San Juan del Sur, where rooms were to be had in the Dime House, the Cosmopolitan, the Lafayette, and the California (93–96, 113).

More insightfully than most other travelers, Cleveland sketched the dialectic of acculturation and resistance that attended the physical and cultural chaos along the route. An old woman "told me with considerable pride," he reported, "that she was an indian puro, señor," but it was pointed out to him "as though it was a great honor" that a six-year-old girl was a mixture of "indian and American." "The circumstances attending her American paternity," Cleveland said, "did not seem to be of the slightest consequence" (40). At the inns along the route between San Juan del Sur and Virgin Bay, the cultural and other costs were much in evidence:

> The presiding damsels in their state of semi-nudity, would laugh and joke with their customers, and try to make themselves agreeable, not a very difficult task under the circumstances, while they beguiled "California" out of as much money as possible. They were not always over[ly] scrupulous or delicate in the means they resorted to to accomplish their purpose. A joke could hardly be too broad or coarse to amuse them. . . . Long and familiar intercourse with "California," as they call all transit passengers, has not improved their morals. (103)

Other women were less complaisant, however, and more aware of the equities and costs of the changes the transit traffic was bringing. In an inn in Castillo, women complain about *el* [sic] *compañía*. To Cleveland's inquiry about why everyone smokes, one replies, "Well, you rich Americans can do what you please, but we poor people could not live without smoking. What would life be worth to us without *cigarros*?" Trying to sell him things to take with him, she asks, "Why does *el presidente* let this company take people through our country, and make so much money, when they won't let the passengers stop and buy our things from us. . . . We will get a new company, and then we will sell our things and make plenty of money" (45).

Nicaraguan people, Cleveland was learning, were coping with the upheaval that enveloped them by means that ranged from thoughtless collaboration to thoughtful resistance. A polyvalently symbolic example of the latter was his *carretero*, who up to a point played the servile, "culturally backward" role demanded of him, but beyond that employed some of the universally proven "weapons of the weak": delay, stubbornness, feigned ignorance, and disinformation.[19] "Our driver was a stupid indian" assisted by a ten-year-old boy, Cleveland reported. "He would not do anything to assist the passengers, except to smoke cigars and eat lumps of sugar and sandwitches [sic], which he downed with great cheerfulness and alacrity. If we requested him to pick us a flower or spring from the roadside, he would shake his head with wonderful gravity, and say, '*No, el es malo*' [No, it is bad] . . . trying to persuade us that it was poisonous. Argument and entreaty were vain. Like our mules he had a will of his own." Indeed the stubbornness of the mules is virtually (though unconsciously, it seems) a cultural paradigm. "They seemed to have settled it among themselves," Cleveland says, "that they would not move faster than the most leisurely walk. For a considerable time they resisted the persuasive logic of blows and curses . . . looking the embodiment of injured meekness, but refusing to hasten their pace" (100).

Mark Twain's account of passing through the transit route in its declining years makes clear that the decline did not necessarily translate into reduced cultural impact, and may in fact have highlighted the cultural contradictions. Arriving in San Juan del Sur from California a few days after Christmas of 1866, Twain reported "hotels" that were in fact "tumbledown frame shanties" and a ragtag collection of broken-down, diseased mules used to ferry passengers in decrepit "ambulances." His account of the procession toward the lake burlesques the disorder and absurdity of American "enterprise":

> Our four hundred passengers on horseback, mule-back, and in fourmule ambulances, formed the wildest, raggedest and most uncouth procession I ever saw. It reminded me of the fantastic masquerading pageants they used to get up on the Fourth of July in the Western States, or on Mardi Gras Day in New Orleans. The steerage passengers travelled on mule-back, chiefly, with coats, oilskin carpet sacks, and blankets dangling around their saddles. . . . Such racing and yelling, and beating and banging and spurring, and such bouncing of blanket bundles, and flapping and fluttering of coattails, and such frantic scampering of the multitude of mules, and bobbing up and down of the long column of men, and rearing and charging of struggling ambulances in their midst, I never saw before. (Walker and Dane 1940, 43)

Some North American travelers themselves were embarrassed by such tragicomic excesses. Upon seeing a sign that said "Try Ward's Shirts" just outside San Juan del Sur, Twain reported, a few travelers indulged in some "round abuse" of "War and plantation bitters men, and all such people, who invade all sacred places with their rascally signs, and mar every landscape one might gaze upon in worship" (Ward and Dane 1940, 40).

For a few North American entrepreneurs who had initiated and controlled the process, however, the commerce was so lucrative that it overrode all scruples whatsoever. Large percentages of their gains were used to bolster their own sense of cultural worth and superiority. Commodore Cornelius

Harbor of San Juan del Sur, ca. 1856.
(From *Frank Leslie's Illustrated Weekly*, 29 November 1856)

Vanderbilt's Accessory Transit Company profits enabled him to buy the new 270-foot steam-powered yacht *North Star*, panel its walls with satinwood and marble, furnish its salons with hand-carved and velvet-upholstered Louis XV chairs, paint the ceilings with medallion portraits of the Founding Fathers, and take along his own personal minister to proclaim the whole ensemble a credit to "American taste and skill" (Folkman 1972, 44, 52).

Unfortunately, the transit traffic was not the only cultural and economic plague of foreign origin that Nicaragua had to suffer at mid-century. On the heels of Squier and the transit route entrepreneurs followed the arrogant and ethnocentric filibuster William Walker, who was restrained by not one iota of nostalgia or respect for lost or threatened cultures.[20]

NEW-YORK AND CALIFORNIA STEAMSHIP LINE.

Via NICARAGUA.

The ACCESSORY TRANSIT COMPANY, (of Nicaragua), Proprietors.

Steerage Ticket No. *126*   Not Transferable, and good for this Voyage only.

BERTH, _____   *New=York,* *Feb 9* 185*6*

Mr. *Richard Jones*

paid for the privilege to go in the Steerage, *with Steerage Fare, from NEW-YORK to PUNTA ARENAS, (the dangers and accidents of the seas and navigation of whatsoever nature and kind, excepted,) in the Steamship* **STAR OF THE WEST,** *to leave New-York this date.*

Dogs will be charged $25 each, and in no case be allowed in the cabins or state rooms. The ship will not be accountable for luggage, goods, or other description of property, unless Bills of Lading are signed therefor. Regulations of the Steamer to be strictly complied with.

(left margin, vertical text:) The holder of this will receive from the Clerk of the Steamer, after leaving New-York, a Ticket of "The Accessory Transit Company of Nicaragua," entitling such holder to a Passage over the route from San Juan del Norte, on the Atlantic, to San Juan del Sur, on the Pacific Ocean.

Accessory Transit Company steerage ticket, 1856. (From Appleton Oaksmith Papers, William R. Perkins Library, Duke University; reproduced by permission)

THE GREY-EYED MAN OF DESTINY: WILLIAM WALKER AS CULTURAL AGENT

"There is a strange tradition current among the Indians of this country," reported *Frank Leslie's Illustrated Newspaper* in March 1856, "which they say has been handed down to them through generations. It is to the effect that a regenerator was to come among them in the future . . . and whom they were to recognise by his large, grey eyes. . . . And they believe that the prophecy is fulfilled. The 'Grey-Eyed Man' [William Walker] has come."

William Walker (1824–1860) was the short, skinny, and shy son of a stern Calvinist father whose antislavery views he first shared and then later renounced.[21] With a medical degree from the University of Pennsylvania, he set up a medical practice in Nashville, then moved to New Orleans where he read law and was admitted to the bar before turning to journalism. After the *New Orleans Crescent* folded in 1849 and his deaf-mute sweetheart died from cholera, he moved to California, the scene of his first filibustering adventure in the Sonora region of Mexico, which ended ignominiously. Soon thereafter, Walker was drawn to Nicaragua through his relationship with Byron Cole, a proprietor of the San Francisco *Commercial Advertiser* (for which Walker worked), who had offered to assist León Liberals in their fight with the Conservative "Legitimists" of Granada by dispatching three hundred mercenaries from the U.S. Walker left San Francisco on 4 May 1855 with a group of mercenaries he grandly christened "The Fifty-Six Immortals."

Battle of Rivas. (From *Frank Leslie's Illustrated Weekly*, 17 May 1856)

Landing late in June, Walker's troops were routed in their first engagement, but within four months had taken Granada, forced the Legitimist commander to surrender, executed the country's minister of foreign affairs, and installed a puppet government. Aided at first by Commodore Vanderbilt's Accessory Transit Company, Walker soon became entangled in a dispute over control of the company, and local elites began to have their doubts about the wisdom of his exploits—doubts shared increasingly by the Conservative governments of Guatemala, Honduras, and Costa Rica, the last of which soon dispatched its own troops against him.

Through a rigged election in late June 1856, Walker proclaimed himself president of Nicaragua and was inaugurated in the plaza at Granada, while a band played "Yankee Doodle." An immediately promulgated set of edicts

Church of Our Lady of Mercy, Granada, where William Walker was sworn in as president of Nicaragua. (From *Frank Leslie's Illustrated Weekly*, 9 August 1856)

proclaimed English co-equal with Spanish as an official language; instituted vagrancy laws, which forced *campesinos* into low-paying jobs; legalized indentured servitude and chattel slavery; promulgated land registration laws intended, as he candidly admitted, "to place a large portion of the land . . . in the hands of the white race"; and provided for the confiscation and sale of the property of anyone who opposed him (Walker [1860] 1985, 253–55, 261, 430).

Less than two months after his inauguration, Walker's troops were defeated by a Legitimist force bolstered by sixty Indian archers from Matagalpa. That engagement produced one of Nicaragua's earliest cultural heroes, Andrés Castro, who—after finding his carbine inoperative—dispatched a filibuster with a rock.[22] Depressed and frustrated by further defeats, Walker torched the indigenous neighborhood of Monimbó near Masaya, and then destroyed Granada.

Many North Americans viewed Walker's escapade as a grand cultural as well as military crusade. "General Walker," said the *New York Times*, "with his usual coolness and bravery, was everywhere conspicuously—the profundity of intellect displayed in his generalship raising him still higher in the estimation of his fellow soldiers."[23] The news that was *not* fit to print, however, was that Walker's drunken soldiers unleashed an orgy of looting and burn-

William Walker war hero Andrés Castro on Sandinista-era 10-córdoba bill.

ing in Granada, wantonly blew up the church on the plaza, and leveled the city. Commander Charles Henningsen — an English mercenary married to a Georgia plantation heiress — left a sign in the smoldering ruins: "Here was Granada." Even Walker himself admitted that the scene "presented more the appearance of a wild Bacchanalian revel than of a military camp" (Bermann 1986, 69; Walker [1860] 1985, 314). Following a series of military reverses after the sacking of Granada, the remnants of Walker's increasingly ill, hungry, and demoralized troops fought for another six months, urged on by his fanatical exhortations, but in May 1857 the bulk of his troops surrendered. A few months after Walker returned to general acclaim in the United States, *DeBow's Review* called him "a man incapable of sordid or selfish motives," an emissary of "a superior culture and civilization."[24] A second expedition aborted and a third, equally unsuccessful, ended with a hero's welcome in Mobile (May 1973, 113, 129). Finally landing again in Honduras in 1860, Walker was captured by British troops and turned over to Honduran troops, who shot him.

The cultural "logic" of Walker's filibustering was straightforward: as a pure rather than mixed race, North Americans were inherently superior to Central Americans, and therefore obligated to bring their civilization and culture to their benighted neighbors, thereby guaranteeing to Nicaragua a dynamic economy, an advanced social order, and high civilization. "The destiny of this region and the interests of humanity are confided to our care," Walker proclaimed. "We have come here as the advance guard of American civilization" (quoted in Bermann 1986, 68). U.S. minister to Nicaragua John H. Wheeler characterized Walker as an "agent of a superior race that [will] replace the allegedly syphilis-infected, feeble races of Central America" (May 1973, 97). Thus filibustering was a cultural as well as military and political crusade, and Walker was determined to shape Nicaragua to his cultural vision.

"[My] first glimpse of [Lake Nicaragua] almost made the pulse stand still," Walker reflected later. He was charmed by the picturesque market women at Rivas, and gratified by the streets full of people in León, "shouting a welcome to their deliverers" (Walker [1860] 1985, 48–49, 217). But Walker's respect for Nicaraguan people—indeed for any non-Caucasians—had narrow limits. With evident disgust he recalled from his Sonora adventure "the skulking form of the half-clothed Indian, relapsing into savagism from which the holy fathers had rescued him." And he was ambivalent about the Nicaraguan troops assigned to him upon his arrival in Rivas. He found one Mariano Mendez courageous and hardened by many years of military experience, but "possessed of violent passions and uncontrolled desires" and thus "utterly unfit for civil life and incapable of being subjected to the rigid rules of military law" (Walker [1860] 1985, 23, 43).

The problem as Walker saw it was that Nicaragua was a nation of halfbreeds. "Instead of maintaining the purity of the races" as the English colonizers had done in the North, the Spanish had "cursed their continental possessions with a mixed race" that could ultimately be lifted to culture and civilization only by a genetic repair job administered by the "robust children of the North," who in the meantime would run the society as benevolent caretakers, providing "exalted intellect and refined taste," technical know-how, iron-willed control and structure, and the vision required for "the real work of revolution" (Walker [1860] 1985, 246, 250, 259).[25]

Walker was confident that he himself possessed the qualities necessary for such a work of social and cultural reconstruction, and that filibustering was an ideal instrument for the purpose (Walker [1860] 1985, 214). A January 1856 article in Walker's newspaper *El Nicaragüense* attributed virtually the entire growth of western society and culture since the Roman empire to filibustering. A few months later *Frank Leslie's Illustrated Newspaper* predicted that in due time Walker would be "invested, like Cortez of old, with . . . glory."[26] Two weeks after Walker's inauguration as president of Nicaragua, the New Orleans *Sunday Delta* carried the analogy to even more lyrical heights. "From the combination of . . . Celtic and Teutonic blood," the *Delta* opined, "a vigorous race sprung into existence." Idealizing Walker's actually unimposing physical aspect, the rhapsody unfolded:

> That blue-gray eye — that full, coarse mouth — that light hair — that [compact] frame . . . that roving disposition . . . that extraordinary faith in the power of a single ship and a small company of hardy followers to destroy nations or to build them up — all these characteristics . . . recall the Vikings who first roused Southern Europe to activity and life. Under the plain Saxon name of Walker we find an energy . . . a confidence in destiny, such as guided the first civilizers on their way. . . . It is a strange thing in this age of dollars and dotage . . . [with] its small passions and narrow ideas, to see the Kinghood of the old Scandinavian sailors . . . reappearing suddenly in our midst.

Seeking a suitable antecedent for the contemplated glorious cultural transformation of Nicaragua, Walker's newspaper *El Nicaragüense* turned to no less than Renaissance Italy, fantasizing that the islands of Lake Nicaragua adjacent to Granada ("the most beautiful and fertile islands it is possible to conceive") would be part of a "future Venice" — a post-capitalist garden of sensual delight bequeathed by capitalist enterprise. Each of the islands, the writer promised, "is in a short time destined to be full of houses, stores and commercial ware rooms. . . . Here canals will occupy the place of streets, and light fairy-like pleasure boats will supersede horses. Here instead of a Wall Street we will have a Rialto; here will be seen and heard señors and señoritas in their gondolas singing love songs in the starlight; and here will be the most pleasing combination of health, convenience and beauty in any city upon which the sun ever shone." [27]

Preposterous as it was, the scenario played well to the public all across the United States. In July 1856, the three-act musical *Nicaragua: or, General Walker's Victories* opened at Purdy's Theater in New York, featuring Jefferson Squash ("a roving Yankee"), Ivory Black ("a superior nigger"), and General Walker ("the hope of freedom"). A year later, *The Siege of Granada: or, Walker and His Men* opened in Sacramento (May 1973, 77; Rosengarten 1976, 144). In the slave-holding states, newspapers celebrated Walker's exploits, and he was given a hero's welcome in several cities.

Meanwhile in Nicaragua, the citizens of burned and plundered Granada condemned Walker and his "mob of foreign ingrates, race of vipers" (*caterva de extranjeros ingratos, raza de víboras*) who laid waste the "pearl of the great lake." In early 1857, Granada's *Telégrafo Setentrional* judged that the

Forrest Theater!

C. E. BINGHAM, ... MANAGER

THE INIMITABLE **MISS**

ALBERTINE!

THE CELEBRATED AMERICAN ACTRESS,

Will appear as

BESS, the Nightingale of the Army

And by particular desire, in her favorite Character of

BOB NETTLES!

The Grand Nicaraguan Drama of The

SIEGE of GRENADA

Having been highly successful in every continued Scene, will be repeated to-night.

TUESDAY EVENING, JUNE 16, 1857,

Will be presented (2d time in Sacramento) the thrilling Drama of

THE SIEGE
—OF—
GRENADA!

Or, WALKER AND HIS MEN!

Gen. Walker, President of the Republic of Nicaragua ...... Mr. MORTIMER
Gen. Henningsen, Commander American Forces in Nicaragua, J. R. PAULLIN
Col. O'Neil, his Aid-de-Camp .... ROGERS
Col. Henry, Acting Quarter Master General, ... JACKSON
Lieut. Ben O'Neil, brother of the Col. .... Miss CARPENTER
Pat. Kenovan, a Broth of a Boy .... DUMPHRIES
Arkansaw, half horse—half alligator .... McGOWAN
Jack of St. Giles, ... POTTER
Negro Pete, ... AUSTIN
Ned, ... **Mr. C. E. BINGHAM**
Bess, Ned's Wife, the Nightingale of the Nicaraguan Army,
Miss ALBERTINE
Ethel, Florence, Jamy and Julien—Ned and Elizabeth's children—Little Rose
Bingham, Little Francis, Julia and James.
SPANIARDS:
Gen'l Belosa, Commander-in-Chief of Native forces .... DENNIS
Price, an American in Spanish pay, ... FERGUSON
Soldiers, Emigrants, Spies, &c. by numerous auxilliaries.

ACT 1.—SCENE 1. Onward is the beacon light of Liberty ! Behind is the
dark gulf of tyranny.
SCENE 2. Four thousand of the enemy surrounding the town—The Charge !
Come on ! brothers.
SCENE 3. Bess—I can, at least, load your rifle for you.
SCENE 4. No quarters! FIRE !
SCENE 5. Now for a glorious Freedom or a lively grave !
SCENE 6. American baricades—Death of BEN O'NEIL !—Three cheers for
Walker and the Lone Star—NED WOUNDED !—That Star will yet be received
as a sister in that glorious family which sheds light and freedom o'er the World.
GRAND TABLEAUX—End of First Act.
ACT 2.—SCENE 1. The baricades—The lookout of the American forces—
Where the Angel of the Plague contends with the Demon of War for the number
of its victims!—Tell them, besides, that AMERICANS never surrender !—Bess
a Prisoner—I will bring her back, or perish with her !
SCENE 2. Ah whiskey, you divil, you were always the death of the Kenovans !
SCENE 3. Spanish baricades—Box make them dance—It's only a little Irish
blackguard, you'll not forget the snuff box jig.
SCENE 4. Returning to the Camp !
SCENE 5. WALKER AND HIS TROOPS ARRIVE !—To the Rescue !
—The blood of our slain Soldiers cries out from the Earth, and echoes through
the vaults of Heaven, Glorious Liberty !—Death of BESS !—her name shall per-
ish only with our Lives and Liberty.
TABLEAUX—End of Piece.

To conclude with the favorite Farce of

BOB NETTLES

Playbill for *The Siege of Granada!: Or, Walker and His Men* at the Forrest Theater, Sacramento, California. (California Historical Society, San Francisco, FN-21365; used by permission)

Goths who sacked Rome should be considered "the very personification of civilization and progress" compared to "the Grey-eyed Demon of Murder and Rapine." Another *Telégrafo Setentrional* article in June said Walker, like Alexander the Great, was *el mayor ladrón en la tierra* (the biggest thief on earth). Reversing its earlier position of support, the *New York Times* began to mock the enterprise, characterizing Walker as a bandit and calling his crusade "paltry ruffianism, masked as enterprise and philanthropy."[28]

CULTURAL RESISTANCE TO CULTURAL CHANGE

Although for the most part the dynamics of expropriation, proletarianization, redistribution of population, and cultural destruction — whether they proceeded from native elites, from intervening foreigners, or (as was frequently the case in Nicaragua) from collaboration between the two groups — were as inexorable in Nicaragua as they were elsewhere in Latin America, the transformation did not proceed without opposition.[29] Opposition took two major forms: organized uprisings — mostly among the indigenous population — and a cleverly masked discourse of opposition embodied in popular literature (both oral and written) and public rituals.

DIRECT OPPOSITION. In Nicaragua, Indian resistance, the origins of which reached back to the conquest itself and to the subsequent opposition to the *encomienda* and the *repartimiento*, continued to crop up throughout the nineteenth century, especially in Indian communities such as Subtiava and Monimbó, and in the highlands around Matagalpa. There were popular insurrections in León, Granada, Masaya, and Rivas in 1811–12. In 1822 Subtiavan artisans joined with students to take over a military post, and uprisings in León and Granada followed. The mid-1840s witnessed another outbreak in the central highlands. Traveling through Matagalpa in the late 1850s, Carl Scherzer found the town "still bleeding from the wounds" of those insurrections (Scherzer 1857, 166; cf. Wheelock [1974] 1981, 68–108).[30]

The last major Indian uprising — the "War of the Communities" — took place in 1881, when Indians around Matagalpa rose up against the expropriation of land, the forced labor on the roads, the low-paid and dangerous work they were compelled to do in the construction of a telegraph line from Managua to Matagalpa, and other cultural harassments, such as being forbidden to make *chicha bruja*, a slightly alcoholic native drink. In late 1881, indigenous people from the area between Matagalpa, El Sauce, and León mobilized about seven thousand troops and carried on a battle against such measures for nine months. About a thousand Indians died in the effort. Refusing to recognize the legitimate complaints of the Indians, or to admit the popular support the uprising had among indigenous people, President Zavala attributed it to the subversive influence of the Jesuit order, which he expelled from the country (Wheelock [1974] 1981, 111–16; Gutiérrez 1981, 2–3; Miranda Casij 1972, 75–82).

But such uprisings were sporadic and of little effect. Most of the time, Indians continued to relate to the dominant elites as they had since postconquest days: doing (or giving the appearance of doing) what they were absolutely required to do, passively avoiding (like the *carretero* Daniel Cleveland encountered on the transit route) whatever demands could be avoided, and keeping to themselves, their families, and communities as much as they could. Having much to lose and little to gain from creating a modernizing, European-style nation-state, they demonstrated little interest in the project. George Byam, who lived in Nicaragua for several years just prior to mid-century, was sensitive to the separatist inclinations of the mass of Nicaragua's "dwellers in the woods and forests." "Generally honest and inoffensive," Baym said, "but bold and hardy, they seem to care as little for revolutions as revolutions do for them. Remote from the cities, they lead a rather uncertain, precarious life, but, with a little hard work for a short time in the year, they can assure subsistence to their families. . . . [They are] altogether . . . superior to the townspeople, both physically and morally" (quoted in Burns 1991, 33).

Most Indians—who constituted perhaps 40 percent of the population—continued to live in 15×20-foot grass-roofed, cane-walled *ranchos* of pre-Columbian form, surrounded by *solares* that included a washing area, gardens, and fruit trees.[31] Travelers who passed through Indian communities frequently observed that some native religious practices survived, though often under a veneer of formal Christianity. By one contemporary estimate, perhaps one Nicaraguan in a thousand knew how to read and write; a majority of the population did not speak Spanish, and perhaps one in a hundred actually understood Catholic doctrine (Burns 1991, 30–31).

NARRATIVES OF SUBVERSION AND OPPOSITION. Overt and violent resistance flared dramatically when it happened, but resistance usually took the more subtle and indirect "everyday" forms Scott has mapped (Scott 1985). Much of that relatively continuous undercurrent of opposition was explicitly cultural in substance and method: jokes, aphorisms, popular narratives, dances, and dramatic performances (frequently in combination).[32]

A large body of trickster tales about "El Indio y el Chapetón" (*chapetón* = Spanish-born) focuses on humorous confrontations in which an Indian outsmarts an upper-class functionary. Many turn on double meanings of words, intentional misunderstandings, and the like. One such tale is called "El Indio Docto que Fue un Doctor" (The wise Indian who was a doctor):

Once it happened that a very intelligent, pure-blooded [*de pura raza*] Indian who had managed to study everything that was necessary to graduate as a doctor in philosophy and canonical law asked to be examined, and his request was granted. But among the examiners was a pure-blooded *chapetón* who was determined by his arrogance not to approve the Indian, even if he was wiser than Solomon.

The Indian's examination was very lucid, but in the secret voting, four examiners who were creoles put a silver "A" in the jar for "Approve," and the *chapetón*—firm in his evil purpose—put in an "R" for "Reject."

But when the president of the examining tribunal announced the results, saying "approved with four A's and one R," the Indian said, "I am satisfied, because I have gotten what I came looking for; I know I am wise [*docto*], and with this 'R' I am a doctor [*doctor*]." (Peña Hernández 1968, 227; cf. 222–42)

Such jokes and stories were mostly swapped in private, but the concerns, angers, and fears they embodied were also acted out in public. Many nineteenth-century travelers in Nicaragua attested to the continuing vitality of festivals and dance-dramas among the Indian communities (cf. Peña Hernández 1968, 79–85, 130–32, 138–42, 149–52). Some—integral parts of church celebrations—had little if anything to do with resistance or protest, but others were witty and satiric expressions of resistance. By far the best known of them, *El Güegüence* (discussed in the previous chapter), continued to be performed throughout the nineteenth century.

But if by performing such examples of cleverly veiled satire as *El Güegüence* ordinary people and the Indian population acted out some of their concerns about how to survive culturally in the face of land loss, community destruction, forced proletarianization, and a general denigration of all non-elite cultural forms and practices, middle-class aspirants for elite status were more likely to concern themselves with what sorts of accommodation and acculturation were likely to assure the quickest and greatest mobility. Those concerns also sometimes took dramatic form.

During the spring of 1873, Managua's *Semanal Nicaragüense* printed a verse play, *El Espíritu del Siglo* (The spirit of the century), which both reflected and caricatured the social and cultural aspects of middle- and upper-middle-class aspirations.[33] The opposition that animates *El Espíritu del Siglo* is between conventional bourgeois Nicaraguan culture and the modernizing currents sweeping over Nicaragua. Additionally, it turns upon women's double (class and gender) subordination and the growing cultural hegemony of the United States.

Formally the play is a conventional comedy of manners built around stereotypes: a *machista* husband (Don Cosme) and his socially ambitious wife (Doña Marcela) contend for dominance both within their marriage and with respect to the choice of a proper mate for their naive daughter Críspula. Don Cosme prefers the stolid and predictable Captain Pancracio, who offers conventional respectability and modest mobility; Doña Marcela prefers the fast-talking dandy Enrique, who promises to take Críspula (and perhaps even her mother and thirty-one-year-old maidservant Eufracia—fearful of spinster-hood—as well) away from the provincialism and parochialism of Nicaragua to the mesmerizing modernity of New York. Críspula, encouraged by Eufracia, is preparing to go—and the parents are at the point of divorcing—when Pancracio recognizes Enrique as the foundling child Martin whom he raised but who stole his hard-earned fortune and fled some years earlier. The happy resolution (parents reconciled, daughter destined to be the captain's lady, chastened maidservant conscious of her naiveté, no one bound for New York, a chorus of prudential aphorisms all around) reaffirms conventional bourgeois values, customary forms, established familial and social relationships, and Nicaragua (whatever it is or is to be) instead of New York.

Despite its trite, contrived plot, the play engages serious cultural issues: technological change, Nicaraguan national versus foreign (in this case North American) culture, the social dislocation induced by rapid cultural change, and shifts in gender definitions, identities, and roles.

Certainly these were not new issues in the 1870s. From the beginning of major U.S. intervention in Nicaragua in the 1840s, local politicians and ordinary citizens alike had debated the wisdom of acquiescing to the wishes and blandishments of the Yankees and other intervenors. By the time of *El Espíritu del Siglo* more than twenty years later, a character as mesmerized as Enrique is by the Yankees ("they are . . . called to govern us," he is convinced) is irresistible bait for satire. In New York, he tells his rapt listeners, there are very strange customs (*costumbres bien estrañas*):[34]

> There nothing is done
> Except by machine.
> Do you have a stomach ache?
> A galvanic machine;
> Are you thirsty?
> The hydraulic machine comes!

More than sixty years before Charlie Chaplin's comical machine-feeding scene in *Modern Times* (1936), Enrique tantalizes Doña Marcela and Críspula with his account of a completely mechanized café:

One goes to a café and enters,
And without saying a word takes a seat;
The waiter comes with the machine
And without opening one's mouth
Or taking a spoon
They put the ingredients in it
And prepare the meal.
In two seconds one is fat. (VI)
When a gentleman goes to a meeting,
One machine takes his hat
Another his cane;
There is a machine to enter,
A machine to leave;
A machine to say things
Without having to talk. (VII)

For Eufracia the news is even better. "Does a girl want to marry?" Enrique asks rhetorically.

It is easy: at six send
A notice to whatever newspaper;
Three minutes later, ten letters
Containing ten proposals
Have arrived at your house
With photo-biographies of the suitors;
Forty seconds pass while you choose.
At seven one goes to the church;
At seven-fifteen one sings.
Victory at eight on the dot.
Now she is a matron; she eats lunch and dances.
At twelve she has a villa
At four coach and servants;
At five she buys a cradle,
And at seven is surrounded
By two chubby creatures. (VI)

"One really *lives* there," Eufracia exults.

How worthless are those of us
Who don't live there.
I would even sell my shirt
To be a citizen

Of the United States.
Long live industry! (VI)

Not to seize such an opportunity is inconceivable to Enrique. "Your father is stupid," he taunts Críspula, reminding her that Don Cosme has never traveled, speaks no English, and worse yet, is going to sacrifice her to a "Hotentot captain."

By comparison with such an automated utopia, Nicaragua is not even a country at all:

> Here there is no peace, no government,
> Neither honor nor good faith.
>
> .   .   .   .   .   .
>
> Of very liberal laws
> The papers attest, . . .
> But they guarantee nothing. (VII)

Culturally, Enrique argues, Nicaragua is a shabby provincial backwater where people live "like savages"—without hotels, roads, canals, theaters, galleries, or vehicles. But "Oh, those Yankees!" he exclaims:

> On Monday they draw the plan
> To build a city
> With that comfort
> That belongs to the American.
> On Tuesday before the sun sets
> There are already a thousand apartments,
> Ten bridges, a hundred monuments,
> And on every corner a street-lamp.
> Wednesday there is a bank;
> Thursday, locomotives;
> Early on Friday
> Palaces of white marble. (VII)

Marcela, enchanted by the vision, pouts about being "buried in this filthy corner" (*rincón inmundo*), which Enrique agrees is "the worst in the world." She has always wanted to go, she says,

> To live somewhere
> Where one may enjoy.
> Where one may [really] live. (VII)

Thus at length the contest between the parents over a suitor for their daughter becomes no less than a contest between two cultures. When Capitán Pancracio emerges as the triumphant suitor, he is also—and more importantly—the representative type of Latin American culture as the culture wishes to see itself: engagingly solid rather than merely stolid, grounded in its own concrete realities (rather than alienated like Enrique), loving and poetic heart balancing commonsensical head.[35] For the thoroughly Latin Capitán Pancracio, "the sea is the great mirror in which we see our lives" (XII); only a deculturated Enrique could be deceived by the smoke and mirrors of New York.

Each confrontation (Enrique/Martin versus Pancracio, Don Cosme versus Doña Marcela, Eufracia versus the parents) stands for a broader historical-cultural conflict. As the rogue and impostor Enrique (New York/the United States) tries to flee, Pancracio (Latin America) exclaims to him in words that evoke a thinly veiled North-South allegory:

> It is in vain!
> Now that I have finally found you,
> You will not escape, Martin,
> From justice and from my hand.
> Infamous one, who when you were young
> Robbed me of my fortune. . . .
> At my cost you elevated yourself. (XIII)

In the final scene, order and tranquillity are reestablished: the father's choice is vindicated, the chimeric and alien culture has lost its allure, parents are reconciled, erring wife and daughter kneel to beg forgiveness, maidservant is reconciled to spinsterhood, shyster suitor is bound for the bar of justice, and honorable suitor is headed for (presumably) the altar.

The anonymous author of the play was not content to leave it there, however. It becomes increasingly clear that the mesmerizing "spirit of the century" is—along with its other menacing characteristics—a direct threat to male prerogative and power, and that hence the order that is ultimately reestablished is explicitly patriarchal.[36]

That the reigning order is patriarchal there is no doubt. Both Críspula and Eufracia, desperate to find husbands, are virtually aflutter in anticipation that they may yet escape the social purgatory of becoming old maids (solteronas [V]). Aging is such a horror that the rejuvenating mirrors of New York are sufficient to create an "earthly paradise" (VII); the women are fascinated by the latest fashions but lack even minimal interest in political affairs. Most importantly, as Don Cosme assures Pancracio, "My daughter will know how to obey" (VII), and "what I say will be done" (X).

Moreover, if Doña Marcela is repulsed by Pancracio's lack of class and fin-ish, Don Cosme is doubtful of Enrique's masculinity. Pancracio smells of tar and talks of ropes, she says; better tar and ropes than pomades, cosmetics, and mincing "good mornings," he counters (XI). Críspula will marry Enrique or we will divorce, she shouts at him; *my* daughter will marry Pancracio, he shouts back. For each, it is a matter both of cultural choice and of dominance, and the stakes are high on both sides: for the women, to break out and enjoy what the other culture appears to offer; for Don Cosme, not to have to admit that his power was insufficient to prevent them from breaking out.

Hence Don Cosme reads the women's agenda as insubordination and a direct challenge to his honor:

> I believed I was head of the house
> And owner of the heart
> Of a docile daughter, submissive
> To the tender voice of her father. . . .
> [But] when women get capricious
> There is no animal more fierce,
> Stubborn, revolutionary. (XII)

Be that as it may, Doña Marcela says, provocatively,

> When we believe we are right,
> And we always do,
> We are made of iron.

Such defiance leaves Don Cosme livid:

> I deny and will always deny
> Such pretension,
> Women are harder
> Than the anvil of a blacksmith.
> More capricious than a child;
> More cruel than Nero;
> More brave than a treasurer;
> More stubborn than a creditor;
> More foolish than a deputy;
> More demanding than a lord;
> More sovereign than Lucifer
> And more dreaded than God. (XII)

For his part, the credulous Enrique is untroubled. "I am the owner of the woman," he says smugly; "a rival means nothing to me."

Thus the unmasking of Enrique/Martin not only rights the cultural balance, but also ends the social nightmare of a potentially inverted gender order. As the final scene opens, Críspula ("as if coming to herself") asks "Where am I? What has happened?" "I am crazy," Doña Marcela laments, to which her angry and imperious husband replies,

> You have always been
> Because it is in your nature,
> And everything that has happened here
> Is your fault.

When his kneeling daughter repents her capriciousness and confesses her deviations (*extravíos*), however, he is finally mollified:

> Very well, then; from today [we have] a new life,
> If you show yourself corrected.
> No more weddings, no more ostentation,
> Which have caused so many bad times.
> And [if you] learn what should be
> The ways of women,
> Honesty and circumspection. . . .
> And let everyone be informed
> Who hears me here . . .
> That here I am the sole owner,
> And as such, I command. (XIII)

Don Cosme's triumphant moralistic peroration leaves no room for misunderstanding:

> He who would place
> On this haughty and treacherous throne
> This daughter of Satan
> This horrible monster
> "The spirit of the century,"
> Will perish with it. (XIII)

Such a "resolution" was no resolution at all, of course, and in any case it abounded in irony and contradiction: the overriding dynamic of the nineteenth century in Nicaragua was precisely the effort of its entrenched and governing elites to restructure the country in the very "spirit of the century" Enrique represented. Far from valuing, empowering, or threatening to free women, that spirit (in either its Latin American or North American version) demanded their continued subordination. At the same time, the continued dominance of Nicaragua's elites depended upon the triumph rather than the defeat of the entrepreneurially developmental part of that spirit—upon their learning to master and channel it in its emerging forms.

The period of elite convergence between the end of the William Walker war and the advent of the Zelaya government in 1893 — the so-called "Thirty Years" of Conservative rule — was characterized by *political* stability, but also by "more drastic . . . modernization than any other period in Nicaraguan history." Hence it was a time of turbulent cultural *in*stability during which traditional peoples and communities were stripped of hereditary lands, proletarianized, and (to the extent the elites could bring it about) forcibly acculturated (Stansifer 1977, 469).[37]

The last Conservative president before the advent of José Santos Zelaya was Roberto Sacasa (1889–93), whose strategies for maintaining political stability were frequently even more draconian and culturally costly than those of his predecessors. His administration was characterized by increased subsidies to coffee growers and a marked buildup of "law and order" facilities, maintained at the cost of large public debt and reductions in public services — costs which always fall most heavily upon the lower classes (Teplitz 1973, 14–21).

The Thirty Years of Conservative rule ended with the accession to the presidency of Liberal José Santos Zelaya (1853–1919) in 1893. Zelaya was himself the son of a coffee planter. Educated in the Conservative stronghold of Granada, he came to the presidency through the support of coffee producers and exporters, Managua's growing middle-class (expanded by the coffee boom), and intellectuals (Teplitz 1973, 49; Booth 1985, 7).

Zelaya's policies benefitted principally those sectors that had put him into power. Even his moves to further separate church and state gave more power to those sectors by expanding the role of government. Increasing foreign investment, commodity export, and infrastructure development further reinforced the economic power and social influence of the already dominant sectors (Teplitz 1973, 38; Booth 1985, 22). Even Zelaya's more "progressive" moves — such as increased attention to education — benefitted the lower class but little. Universities continued the Latin American tradition of serving principally to provide attorneys and physicians for the upper class, and a system was created to pay up to fifty dollars per month each in gold to send the children of the elite abroad for their education — an amount that was double the entire national budget for other social welfare purposes (Teplitz 1973, 173–74).

Some of the cultural results of such a skewed allocation of resources were evident to Gustavo Niederlein, chief of the scientific department of Philadelphia's Commercial Museum. What Niederlein saw when he traveled in Nicaragua near the turn of the century was a social and cultural infrastructure in shambles: few paved streets even in León and Granada, street cleaning "left to the rain or the wind, to the pigs," most roads in rural areas impassable during the rainy season (and none passable year-round). Although the higher class of *ladinos* tried to "imitate European usages," there were no clubs, coffee houses, theaters, promenades, and few plazas "of cultivated aspect." The inspector general of public instruction lamented, "We have no teachers, we have no furniture, we have no equipment, we have no buildings; in a word, the school does not exist in the Republic" (Niederlein 30, 48, 55ff., 65, 84–89).

Detailed information on the Zelaya administration's active promotion of elite culture is not plentiful, but it appears that European cultural forms continued to be preferred. Gilberto Vega Miranda's brief biographies of several dozen Nicaraguan musicians born between 1812 and the turn of the century report that Zelaya ("a benefactor of music and of musicians") gave state aid to departmental bands and orchestras, that "schools of music" were started, and that medals and prizes for artistic accomplishment multiplied (Vega Miranda 1982, 51–72).

Vega Miranda's biographical vignettes suggest that the middle and upper classes in Nicaragua had a flourishing musical life that reflected primarily European cultural forms and values. Among the country's "serious" musicians, European training (or study under European-trained teachers) and a consequent orientation toward European art music was the norm. Tránsito Sacasa (1862–1936) studied painting, sculpture, and music in Italy and taught many students. Alejandro Vega Matus (1875–1937) received his training in European art music at a conservatory in Guatemala. The younger Fernando Midence (1889–1935) studied piano in Milan.[38]

Unfortunately, Zelaya's support of the elite arts was not balanced by a concern for the culture of the majority. As Teplitz has noted, "Virtually the entire cost of mobilizing agrarian resources for modernization was placed on the lower class," as it had been during previous decades (Teplitz 1973, 233). The so-called "first fruits levy"—instituted in 1893 on the eve of Zelaya's term—functioned as a tax shelter for (white) capitalists but burdened communal farmers (Indians) heavily, and big growers were given preferential freight rates. A variety of laws (vagrancy laws, for example) forced all those over fourteen years old to work on large estates. Titles to common (ejidal) lands continued to be abolished, and more than two million acres of such lands were sold during the Zelaya administration.[39] Since some of the proceeds were returned to the Indians for educational purposes, and since the schools under Zelaya emphasized a Positivist, modernizing perspective, the Indians were in effect forced to sell their land in order to pay for their own Europeanization (Teplitz 1973, 85, 155, 183–229).

Like the Matagalpan Indians in 1881, some indigenous people tried to resist the Zelaya restructuring. They responded to the forced labor drafts, for example, by fleeing, refusing to register, registering under aliases, and signing with several growers at once in order to get several of the allowed cash advances. But such tactics availed as little as they had earlier. Indigenous communities were dissolved, populations were dispersed, and passivity followed—as Thomas Belt had already observed in the mountainside hut at Ocotal (Teplitz 1973, 198–219).[40]

If Zelaya's domestic policies reinforced the elite culture of the *cafetaleros* and the emerging coffee- and banana-linked bourgeoisie at the expense of indigenous communities and other *campesino* populations, his policies on foreign investment—particularly from the United States—continued to smooth the way for long-range North American cultural influence in Nicaragua. Despite the elites' growing ambivalence concerning North American intervention, signs that it was now virtually unstoppable were plentiful. Those signs became especially evident on the Atlantic coast, where the coming of independence had not brought an end to foreign control as it had (however temporarily) on the opposite coast.

The partial (1821) and then complete independence of the United Provinces of Central America (1823) left the Atlantic coast free of Spanish control, but thereby open again to the British (Vilas 1989, 20; Naylor 1989, 103–17). A dozen years later, a British attempt to plant a sizeable colony met little opposition because the "united" Central American states were by then embroiled in internal conflict and Nicaragua's own Liberals and Conservatives were fighting the first of their many civil wars (Dozier 1985, 30–35).

Relatively unimpeded in their enterprise of indirect rule and intensive trade, the British continued through mid-century to build a series of trading posts up and down the coast. After a brief period during which the U.S.-British (Webster-Crampton) treaty of 1852 established the so-called Mosquito Reserve between the Rama River in the south and the Coco in the north, the British finally relinquished all claim to the Mosquito coast in 1860 (Vilas 1989, 26–27; Bourgois in Walker 1982, 308; Nietschmann 1973, 38; Naylor 1989, 168–97; Dozier 1985, 52–75). Thenceforth the territory was officially a part of Nicaragua, but efforts to make it so completely and in fact were to stretch over more than another century. Indeed, by the time the British departed, North American commercial incursions (related primarily to the transit route) had already been under way for a dozen years (cf. Dozier 1985, 76–106).

What looked in the late 1840s like the beginning of another sustained period of foreign commercial and political intervention into Atlantic coast affairs proved relatively short-lived, however. The William Walker filibuster war, the onset of the Civil War in the United States, the opening of the transcontinental railroad a few years after the war ended, and the coming of a thirty-year period of stable Conservative rule in Nicaragua brought a virtual end to the transit traffic and to commercial development.

The departure of the transit traffic and most of the entrepreneurs did not, however, leave the coast free of foreign cultural and social influence. With the opening of the transit route, in fact, came the missionaries of the Moravian church, who settled permanently. Welcoming them partly because they spoke English, the British granted the Moravians land for their work (Dozier 1985, 64). Confident that they could both save the souls of the Miskitos and show them better ways to live, the Moravians encouraged them to raise their houses on stilts, enclose them with sawed lumber, use cooking platforms made of wood and clay rather than their accustomed fires on the ground, and replace the communal pot with individual eating vessels. Breadfruit trees were introduced, as were new varieties of rice. Young women used to marrying at twelve now had to wait until they were eighteen, and monogamy became the new rule. The traditional fermented drink of pineapple and sugar cane (*mishla*) was proscribed as inimical to the sober life of hard work and self-denial favored by the missionaries. Native shamanic practices were frowned upon, Moravian "lay pastors" became key members of the social structure, and Moravian doctors endeavored to replace traditional remedies with pills and injections. Increasingly settled into villages for more effective proselytizing, the traditionally semi-nomadic Miskitos adopted matrilocal residence as women stayed at home to tend children and garden plots while men hunted, fished, and traveled to trading stations (Helms 1971, 22–26, 51, 70–71, 145; Vilas 1989, 34; Dennis 1981, 217–20, 277).

The proliferation of trading stations in the late nineteenth century was an outgrowth of another profound systemic change on the coast: large-scale corporate exploitation of natural resources (rubber, mahogany, gold and silver, bananas, and—last in the series—enormous pine forests). By the 1880s, 90 to 95 percent of all east coast trade in such commodities was controlled by U.S. corporations and citizens. In 1884 the John D. Emery Company of Boston gained access to tropical woods in 10 percent of the entire province (Dozier 1985, 142).

The first few hundred bunches of bananas were shipped in 1883, but by 1891 the total had reached 1.2 million bunches. That same year, five thousand ounces of gold left the coast, along with six hundred thousand pounds of rubber. Two years later, four steamboat loads of lumber were leaving the WaWa River area every month. The "banana era" lasted until it was curtailed by disease and soil exhaustion in the 1930s (Helms 1971, 25–29; Vilas 1989, 29, 45–46; Dozier 1985, 142). In the opinion of the U.S. Consul in 1893, the port of Bluefields, which had doubled in population over a short time, was "American to the core" (Hale 1994, 41). U.S. residents built homes like they were accustomed to, had their own English-language newspaper and Protestant churches, bought U.S. goods in the stores, insured themselves with

U.S. companies, drank ginger ale and lemonade bottled in their own local bottling company, relaxed in the lounges, reading rooms, gymnasiums, and shower baths of their German Club, and (when the notion struck) availed themselves of bi-weekly passenger service by steamer to New Orleans (Dozier 1985, 145–46).

President Zelaya granted so many concessions to U.S. capitalists (even while denying in principle that the United States had any right to intervene in Nicaragua's affairs) that by the end of his administration U.S. companies had a monopoly on the rivers through the banana country west of Bluefields. U.S. companies were growing bananas on a vast tract of government land near Las Perlas, and one U.S. company was exploiting some eight thousand acres of east coast timber rights. Other U.S. companies had substantial mineral rights, an American company owned all the port facilities at Corinto, and another U.S. company had exclusive rights to manufacture ice in Nicaragua. As a result, control of virtually all the country's principal exports (gold, coffee, bananas, lumber) came into the hands of U.S. companies (Macaulay [1967] 1985, 22).[41]

The cultural transformation of the coast, although quite continuous in some respects, proved to have a wavelike character because entrepreneurs and corporations shifted their attention from one resource to another as demand for individual commodities went through boom and bust cycles. Regardless of the resource or point in the cycle, however, every wave swept local people up and down the coast as they followed the available work, swapped their wages for goods in the commissaries, negotiated necessary social and cultural changes, and made accommodations in their lives.

The necessity to make such changes and accommodations increased considerably after Zelaya's accession to the presidency. Determined to incorporate fully into Nicaragua what had officially been an autonomous territory under Nicaraguan protection since the 1860 agreement with Great Britain, Zelaya gave orders to "occupy Bluefields militarily; dispose the Mosquito Chief and leave the consequences to me" (Hale 1994, 41). He then declared martial law, renamed the region the Department of Zelaya, and granted major resource-extraction concessions to foreign corporations. He talked with the British about a railroad and the Japanese about a canal; the Dietrick Company acquired lumber, mining, and infrastructure development rights to a seventy-mile-wide strip (equal to nearly one-quarter of the entire land area of the country). New companies rushed in, and older ones expanded: Standard Fruit, Nicaraguan Long Leaf Pine Company, Wrigley's, Rosario and Light Mines (Canada), and the Japanese-controlled Atlantic Chemical Company (Vilas 1989, 43; Bourgois 1981, 25).

Wave followed upon wave from the 1890s onward. Bragman's Bluff Lumber Company began large-scale lumbering of pine on a fifty-thousand acre concession in the northern savannas in the early 1920s, building one of the largest sawmills in Central America as well as its own electric and ice plants. Bragman's paid almost no taxes, kept no formal books, and paid workers in vouchers good only at its own commissaries. At its peak it was shipping fifty-five thousand board feet of lumber every day (Nietschmann 1973, 40–48; cf. Bermann 1986, 127–40). Environmentally the convulsive period was a disaster. Forests and their wildlife disappeared, turtle beds were exploited beyond their capacity, soil was exhausted and water polluted.

President Zelaya was forcibly removed from power with the help of four hundred U.S. Marines in 1909 (Bermann 1986, 123–50; Woodward [1976] 1985, 192–96). He was replaced as president briefly by José Madriz, but Madriz also ran afoul of the United States, and his government lasted only a few months. He was followed by Adolfo Díaz—corporate secretary of La Luz and Los Angeles Mining Company in Bluefields—whose accession was conceived and managed by the U.S. government. The corrupt and weak Díaz government found itself with a major revolt on its hands as a result of giving away national resources to U.S. interests, and of compromising the country's sovereignty. Díaz asked for U.S. troops, which quickly recaptured the west coast cities except for Masaya (Bermann 1986, 151–74). Politically as well as culturally, the message was that the United States' interpretation of its interests in Nicaragua could be opposed only at great peril.

RETROSPECTIVE: LETTERS HOME

This chapter—drawing heavily upon cultural observations made by tourists, fortune seekers, government emissaries, writers, entrepreneurs, scientists, and engineers—has focused on the cultural impact upon Nicaragua itself of both elite agendas for change and intervention from outside. The cultural changes that were happening *within* Nicaragua constituted but one pole of a political-cultural dialectic, however; the other consisted of changes in the images people *outside* Nicaragua had of a small, poor, and conflicted country. In that regard, one must bear in mind that the accounts written by such travelers as E. George Squier, Daniel Cleveland, Thomas Belt, Captain Pim, and others were also "letters home" that helped shape outsiders' attitudes toward expectations of Nicaragua.[42]

The reports of E. George Squier were among those taken most seriously back home.[43] Arriving at the mouth of the San Juan river in June 1849, Squier judged the local Indians to be "the most squalid wretches imaginable," with "faces void of expression, and altogether brutish." "They use time in Central America as if each man had an eternity in store," he reported, "and the stranger, accustomed to the . . . energy of other countries, is confounded, amazed, in fact almost crazed by the hateful inattention and car[e]lessness of the people."[44] Such "squalid and brutish" savages, Squier said, had little thought that "the great world without was meditating the Titanic enterprise of laying open their primeval solitudes, grading down their hills, and opening . . . a gigantic canal, upon which the navies of the world might pass, laden with the treasures of two hemispheres!" (Squier 1852, 1:69–70).

In such a case it was reassuring to note, Squire observed, that "the Indians of Nicaragua . . . are singularly docile and industrious, and constitute what would, in some countries, be called an excellent 'rural population'" of workers (Squier 1852, 1:284). Even better, he added later, the Nicaraguan Indian "retains his traditionary deference for the white man, and tacitly admits his superiority. . . . [Jealousy of caste] has never displayed itself in any of those frightful demonstrations which . . . threaten the entire extinction of the white race in Yucatan," but which could be avoided in Nicaragua by "the judicious encouragement of white emigration" (Squier 1852, 1:294).

Logically, then, Squier viewed himself as an official representative of a superior civilization, bearing cultural light and truth "amongst races of lesser vitality" and girding the world "as with a hoop, to pass a current of American Republicanism, vivifying dead nations and emancipating mankind, over the continent of the earth" (Squier 1852, 1:xvii, 8). He found it fitting and proper that "cheerful and enthusiastic assemblages, which the presence of an Envoy of the Great Republic of the North had inspired with passionate hopes of their own future glory and prosperity" greeted him in the cities. Arriving at Granada, Squier's party responded to the sentinel's challenge with "*americanos del norte*" — "magic words," he said, "which opened every heart and every door in Nicaragua." Granada and León welcome both him and the culture he brings. "We only want an infusion of your people," the local bishop told him in León, "to make this broad land an Eden of beauty, and the garden of the world" (Squier 1852, 1:150, 247).

The biblical drama of Squier's vision was heightened by his report on the Nicaraguan government's capture and execution (less than a month before Squier's arrival) of its most charismatic antagonist Bernabé Somoza. In Squier's view, the lesson of the struggle — characterized by the government as pitting "the civilization of the nineteenth century against the barbarism of the thirteenth" — was that the characteristic strain of Latin passion and lawlessness embodied in Somoza would inevitably be subdued and controlled by the forces of order, and that in supporting those forces the United States was clearly on the side of order, progress, and civilization.

The reality was more complex than that, however. Although Somoza first turns up in Squier's account as a "lawless, reckless fellow" who spreads random havoc for the shèer excitement and meanness of it, Squier is nevertheless fascinated by secondhand accounts of his passionate bravado and grace: A local man traveling in a boat with "an old nigger, a fat wench, and two naked picaninnies" is startled when another boat pulls alongside with "a tall, graceful man, with a feather in his hat, a red Spanish cloak hanging over one shoulder, a brace of naked pistols stuck in his belt, and a drawn sword in his hand" standing in its prow. But instead of a fearsome terrorist, Somoza turns out to be a gallant, elegant, graceful, and generous man who greets the traveler civilly (in broken English), embraces him, delivers an "energetic oration" in Spanish, attempts to give him a "splendid ring," parts "with much kindness," returns to his own boat, and pulls away (Squier 1852, 1:121, 155, 164, 166–67).

Titillated as he is by such accounts, Squier's sympathies lie with the government, which he reports to be "taking the most efficient means in their power" to put down an insurrection led by a "malefactor" surrounded by "reckless characters" aiming blows "at all order." Against a threat whose "real objects [are] revenge and plunder," mere "party distinctions [are] forgotten" and everyone pulls together to "restore the public peace" (Squier 1852, 1:168–69). Governmental decrees aimed at establishing the official demonic image of Somoza, he was at pains to point out, "were of necessity adapted to touch the popular mind." The principles at stake, said the decrees, were those "of order, of liberty, and of humanity," of God and religion, of honor, valor, and patriotism. The "wanton atrocities" of the "Vandalic horde" (anarchy, barbarism, savagery, chaos, hatred, "incendiarism, pillage, and bloodshed") were threatening the very existence of "the supreme government, the centre of order." One military commander, employing an equally melodramatic figure, warned that "the lava of sanguinary destruction threatens to overflow our dearest interests" (Squier 1852, 1:169–75).

Less than a month after Squier arrived in Nicaragua, Somoza was hunted down and captured with his principal lieutenants. "It is hardly necessary to add," Squier notes, "that they were tried by court-martial, and shot," quoting at length the statement of the commanding officer, who one last time, for good measure, called Somoza "a monster." "The robber," the commander said, "the incendiary, the desecrator of temples, the violator of female innocence, the murderer, has passed from beneath the sword of human justice to the awful presence of an offended God!" "Thus has triumphed," he assured his troops, invoking the explicit language of Liberal-Positivism, "the cause of order, of progress, and of reason!" (Squier 1852, 1:296–97). "Thus ended the insurrection of Somoza," Squier reported. "The conduct of the government, from its commencement to its close, was marked with great justice and moderation" (Squier 1852, 1:299).

British mining engineer Thomas Belt sent similar (if less dramatic) "letters home" in his book about Nicaragua. For all his sympathy for the Indian family marooned in the mountains of Chontales, for example, Belt's racism, elitism, and ethnocentrism were quite evident, and their summary message was that European (more specifically Anglo-European) culture was best. The typical east coast Nicaraguan black, he reported, "will work hard for a short while, on rare occasions, or when compelled to by another, but is innately lazy. . . . [He is] talkative, vicious, vain and sensual. . . . [He] seldom [works] either in [the mines] or in any other settled employment, unless compelled as a slave, in which condition he is happy and thoughtless." After a trip into Nueva Segovia, Belt lamented the cultural "stagnation" of Matagalpa, and noted that the "utter absence of aim or effort in the people" was distressing to "a foreigner used to . . . European cities." All the work he saw going on, he said, was "a few women washing in the river, or making tortillas or cigars in the houses." The valued markers of European culture were distressingly absent: there were "no libraries, theatres, or concert rooms; no public meetings or lectures. Newspapers do not circulate among the people, nor books of any kind. I never saw a native reading" (Belt [1874] 1985, 63–64, 234).

Such lifeways, Belt judged, had a characterological and cultural origin, rather than structural and systemic. The "ignoble reason" for the Indians' immobility, he concluded, was simply "their confirmed and innate laziness." During the two generations one house he visited had been occupied, he noted, no one "had brought in even a log of wood for a seat," and the only fruit tree in the vicinity had been nearly destroyed by target practice (Belt [1874] 1985, 243–44).

Thus Belt looked forward unabashedly to the time when Anglo-Americans would take over Central America, covering it with cattle ranches and plantations, and criss-crossing it with railroads "to keep up a healthful and continuous intercourse with the enterprising North." "The sluggard and the sensual," he said, will finally "not be able to stand before the competition of the vigorous and the virtuous." Overjoyed to return to England, Belt celebrated it as "the centre of science, philosophy, literature, and art of the Anglo-Saxon race—that race whose sons all over the globe will then look up to her with loving reverence as the mother of nations, the coloniser of the world, the pioneer of freedom, progress, and morality" (Belt [1874] 1985, 387).

A final message most travelers sent home—perhaps the most tantalizing of all, though expressed more subliminally by some than by others—was that the economic and political domination that would ensue from the triumph of order, progress, and reason over "races of lesser vitality" might be sweetened by sexual conquest as well. E. George Squier was far from alone in sketching for home-town readers the allure of the bare-breasted brown maidens of Nindirí. "There are plenty of brown damsels," the traveler Carl Scherzer reported in the mid-1850s, "with their raven hair twisted carelessly round their heads . . . and gold or mock gold ornaments on their high, somewhat too full bosoms, which they display with liberality far exceeding even that of our ball costumes" (Scherzer 1857, 1:23). Two years later Peter Stout eyed the women vendors in a street market and sent word home to Philadelphia that "the dark-eyed daughters of Seville, and the nut-brown lasses of Nicaragua, have the same origin," and that the sweet smiles that "wreathe the pouting lips of Nicaragua's daughters . . . [are] sufficient to bewilder any poor devil who, for the first time, dallies by their side" (Stout 1859, 34).

Even Mark Twain, who was more sensitive than most travelers to the cultural subtexts and the wake of corruption that followed transit-route entrepreneurs and curiosity seekers, echoed the sentiments of other leering male travelers on this subject. "About every two-hundred yards," he told his readers,

we came across a little summer-house of a peanut-stand at the roadside, with raven-haired, splendid-eyed Nicaraguan damsels standing in attitudes of careless grace behind them — damsels buff-colored, like an envelope — damsels who were always dressed the same way, in a single flowing gown of fancifully figured calico, "gathered" across the breast (they were singularly full in the bust, the young ones), and ruffled all round, near the bottom of the skirt. They have white teeth, and pleasant, smiling, winning faces. They are virtuous according to their lights, but I guess their lights are a little dim. Two of these picturesque native girls were exceedingly beautiful — such liquid, languishing eyes! such pouting lips! such glossy, luxuriant hair! such ravishing, incendiary expression! such grace! such voluptuous forms, and such precious little drapery about them! (Walker and Dane 1866, 41)

That in the national experience of Nicaragua during the nineteenth century, political and military intervention, cultural manipulation, and sexual adventure were linked in perverse symbiosis was a truth that even the most romantic and ethnocentric of nineteenth-century travelers admitted in their more candid moments. Riding into Chinandega at breakfast time at the beginning of the North American decade, E. George Squier reported that

we found a considerable party of Americans from California, homeward bound, "with pockets full of rocks," who, taken with the luxuriant climate and country, and oriental habits of the people, had rented a house, purchased horses, and organized an establishment, half harem and half caravansary, where feasting and jollity, Venus and Bacchus, and Mercury and Momus, and half of the rare old rollicking gods, banished from refined circles, not only found sanctuary, but held undisputed sway. [The Americans] were popular amongst the natives, who thought them "*hombres muy vivos*," and altogether prime fellows, for they never haggled about prices, but submitted to extortion with a grace worthy of Caballeros with a mint at their command. (Squier 1852, 2:152–53)

Beneath their elevated rhetoric of order, progress, and civilization, one gathers, local elites, entrepreneurs, and foreign emissaries alike shared symbiotic agendas in which savior and exploiter fuse, moralistic and Puritanical Yankee savior-exploiter is seduced by what he has come to condemn, and exploiter and exploited swap places phantasmagorically.

EPILOGUE

Surveying the political drama in Central America at the close of World War I with a culturally critical eye, the North American writer O. Henry noted that military adventure and predatory cultural invasion were both a concomitant of and an analogue for higher-order machinations. And as in many a tale of yore, he cast the drama as a quest for (and conquest of) the fairy princess of a far-distant land. "The game still goes on," he said,

The guns of the rovers are silenced; but the tintype man, the enlarged photograph brigand, the kodaking tourist and the scouts of the gentle brigade of fakirs have found it out, and carry on the work. . . . Gentlemen adventurers throng the waiting rooms of [a country's] rulers with proposals for railways and concessions. The little *opera-bouffe* nations play at government and intrigue until some day a big, silent gunboat glides into the offing and warns them not to break their toys. And with these changes comes also the small adventurers, with empty pockets to fill, light of heart, busy-brained, the modern fairy prince, bearing an alarm clock with which, more surely than by the sentimental kiss, to awaken the beautiful tropics from their centuries' sleep. (O. Henry [William Sidney Porter] 1919, 8)

O. Henry was wrong only about the centuries of sleep, for if it was a sleep then it was a nightmarish one at best.

Indeed a half-century before O. Henry wrote his parable, Captain Pim recounted a visit to Mosquito king George Augustus Frederic, which made it clear that the ironies, paradoxes, and contradictions of the process were evident to at least some Nicaraguans. The king was himself far from unacculturated. Educated in Jamaica, he was living in "a very commodious American lumber-house" raised on stilts. He spoke perfect English and had a "good assortment of books" including (Pim was pleased to note) the "best English

Caricature of Mosquito
Captain Drummer.
(From "Something
about the Mosquito,"
*Harper's New Monthly
Magazine*, 1855)

CAPTAIN DRUMMER.

authors" (Shakespeare, Byron, Sir Walter Scott). Also on his shelves, however, were travel narratives such as Cockburn's *A Journey Over Land* (1735),
Orlando W. Roberts's account of his journey up the San Juan river in the
1820s, and E. George Squier's pseudonymously published, ethnocentric, and
racist novel *Waikna, or Adventures on the Mosquito Coast*. The King told Pim
he couldn't believe anyone could "string together for any purpose such a
pack of lies," and that he hoped Squier's other books were written "with a
greater regard to accuracy and truth." Perhaps sensing that the Englishman
Pim would be sympathetic to anti-American sentiments, the king told of a
foreign trader from Matagalpa who called Squier "a playful liar" ("*un alegre
menteroso*" [*sic*]). As a boy, the king said, he looked on Yankees as "next
to Englishmen, the most honest and truthful people in the world," but now
scarcely knew how to express his contempt for such people, who are concerned only with "how best to advance their interests by lying and cheating."
He assured Pim that he would "far sooner be a 'poor Indian' than the best
Yankee gentleman" (Pim 1869, 267–72).

Ironically, it appears that beneath his veneer of rationality and cultural superiority, the British Museum's collector Frederick Boyle knew that the Mosquito king was right. Not able to trust himself to permit that truth to emerge into the light of day, he embodied it in scene of mythic, chthonian power. "Our friends had already set three or four fires alight," Boyle reported,

> and were deep in a laughing war with the Indian girls who had come down [to the lake] to fill their pitchers. . . . Verily, though the skin of our English love be white as her innocence, and red as bright blood can stain, yet in the gay firelight, under the dusky forest trees, it shall not make so fine a show as the golden bronze of an Indian dryad. The eyes of our love may softly shine with all the virtues; but whilst the azure smoke curls up amongst the leaves, a laughing glance and a wicked jeer will be more apt to move the pulse. White faces, low glances, and ribands of maidenly blue, are pretty things enough under the trees of Richmond; but in those picnics where the gentlemen stride about the fire in knee-boots, and flirt while polishing their revolvers, such delicate charming would, in all innocence, be cut out by the first yellow nymph whose wild black eyes sparkled within the red circle. (Boyle 1868, 62)

These "wild black eyes sparkl[ing] within the red circle" in a primordially dark wood focus a set of truths laced with irony and paradox: that what has passed for civilization turns out to be less compelling than what civilization has called savage; that civilization's dominant male paradigm of conquest (kneeboots and polished revolvers, swagger and flirtation) is here self-parodying and mawkishly beside the point; that the gentlemen's anticipated sexual conquest in fact betokens a multileveled capitulation, since these women—both as women and as sexually, psychically, and culturally other—embody (em-body) both knowledge and power the gentlemen know not of. Most tellingly, the colonizer-civilizers will fail in their political and cultural project at the very moment of their "success" with the wild black-eyed nymphs, whom they have manifestly chosen over the finest flower of their own culture—the "white faces" encircled with "ribands of maidenly blue." Since according to their own formal values it is precisely those ribands that hold their civilization together and invoke "all [its] virtues," the jig is up—for Englishmen and Yankees alike. Unfortunately for Nicaragua, the resolution of the cultural logic took far longer to play itself out historically than symbolically.

The cultural-political drama of that process continued uninterruptedly, of course, from the fall of the Zelaya government in 1909 to the advent of the Somoza regime in 1936.[45] We shall in due time return to some important aspects of the cultural politics of that interregnum. Part of Chapter 6 will carry forward the political-cultural dialectic between the Atlantic and

Pacific regions of the country; Chapter 9 will focus on the crusade of General Augusto C. Sandino's "crazy little army" (1927–33) against the first of the Somozas before he ascended to the presidency from the leadership of the National Guard; and Chapter 10 will address the rise of the Nicaraguan women's movement, which was well underway by the time the first Somoza came to power. But at this juncture we pass directly to the cultural politics of the regime from 1936 to 1979, tying the analysis as necessary to relevant developments prior to and during the interregnum.

CHAPTER 3 HE HAD AN ODD ACCENT IN SPANISH

CULTURE AND THE SOMOZA DICTATORSHIP

. . . .

[Somoza] was always behind a glass case like a watch display. He never shook hands with the people.

He was always protected. . . . [He] spoke in another language, almost always in English. He had an

odd accent in Spanish. — Omar López (Hart 1990, 58–59)

. . . .

Long dictatorships in Latin America, Jean Franco has written, "reduced to cultural deserts the countries subjected to them" (Franco 1967, 217). Certainly that was true of the forty-three-year dictatorship of the three Somozas (father and two sons) in Nicaragua (1936–1979). But Franco's desert metaphor does not fully comprehend the complex relationship between culture and the agendas of dictators. For it is not only a matter of turning a richly textured cultural landscape into a barren and arid wasteland. In a period characterized by urban life, mass communications, cultural consumerism, technically skillful and psychologically subtle image making, elaborate bureaucracy, finely tuned police power, and intricate international relations, it is also a process of manipulating and reshaping the features of that landscape: of legitimation and delegitimation, of co-optation, of deformation, of substitution and alienation.

To comprehend the cultural politics of the Somoza years, one must attend a half-dozen processes: (1) the development of Managua as the cultural (as well as political and economic) center of the country in the years prior to the advent of the regime; (2) the elaboration of the regime's own politically manipulative cultural agenda; (3) the transformation of traditional cultural systems as a result of elite-oriented economic development schemes such as cotton growing and other export-oriented agriculture; (4) the increasing penetration of Nicaragua by the consumer culture of the United States, linked in turn to systematic U.S. cultural intervention and the use of culture as an instrument of larger policy objectives; and (5) the private cultural initiatives that arose in response to the Somoza regime's neglect, manipulation, and repression.

THE MANAGUA STAGE

The Somozas built their fortunes and political power in Managua, which had slowly been increasing in importance since the 1850s, and which afforded a more hospitable stage for a megalomaniacal drama produced by a crude, upstart family than did León or Granada—the historic centers of cultural prestige, economic power, and political status in Nicaragua, dominated as they still were by entrenched elite families.

Although Managua's forty thousand inhabitants made it the largest of the pre-conquest provincial centers, the chronicler Oviedo, who saw it soon after the conquest, said it lacked "the body of a town" such as was evident in León and Granada, but instead was strung together like "a rope along the lake" (Newson 1987, 48–49). Three centuries later, the city still had a long way to go. A cholera epidemic in 1838 carried off six hundred out of a population of perhaps twelve thousand, but a dozen years later, U.S. emissary George Squier observed presciently that Managua's "position, beauty, salubrity, and capacity for production" made it "the most favorable point for the commencement of any system of colonization from the United States or from Europe" (Belcher [1843] 1970, 1:172; Squier 1852, 1:415).

By the time Squier spoke, Managua had already become (in 1846) the official capital of Nicaragua, but it would not be the center of Nicaraguan political and cultural life for some time to come. Riding through the city in the late 1860s on his search for antiquities for the British Museum, Frederick Boyle described it as still "a dirty little town" with unpaved streets, huts of cane, a wooden national palace that looked like "an ornamental barn," and "a reputation for turbulence, noise, and immorality which it has justly earned" (Boyle 1868, 2:152–56). Six years later Managua was still lighted by kerosene. By 1876 it got its first telegraph, and a decade later the railroad arrived, followed by telephones the next year. But in 1896 Richard Harding Davis found

Managua still little changed from the time of Boyle's visit. "A most dismal city," he called it, "built on a plain of sun-dried earth, with houses of sun-dried earth, plazas and parks and streets of sun-dried earth, and a mantle of dust over all. Even the stores that have been painted in colors and hung with balconies have a depressed, dirty and discouraged air. The streets are as full of ruts . . . as a country road, the trees in the place are lifeless, and their leaves shed dust instead of dew, and the people seem to have taken on the tone of their surroundings" (Davis 1896, 178). Electric lights were not turned on until 1900. As late as 1915, the city's streets were still unpaved and full of holes, and automobiles had not yet arrived. Few houses had glass windows, and the wooden cathedral's masonry facade evoked frontier-town pretense (Munro 1964, 17–19).

The cultural development of Managua was in some respects moving a bit faster than its physical transformation, however, and most of that movement had to do with competition for status as a center of the same elite (North American and European) culture that was so important to other Latin American cities' drives to modernize. As early as 1867, Nicaragua's ambassador to Great Britain had returned to Managua with the first piano ever seen there. During the Zelaya period El Teatro Castaño was constructed, and touring *zarzuela* companies as well as Italian and Cuban theater companies performed regularly. A little later, El Teatro Variedades, with support from the Díaz government, was hosting dance companies from Spain and opera companies from elsewhere in Europe (Halftermeyer [1946?], 99, 116, 143–50, 204, 338; Arellano 1982a, 48).

Shortly after the turn of the century a fairly lively literary scene also developed in Managua, aided by the waning of León's cultural influence after the death of its most famous native son, Rubén Darío, in 1916, and nourished by such journals as *Alma joven* (Young soul) and *Albores* (Beginnings) (both 1907), *Esfinge* (Sphinx) (1908), *Atlántida* (1911), and, most importantly, *Letras* (Letters) (1913). *Pinolandia* (1916), *La Semana Gráfica* (Graphic week) (1917), and *Los Domingos* (Sundays) (1918) followed during and after World War I (Arellano 1982a, 48–49). In the mid-1920s Managua's *El Diarito* reported on its front page that a ten-piece orchestra "in the Yankee style" had been formed; a month later it announced that "the national orchestra is the pride of Managua."[1] Although the apparently rather substantial theater scene in Managua was already tapering off with the arrival of moving pictures in the 1920s, it was the earthquake of March 1931 that dealt it the severest blow by destroying El Teatro Variedades and several others.

The first of the Somozas thus arrived upon the scene in Managua at an opportune moment: the city was the acknowledged political and cultural center of the country (not least because for decades it had been the seat of the embassy of the United States, from which for much of the time the country had in effect been run), and the earthquake provided an unexpected opportunity to reconstruct it in accord with some (powerful) individual's personal vision or fantasy.[2]

THE CULTURAL AGENDA OF THE FIRST SOMOZA REIGN: 1936–1956

The politics of culture during the regime of the first of the Somozas were complex, multifaceted, and frequently contradictory. Anastasio Somoza García (1896–1956), although a crude, venal, and supremely greedy man, had an intuitive grasp of the nuances of culture and of their potential political uses. He routinely allied himself with local elites and their cultural forms and values. But at auspicious moments he also sought alliances with Nicaragua's working-class people, fawning over their culture. And perennially, he steeped himself in (and shaped himself in accordance with) the popular culture of the Colossus of the North.

Anastasio Somoza García was the son of a Conservative coffee planter from San Marcos, a few miles southwest of Masaya. His father sent him to school in Granada and then, after he got the maid pregnant, to Philadelphia to live with his uncle. He attended business school and worked at various jobs before returning to Nicaragua fluent in colloquial English and an ardent Phillies fan. In between failing in various business ventures (storekeeper, automobile dealer) and working as an outhouse inspector for the Rockefeller Sanitary Commission, Somoza married Salvadora Debayle Sacasa, whom he met in Pennsylvania while she was a student at nearby Beechwood College and whose father (wealthy León Liberal doctor Luis H. Debayle) considered him unworthy of her (Bermann 1986, 219–20; Diederich 1981, 10–11).

Gratus Halftermeyer's fawning history of Managua makes the early years of Somoza García's rule sound like a cultural renaissance: the city got an Academia de Bellas Artes, a music academy, a library (Biblioteca Centroamericana), "temples of music," and painting studios in two parks (Halftermeyer [1946?], 134).[3] In the early 1940s Somoza's minister of public instruction published a school music book that included—among its saccharine hymns to the Junior Red Cross, sanitary inspectors, firemen, and the Archbishop—two or three traditional songs and a hymn to Bolívar (Ministerio de Instrucción Pública 1943).[4] In 1950 Somoza looked benignly upon the first meeting of the Congress of Nicaraguan Intellectuals (organized by the Catholic *cofradías*) and later provided state funds for a symphony orchestra.[5]

But insipid school music books, aspiring academies of the *bellas artes*, and romantic temples of music were little more than superficial public relations gestures. More representative aspects of the regime's cultural agenda were evident in its neglect of the struggling National Museum, its control of radio and television broadcasting, its censorship and repression of writers, and its blindness to the cultural fate of rural working-class people as Nicaragua's economy changed in the post–World War II period.

AN ORPHAN NATIONAL MUSEUM. Nicaragua's National Museum had fallen on hard times soon after its creation by the Zelaya administration at the turn of the century. Zelaya's successor, President Madríz, had wanted to close it, but director Diocleciano Cháves agreed to continue on as a caretaker on minimal salary.[6] Cháves personally renovated for museum use a former school building (*La Momotombo*) located next to a women's prison and a military barracks, even turning a tiny patio into a zoological and botanical garden. When U.S. puppet Adolfo Díaz became president in 1911, Cháves went without salary for a year. Neither of the two assistants Díaz's successor gave him knew or cared anything about museum work, so Cháves began to train and work with his own children. Despite his almost total lack of resources, he conducted archaeological, botanical, and zoological investigations, published scientific papers, and established collaborative relationships with major museums in the United States and Europe.[7]

During the war with Sandino (1927–33), when the government wanted to use *La Momotombo* as a hospital for Somoza's National Guard, the U.S. Marine Corps ordered Cháves to store his collection and move elsewhere. The museum later returned to *La Momotombo*, which was subsequently reduced to rubble by the earthquake of 1931. Five years later—just as the first of the Somozas assumed the presidency—Cháves died at the age of ninety-two, and the museum (then housed, appropriately enough, in one wing of a former orphan's home) was taken over by his daughter Crisanta. Two of her handwritten letters that survive from 1939 limn the desperate situation: virtually no salary, no staff, no money to do curatorial or investigative work, no assistants, and private entrepreneurs looting archaeological sites to sell artifacts to the museum.[8]

BROADCAST MEDIA: SPREADING THE GOOD GOSPEL OF AMERICAN GOODS. Controlling the radio and television broadcasting industry in Nicaragua was far more crucial to Anastasio Somoza García's political project, however, than the tiny National Museum (or any specifically cultural institution or program) could possibly be. As it turned out, his drive to control it dovetailed well with both the expansionist aspirations of the nascent U.S. broadcasting industry and the strategy of containment and manipulation being pursued by the U.S. government in Central America.

Somoza's interest was captured first by the radio network built by the U.S. Marine Corps and the National Guard (created by the United States in May

1927).[9] Marine Corps Captain James Smith began training the Guard's first telegraphers in June 1929, using Westinghouse equipment, and eighteen days later they were sent into the field with government troops fighting Sandino's army. During the next two years, technicians created a radio network (*Radio Nacional*) linking Guard installations. In 1931, radio operators who were veterans of the campaign against Sandino returned to form the Guard's Office of Communications (Hernández 1969). In December, *Radio Nacional* began transcontinental service from a station located at Bonanza, an American-owned mining center (Millett 1977, 76).

By the time he became head of the Guard in January 1933, Somoza García had a firm sense of both the military necessity and the political potential of the new medium (Millett 1977, 92, 110–11, 132–35). Within a few months he created a formal radio school, headed by former Marine Lieutenant Hugh James Phillips. Phillips's students sat on wooden benches and shared scarce books and equipment during a spartan ten-month course. For political emphasis, Phillips displayed in his office a skull he said came from a person killed by Sandino's men, and a copy of Sandino's own order ordering Phillips's death if he were caught.

Somoza's strategy was to fuse the Marine Corps–National Guard system with Nicaragua's fledgling commercial radio stations, the antecedents of which came to Nicaragua through the United Fruit Company, which had begun experimenting with radio communications among its Central American producing areas, shipping stations, and ships as early as 1904. By 1906 the company had constructed primitive stations on Nicaragua's east coast (Bluefields and Rama), and in 1911 had formed its Tropical Radio Telegraph Company subsidiary. Political and military developments thereafter (the Panama Canal, the Mexican Revolution, World War I) intensified the U.S. government's interest in controlling the involvement of Central American states in commercial radio. In 1921 (after some years of trying) Tropical Radio Telegraph — by then linked to the new Radio Corporation of America trust — signed a contract to open commercial stations in Nicaragua (Managua, Bluefields, and Cabo Gracias a Dios), and opened the first one in 1925 (Hernández 1969, 96; McCreery 1993, 26–34). The five-hundred-watt commercial station YNOP went on the air in February 1933 as *Radio BAYER*; *Radio Rubén Darío* and *The Voice of Nicaragua* followed within the next year or so.

By 1936 Somoza had fused what were by then the Guard's fifty radio stations with the new private ones to create *Radio GN y Nacional* (Radio National Guard and National) — in order, he said, that "the entire citizenry of our country may feel that they live and vibrate to a single high ideal marked by evolution toward progress, culture, and peace" (Hernández 1969, 49). In fact what the public was being offered was small doses of Latin American programming and large ones of the popular music of Bing Crosby and Tommy Dorsey, Hollywood film-star gossip, "Amos 'n Andy," and the like.[10] Clearly, radio was, as New York Congressman Emanuel Celler reminded President Roosevelt in 1937, "of intense utility and value to us for spreading the good gospel of American goods." Radio could be used, Celler added, "to cement our neighborly relations with South and Central American countries."[11]

Between 1933 and 1968, 135 radio stations were licensed in Nicaragua. The earliest ones were all in Managua, but by 1940 others were operating in Masaya, León, and Bluefields. Matagalpa (in the mountains) and Chinandega (near the northwestern border with Honduras) got stations in 1947 and 1953, but Estelí (in the far north) and Rivas (near the southern border) had none until the 1960s. Several stations were devoted explicitly to cultural programming: Diriamba's *La Voz de Diriangén* (YNDX, 1950) and *Radio Cultural* (YNRC, 1957), and Managua's *Radio Güegüense*.[12]

Commercial radio developed in Nicaragua, it is important to note, within the interwar climate of growing nationalist (and fascist) sentiment. Under the banner headline FASCIST REGIME IMPELS PROGRESS IN ITALY, Granada's *El Diario Nicaragüense* quoted from the *New York Times* Mussolini's taunt that "what we have done is nothing compared with what we are still going to do." During the early 1930s, Nicaragua had its own European-style fascist *camisas azules* (blue shirts), trained by National Guard troops who praised the killing of Sandino and held rallies in support of Somoza's emerging power. Luis Alberto Cabrales, former director of the *Camisas Azules*, was appointed inspector of public instruction in 1933. Radio broadcasting schedules published in Managua's newspaper *La Noticia* in late 1934 included four hours of programming (in German and Spanish, via shortwave) from Germany, including an offering called "Why we have faith in our Führer." In the same spirit, Nicaragua's immigration law prohibited entry of any person who "propounds doctrines dangerous to the social welfare, morality or public order," anarchists and those who "teach the destruction of the regime of private property," as well as Chinese, Turks, Arabs, Syrians, Armenians, Negroes, gypsies, and "those individuals called 'coolies.' "[13]

Within such a climate, Somoza moved swiftly to control broadcasting over the radio network his National Guard had established. After December 1935, all radio stations were subject to Executive Decree No. 284, based on the international radio broadcasting conventions of 1927 but also altered to serve explicitly political ends. Article 31 of Decree No. 284 allowed the government to prohibit any transmission or to interrupt any private telephone conversation or telegraphic communication "which may be dangerous to the security of the State . . . to public order or to good custom." Article 47 specifically prohibited the transmission of "Marxist propaganda concerning the abolition of private property or militant atheism," or other propaganda that "might stimulate strikes having political ends." Nor did control wane with the passing of the years. When Lieutenant Phillips departed in 1943, after heading the National Guard radio school for ten years, Somoza appointed his nephew Captain Rodríguez Somoza as its new director. After Somoza's death in 1956, his sons continued the tradition: of the nine heads of the various operating sections of *Radio Nacional* in 1969, seven were uniformed National Guard officers; all ten of the higher-ranking officials were as well (cf. Walter 1993, 81–82). The National Director of Radio and Television was Lieutenant Colonel Armando Monge González (Hernández 1969, 14–15).

During its early days, Nicaragua's fledgling television industry was not controlled quite so tightly by the Somoza government as radio had been. To an even greater degree, however, it developed as an extension of North American media interests, commercial products, and cultural styles and values.

As early as 1934, the Radio Corporation of America informed its stockholders that "street scenes and studio performances have been satisfactorily transmitted and received by television, on an experimental and laboratory basis."[14] The foreign extension of the U.S. television industry began in 1939 when RCA sold a transmitter to the U.S.S.R., but it was nearly twenty years until it reached Latin America (Wells 1972, 94). Emerging first in Mexico, Argentina, Brazil, and Venezuela in the early 1950s, television did not reach Nicaragua until the 1960s (Tunstall 1977, 175). As long as the U.S. market was still not saturated, U.S. commercial television networks were reluctant to invest heavily in Latin America, but by 1960 that market saturation was evident and investments grew rapidly. In the decade after 1955, the number of television stations in Latin America increased from 32 to 217 and the number of sets from 600,000 to 6.6 million. By 1972, there were nearly 17 million sets and close to 80 million viewers (Nordenstreng and Varis [1974] 1985, 13; Wells 1972, 174).[15]

Once it began, the merchandising of North American (primarily U.S.) programming moved aggressively into Latin America. Prohibited by FCC regulations from exporting as freely as they would have preferred, U.S. television networks collaborated with major film companies (not similarly restrained) to form such exporting entities as the Motion Picture Export Association of America (MPEA), Viacom International, and ABC Worldvision. Together with Screen Gems, MCA, and Twentieth Century–Fox, these merchandisers supplied the bulk of Latin American television fare: Screen Gems' *Flintstones* and *Father Knows Best*; MCA's *Leave It to Beaver*; Twentieth Century–Fox's *Peyton Place*; Viacom International's *Wild, Wild West* and *Perry Mason*; ABC's *Invaders*; and NBC's *Bonanza* (already by 1965 the network's top export, watched by 350 million viewers in sixty countries) (Nordenstreng and Varis [1974] 1985, 32–33; Schiller 1969, 82). By 1965, U.S. commercial television networks were selling $80 million worth of programs a year in Latin America (80 percent of all programs broadcast there) (Wells 1972, 120–21). Taken together, U.S. television stations were broadcasting some five million hours of programming annually by 1972, less than 30 percent of it news or educational programs. Between 100,000 and 200,000 of those hours were being exported to other countries, approximately a third of them to Latin America. Some 26 percent of what Latin American viewers saw on television consisted of commercial advertising (Nordenstreng and Varis [1974] 1985, 15, 19, 32).

Managua's first television station (YNSA-TV, Channel 8) became operational in 1956. In 1960 ABC linked Nicaragua to its *Cadena Centroamericana* network, and thence to its larger Worldvision network by buying YNSA-TV. Agreements required the stations to accept whatever ABC offered in programs and advertising. By 1962 a second station (Televisión de Nicaragua) was on the air, and in the late 1960s ABC controlled four stations in Nicaragua. The number of sets in use grew rapidly: from about 6,000 in 1964 to 19,000 three years later, to 35,000 in 1970, and to 68,000 in 1975 when YNTCN (Telecadena Nicaragua, the last of the Somoza-era stations) went on the air. By the time the regime fell in 1979, there were 115,000 sets in the country (Frappier 1969, 1–7; Wells 1972, 102, 177).[16] During the Somoza regime's final days, big-league sports, game shows, soap operas, crime shows, and the newly popular PTL (Praise the Lord) Club of fundamentalist evangelist Jim Bakker were as accessible to Managua viewers as to those in any U.S. city.[17]

Hence Nicaraguan media developed as they did during the Somoza period partly because of the powerful expansionist capacities of the U.S. media industry (supported in many instances by official U.S. foreign policy), but also because of the Somozas' cultural and political sycophancy, their own rapacious drive to reap the economic benefits of a rapidly expanding new technology, and their cynically perspicacious grasp of the media's political usefulness.

REPRESSION AND CENSORSHIP. While the Somoza regime starved the National Museum through neglect and built a broadcast media system tailored to its own interests and those of North American corporations, it also engaged in direct repression and censorship against many writers and artists.

Concern about violation of citizens' rights had arisen as early as January 1933, immediately after Somoza became head of the National Guard, when some members of the National Assembly demanded an investigation of reported torture by the Guard. During the ensuing months President Sacasa repeatedly declared states of siege that limited constitutional freedoms. As the election of 1936 approached, the Guard took an increasingly active role in pro-Somoza rallies, imprisoning supporters of Sacasa. To offset criticism in *La Prensa*, Somoza started his own newspaper *Novedades* in 1936.[18]

Openly declaring his admiration for Mussolini, Somoza projected himself as a "strong *caudillo*" redeemer of Nicaragua, and moved to take over municipal governments. To the National Assembly in January 1937 he proclaimed that his government would prohibit "the expression of *ideas exóticas*." The constitution of 1939 made it illegal to "make statements contrary . . . to the fundamental institutions of the state," to the established social order, or "to public morality and proper behavior" (*la moral y las buenas costumbres*). It guaranteed freedom of the press, but provided for preventive detention and martial law. As World War II approached, a new Law for the Defense of Democracy prohibited the diffusion of "all ideologies and political and social systems contrary to the country's 'republican and democratic system' and against established social order." It led to the closing of the labor newspapers *La Verdad* and *Hoy* in 1941–42 (Booth 1985, 51–63; Walter 1987, 80–88, 98, 125, 166–95). As soon as Nicaragua entered the war, Somoza declared a state of siege that remained in effect for four years. Anti-Somoza demonstrations in mid-1944 led to the ironically named *Ley de libertad de emisión y difusión del pensamiento* (Law of freedom of broadcast and diffusion of thought) of September 1944, which gave the media free postage and tax exemption but prohibited propaganda to subvert public order, to call for civil disobedience, or to insult the fundamental institutions of the state (Walter 1987, 166, 184, 194–96, 229–42).

The end of the war brought little relaxation in the repression. The National Guard became larger rather than smaller—from about thirty-six hundred in 1946 to nearly forty-four hundred in 1956, and many Guard members became wealthy through working in Somoza family businesses and participating in the many forms of graft and corruption in which the Guard was regularly involved (Booth 1985, 54–57; Walter 1993, 214–15).[19] The university student newspaper *El Universitario* was harassed continuously by the Guard throughout its short life until it was closed down early in 1947. A new law passed in September 1953 made it a crime for anyone to criticize established authorities or friendly foreign governments, or for anyone belonging to a "political party with international connections" to own a printing shop or newspaper. An executive decree of February 1955 prohibited the circulation of any printed "communist propaganda," and reporters and publishers of newspapers were regularly paid off to hew the regime's line (Walter 1987, 244, 353, 372).

One of the first Nicaraguan writers to feel the repression was Manolo Cuadra (1907–57), who had worked as a journalist in Managua before fighting with Somoza's troops against Sandino. He soon became disaffected, however, and was jailed in León's infamous *La Veintiuno* prison for participating in an uprising in the army against Somoza. Subsequently accused of being a Communist, he was confined for ten months to Little Corn Island off the Atlantic coast. He was also jailed for political activity in Managua's *La Aviación* prison in 1943 and on the island of Ometepe four years later (Cuadra 1982, 11, 171).[20]

Following the assassination attempt against Somoza García in April 1954, artists, writers, and intellectuals felt increased pressures to conform or keep silent. Poet Ernesto Mejía Sánchez, rumored to be the "intellectual author" of the 1954 plot, had to leave the country for ten years after Somoza was assassinated in 1956. Father Ernesto Cardenal—a participant in the 1954 plot— found all of his books prohibited in Nicaragua, as were those of virtually any Russian writer (even Tolstoy) and any books by or about Fidel Castro or Che Guevara (White 1986, 38–39, 61). Cardenal's mail was also intercepted and opened, and he was harassed by customs officials when he returned to Nicaragua from travels abroad (experiences recounted in his poem "La Llegada") (Cardenal 1983b, 240–41; Zwerling and Martin 1985, 45; Borgeson 1977, 36, 77).

WORKING-CLASS CULTURE AND BOOM DEVELOPMENT

From his earliest days in public life, Somoza García showed himself to be quite aware of the political value of venerating working-class or *campesino* culture—particularly those portions of it that were, or could pass for, indigenous. So as not to function as a barrier to elite visions of economic and cultural progress, however, such culture had to be defined and positioned carefully. For elite purposes, romanticized characterizations of indigenous culture proved more deployable—more palatable to the elites, more easily assimilable to nationalist purposes, less burdened by paradox and contradiction—than were the disagreeable realities of working-class and *campesino* life.[21] Thus, sensitive to the pacifying potential of such cultural constructions in the 1940s, the massive San Antonio sugar mill (which employed half of all of Nicaragua's industrial workers and produced three-quarters of its sugar) staged a ceremony featuring cane-cutting contests among its workers (upon whose ancestral lands its cane fields were located), and *La Prensa* hailed it as "the solution to the social question" (Gould 1990a, 58–59; Walter 1987, 338n.).

This divided agenda of veneration and manipulation was evident in Nicaragua's Instituto Indigenista Nacional, founded in December 1941 for the ostensible purpose of studying "the indigenous problem in Nicaragua . . . toward the end of improving the conditions of life for Nicaraguan Indians," and proposing protectionist legislation.[22] Voicing alarm that "groups of purely indigenous people" (*grupos de indígenas puros*) were disappearing, that the few remaining ones for the most part had lost their primitive languages and their customs, and were adapting themselves more and more to "western civilization," the institute called its members to the "high social labor" of "the culturation of our indigenous masses" (*la culturación de nuestras masas indígenas*).

The term *culturación* was somewhat ambiguous in the context, but appeared to refer to socializing Indians back into primary relationship to their own culture, rather than *acculturation* to the dominant mestizo society. It soon emerged, however, that despite the culture-sensitive rhetoric, acculturation was what was intended. Early in 1947, the institute's Director General Carlos reported to his Instituto Indigenista Interamericano colleagues that eight to ten thousand Sumo Indians who were still living *la vida primitiva* in central Nicaragua were to be moved into new "urban centers" where they could be "incorporated better into civilization."[23] Subsequent issues of the journal carried many articles on the problems of "incorporating" the indigenous population into national life and culture, but virtually nothing on protective legislation.

The majority of the benefits of the "high social labor" of the institute were intended to flow, in fact, to the Somoza regime rather than to Nicaragua's remnants of indigenous people. The institute proclaimed its independence of the government, but its executive committee was made up largely of heads of government ministries (even including the Ministry of Marine War and Aviation). The third issue of *Nicaragua Indígena* (January 1947) carried a picture of Somoza on its cover.

Later issues contained substantive articles on both pre-Columbian and indigenous language, place names, legends, and customs, but the institute's political debts and agenda were evident. The issue following Somoza García's assassination in 1956 carried another full-page photo of him in full military dress, and acknowledged him as its founder and "a great statesman" (*un gran estadista*). The institute itself was proclaimed to be "the fruit of [the] noble concerns" of one who was "ever vigilant for the growth and prestige of Nicaraguan culture." Another issue a year later recalled Somoza as "our unforgettable leader" and praised his efforts to "rescue aboriginal peoples from a tangential and painful life, giving them the light of civilization and exalting them to the effective enjoyment of their Nicaraguan nationality."[24]

Just how little Anastasio Somoza García actually valued traditional or *campesino* culture became clear during the post–World War II economic boom. He had taken office at a time of serious financial crisis for Nicaragua: inflation was rising (the U.S. dollar that would buy only one *córdoba* in late 1934 would buy nearly six in 1938) and the price of coffee (hence export income) was falling. After World War II, however, coffee prices increased dramatically again, raising coffee export income from $4.3 million in 1946 to $23 million in 1956, and overall export income from $18 million to $65 million during the same period (Walter 1987, 75, 128–32, 293–95; 1993, 180–81).

The most important boom crop from the late 1950s onward, however, was not coffee but cotton. In the early 1940s, all five Central American countries had produced only about twenty-five thousand bales of cotton, but post–World War II demand, coupled with favorable soils and climate, new insecticides and fertilizers, new technology, and new roads, boosted production. Nicaragua's Banco Nacional provided the highest loan subsidies to growers of any of the Central American republics, and cotton export sales rose from less than $150,000 in 1946 to $23.5 million a decade later. Between 1949 and 1955, Chinandega area cotton growers tripled their acreage, and the number of tractors in Nicaragua rose from five hundred to twenty-five hundred, virtually eliminating oxen as draft animals. Production rose to 450,000 bales in 1958, and to nearly triple that in 1965. Half-page newspaper advertisements offered the vehicles, machinery, and pesticides that would guarantee the new cotton fortunes: Caterpillar bulldozers and harvesters and Land Rovers, Bayer's E-605 and Shell's Aldrin. By the early 1970s, 45 percent of all Central American cotton was coming from Nicaragua (Walter 1987, 293–95; Gould 1990a, 165–66; Williams 1986, 13–15, 26–28, 40, 166).

The new infusion of money meant that life for Managua's expanding middle class and a new sector of cotton-growing oligarchs improved steadily.[25] *La Prensa*'s advertisements for cosmetics, fancy clothing, and English classes beckoned daily, and much of the new disposable income in consumers' hands went to buy social and cultural status. Social and political contradictions were stark: in one May 1955 issue of *La Prensa*, photos of Nicaragua's newly crowned Queen of Tobacco and Agriculture vied for the attention of readers beguiled on the next page by the quintessential cultural models for such queenery: voluptuous Jane Russell and Marilyn Monroe in an ad for *Gentlemen Prefer Blondes*.[26]

In the process of such a transformation, rural agricultural workers fared poorly, both economically and culturally—especially those caught in the burgeoning cotton industry. As more and more land was converted to cotton production, tens of thousands of *campesinos* lost their traditional jobs on *haciendas*, and the majority of the agricultural labor force became seasonal rather than year-round (Gould 1990a, 87, 98, 134). Although Nicaragua had a higher than average percentage of small growers, 60 percent of its cotton came from farms larger than 364 acres. And as elsewhere in Central America, the largest share of the wealth went to a few dozen families (Williams 1986, 31–32, 51).[27]

As Gould has shown, the implications of such a transformation for rural agricultural workers and their traditional cultural system were especially evident (but not uncharacteristic) in the small village of Tonalá near Chinandega. Of the ten thousand acres of communal land distributed to individual Indian families in the area by the Zelaya government at the turn of the century, most had quickly ended up in the hands of Liberal politicians, leaving the Indians eking out a living in subsistence agriculture. A new railroad into the area in 1938 spurred a development boom oriented toward agroexport production. To boost his standing with local *campesinos*, Somoza García donated land for the village of Tonalá, which was established in the late 1940s. But when the cotton boom came, it brought large expropriation of lands from the *campesinos*, whose fields were taken over and whose orchards were plowed up (Gould 1990a, 157–77). The transformation of life and labor was dramatic:

> The view from the village changed from verdant, lush forests and hilltop pastures into brown, barren hills and blinding white fields of cotton. Where a few years earlier, men had hunted birds to provide extra protein for the family diet, small propeller planes sprayed insecticide, poisoning men, women, children, animals, and water supplies, and, indirectly, the milk of nursing women. In one boom year alone, several hundred cotton pickers died from inhalation of the poisonous fumes; but the cotton buds sprouted and the *hacendados* prospered beyond their forefathers' wildest dreams. (Gould 1990a, 164; cf. Williams 1986, 48–52; Incer 1977, 29)

Ecological impacts of the transformation were devastating: air, land, and water were fouled; new insecticide-resistant insects multiplied; and soil was depleted by the nitrogen-hungry cotton plants.

Meanwhile, Tonalá itself was being turned into a sordid center of gambling and prostitution (controlled by Somoza functionaries) for migrant agricultural workers. Indeed, cultural domination by the oligarchy and denigration of working-class culture was so great in some rural areas that a field laborer who met his landlord was obliged to step into the street, press his hands into a praying gesture, and ask the blessing of his *Santito patrón* (Gould 1990a, 73). Moreover, as Williams (1986) has pointed out, the social and cultural impacts of the agroexport conversion associated with cotton were not reversed (or indeed, reversible) when the world market turned downward in 1964. Peasant family and community life had been permanently transformed, cotton lands and machinery were turned to other crops, labor had been proletarianized, and banks channeled their funds into similar new ventures (Gould 1990a, 177–78; Williams 1986, 66, 71). Meanwhile, reassuring romantic articles on traditional culture appeared regularly in *La Prensa*.[28]

CULTURAL INTERVENTION FROM THE NORTH

Both the system of cultural neglect, manipulation, censorship, repression, and transformation put into place during the early decades of the Somoza dynasty's rule and subsequent culturally destructive cotton-boom economic development were problematic to the people of Tonalá and scores of other communities across Nicaragua. That was so in the first instance because such transformations were directly inimical to non-elite ways of life. But those transformations were also exacerbated by the increasing cultural intervention of U.S. culture through print and broadcast media, a flood of consumer products, and what in diplomatic parlance was called "cultural exchange." Although the U.S. Marines left Nicaragua in January 1933 and Managua celebrated its own national culture by raising a monument to poet Rubén Darío in September, the presence and influence of U.S. culture continued to increase for the next forty-six years, both because U.S. corporations and the U.S. government urged it, and because of the Somozas' sycophantic attraction to U.S. cultural values.

CONSUMER CULTURE. As the previous chapter suggested, North American products, styles, values, and institutions were already abundantly in evidence to travelers who sailed up the San Juan River in the 1850s. By the early 1920s the tide was in full swell. León's *El Centroamericano* of 1922 carried only a few advertisements for U.S. products (Sloan's liniment, Bayer aspirin, and Dewitt's liver pills), but advertisements in other newspapers in succeeding years offered a cornucopia of such products: Arrow shirts and Stetson hats, Johnnie Walker and Black Cat whiskey, Fisk tires, General Electric and Westinghouse electrical appliances, Vick's Vaporub and Mentholatum, Gillette razors, Quaker Oats and Royal baking powder, Flit insect spray, Victrolas and Atwater-Kent radios, Ford and Nash automobiles, Camel cigarettes, and

Bailará como nunca lo ha hecho antes…al compás de la *Nueva* Victrola Ortofónica

Las notas profundas, rítmicas y fascinadoras de los bajos y las vibrantes notas agudas de los instrumentos—tonos y variaciones como nunca se han oído antes—son elementos muy importantes de la música de baile que ahora son reproducidos por la *Nueva* Victrola Ortofónica en toda la belleza característica de estos instrumentos.

Adquiera uno de estos maravillosos instrumentos para su hogar. Es lo mismo que si tuviera a su disposición las orquestas más famosas del mundo. Bailará como no lo ha hecho nunca. Acuda a un comerciante Victor y pídale que le toque sus piezas favoritas. Sólo con una audición podrá darse cuenta de la absoluta perfección de la *Nueva* Victrola Ortofónica.

La *Nueva* **Victrola** *Ortofónica*

VICTOR TALKING MACHINE Co.   CAMDEN, N. J., E. U. de A.

Vendidas exc'usivamente — por — La⁺ern & Thompson en Gran'da

Modelo *Colony*

Victrola advertisement. "You will dance as never before . . . to the new Victrola. . . . It is as if you had the most famous orchestras in the world at your disposal." (From *El Diario Nicaragüense*, 9 July 1926)

Waterman pens. "You will dance as you have never danced before," promised an ad for Victrolas in 1926; phonograph records reorganized social life ("It is much more comfortable and agreeable to dance at home," said a Victrola ad in a Managua daily).[29] A later Victrola advertisement that offered the "divine art . . . of the music of the whole world" was illustrated with images of Latin instrumentalists and dancers, but the text referred solely to European performers. By contrast, virtually no analogous products from European countries were to be seen. Writing in the late 1930s, Gratus Halftermeyer spoke proudly of Managua's "beautiful Roosevelt Avenue, where one encounters the Executive Power, the National Bank and the Bank of London, the best

● Pida Avena Quaker a donde-
quiera que vaya . . . así obtendrá
siempre la fuente natural de nu-
trición más completa y económica para provecho de su propia
salud! Cómala habitualmente,
recuerde que la Avena Quaker
es el cereal más rico en energía
alimenticia, proteína y vitamina
B1. Además su exquisito sabor
halaga el paladar.

FÁCIL DE PREPARAR Hierva
2 tazas de agua. Añádale
sal.Cuandoestéhirvien-
do agregue 1 taza de
Avena Quaker. Coci-
nela meneando, por
2½ minutos. Eso es
todo.

Quaker Oats advertisement as a late
example of colonialist themes in
advertising. "Don Facundo never
penetrated into anywhere without being
served Quaker for breakfast." (From *La
Prensa*, 18 May 1949)

department stores . . . and elegant buildings. . . . This avenue is today the
Wall Street of Nicaragua." By 1940, nearly 60 percent of Nicaragua's imports
came from the United States (Halftermeyer [1946?], 117; *Nicaragua. Guía general ilustrada* 1940, 15). Both the products themselves and the advertising that
accompanied them were freighted with cultural messages—frequently with
subliminal political messages.

With the development of the Pan American highway and direct air links
to the United States, the flood of beguiling U.S. products, styles, and values
was further reinforced by tourist traffic in both directions. Pan American
Airways made its first Key West–to–Havana flight in 1927 and by 1929 was
flying to Puerto Rico with intermediate stops in all the Central American
capitals.[30] A 1941 edition of the airline's Spanish-language public relations
magazine (*Caminos del Aire*) was dedicated to Somoza, whom it called a
"heroic champion of peace and pure idealist, whose goals . . . have been to
channel . . . Nicaragua along the paths of progress." By the late 1940s, Costa

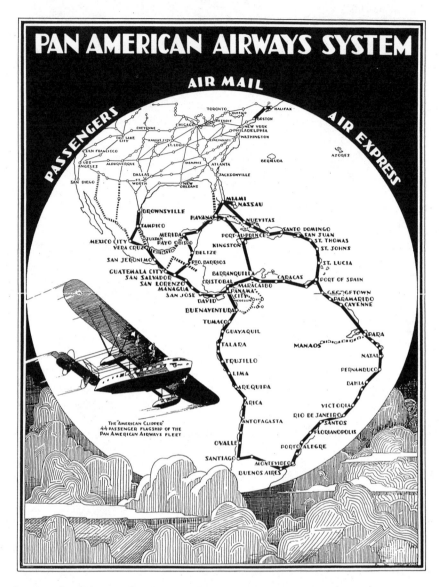

Pan American Airways advertisement, 1933. (From *Sixth Annual Report to Stockholders of the Pan American Airways Corporation, 1933*, Franklin D. Roosevelt Library)

Rican TACA Airlines was offering direct flights to New Orleans and Miami, and $149 roundtrips to Mexico City. Pan Am countered with four flights daily to Guatemala. The Pan American highway, first proposed during the 1920s and developed during the 1930s and 1940s, finally opened completely in 1948.[31]

It was not merely the taste-shaping presence of U.S. products on the mar-

"Kill Him!" Advertisement for Bayer Aspirin. Text reads in part: "When the adversary did not deserve grace, the thumb of the Caesars ordered the triumphant gladiator, 'Kill him!' When a man is assaulted by physical pain, his whole organism, impelled by the powerful instinct of defense, gives him the same definitive and unappealable mandate, 'Kill him!'" (From *Los Domingos*, 31 December 1922)

ket in Nicaragua that had such a cultural impact, however, but the fact that their use inevitably affected long-established cultural practices and values. The availability of patent medicines changed both notions of health (particularly of women's health) and methods for treatment; electrical appliances reorganized domestic design, decoration, and daily routines; baby formula

Los dolores y las enfermedades son una barrera entre Ud. y su felicidad. ¡Destrúyala! La ciencia moderna ha puesto a su alcance la fuerza necesaria para ello perfeccionando la Aspirina hasta convertirla en un analgésico absolutamente seguro: la **Cafiaspirina,** o sean las Tabletas Bayer de Aspirina y Cafeína (identificadas por la Cruz Bayer). Con dos Tabletas de **Cafiaspirina** puede Ud. destruir en pocos instantes el sufrimiento causado por los dolores de cabeza, muela, garganta y oído; las neuralgias; las jaquecas; los resfriados, etc., y devolverle la energía y el bienestar a su organismo.

"Destroy!" Advertisement for Bayer Aspirin. (From *Los Domingos*, 4 February 1923)

changed both the relationship between mother and child and other traditional aspects of child care. Other advertisements employed remarkably explicit appeals to gender stereotypes to enhance the appeal of products. A series for Bayer's Cafiaspirina in the early 1920s featured one-word large-type imperatives illustrated with images of forceful Aryan-looking males: a sword-wielding gladiator standing triumphantly with one foot on his dead opponent (*MATALO!* [kill him!]); a nearly nude, muscular male breaking through a

"Create!" Advertisement for Bayer Aspirin. (From *Los Domingos*, 25 February 1923)

barrier of stone letters (*DESTRUYA!* [destroy!]); and a burly sculptor gazing
(hammer and chisel resolutely in hand) at a sculpture of a nude female who
is leaning on a rather insistently phallic-looking support (*CREA!* [create!]).
A parallel series drew upon explicit and subliminal images of women: three
flaxen-haired and begowned maidens stretched upon the rocks in a mountain
pass, pouring *La Fuente Primitiva* (the primitive fountain) from their hands
into the peaceful valley below; and another naked, muscled Aryan male forc-

LA FUENTE PRIMITIVA

No existe sino una Aspirina. Surgió ella de la fuente Bayer y ha extendido su fama por el mundo entero. Quien hable de Aspirinas esta, por tanto, en un error fundamental.

De la misma fuente salió la Fenacetina, y las dos, asociadas, formaron una corriente poderosa (Tabletas Bayer de Aspirina con Fenacetina) para combatir catarros, resfriados, gripe, etc.

Un tributario de gran importancia, la Cafeína, unida en dosis terapeutica a la Aspirina (Tabletas Bayer de Aspirina con Cafeina,) formo otra corriente de fuerza incomparable para vencer, de modo seguro y rapido, los dolores de cabeza, muelas y oido; las neuralgias; las jaquecas, etc.

The Primitive Fountain (earlier version). Advertisement for Bayer Aspirin. (From *Los Domingos*, 10 April 1921)

ing kneelike rocks apart with his bare hands to allow the Primitive Fountain to flow.[32]

HOLLYWOOD FILM AND U.S. POLICY. In some sectors, the aggressive promotion of U.S. commercial culture was bolstered by U.S. government policy. The marketing of U.S. commercial films, for example, depended upon close coordination between Hollywood and Washington, and the proliferation of

The Primitive Fountain (later version). Advertisement for Bayer Aspirin. (From *Los Domingos*, 22 May 1921)

U.S. comics in daily newspapers benefitted from Walt Disney's enhanced prestige as a producer of (and spokesperson for) U.S. cultural and political propaganda from the early 1940s onward.

From at least a dozen years before the advent of the Somoza regime, U.S. commercial filmmakers were peddling their wares successfully in Nicaragua, as they were throughout Latin America. As early as 1926, Managua had at least three movie theaters, and U.S. films were their staple fare.[33] The earthquake of 1931 destroyed some theaters, but new ones (the Palace, the González, Teatro Clamer) opened soon thereafter. It was almost as easy for Managuans as for North American audiences to see Clara Bow ("more beautiful and seductive than ever") in *Savage* ("an impetuous romance, full of passion"). On the same day that El Teatro González was offering viewers Charles Boyer and Olivia de Havilland in *The Golden Door*, and Mickey Rooney in *Harmonies of Youth* with the Paul Whiteman orchestra, Carole Lombard and Victor Mature graced the screen of the América.[34]

With the advent of the Franklin Roosevelt administration in 1933, film and its effects upon public attitudes and its consequent implications for policy began to receive more governmental attention. Only a few months after the inauguration, Senate majority leader Joe T. Robinson wrote to Roosevelt to advise him that "a subtle campaign is being started through the media of moving pictures designed to render the Administration unpopular." Robinson was concerned that former Republican National Committee chairman Will Hayes's increasing power in the film industry promised that more and more clips of out-of-work people would show up on movie newsreels.[35] Roosevelt's papers reveal him to have maintained a keen interest in film: its educational and entertainment value, its potential political uses relative to economic recovery and to partisan politics, and its technological development.

In order to maintain good relations with the motion picture industry, the administration worked to facilitate the distribution of Hollywood films in Latin America. In late 1938, U.S. Vice Consul H. Bartlett Wells wrote to his superiors in Washington about gaining concessions from the Somoza government that would make U.S. films more competitive with films from Mexico, Germany, and Great Britain.[36] His efforts paid off. Of the nearly fifty films shown during November 1941, thirty-six (72 percent) were from the United States.[37] In mid-1941, Managua's Teatro Margot had screened *The Duke of West Point*, starring Joan Fontaine and Louis Hayward—a timely offering in view of the fact that Somoza's elder son would shortly enter West Point as a student.[38] Viewers were promised "a brilliant and grandiose film developed in the famous academy of West Point, with its joys, its nobility, its patriotic ideas, its immortal romances and its impressive parades." By the end of the 1940s, Managua could offer Paramount, United Artists, and other U.S. film companies more than a dozen theaters for screening their creations, and the U.S. embassy reported that of nearly 250 feature films shown in Nicaragua during the first six months of 1950, 177 (73 percent) were from the United States.[39]

The U.S. government also attempted to insure that the films screened would reflect favorably upon the United States, especially during World

United Artists movie advertisement for
The Duke of West Point. (From *La Prensa*,
19 July 1941)

War II. In mid-1942 Coordinator of Inter-American Affairs Nelson Rockefeller chartered as a Delaware corporation Prencinradio, Inc., all of whose
officers and employees were Rockefeller's own employees in the Office of the
Coordinator. Rockefeller's letter of 18 July 1942 to the general counsel of the
Office of the Coordinator argued that forming the corporation was essential
"in view of the practical difficulties in having the Government participate
directly in foreign countries in activities of a confidential nature designed to
improve existing media and to create additional media."

Prencinradio's confidential first annual report described its two principal
activities. The first was "to stimulate development of the Mexican motion picture industry" in order to support the war effort and hemispheric solidarity
and to "combat Axis Spanish-speaking pictures," and forestall development of
the industry in Mexico by interests unsympathetic to the U.S. war effort. The
United States sold equipment to two Mexican companies (Azteca and Clasa
studios), and provided training, underwrote some production costs, and co-
operated in distribution. The second activity was referred to cryptically as "a

radio project of a highly confidential nature" for which funds appear to have been laundered through commercial banks. Although the initial film-related activities of Prencinradio were carried out in Mexico, Rockefeller informed its board of directors shortly after it was formed that "this program designed for Mexico is but one of a broad plan to develop the motion picture industry in some other Latin American republics for the same purpose." "It is believed," wrote an official of the Motion Picture Division of the Office of the Coordinator, "that the plan will serve the important purpose of cultural and educational interchange between the other American republics themselves"; that it would be a "local industry" that could do a better job than the United States itself; and that it "would carry their message in the native tongue of the republics." [40]

The U.S. government's interest and involvement in film in Latin America continued unabated after the war's end. A confidential 1950 memo referred to the embassy's interest in gathering "information on newspaper reviews, public criticism and informal evaluation . . . of the effect on local audiences of American motion pictures and in particular in cases where . . . [films] might be offensive to the customs, languages and institutions of foreign peoples." [41] The embassy was concerned, however, not about offending foreign sensibilities but about embarrassing revelations of racism in the United States. At issue were two Twentieth Century–Fox films in particular: Elia Kazan's *Pinky*, and *No Way Out*, both of which treated "the negro question in the United States." The embassy admitted that both films were "remarkably fine productions from an artistic point of view," and that the latter was a "truly fine picture." Moreover, they were "honest portrayal[s] and interpretation[s] of an American problem." Nevertheless, the embassy argued, "both are equally inappropriate for showing in Managua." But why? Weren't local people capable of judging whether or not the films were offensive? The embassy spokesperson argued that *No Way Out* was "a very dangerous picture to be shown abroad in almost any country and certainly in countries where mixed blood, negro or Indian, is the rule." Why? Because racial tensions were so high in Nicaragua? That couldn't be it, because—as the writer admitted—"the problem with which [the film] deals does not exist in this country . . . and racial prejudice is virtually unknown." Then why? The problem, it turned out, was that the film "has been prejudicial to . . . [U.S.] interests . . . [and] can be used as ammunition by communist elements." For their own part, Nicaraguans seemed indifferent to the potentially dire consequences of showing the films; there have been, the embassy admitted in conclusion, "no press reviews or comments." Even back home in the United States, *Commonweal* called *Pinky* one of the year's best films and *Newsweek* noted that "what little press criticism there was . . . was either tactfully oblique or ironic." The film played without incident in many southern cities, although Houston's blacks and whites had to attend separate showings.[42]

Fortunately, the embassy was persuaded, there were safer means of achieving "cultural understanding" than promoting Hollywood films that treated "the negro problem" so candidly—such as promoting a "cultural exchange" of baseball players. Since its introduction to Nicaragua decades earlier, baseball had become the national sport, and earlier U.S. functionaries had been well aware of its pacifying political potential. From his position as Collector General of Customs in Nicaragua, North American Clifford D. Ham commented in 1916 on the "moral influence" of the marines and the political impact of baseball upon Nicaragua. Middle-class working people who initially resented the presence of the marines, Ham said, got interested in watching them play baseball, and then formed their own teams "under the patronage of the President and the Archbishop." "The American marines are now very popular," he reported, and "baseball has done it. It would be a crime to withdraw the marines and stop the baseball craze in Nicaragua. It is the best step towards order, peace and stability that has ever been taken. . . . People who will play baseball and turn out by the thousands every week to see the match games are too busy to participate in revolutions" (Ham 1916, 187–88). "Anything to do with baseball and anything that would tie Nicaraguan and American baseball in the public consciousness," the embassy was still convinced more than thirty-five years later, "would pay off heavily in the promotion of good will."[43]

The cultural planners envisioned a "traveling exhibit" of baseball paraphernalia that could be given as trophies to local teams after exhibition games. "The appearance of two or more well-known baseball names . . . heralded by good advance newspaper and radio publicity," they assured the State Department, "could make a greater sensation in this country than the visits of top ranking movie stars." The problem of the "language barrier" could be easily solved: Nicaraguan players from the Atlantic coast spoke English, albeit of "a somewhat peculiar variety." And U.S. players put off by the lowly "social status" of Nicaraguan players could be mollified by arranging visits "to the Presidential Mansion, to General Somoza's residence, and the like." Visits by U.S. players to Nicaragua would be preferable, moreover, to visits in the other direction, because they "would yield considerably smaller returns on the money invested" and because "many of the top flight local players have colored blood" and (incidentally) would find it "very hard on their finances to provide themselves with suitable clothes for a visit to the United States."

THE CULTURAL POLITICS OF COMIC STRIPS. The growing importance of Hollywood movies and the promotion of U.S. big league sports (together with their associated politics) was paralleled by the proliferation of U.S. comic strips in Nicaraguan newspapers.

The contemporary newspaper comic strip's most recognizable predecessors emerged in the 1890s in the Hearst and Pulitzer newspapers. The *Katzenjammer Kids* dates to 1897 and *Mutt and Jeff* to 1907, but many others appeared in the 1920s and 1930s: *Little Orphan Annie* in 1924, *Tarzan* and *Buck Rogers* in 1929, *Dick Tracy* in 1931, *Terry and the Pirates*, *L'il Abner*, and *Flash Gordon* in 1934, and *Superman* in 1938.

Although an early form of *Aventuras de Chico Rosita* ran as early as 1922 in *Los Domingos*, comic strips were rare in Nicaraguan newspapers until the 1930s. *La Prensa's El Agente Secreto X-9*, which appeared on 1 January 1934, ran only a few months, but others soon became staples of the daily newspapers. *Aventuras de Sherlock Porras* and *El Temporal* appeared in January 1935 and were followed by several short series produced by Ed Wheelan for Editors Press, another of whose series created by J. Carrol Mansfield featured U.S. military actions against "redskins" (*pieles rojas*).

Following a hiatus during World War II, the comics became more numerous. *La Flecha* had *Felix the Cat* by late 1947, and by at least the early 1960s, *La Prensa* and *Novedades* readers could follow such characters as Mutt and Jeff (*Benetín y Eneas*), Buck Rogers (*Buck Rogers en Guerra Interplanetaria*), El Jincho Inteligente (featuring a stereotypical sombreroed Mexican *indio* [mispronounced "jincho" for a denigratingly comic effect]), Sherlock Holmes, the Katzenjammer Kids (*Maldades de Dos Pilluelos*), Maggie and Jiggs (*Educando a Papá*), Tarzan, Superman, Dick Tracy, Blondie and Dagwood (*Lorenzo y Pepita*), Popeye, and Walt Disney's Donald Duck and Mickey Mouse (*El Ratón Miguelito*).[44]

Especially in countries undergoing socially and culturally destabilizing pressures — rapid urbanization, the disturbance of traditional patterns of rural life, a major influx of consumer culture from outside, or the rise of a dictatorship — so apparently benign a cultural detail as newspaper comics is by no means devoid of political effect. The political and cultural implications of the Walt Disney comics in underdeveloped countries, and especially their links to larger U.S. interests, are particularly suggestive in this regard.[45]

The emerging Disney empire in fact almost died during the late 1930s, and probably would have done so had its resuscitation not been aided by the U.S. government (Schickel [1968] 1986, 229–30; Eliot 1993, 81–118). When World War II cut off Disney's lucrative European market (and thus half his income), the government rescued him by commissioning training and propaganda films that became a mainstay for his nearly bankrupt studio. A parallel

Aventuras de Chico Rosita comic strip. (From *Los Domingos*, 3 December 1922)

effort turned Disney toward developing Latin American markets for his films and comics.

At a critical moment when Disney was trying to settle a long and costly strike among his employees, Nelson Rockefeller, as Coordinator of Inter-American Affairs, arranged for him to go on a six-week tour as a "good-will ambassador" to Latin America, which coincidentally helped divert public attention from the strike (Schickel [1968] 1986, 263; Mosley 1985, 205; Eliot 1993, 148–50).[46] Disney's subsequent Latin American films *Saludos Amigos* and *The Three Caballeros*, which depicted a stereotypic Latin America of comic parrots and goofy gauchos (together with a lecherous Donald Duck and a sequence of animated phallic cactus plants), were panned by the critics (Schickel [1968] 1986, 275; Eliot 1993, 180–83).[47] But the critics had one view, and the public had another: the Disney empire flourished, and by 1962, the monthly circulation of Disney comics had reached fifty million in fifteen languages in fifty countries, including four Spanish language editions.

As Dorfman and Mattelart amply demonstrate, the political and cultural world projected in the Latin American versions of the Disney comics features degrading cultural stereotypes and reactionary politics. Third-world countries (Inca-Blinca, the Republic of San Bananador, Aztecland, Unsteady-stan, and Outer Congolia) are burlesqued and trivialized. The typical Disney Latin American, Dorfman concluded after looking at hundreds of examples, is "somnolent, sells pottery, sits on his haunches, and has a thousand year-old culture" (Dorfman and Mattelart [1971] 1984, 54). Women are unfailingly subordinate to men; their only power derives from their role as seductresses. In the Unsteadystans of Disney (ruled by leaders with names like Prince Char Ming and Soy Bheen), power relationships are sharply defined by patterns of obedience, submission, discipline, economic domination, and physical repression. When Unsteadystan citizens get up off their haunches and rebel, Dorfman and Mattelart note, their rebellion "is immediately turned into an incomprehensible game of someone-or-other against someone-or-other, a stupid fratricide lacking in any ethical direction or economic *raison d'être*" (Dorfman and Mattelart [1971] 1984, 56).

Disney's own real-life politics mirrored those of his comic strips, and even as he shipped politically and culturally reactionary movies and comics south of the border, he placed those politics directly in the service of the similarly reactionary elements of U.S. life. From late 1940 onward, as Eliot demonstrates from FBI files obtained under the Freedom of Information Act, the openly anti-Semitic Disney was a valued collaborator of the FBI and (later) of the House Un-American Activities Committee. He also served as vice president of the anti-Communist Motion Picture Alliance for the Preservation of American Ideals from its formation in 1944, working to blacklist "communist sympathizers" in the industry (Eliot 1993, 168–97; cf. Tunstall 1977, 140). Thus within repressive, increasingly anti-Communist *Somocista* Nicaragua, the Disney intervention was in no way benign.[48]

CULTURAL POLITICS AND "CULTURAL EXCHANGE." The U.S. government's promotion of the Disney version of Latin America was neither coincidental nor divorced from larger political-cultural strategies. Indeed, as Ninkovich has shown, those strategies were developing during precisely the two decades in which the United States deposed Nicaraguan President José Santos Zelaya, imposed a series of puppet presidents, sent in the marines against Augusto César Sandino, and launched the career of the first Somoza.

The roots of the U.S. government's cultural policies in the international arena reach back to the formation of the private Carnegie Endowment for International Peace in 1910. Naively conceiving of international relations as taking place in something resembling a "hemispheric fraternity house" in which conflicts were caused by nothing more serious than culturally based misunderstandings, the Endowment urged that cultural relations be tied to foreign policy objectives. Although the Endowment's own efforts to construct such ties proved to be uncritically liberal and elitist, it was not alone in its vision of linking culture to foreign policy objectives. The Rockefeller Foundation, founded in 1913, also began to take a major interest in cultural relations in the 1920s, and in the 1930s the Simon Guggenheim Foundation began trying to intervene in what it called "the commerce of the mind" by granting fellowships for study in Latin America (Ninkovich 1981, 8–15).

Much of the United States's cultural intervention in Central America after 1932 occurred as President Roosevelt's Good Neighbor Policy proliferated committees, commissions, and leagues formally oriented toward improving cultural relations; but in fact, as Black observes, these were concerned mainly with "a reaffirmation of the United States's faith in its own virtue . . . [and] guaranteeing the stability of [its] 'ignorant, quick-tempered' neighbors through . . . indirect controls" (Black 1981, 61).

The "boldest symbolic expression of Roosevelt's vision of a future world of Good Neighbors," Black observes, was Somoza's 1939 trip to Washington. The Roosevelt administration was in fact rather wary of Somoza. A document labeled "Confidential Biographic Data on President Anastasio Somoza and Members of His Party" prepared by the State Department for the visit noted that he was "not considered — even by his friends — to be a very forceful character," and that "his rise to power in Nicaragua may be attributed principally to his political acumen and his pleasing personality rather than to any profound abilities or outstanding qualifications for office."[49] These reservations notwithstanding, President Roosevelt rode with Somoza in an open car to the White House, the route lined with five thousand full-dress troops and thousands of federal employees given the day off to swell the crowd. A twenty-one gun salute and a fly-over by several dozen airplanes completed the public celebration, and a formal dinner for the entire cabinet, the Supreme Court, heads of New Deal agencies, and selected members of Congress followed.[50] Somoza returned to Nicaragua to a huge welcoming ceremony: leaflets distributed weeks ahead of time promised train tickets and a free lunch in Managua to all who came, and seventy thousand people (including the diplomatic corps, members of the National Assembly, the National Guard general staff, sports teams, and Boy Scouts) lined the route from the airport.

During the ensuing years, Somoza went to great lengths to ingratiate himself with the U.S. president. He renamed Managua's main thoroughfare Avenida Roosevelt and built a huge monument to him.[51] In mid-July 1940 he wrote to Roosevelt, "Each day I congratulate myself more on having personally known you, on calling myself with pride your faithful and sincere friend, on having shaken your hand, on having discussed [matters] with you and listened to you think out loud in regard to the problems of our nations. . . . If I have had any aspiration in my life as a rule, it is to try to imitate you, although on a small scale, in all the great and good things that Your Excellency has done. . . ."[52] In subsequent months and years, Somoza declared Roosevelt's birthday a national holiday, named a boys' school for him, and arranged for a park in Granada to be renamed for him and for the National University in León to confer an honorary degree upon him.[53]

Less ephemeral and more structurally important than ad hoc regime-legitimizing cultural gestures, however, was the systematic development of official cultural programs as an arm of U.S. foreign policy (not only in Nicaragua but throughout Latin America). Except for minor efforts by the Library of Congress and the Smithsonian since the mid-nineteenth century, the United States had done virtually nothing of the sort prior to the mid-1930s, when Assistant Secretary of State Sumner Welles proposed a Convention for the Promotion of Inter-American Cultural Relations to the 1936 Inter-American Conference for the Maintenance of Peace in Buenos Aires (Scott 1959, 179–89; Shuster in American Assembly 1968, 2).

Within the State Department, policy development followed Welles's conception of cultural relations with Latin American countries as "a problem in the dynamics of cultural lag." It was not possible, Welles thought, for Latin American republics "to absorb the theory and the principles and the spirit that underlies the structure of free government" unless and until they had absorbed certain values to be inculcated through cultural offerings (Ninkovich 1981, 24–30). To try to bring such benighted republics up to cultural speed, the Office for the Coordination of Commercial and Cultural Relations Between the American Republics was established by presidential order in August 1940 with the specific mission of overseeing the commercial and cultural aspects of hemisphere defense. It was headed by Nelson Rockefeller. The Office seems not to have been overly effective in its work, especially with regard to mass communications issues; by the spring of 1941, the Director of Radio for the Democratic National Committee was of the opinion that it had "bogged down almost completely." [54]

The Office for the Coordination of Commercial and Cultural Relations was replaced in July 1941 by the Office of the Coordinator of Inter-American Affairs (CIAA), also headed by Rockefeller. [55] Earlier planning discussions had emphasized that reciprocal exchanges and understanding were to be stressed over propaganda, in order to avoid "the slightest suggestion of the imposition of one people's culture upon another" (Scott 1959, 39–43).

Rockefeller rejected the idea of working for reciprocal benefits in cultural programs, emphasizing instead the interpretation of the United States to Latin America. Top positions in the agency went to the social and cultural elite, linked in turn to private arts booking agents. A series of Latin American tours by elite performers followed (singers Helen Traubel and Lauritz Melchior, violinist Yehudi Menuhin). Early touring art exhibits arranged by critics attached to major New York museums featured contemporary and modern art. [56] The strategy was well calculated to serve those ends of "cultural relations" later cataloged by Pendergast:

> to permit policy gradualism, consolidate hinterlands and secure political alignment of client states, prepare for commercial expansion, mitigate political quarrels, attenuate resentments and dissatisfactions among domestic constituencies, manipulate public opinion, secure policy flexibility for the elite, and (despite the lack of convincing evidence) reinforce belief in the formal efficacy of direct popular exchanges ... [thereby] institutionaliz[ing] popular ambivalence and susceptibility to manipulation ... [and increasing] policy latitude and flexibility. (Pendergast 1973, 683–93)

The advent of World War II introduced an additional element of *realpolitik* into the operation of U.S. cultural programs in Latin America. By late 1941, Rockefeller was spearheading what Ninkovich calls "a near craze for Pan-Americanism"—a plethora of institutes, seminars, essay and poster contests, and efforts to rally the academic community. As the war heated up, "national security justifications came to dominate student exchange programs," and the Office of the Coordinator of Interamerican Affairs began to maintain "a sharp eye . . . for the ideological purity of cultural grantees." The Office appears to have operated simultaneously at two levels, one functioning as a formal cover for the other. At one level it promoted such innocuous events as "Inter-American Music Day," tried to popularize Latin American handicrafts in the

United States, and promoted the idea of vacations in Mexico rather than in Europe.[57] But another level of operation is suggested by President Roosevelt's directive to the attorney general in early 1941 that the facilities of the FBI should be made available to the Coordinator for "carrying out Coordinator's program of contacting limited number of executives of American business for purpose of soliciting their cooperation in eliminating totalitarian agents who represent their organizations in the American republics."[58]

U.S. cultural relations activities were folded into the Office of War Information, acquiring thereby an even more conservative and propagandistic cast, especially in the new Voice of America radio broadcasts (1942). Leftist Chilean poet Pablo Neruda was denied a visa to enter the United States, and U.S. playwright Thornton Wilder opined, "In the long run the adherence of these republics must be gained by force. They will continue to make the charge of imperialism, but they are not ready for any other method" (Ninkovich 1981, 44; Shuster in American Assembly 1968, 7–8).

As the months passed, in any case, the United States's formal commitment to lofty cultural enterprises (of whatever character) outstripped its willingness to pay for them. By March 1942, the U.S. chargé d'affaires in Managua, embarrassed by lack of funds for cultural goodwill gestures, was begging the secretary of state for a few hundred dollars to reproduce public relations photographs (as the British seemed to be doing so freely, he noted) and buy some flags to hand out to callers. "An individual who comes here to ask for three items can usually be satisfied if he is given one," he reported, "but it creates a most unfortunate impression if he must always be turned away empty-handed." Two months later, the chargé got his three hundred dollars for flags.[59]

The situation took a more welcome turn in August 1942, when the North American Cultural Institute of Nicaragua was opened by Ambassador James B. Stewart.[60] At the opening ceremony, Somoza's National Guard band played the U.S. and Nicaraguan national anthems, a color portrait of George Washington was unveiled, and Dr. Rodolfo Rivera, director of the American Library of Nicaragua (as yet unopened because it had no books), presented the institute a thirty-volume set of Washington's collected works. Stewart eulogized Washington and spoke blandly of brotherhood, peace, and mutual understanding, but in Rivera's response the political subtexts underlying the institute pushed a bit closer to the surface. Rivera characterized General Washington as a no-nonsense man of business — a prototypical free-enterpriser who was a landowner, farmer, nurseryman, animal breeder, and "one of the richest tobacco growers in Virginia." "Industrious, punctual, efficient, and economical," Rivera's Washington disapproved of slavery for social and economic reasons rather than moral ones, and treated his own slaves well. He was moreover a military man, and a most reluctant revolutionary.[61]

The institute's first few months produced mixed results. Putting the best face on matters, it reported sixty members (including Somoza) attending semimonthly meetings for lectures and discussions. A series of teas and smokers was contemplated to provide "an opportunity for an exchange of ideas between interested Americans and the intellectuals and thinking people of Nicaragua." The American Library was belatedly reported to be "a going institution" with eighteen hundred books housed in a building provided by the Somoza government, and there were some four hundred students in English classes.[62]

But in fact the American colony in Nicaragua was not much interested in the institute, which as a mere adjunct of the American Library was always short of funds.[63] Motion picture showings were confined mostly to Managua, and projected radio broadcasts were few, but a few books and pamphlets were being distributed. Plans to establish an American school in Managua were still on the drawing board, and a collection of "cultural objects" was apparently limited to a framed photograph of President Roosevelt hanging beside one of Anastasio Somoza. The elite-oriented embassy staff reported disappointedly that there was a "steady stream of . . . would-be artists, writers, and poets, who bring in works which they wish to have sent to the United States," but in most cases "the work is inferior and would be of little interest [there]."[64]

To complicate matters further, a contemplated exchange of students, professors, and "intellectual leaders" was producing paltry results and considerable ill will. The student exchange program had brought no U.S. students to Nicaragua, and of the twenty-eight Nicaraguans who were studying in the United States, half were training as pilots or mechanics, or studying "radio detection and monitoring." Only one U.S. professor (of architecture) was sent to Nicaragua for two weeks, and he made a very unfavorable impression because he spoke no Spanish. His Nicaraguan counterpart, Dr. Salvador Mendieta (1879–1958), rector of the Central American University and also director of the institute, wrote an article upon his return, which made "what was generally interpreted" (said the anonymous writer of the institute's January 1943 report) as "a shielded attack" upon Guatemala's dictator Jorge Ubico. Mendieta's remarks produced such a strain in Nicaraguan-Guatemalan relations that Somoza asked him to resign as rector of the university.[65]

Not surprisingly, the fortunes of the North American Cultural Institute of Nicaragua declined precipitously; on its first anniversary, it reported having no permanent employees, and activities were at a low ebb.[66]

For a brief time following the end of World War II, the State Department adopted a putatively benign strategy of using cultural policy and institutions to "cover the world with truth," but with the advent of the Cold War reactionary elements surged to the forefront of U.S. cultural policy throughout the world (Scott 1959, 68–75, 100–106). Ninkovich has characterized William Benton, who became Assistant Secretary of State for Public and Cultural Affairs in 1945, as viewing cultural programs "as chores in international salesmanship, as a sort of educational Muzak or pleasant background noise against which to conduct foreign relations," but the State Department itself became suffused with an anti-Communist anxiety that strongly marked all its cultural programs. Fears of Communist subversion within UNESCO (founded 1945–46) soon reached hysterical levels. "Let us face it," Assistant Secretary of State George V. Allen said in early 1949, "we are in the business of international propaganda" (Scott 1959, 106).

By 1950, Ninkovich concluded, "American cultural programs of all kinds were deeply committed to waging the Cold War" (Ninkovich 1981, 35–46, 87, 100, 118–20, 134–39). Cultural ambassadors from the United States and potential ones from Latin America were carefully screened. Taken together, Latin American tours by the (black) Howard University choir and the musical *Annie Get Your Gun* in the early 1960s presented a somewhat garbled political message, but many other cultural emissaries to the south were safely bland: the San Francisco Ballet and the American Ballet Theater, José Limón and Paul Taylor.[67]

Somoza's Nicaragua was fertile ground for such an agenda. By late 1947, Managua's *La Flecha* was carrying almost daily articles on Communists in the Hollywood film industry—"news" that owed much to the anti-Communist hysteria in Hollywood led by Walt Disney and others.[68] Somoza's staunch anti-Communist stance helped him maintain cordial relations with the United States and get his share of the largesse from military assistance programs (Bermann 1986, 240). "The Fourth of July is celebrated enthusiastically throughout Nicaragua," Secretary of State Dean Acheson reported in 1952, and in February 1955 *La Prensa* heralded the visit of Vice President Richard Nixon with a photo of Nixon ("one of the most brilliant political careers in the U.S.," said the caption) arm-in-arm with Somoza.[69] In the issue of *La Prensa* that covered the funeral of the assassinated Anastasio Somoza García in late 1956, upwards of 90 percent of advertised products were of U.S. origin; sports news focused on U.S. major league baseball, boxing, and golf. Had it not been written in Spanish, most of it could have emanated from any sizable city in the United States.

SECOND-GENERATION SOMOZAS:
TOLERANCE, REPRESSION, AND CULTURAL HEGEMONY

A twenty-one-gun salute by U.S. troops boomed as Anastasio Somoza García's body left the Canal Zone on a U.S. military C-54 with an escort headed by the Caribbean command's chief of staff (Diederich 1981, 48). Secretary of State John Foster Dulles—having only recently masterminded the CIA coup against Guatemala's progressive Arbenz government—assured Somoza's widow that "his constantly demonstrated friendship for the United States will never be forgotten." Even though a planeload of U.S. doctors headed by President Eisenhower's own surgeon had not been able to save the dictator's life, the second generation had long been groomed to carry on. It did so with the continued backing of the United States, and with the same implications for cultural life in Nicaragua, where anti-Communist ambassador Thomas Whelan worked to insure that business would indeed continue as usual (Bermann 1986, 3, 242–43).

Neither of the Somoza sons who followed their father as head of the dynasty—Luis (b. 1922) and Anastasio Somoza (b. 1925) Debayle—was disposed to question or break their father's ties to the United States, where both had been schooled. Both were rushed through the ranks of the National Guard while very young: Luis was a colonel at twenty-eight; Anastasio was already a captain by the time he entered West Point at seventeen.

Luis Somoza Debayle, who had served an apprenticeship under his father as the caretaker of the National Assembly and of the *somocista* PLN (*Partido Liberal Nacionalista*; Liberal Nationalist Party), took over the presidency within eight hours after his father's death, and remained in control until his own death in 1967 (Diederich 1981, 50–51). Slightly less repressive in some respects than his father had been and than his brother would be after him, Luis eased up somewhat on press censorship and granted autonomy to the National University in 1958, after which it entered upon a period of unaccustomed vitality under progressive rectors Mariano Fiallos Gil (1957–64) and Carlos Tünnerman Bernheim (1964–74). But the university's autonomy had its limits. On 23 July 1959, the Guard (headed by Anastasio Somoza Debayle) shot and killed four university students during a political protest (Bermann 1986, 243–45).

The advent of the overtly political U.S.-backed Central American Defense Council (CONDECA) in 1964 further stepped up military arms and training to the repressive National Guard. During the presidential campaign of anti-Somoza candidate Fernando Agüero in 1967, the Guard gunned down forty demonstrators at a Managua rally (Bermann 1986, 246–52; Diederich 1981, 64–79). To no one's surprise, Anastasio Somoza Debayle (who had stepped into the race after the regime's hand-picked candidate, René Schick, died during the campaign) won the election. Continued close and friendly relations with the United States were assured when President Nixon appointed Turner B. Shelton as ambassador—in which post, recalls journalist Bernard Diederich, he "soon outshone the memory" of Thomas Whelan, Anastasio Somoza García's poker-playing buddy, as a "Somoza lackey" (Diederich 1981, 88).

Meanwhile, those few public cultural institutions that had managed to survive through the first several decades of the Somoza regime were falling to pieces. The $14 million (U.S.) national budget for 1950–51 allocated less for education and health put together than it did for the Ministry of Marine War and Aviation, which took up nearly 12 percent of the entire budget. It included $5,285 (U.S.) for the national library and archives (whose total staff of four had an annual office expense budget of $3.57 [U.S.]), a school of music, several municipal librarians' salaries at $3.50 to $14.25 per month (U.S.), and the grandly named *Escuela de Bellas Artes* (School of Fine Arts).[70]

Such neglect continued through the 1950s and 1960s. In 1968, cultural matters were being handled by a total staff of eighty-nine in the "cultural extension" section of the Ministry of Education. The National Museum had a staff of only five and an annual budget of approximately $2,000 (compared to the president's own salary of $15,000, and a $54,000 budget for the military bands of the National Guard).[71] Even an official tourist guide of 1971 admitted that the museum was located in an "inadequate" building and could not be considered "a true museum in the strict sense of the term" (Rizo 1971, 68). The directors of the National Library, the School of Plastic Arts, Theater, and Dance, and the National Conservatory earned $5,000–$6,000 a year, but the other seventeen staff members of the library averaged only about $1,000 each. A "school of folklore" in Masaya had an annual budget of less than $2,500 and was open only seven months of the year. Its director earned less than $900 and its only "professor" less than $600 (slightly more than a drummer in the National Guard band). Three traditional musicians were paid $225 each. The same 1968 budget set the salary of the head of the National Guard at $8,571.[72]

Contrasts in the next year's 659 million *córdoba* budget were also sharp: all cultural programs combined received 0.20 percent. At the same moment when the regime was bestowing the *Orden de Rubén Darío* upon its cultural favorites, the tiny Rubén Darío memorial (*Casa Rubén Darío*) had a staff of two, each of whom received an annual salary of about $85 U.S.[73] Meanwhile, the government was announcing to potential tourists a projected *Centro Cultural* that would include new buildings for the National Library and National Museum (Rizo 1971, 68).

This grandiose plan reflected the cultural vision not of Anastasio Somoza

Debayle, however, who preferred boxing, baseball, horses, fancy cars, war movies, illicit liaisons with women, and drinking, but of his American-born wife (and first cousin), Hope Portocarrero. As a graduate of Miss Harris's Girls' School in Miami, Barnard College, and Georgetown University Foreign Service School, she considered herself a woman of high culture. She carefully maintained her U.S. citizenship, insisted that her children be born in the U.S., and was determined to reform her boorish and uncultured husband. She wanted him, a friend reported, "to fit in Newport Society, eat caviar and drink champagne and watch his language and manners." A woman reporter who saw her bedroom shortly after the Managua earthquake of 1972 found it "littered with fashion magazines from Neiman-Marcus" and Hope herself "look[ing like] the smart American woman she was" (Diederich 1981, 39, 75, 82, 88).[74]

One of Hope Portocarrero Somoza's pet cultural projects was in fact the thirteen-hundred-seat Rubén Darío National Theater (centerpiece of the announced Centro Cultural), whose opening performance by the *Ballet Folklórico* of Mexico in 1969 she anticipated with great pride. Unfortunately her husband made a public fool of himself by getting drunk and spending the evening eyeing his mistress in the audience (Diederich 1981, 88). Hence it was ironic that the National Museum acquired the best quarters it had ever had when Somoza renovated a modest house (donated to the government by Swiss architect Paul Dambach) for museum use in 1977 as a birthday gift to his wife, who for years had been rumored to be selling Nicaraguan archaeological artifacts through a boutique in Miami, and who in any case had separated from him the year before (Stansifer 1981a, 9; Diederich 1981, 116).

Fortunately, from the early 1960s onward, the void created by the paucity of significant public cultural policy and programs began to be partially filled by private initiatives. The new Central American University established an Institute of Historical Studies and a historical archive, published a major collection of colonial documents, and began publishing a cultural magazine (*Encuentro*). In 1960, Joaquín Zavala Urtecho began to edit the preeminent journal *Revista Conservadora* (later the *Revista Conservadora del Pensamiento Centroamericano*) (Stansifer 1981a, 5–9). The influential literary magazine *El Pez y la Serpiente* appeared the following year, edited by a group that included Pablo Antonio Cuadra, José Coronel Urtecho, Ernesto Cardenal, Fernando Silva, and Ernesto Gutiérrez.[75]

In the first issue, the editors invoked the polyvalent symbols of water (Nicaragua's lakes and rivers, its annual rainy season, the water-borne *conquistadores*, and Christian baptism) and serpent (the plumed serpent of aboriginal myth, the serpent Moses raised in the wilderness), and of their oppositional tension (the struggle between Good and Evil, "the agony of

Nicaraguan National Theater, Managua. Designed by Edward Durrell Stone as copy of John F. Kennedy Center in Washington, D.C. (Photograph by author)

the contemporary writer in his/her difficult and dramatic testimony").[76] The first issues carried anti-imperialistic pieces by Ernesto Cardenal and Ernesto Gutiérrez, and later ones contained poems by young women poets (Ana Ilce, Yolanda Blanco, Rosario Murillo), articles by exiled anti-Somoza writers such as Sergio Ramírez and Lizandro Chávez Alfaro, and lengthy pieces on Cardenal's experimental Solentiname community (to which I return in a subsequent chapter).

The breadth of the anti-Somoza coalition after 1972 was suggested by the fact that *El Pez y la Serpiente*'s sponsors came to include large banks and insurance companies, Esso and Shell oil companies, Nabisco and Quaker Oats, Datsun, and the huge San Antonio sugar mill. The same issue that listed those sponsors also carried poems by Ernesto Cardenal satirizing nineteenth-century U.S. intervention, the mistreatment of Indians by the U.S. government (*Grabaciones de la pipa sagrada*), political torture and repression in Latin America, the political agendas of multinationals such as Kennecot and Anaconda, and death squads.[77] Even in the heavily repressive cultural climate of the regime's latter days, *Centroamericana*, edited by Pablo Antonio Cuadra, was publishing articles by some of Latin America's best-known oppositionist writers (Gabriel García Marquez, Roque Dalton, Ariel Dorfman, Eduardo Galeano, Julio Cortázar, and Pablo Neruda).[78]

Like many banks throughout Latin America, Nicaraguan banks also began to develop an array of cultural activities. Banco Central established the best library in the country, bought paintings and other art objects, inaugurated a publication series in 1964, hired scholars to do archaeological research, and established both the Masaya National Park and a National School of Ceramics. The private Banco de América supported a publications series that grew to more than fifty titles. Its *Fondo de Promoción Cultural* published Bovallius's *Nicaraguan Antiquities* and Bransford's *Archaeological Investigations in Nicaragua*, historical documents and studies (including important ones on the conquest), works of Nicaraguan writers (Salomón de la Selva, Enrique Guzmán), and others in "human sciences" (Ernesto Mejía Sánchez's *Romances y corridos nicaragüenses* and Francisco Pérez Estrada's essays on Nicaraguan folklore). In 1977 it also produced several LP phonograph records prepared by Salvador Cardenal Argüello, who had for years been collecting, documenting, and presenting Nicaraguan traditional music to the public through his own radio program (Stansifer 1981a, 5–7).[79]

The fragile fabric of cultural activity that such private efforts were slowly weaving—whatever its merits or deficits—was torn asunder both literally and metaphorically by the December 1972 Managua earthquake, which destroyed virtually the entire center of the city, leaving eight thousand dead and tens of thousands wounded and homeless. As cultural institutions began to dig themselves out, it was clear that their losses were great. The National Library managed to salvage fewer than eight thousand of its eighty thousand books (Stansifer 1981a, 9). The Old India Cafe, long a meeting place for poets and writers, was gone. Private galleries disappeared, many never to reopen, and many middle-class patrons of Managua's artists were bankrupt. Dozens of intellectuals scattered to Costa Rica, the United States, and Europe, and some journals and literary magazines ceased publication.

To the cultural sector, the regime responded only with sanctimonious rhetoric. Nicaragua, Somoza opined lamely, "has little time to worry about artists, writers, and musicians at this time. . . . In a disaster of this type, men are separated from boys. . . . [Everyone] has his job to do and the artists could help their people by portraying the tragedy of this country through murals, poems, and essays."[80] Such a platitudinous remark combined irrelevant *machista* posturing and ignorance about the cultural costs of the earthquake in order to mask the regime's own cynical greed at such a tumultuous moment.

More important, from Somoza's point of view, the earthquake provided another opportunity to declare a state of emergency (Diederich 1981, 97). Reconstruction (hence a lifting of emergency powers) was delayed for years because the regime stole relief supplies and sold them for profit, bought up construction sites and resold them to the government at huge markups, pocketed much of the international reconstruction aid that poured into the country, and doled out much of the rest to cronies.

The state of emergency also brought renewed censorship of creative activity. Writing in the autumn of 1976, Nicaraguan poet Ernesto Gutiérrez framed succinctly the dilemma he and other writers faced during the last tortuous years of the regime:

> Screwed! [¡Jodido!] I cannot publish, and now I read my poems in the library of my house to some young poet friends who visit me. I am afraid of the state of siege and police control of the press, and moreover I have no money and I have four children and a wife. And if they kill me in jail, who is going to look after them? And if they fine me, how am I going to pay if I have nothing but the furniture in my house and an old automobile worth maybe three thousand córdobas? I definitely cannot publish; I don't have that valour; nor am I alone; I have to look out for others. And if they torture and murder me? Frankly, I cannot publish.

Carlos Mejía Godoy and other young musicians—influenced by and partici-pating in the *nueva canción* (new song) movement—were watched, followed, and harassed, and Mejía Godoy himself was jailed.[81] Sergio Ramírez recalled that one Nicaraguan citizen went into exile in Costa Rica to escape a prison sentence given him for carrying Jaime Wheelock Román's *Imperialismo y dictadura* in his bookstore (Leiken and Rubin 1987, 171).

Meanwhile, despite the turmoil of the earthquake, the ranks of consumers with disposable income continued to grow steadily throughout the turbulent 1970s, and markets for U.S. goods and their accompanying cultural styles and values seemed insatiable.[82] A 1971 official tourist guide to Nicaragua ad-vertised that the club La Cave featured *espectáculos de streap-tease* [sic]. The Cuesta and Nejapa country clubs offered tennis and golf, and the Club Social de Managua boasted of *vistosas lámparas de cristal* (showy crystal lamps) in its great dance halls (Rizo 1971, 37).

In his "Managua de tarde" (Managua in the afternoon) of late 1975, Fer-nando Antonio Silva burlesqued Nicaraguans' decadent hunger for U.S.-style consumer products, and the eagerness with which Nicaraguan young people conformed to the alien and idealized images in commercial advertising:

> The city grows with its by-pass
> and its giant shopping centers
> inaccessible
> to those who don't use CRED-O-MATIC
> MASTERCHARGE or some other backup capital
> great show windows brilliant lamps
> ARROW and GIVANCHY [sic] shirts
> perfumes (they look pretty in their boxes)

and the pretty girl with her eyelashes
caked with Maybelline or eyeliner
dressed in her long skirt
(the last word in fashion)
and high heels
(because she is a bit short)
with her sweet little voice she shows you all the things
in the store
and they look like they
have no price.

The afternoon passes bowling
seeing girls walking agitatedly
moving rhythmically, their hips delineated
by LEVI'S tailoring
from one side to the other, from one game to another
swapping coquettish glances
with long-haired boys in sexy haircuts
faded blue-jeans and peasant shirts.[83]

Even during the final few days before the Somoza regime fell in mid-1979, mass popular culture in Managua evoked an eerie stasis reminiscent of the daily newspapers thirty years earlier. Even the prestigious *La Prensa Literaria* supplement had been cut back: it was being printed on newsprint, serious articles were less numerous, and U.S. comic strips (Dagwood, Mutt & Jeff, Maggie and Jiggs, Popeye) had reappeared. Soap operas and commercials for consumer products from the U.S. continued to proliferate on television; Disney cartoons and major league baseball filled the newspapers; Hollywood films (*War of the Galaxies*, *You Light Up My Life*, Bruce Lee) were showing in seventeen out of thirty-one movie theaters.[84]

In sum, the economic and political transformation of Nicaragua under the Somozas (the focus of most existing analyses) was paralleled by an equally pervasive cultural transformation. Mobilizing all of the structures and processes of the modern state—the symbolic stage of the central political capital, media technology, censorship and police powers, consumer merchandizing, international cultural relations—the Somoza regime was able to shape most of the cultural development of the country to its own purposes. The cultural costs to non-elites—especially those associated with the boom in agroexport production—were both great and for the most part irreversible.

And yet, there were unquenchable resources of autonomy, vitality, and resistance within the culture, and visions of other and better ways to live. If the Somozas demonstrated that culture could be censored and coerced, repressed and manipulated, bought and sold like so much coffee or cotton, tens of thousands of ordinary Nicaraguan people—as well as those who consciously considered themselves artists—proved that it could also be mobilized for resistance and survival.

CHAPTER 4 ANYTHING BUT FLOWERS CULTURE

AND RESISTANCE TO THE SOMOZA DICTATORSHIP

If Somoza hadn't permitted anything but flowers, then talking only about flowers we would have been able to denounce him.

— Nicaraguan musician Luis Enrique Mejía Godoy, 1988

In his analysis of the Somoza regime's organization and use of state power, Knut Walter argues persuasively that opponents of the regime fell into two groups. First, there were the political conservatives and much of the oligarchy who were essentially loyal to the regime, but who insisted upon sharing power as well as the spoils of power. The second group included those whose opposition was more principled: mainly independent liberals and university students. Among them, Walter explains, they employed several oppositional strategies: "civic" opposition (mainly party and electoral politics); "exiled" opposition, which was mostly middle class and reformist (the Nicaraguan Revolutionary Committee [*Comité Revolucionario Nicaragüense*] in Mexico, the Patriotic Nicaraguan Abstentionist Committee [*Comité Patriótico Abstencionista Nicaragüense*] in New York, and others in Costa Rica); and armed opposition, which arose embryonically as early as the

1940s and came to fruition in the FSLN, which began to form in the early 1960s (Walter 1987, 244, 357–65, 374–78; 1993, 216–35).

Absent from Walter's otherwise useful typology, however, is cultural opposition, which plagued the regime from its earliest days, took a multitude of creative forms, and was—even in its more subliminal guises—an essential aspect of most other types of opposition. As the previous chapter suggested, the Somoza regime, for all its cynicism, skill, and effectiveness in manipulating, appropriating, and controlling culture, was beset with cultural resistance—both organized and unorganized, and from many quarters—throughout its more than four decades in power. Important generative centers of that resistance were (1) the politically divided *vanguardia* movement of the early 1930s; (2) the Generation of 1940; (3) the cultural movement among students from the mid-1940s onward, but especially in the 1960s and 1970s; (4) oppositional literature and music, especially from the 1960s onward; and (5) the insurgency of the indigenous *barrios* in the mid-1970s.[1]

WOBBLING TOWARD CLARITY: THE VANGUARDIA

Opposition to the Somoza regime itself was linked to two larger agendas that both antedated and lasted beyond it: the task of redefining and reestablishing Nicaraguan national identity (especially those aspects of it that lay—or could be argued to lie—within the lifeways of indigenous people); and the effort to counter growing U.S. hegemonic domination of Nicaragua. Although Nicaragua's *Vanguardia* movement was ultimately (as Beverley and Zimmerman observe) "ideologically incoherent and unstable"—hence confused in general about the best approach to national revitalization and about the merits of the embryonic Somoza regime in particular—its members directed much of their energy to these larger agendas. By spearheading the rediscovery and revalorization of Nicaraguan traditional culture, resuscitating public discourse concerning national culture, and contributing to the broad opposition to U.S. intervention (and consequently supporting Sandino's nationalist struggle), they helped prepare the way for later and more focused opposition to the Somoza regime (Arellano 1982a, 57–74; Beverley and Zimmerman 1990, 61).[2]

Among the many strands of *vanguardista* thought and writing, five are especially pertinent here: their generally anti-bourgeois spirit, their interest in national literature and culture, their anti-interventionist posture, their admiration for General Sandino, and (however contradictory) their effectively fascist support of nascent dictator Anastasio Somoza García.[3]

The early formation of most of the *vanguardistas* was profoundly conservative. As Arellano has noted, except for Luis Alberto Cabrales (1901–1974),

José Coronel Urtecho (b. 1906), and Manolo Cuadra (b. 1907), they were all young (between sixteen and twenty years old). All, regardless of age, were from traditional Granada families recently eliminated from political power. In Jesuit schools they had studied Latin and Greek and what was understood at the time to be the best of "western culture"; all were therefore Catholic in religion and scholastic in philosophy (Arellano 1982a, 65).[4]

But other contemporary currents of thought and expression beckoned in other directions as well. Living temporarily in San Francisco in the mid-1920s, Coronel Urtecho was excited by the "new poetry" of the period: the familiar language and compact style of Edwin Arlington Robinson; the exactness, rigor, and psychological insight of Edgar Lee Masters; Robert Frost's "fidelity to facts and objects"; Carl Sandburg's "direct and dynamic realism"; and the "prodigious variety" and tonal richness of Vachel Lindsey's folk-based poetry. Cabrales returned from France enthusiastic about the fresh expressive possibilities of contemporary French poetry, and the group hungrily devoured as much of *lo nuevo* as it could lay hands on, especially avant garde French and Spanish books, newspapers, and journals (Coronel Urtecho 1985b, 139–50; Arellano 1982a, 67–69).

Energized by these currents and eager to demonstrate their nonconformity and to destroy what they considered to be derivative, sterile, sentimental, and dead (especially the legacy of the nineteenth century), the *vanguardistas* set about challenging their bourgeois and upper-class parents' lives and cultural preferences—"an old literature, an old politics of stupid ideas," as Pablo Antonio Cuadra put it in 1931. Death is preferable, they said, to "their stupid and deceived lives." "We want to have done with the weepy generation [*generación llorona*]," they said. "May a free and happy generation arise." Their first formal manifesto asserted that they would use any means including "dynamite and the literary rifle" to make their revolution (Cardenal in Coronel Urtecho et al. 1979, 12–15, 25–28). At the first public presentation of *vanguardista* poetry, sixteen-year-old Luis Downing recited from a staircase with a hammer and nail in his hand, and eighteen-year-old Pablo Antonio Cuadra read his poem "Stadium" with boxing gloves on his hands, swinging dramatically. Cuadra later dressed like an Indian for several months, Coronel Urtecho went about with his head shaved, and Downing sallied forth to hunt wild animals in the mountains of Chontales. "Beside our ancestors," they said, "let us go against our fathers" (Arellano 1982a, 57–67).[5]

By the spring of 1931, the *vanguardistas* had created what they called the Nicaraguan Anti-Academy as a direct challenge to the "sterile and formalist spirit" of the country's Nicaraguan Academy of Language, and more broadly to the culturally and politically dead hand of the nineteenth century (Coronel Urtecho et al. 1979, 36–53). Pushing beyond mere syncretism, they intended to generate a new and authentically Nicaraguan literature — autochthonous, vernacular, personal, "truly free," and youthful (*juvenil*). Reaching back beyond the nineteenth century, they wanted to discover, they said, "every Nicaraguan artistic manifestation of the past which pertains to the pure vein of our national tradition" (Cardenal in Pasos 1986, 11). The group began to publish a rather pugnacious column called the Vanguardia Corner (*El rincón de la vanguardia*) in Granada's newspaper *El Correo*, declaring that they would hurl their images "like projectiles." The column was short-lived, but the group's separate publication *Vanguardia* appeared in April 1932.[6]

A central concern for the *vanguardistas* was to recover and revitalize those elements of indigenous and traditional culture they considered a better basis for national cultural revitalization than the desiccated bourgeois borrowings of their parents.[7] It was partly this interest in reviving and revitalizing indigenous and national culture that drew the *vanguardistas* into active opposition to U.S. military and cultural intervention, which one after another of them satirized: Coronel Urtecho penned "Mr. Hoover me visita" (Mr. Hoover visits me) in mid-1928; Pablo Antonio Cuadra wrote "USMC"; and Joaquín Pasos wrote (in English) "Peggy O'Neill: lo único aceptable de la Intervención Americana" (Peggy O'Neill: The only thing acceptable about American intervention), about the daughter of an American official who stayed nude in her house because of the Managua heat (Arellano 1969, 68–69).

Indeed an imitation of anything Yankee, wrote *vanguardistas* Joaquín Pasos and Joaquín Zavala in 1932, is "bastard and spurious, besides being unadaptable to our circumstances" (Coronel Urtecho et al. 1979, 28, 68). "Yankees get out," Pasos wrote in another poem, and José Román burlesqued the transformation of Managua under the U.S. military presence:

> Many uniforms, chests with medals,
> The canal, the yankees and the liberals, the conservatives
> and all politics, crazy illusions . . .
> Pasteurized milk and Club and Jazz Band
> and English spoken everywhere.
> "How many million souls will be speaking English."
> Yes Sir. . . .
> Managua, Managua now you are civilized.
> Your suit of khaki; your people, everything is foreign
> even your cathedral is imported.
> Soon we will see an English-speaking God in it.
>   (Coronel Urtecho et al. 1979, 119–20)

More specifically, the majority of the *vanguardia* took the next logical step of supporting the guerrilla campaign of General Sandino against the U.S.

Marines (hence, not incidentally, against General Somoza) (cf. Arellano 1969, 69–70; Coronel Urtecho et al. 1979, 75–76).[8]

Thus in their determination to go against the grain, to revitalize what they considered to be the authentic best of Nicaraguan thought and culture, to learn from and appropriate the freshest cultural currents from elsewhere, and to oppose North American cultural intervention, the *vanguardistas* showed considerable promise. But much of that promise was unfortunately diverted and delayed by a fatal tropism several of them developed for the emerging Somoza regime.

Like the European fascist leaders he openly admired, Somoza began his rise to power partly by railing against the traditional political parties (with which the *vanguardistas* had already so dramatically expressed their discontent, albeit for markedly different reasons) and by promising to exalt the "national soul." Such a combination of iconoclasm, nationalism, and cultural pride (whatever its ideological bases or political motives) proved attractive to some of the *vanguardistas* (Pablo Antonio Cuadra and Coronel Urtecho in particular), as it did at the same time to poets such as Ezra Pound. Cuadra's struggle with the relationship between the immediate vicissitudes of Nicaraguan cultural-political life and their roots in its history illustrates rather starkly the logical and cultural linkages that made Somoza temporarily attractive to a group of young writers and intellectuals who had every reason to know better.[9]

In his *Poemas nicaragüenses* (Nicaraguan Poems) of 1934, Cuadra (like most of his *vanguardia* associates) was preoccupied with the strength and perdurability of indigenous people and their culture. His poem "India," for example, celebrates an Indian woman—strong, grounded in physical realities, able to cope with both life and death. Several other poems draw vocabulary from the ancient nahuatl.[10] Four years later in *Hacia la cruz del sur* (Toward the southern cross), he proclaimed that "America still lives, spread out, it is true, like a dead person beneath the agitated swooping of the eagles of prey. . . . We have to discover America again. The rediscovery . . . will be in the hands of poets" (Cuadra 1938, 17, 25).

The central metaphor—historical, cultural, political, religious, sexual—for Cuadra's quest is a journey through Latin America. Panama is a "hermaphroditic" nation (Saxon and Latin) whose canal embodies the imperial essence of a materialistic culture whose supreme ideal is comfort. "America abandoned its America," Cuadra says, "to adore the machine, the great hotels, the dance halls, the movies, tourism—in a word, the superficial luxuries of a material civilization" (28–31).

Passing through Bolivia, Cuadra comments bitterly on the "tragic international farce" of panamericanism, conceived and directed by the United States, which wraps the brute fact of its economic domination in the "halo of demo-cratic holiness" (61–64) of Rooseveltian Good Neighborism and Rockefeller-style Inter-American Cultural Relations. Finally on the Argentine pampa, he finds what he has been looking for, "the countryside and country people" (*el campo y el campesino*): "Here is the elemental and urgent return. The first step for America to recover its vigor and value. . . . The *campo* is land in which to root oneself. Continuity and perseverance. Primacy of the familiar" (113–14).

Such an emergent (in Raymond Williams's term) perspective offered Cua-dra and his fellow *vanguardistas* the potential to develop a nationalist, anti-imperialist, democratic, culturally progressive politics of opposition to the Somoza regime's greedy and sycophantic policy of urbanization, moderniza-tion, agroexport development, forced acculturation, and fascist-centralized control. Unfortunately, other residual elements (again, Williams's term) of Cuadra's politics — romanticism, reactionary conservatism, Catholicism, elit-ism, anti-communism, even anti-Semitism — aborted that potential.[11]

As he moves southward, Cuadra becomes more and more reactionary. The Spanish conquest, he argues, was not a crime and a tragedy but a beneficent and progressive event whose arch-fiend was not one or another of the *con-quistadores* but (amazingly) Bartolomé de las Casas, whose efforts to protect the Indians made him in fact their "first enemy" (57). "We were not colonies of Spain," Cuadra maintained. "We belonged to an empire. In an empire all members are equal and the head directs. Under imperialism the head enslaves the members." For Cuadra, the Empire "was founded in God" and guaranteed justice, order, love, service, and brotherhood; it was "universal and Catho-lic," while imperialism is "international and Jewish." Hence the tragedy of the conquest was not that it occurred but that it was only partial, that "the light of hispanicity" and "the grace of Catholicity" (*la gracia de Catolicidad*) did not succeed in establishing a universal *Imperio Cristiano* in Latin America (18–21). The opposition between Spanishness (*hispanidad*) and barbarism (*barbarie*) was stark, since "the glory of *hispanidad* was the glory of God" (48).

From such a perspective, *indigenismo* was but a bourgeois conceit, a liberal-Marxist confusion emanating from "the low literature of American communism," and terminating inevitably in the barbarism "that sleeps in every man."[12] "Every flight from *hispanidad*," Cuadra asserted categorically, "leads to cannibalism." Indeed because Nicaragua's Atlantic coast was never conquered by the Spanish, Cuadra argued, the Indians there are "still Indians, wandering in barbarism, waiting for *hispanidad*" (50–52, 58).

When Cuadra returned from his southern trip in March 1934, some key members of the *vanguardia* (by then virtually extinct as a literary group) had in fact already launched a flagrantly anti-democratic political project. As early as 1929, Coronel Urtecho had proclaimed that the democratic idea was "false in itself and therefore impracticable" — an instrument of deceit used by the ambitious to slaughter people, "a principle of disorder and chaos." Hence dictatorship, he added in 1932, was "the *natural* regime for an independent Nicaragua" (Arellano 1969, 55).

As enemies the reactionary *vanguardistas* selected liberalism and democracy, which they conflated as "a system invented to allow the exploiters to exploit the disorganization of the people" (Arellano 1969, 53–54). With the first issue (April 1934) of the pro-Somoza journal *La Reacción*, edited by Cuadra and Coronel Urtecho, the pro-fascist strain of *vanguardismo* emerged in full light. In the lead article, Coronel Urtecho charged that liberal philosophy and democracy were "a failure," and that the principle of the freedom of thought was a "liberal myth." In the next issue he predicted that within twenty years "we will have imposed reactionary thought in Nicaragua and created a favorable climate of opinion so that a free and strong authority can reorganize us." Ten days later he was even more direct: to his own rhetorical question "What do we reactionaries want?" he answered, "The reorganization of the country by means of the dictatorial instrument."[13] As Somoza gained power, Coronel Urtecho jubilantly proclaimed that "the dictatorship comes flying. There are signs in the skies and the atmosphere." Prior to the 1936 elections, Coronel Urtecho praised Somoza as "the candidate of the people" (Arellano 1969, 56).

Thus the *vanguardistas* ("lyrical fascists," poet Ernesto Mejía Sánchez later called them, except for Cabrales, a "true fascist") continued to develop their reactionary program for the country throughout Somoza's first bid for the presidency, promulgating their ideas (and his candidacy) in a series of periodicals: *Trinchera* (1935–36), *1937*, *1938*, *Orden*, *Gris* (Gray), and *Jornal*. When Somoza took office in January 1937, he rewarded some of the *vanguardistas* with minor offices, but their larger hope for political power was not to be realized (White 1986, 40; Arellano 1982a, 74). Nevertheless, some (especially Cuadra and Coronel Urtecho) continued to serve it for years, both in various official capacities (Coronel Urtecho as sub-secretary of external relations and Cuadra in the statistical unit) and by providing cultural rationales for its policies (Arellano 1969, 56).[14]

The younger *vanguardista* Joaquín Pasos (1914–47) initially followed Coronel Urtecho and Pablo Antonio Cuadra in their pro-Somoza fantasy, but soon shifted to the opposition. After founding the literary-political review *Opera Bufa* in mid-1935 (a journal so reactionary it was repressed by the Liberal Sacasa government), he served briefly in the Somoza government as Secretary of Protocol, but quickly became disillusioned and thereafter attacked Somoza repeatedly in the same periodical. Pasos later worked with Alberto Ordóñez Argüello on the journal *1938*, and with Manolo Cuadra and others on the humor magazine *Los Lunes de la Nueva Prensa*, whose sole purpose was to attack Somoza. In return, the regime periodically suppressed *Los Lunes*, and Pasos spent time in jail because of his association with it (Arellano 1969, 14–16). For several other *vanguardistas* the fascination with Somoza was also short-lived. Ordóñez Argüello lived in exile for many years because of his opposition to the dictatorship.

The most consistently and colorfully implacable anti-Somoza *vanguardista* was Manolo Cuadra, who entered the group at the advanced age of twenty-four. The multifaceted Cuadra—boxer, telegrapher, radio operator, folk healer (*curandero*), writer—opposed Somoza from the beginning. With only a third-grade formal education, Cuadra had an innate grasp on political realities in Nicaragua. "If I had to be one-eyed," he said, "I would ask that they leave me the left one" (Calatayud Bernabeu 1968, 11). Although he entered the National Guard (essentially as "a mercenary in a promiscuous army," he said) and fought against Sandino for three years, he used the experience as a basis for a collection of stories, *Contra Sandino en la montaña* (Against Sandino in the mountains), in which his purpose—as he wrote to Pablo Antonio Cuadra in 1934—was to "exalt the guerrilla spirit of the Nicaraguan Indian. Venerate that natural valor which animated their men [those of Sandino]—silent, fierce, a possible inheritance from the days of the conquest" (Calatayud Bernabeu 1968, 46; Cuadra 1982, 14).

Cuadra's opposition to the regime got him into trouble in short order (Calatayud Bernabeu 1968, 44–50). In 1935, after his brother participated in an uprising in the National Guard against Somoza, he was jailed and declared a Communist, and later confined for nine months on Little Corn Island off the Atlantic coast. Cuadra's *Itinerary of Little Corn Island* (1937) typifies his oppositional cultural strategy: to refuse to take the regime seriously, to mock its pompous self-importance, and (when the occasion offered) to burlesque its prudish rigidity, its very joylessness.

"Ah, this joy of living!" Cuadra proclaimed as he recounted the National Guard's response to one of his more outrageously taunting Corn Island exile escapades: for the purely joyful devilment of it, it seems, Cuadra had climbed to the platform atop the lighthouse one calm May evening, doffed his clothes, and struck a series of dramatic statuesque poses (one like *Victory of Samothrace*, he confided, another like a dimly remembered Monet drawing, still another like "Ana Pavlova with a beard"), timing his performance so as to be sure to be seen by the islanders. And indeed in one of his arresting poses he was spotted by a local female resident—calmly gathering crabs on the beach—who when she recovers from her astonishment carries the news forthwith to her neighbors. The news of "the funereal nudist of Coconut Beach" spreads like wildfire across the island "as if it were a Biblical miracle," and comes—as he had calculated it would—to the local National Guard commander. "If you don't like it, go back to Managua," Cuadra taunts him, and in a subsequent fantasy imagines that a week later the boat brings a letter from the Guard's Corn Island *comandante* to "Prisoner Manolo Cuadra, *comunista*" concerning his "nudist relapse." In a single page of wickedly evocative prose, Cuadra's rendering of the letter deploys a dense array of linked cultural resonances — indigenous as well as bourgeois and elite — to burlesque the Guard's charges against him:

1st: Fifteen negro inhabitants, the most outstanding on this little island, have complained to the *comandante* that last week a strange "statue" appeared unexpectedly on the lighthouse.

2nd: The statue displayed, against all the rules of sculpture, several months growth of beautiful beard, and from the time when the negress Lily Doublette told the other inhabitants until they arrived, the statue had changed positions.

3rd: Examining afterwards the place where the apparition took place, Guard officer Frederick Clofth found fresh human excrement at its base.

4th: The public voice of the island accuses you unanimously, both for the beard and for the excrement, and

5th: I ALSO accuse you. In your official record as soldier (1934) is noted a punishment imposed upon you by the *Comandante* of Quilalí, for having gone out in the village at night to dance strange dances in the nude. . . .

These two facts, isolated in time but concatenated by psychopathological deformities peculiar to certain individuals, indicate to me that the "statue" was none other than you. Stop your clowning (*Déjese de payasadas*). Today I have sent orders to officer Clofth that without regard to beards, he shoot to pieces whatever "statue" appears on the lighthouse. . . .
PATRIA Y LIBERTAD.

Luis Emilio Pérez, *Comandante* of Little Corn Island
Lieutenant, *Guardia Nacional*. (Cuadra 1982, 31–33, 57–59)

For repeated instances of such penetratingly satiric writing (and behavior), Cuadra was later imprisoned by the regime in Managua's *La Aviación* prison (1943) and on the island of Ometepe (1947). In his novel *Almidón* (Starch) of 1944, he roundly ridiculed life in Somoza's Nicaragua and all its institutions, including both the Conservative and the Liberal (PLN) parties. At one point in the novel, a letter from the former carries the party legend "Alienation of national lands. Torture to the taste of the client. Order — Religion — Illiteracy"; the answering PLN letterhead says "Monopolies — Electoral frauds. Tortures at home. Dictatorship" (Cuadra 1982, 121–22). In a series of newspaper articles during the 1950s Cuadra kept the pressure on. When a Managua newspaper asked its readers what should be the "national dish" of Nicaragua, he responded that it should be a plate of slobber or slime (*baba*) because it was "the plate of the day, the plate of the year, and the plate of forever," the only one that every Nicaraguan eats "with as much excess of enthusiasm as lack of modesty, daily, voluntarily, never tiring."[15]

THE GENERATION OF 1940

During the 1940s and 1950s, the center of cultural opposition to the Somoza regime passed from *la vanguardia* to a group of writers who became known as the Generation of 1940. The most important of them were Ernesto Mejía Sánchez (b. 1923), Carlos Martínez Rivas (b. 1924), and Ernesto Cardenal (b. 1925), but at various times the group also included Enrique Fernández Morales and María Teresa Sánchez (both born in 1918), Guillermo Rothschuh Tablada (b. 1928), and Ernesto Gutiérrez (b. 1929). Oddly enough, the group had first begun meeting with arch-conservative Pablo Antonio Cuadra in Granada to read poetry and talk about literature (Beverley and Zimmerman 1990, 64–65; Borgeson 1977, 5).[16]

The Generation of 1940 produced a steady stream of anti-Somoza writing, much of it inspired by the guerrilla campaign of Augusto Sandino. "We want Sandino to be reborn among us," wrote Mejía Sánchez in 1954, and Mario Cajina Vega's poem "¡Sandino!" concluded with a reference to his traitorous assassination by Somoza García (Asís Fernández 1986, 89, 150–51). Following the assassination of Somoza García himself in 1956, Mejía Sánchez—forced into exile as the "intellectual author" of the failed 1954 coup attempt—fashioned his bitterly ironic poem "La muerte de Somoza" (The death of Somoza) around President Eisenhower's eulogistic statement that the dictator had been "a great friend of the United States." His 1959 poem "La cortina del país natal" (The curtain of my native country) invoked contemporary discussions of the iron, bamboo, and other curtains surrounding totalitarian countries to observe that "no one talks about / the Curtain of Shit / around my native Nicaragua" (Mejía Sánchez 1985, 114–16; cf. White 1986, 37–41).

One of the most frequently reprinted of the anti-Somoza poems was Ernesto Gutiérrez's clandestinely published "Mi país es tan pequeño" (My country is so small), which burlesqued the paranoid pettiness of the dictatorship:

> My country is so small
> that 2,000 National Guardsmen sustain the government.
>
> My country is so small
> that private life

has to be in favor
or against the government.

My country is so small
that Mr. President
personally settles
even the arguments in the streets.

My country is so small
that with the rifles of the Guard
any imbecile can govern it.[17]

The largest body of anti-Somoza poetry to emerge in the 1950s was written by Ernesto Cardenal.[18] Born in Granada, Cardenal received his first schooling with the Christian Brothers in León, but graduated from high school at the Jesuit Colegio Mayor Centroamericano in Granada. Although he studied and lived outside the country between his seventeenth and twenty-fifth years — first in Mexico (1943–47), later at Columbia University in New York (1947–49), where he perfected his English, and then in Spain (1949–50) — Cardenal maintained a strong commitment to Nicaragua. In Mexico City he participated in political activities organized by Nicaraguan exiles (including Mejía Sánchez) against Somoza and other Latin American dictators (cf. Mejía Sánchez 1985, 112–14).

Returning to Managua in mid-1950, Cardenal opened a bookstore he called *El Hilo Azul* (The blue thread), formed a small publishing firm with ex-*vanguardista* (and relative) José Coronel Urtecho, and continued to write poetry. Influenced by Pablo Neruda, St.-John Perse, and Ezra Pound, Cardenal's early poetry focused primarily on love, but he turned increasingly to more political themes and (like the *vanguardistas*) to an exploration of indigenous culture and native resistance to domination. His *Proclama del conquistador*, which included a dialogue between a *conquistador* and an Indian *cacique* whose lands were to be taken, appeared as early as 1947, and his long poem "With Walker in Nicaragua" was published in 1952 (Cardenal 1983b, 20–36). A number of his epigrams burlesqued the Somoza regime: the dictators' self-important posturing (*Somoza desveliza la estatua de Somoza en el estadio Somoza* [Somoza unveils the Somoza statue in Somoza stadium]), the regime's repressiveness (*La Guardia Nacional anda buscando a un hombre* [The National Guard is looking for a man]), its censorship (*Nuestros poemas no se pueden publicar todavía* [Our poems still cannot be published]), and its falsification of language (*Nos has leído, amor mío, en Novedades?* [Have you read to us, my love, in *Novedades*?]). One such epigram (*En Costa Rica cantan los carreteros*) caused Somoza to order Cardenal's arrest, but he was tipped off and was able to hide until the crisis passed (Cardenal 1983a, 15–24; Borgeson 1977, 35–39).

In 1954 Cardenal participated in the so-called April rebellion against Somoza. Mounted by the National Unit of Popular Action (*Unidad Nacional de Acción Popular*), the plot failed after being discovered by Somoza. Following the coup attempt, Cardenal went into hiding and then into exile as repression became more intense after the assassination of Somoza García in late 1956. One major result of his period of personal turmoil was that he decided — as he later described it — to yield himself to God.

The great preoccupations of his youth and young adulthood, Cardenal admitted, had been drinking, women, and parties. "He had loved so much," Arellano has observed, "and so many women that could never satisfy that love, or rather the love that subjugated him." "It was in reality an absolute thirst for an infinite love that human love could not satisfy," Cardenal said. "But I did not know it" (Arellano 1979, 40). In May 1957 he joined the communal life of silence, prayer, and contemplation in a monk's unheated cell at the Trappist monastery at Gethsemane, Kentucky. During his two years there, Cardenal became the protegé of Thomas Merton — a relationship that reanimated his interest in indigenous culture and brought further reflection upon the possible forms of political action (Borgeson 1977, 48–50; Arellano 1979, 40–42).[19] Understanding from Merton that a contemplative life may impel one to identify with people who have no rights and who live in misery, Cardenal left the monastery in 1959 and published *La hora zero* (Zero hour). Borgeson has called this long poem "an act of social conscience . . . [that represents] the political Cardenal at his best," and Beverley and Zimmerman see it as "the founding text" of the "literary *Sandinismo*" that flourished later with the birth of the FSLN (Borgeson 1977, 40–44; Beverley and Zimmerman 1990, 66). Casting revolutionary activity as a means of continually renewing life, it included sections on the 1954 coup attempt, the collusion between North American corporations (especially the fruit companies) and Central American dictators, and the collusion between Somoza and the U.S. ambassador to assassinate Sandino.

After two more years of study at Cuernavaca, Cardenal went to Colombia in 1961 to study for the priesthood. He was ordained in 1965, a year after he had published his *Salmos*, an idiomatic, colloquial Spanish version of Psalms, which he rendered in terms of contemporary political, economic, and cultural realities. In the *Salmos* Cardenal moved, as Borgeson has observed, from didactic poetry to "a contemporary poetry of prophecy" (Borgeson 1977, 136).

Both his discussions with Merton and his later anthropological studies at Cuernavaca reinforced Cardenal's interest in primitive American poetry and corrective social-political paradigms drawn from pre-conquest native society.

He had extended those interests during his years in Colombia, and after 1963 spent some time in the Amazon region as well, looking for "old America, which is for me the America of the future."[20] During the late 1960s, he attended ever more carefully to the history of pre-conquest and indigenous society in Latin America. His long poem sequence *Homenaje a los indios americanos* (Homage to the American Indians) of 1969 emphasized the beauty and integrity of those ancient societies, whose political and religious truths seemed to him a unified whole.

Soon after publishing *Homenaje*, Cardenal traveled to Cuba to observe and write about revolutionary cultural programs. His 1971 anthology *Poesía nicaragüense* (Nicaraguan Poetry) included a liberal sampling of anti-Somoza poetry, and he dedicated his *Canto nacional* (National Hymn; 1972) to the FSLN. His long historical poem "Oráculo sobre Managua" (Oracle over Managua) focused on the life of the martyred Leonel Rugama and treated the 1972 earthquake and the heightened cynicism and repression of the dictatorship.[21]

CULTURAL RESISTANCE AMONG STUDENTS

The granting of autonomy to the Universidad Nacional Autónoma de Nicaragua (UNAN) helped shift the locus of cultural opposition to the regime from the Managua- and Granada-based *vanguardistas* and their Generation of 1940 successors to a group of young university students in León.[22]

Direct political action by university students had deep historical roots in Nicaragua. As early as 1822, students in León had joined artisans in the indigenous *barrio* of Subtiava to take over a military headquarters. In the early 1890s, secondary school students in León and Granada rioted. More recently, during the U.S. military operations against rebel nationalist General Sandino in 1929, Mariano Fiallos Gil and other National University students formed the group "Cultura" to seek, as they phrased it, "our own values in the face of the foreign, forming a concept of rural and indigenous America as the only valid one" (Wheelock Román [1974] 1981, 90–91; Teplitz 1973, 17; Ramírez 1971, 27). Two years later, one of Sandino's manifestos that celebrated the lion (*león*) as both king of the beasts and symbol (as Darío noted) of the twenty-one growing lion-cub states of Latin America, caught the attention of students in León, who were sympathetic to Sandino's crusade against the marines, and who—with other students in Managua and Granada—were trying to establish a Federation of Nicaraguan Students (Ramírez 1971, 28). When the León students printed and distributed the statement, the regime disparaged them as "deceived by the false halo of patriotism" (Macaulay [1967] 1985, 226; Ramírez 1974, 2:198–99).[23] In 1944, emboldened by student agitation against other Central American dictators, anti-Somoza Nicaraguan students issued the first call for a university "unique, autonomous, and popular." Student demonstrations in Managua and León at mid-year were broken up by the National Guard, which imprisoned scores of them. Four years later Managua students organized the anti-Somoza National Union of Popular Action (*Unión Nacional de Acción Popular*), and in the early 1950s students in law and social sciences raised the university autonomy issue again. In 1955 they formed a Permanent Committee for University Autonomy (Ramírez 1971, 49, 88–89; Walter 1987, 213–23, 364; Walter 1993, 111, 125, 130–31). Meanwhile Somoza confided to intimates, "I don't want educated people; I want oxen" (LaFeber in Cabezas [1982] 1985, 227). In 1957, a year after Somoza García had been assassinated by poet and university student Rigoberto López Pérez, the new president Luis Somoza Debayle (slightly less repressive than his father) named Mariano Fiallos Gil (1907–64) rector of the National University.

Fiallos was — given his politics — something of an odd political choice but a fortunate one, and he proved remarkably effective.[24] Having entered the university himself in 1927 when students merely matriculated and appeared for final exams, Fiallos had finished law school in 1933 and retired to the country to read and write until he was named to a high post in the Ministry of Education by the new Somoza government. After serving in several such posts, he returned to the countryside before he found himself drawn into the 1947 Leonardo Argüello presidential campaign against Somoza. Through manipulation and fraud, Argüello won the election, but was forced out by the regime after he dismissed Somoza as head of the National Guard; he fled to Guatemala, where he formed a government in exile and named Fiallos minister of foreign relations (Bermann 1986, 236; Booth 1985, 59).

Fiallos became rector after a solitary and frustrating period in his life. Returning to Nicaragua from exile in Guatemala (which under President Arévalo had become a haven for Central American oppositionist groups), he had supported himself by occasional work as a journalist. He then went to Washington, where a promised job with the Panamerican Union was blocked by the Nicaraguan embassy. For a while he looked for work in New York and Washington, supporting himself by playing piano in a cheap bar, and then went home to his farm in Nicaragua again to read and paint.[25] It was there that the call came to him to take over the university. Unfortunately, the university Fiallos took over was little more than a mere shell: the student body totaled 919 (out of more than 160,000 college-age students in the country), and only forty or so were graduating each year. Most of the faculty were private lawyers and doctors who rarely came to classes, all of which were held in the university's sole building.

Fiallos's reform efforts stimulated student-based cultural resistance to the Somoza regime. Supported by a niggardly government salary of less than $200 (U.S.) per month, he set about freeing the university from what he called its "ancestral vices of preconceived ideas, bookish teaching . . . disequilibrium between science and the humanities . . . [and] disconnection from the situation in which one is living" (Fiallos 1965, 63; Ramírez 1971, 93). Practically, he focused on upgrading all aspects of the university's work, moving aggressively to expand programs, improve the faculty, and provide free medical and other social services to the public. He was particularly committed to expanding both the conception and the role of culture in university life. His first press release announced the formation of an experimental theater, and he moved quickly to institute literary and artistic courses and conferences, and to establish a museum of popular culture. At El Salvador's National Cultural Contest the following year, he noted with envy that El Salvador's national university was "the center of cultural attraction."

Fiallos's vision of such a university was linked to his long-time commitment to progressive movements. His "dynamic liberalism," as Ramírez characterized it, was oriented "not to the contemplation of the world, but to a participation without reserve in order to transform it into a more habitable one." Within that conception, the role of the university was to be the conscience of the nation (Ramírez 1971, 188–89). "The university," Fiallos told students, "should be at the service of democracy and never of despotism." "Take possession of it," he advised them (Ramírez 1971, 94, 101–2, 106; cf. Fiallos Gil 1965). Students took him at his word, organizing soon thereafter to prevent President Eisenhower's brother Milton, who had facilitated friendly relations between the United States and the regime, from receiving an honorary degree from the university (Diederich 1981, 55–58).

After the Castro triumph in Cuba in January 1959, UNAN students organized and demonstrated with renewed vigor. Called in a few months later by the government to quiet a large demonstration, the National Guard fired on them, killing several and wounding more than eighty. "That contributed," recalled former student Sergio Ramírez, "to our violent process of maturation" (Ramírez 1971, 115, 137; cf. Ortega Saavedra 1979, 75, 93, 115). Student organization continued to develop rapidly as the leftist Student Revolutionary Front (Frente Estudiantil Revolucionario [FER]) gained control of the largest student organization, news of plots against Somoza filtered in from Mexico and Venezuela, and abortive armed resistance movements were attempted (including a dramatic one at El Chapparal in June, 1959, in which the future founder of the Frente Sandinista de Liberación Nacional [FSLN], Carlos Fonseca, was wounded).[26]

Far from monolithically united, the student generation of the 1960s was actually deeply divided, with the progressive and leftist students at UNAN—the *Ventana* (Window) group—opposed by a Managua-based group (led by Roberto Cuadra, Edwin Yllescas, Ivan Uriarte, and Beltrán Morales) that called itself the Betrayed Generation (Ramírez 1985a; Morales 1970; Randall 1983c). The Betrayed Generation's cultural politics—in some ways analogous to those of the Beat Generation in the United States, although more bourgeois—resembled the apolitical elitism of *La Prensa Literaria*'s rather pontifical editor Pablo Antonio Cuadra, who insisted that literature not be contaminated with ideology. They therefore concerned themselves with a type of literary innovation and experimentation they hoped would "rescue the purity" of Nicaraguan literature, threatened by consumerism and the attendant mass-cultural pathologies of modern urban life. They agreed with Cuadra that political commitment and literary-cultural rejuvenation were antithetical and incompatible.[27]

The *Ventana* students, on the other hand, were in no way disposed toward a Cuadra-like apolitical aestheticism and "alienating ideology." "We are not the betrayed generation," they proclaimed. "We are the generation that should not betray Nicaragua." [28] From the *Ventana* perspective, the Betrayed Generation was confused by "colonialist worries distant from Nicaraguan realities." Betrayed Generation students in turn accused the *Ventana* group of impoverishing literature "with themes that are too prosaic" when they wrote of Siuna miners suffering from silicosis or the poor of Managua's Acahualinca community (Ramírez 1985a; White 1986, 80–81).

Undeterred by such arguments, Sergio Ramírez suggested to some student friends during the summer of 1960 that they start a small cultural magazine. No one responded except anti-Somoza student leader Fernando Gordillo, noted for his grasp of the cultural-political history of Nicaragua.[29] Securing a small subvention from university rector Fiallos, Gordillo and Ramírez became co-directors of a journal they called *Ventana* (Window). Printed on a press owned by the Christian Brothers, the twelve-page, yellow-covered five-hundred-copy first issue challenged Pablo Antonio Cuadra and the Betrayed Generation aesthetes, and proclaimed a "literary attitude of commitment." "No one dare interfere" in what the *Ventana* students are doing, proclaimed an editorial by Mariano Fiallos, and the students themselves promised that "we are going to open a new breach into the heart of the university . . . [and] inject a new hormone into our flesh." A people without literature, they argued, is "a people without poets, zombies without a future and with the same past." [30] Gordillo's "anti-editorial" in the next issue affirmed that "to publish a poem, a story, an essay . . . is to try to encounter our human reality, and not to contribute to the personal happiness of anyone." A wood-

Cover of *Ventana*, student magazine at the Universidad Nacional Autónoma de Nicaragua, León, honoring martyrs of the National Guard's attack on university students.

cut of a scene from the massacre of university students by the National Guard illustrated an essay by Ramírez and poems by Gordillo on student martyrs.[31]

By the fall of 1960, *Ventana* had become a substantial magazine, and its politics had toughened and become even clearer. In the following issue, an "anti-editorial" asserted that literature is "neither pastime nor diversion, but a vehicle of culture, a road of life and truth."[32]

Later issues of *Ventana* carried the poetry of Thomas Merton, Langston Hughes ("the defender of his people against the aggressions of racism"), the Beat poets, Ezra Pound, Robert Frost, Salomón de la Selva, and Ernesto Cardenal, an interview with William Faulkner, North American Indian love poems, and others translated from Quechua and Chinese.[33] However eclectic the sources, themes and emphases were consistent: *Ventana* featured writers who spoke for subjugated people and their culture, and against their oppressors; who understood the music and power of vernacular language; whose aesthetic experimentation was inseparable from political criticism and opposition; and who above all comprehended the inescapably political dimensions of culture. "We don't believe in exile," *Ventana* proclaimed. "We know that we are on a field of battle. . . . The clamor of our people strikes at our hearts. . . . We know that beans are more important than chewing gum. Therefore we write of beans rather than chewing gum. . . . We know it is necessary to destroy. We want to destroy. But [it is] the destruction of the seed that rots itself in order to produce a new plant. . . . We believe poetry is the voice of the people."[34] At an autumn 1961 *Ventana*-sponsored "Culture Week" series of performances and discussions, students talked about how to avoid a rupture "between the poet and society," whether there was a tradition of struggle in Nicaraguan literature, whether indigenous materials should be integrated into poetry, and how writers might speak against human pain and misery without lapsing into mere propaganda.[35]

By the mid-1960s, the Ventana group of students had graduated and dispersed, and *Ventana* ceased publication, but students continued to be active in other cultural sectors. In August 1963, painter Alejandro Aróstegui founded Grupo Praxis with other painters and writers to forge closer relations between artistic production and national political and social realities, and to enlist creative artists in "the struggle of the people against the Somoza dictatorship."[36] As editor of UNAN's *Cuadernos Universitarios* (University Notebooks), poet Ernesto Gutiérrez encouraged a new generation of students to publish their own journal, independently of the university, and gave them paper to print it on. *Taller* (1968) was the result; it published a lot of anti-Somoza writing Gutiérrez dared not publish in the official *Cuadernos Universitarios*.[37]

Taller began more cautiously than *Ventana*: "To link cultural work to social action seems incongruent," said the editors in the first issue. But the *Taller*

Parish church in Indian community of Subtiava, 1988. (Photograph by author)

students, like their *Ventana* predecessors, soon became unabashedly political and militant.[38] Leoncio Sáenz's cover for the third issue showed three naked prisoners hung by their ankles for torture; the next was dedicated to militant poet Leonel Rugama, killed by the National Guard in 1970. Scattered through the twenty issues of the next decade were an essay by former Betrayed Generation writer Beltrán Morales on *Ventana* founder Fernando Gordillo, a selection of Cuban poetry edited by Ernesto Cardenal, an essay by Salvadoran poet Roque Dalton, and poems of Leonel Rugama, Daniel Ortega (sent from jail), and Mao Tse-tung. Young Nicaraguan poets found *Taller* especially open to them and to attempts to ground Nicaraguan poetry in the country's "underdeveloped and dependent" circumstances. "The life of the people," an editorial asserted in 1975, "is the only inexhaustible source from which true art arises."[39] Student José Fonseca juxtaposed the ancient culture of his indigenous *barrio* of Subtiava with the social and political ugliness of life under the dictatorship. Subtiava, he wrote,

> An ancient church
> And a hermitage equally ancient . . .
> A school and a small
> Police station . . .
>   Two rivers
>   Pardon —

> One is still a river and
> The other is shit. . . .

> A language
> That nobody remembers.[40]

Between them, *Ventana* and *Taller* provided a forum for several generations of student writers and intellectuals — many of them formed intellectually, politically, and culturally in the caldron of *somocismo* repression and
violence. Some of them (Leonel Rugama, Ricardo Morales Avilés) lost their
lives in the armed struggle; others (Sergio Ramírez, Jaime Wheelock Román)
went on to high positions in the post-1979 Sandinista leadership, from which
they continued to shape both the discourse about culture and the cultural
policies of the new government.

Among the most important oppositionist writers of the late 1960s and
early 1970s were Ricardo Morales Avilés, Leonel Rugama, and a group of
young women writers. During his imprisonment by the regime between 1968
and 1971, Morales Avilés wrote a small body of poems (rejected by Pablo
Antonio Cuadra's *La Prensa Literaria*) and a group of important theoretical essays asserting the pivotal necessity of political clarity and revolutionary
commitment among cultural workers in Nicaragua (Morales Avilés 1983).
Rugama wrote relatively little poetry, but what he wrote was profoundly influential — especially his "La tierra es un satélite de la luna," which dramatizes
the ironic contrast between the vast sums spent on the U.S. space program
and the elemental needs of Nicaraguan slum dwellers (Rugama [1978] 1985).

One of the earliest and most important pieces written by women during the insurrectionary period was Michele Najlis's *El viento armado* (The
armed wind; 1969).[41] It was not only (as Beverley and Zimmerman observe)
"one of the most important literary expressions the insurrectionary period
produced," but also the opening volume in what became a large body of
important revolutionary poetry by young women writers (Gioconda Belli,
Vidaluz Meneses, Rosario Murillo, Daisy Zamora, Ana Ilce, Yolanda Blanco,
and others) (cf. Randall 1984, 21–40, 109–19, 141–54). The poems of *El viento
armado* were precocious in their grasp of the central psychic challenges of the
still embryonic and fragile guerrilla campaign against Somoza: the solidarity
and will to persevere paradoxically engendered by brutal torture and martyrdom ("Nos persiguieron en la noche" [They pursued us in the night] and
"Con toda la ira de tu muerte" [With all the wrath of your death]), the sense
of continuity with past struggles ("Los inocentes alzaron los fusiles" [The
innocents lift the rifles]), the confidence in victory despite the odds ("Ahora
que andas por los caminos de la Patria" [Now that you walk the country's
roads]), and the sexual-political syllogism the earth = woman's body = the

yearned-for wholeness and joy of the liberated and reconstructed homeland ("Si me ves en las calles llena de sonrisas" [If you see me in the streets full of smiles]) (Najlis 1969, 31, 35, 39, 45, 71).[42]

Except for an expression of relatively mild nostalgia for indigenous culture in its final poem, Belli's *Sobre la grama* (Upon the grass) of 1974 was not explicitly political. But in its frank and joyous celebration of a woman's sexual desire, energy, and power, it went beyond Najlis's *El viento armado* in challenging the old patriarchal order of which the Somoza regime was the most palpable present example. "When we are together," one poem proclaimed,

> I want to turn myself into laughter,
> Full of joy,
> Frolic on beaches of tenderness
> Recently discovered . . .
> Love you, love you
> Until we forget everything
> And know not who is who.[43]

By the time Belli's *Línea de fuego* appeared in 1978, the insurrection was in its final phase, and the politics of her poetry had become much more explicit. The aggressive sexuality of *Sobre la grama* was still present ("My body seems always to have loved you / to have been waiting for you" confided "Manuscrito"), but was now elaborated in a sexual-political-insurrectionary metaphor in which moments for love are stolen from the tasks of war ("Como será buscarte en la distancia" [How it will be to look for you in the distance]), the beloved's body is a map of the imagined post-revolutionary body politic ("Recorriéndote" [Exploring you]), making love and making war are fused into one totality ("Mi amor es como un río caudaloso" [My love is like a swelling river]), the tragedy and loss of war are acutely personal (*Al comandante Marcos* [To Comandante Marcos]), and children are born to follow in the steps of the *guerrilleros* ("Engendraremos niños" [We shall engender children]). Similar themes animated Ilce's *Las ceremonias de silencio* (1975), Meneses's *Llama guardada* (1975), Murillo's *Gualtayán (Amar)* (1974) and *Sube a nacer conmigo* (1976), and Blanco's *Cerámica sol* (1977) (Beverley and Zimmerman 1990, 90).[44]

Closely linked to the oppositional poetry, both implicitly in spirit and frequently explicitly through their titles, were the *testimonios*—first-person, usually nonfictional narratives that had deep roots in earlier literary forms in Latin America and in which the narrator's testimony concerning her or his experience stands for that of an entire community, ethnic or other group, or class.

In Nicaragua, the *testimonio* appeared in its earliest forms in the 1930s

Caricature of dictator with ceremonial medals representing American corporations. Pen and ink drawing by Lenin Cerna, Tipitapa Prison, 1974. (From Carlos José Guadamuz, *Y . . . "Las casas quedaron llenas de humo,"* 1982; reproduced by permission of Editorial Nueva Nicaragua)

with Hernán Robleto's *Sangre en el trópico* (Blood in the tropics; 1930) and *Los estrangulados* (The strangled ones; 1933), Pedro Joaquín Chamorro's *El último filibustero* (The last filibuster; 1933), and José Román's *Maldito País* (Cursed country; 1934) (Beverley and Zimmerman 1990, 172–80; Ramírez 1972). Carlos José Guadamuz's *Y . . . "Las casas quedaron llenas de humo"* (And . . . "the houses remained full of smoke"), which Beverley and Zimmerman call "the pioneer work of Nicaraguan *testimonio*," was written in prison in 1970, smuggled out, and circulated clandestinely in mimeographed form (Beverley and Zimmerman 1990, 183–84). Guadamuz's *testimonio* was followed by Doris Tijerino's *"Somos millones . . .": La vida de Doris María,* combatiente nicaragüense ("We are millions . . .": The life of Doris María, Nicaraguan combatant; 1977), whose title came from a poem by Morales Avilés; Tomás Borge's *Carlos, el amanecer ya no es una tentación* (Carlos, the dawn is no longer beyond our Reach; written in the late 1970s but not published until 1980); and pre-eminently—Omar Cabezas's *La montaña es algo más que una inmensa estepa verde* (The mountain is something more than an immense green steppe) (Cabezas [1982] 1985).

One of the most arresting images of Cabezas's *testimonio* located additional roots (and possibilities) of resistance within indigenous communities. As a young student in León, Cabezas was awed by political demonstrations in the city's indigenous *barrio* of Subtiava: "The Subtiavans . . . before coming out to demonstrate, played their *atabales* [drums] . . . *parangan-parangán-parangan-parangán*. And they looked to neither side, but went straight ahead, *parangan-parangán-parangan-parangán*." Resonating from deep within the culture, the *atabales* were different, Cabezas noted, from "the merrymaking of [demonstrating] students who screwed around and invented sounds" (Cabezas [1982] 1985, 52–53). Indeed the oppositional potential of the culture's complexly resonant stock of cherished sounds, of music itself, was even clearer to some of Cabezas's contemporaries than it was to him.

MUSIC AND RESISTANCE

The politics of musical preferences in Nicaragua ran deep, and had always been contested. Exiled on Little Corn Island off the Atlantic coast in the 1930s, Manolo Cuadra listened to the song of Lola, a black woman: "Lola sings with much spirit. Hearing her, I have felt for the first time on this little island a real sadness. They are songs of black love, across whose epidermis—sensible like the epidermis of almost all the songs—passes the warm breeze of animal melancholy. But melodious and soft. The last song, as best I could understand, was about a prisoner who was crying for the loss of his liberty. She offers to repeat it the day I go, the day I am again a free man" (M. Cuadra 1982, 22).

Although early travelers such as Squier, Froebel, and Stout had commented briefly on music in Nicaragua, little was known about non-elite musical production until the *vanguardistas* began to collect a few traditional song texts, some of which they published in the cultural supplement to *La Prensa* in the early 1940s. In *Hacia la cruz del sur* (Toward the southern cross), *vanguardista* Pablo Antonio Cuadra declared that "only through music can we unite with the past. Only music has the power to evoke the spirit and poetry that circulated in our ancestors' veins, and which . . . emerges in our hearts today. . . . A single lullaby coos the entire infancy of America" (Cuadra 1938, 35). By

1946 Ernesto Mejía Sanchez had published texts of several dozen songs, including a few collected among Sandino's guerrillas, but serious and sustained attention to native Nicaraguan music was lacking (Mejía Sánchez 1946).

Popular musical taste during the Somoza period was oriented mostly toward Latin American and North American popular music—especially that to be heard on radio, mass-market phonograph recordings, and in Hollywood films. Elite taste deferred to the programming of European and North American touring performers and a few Nicaraguan composers. Among the latter, the most influential was classical composer Luis Delgadillo, who recorded for Odeon in the United States and founded a small conservatory in Managua that eventually became the National School of Music. Devoted as he was to elite musical models in the late 1950s, Delgadillo was troubled by what he saw as "a crisis in American music" deriving from the introduction of an *elemento negroide* that was driving out higher "European influences" and thus frustrating the "natural advances in musical art" that might otherwise be expected.[45]

Fortunately, some students at UNAN were moving in musical directions more promising than those delineated by Delgadillo. By the mid-1950s, their anti-Somoza songs were circulating clandestinely:

> With the head of Tacho
> We will make a ball
> To play football
> From Managua to León.

Another student-written song commemorated the student uprising and massacre at UNAN of July 1959 (López 1982, 9, 14).

Students' explorations of the political uses of music received a major impetus from the *nueva canción* (new song) movement that developed in Chile in the mid-1960s and spread throughout Latin America. Opposing the increasing domination of popular music by "disposable consumer songs," *nueva canción* composers drew upon traditional musical forms and rhythms and employed indigenous instruments to create songs oriented toward progressive political and social change, some of which played a major role in Salvador Allende's Popular Unity campaign. Outlawed during the "cultural blackout" that followed the Pinochet military coup, and suppressed by media bans, blacklisting, and exiling of performers, and even prohibition of certain instruments, *nueva canción* went underground and became necessarily more metaphoric and less overtly political in its lyrics. The music reemerged slowly as cultural controls were relaxed and the new technology of cassette recorders facilitated hand-to-hand dissemination (Morris 1986; cf. Luzuriaga 1978, 417–18).

Especially active in grafting the *nueva canción* movement onto the roots of resistance in Nicaragua were the brothers Carlos and Luis Enríque Mejía Godoy. Sons of a marimba maker, the Mejía Godoys came from an economically marginal family of composers, musicians, and instrument makers who had long been involved in progressive activities in their community near the Honduran border. Both of them spent much of their adolescence and young adult years in Costa Rica, but returned to Nicaragua frequently and began to integrate themselves into the emerging anti-Somoza political struggle in the late 1960s. Attracted by the currents of *nueva canción* as early as 1970, Carlos began writing musical parodies of Somoza and setting the political poems of Pablo Antonio Cuadra and Ernesto Cardenal to music. Soon he was taking his songs to music festivals in Costa Rica (1973) and Panama (1976). His younger brother Luis, at first a singer of popular romantic songs, helped establish *nueva canción* in Costa Rica. Forced to leave Nicaragua after the FSLN "Christmas party raid" of 1974, Carlos continued to work clandestinely with political groups in Nicaragua and Chile and elsewhere in Latin America.[46]

Through the efforts of the Mejía Godoys and other composer-performers —working at times with traditional *campesino* musical groups (such as Los Soñadores de Sarawas, a group of blind musicians from Jinotega) — the *nueva canción* movement began in earnest in Nicaragua in 1973 (at the time of the Pinochet crackdown in Chile). Called *volcanto* (from *volcán* [volcano] and *canto* [song]), the movement intensified as pressure against the Somoza regime stepped up in the mid-1970s.

Students at UNAN organized the performing group Grupo Pancasán in 1975 (named for one of the FSLN's militarily unsuccessful but symbolically important military actions in 1967). The Costa Rican company INDICA released at least one long-playing record by the group (Marlene Alvarez, Francisco Cedeño, Martín Fonseca, and Agustín Sequeira) on the Sonorama label (PP-445) (Pring-Mill 1987, 180). Arranged for voices, guitar, flute, percussion, and *quena* (an Andean instrument prominent in *nueva canción* in Chile), its intensely political songs included "Canción del hombre nuevo" (Song of the new man), "Toma la tierra" (Take the land), "Se está forjando la patria nueva" (A new country is being forged), "Trabajadores al poder" (Workers to power), "General de hombres libres" (General of free men, Pancasán's hymn to Sandino), "La hora zero" (Zero hour, a fragment from Ernesto Cardenal's long poem), and "María Rural" by young FSLN martyr Arlén Siu.

Returning to Nicaragua in 1977, Carlos Mejía Godoy helped to organize the Talleres de Sonido Popular (Popular sound workshops) — a loosely structured aggregation of performing groups (Nueva América, Ocho de Noviembre, Mejía Godoy's Los de Palacagüina, Libertad, and others) — to carry the work forward in his own country. By mid-1977, a number of such performing groups had been organized; most concentrated upon *nueva canción/volcanto* and drew heavily upon Nicaraguan traditional repertoire. Several years before the fall of Somoza, three thousand people heard Soñadores de Sarawaska, Grupo Pacaya, Grupo Pancasán, Pánfilo Orozco, Luz y Verdad, Nueva América, the Mejía Godoys, and others perform *nueva canción* and *volcanto* at a Festival of Human Rights in Managua.[47] Despite the ongoing climate of repression, young musicians managed to mobilize their creative energies in such a way as to both dramatize their opposition and reserve to themselves a margin of protection.

As student and popular uprisings intensified after the Somoza regime assassinated *La Prensa* editor Pedro Joaquín Chamorro early in 1978, more militant songs continued to appear, and a number of Nicaraguan groups took the songs of the revolution to the eleventh World Youth Festival in Havana. Paradoxically, the intensification of the conflict that provided a constant stream of material for song-writers and performers also fragmented the performing groups themselves (including the Talleres de Sonido Popular groups, which had managed to organize themselves briefly into a national federation) as young musicians were drawn into the revolutionary process either as combatants or in other roles that made it difficult to maintain the performing groups intact.[48]

Working with recording companies outside Nicaragua during the final two years of the insurrection—and linking themselves with movements of resistance and liberation throughout Latin America and beyond, the Mejía Godoy brothers continued to produce insurrectionary music on long-playing records. Although importing such records into Nicaragua was forbidden by the regime, planning, recording, and producing them were politically important for the artists. The process sharpened images and generated patterns of sound as charged with social and political meaning as were the *atabales* of Subtiava.[49]

Although many of the songs recorded by musicians in opposition to the regime were explicitly political in the sense that they employed overtly political texts, their oppositional qualities were not confined solely to those texts. Within a cultural situation such as that which pertained in Nicaragua from at least the mid-1970s onward, merely to seek (through performance or recording) to relegitimize long depreciated and marginalized expressive forms was itself an important political act. Moreover, within a cultural climate increasingly overlaid with the commercial culture of the United States—the preferred culture of the regime itself—to resurrect and broadcast the submerged instruments, vocal styles, and song forms characteristic of Nicaraguan culture was also an act of opposition. Indeed in this sense even a purely instrumental performance could take on a political meaning.

Fortunately, recordings issued by the Mejía Godoys and others offer insight into the nuances of the cultural-political ferment of 1970s Nicaragua that is difficult to gain in any other way.

The control exercised by the Somoza regime over cultural and political life in Nicaragua forced musicians to go outside the country to produce their records. Recorded in Spain by Carlos Mejía Godoy's group Los de Palacagüina, *El son nuestro de cada día* (Our everyday song) was released in 1977 by the Mexican subsidiary of CBS. Except for one traditional piece, all of its songs were written and arranged by Mejía Godoy. Included among a number of humorous and romantic songs were the overtly political "Juancito tirador" (about a landless *campesino*), "El Cristo de Palacagüina" (about a young Nicaraguan Jesus whose mother wants him to grow up to be a carpenter, but who prefers to be a guerrilla fighter), and the subtle and paradoxical "María de los guardias." [50]

More decidedly political was *La nueva milpa* (The new field) of 1978, recorded in Madrid, pressed by INDICA in Costa Rica, and released by the Madrid subsidiary of CBS (CBS 100406). The jacket featured an FSLN flag and combatant faces in a cornfield. "El solar de Monimbó" promised that "the land will be ours when the Revolution triumphs"; "Flor de pino" nostalgically recalled the wedding of Sandino; "La viejecita de Mozambique" (The old lady of Mozambique) asserts "how important is the one who dies rifle in hand, defending the liberty of his country, like the one who dies in exile dreaming of returning to her." To the query "Where is the tomb of the guerrilla?" another song answers that "Your tomb is our whole territory." Like the guerrilla, the proud child warrior in "Quincho Barrilete" joins in the struggle with his poor *campesino* countrymen. The album's final song, a macabre setting of Ernesto Cardenal's poem "Las campesinas del Cuá," memorializes the terror *campesina* women of Cuá suffered at the hands of Somoza's National Guard. [51]

The tempo of the insurrectionary struggle during the early months of 1979 severely curtailed the production of more phonograph albums. [52] Many writers, composers, singers, and other cultural workers had already been imprisoned, tortured, and killed by the National Guard, and others had fallen in combat. Those who escaped were forced underground or into exile during the final months of the insurrection, and many insurrectionary cultural organizations disappeared (Beverley and Zimmerman 1990, 92). Perhaps the last album to appear before the July 1979 triumph was the militant *Guitarra armada* (Armed guitar), which presented songs by the Mejía Godoys designed to teach combatants to use arms and explosives: the outdated but

Jacket design for phonograph record *Guitarra Armada* (ENIGRAC, MC 015, n.d.).

effective U.S. Garand ("among all rifles the Garand is the law"), the later M-1, the Israeli FAL, and even .22 caliber sporting rifles.[53]

REVOLT IN THE INDIGENOUS BARRIOS: SUBTIAVA AND MONIMBÓ

However important in themselves, the student writers of *Ventana* and *Taller* and other young writers and musicians of the late 1960s and 1970s were also constituent parts of broader processes of cultural opposition to the Somoza regime. For example, as earlier chapters have suggested, Nicaraguan writers and intellectuals had long been bringing to public awareness the record of the spirited resilience of—and defiance mounted by—the country's remnant groups of indigenous people. Through their imaginatively conceived and heroically executed movements of resistance in the 1960s and 1970s, certain traditional communities in Nicaragua taught not only the larger public but most especially writers, intellectuals, and the putative FSLN "vanguard" itself the depths, strengths, and uses of traditional culture in processes of social and political change and reconstruction.

Whatever revaluing and repositioning of traditional culture in the insurrectionary process was to be done in Nicaragua, however, had to be done against the preponderant weight of popular opinion. Despite the formal (and as I have suggested, intensely politicized) earlier gesture of the *Instituto Indigenista Nacional*, the low social and cultural status of Nicaraguan Indians had long been evident in popular culture. Of someone who lost his temper it was said *Se le subió el indio* (the Indian came out in him), and an educated person who behaved badly was chastised as "pure Indian." Like snakes and other pests, Indians could be killed with impunity (*Al indio, la culebra y el zanate, dice la ley que se mate* [The Indian, the snake and the pesky bird, the law says kill them]), and decent people admonished each other not to allow (literal or figurative) Indians to eat from china plates, lest they think themselves equal to their betters (*No hay peor cosa que poner a un indio a comer en plato de china*). A brutish, odious, ignorant person was a *jincho* (a slang pronunciation of the Spanish *indio*). To gain position in an argument, a member of the León elite might exclaim *¿Y vos qué sabés? ¿Acaso no sos vos de Subtiava? ¿No sos indio?* (And what do you know? Are you by chance from Subtiava? Are you an Indian?).[54]

Indeed the conventional wisdom (despite the virulent pertinacity of the stereotypes) was that except for the Atlantic coast—still effectively a separate country—Nicaragua's indigenous population and culture had ceased to exist, a judgment reinforced by some putatively objective outside observers.[55] In his 1957 cultural survey of Central America, Adams reported that although the *barrio* of Subtiava was "always thought of as an Indian town," there was "very little to distinguish [its] culture . . . from the general small-town and rural culture to be found elsewhere."[56] Subtiavans spoke Spanish and had adopted Spanish customs, he said, wore the same clothing as everyone else in León, and "in most ways act just like other mestizos." For Adams, the evidence pointed to a marked process of what he called "deculturation" in Nicaragua (Adams 1957, 238–41).[57]

As subsequent events were to demonstrate, however, Adams failed to appreciate the ability of indigenous people to appropriate selected elements of a dominant culture (language, clothing) — in order to survive economically, for example, or to avoid stigmatization in their daily life or work — while at the same time retaining and elaborating elements of their own culture. The most likely candidates for retention were those that were especially cherished and could be retained at low risk within the privacy of the family or community, those that carried little risk of stigmatization if exhibited in public, and those that were guarded in a passive or dormant secrecy in normal times, and reactivated when the group or community came under threat.[58]

Indeed Adams himself, despite his conviction that a broad "deculturation" was under way in Nicaragua, observed much evidence of the survival of cultural diversity and of the vitality of many traditional cultural practices. Tractors were proliferating on the coffee *fincas* and cotton plantations, but ox-drawn plows and digging sticks were also being used on small farms. Traditional ceremonies both sacred and secular were to be seen on virtually all public occasions. Traditional music, foods, and *artesanía* (textile production, tile-making, house construction, and musical instrument making) were still much in evidence. Native healers (*curanderos*) still treated *pujo* (constipation) — caused, they believed, by too much sun — by spitting in the navel. *Empacho* (joint inflammation) received massage, and there were as many cures for *mal de ojo* (evil eye) as there were symptoms and forms of it. More than a decade after Adams's survey, in fact, Peña Hernández presented evidence of the survival and vitality of traditional culture in the environs of the old elite cultural centers of León, Masaya, and Granada (which in turn had been centers of pre-Columbian culture): food, clothing, *artesanía*, proverbs and legends, music, theater, games and toys, and ceremonies (Peña Hernández 1968).

Hence traditional and indigenous culture survived in manifold ways in Nicaragua — however damaged, warped, and redefined by four and a half centuries of foreign intervention and a few decades of the Somoza-style, Managua-based cultural hegemony that took many of its major cues from U.S. popular culture. Two places where the resistant capacities of traditional culture flared out in dazzlingly imaginative and effective ways during the

El Tamarindón, the tree from which Cacique Adiac was hanged by the Spanish. Still standing in 1988. (Photograph by author)

latter days of the insurrection were Subtiava (a *barrio* of León) and Monimbó (adjacent to Masaya).

The harsh facts of domination were symbolized daily for Subtiavans by the tree—*el tamarindón*, still standing in the community—on which their *cacique* Adiac had been hanged by the Spanish. In 1681, provoked by increasingly harsh treatment at the hands of the Spanish in León, Subtiavans rose in rebellion. Forty years later, after the Spanish magistrate of León expropriated portions of their properties and sequestered all their corn and other produce except what they had to have for bare subsistence, they rebelled again. In 1822, Subtiavan artisans joined university students in taking over a military headquarters (Wheelock Román [1974] 1981, 52–55, 90–91, 97). The return of Liberals to power in 1893 brought renewed assaults upon the community's identity and integrity: by the church, which was pushing the sale of *cofradía* lands and trying to eliminate community control of religious symbols and ceremonies, and by the León elite, which hoped to turn the community's internal class and occupational divisions to its own advantage. By 1900, few distinctive cultural attributes remained evident; only a handful of older people remembered the language, and even they were reluctant to speak it in public. Virtually all that remained to the community, it appeared, was its coveted status as a separate, autonomous municipality, and the elite had designs upon even that. As early as 1877, the León elite, covetous of the Subtiavans' lands, were proposing that the community be annexed to the city; by 1902 they had gained their objective (Gould 1990b, 70–96).

The struggle was far from over, however. In the wake of the overthrow of Liberal President Zelaya in 1909, Conservatives sought to broaden their political base partly by annulling Zelaya's abolition of indigenous communities. Both legal status and rights to traditional lands were returned to them. The León elite objected strongly, arguing (with wondrously self-serving illogic) that the community had no land, therefore did not exist, and therefore could not be granted legal status (Gould 1990b, 85). The various dimensions of the struggle (including cultural ones) were dramatized in a conflict over the elites' determination to build a highway through Subtiavan lands to the increasingly popular beach at Poneloya. When the government approved construction monies and a prominent León citizen added insult to injury by proposing that ox-carts be barred from the highway, a hundred armed Subtiavans took over portions of the highway and extracted a compromise (Gould 1990b, 86–88, 93, 100). The struggle over the highway was, Gould has shown, merely part of a larger "legal, political and ideological offensive" mounted by the elites against the continued existence and cultural identity of the Subtiavan community, which it stigmatized as *la raza rebelde* (the rebellious race): uncivilized, barbarous, "static in time," and "unable to evolve in an autonomous manner." The effect of the elites' arguments and machinations proved, however, to be exactly opposite to what they had intended: "the cumulative effect of six years of struggle against the elite," Gould observes, "was a decisive reaffirmation of Subtiavan ethnicity, precisely when other Nicaraguan Indians were rapidly losing their identity." Against the political, cultural, and economic assaults of the following decades, Subtiavans managed to maintain control over their own local educational and cultural institutions, and their drums continued to call citizens to clean the cemeteries and carry food to departed ancestors upon ritual occasions (Gould 1990b, 91–99).

Subtiavan resistance virtually disappeared for several decades following the liberal revolution of 1920. Their local market—long a focus for reinforcing cultural cohesion—was overshadowed by a new central one in León, which had an opposite, acculturating effect. An increasing number of Subtiavan men and women went to work in León—in textile factories, as domestics, as construction workers—and the cotton-boom-driven expansion of credit in the 1950s led to the sale of more and more Subtiavan lands (Gould 1990b, 98–101). But *la raza rebelde* (the rebellious race) was not dead; it was biding its time. In 1954, Subtiavans renewed the battle against the local Sacasa family and the San Antonio sugar mill after the latter developed the ten-thousand-acre *El Polvón* sugar plantation on land Subtiavans had long used for hunting and subsistence farming. In 1958 they undertook night fence-cutting attacks against both the Sacasa *hacienda* and *El Polvón*, which brought severe reprisals: *haciendas* were militarized, National Guard troops were put in as foremen, and stables were turned into jails (Gould 1990a, 96; 1990b, 103–7).

One crucial effect of the decades of struggle, Gould points out, was to change the conceptual base of solidarity within the Subtiavan community. The community's practice of accepting single Subtiavan women who returned from working as domestics in León and who brought illegitimate children with them helped to generate a new historical and ideological base for solidarity to replace the traditional endogamous one, disrupted by the forces of irresistible change. Such experiences, Gould argues, taught Subtiavans that "the nucleus of their ethnicity was located in an ideology of resistance more than in a system of endogamy." Consequently they learned "to project a vision of a rebellious and anti-capitalist culture which was able to mobilize other dispersed indigenous communities in defense of their historic rights" (Gould 1990b, 98, 109). Learning this enabled them to bridge their internal divisions, absorb change in a less destructive manner, and keep clear in their heads about the nature of the opposition. When the Somoza regime (with which they had not infrequently collaborated in their struggle against local elites) tried to buy them off with indigenist rhetoric or gifts of tractors, they saw it correctly as a ruse to entice "the poor and dispossessed to taste the slobber [*baba*] of the powerful" (Gould 1990b, 107).

Thus two decades after Adams wrote off traditional culture in Subtiava, critical elements of it were thriving and available to the community as a source of strength, cohesion, and resistance in times of crisis. Omar Cabezas's account of work by the emerging FSLN in Subtiava in the early 1960s admits that when the FSLN began (albeit belatedly) to understand the power of Subtiavan ethnic identity, political work in the community took a major leap forward. In Cabezas's account, the ancient symbols of drums and bonfires and the ancient ritual of night marches focused and intensified resistance in the *barrio*. The marches were illuminated by pitch-pine torches and bonfires, and the surging power seemed linked to all resistance movements in Latin America, in all times and places:

> When we saw the Subtiavans march, and heard their drums ahead of them . . . we also saw the stone faces of indigenous people . . . with the repressed rage that was beginning to come out. We saw that within hearing of the drum there was a unity . . . which began to strike fear into the bourgeoisie because rebellious indigenous people were waking up. . . . When we saw hundreds of Indians marching in that way . . . we imagined that it was a march not only in Subtiava, but a march of indigenous people projected throughout Latin America. (Cabezas [1982] 1985, 53–54)

Although Cabezas and his *compañeros* in the FSLN were mistaken about how recently Subtiavans had begun to wake up, they nevertheless understood how important traditional culture was in sustaining, galvanizing, and organizing the Subtiavan community. Cabezas's autobiographical narrative also reveals how important the culturallly based solidarity of such indigenous communities was in breaking through the cultural alienation and disorientation of the emerging young FSLN leaders, a majority of whom had been born in the late 1950s or early 1960s, at precisely the time when such communities were under intense pressure to acculturate and capitulate to the multidimensional transformations attendant upon agroexport development. Thus when he went to join the guerrillas in the mountains, Cabezas said, "It was not only the march of the Indians that I carried with me, but also an unleashing of fire . . . of cries in all the barrios, of conspiracy, of rebellion that accompanied me" (Cabezas [1982] 1985, 58).

As resistance to Somoza mounted during the 1970s, dramatic uprisings also occurred in Monimbó, an indigenous community of about fifteen to twenty thousand people adjacent to Masaya that had had more than its share of prior disturbances. Monimbó had been burned without provocation by William Walker in the 1850s, and General Benjamin ("El Indio") Zeledón was killed there in the hilltop fortress of El Coyotepe (Bermann 1986, 69; Black 1981, 113–15). But until early 1978, the community remained solidly pro-Somoza— coming out in force to demonstrate for him, and having pro-Somoza organizations of women and young people and a unit of AMROCS, his paramilitary organization (Black 1981, 240).

With the assassination of popular *La Prensa* editor Pedro Joaquín Chamorro on 10 January 1978, the FSLN offensive increased dramatically in intensity—partly leading and partly being led by spontaneous insurrections in many cities and neighborhoods. Those in Monimbó, some of the most heroic and dramatic of them all, began in early February with the first demonstrations by young people and the raising of the first barricades.[59] Within three weeks the community was put under siege by the National Guard, water and electric service were cut off, and the death toll mounted daily. The fighting and bloodshed continued throughout the rest of 1978 and early 1979, culminating in the early June final offensive in which the FSLN gained complete control of Monimbó and Masaya.

As it had in the Subtiava, Matagalpa, and other uprisings of earlier periods, the traditional culture of the Indian community of Monimbó played a decisive role both in its capacity to resist and in the forms that resistance took. Long known as skilled artisans (weaving, carving, wood and leather work, embroidery, pottery), the people of Monimbó turned their skills with their hands to the fabrication of homemade weapons as National Guard violence

Traditional house in Monimbó, 1988. (Photograph by author)

increased in the community.[60] An anniversary demonstration commemorating the Guard's attack on the community of February 1978 was integrated with traditional religious observances and rituals that the Guard was bound to respect and that therefore offered protection. Traditional dances that had first been used to satirize the *conquistadores* (*El baile de las negras* [the dance of the black women], *Los diablitos* [the little devils], *El torovenado* [the bull-deer]) were used similarly against the Guard and the Somoza regime. Masks normally seen during the fiesta of the patron saint became useful as disguises during street demonstrations. Drums that had served traditionally to call people to public duties were used during the insurrection to warn of danger, to commemorate the fallen, and to echo protest. A long-established system of interconnecting patios or yards in the community allowed people to circulate and regroup quickly, keeping the Guard off balance and confused (Miranda de Peña 1979, 119–35; Ministerio de Cultura 1982a, 243).[61]

SOLENTINAME: PILOT PROJECT FOR SANDINISTA CULTURAL POLICY

A quite different approach to mobilizing traditional culture within a larger process of resistance was Ernesto Cardenal's experimental community of Solentiname (1965–77) on Mancarrón island (part of the Solentiname archipelago of Lake Nicaragua), which he organized at the same time that he was writing some of the most pointedly political poetry of the late 1960s. The community was destroyed by the National Guard in 1977 after some of its members participated in an armed assault on the National Guard garrison at San Carlos, but during its brief life it served as a laboratory for approaches to cultural resistance and reconstruction that were later to form much of the foundation for Sandinista cultural policy.

As Cardenal has often explained, the idea for an experimental community such as Solentiname ("a little hermit colony," he called it in a 1965 letter) came originally from Thomas Merton. It was to be an experiment in Christian communism in which all property would be held in common, each member would work for the common good and receive according to her/his needs in "an ambience of silence, reading, reflection and meditation," a "religious attitude" would predominate but not be obligatory, and in which a primary aim was revolutionary *concientización* (Randall 1983a, 41–45; Cardenal [1982] 1984, 5; Borgeson 1977, 64–67).[62]

Combining money from a literary prize with donations from friends, Cardenal bought land and arrived with construction materials, food, and medicine in 1966. Local people (like most of the six hundred or so people on the twenty-one islands) were poor and lacking in essential services: they were seven hours away by rowboat from San Carlos, the closest place they could go to sell their farm produce, and they had neither schools nor medical facilities (Randall 1983a, 46–56; Field 1987, 240; Pataky 1957, 35–36). During the ensuing months and years Cardenal and local people, while sharing communal meals and the physical tasks of building the community, joined in theological and political discussions oriented toward the larger national task of revolutionary transformation (Randall 1983a, 62–79).[63]

Most immediately pertinent to Cardenal's later work with the Ministry of Culture were his efforts to stimulate painting and poetry writing among the people of the Solentiname community. The idea for the *pintura primitivista* (primitivist painting) project, Cardenal said, came to him after he saw some beautiful carvings and drawings done by a local man. Bringing in skilled teachers, Cardenal slowly built up a group of local painters who took their subjects from the landscape and life around them, and many of their themes from the community's political-theological discussions. Herod's massacre of the innocents was portrayed as an assault by the National Guard on a peasant community; the interrogation of Jesus before the court of Caiphas was rendered as the interrogation of a Somoza opponent by a military court (Cardenal 1982e, 18–19, 55–56).

Subsequent efforts extended to pottery, leather, and metal work, but as one resident later commented, "Painting was what worked." Soon a steady stream of primitivist paintings flowed from the island, first to local markets but increasingly to international ones, and foreign visitors flocked to Solentiname to see for themselves what God, Cardenal, and local *campesinos* had wrought (Cardenal [1982] 1984, 6–10; Randall 1983a, 58–60).

As a poet rather than a painter himself, however, Cardenal was naturally intrigued by the possibility of extending the experiment into poetry. He had observed literary workshops in Cuba in the early 1970s, but was unsure whether he could make them work in Solentiname until he met Costa Rican Mayra Jiménez, who had experience in similar efforts with children, and who agreed to come to Solentiname (White 1986, 106; Cardenal [1972] 1974, 212).

In her first sessions with the people on Solentiname, Jiménez read and discussed the work of established Nicaraguan poets (José Coronel Urtecho, Pablo Antonio Cuadra, Cardenal, Ernesto Gutiérrez, Leonel Rugama, and others). But soon they began to write their own poems. "At first it didn't make any sense," one student recalled later; "it was only for great persons . . . but [t]hey said poetry is in the fields, in everything you live everyday. And then I knew poetry was something we could do ourselves" (Jiménez 1980, 7–10; Randall 1983a, 61). "Poetry appeared," Jiménez said, "like a miracle." As the writing continued and poems were discussed collectively, themes shifted — in what Jiménez insisted was a logical and organic way — from "the relation man-nature" (in which the poems featured the landscape, flora, fauna, and daily life of the island) to "man-insurrection" (hunger, exile, death, combat, the enemy, revolution, victory). Solentiname poems, Jiménez said, "were full of the people . . . without artifice, without metaphysical images. . . . This *campesino* poetry will be an example for the proletarian classes of the world. [It] is an excellent example of the function of true art."

As example par excellence, Jiménez cited the poetry of Felipe Peña ("so disciplined in combat, so constant in his poetry"), later assassinated by the National Guard. Some of Peña's poems are simple love lyrics ("Te vi" [I saw you], "Marina" and "Lucrecia"); others are about life under the Somoza dictatorship, and the insurgency ("Nostalgia desde la cárcel" [Nostalgia from prison], "Día de liberación" [Day of liberation], "Las visitas a la cárcel" [Visits to prison]); some of the most moving deal with the personal costs and pain of the revolutionary struggle ("Visita de una amiga" [Visit from a woman friend in prison], "Despedida del padre" [Goodbye to father]). The short lyric "Vos crees" (You believe) sets personal romantic attachment into the context of the wider struggle for liberation:

> I ask that you think what a guerrilla
> who goes splashing through the mud
> on mountain roads, sleeping on beds of twigs

or wrapped in plastic on the floor
can offer you? What can I offer you
if I have offered my life to the people?
I have nothing but my rucksack, my rifle, some cartridges
and my olive-drab uniform.
(Jiménez 1980, 20 [my translation]; cf. Jiménez 1979, 110–22)

Like the primitivist painting, the poetry of the Solentiname poets soon brought them international acclaim, but it also drew less welcome attention from the Somoza government. Cardenal gradually abandoned his long-held opposition to violence as a tool of political change, and as the years passed both he and other Solentiname residents were drawn into active roles in the FSLN opposition to Somoza. By the mid-1970s the *Guardia Nacional* was bringing pressure to bear on the community, and after some residents participated in an armed attack upon nearby San Carlos, the community was destroyed and some of its guerrilla members captured and tortured (Randall 1983a, 81–91).[64]

Scarcely had the Solentiname enterprise been destroyed when the instrumental mythicization of the experiment — so important to the later Sandinista government's project of cultural reconstruction — began. Cardenal characterized the community in retrospect as a "near paradise" of pleasure, cooperation, creativity, and political clarity: there was "a great library," he recalled, and "pictures, sculptures, books, [phonograph] disks, classes, smiles of beautiful children, poetry, song" (White 1986, 72; Cardenal 1976, 2:254 and [1982] 1984, 8).[65]

For Cardenal, Solentiname had indeed become a visionary model for the larger project of liberating and reconstructing the entire country. The painting and poetry experiments suggested powerfully, he argued, that there was great untapped intellectual and creative potential in Nicaragua's *campesino* population, that their daily lives were full of expressive possibilities to which they were at least latently sensitive, and that a collective process of *concientización* could liberate that potential and both link them to their accustomed environments and draw them into larger processes of political understanding and transformation. Solentiname "has become truly important," he said in 1981, "because . . . the same work must be done throughout the country" (Cardenal 1981a, 206).

Doing the same work (or some version of it) throughout Nicaragua would prove a daunting task indeed. So immense and bewildering in its complexity was the task that faced the Sandinistas on 19 July 1979 that it was, as poet Daisy Zamora later said, "like talking about the creation of a world" (White 1986, 96).

CHAPTER 5 CULTURE AS REVOLUTION, REVOLUTION AS CULTURE THE SANDINISTA CULTURAL PROJECT

Esta revolución es cultura.

—Julio Cortázar

With songs like these, it was impossible not to have a revolution . . . [and] with a revolution like ours, it was impossible not to have songs like those we have. — Tomás Borge, May 1980

The triumph of a revolutionary process brings with it a collective sense that old pains, fears, and frustrations have been conquered and banished, that structures have been changed fundamentally, and that the future is full of new hopes, energies, and possibilities. Certainly for the Sandinistas the need for a clean break with the past and an apocalyptic glimpse of a future wholly new were strong. The four-and-a-half-century history of the conquest, of the colonial period, of new imperialism after independence, of nearly three-quarters of a century of U.S. political and cultural hegemony, and of the neglect, repression, cultural philistinism, and sycophancy of the Somoza dictatorship argued for the cleanest possible new beginning.

In some respects, such dramatic breaks occurred after 1979 as decisively as Somoza's statue was toppled and broken apart. Impressive cultural developments in Nicaragua came quickly after 1979. A few months after the triumph, Minister of Culture Ernesto Cardenal characterized the transformation optimistically as the difference between "the horror and a smile, between those who tortured and assassinated and those who now write poetry and love." Before, he said, "we had a culture of oppression; now we have one of liberation" (Cardenal 1982c, 8–9). International interest in and optimism about the Nicaraguan cultural project were also high. Even during the darkest days of the insurrection, many writers of international stature (Uruguayan novelist and essayist Eduardo Galeano, Chilean writer Julio Cortázar, Colombian novelist Gabriel García Marquez, and many others) had already lent their voices and pens to the project (Galeano 1981; Cortázar 1983a, 1983b, 1985; García Marquez 1983; cf. S. Ramírez 1984a, 1985b). Cortázar in particular waxed lyrical concerning the promise of the new cultural initiatives:

> [The new government] has pushed the word culture into the street as if it were an ice cream or fruit cart; they have put it into the hands or the mouth of the people with the simple and cordial gesture with which one offers a banana. . . . [It] is no longer the privilege of those who write well, or sing well, or paint well; that partial notion of culture has exploded into thousands of pieces which are recomposing themselves in a synthesis more and more visible, and which entails thousands of wills, of feelings, of options, of acts. (Cortázar 1983b, 49)

But because human beings have a limited tolerance for total discontinuity, the necessity for some sense of continuity in the midst of the reality and power of such moments of sharp transformation surges forth. Hence such intervals and processes of radical transformation are also likely to generate efforts to reconnect with the past.

Or rather with *a* past—frequently a past defined in cultural terms. And since the culture of the immediate past likely appears inseparable from the oppressive political and social order so lately overthrown, a powerfully tempting option is to leap further back into a more remote past that is understood to antedate the perversions and distortions of the deposed regime, and thus to be antithetical to it. To a past, one might say, that predates the cultural fall. Hence the cultural dynamics that follow revolutionary triumph are likely to have a Janus-like quality: one face hopefully toward a still only dimly imagined future, the other nostalgically toward a prelapsarian cultural past which promises guidance toward that future. Moreover, the psychic need for continuity is paralleled by structural inertia in the social and (particularly) cultural order, so that at some level the Janus-like longing for a remote and revitalizing past may bespeak a liminal awareness that the perceived and projected cultural break represented by the revolution is and must be less than complete (cf. Williams 1979, 128–29).

It soon became apparent, in any case, that Cardenal's optimistic expectation that cultural transformation would be both rapid and radical was not fully warranted—in the first instance simply because the country itself was a shambles.[1] For most people, there was in effect no health care system. Industry and agriculture were wrecked; the cotton crop (on which the country depended for much of its foreign exchange and for which, as was suggested earlier, it had paid such a high cultural price) was a small fraction of what it had been before the insurrection began (cf. Conroy in Walker 1985, 219–44). Tens of thousands had been killed in the fighting and thousands of children orphaned. Schools had not operated regularly in several years, and buildings and equipment were in disrepair. The hulks of buildings shattered by the earthquake of 1972 were still scattered over central Managua, and cows grazed where blocks of commercial buildings once stood. Bombed-out buildings in cities like León, Masaya, and Estelí were mute reminders of the ferocious fighting of the latter days of the insurrection. The country had been bankrupted by Somoza and his cronies as they fled, and was left holding a $1.6 billion debt. Vital infrastructural systems—roads, sewer and water lines, telephones, public transport—were antiquated and falling apart. With virtually every sector demanding attention immediately and on a massive scale, budgetary and psychic capacities for response were stretched to the limit. The country faced, as poet Gioconda Belli put it ten months after the Sandinistas came to power, *una tarea gigantesca* (a gigantic task) (Belli 1980, 62). Hence there were few resources to commit to cultural institutions and programs.

Cultural values, structures, and practices that were themselves obstacles to rapid change were everywhere evident as well. Some scholars and writers whose knowledge might have been useful in designing cultural policy, institutions, or programs had been forced to flee the country during the Somoza period, and many did not return after 1979 (cf. Mejía Sánchez in White 1986, 37–41). Other cultural problems and obstacles had roots that reached back much earlier. The centuries-old cultural division, distrust, and hostility between eastern and western Nicaragua (to which I return in the next chapter) had been exacerbated by the years of political struggle. The Catholic church was politically split, and gender conflict (the subject of my final chapter) was much in evidence. And despite the banks' substitutionary scholarly publication programs, some of the most basic tools of scholarship—biographical dictionaries, archival collections, primary ethnographies, synoptic histories—for

Earthquake damage to Managua Cathedral in 1972, still unrepaired by 1988. (Photograph by author)

the most part still did not exist. Book-length studies of Nicaraguan cultural history and life written by Nicaraguans were few and of very uneven quality.[2] Some of the most substantial work—like Carlos Mántica's on Nicaraguan language (Mántica 1973) and Jaime Incer's (Incer 1977) on geography—was sparse and of limited immediate usefulness for policy purposes.[3] Scholarship on Nicaraguan culture written by non-Nicaraguans was also minimal.[4]

In the more than a century and a half between independence and 1979, moreover, Nicaragua had never established an even rudimentarily adequate array of public cultural institutions or programs. As early as 1874 the Colegio de Granada had a small museum and meteorological observatory, and in 1881 the scientific and literary society El Ateneo in León was offering classes in aesthetics, holding conferences, and editing a journal. Just after the turn of the century, others in León organized the Academia de Bellas Artes (Arellano 1982a, 28, 41). The country's few other institutions were centered in a half-dozen Pacific coastal cities and oriented for the most part toward the elite sector. Except for the church, there were few cultural institutions of any sort in the countryside. The Zelaya administration and its mostly short-lived successors had done little toward creating such institutions, and the four decades of the Somoza regime had—as we have seen—not improved the situation substantially. Instead of fostering public awareness that culture could (or should) be a legitimate policy sector, it had most often neglected, short-budgeted, pilfered, and made the country's few public cultural institutions

One of many earthquake-damaged buildings in Managua still being used as makeshift housing, 1988. (Photograph by author)

Remains of building in León damaged by Somoza bombing raids during Sandinista insurrection. (Photograph by author)

a dumping ground for ignorant and greedy political appointees. Within less than a half-century, both public and private cultural institutions located in Managua (the majority of them) had also been twice ravaged by earthquakes (in 1931 and 1972). The few institutions of higher learning—bearing the scars of those earthquakes and of the insurrection—were rudimentary.

Thus when they arrived at their offices on 20 July 1979, new Sandinista government officials faced a formidable task in elaborating a comprehensive cultural policy. Virtually every new program had to be conceived and designed detail by detail; every new institution had to be built from the ground up. Prior to the problem of what policies to put in place, what institutions to construct, and what programs to implement was the problem of merely mapping the Nicaraguan cultural landscape: the surviving elements of indigenous or traditional culture, the needs of the country's creative artists and performers, the murky boundaries between the popular and elite cultural sectors, the surviving bases of cultural stability and continuity, the useful agents of cultural change. There were far more questions than answers: To what cultural initiatives might any given sector of the population respond positively? How might the energy released through cultural activities during the insurrection be encouraged, organized, and deployed for reconstruction? Where could suggestive models of cultural policy be found? How could mutually supportive relationships between the cultural policy sector and other policy sectors be constructed? What should be the role of culture in the broader process of national reconstruction?

Fortunately there were some positive elements in the mix as well. The cultural dynamics of the final months of the insurrection had fomented cultural pride among the general population, and an awareness of culture as a resource for reconstruction. Embryonic groups and organizations (in theater, music, dance, graphic arts, poetry) had sprung up. The vitality of Nicaraguan culture had been brought to international attention. Vice President Sergio Ramírez even suggested that it amounted to a negative advantage that Somoza had been "unable to consolidate a cultural model with an articulated ideology and with organic instruments." In the long run, this failure was fortunate, since "it would have been difficult to destroy a firmly entrenched somocista cultural apparatus" (Ramírez in White 1986, 82).

CREATING THE WORLD: GENESIS OF THE SANDINISTA CULTURAL PROJECT

The core ideas and paradigms for the Sandinistas' cultural project came from a variety of sources, ideological directions, and bodies of historical experience: from the historical-cultural examples of Rubén Darío and Augusto C.

Sandino (cultural nationalism as analogue of national liberation, a pride in *mestizaje*, awareness of the cultural dialectic between north and south in the Americas); from the *vanguardia* (recovery and revaluing of indigenous culture, anti-bourgeois orientation, awareness of the regenerative possibilities of cultural syncretism); from the Generation of 1940 (political commitment as organic to cultural work); from Italian Communist theoretician Antonio Gramsci (the notion of cultural hegemony, and of culture as a primary arena of political struggle); from the student resistance movement of the 1960s (anti-imperialism, cultural work as organic sector of revolutionary resistance and primary instrument of social reconstruction); from Marxist cultural theory; and from Ernesto Cardenal, who at each way-station of his own political-cultural odyssey gathered ideas and bits of models.

Previous chapters have explored most of these strands of the history. This chapter schematizes the pivotal ideas about culture that the Sandinistas distilled from these disparate sources and made central to their own cultural project; it also surveys and evaluates the practical cultural work they undertook amidst the physical, economic, and cultural rubble bequeathed to the country by the Miami-bound Somozas and their entourage.

Even before the birth of the FSLN itself, culture had bulked large in young anti-Somoza Nicaraguans' visions of what a post-Somoza Nicaragua might look like. Carlos Fonseca's studies and travels in the USSR in the late 1950s left him awestruck over what he perceived to be the healthy intensity of cultural activity. Ecstatically he reported that the USSR had more musicians than any other country, that artists were supported and protected economically by the state, that scores of theaters were accessible to everyone, that parks with trees, benches, and statues abounded, and that factories had their own performing groups and theaters. At the Sixth Festival of Youth and Students for Peace, he watched Chinese students (in rural dress) present a dance performance called "Cooperation" (Fonseca Amador 1981, 1:27–96).

However naive and romantic Fonseca's evaluation of the politics of culture in the Stalinist USSR, his excitement over the possibility of both using culture as an instrument in the revolutionary process and of making a rich cultural life for ordinary citizens a central aim of revolutionary reconstruction was infused into the program of the *Frente Sandinista de Liberación Nacional* he helped found three years later. In its program statement of 1969, the FSLN promised a "revolution in the culture" that would establish the basis for the development of national culture, extirpate "neo-colonial penetration in our culture," "rescue progressive intellectuals and their works . . . from the neglect in which they have been maintained by the anti-people's regimes," and "rescue the university from the domination of the exploiting classes, so it can serve the real creators and shapers of our culture, the people."[5]

Ten days before they came to power in mid-1979, the Sandinistas' projected Program of the Governing Junta of National Reconstruction vowed to stimulate literary, artistic, artisanal, and folkloric production in order to "consolidate a true Nicaraguan popular culture" and recover national cultural values. Toward those ends they promised to create arts training schools, foment artistic and performing groups, publish "massive editions" of books, protect the artistic, cultural, and historical patrimony, and create libraries, archives, and museums (Programa de la Junta de Gobierno de Reconstrucción Nacional de Nicaragua 1979, 835–42, section 3.9 a–d).

For such ambitious endeavors the Sandinista leadership was not entirely lacking in experience. During their twenty-year struggle to depose the Somoza regime, many of them had written and published (clandestinely or otherwise) poems, novels, stories, and plays, composed and recorded songs, performed plays, published newspapers and journals, and created cultural organizations. But the new challenge was to draw those fragmented experiences into the service of an overarching cultural vision and give it institutional and programmatic form at local, regional, and national levels.

Although a substantial number of the Sandinista leadership had thought for years about the relationship between culture and political transformation, they were nevertheless in some respects ill prepared by their own cultural formation to deal with the cultural system in Nicaragua. Those lacks were especially evident with regard to two salient elements of the post-Somoza cultural agenda. The first was to recover, revitalize, and mobilize traditional culture (however defined) among the *campesino* and working-class population that was the Sandinistas' putative legitimizing link to authentic national culture. The second necessary element was to define and forge — in a country historically divided along several gaping fault lines — a "national" culture as a foundation for national identity and political unity.

Through its pamphlet series of popular biographies of heroes and martyrs of the revolution, the FSLN made as much as it could of its working-class base.[6] Child martyr Luis Alfonso Velasquez (#1) was described vaguely as being from a proletarian background; Juan de Dios Muñoz (#2) was "of very humble origin . . . where misery is common"; René Cisneros Vanegas (#3) was from the poor barrio of Acahualinca, symbolically important site of a set of prehistoric footprints preserved in volcanic deposits; Francisco Gabriel Meza Rojas (#9) was the son of "working people" (*gente trabajadora*); Sandinista poet Leonel Rugama (#13) was born "in the midst of proletarian conditions . . . of a carpenter father and a schoolteacher mother"; female martyr Luisa Amanda Espinosa (#17) was the daughter of a "humble woman, who washed and ironed to help her family survive." Thus the prototype was clear; the problem was that most of the post-1979 Sandinista leadership in fact came from higher social strata.

A substantial number of the founders and earliest members of the FSLN had indeed come from lower- and lower-middle-class families. Health Minister Lea Guido's mother was a meat seller in Managua's Eastern Market and her father had begun his working life as a bricklayer; guerrilla commander Monica Baltodano's parents were both from working-class families. But as the student movement emerged in the middle and late 1960s, an ever higher percentage were from more privileged backgrounds (Black 1981, 66; Booth 1985, 151; Randall 1981, 1, 59).

Indeed most students who joined the oppositionist university community of Father Uriel Molina in Managua's barrio of El Riguero in the middle and late 1970s—the spawning ground for many members of the future Sandinista government leadership—were from bourgeois families who preferred that their children go abroad to study (to groom them for social position, to shield them from turmoil and alien ideology). And indeed many of them actually went—a fact that paradoxically both increased their social and cultural distance from the lives of a majority of their countrymen, and at the same time sharpened their emerging sense of contradiction. Gloria Carrión, later general coordinator of the FSLN women's organization, took a degree in education in the United States, and her brother Luis (later a member of the FSLN national directorate) also spent two years studying in the U.S. (1969–70). Bayardo Arce (also destined for the national directorate) took a law degree in Chile; Sergio Ramírez studied for two years in Europe (1973–75); poet and FSLN militant Rosario Murillo—later Daniel Ortega's wife and head of the Sandinista Association of Cultural Workers—was educated in the United States and Europe. Nora Astorga, later Sandinista ambassador to the United Nations, recalled that her parents sent her to live in Washington to get rid of her "crazy ideas." Poet Gioconda Belli, who described herself as coming from a comfortable family from high society (*una familia acomodada, de la alta sociedad*), went to Europe and the United States to study before entering a "good" marriage at eighteen.[7]

Hence by the time of the triumph in 1979 most of the top Sandinista leadership and its core group of supporters—including those who would lead its cultural programs—consisted of people who had grown up isolated from most aspects of the traditional, rural, or working-class culture they projected as their major political base. Daniel, Camilo, and Humberto Ortega were from a middle-class family (their father ran a small export-import business and their mother was a cashier for a mining company); their grandfather had been rector of the Pedagogic Institute of Granada. Vice President Sergio

Ramírez described himself as the son of a petit bourgeois family; his father wanted him to grow up to be a lawyer in Masatepe. Sandinista poet Daisy Zamora recalled that her parents spent their lives "flit[ting] from social affair to social affair." Guerrilla commander Dora María Tellez (later a member of the Council of State) described herself as having been "born into a petit bourgeois, comfortable family . . . [in which] what mattered was to have friends who belonged to the country club." Vidaluz Meneses was the daughter of a National Guard lieutenant who later served as Somoza's ambassador to Guatemala (Diederich 1981, 85; Randall 1983c, 7; Randall 1981, 41; Randall 1984, 42–47).

The Sandinista leaders were thus acutely aware of their class and cultural origins, of the distance that separated them from those lower down in the social-cultural hierarchy, and of the political contradictions that resulted. Indeed the distance was evident to those on both sides: "It was clear they . . . were from rich families," recalled one poor man from the El Riguero *barrio*, and that "they wanted to integrate into . . . our poverty, our need." "For me," reflected student Salvador Mayorga from the other side of the divide, "it meant . . . breaking with a [bourgeois] life I rejected." Daisy Zamora recalled feeling "uncomfortable with the customs of my social class" during her adolescence and saw herself as a confused "product of my class origin" during her university years (Randall 1983a, 132, 137; 1981, 41, 97).

Such young people in fact frequently traced their earliest political formation to a childhood or adolescent sense of such class and cultural differences, and they recalled the pain and confusion of moving hesitantly into political action. Tellez recalled grieving, already at the age of six or seven, for the cleaning woman who could not enter the country club where her family went; Nora Astorga said the fact that she "always felt privileged" in her economically comfortable family made her "feel obliged to help others." Daisy Zamora admitted being "very confused about my petit bourgeois background" and talked of her long struggle toward political commitment, of "how hard it was for me to get over the inferiority I felt about my class background." Gioconda Belli encountered a moment when she knew that she could not go on "living well and nothing more"; increasingly she was shocked by the "enormous contradictions" between "the life I was living and that which I saw happening around me." It was, she recalled, "a difficult process, because I had to break with a whole way of life, a whole series of values."[8]

Some parents responded understandingly if anxiously to the transformations they were witnessing in their children; the outraged responses of others highlighted the cultural contradictions in stark relief. Gloria and Luis Carrión's father, a wealthy landowner, stormed at Father Molina, "You are my class enemy. You are forcing our children to change so that they'll . . . leave behind the culture of their own class" (Randall 1983a, 154). More dramatic yet was a televised encounter between guerrilla Martha Cranshaw and her father, who was Somoza's director of police. Captured in the mountains after fighting for two years with the FSLN, Cranshaw was brought blindfolded into a room filled with newsmen; when the blindfold was removed, she confronted her father before being thrust into a television studio to repent before a national audience. The elder Cranshaw, sharing Sr. Carrión's outrage at Father Molina, stormed that it was "time to start killing priests" (Randall 1983a, 180–82).

Removing Martha Cranshaw's blindfold was in one sense an appropriate metaphor: it signified the abrupt and brutal confrontation between dominance and defiance; it dramatized difference and discontinuity. But in another sense the metaphor was misleading: to move instantaneously from not seeing to seeing is one thing; to move from one deeply ingrained cultural formation into empathy for, understanding of, and commitment to another radically different one is quite another. It is, as Gioconda Belli put it, "a process of internal revolution . . . because it is the search for revolution at deeper levels. . . . The revolution from within outward, the search for a consequential identity, for new human relations which are difficult because one knows one has to destroy the past, but we do not know very well . . . what we are going to substitute for the traditional relations."[9]

THE MINISTRY OF CULTURE

The Ministry of Culture was created on the first day after the Sandinistas entered Managua on 19 July 1979, and its leadership was entrusted to Father Ernesto Cardenal, who in the twenty-five years since his participation in the 1954 coup attempt against Anastasio Somoza García had become (except for Rubén Darío) Nicaragua's best-known writer (Ministerio de Cultura 1982, 277).

Poet Daisy Zamora—one of the original group of five who began to put together the ministry—recalled later, "[We] were generally clear about the importance of culture," she recalled, "but we didn't know how to give it a concrete form. . . . [The] only starting point for us was the new reality of Nicaragua. We couldn't refer to the past, and that was the hardest part. It was a new reality and we had to create an entire project with hardly any direction or orientation because at the time we were told, 'Let's see what you can create'" (White 1986, 95–98). The early days of activity were "chaotic," Zamora recalled: the house given to the ministry for office space (formerly owned by Somoza) had been "totally ripped apart" in revenge after the triumph. There were no desks, chairs, or typewriters. Many of those assigned to the ministry—some of whom didn't even know each other—wandered around waiting to be told what to do. Meanwhile, "people rained down on us from all over the country. People came with their guitars. . . ; people came who told us they were sculptors, writers, painters, all associating themselves with us because they were artists. . . . They sent us people just because it said on their identification card 'I like to paint' or 'I like to play the guitar.' They were told, 'To the Ministry of Culture!' "

Only a few things seemed clear in the first weeks and months: these disparate and unorganized energies had to be channeled into cultural activities, some structures and institutions had to be created, and the whole enterprise had to be integrated into the broader process of reconstruction. A statement the ministry distributed through UNESCO during its early months laid down five lines of strategy:

(a) recovery and affirmation of national cultural identity;
(b) opening of Nicaraguan culture to Latin American and universal culture;
(c) promote the highest degree of artistic excellence;
(d) promotion of the cultural development of the people in its two dimensions: access and participation of the masses in culture;
(e) fomenting creativity and supporting artistic creation.[10]

It was a large order, but during the first several years after 1979 the government was seriously committed to building strong policy and programs in the social sector, within which culture was more than a peripheral concern. The ministry's budget was five times larger in 1980 than it had been in 1979, although it still claimed only about 2 percent of the total expenditure for social programs.[11]

Hopes and expectations were high, nevertheless. Inheriting no functioning cultural institutions from the Somoza regime, having few financial or technical resources, facing urgent demands in every other policy sector, and hampered from 1982 onward by a disruptive and costly counterrevolutionary war, the Ministry of Culture managed to establish Nicaragua's first significant system of public cultural institutions, to generate a serious and sustained public discussion about culture, and to design a set of cultural policies and programs far more elaborate than any the country had ever had. The effort drew attention and support from Latin America (Mexico, Venezuela, Cuba), Europe (France, Holland, West Germany, Bulgaria, Hungary), Asia (Korea and Vietnam), the USSR, UNESCO and development programs of the United Nations, and the Organization of American States. Technical and financial support provided assistance for cultural planning, conservation, technical training, and development; cultural institutions; performance and media;

and research, documentation, and publications (Ministerio de Cultura 1982a, 293–319). A 1982 ministry organizational plan showed five divisions: Arts, Libraries and Archives, Historical Patrimony, *Artesanía*, Centers for Popular Culture. There were also two institutes (sports and film), plus a Cultural Corporation of the People apparently charged with selling and distributing cultural products and managing cultural events. Not wholly intelligible data suggest that perhaps six hundred people were working for the ministry.[12]

The range of the ministry's endeavor — and the problems it encountered — can be comprehended by looking at its efforts to create a series of dispersed and democratic popular institutions (Centers for Popular Culture, poetry workshops, libraries, and museums), to build a film and television system, and to foment new creative vitality in the performing arts (dance, theater, music, and sound recording). In each sector, the results were mixed. The Centers for Popular Culture were congruent with the idea of a democratic, grassroots-based culture, but they proliferated and dispersed beyond the government's capacity to support them. The poetry workshops engendered intense controversy, and the library effort foundered for lack of funds. Museums, which had a narrower mission more easily shaped to the Sandinista political project, fared better, but remained short of funds, staff, and adequate facilities. Bolstered by early international cooperation and technical support, film and television looked promising initially, but the difficulties of building an expensive national system from the ground up and of shaking off decades of North American media influence were daunting. Less expensive to support and with a broader social and cultural base, dance and theater flourished but had to contend nevertheless with deeply ingrained elite bias. Mostly unimpeded by such bias, music performance blossomed and played a major role in the process of reconstruction. The production of sound recordings was a major element in the process, but the recordings that were produced proved less overtly political than those that had appeared during the final years of the insurrection, and more accommodated to the popular, mass-market aesthetics they were intended to supplant.

EARLY EFFORTS: CENTERS FOR POPULAR CULTURE AND POETRY WORKSHOPS

The Ministry of Culture's first cultural programming efforts focused on Centers for Popular Culture and workshops (*talleres de poesía*) to foster poetry writing among all social sectors. Both proved successful in some senses but problematic in others: the former provoked controversy over the structural relationships between the various entities engaged in cultural work; the latter drew fire from those who felt that the effort to integrate culture into the process of revolutionary reconstruction would inevitably limit expression to a few insufficiently flexible paradigms.[13]

CENTERS FOR POPULAR CULTURE. The idea for the Centers for Popular Culture was not original with the Sandinistas; such institutions had existed in Europe for decades. France had its *maisons de culture*; Sweden had its cultural "activity houses"; socialist countries such as Hungary had "houses of culture" in factories. A *Casa del Obrero* (workers' house) established for Chinandegan sugar workers by Somoza García in 1945 was later converted by the Socialist Party (PSN) into a "culture center for the working class" that featured lecturers brought in from Managua, weekend dances, and the like. A *casa de cultura* also operated briefly in Managua around 1950 (Nilsson 1980, 30; Vitányi in Huszá, Kulcár, and Szalai 1979, 271, 280; Arellano 1982a, 78; Gould 1990a, 73). In the early 1970s the model had again been proposed by Horacio Peña in a talk at Managua's Alliance Francaise. Noting that French Prime Minister André Malraux had started such institutions as a way of "saving" culture in the provinces, Peña compared Paris and Managua as cultural metropolises whose duty and destiny it was to "irradiate" the cultural outback, where — he averred — cultural life was absent. He envisioned the benefits that would flow to provincial cities from "the presence, for one night, of some of [Managua's] theater groups." Indeed, Peña reported, some Franciscan monks were already operating a "house of culture" in Matagalpa (Peña 1973, 3–7).

The mission of the Sandinista Centers for Popular Culture was not to carry putatively ennobling elite culture to the benighted outback, however, but to support and foster the cultural forms and practices that were already there, and thus contribute to the democratization of culture.[14] León's CPC was founded scarcely a month after the July 19 triumph; it and the Granada CPC had the largest and best facilities of any.[15] By mid-1982 there were twenty-six CPCs operating on some scale or other with modest administrative support from the ministry, plus six *casas de cultura*, supported entirely by local communities. Both were conceived of as "true mass laboratories of popular culture."[16]

The CPCs and *casas de cultura* fostered a wide array of activities: Juigalpa had a plastic arts workshop; Jinotepe had poetry readings; Managua had films, dance, and puppets; Estelí mounted an exhibition of the works of Darío; Masaya arranged a photographic exhibit; Boaco organized a seminar on theater; tiny Bonanza in the northeast established workshops on painting, music, and dance. Others opted for "culture weeks," sporting events, children's cultural events, and film festivals.[17] More than four hundred dance groups and ninety-two theater groups were reported to be using CPC facilities. The ministry also talked of using the CPCs to train people to do scientific cultural documentation, but apparently the effort came to nothing.[18]

By mid-1985, after protracted and sometimes heated public debate, it had been more or less agreed that the mission of the CPCs was to rescue "the popular cultural traditions" of the country, to support and elaborate the artistic activity that had developed during the struggle against the dictatorship, to "massify" creativity among the people, and to provide mass recreation.[19]

POETRY WORKSHOPS. The ministry's second early activity was the poetry workshops, an outgrowth of Ernesto Cardenal's work on Solentiname. The workshops eventually evoked considerable anxiety among some respected Nicaraguan writers, but during the early post-Somoza months of reconstruction they flourished and drew much attention beyond Nicaragua's borders. To the earliest critics Cardenal responded that in fact Nicaragua had always had poetry workshops, because it had been the custom for older poets to teach younger ones—as José Coronel Urtecho (b. 1906) had taught Pablo Antonio Cuadra (b. 1912). To establish the workshops was therefore, he said, the first idea he had after being named Minister of Culture (Ministerio de Cultura 1982a, 225–32).

Once they began to be established (the first two in the indigenous barrios of Monimbó and Subtiava—famed for their insurrectionary bravery), the workshops multiplied quickly. Representatives from some thirty-three workshops (all on the west coast except for one in Bluefields) attended the first national meeting of the workshops in December 1981. There were representatives from workshops in the army and the air force, the unions, the embassy police, and Managua's transit police, as well as from Sandino's and Darío's birthplaces (Niquinohomo and Ciudad Darío), and small cities and *barrios* whose brave insurgency had been crucial during the insurrection (Masaya, Monimbó, Subtiava, Palacagüina).[20]

Cardenal's address to the first national meeting stressed the international notice the workshops were drawing, their rapid proliferation, and the praise they were eliciting from the Sandinista leadership. Vice President Sergio Ramírez trumpeted their "magnificent results," and Interior Minister Tomás Borge judged the poetry to be "so luminous and moreover so original, and at the same time so simple . . . like a sun recently born." By mid-1982, Mayra Jiménez reported fifty-three workshops operating and estimated that more than five hundred aspiring poets had passed through them (Ministerio de Cultura 1982a, 225–32; White 1986, 111; Jiménez 1983).

As early as mid-1981, the ministry began to publish the small journal *Poesía libre*—printed on kraft paper and tied with hemplike twine to emphasize the project's loyalty to the grassroots—to highlight the poetry being written in the workshops as well to codify and explain the aesthetic and politics that underlay their work. In the first issue, editor (and poet) Julio Valle-Castillo promised a monthly publication that would welcome "every creative word, every creation of words." The slender twenty-five-page issue contained three unpublished poems by the martyred poet Leonel Rugama, poems from the workshops, and a poem by two Palestinians jailed by the Israelis.[21] The second issue (nearly three times larger than the first) was dedicated to poetry from the workshops. Such poetry, Valle-Castillo said, "is a direct and profound poetry; it is the life of the people with their language; it is physical geography; it is the history of our Sandinista Revolution written in verse. A poetry full of emotions, of testimony (of combat, of love). . . . [It] is poetry written by *campesinos*, by workers, by militia, by *brigadistas*, by the people."[22]

Already it was clear that *Poesía libre* would gather its materials rather widely: from the workshops; from other Central American, Caribbean, and Latin American poets; from established Nicaraguan poets (especially Cardenal); from Europe (Brecht, for example); from South Korea; from Japan (Spanish translations done from Kenneth Rexroth's English translations); from the Pacific (Hawaii, the Philippines, Melanesia, Australia, and New Guinea). Selections from the poetry of the United States also frequently appeared, all of them chosen for their spirit of unity with struggles against oppression. Ernesto Cardenal's early favorites (Whitman, Sandburg, Pound, Masters, Williams) figured prominently, but the list also included Ginsberg, some Sioux Indian poets, and Chicana writer Gina Valdés. Whitman appealed as "a free voice, in agreement with the absolutely free poetry of Free Nicaragua, in spite of his being from the country from which come aggressions against our liberty." Sandburg ("socialist, journalist . . . collector of the folklore of his people") was characterized as one who wrote "for the common people" despite being depreciated by aestheticist and Eurocentric North American critics who considered his poetry "too easy."[23]

Hence during the ministry's early months the poetry workshops were a prime exhibit: vibrant evidence that it might indeed be possible to replicate the energy and revolutionary idealism of the Solentiname experiment on a national scale, that soldiers and sanitation workers, housewives and market vendors, clerks and taxi drivers could write what Cardenal called "good modern poetry" (*la buena poesía moderna*), unburdened by cloying romanticism (Ministerio de Cultura 1982a, 229). As we shall see in the following chapter, however, not everyone was equally pleased by the experiment.

As has been noted in previous chapters, prior to the Sandinista period, Nicaragua had never had a substantial system of either libraries or museums worthy of the name. Although it was not in fact to acquire such a system under the Sandinistas, either, the Sandinista government's efforts to create one surpassed any that had gone before.

LIBRARIES. If Nicaragua was truly to become a "nation of poets," it would have to become also a literate nation of readers with ready access to books. The need for literacy led to the massive national literacy campaign of 1980 (cf. Stansifer 1981b; Miller in Walker 1982, 241–58; Hirshon and Butler 1983; Miller 1985; Arnove 1986), and thence to an effort to develop a national system of public libraries, which the country had never had.

Two brief turn-of-the-century references to the National Library of Nicaragua, founded in 1882, say that it had between six and eight thousand volumes, and was the only such institution in the country (Halftermeyer [1946?], 153; Niederlein 1898, 87).[24] What sorts of books it had, and to whom they were accessible, is uncertain, but Watland's report that the majority of its books (bound in Spanish leather and gold-embossed) were chosen by Spanish Liberal Emilio Castelar suggests that it was probably intended for and used principally by the elite (Watland 1965, 67, 73). The library grew modestly during the ensuing decades but was heavily damaged in the 1931 earthquake and virtually abandoned thereafter (Stansifer 1981a, 3).[25] Other libraries were few and small. Except for some collections made by private banks in the 1960s (discussed in an earlier chapter), the only ones of any consequence were in private hands. One of the greatest (that of poet Ernesto Mejía Sánchez) accompanied its owner into exile in Mexico City during the Somoza period. As late as the 1960s, the library of the newly autonomous National University in León consisted of one tiny room that contained current newspapers, some encyclopedias, and a few reserve reading materials deposited by professors for specific courses. The situation in nearby Chinandega (the next largest city on the northern Pacific coast) was worse. The only "public library" consisted of a few books in the private residence of a local *somocista* functionary who maintained the service (used by virtually no one) in exchange for the rent-free house provided by the city.[26]

Six months after the Ministry of Culture was established, Ernesto Cardenal characterized the National Library as "a nest of rats feeding on the classics." But Nicaraguan people have "a great hunger for books," he said, promising that a "great national library" was to be constructed in Managua's Luis Alfonso Velásquez park. Eighteen months later the ministry's full-page ad

Sandinista-era mural, León, featuring literacy campaign and anti-imperialistic themes. (Photograph by author)

Only library open to the general public, León, 1988. (Photograph by author)

in the party newspaper *Barricada* announced a National Library campaign, urging citizens to contribute money, books, and equipment.[27]

The 1982 organizational plan for the Ministry of Culture included a Division of Libraries and Archives and envisioned "the endowment of public libraries in the entire country," capped by the Rubén Darío National Library in Managua and a National Archive as "the depository of the collective memory of the nation" (Ministerio de Cultura 1982a, 279–80). The ministry reported thirty-four public libraries already operating but offered no data on the size of collections. Since the entire Division of Libraries was then receiving less than 8 percent of the ministry's tiny budget, however, it is unlikely that such institutions were libraries in much more than name only. In 1982, the total budget for libraries was 4.3 million *córdobas*. Assuming that perhaps 25 percent may have gone to the Rubén Darío National Library, and dividing the rest equally among thirty-two libraries, each would have received perhaps ninety-five thousand *córdobas*. At the prevailing exchange rate of forty-five *córdobas* to the dollar, such a budget (ca. $2,100 per year) would have been insufficient to build even small local libraries.[28] A half-dozen years later, the situation had not changed appreciably. The only "public library" in León consisted of a single dingy room with a random assortment of a few hundred tattered paperbacks.

The National Library in Managua was a two-hundred-square-foot building of one floor, open to the air. The entire author catalog of cards (soiled and thick at the edges from use) fit easily into sixteen loosely filled file drawers, and the books (perhaps thirty-five thousand at most) stood on industrial steel shelving topped with plastic sheeting to protect them from bird droppings. A few outdated and incomplete sets of encyclopedias and the like comprised the reference section. A small collection of journals and periodicals was housed blocks away in the Hemeroteca Nacional, whose tiny unairconditioned reading room fronted on the dusty and smoky Masaya highway.[29]

To create a substantial, functioning, accessible national system of libraries clearly required a degree of political stability and economic solvency that Nicaragua did not possess even during the opening years of the 1980s, and the situation deteriorated steadily as the months passed and the toll of the U.S.-financed contra war increased. Unfortunately, the situation with museums mirrored that of libraries.

MUSEUMS. As previous chapters have suggested, the early history of museums in Nicaragua was no less than shameful. A few belated private efforts to start museums during the Luis Somoza era (1956–67) had not come to much. Early in 1958 the journal *Nicaragua Indígena* proposed founding an Indigenous Museum of Nicaragua, and soon announced the opening of a Library and Archaeological Museum of Pre-Columbian Ceramics (later referred to as the National House of Indigenism), but the effort apparently did not flourish.[30] National University (UNAN) rector Mariano Fiallos Gil and others attempted to open a Museum of Popular Art in León the same year, but it apparently foundered for lack of public interest and support. On the hundredth anniversary of the heroic Battle of San Jacinto (of the William Walker war) in 1959, *La Prensa* announced that there were plans to reconstruct a period house as a museum, but there was no subsequent indication as to whether the task was actually undertaken.[31] In the 1960s the tiny, poor, ill-equipped, and ill-housed private Museum of Nindirí (a village near Masaya) had a substantial collection of ceramics, stone statues, musical instruments, and masks that folklorist Enrique Peña Hernández suggested ought to attract state support, but such support was not forthcoming (Peña Hernández 1968, 110, 153).

In mid-1979, therefore, the field was wide open to the Sandinistas to develop a system of museums that the country needed but had never had. Both of the most venerated heroes of the revolution—Augusto César Sandino and Carlos Fonseca—had been fascinated by the links between museums and projects of national reconstruction. Sandino told José Román of storing hundreds of pounds of documents in his hometown of Niquinohomo and of hiding materials at various places in the mountains for "our archive and museum": documents, maps, flags, airplane propellers, and photographs

Museum of Nindirí, 1988. (Photograph by author)

taken after victories over the U.S. Marines. All were the property of the nation, he said, and would be shown to the public when the war against Somoza and the U.S. Marines was over (Román 1983, 142–43). In November 1933 Sandino told Nicolás Arrieta of his wish to establish a "workers' house" — like those in Mexico — for his archive, so that "all Nicaraguans may see documents and photographs of our whole campaign and of our ideals, the offerings and threats of those [Yankee] dogs, so as to destroy all the lying and calumny and also to enliven the patriotism of the people" (Ramírez 1984b, 2:362–63).

After his late-1950s trip to Russia, Carlos Fonseca wrote almost lyrically of the museums he reported encountering "in every corner" of the country. "All over Russia," he said, "there are museums of art, history and science." Fonseca was especially moved by Kiev's museum to the poet and painter Taras Sechenko, who depicted the sufferings of the Ukrainians under the czar. In Leningrad (home of the Hermitage Museum), he reported, czarist prisons had been converted into museums that "denounce Czarist atrocities." There was a small museum to Lenin and a defense museum that honored the people's defense of the city during World War II. The cruiser *Aurora*, from which shots were fired announcing that the Bolsheviks had taken power, was also turned into a museum. On a side trip to Poland, Fonseca visited Auschwitz, where he said the government had established a museum "so that the future may view the crimes of the past." After visiting Dresden, he reported that the Red Army had respected its cultural treasures during World War II — carrying them to

Russia to protect them and returning them after the war ended (Fonseca 1981, 1:60, 80, 84, 91, 93–94).

Because of the capacity of museums to convey certain constructions of the past and their consequent usefulness in the general reformation of consciousness that the Sandinistas conceived of as central to a broader social reconstruction, the Sandinista government put more energy and imagination into museums than into libraries, and consequently produced earlier and more dramatic results.

Scarcely six months after the triumph, Ernesto Cardenal reported that the Ministry of Culture had recovered great quantities of archaeological, artistic, and historical pieces from the homes of *somocistas*, and that they were destined to be put in a national archaeological museum already being prepared. By early 1982 there were plans for no fewer than forty new museums (Ministerio de Cultura 1982a, 173, 243). The idea was not merely to proliferate museums, however, but rather to create a new type of museum congruent with the revolutionary process. Cardenal disparaged elitist museums of the past that presented "mummified culture" to a passive public. The Sandinistas' museums were to be *centros culturales*, created in active cooperation with the communities they were to serve. They were to function as "a true means of cultural socialization," presenting not only memories of the past but "the necessities of the present and dreams of the future." "We believe," Cardenal concluded, "that if a people were able to make a revolution, they are capable of making their own museums" (Cardenal 1982c, 1–20; Ministerio de Cultura 1982a, 245–46).

Although the ministry's 1982 organizational plan included no unit specifically charged with developing museums, some ambitious projections were nevertheless being made. Early in that year, there were reports that the ministry intended to establish "community teaching museums" (*museos didácticos comunitarios*) in the Centers for Popular Culture throughout the country; one had already opened in Camoapa in March, and by mid-year small "galleries of heroes and martyrs" were reported in several other CPCs. Estelí had its own Museum of the Insurrection, and the CPC in Masaya announced plans for a National Museum of *artesanía*.[32]

One of the earliest and most elaborate museums actually constructed and opened was the National Literacy Museum (*Museo Nacional de la Alfabetización*), which dramatized the history of the National Literacy Crusade (1980–81).[33] Several large rooms of well-designed exhibits (maps, text, photographs, and artifacts) presented the various stages of the crusade, from planning onward. Photographs of the sixty thousand literacy *brigadistas* leaving by bus, boat, truck, and foot for their assignments in the countryside conveyed a sense of the massive scale of the operation; other photographs and artifacts

Museo de Alfabetización (Literacy Museum), Managua, 1988. Rock wall of *adoquines* (paving stones) manufactured by Somoza-owned factory; used by Sandinista militants during insurrection to construct barricades in the streets. (Photograph by author)

(such as letters home) suggested the hardships the *brigadistas* endured and the meanings they attached to the experience.

Given more resources because of its closer relationship to the political project was the Museum of the Revolution, next door to the impoverished National Library at the Huembes market.[34] At least with Minister Cardenal, the idea for such a museum went back nearly a decade. Following his visit to Cuba in the early 1970s, he had written passionately of a poor bootblack who after the Castro revolution had grown up to teach philosophy at the University of Havana and who had his own "revolutionary archive" in a corner of his house. Moved by the encounter, Cardenal returned to Nicaragua carrying samples from the young man's personal museum (Cardenal [1972] 1974, 67–70).

The entrance to the Museum of the Revolution (opened in 1981) was flanked symbolically by a U.S.-made armored personnel carrier of the Somoza era and a home-built Sandinista tank fashioned from steel boiler plate welded around a pickup truck body. Inside, well-mounted displays dramatized the country's long history of military and political conflict, concentrating (naturally enough) upon the Sandino period, the Somoza regime and its National

Museo de la Revolución, Managua, 1988. The U.S.-supplied tank in foreground was used by Somoza's National Guard; the homemade FSLN "tank" in background was made from a pickup truck shielded with steel armor plate. (Photograph by author)

Guard, and the Sandinista insurrection.[35] Photographs from the end of the nineteenth century onward illustrated the history of U.S. intervention in Nicaragua and the sycophancy of the Somoza regime. The Sandino resistance effort was evoked by Sandino's jacket, photographs, letters and documents, obsolete weapons, and other crude equipment used by Sandino's army. Such items contrasted sharply with photographs and artifacts of the late-1920s airborne United States Marine Corps. Somoza-era repression was dramatically illustrated by photographs of radical students in detention (including one of President Ortega), their notes and letters from prison, Somoza García's engraved pistols, medals from Anastasio Somoza Debayle's jacket, weapons captured from the National Guard, instruments of torture and part of a wall from a prison where the tortures occurred, and parts of destroyed statues of the last Somoza. The rise of the FSLN and the insurrection was evoked by Carlos Fonseca's typewriter, false documents used by insurrectionists in the mountains, photos of demonstrations in indigenous communities, sketches of plans of attack, homemade weapons, and masks made of screen wire and painted with faces. The final section of the exhibit juxtaposed photographs of Somoza's flight from the country and the triumphal entry of the Sandinistas into Managua.[36]

National Museum of Nicaragua, Managua, 1988. (Photograph by author)

In sharp contrast with the Museum of the Revolution, the National Museum languished, as it continued to do throughout the remaining years of the Sandinista government. Nine years after the triumph, it was still housed in a small building of seven or eight unairconditioned rooms in the Colonia Dambach. In the entry hall an otherwise carefully prepared photographic exhibit on traditional *artesanía* dramatized the museum's poverty: uncovered photographs were tacked with straight pins to panels constructed of cardboard affixed to rough wooden frames. The largest room held a collection of a hundred or so small pre-Columbian artifacts; another displayed a half-dozen small monoliths; in another stood a single skeleton and a small case of mineral specimens.[37]

Even as late as December 1987, the Sandinista government — by then fighting imminent financial disaster as a result of the contra war, its Ministry of Culture in its last days as a separate entity — opened a mini-museum (a "historical corner") in the upper-class Managua neighborhood of Los Robles. Designed by the political office of the Ministry of the Interior, it was located at the site of the celebrated Sandinista takeover of a Christmas party in honor of U.S. Ambassador Turner Shelton in 1974 — a daring and dramatic event aimed at seizing hostages to be traded for Sandinista leaders being held in Somoza's prisons.[38] The historical corner (named for Comandante Eduardo Contreras, who had led the raid and was later killed by the National Guard) included maps, photographs, personal effects of the guerrillas, and a video viewing room.

Taken together, the Sandinista government's accomplishments with museums were impressive (if modest by the standards of wealthier countries). The Sandinistas at least managed to create an array of museums of varied character and focus in an impoverished and embattled country. This proved possible partly because the collections and exhibits that interested the Sandinista government were not of the sort that had to be acquired in the high-stakes international art market. Ultimately, however, Sandinista accomplishments fell far short of the hopeful projections of the first days after the fall of the Somoza regime.

MEDIA

Three purposes were central to official planning concerning film and television during the early days of the Sandinista government: to end North American domination of the media; to offset its accumulated social, cultural, political, and psychological effects; and to design alternative media to reflect and support revolutionary change.[39] It was an enormous task, and resources were few.

FILM. As a previous chapter explained, Nicaraguan social and cultural life had been penetrated so early, so deeply, and for so long by North American commercial film that in attempting to change the situation the Sandinistas faced a daunting task. Because the country had deferred for so long to North American corporate producers for their media fare, the local base of experience and technical expertise in filmmaking was thin. The Somoza government's small film production company (PRODUCINE) had acquired equipment to make National Guard training films and propaganda films, but in late July 1979 young Sandinista film technicians found PRODUCINE "an empty shell." Some missing equipment turned up in packing crates at the airport, left behind by the fleeing Somoza entourage, but much of it had already been spirited out of the country. Several hundred hours of footage shot by Somoza's film crews remained as possible salvage material for documentaries on the dictatorship, but that was all (Mattelart 1986, 41–45; Burton 1986, 69–79). Thus it was not surprising that during the autumn of 1979, several months after the triumph, Managua theaters were still offering such commercial trivialities as *10* and Bruce Lee movies.[40]

Hopes and expectations for the role of film in the new Nicaragua were high, nevertheless. "The Revolution," said one spokesman during the early days of the new government, "plans to divest the cinema of its mystifying mercantile character and make it a product within reach of everyone."[41] Toward that end, the Ministry of Culture established the *Instituto Nicaragüense de Cine* (Nicaraguan Institute of Cinema; INCINE) two months after the triumph.

In the beginning, INCINE had almost nothing to work with. The FSLN's tiny War Correspondents Corps—not even formed until April 1979—had included a dozen photographers and filmmakers, but most of them were visitors from elsewhere in Latin America. Even among those charged with establishing INCINE, experience was limited. The cooperation and advice of filmmakers drawn from international solidarity groups was crucial during INCINE's early days, but few of them stayed to work with the institute.

Creative possibilities were as great as resources were limited. "The riches are there" in the streets, insisted INCINE's María José Alvarez; "what we have to do is capture them." [42] Poet Gioconda Belli argued that "the necessity is to create a whole mythos (*toda una mística*) . . . which will allow [us] . . . to confront the enormous problems we have . . . with a collective sense and a . . . view toward the future, [so that people will] realize that they are investing in their own history, in their own future." For Belli the fundamental task of INCINE was to "help create this public mythos." [43] Belli's argument paralleled Dorfman and Mattelart's about the reactionary intent and effects of Disney comics in Latin America: if culture (especially popular culture) is a key agent in the social reproduction of consciousness, then any serious project of social and cultural reconstruction has to engage in that process positively as well as reactively.

How best to do so was not clear, however. The earliest borrowed offerings of the *Sistema Sandinista de Televisión* (SSTV) were not particularly promising: *Maratón otoñal* (Autumn marathon) described as "a Soviet film in full color"; a *Grandioso Festival de Dibujos Animados Socialistas* (Grandiose festival of socialist cartoons); a documentary on the CIA; and Dustin Hoffman's *Midnight Cowboy* (Perdidos en la noche), advertised as a film about New York ("a decadent city that crushes humanism"). [44]

What was produced locally during the new government's earliest days was very rudimentary. Bits of footage shot during the tumultuous insurrectionary autumn of 1978 were edited into two short documentaries: *Patria libre o morir* (Free country or death) and *Victoria de un pueblo en armas* (Victory of a people in arms). Internationalists working with Nicaraguan filmmakers wanted to move toward commercial fiction films (partly to generate much needed foreign exchange)—perhaps one on Sandino starring Robert De Niro, or others with Jane Fonda or Anthony Quinn. But the Nicaraguans, not convinced such commercial films would be feasible, preferred more modest projects dedicated to reinforcing "the visual historical memory of our people." [45]

Only a few months after the triumph, Minister of Culture Cardenal optimistically reported substantial advances in film and video, including the appearance of the first locally produced documentaries and news programs. Two weeks later, Junta member Bayardo Arce suggested that the effort was aimed against all the modern techniques that had allowed "ideological values distant from our reality and our interests" to be seen as normal (Ministerio de Cultura 1982a, 175 and 20).

Actual progress in film and television proved to be both less encompassing and more fraught with difficulty than Cardenal's and Arce's sanguine projections, however. Production facilities consisted only of a small studio, editing room, darkroom (for stills only), and a recording studio. There was neither a sound studio nor a film laboratory. Cameras were few and mostly antiquated, and INCINE director Ibarra was traveling in the United States and Canada to beg for equipment. The shortage of equipment was particularly frustrating in view of the surplus of personnel: within a few months, INCINE had put together a production staff of twenty-five. Another twenty were working in distribution, focusing their efforts on a mobile cinema program that sent films from town to town. Climbing aboard public buses with projector, film, and takeup reel, projectionists traveled to smaller cities and remote areas to screen European and Latin American films (Burton in Mattelart 1986, 43–44; Dratch and Margolis 1987, 27).

INCINE's most substantial products during its first two years resulted from international collaboration. German television documentary filmmaker Peter Lilienthal, working with ISTMO-Film in Costa Rica, began as early as November 1979 to film *The Insurrection* in León. Some of the extras posing as FSLN troops were still so traumatized by the war that when other extras dressed in National Guard uniforms appeared in the streets, they fired on them instinctively (Lilienthal 1981, 165–68).

Also filmed with international assistance was the full-length fiction film *Alsino y el cóndor* (Alsino and the condor). Cuba sent a production group and photographer-director Jorge Herrara; Mexico sent three actors; the Nicaraguan government supplied troops and a helicopter in addition to meager funds.[46] Described by Gabriel García Marquez as a story about a "tropical Icarus," *Alsino* is an allegorical tale about a Central American boy—maimed after jumping out of a tree, trying to fly like a condor—who is rehabilitated through the psychic and social trauma of a guerrilla war.[47] The war in which young Alsino finds himself caught up is set specifically in Nicaragua, but its most salient aspects are typical of the ongoing political-military-cultural holocaust of the late twentieth century in Central America: a traditional *campesino* culture stubbornly persisting amidst social and economic chaos; U.S.-directed and funded repression against the native population ("We're going to whip these assholes into shape and put some order back into this

216 BUILDING A CULTURAL APPARATUS

place," says one U.S. advisor to a National Guard lieutenant); mass executions and the burning of bodies; guerrilla forces armed with homemade weapons; bewildered old people and children fleeing the conflict. *Alsino*, as Christian Klaist observed, straddled the line between fiction and documentary, "authentic testimony and imaginary recreation" (Klaist 1981, 169–74).

Surveying the first four post-Somoza years of film showings (both public and private) in Nicaragua, INCINE director Ibarra did not find the situation encouraging. In private theaters, nearly half of the seventy-nine films shown originated in the United States; most of the other half were from Mexico and Italy. Nearly 10 percent were pornographic, and 15 percent were horror films (Ibarra 1983, 7). Clearly, there was a long way to go.

Unfortunately, a sizable portion of the resources available to INCINE went into the making of a film on the William Walker filibustering episode, directed by Alex Cox (*Repo Man*, *Sid and Nancy*) and starring Ed Harris (of Tom Wolfe's *The Right Stuff*) and Oscar winner Marlee Matlin. The script was approved personally by Vice President Sergio Ramírez, and the Sandinista government provided building materials, workers to reproduce period sets, and other technical support. The subject was ripe with potential both for appealing to popular audiences and for helping those audiences (especially North American and European ones) comprehend some of the essential features of Nicaraguan political, social, and cultural history. Unfortunately neither potential was realized; the film was in most respects a disaster. Former INCINE director Carlos Vicente Ibarra defended *Walker* after it appeared, arguing that its political value (its emphasis on the parallels between the barbarities of the Walker episode of the 1850s and those of the contra war of the 1980s, for example) had to be evaluated separately from its all-too-apparent cinematic weaknesses. But a convincing defense was difficult to come by.[48]

TELEVISION. In television the Sandinista government also faced the challenge of replacing a system dominated by foreign commercial interests with a reasonably autonomous national one oriented toward education and reconstruction. Again the prospect was not encouraging. Equipment and facilities left over from the Somoza period had received little or no maintenance during the last couple of years of the insurrection, and trained technicians were scarce. Two years after the triumph, the two operating channels of SSTV were on the air only five to seven hours a day, and much of the programming was still from the United States. Throughout the early 1980s, television production remained fragmented, and INCINE (hence the Ministry of Culture) was not centrally involved in it. Lack of money, equipment, and expertise delayed changes in public television programming. A weekly series of half-hour documentaries from western Europe and the Soviet bloc did little to relieve the tedium.[49] SSTV director Ivan García complained of the parallel difficulties of either getting good programs from abroad or of producing them at home. Some efforts were being made to raise the quality of the *telenovelas* (soap operas) above that of the *lloronas* (weepers) to which people were habituated. Technical assistance from many countries (Cuba, Mexico, Spain, France, Holland, Czechoslovakia) was relatively plentiful, but fiscal restraints were tight. The problem was made more urgent by the easy availability of conventional (and usually politically reactionary) programming beamed in from Honduras and Costa Rica.[50]

Despite the difficulties, by mid-1983 at least five television production centers had evolved in addition to SSTV: *Comunicaciones Midinra* of the Agrarian Reform Ministry, the *Talleres Popular de Video* (Popular Video Workshops) of the *Central Sandinista de Trabajadores* (Sandinista Workers' Union; CST), the Ministry of Education's Pro-TV, the audio-visual section of the Department of the Interior, and INCINE.

As in film, limitations upon equipment and other resources were severe, especially outside SSTV. Virtually all the video production units were using donated equipment, and most training was being provided by international visitors. Seventy people working in video for Midinra shared a single telephone; donated lighting equipment overloaded antiquated electrical circuits; repair parts were nearly unobtainable. Four years after the triumph, the lack of coordination among the bureaucratically separate units still often forced one unit to cancel a project for lack of equipment that another had sitting idle (Halleck in Mattelart 1986, 113–19).

Limitations and complications notwithstanding, some impressive and imaginative television programming emerged. Focusing most of its resources on the agricultural issues central to the Agrarian Reform Ministry (land reform, cooperatives, ecology, social services in rural areas), Midinra also ventured into a documentary on the life of Sandino and produced a humorous popular documentary ("What's Up with the Toilet Paper?") dealing with the shortages of essential products. The Popular Television Workshop—an outgrowth of a Super 8 workshop initiated by international visitor Julia LeSage in 1981—produced a variety of engaging character sketches of Nicaraguan people, who collaborated in planning and shooting them. The Ministry of Interior's video unit produced the much-touted series *Cara al pueblo* (Facing the people), in which members of the Junta or local officials responded to (frequently highly critical) questions from citizens. By comparison, INCINE's early accomplishments in video were modest; the potential of their large staff and (except for Interior's video unit) superior equipment was frustrated by a somewhat elitist attitude toward programming and a predilection for grandiose projects prone to get stalled in practical details.

The accomplishments of the first nine years of video production in post-

Somoza Nicaragua were evident in the first Festival of Nicaraguan Video held in early 1988. From hundreds of submissions, approximately 150 were chosen for six categories of competition (documentary, fiction, reporting, music videos, children's programs, and television spots). About a third of them were from SSTV, and the rest were scattered among independent producers, the Ministry of the Interior, INCINE (only four entries), and other government agencies. The documentaries ranged broadly over such topics as pre-Columbian art, martyred international volunteer Benjamin Linder, captured CIA airman Eugene Hasenfus, and the problems of providing social services.[51]

PERFORMING ARTS

Creating programs and institutions for the performing arts was in some respects less daunting than similar efforts in film and television, because dance, theater, and music were deeply rooted in local communities, and more could be done with modest cash and equipment resources.

DANCE. At the end of the 1960s folklorist Enrique Peña Hernández cataloged the abundance of traditional dance thriving in Nicaragua, usually in connection with the religious festivals of patron saints of towns and villages, which had continued uninterrupted through the culturally turbulent years before and after World War II. Grenada had its Christmas Eve festival. In Masaya one could see *El baile de las inditas* (Dance of the Indian girls) — about the courting of a Nicaraguan girl by a Spanish man, *El baile de los diablitos* (Dance of the little devils), *El baile de los negros* (Dance of the Negroes), and other dances on the Feast of San Jerónimo.

León had several festivals that incorporated traditional dance: its *barrio* of Subtiava celebrated its Fiesta de San Jerónimo on September 30 with the *Baile del toro* (Dance of the bull); on December 7 (the feast of the Purísima) one could see *El baile de la gigantona* (Dance of the great giant, also performed in Chinandega); a week later came another festival with *El baile de los Mantudos* (Dance of the wingless birds). At its Festival de Santiago y Santa Ana, Nindirí presented *El baile de los chinegros*, and in Boaco was the only surviving example of a *comedia-bailete* dramatizing the conflict between the Christians and the Moors. Even cosmopolitan Managua regularly celebrated its Fiesta de Santo Domingo de Guzmán, with its elaborate *Baile de la vaca* (Dance of the cow) (Peña Hernández 1968, 71ff., 149–55, 160–69; López Pérez 1960, 15).

Efforts to encourage traditional dance in Nicaragua reached back at least into the mid-1960s, when the indefatigable Irene López began working with composer Camilo Zapata of Managua's Radio Mundial to draw attention to Nicaragua's traditional culture — especially the dance of the patron saints' fes-

Christmas Eve religious festival, Granada, 1932. Note U.S. military officer at extreme right. (Photograph by Newell F. Johnstone; © National Geographic Society)

tivals—which was generally ignored or depreciated by the cultural elite of the capital. López formed a small dance school and began to teach traditional dance to a few young students. Except for her fledgling effort, there were only expensive private schools of dance in Managua, dedicated to elite European dance forms.[52]

For fifteen years, López endeavored to gain recognition for Nicaraguan traditional dance—a solitary effort until the Sandinistas came to power in 1979. After experimenting briefly with a small school of dance in the *barrio* La Tenderí, the Ministry of Culture formed the National School of Dance and named López as its director (Ministerio de Cultura 1982a, 172). With several other teachers, López began giving classes to children whose school teachers were away during the Literacy Campaign. After the campaign ended, the ministry brought in Cuban and Soviet dance teachers, but Nicaraguan dancers who had taken it upon themselves to study the tradition proved more useful. One of the best was Bayardo Ortiz, who had danced since the age of seven in his native Masaya, and who while working in a shoe shop became a self-taught scholar and historian of Nicaraguan culture. In his early thirties Ortiz had started his own radio program, featuring Nicaraguan music, tales, and legends. Shortly thereafter, López invited him to assist with one of her early dance groups, which subsequently traveled and performed all over Nicaragua and elsewhere in Central America. Having gained recognition out-

Masked dancers of Masaya at Feast of San Jerónimo, 1944. Note traditional marimba player. (Photograph by Louis Marden; © National Geographic Society)

side Nicaragua, the group was embraced by the elite who controlled cultural programming at Managua's Rubén Darío Theater after it opened in 1969.[53]

The first year curriculum at the National School of Dance concentrated on dances associated with the marimba, by all odds the most popular traditional instrument in Nicaragua in the post-Somoza period.[54] Students then moved on to study the waltz, mazurka, and polka, all elite eighteenth- and nineteenth-century European dances that had (in Nicaragua as in much of Latin America) dispersed into the culture of the lower classes, where they remained popular long after they were considered passé by the elite.[55] From such popular dances they proceeded to those of the patron saints' festivals (Morales Alonso 1983, 8–9; Galarza 1985, 14–15).

By 1982, the National School of Dance had more than a hundred students, and other organizations were developing their own troupes. The Experimental Workshop of Folkloric Dance, associated with *Juventud Sandinista* (JS; Sandinista Youth) and with the *Asociación Sandinista de Trabajadores Culturales* (ASTC; Sandinista Association of Cultural Workers), had a group of twenty-seven dancers aged sixteen and seventeen years old (Alegría and Flakoll 1982, 7; Cedeño 1982, 6). A festival of traditional dance held at the Rubén Darío Theater in early 1988 attracted dozens of groups from all over the country. The director of the National School of Dance was determined

Participants in *El baile de los chinegros*, Nindirí, in procession on highway to Masaya, 1988. (Photograph by author)

that Nicaraguan dance would never lose its "folkloric roots," but her efforts to insure their survival were suffering as the budgetary constraints of the contra war increased and the number of students dwindled.[56] Concurrently, dancers within the ASTC were moving in precisely the opposite direction by forming an Experimental Workshop of Classical Dance with assistance from the National Ballet of Cuba. Already working with more than a hundred students nine to twelve years old, ASTC dancers hoped to form Nicaragua's first professional ballet company.[57]

THEATER. Numerous commentators have remarked upon the prominence of European norms and repertoire in the history of theater in Latin America, the relative lack of native dramatists, and the late emergence of theatrical productions based upon native materials and local social and political themes. Although Picón-Salas notes that as early as 1548 Cristóbal de Llerena of Santo Domingo composed a skit that gave voice to popular protest against lawyers, merchants, and speculators, Franco judges that the first modern attempts to create a theater "relevant to the contemporary . . . scene" arose in Mexico in the 1930s (Picón-Salas [1944] 1962, 69; Franco 1967, 233).

At the time of the first Congress of Latin American Theater in Mexico

Participants in Fiesta de Santo Domingo, Managua, 1988. (Photograph by author)

City in 1957, Managua's *La Prensa* lamented the absence of a theater tradition in Nicaragua, and two decades later, in his history of Nicaraguan literature, Jorge Arellano agreed that "the theater in Nicaragua has not constituted a tradition, much less produced anything of universal value."[58]

Nevertheless, as I have suggested earlier, the roots of protest in Nicaraguan drama reached centuries back. Dramatic pieces such as *El Güegüence* and *Loga del Niño Dios* of the colonial period mixed native vernacular language with Spanish and native music and dance with Spanish verse forms to challenge and mock the *conquistadores*. Other religious enactments associated with Christmas and Holy Week, fashioned upon models drawn from medieval Spanish theater, were frequently cast in an idiomatic Nicaraguan Spanish infused with indigenous rhythms and expressions. But the ritual enactments of the patron saints' festivals constituted Nicaragua's only theater tradition—of whatever political character—until the nineteenth century. Traveling through in the late 1850s, Peter Stout found them still nearly ubiquitous, but they were getting competition from the *zarzuelas* and comedies that Spanish touring companies were beginning to perform in the principal cities, as they continued to do at least into the 1880s (Stout 1859, 71–73). The taste for theater the touring companies stimulated led to the formation of the first Nicaraguan performing company (the Dramatic Company of Aficionados) in Masaya in 1859 (Arellano 1982a, 152).

Although Rubén Darío and Nicaraguan writers of lesser stature began to write occasionally for the theater in the mid-1880s, not until the advent of Salvadoran-born Felix Medina after the turn of the century did Nicaragua have a dramatist who produced regularly. At the close of the first decade of the century, Anselmo Fletes Bolaños's *The Raffle* satirized the social prejudice and corruption of the Zelaya period. By the 1920s and 1930s, *modernista* and *costumbrista* writers such as Adolfo Calero Orozco and Hernán Robleto were exploring the dramatic possibilities of native materials and themes (Arellano 1982a, 152–55).

The move toward a vernacular and socially engaged theater received a boost from the *vanguardista* writers of the 1930s. *Chinfonía burguesa*, based on a poem by Joaquín Pasos and José Coronel Urtecho, employed popular superstitions, aphorisms, children's songs, and other colloquial materials in a humorous satire of the money-grubbing philistinism of the bourgeoisie. Pablo Antonio Cuadra's *Por los caminos van los campesinos* focused on the country people of Nicaragua, caught again and again in civil war. Set at the time of the U.S. Marine occupation, the play was written as street theater to "carry the message of rebellion against the political routine" of changes of government (which almost invariably visited more pain upon ordinary people). It features the *campesino* Sebastiano, the Indian girl Rosa, Dr. Fausto Montes (a petty and malicious small-town lawyer), and Lieutenant Comfort of the U.S. Marine Corps. The lieutenant, who talks of protecting and civilizing the natives, proclaims, "I am the law here," and colludes with the sycophantic lawyer, who assures him that "there are good opportunities to exploit here; what we need is men with initiative, energetic men like you." Sixteen-year-old Soledad's resistance to the lieutenant's attempt to seduce her becomes a metaphor for the country's determination not to yield to Yankee domination and exploitation (Cuadra [1937] 1981, introduction [unpaginated], 78–82). José Coronel Urtecho's *La Petenera* (1938) and Pablo Antonio Cuadra's *Bailete del oso burgués* (Dance of the Bourgeois Bear, 1942) were also important contributions.

Concurrently with the *vanguardistas'* experiments, a group of students at the National University (UNAN) in León were mounting guerrilla theater presentations (such as a public burial of the national constitution) that ridiculed government figures and policies. Among the students was Mariano Fiallos Gil, who became rector of the university in 1956. Immediately upon assuming the rectorship, Fiallos formed an experimental student theater and hired a director (Ramírez 1971, 28, 94, 101).

From its earliest days, the FSLN was intrigued by the political possibilities of theater. On a visit to the USSR in 1957, UNAN student (and later FSLN founder) Carlos Fonseca was moved nearly as much by the possibilities of theater as he was by those of museums. Having seen the Bolshoi Ballet on film in Managua, Fonseca was enchanted to sit in a velvet-upholstered seat in the Bolshoi Theater and view a majestically staged *Swan Lake*. In Moscow, he reported, "there are theaters in great quantity which present ballet, drama, and performances of dance and song. . . . And in almost every factory there are halls for film or theater" (Fonseca 1981, 44–45, 61).

Fonseca's remarks on the socially reconstructive possibilities of theater struck a responsive chord with later UNAN students. As the *Ventana*, *Gradas*, *Praxis*, and *Taller* groups focused the energies of students interested in using fiction, poetry, and painting for purposes of political resistance, other radical students explored the possibilities of theater. By the early 1970s, Carlos Vicente Ibarra (later director of the Sandinista film unit INCINE) and others were delving into *El Güegüence*, the plays of the patron saints' festivals, the *vanguardista* plays, and other early Nicaraguan drama for ideas and models as they developed their revolutionary work. A patron saints' festival piece favored for its relatively overt politics was *El torovenado*, whose central half-bull, half-stag figure reflects the colonial syncretism of Nicaraguan culture. Blending the most salient attributes of the Spanish bull (strength, haughtiness, brutishness) with those of the Indian stag (alertness, sagacity, agility), *El torovenado* dramatizes the capacity of indigenous people to resist cultural domination by incorporating into their own culture the very instruments and symbols of their domination. Thus *El torovenado* is intended, as Carlos Alemán suggests, "to protest, to denounce, and to explain to people how things are." It limns "the cultural stance against conquest, cultural penetration and political opportunism" (Alemán Ocampo 1981, 2–3).[59]

Thus it was not surprising that during the final 1978–79 insurrection, guerrilla theater performances were to be seen regularly in the *barrios*, in the streets of major cities, and amongst the fighting troops. Following the triumph, theater groups continued to proliferate both among the general population and among the armed forces.[60] Vice President Sergio Ramírez declared that such groups should come to be not only "the highest example of popular cultural organization" but also "the best example of creative liberty" (Ramírez in Ministerio de Cultura 1982a, 165). Performances scheduled by the Ministry of Culture for the Rubén Darío National Theater soon after the triumph—such as those by the Wallflower Order Dance Collective (a group of five women) and Catalan political singer Joan Manuel Serrat—suggested that the "great white mastodon of a super-elitist theater," as Minister Cardenal called it, would be reoriented toward new performing groups and new audiences.[61]

One of the most impressive local theater companies to emerge after 1979 was the Colectivo Nixtayolero, formed during a coffee harvest crisis in late 1979 when the Ministry of Culture sent a group of actors and writers to live among coffee pickers on the Hacienda Laguna. Directed by Alan Bolt but dedicated to a collective process of creation, the group focused upon recovering popular traditions and using them to develop "a theater which reflects the struggle, problems and victories of our people." Fittingly, their first production was *El corte de café* (The coffee harvest).

Member Socorro Molinares explained that the collective began with the intention of not provoking a "cultural invasion," but instead went to the countryside, investigated what was important to people in a particular place, and selected data and incidents upon which to elaborate a production to be taken back into the community. To ground their creative work in the realities of workers' lives, members of the collective moved to the mountains to live among agricultural workers. They spent months studying the habits, customs, and traditions of local people and then developed characters as faithful as possible to their ways of walking, gesturing, thinking, and speaking. Five years of such work produced a stable performing group of eight with a repertoire of eighteen plays, many of which incorporated poetry and traditional music and dance. Relatively unencumbered by the self-absorption and elitism frequently encountered among professional performers, members of the collective saw themselves as merely "adding a grain of sand to the great mountain we are all building."[62]

MUSIC AND RECORDING. As with libraries, museums, television and film, and dance and theater, the Sandinista government had to make difficult choices concerning which of a wide array of already existing musical preferences and activities might most advantageously be encouraged with the limited resources available. European classical music, studied and performed seriously if not widely in Nicaragua since the mid-nineteenth century, had an audience in the major cities. Traditional instrumental and vocal music flourished in smaller towns and in the countryside. On the west coast, marimbas and guitars predominated and the songs were in Spanish; on the east coast, steel drums, brass, and Caribbean rhythms were the norm, and lyrics were as likely to be in English as in Spanish. Both conservative and liberal wings of the Catholic church had their music, as did the growing number of fundamentalist Protestant churches (Moravians on the east coast, and Baptists, Nazarenes, and Pentecostals on the west). Contemporary Latin American popular music as well as rock wafted from the radios of the majority of houses.

Closer to the heart of the Sandinistas' political project, however, the politically committed musicians who had been so deeply engaged in the struggle against Somoza preferred music likely to be useful in revolutionary re-

Marimba de arco and guitar duo, Fiesta de Santo Domingo, Managua, 1988. (Photograph by author)

construction. By the time Nicaraguan musicians organized themselves into a union under the ASTC in early 1982, it was clear that the new political currents in song were quite vigorous. In a series of articles that ran for months in the Sandinista newspaper *Barricada* in 1982–83, spokespersons such as poet and ASTC director Rosario Murillo and *nueva canción* veteran Wilmor López saw the new currents as vital and essential. Political song, Murillo insisted, "was the first line of fire in the fight against the dictatorship. It was tool, hammer, firearm; it participated in combat, occupied the trenches, sprang into the mouths of the machineguns . . . and lasted until victory." In April 1983, politically conscious musicians from Latin America and elsewhere gathered in Managua for the second international festival of *nueva canción*.

As in film, the Sandinista government had to build its sound recording and record production effort from the ground up, for little was left from the Somoza period. The regime's own record company SISA (Sonido Industrial, S.A.) merely marketed records licensed from transnationals (such as CBS and Onda Nueva), a number of which had offices in Nicaragua.[63] In an effort

MARIMBA DE ELIAS PALACIOS

Cover illustration for phonograph album *Marimba de Elias Palacios*
(ENIGRAC MC-018, 1982)

to repopularize Nicaraguan music in the mid-1950s, Salvador Cardenal Argüello formed CENTAURO to record and release it on discs. Unfortunately
Cardenal chose to record traditional music in performances by professional
singers and instrumentalists who, for example, insisted upon playing large
manufactured marimbas rather than the small wooden *marimbas de arco* used
by *campesino* musicians. The few discs CENTAURO managed to produce—
perhaps the only sound archival record of traditional Nicaraguan music that
survives from the Somoza period—were dismissed by Carlos A. María (a
medical doctor who also composed popular music) as offering music that was
"extremely poor, sadly insipid."[64]

To record and market the music of the new Nicaragua, the Ministry of Culture created the Empresa Nicaragüense de Grabaciones Culturales (Nicaraguan Cultural Recordings Co.; ENIGRAC). Compared with the rather paltry

efforts that had preceded it, ENIGRAC's immediate post-Somoza output was impressive: some seventy-five LP albums and numerous 45s during its first half-dozen years of operation.[65] Virtually all of ENIGRAC's recordings were political—either implicitly in that they presented Nicaraguan traditional music as a counter to both native elitism and the hegemony of U.S. popular culture that had characterized the Somoza period, or explicitly in that they offered music with obviously political lyrics.[66]

The popularity of the marimba among traditional Nicaraguan musicians and the public moved ENIGRAC to devote three LP discs to Masaya marimba maker and player Elias Palacios (MC-018 [1982], 033, 036). Although the albums were strictly instrumental, both the symbolic status of the *marimba de arco* as quintessentially Nicaraguan and the political-cultural resonances of the titles of certain tunes (e.g., "El indio de Monimbó" [The Indian of Monimbó]) gave Palacios's performances a political edge.

Similar in its muted politics was an album by Chinandega popular/traditional singer Jorge Paladino. Paladino had begun performing (with two friends as "Trio Cosigüina") on Radio Occidental in Chinandega in 1961. Salvador Cardenal Argüello arranged for Paladino to record his first two songs, one of which—"Para vivir sólo contigo" (To live only with you)—became very popular in both city and countryside. Paladino performed with a half-dozen or more groups and eventually recorded dozens of songs, but finding himself repeatedly exploited financially in the process, he stopped performing until after the fall of the Somoza regime.[67] In November 1985, ENIGRAC brought Paladino into its studios in Managua to record the album *Soy campesino* (I Am a Campesino; CHLP-6007). Most of its songs are simple romantic *cumbias* and *boleros*, but the much-celebrated heroism of the *campesino* populace during the anti-Somoza insurrection gave the title cut a political edge, and two others come through Paladino's consummately nuanced singing as gently, almost exquisitely political. *Yo canto a los niños* (I sing to the children), addressed to "the children of my beloved country," refers fleetingly to the coming of a cultural *brigadista* to teach them to read; *Anhelando la paz* (Yearning for peace) is a song of love deferred by the necessarily prior process of reconstruction. Yearning for love is inseparable from yearning for the peace that will make possible the tranquillity love needs, and is in tension with the struggle that gives meaning to both:

> I want to tell you that if there were peace
> I would quietly talk to you of love.
> I would take you many places,
> But I have not had the time. . . .
> Please wait for me . . .

One must struggle to achieve peace
To build the country
and a new society.

The political point was even more muted with an album from a festival of romantic song (CHLP-003 [1983]) held in Managua. Although introduced by the observation that the festival "carries out one of the purposes of our Popular Sandinista Revolution, the rescue of the artistic and cultural values of our people," the album included only sentimental love songs backed by pop orchestrations. Nevertheless, to stage a festival of popular music in the previously elitist Rubén Darío Theater was itself a political statement. Similarly, a note on *Los Girasoles* (CHLP-006 [1983]), featuring a similar repertoire, explained that Nicaraguan romantic music had been displaced in the 1960s and 1970s by an "an avalanche of the so-called 'new wave' music produced by large recording companies in Spain, Mexico, Argentina and the United States." Such music was "inundating radio, conquering the 'hit parades,' and conditioning public taste." ENIGRAC felt proud, it said, to "rescue from being forgotten these old and new songs."[68] In their doo-wop vocals, smooth phrasings, and barbershoplike harmonic progressions, however, the stylings of the performances themselves attested to the power and pervasiveness of the very influences being protested.

ENIGRAC's two *mariachi* albums highlighted more convincingly the creative syncretism characteristic of traditional musical culture in Nicaragua, the persistence of traditional forms and styles, and the political usefulness of a variety of musical idioms. The cover of *Música nicaragüense: Mariachi internacional* (CHLP-001 [1982]) featured—against the background of Lake Nicaragua and the volcano Momotombo—a *mariachi* band dressed in stylized but unmistakably Mexican *sombreros* and *sarapes*. The music was a *mariachi* rendering of some political texts written and recorded previously by Carlos Mejía Godoy and others. Three years later the album *Mariachi Cocibolca* (CHLP-6002) presented nonpolitical songs but carried on the front of the jacket a photograph of the band gathered around the base of Managua's larger-than-life statue of Rubén Darío (toga-clad with a spread-winged angel perched on his shoulder) against the backdrop of the Rubén Darío National Theater. The image was powerful and polyreferential: traditional and popular music as fulfillment of Darío's championing of Latin (as opposed to North) American culture; tradition-based *sandinista* culture versus the cultural elitism of the *somocistas* and others who had caused such sentimental statues and sycophantic architecture to be created; the right of the Sandinistas to rank themselves culturally with the highest exemplars of Nicaraguan culture; the continuity between *sandinista* culture and both Nicaraguan classical culture (as embodied in Darío) and its deep historical roots (as expressed in some of Darío's poetry).

As part of the Sandinista government's effort to reunify the country's long antagonistic east and west coasts, ENIGRAC also committed substantial resources to Atlantic coast music. Although relatively little of it was explicitly political, it promised to help soothe the wounds caused by the Sandinista government's early political and cultural bungling of the historical east-west division in the country (to which I return in the next chapter). Both the earlier history and the more recent policy bungling made it essential to honor and promote Atlantic coast culture, of which music and the *Fiesta del palo de mayo* (Maypole festival) were dramatically attractive examples.

The music of Nicaragua's mainly black, heavily English-speaking, Protestant, Atlantic coast population differs starkly from that of the west coast. The English (sometimes Miskito, and much less frequently Spanish) lyrics are set to Caribbean calypso and reggae rhythms, and the most likely instruments are brass, bongoes, saxophones, keyboards, and steel drums rather than guitars and wooden *marimbas de arco*. Several years after the triumph, ENIGRAC inaugurated its Chilmate (CHLP) series of "danceable" music, and began to record Atlantic coast groups: Macondo (CHLP-007 [1984]), Run Down (CHLP-6005 [1985]), Happy Land (CHLP-6010 [1986]), and the better-known and more professional Cawibe (CE-6001 and 6016 [1987]) and Dimensión Costeña (CE-6004 [1984] and CE-6009). ENIGRAC's jacket notes on Run Down's *Great Celebration Day* album of 1985 spoke in a somewhat fawning and self-congratulatory way of "our coastal people, our beloved and unknown coastal people. . . . Our exploited, unknown and oppressed people, leaping in joy and happiness. Their revolution, our Revolution. The real possibility, the only possibility of returning to our roots." Songs on the two albums evoked the polymorphous sensuality of the Maypole festivals, the era of the great foreign-owned banana plantations, the multiracial and multilingual character of the people, the lives of fishermen, and the Caribbean and African orientation of the culture.

Other albums—especially those featuring the performing groups headed by the Mejía Godoys—were situated still closer to the ideological center of the Sandinista project. A long-playing album of Literacy Crusade songs produced in 1980 (MC-002) included the marching song of the *brigadistas* ("Hymn to Literacy"), an alphabet-learning song, and others linking the literacy effort to the broader revolutionary task (e.g., "Hay que aprender a leer" [One must learn to read], and "Salgamos juntos de la ignorancia" [Together we will leave ignorance behind]).[69] More symbolic but no less political was ENIGRAC's *Somos hijos del maíz* (MC-016), which presented songs performed at a corn festival organized by the Ministry of Culture in response to the

Reagan administration's embargo on wheat sales to Nicaragua in 1982. Luis Mejía Godoy's "Somos hijos del maíz" (We are children of corn) linked the current struggle to those of the colonial period.

During the revolution's fifth-anniversary year of 1984—also the fiftieth anniversary of Sandino's death—ENIGRAC produced at least four pointedly political albums.[70] Mejía Godoy's *Yo soy de un pueblo sencillo* (I come from a simple people; MC-021) resulted from a collaboration among Nicaraguan, Dutch, and other Latin American musicians and was coproduced by ENIGRAC and the Latin American Cultural Collective of Utrecht (KKLA). It mixed romantic songs with revolutionary ones of "the people of Sandino and Zeledón" and employed traditional instruments as well as synthesizer.[71] The Sandino anniversary album *Sandino: General de hombres libres* (Sandino: General of free men; NCLP-5002), recorded by a half-dozen Nicaraguan groups, included anonymous songs from the Sandino campaign itself (such as "Somos los libertadores" ["We are the liberators"]) and newly composed ones based on texts drawn from a variety of sources. "Somos los libertadores" also appeared on Mexican political singer Oscar Chávez's *Nicaragua vencerá* (Nicaragua will triumph; NCLP-5003) together with other songs of the Sandino period and newer ones of the struggle against Somoza. "La mama Ramona" harked back to the William Walker filibustering war of the 1850s. Recorded in Holland in February 1984 and released by ENIGRAC a year later, Mancotal's *A pesar de usted* (In spite of you; NCLP-5008) blended tender feeling for homeland with revolutionary commitment ("This song is a shot into the heart of imperialism, the enemy of peace") and the defiant challenge of "En tierra de Fonseca" (In the land of Fonseca):

> We will build the country we have dreamed of
> We will never allow them to tie our hands
> We will make a country without doors or windows
> We will not allow them to clip our wings.

ENIGRAC's most ambitious releases during its first half-dozen years were *La misa campesina nicaragüense* (1981) and Carlos and Luis Enrique Mejía Godoy's *Canto épico al FSLN* [Epic song of the FSLN] (1985). *La misa campesina* drew together the post–Vatican II theology of liberation, the political poetics Ernesto Cardenal had worked out during the past twenty-five years, and the terrifying and exhilarating experience of the insurrection and the triumph. It blended the traditional forms and rituals of the Catholic mass with the colloquial language and quotidian imagery of Nicaraguan peasant and working-class life.

The God of *La misa campesina* addressed in the "Canto de entrada" is

Cover illustration for phonograph album by Oscar Chávez (ENIGRAC NCLP-5003, 1984)

> the God of the poor
> the simple and human God
> the God who sweats in the street.

"I have seen you in the gasoline stations," the Entrada continues, "repairing the tires of a truck." The Kyrie implores Jesus Christ to

> enter into solidarity
> not with the oppressor class
> that squeezes out and devours
> the community
> but with the oppressed.

The Gloria, then, is sung to a Christ "who fearlessly denounces injustice . . . / and gives his life combatting the oppressor," and the Pilate of the Credo is *el Romano imperialista*, who crucifies the "worker Christ" (*Cristo obrero*), the "rebel Christ" of the "Canto de meditación." Those who praise him, in turn, are the working class—bricklayers, carpenters, tailors, stevedores, and bootblacks in the park, and their language of praise is the colloquial, richly imagistic, and metaphorical language of everyday life.

Composed by the Mejía Godoys to commemorate the second anniversary of the triumph and recorded in Mexico (1982–84), *Canto épico* is based upon texts drawn from Nicaraguan poetry, traditional song, and the testimony of combatants in the insurrection. Its three dozen songs are set as *corridos*, polkas, *habaneras*, mazurkas, and other forms drawn from the country's most characteristic celebrations: Easter, *Purísima*, and the Atlantic coast's *Palo de mayo* festival. The whole was intended to "recover from the soil of Nicaragua itself and from the blood of our most heroic brothers all of their inspiration, vigor and purity. It is a Nicaraguan song that arises from the warbling of the birds that gave joy to the guerrillas' mornings and saluted their fall, that is nourished by the sap of our centuries-old trees, witnesses of their exploits, prowess and heroism—the heroism that forged the new era." [72]

Canto épico opens with the gemlike lyric "Nicaragua, Nicaragüita" (which soon became the country's unofficial national anthem), a hymn to Sandino, and a commemorative song on the birth of the FSLN. Eight brief songs (some little more than fragments) on the trees of Nicaragua evoke the country's energy, creative vitality, combative spirit, and ability to survive. Later ones commemorate epic battles of the insurrection (Pancasán, Matagalpa, Estelí). Half the remainder memorialize fallen combatants (poet Leonel Rugama, Luisa Amanda Espinosa, FSLN founder Carlos Fonseca, Camilo Ortega, Germán Pomares, Comandante Marcos). The closing section focuses on pivotal symbolic moments in the latter days of the insurrection—the August 1978 assault on the National Palace, the general strikes of 1978–79, the secret nighttime evacuation of tens of thousands from Managua to Masaya—and concludes jubilantly and defiantly: *A veinte años de la lucha inclaudicable / juramos defender nuestra victoria* (After twenty years of struggle that could not go wrong / We pledge to defend our victory).

The *Canto épico* and *Misa campesina*'s jubilant celebration of the history of struggle against the Somoza regime was inspired and energizing, but the months and years ahead were to prove frustrating and full of disappointment—in the area of culture as in most others. Indeed despite the undeniable gains and achievements of Sandinista cultural policy and programs, the enterprise of cultural reconstruction had been freighted with problems from the beginning.

In mid-January 1981, only a few months into the revolution, Tomás Borge — the oldest member of the Junta and a veteran of more than three decades of struggle against the dictatorship — had stood in the house where Rubén Darío was born in Metapa (now renamed Ciudad Darío [Darío City]) and declared, "To build the House of Culture we have to continue making the bricks. . . . The House of Culture will not be a building of steel and cement, but a historical attitude — a culture popular, anti-imperialist and democratic like the Revolution. . . ; a culture that copies neither Michelangelo nor the Beatles, but which is able to understand [all] artistic production with Nicaraguan eyes" (Ministerio de Cultura 1982a, 67). During the eleven years they were in power, the Sandinista cultural workers made a lot of bricks, reared some impressive edifices, and mounted some admirable programs, despite the shortage of money and even the most rudimentary materials, the disruption and destruction of the contra war, and constant financial crisis. But it turned out that historical attitudes lagged behind the construction of buildings and the operation of programs, that roots ran in many directions and sent up trunks and branches of diverse types, that not all "Nicaraguan eyes" saw culture in the same way.

CHAPTER 6 POLITICAL THEORIES AND CULTURAL REALITIES OPPOSITION TO SANDINISTA CULTURAL POLICY AND PROGRAMS

....

The first duty of every revolutionary is to make the Revolution.

—Rosario Murillo (1982)

....

We had difficulty grasping the ethnic character of the Miskito problem.

—Tomás Borge (1984)

....

A distinguishing mark of the Sandinistas' approach to culture was their belief that culture was central to their larger effort and thus that cultural policies and programs had to be fully integrated with those in other sectors. The Ministry of Culture was charged not only with creating a full array of cultural institutions and programs, but also with insuring that both each one and the whole contribute optimally to the larger task of revolutionary reconstruction. The national and international arena in which that larger task was situated, moreover, grew increasingly perilous as U.S. pressure on the government siphoned money from all nonmilitary sectors and correspondingly increased social dislocation and heightened cultural stress.

As the months became years and the pressures mounted, the cultural project was not spared the turmoil and controversy that swept over other policy sectors. Memories of the cultural wasteland of the Somoza years, however keen and painful, did not preserve from criticism the Sandinistas' efforts at cultural reconstruction. From the outset, there was structural competition and policy and program disagreement between the various operating units of the ministry. Some of the most problematic of them derived from disagreement about the proper role for culture in the larger process of reconstruction, and about whether the revolutionary situation did or did not justify placing constraints upon artistic creativity. Intense disagreements centered on a network of workshops intended to help ordinary people write poetry and on the ministry's work with traditional artisans. As the months and years passed, the ministry's inability to institutionalize its policies and operate its programs effectively—however thoughtfully and imaginatively designed—also became increasingly evident. And most problematic of all was the deepening political-cultural conflict between the Atlantic and Pacific coastal regions. That conflict reached far beyond the Ministry of Culture itself, engaged virtually every part of the governmental apparatus in some way, and threatened not only cultural harmony, but also national unity and tranquillity.[1]

STRUCTURAL DIVISION: THE MINISTRY OF CULTURE AND THE SANDINISTA ASSOCIATION OF CULTURAL WORKERS

The costs and stresses of placing severe demands upon the meager funds and inexperienced staff of the Ministry of Culture manifested themselves in short order. An early symptom was a festering conflict with one of the ministry's own creations, the Asociación Sandinista de Trabajadores Culturales (ASTC; Sandinista Association of Cultural Workers).

ASTC, founded in February 1980, was conceived as a Sandinista mass organization (structurally similar to mass organizations of farmers, workers, women, and other groups) made up of unions or guilds of practicing artists—both the professionals and the most outstanding amateurs (*aficionados más destacados*).[2] As described in early 1982 by the ministry, ASTC consisted of six unions of artists and performers (writers, plastic artists, musicians, dancers, actors, photographers) and a *sindicato* of circus workers and artists.[3]

ASTC's aims were both practical and political. On the one hand, it was created simply to help artists do their work: supply them with materials, help with publication and exhibition, provide mutual support, define and apply professional standards, foment artistic development within communities and the armed forces, and arrange international cultural exchange. On the other hand, like all of the ministry's operating entities, it was charged with organizing, orienting, and mobilizing artists in the larger revolutionary process

(Ministerio de Cultura 1982a, 285–86). In theory, the two sets of aims were not only compatible, but mutually reinforcing. As it happened, events severely challenged theory.

The first problems to emerge were practical rather than political, however, and lay within ASTC itself rather than between it and the ministry. ASTC was slow to establish itself as an effective organization, its widely dispersed activities were not adequately coordinated, and it was relating but poorly to cultural activities being promoted by other entities.[4] By mid-1983, however, there were seven unions, bringing together nearly nine hundred artists in the various genres, and ASTC was sponsoring lectures, conferences, readings, editions of literary works, exhibitions, and performances. By addressing such issues as wages and royalties, it was trying to improve the professional standing of artists.

On the negative side, in spite of its revolutionary determination to break with the reactionary bourgeois and elitist cultural politics of the Somoza era, some of ASTC's policies signalled that aspects of the cultural dialectics of that era were still deeply embedded in Nicaraguan cultural life. Designating about half of its members as *destacados* (outstanding), for example, preserved the cleavage between elite, "good," "serious" art on the one hand, and everything else on the other, and hence between trained professional artists and both amateur artists and the general public. Both distinctions ran directly counter to Sandinista ideology, which held that "the people" were the real creators of art, its sole legitimate audience, and ultimately its most reliable judges.

Originally, the ministry planned for its Division of Artistic Promotion (Fomento del Arte) to have responsibility for both professional and amateur artists (*aficionados*), but by the time the ASTC was actually established a few months later, a de facto partition between the two had developed (despite official explanations to the contrary), with professionals making up the bulk of the ASTC and *aficionados* shunted to the organizationally more distant and shaky Centers for Popular Culture (Meneses 1985).

The elite/professional versus *aficionado* cleavage was particularly evident in ASTC's relationship with the Campesino Movement for Artistic and Dramatic Expression (*Movimiento de Expresión Campesina Artística y Teatral*; MECATE). Founded in April 1980, only a few weeks after ASTC, MECATE by late 1981 had organized some eight hundred people into nearly fifty theater and music groups. But its work was not well known in Managua where ASTC was most active, partly because of a prejudice against the presumed cultural backwardness of the countryside and ASTC members' corollary conception of themselves as the cultural-political vanguard.[5] In some respects, however, MECATE was linked more closely and organically to the revolutionary process than was ASTC. For their presentation at the first Central American

Festival of Popular Theater in 1982, five MECATE groups developed theater pieces on agrarian reform (e.g., landowners' resistance to the revolution, the work of cooperatives).[6]

As the months passed, ASTC tried to restructure its relationships with MECATE and other cultural organizations. But at the same time it was having repeated intense conflicts with the ministry—periodic proclamations of revolutionary solidarity to the contrary notwithstanding: over the issue of "quality" versus popularization; over hierarchical control and direction versus wholly autonomous artists organized collectively; over freedom of expression versus the privileging of certain aesthetic (and ideologically linked) models; over maintaining a workable and politically viable balance between artistic freedom on the one hand, and situating culture in the service of revolutionary transformation on the other.

From the outset, in fact, there had been two views concerning the Sandinista cultural project. Some argued that culture must be placed principally (that is, instrumentally) in the service of revolutionary reconstruction; others maintained that doing so would endanger the vital creative process of cultural development—not only under the hopefully short-term pressures of revolutionary reconstruction, but over the long haul as well.

Convinced that the instrumentalist position was demanded by circumstances, poet Gioconda Belli argued that the welter of problems the country faced called for no less than "the formation of a new national consciousness," and that culture must play "a fundamental role" in the process. She conceived of that role as strongly ideological. Culture, Belli maintained, would "recover and synthesize for historical memory the rich experience of the years of struggle . . . and [stimulate] the formation of social values leading to the construction of the new man" (Belli 1980, 63).

Formal statements of purpose attached to the ministry's earliest budgets suggest that Belli's view was dominant. "The cultural task," said the ministry's 1981 statement, "is an ideological activity which will carry with it a profound restructuring of the character, functions and ends of the culture. . . . For the period of transition, the Ministry of Culture positions itself between the Nicaragua we inherited—dispossessed and distanced from its own identity—and the Nicaragua of the new man, owner of his own culture, owner of his own values." The immediate objectives, the ministry continued, were to "neutralize the paralyzing cultural influences inherited from the past by rescuing our cultural values according to our national identity . . . [and] develop on the basis of our own values a culture . . . in which the people will cease to be simple receptors of cultural values and will become makers of culture."[7]

It was a laudable aim. Putting such an ideal dramatically into practice, "mobile cultural brigades" had carried music, dance, and theater into the countryside during the literacy campaign of mid-1980. The cultural brigades (formally, the *Movimiento Cultural "Leonel Rugama"*) helped form and guide Assemblies of Amateur Artists (*Asambleas de Artistas Aficionados*) in the countryside, producing festivals, dance and theater events, workshops, and classes.[8] Tired, dirty, insect-bitten and ill from unfamiliar food, cultural *brigadistas* returned from their second (1983) mobilization telling of sixteen-hour days in which performances alternated with testimonies from combatants around campfires. They were enthusiastic about "trying to make culture the patrimony of everyone and not of the privileged classes." "Our labor as revolutionary artists in the cultural brigades," *brigadista* Roberto José Layva proclaimed lyrically, "is to seek the autochthonous, dig it up, and return it to the source from which it came: the people. . . . [We are carrying on a] struggle against ideological diversionism in the field of art, responding firmly and with . . . an art which has to be better, which has to be more beautiful . . . than whatever art has been produced by the bourgeoisie. . . . Our charge of love in the mountains was . . . [to create an] art for the poetry of life, against aggression and death."[9]

As a response to the urgent exigencies of the literacy campaign and the hunger for cultural activities in the countryside, MECATE's strategy was both admirable and functional, and it demonstrated that culture could indeed be placed directly in the service of broader reconstruction. The larger, long-term political-cultural project demanded, however, that the needs of individual artists for creative freedom and support—whatever the circumstances—be brought into sustainable harmony with the drive of the state for stability and legitimacy vis-à-vis both its own people and the international community. By the time of the ASTC's second annual assembly in February 1982, conflicts with the ministry over these issues were beyond hiding.

Trying both to pull themselves together and to heal the rift, ASTC members focused much of their attention during the assembly on the relationship of culture to the larger revolutionary process. ASTC director Rosario Murillo (also wife of President Daniel Ortega) asserted categorically that "the first duty of every revolutionary is to make the revolution" (Murillo 1982, 12). But the syntactical balance of her assertion helped mask its essentially tautological character, and its programmatic implications were obscure at best.

In any case, ASTC members insisted upon ventilating their differences with the ministry. Writers' union members attending the 1982 meeting charged that the ministry had failed to respond to the "inquietudes" of the association's membership. Noting a general breakdown in communication and cooperation between the two, the writers granted that the ministry should be "the great organizer of cultural activity," but insisted that it should "abstain from intervening in or influencing the forms chosen by those who create, . . . [and] favor a creative ambience without trying to make creative activity uniform or official." While pledging solidarity with the revolution in general and the ministry in particular, they argued that neither should "promote, with a paternalistic attitude, an art valued simply for its origins in a certain class" (Union of Writers 1982, 10–11).

In the meeting's closing statement, ASTC took care to locate itself in the lineage of those Nicaraguan patriots — Rubén Darío, Augusto C. Sandino, the students of the 1960s and 1970s, the cultural *brigadistas* of the insurrection — who had best understood that culture could and must serve the ends of liberation. Claiming as its first obligation the defense of the national sovereignty won through the revolution, ASTC also noted pointedly that the *Revolución Popular Sandinista* had consistently promised "the total and absolute liberty Nicaraguan creators have to develop their artistic activity." It explicitly rejected "whatever thesis of official art." The political delicacy of such a position was patent, however, especially at the opening of the second year in office of a U.S. president who had sworn to remove the Sandinistas and end the revolution. Hence ASTC's commitment to promoting *todas las formas de expresión artística* (all forms of artistic expression) contained the crucial qualifying phrase *que sirvan para mostrar la riqueza de un proceso de liberación nacional* (that serve to show the richness of a process of national liberation).[10]

In any case, beneath such carefully crafted rhetoric, the ministry continued to pursue an avowedly instrumental agenda for culture that was at odds with ASTC's demand for artistic freedom. Indeed, fears were widespread that the parallel emphases upon cultural production and "popular" art (i.e., arts "of the people") were leading irreversibly to a decline in quality. In July 1982, Pablo Antonio Cuadra — while admitting the "brilliant results" of the ministry's efforts to democratize culture in Nicaragua — charged that the "overpowering . . . cultural *dirigismo* [state control]" that had come to characterize the Sandinista cultural project demanded "that arts and letters place themselves at the service of the Revolution."[11]

The controversy lingered for more than a year after the 1982 assembly. "In no way do I like the idea that within our revolutionary process there is a confrontation between two revolutionary institutions," Luis Rocha declared, but despite repeated attempts on both sides to heal the wounds and find mutually acceptable language to describe shared commitments, the two organizations remained at odds.[12] Paradoxically, the disagreement was at one level a conflict between two forms of elitism. The ministry, for its part, professed a proletarian commitment to "the people," but manifested an elitist paternalism in designing programs for them (such as the poetry workshops). Similarly, the ASTC's rebellion against that particular form of elitism arose partly because it was in conflict with its members' own customary elitist conception of themselves as a special category of autonomous "artists."

ASTC was determined, Director Murillo recalled later, not to "require, limit or establish forms or styles. We open all the doors of imagination." [13] But the politics of the situation required that there be no ambiguity about ASTC's commitment to the goals of the revolution. Nearly five years after the Sandinistas came to power, Murillo still felt it necessary to insist that "it doesn't matter what style or form [artists] choose to express themselves. Their work is revolutionary because it comes from a human being who's living the Revolution in all its manifestations. . . . All the doors to individual creativity *based on the collective experience* are open. . . . One's individual work has to be the product of one's personal experience *within the collective experience*" (White 1986, 126–27; italics added). Significantly, the mollifying phrase "collective experience" no more solved the problem than had ASTC's similarly inventive language two years earlier.

The concrete implications of the institutional argument were evident in a minor way among musicians, and in a major one in the argument over Cardenal's cherished poetry workshops (*talleres de poesía*).

Luis Mejía Godoy, veteran of years of activity in the *nueva canción* movement and leader of one of Nicaragua's best-known performing groups, found the thoughtless "revolutionary" imitativeness of some younger musicians and their at-times merely propagandistic music "a great weight" on his conscience. Both Mejía Godoy and Pancho Cedeño urged that musicians do their own serious historical research in order to go beyond romantic and "touristic" readings of Nicaraguan music and culture. [14] Younger rock- and jazz-oriented musicians were impatient with both the folkloristic orientation of older musicians and with imitative, propagandistic "revolutionary" music that denied the rich syncretistic musical creativity which reached across political boundaries. As early as 1981, musicians of the Sandinista Youth Movement had organized a festival of electronic music whose aim was to "erase in young people the idea that . . . electronic music is bad, or that it should be understood as an imperialist and counterrevolutionary invasion. . . . [Jazz] was born among negro slaves as a movement of emancipation. . . . Imperialism is one thing, but the music of Diana Ross is another. Cultural penetration is one thing, but Louis Armstrong, Janice [*sic*] Joplin and Chick Corea are another" (Murillo 1981). [15] To a Sandinista cultural establishment for which one of the cornerstones was to create an "anti-imperialist" culture in the new Nicaragua, such arguments were hardly welcome, however paradoxically they mirrored the interest of Nicaragua's *vanguardistas* a half-

National School of Music, Colonia Dambach, Managua, 1988. (Photograph by author)

century earlier in the then-new North American poetry of Frost, Sandburg, Masters, and Pound.

Other complicating perspectives emanating from among musicians blended the issues of elitism and instrumentalism. A quite unrevolutionary elitism was especially evident among those in charge of the National School of Music.[16] Initially projected by the Ministry of Culture as open democratically to all comers, including adults and those without prior musical training, the school quickly became more oriented toward younger students who could be trained according to classical models. To the political argument that art not comprehended by "the people" was not art at all, the school's director responded, "We are not going to lower art so that people can understand it. What we want is for the people to rise in their cultural level so that they can understand art. . . . That would be the ideal."

Hence within the single sector of music, the policy choices were complicated. It was one thing to promulgate a new "popular" and "democratic" culture "of the people." It was quite another to admit (and deal practically with) the fact that separate groups of musicians clearly preferred distinctive repertoires and employed sharply contrasting performing styles: traditional *campesino* musicians (both political and nonpolitical), politically committed *nueva canción* and *volcanto* musicians, classical performers oriented to elite

European music, and younger musicians (some politically engaged, some not) attuned to North American jazz and rock.

The site of the most intense conflict, as it turned out, was Minister of Culture Ernesto Cardenal's cherished *talleres de poesía* (poetry workshops), the value of which he considered to have been conclusively proven through the Solentiname experiment. In early issues of *Poesía libre*, the magazine of the poetry workshops, editor Julio Valle-Castillo proclaimed that the magazine would be absolutely open to all forms of poetic expression.[17] His proclamation was to some extent misleading, however, for in fact certain preferences were in evidence, certain paradigms favored: assurances of creative freedom notwithstanding, Cardenal himself described the workshops as places "where carpenters and masons are learning *the correct techniques* for writing *good modern* verse" (Cardenal 1981a, 205 [emphasis added]). The "correct" techniques were those of Cardenal's *exteriorismo*.

That emphasis soon produced heated controversy among writers from both inside and outside Nicaragua. In early 1981, poets Rosario Murillo and Francisco de Asís Fernández, Uruguayan novelist (and staunch supporter of the revolution) Eduardo Galeano and others voiced their fears: that poets would be obligated to write solely about the revolution, that the creative process would be limited, that there was a danger of developing a cultural "line," and even more specifically that the *exteriorismo* of Cardenal would become the most (or only) valid model.[18] A week later, some sixty poets with experience in the workshops responded that the revolution was far from the only focus of the poetry being written in the workshops, that there were no limits on creativity, and that in addition to the poetry of Cardenal, that of many other Nicaraguan (and even North American) poets was being studied.[19] The next week, however, Nicaraguan poet (and later associate minister of culture) Vidaluz Meneses countered that she had attended the organizing session of one workshop in the Atlantic coast city of Bluefields with Mayra Jiménez, and found her attitude sharp and cutting (*tajante*) with respect to the kinds of poetic language preferred and the necessity to eliminate all metaphors and similes as "obscurantisms" (cf. Heyck 1990, 227–42). Jiménez paid little attention to the lives and experiences of the aspiring poets who attended, Meneses recalled.[20]

Despite the surging controversy, Jiménez continued to insist that "there really [isn't] a conflict, just different ideas about what art should be." The workshops were producing "eminently revolutionary" poetry simply because the poets, "owing to their proletarian origins, use a concrete, simple, and direct language . . . closely related to [their] immediate reality." As for proscriptions against figurative language, she said, "We don't have anything against the metaphorical or the conceptual." Their absence is "simply a [natural] phenomenon," since "the language [the poets] use is the language they use in their everyday lives. They write that way and nobody tells them they have to. . . . What we do . . . is give the language the profundity it needs to become art." Reminded of the apparent paradox that the language of such people (for example in their oral legends and stories) is richly metaphorical, Jiménez explained that such language did not show up in poetry from the workshops because most of the poets were young people whose recent experience as combatants in the revolution was primary: "They haven't looked for ways to bring to their poetry that other world related to legend and myth, superstitions, [and] symbols. . . . That's the way these young people write and there's no reason to force them to change. It wouldn't be natural for them to look for that other world" (White 1986, 106–13).

As experience with the workshops accumulated, Cardenal himself became even more candid in his insistence that what they were doing was not only justified, but essential and correct. "The poetry which our people write," he insisted early in 1982, "is bad when they have not been taught how to do it. In all of the poetry contests conducted by the mass organizations, when poets from the workshops have not participated, all the poetry has been bad" (Cardenal 1982d, 12–13). Many people send poems to the Ministry of Culture, often with revolutionary themes, he continued, but "they are always bad." Thus the contradiction was fundamental: on the one hand, Mayra Jiménez and other partisans of the workshops argued that "art is from the people, should come from the people, be enjoyed by the people, and be produced by the people," but on the other hand they declared that the art "the people" in fact produced when they followed their own aesthetic was bad (White 1986, 113).

On the other side of the argument, meanwhile, some of Cardenal's critics charged that his approach to creativity both lacked the traditional roots he claimed for it and produced mediocre art. The putatively traditional primitive painting (*pintura primitivista*) of Solentiname was in fact, they argued, imposed by Cardenal as his personally preferred graphic analogue to *exteriorismo* in poetry, and in any case it was not an art form worthy of serious attention. Even painter Roger Pérez de la Rocha, who had helped teach some of the Solentiname painters, dismissed it as "postcard art."[21] Cardenal's own accounts of the early experiments in primitivist painting on Solentiname consistently emphasized that his efforts were directed toward elaborating wholly autonomously engendered artistic activities already in evidence among the island's inhabitants. Unfortunately, the history of non-elite graphic art in Nicaragua is not sufficiently documented to settle the issue of origins and models, but some evidence suggests that at least Cardenal himself had long-established models in mind as he guided and developed the Solentiname painters. Cerutti asserts that José Coronel Urtecho discovered primitivist painter Salvadora Henríquez de Noguera in San Carlos in the 1940s, and that by the 1960s her paintings were represented in the Banco Central's collection. Self-taught Granada painter Asilia Guillén (1887–1964), abandoned by her husband with three young children, and having had no formal artistic training, began to paint about 1950, concentrating on landscapes of the islands in Lake Nicaragua. Her work was exhibited in Washington, Belgium, and São Paulo (Fernández Morales 1961; Cerutti 1984d, 22).

INSTITUTIONAL INEPTITUDE: POTTERS AND THE POLITICS OF CULTURE

Some of the most dramatic evidence of the problematics of Sandinista cultural thinking and strategizing—and of both the ministry's insecure grasp on the country's cultural situation and its inability to operate its programs effectively—emerged in the course of the ministry's work with traditional artisans.

Despite the Instituto Indigenista Nicaragüense's formal proclamations of the irreplaceable worth of traditional culture, the Somoza years had been difficult indeed for the country's traditional artisans. The manufactured consumer goods that had begun to flood into Nicaragua as early as the mid-nineteenth century steadily reduced public demand for handwrought products. Later decades multiplied the threats: some local materials had become scarce and imported ones prohibitively expensive; the artisans' local communities were disturbed by the agroexport booms in cotton and coffee; some artisans (such as weavers) who offered competition in markets in which the Somozas and their associates had interests were actively harassed.

The situation was particularly acute among traditional potters.[22] A study commissioned by Banco Central during the latter years of the Somoza regime found 99 percent of the country's pottery workshops with only broken and inadequate tools, and lacking kilns and machinery routinely used by traditional artisans in other countries. A series of consultants brought in to implement some of the study's recommendations—despite their disagreement about the relative merits of traditional and modern designs and techniques—managed to introduce new machinery and techniques. Other Banco Central efforts led to the paving of roads necessary for access to materials and markets, and to the formation of a pottery cooperative, from which the bank encouraged its large restaurant and resort customers to order ceramic items (Field 1987, 63, 94–99).[23]

The Sandinista government's approach to traditional artisans contrasted sharply with that of the Somoza regime. The active and even heroic participation of Nicaragua's traditional *barrios* and rural communities in the final stages of the 1978–79 insurrection had made young Sandinista partisans aware (many of them for the first time in their lives) of the variety and vibrancy of traditional life and culture in the country. More importantly, a major cultural policy commitment to valuing, revitalizing, and promulgating traditional artisanry appeared to offer the Sandinistas large practical and political returns: it was congruent with both their claim that the Sandinista revolution was a popular (in the sense of being *of the people*) revolution and their consequent commitment to fomenting a new *popular* culture; it could capitalize on the international taste for the marketable products of Nicaraguan traditional artisanry that Ernesto Cardenal's pilot work on Solentiname had already demonstrated; it might help modulate the threat of rapid revolutionary change by associating the Sandinistas with the deepest historical layers of traditional culture; and — not unimportantly, some argued — it might even ease the national debt situation slightly by substituting inexpensive locally made items for expensive imported ones.

Thus a commitment to Nicaragua's traditional artisans appeared to offer the Sandinistas potentially large returns on a modest investment. It promised, as had *campesino* and *barrio* militancy during the latter days of the insurrection, to "[weave] the threads of Indian heritage, artisanal production and revolutionary struggle into a tight and brilliantly colored fabric." Embodying "both tradition and revolutionary struggle," as Field puts it, Nicaragua's *artesanía* wedded "the possibility of revival of the past and [the] creation of the future" (Field 1987, 69, 253–59). As Minister of Culture Ernesto Cardenal optimistically told an interviewer, "This rediscovery of indigenous culture causes a complete change of mentality for the people" (Zwerling and Martin 1985, 44).

Unfortunately, the leaders of the Sandinista cultural project were less prepared culturally than they should have been to make the modest investment. Field's evaluation of the cultural orientation of that leadership corroborates the broader ones advanced in earlier chapters here concerning the Sandinista leadership in general: they were drawn in large part not from the working class, or from *campesino* life, but from the middle class upward. The Ministry of Culture in particular, Field concluded, "coalesced a group of intellectuals who purported to represent . . . the poor masses of Nicaraguans," but whose "die-hard [petty bourgeois] attitudes" made it difficult for them to work with traditional artisans (Field 1987, 271–72).

As an early prime site for work with traditional artisans, the Ministry of Culture chose the San Juan de Oriente pottery cooperative, established by the Banco Central project in 1978. Although the technicians and consultants hired by the bank had introduced new technologies and designs, the people of the area were known for their supposedly "pure Indian blood," and the area itself was popularly understood to be a center for "Indian" ceramics. Hence San Juan de Oriente seemed a propitious place to begin the "lively process of myth making" which Field concluded that the ministry undertook in order to establish the desired cultural-political linkages (Field 1987, 71–87).

By late 1984, an article in the FSLN newspaper *Barricada* was reporting that "with the revolutionary triumph . . . *artesanía* received a special stimulus. . . . One expression of this is the transformation of a place which once was a school workshop and which became the Ceramics Cooperative of San Juan, where the members now work in dignity thanks to the help the Revolution brought."[24] Not only had the revolution and the Ministry of Culture had nothing to do with establishing the co-op, however, but government policies and agencies had (as we shall shortly see) actually complicated and frustrated the artisans' work and denigrated them personally and collectively.

In its efforts to survive and flourish following the fall of Somoza, the co-op dealt with the ministry's *Dirección de Artesanía* (DA; responsible for policy and training), its *Empresa Nicaragüense de Arte* (ENIARTE; its marketing arm), and the *Unión Nacional de Artesanos Diriangén* (UNAD; the artisans' union), which was part of ASTC rather than the ministry. Originally organized and headed by U.S.-educated Marta Zamora, DA purchased raw materials for resale to artisans at modest cost and established training centers where artisans learned new techniques and technologies. Providing such desperately needed services was complicated by the requirement that the agency had to allocate some jobs so as to pay off individual political debts, and to channel money into certain quarters (such as the heroic indigenous *barrio* of Monimbó) to pay off collective ones. Consequently there were never enough raw materials to go around, some training workshops operated below capacity, and others had to be closed. Frustrated with the constraints and political distortions, Zamora left DA and took over the direction of ENIARTE in 1981 (Field 1987, 151–55; Ministerio de Cultura 1982a, 280).

The original purpose of ENIARTE was to buy *artesanía* from traditional artisans for resale, thus assisting them with the critical problem of effective marketing. In fact much of what it did, however, was to bring non-artisan unemployed people into state-owned artisan workshops, provide them with nontraditional designs, and train them in modern production techniques. The result, as Field puts it, was "a policy of artisanal development that often had little to do with revival but everything to do with official promotion of marketable, and often mass produced, artisanal goods" (Field 1987, 213).

Not surprisingly, legitimate traditional artisans came increasingly to see ENIARTE policies as hostile to both their interests and their sense of themselves as creative artists. As a condition of receiving aid, for example,

ENIARTE demanded that the co-ops sell exclusively to them, and then bought *artesanía* in bulk from the co-ops and resold it at 100 percent markup, failing to return a fair share of the profits to the artisans. Hence by the time the ministry was reporting in *Barricada* that artisans were working in "new dignity" thanks to the revolution, the San Juan de Oriente potters had concluded that ENIARTE was a "corrupt and graft-ridden institution." Many of them refused to sell what they made through ENIARTE's Culture House sales outlet in Masaya (located in a building built by Banco Central for the purpose a few years earlier). Following a running series of disputes with the ministry, Zamora was removed as head of ENIARTE. She went on to help found UNAD, the artisans' own union, which became a focus for her ENIARTE successor's suspicion and hostility (Field 1987, 155–70, 209–13).

Granted legal status by the National Assembly in early 1985, UNAD was allowed to import machinery and engage in other activities similar to those earlier granted to DA and ENIARTE. Its markup on artisanal goods bought from the co-ops was 20 percent rather than 100 percent, and it worked diligently to keep the San Juan de Oriente co-op from collapsing under the mounting pressures of the contra war: lack of raw materials, family and community disruption, and labor shortages caused by the military draft (Field 1987, 169–72).

The creation of UNAD produced what was in effect a three-way struggle (UNAD versus DA versus ENIARTE) for power to direct artisanal development in the new Nicaragua. DA was less hostile to UNAD than was ENIARTE, but still insisted upon retaining the leading role in the effort. Recognizing that its own survival depended upon ENIARTE-supplied funds from sales, DA supported ENIARTE's marketing function, thus tacitly endorsing procedures that UNAD artisans themselves found exploitative. DA policy also insisted that UNAD be "a political organizer of the artisans in support of the government, the SMP [military service], and the economic development of the country." In the long run, DA was in fact committed to a network of totally state-run artisanal workshops, a model of which was constructed in Managua to train unemployed young men and women to make utilitarian ceramics that DA hoped would have a substantial positive economic impact. President Daniel Ortega's appearance at UNAD's second national assembly legitimized the organization, but came at the price of UNAD's reciprocal guarantee to make "defense of the revolution" a first priority. The effect of that guarantee was, as Field observes, to insert UNAD into "the mythology the Sandinistas [had] created for themselves" (Field 1987, 214, 219–21, 231).

Paradoxically, the conflicted post-Somoza process of artisanal development in Nicaragua both revealed and produced political dynamics that were neither planned nor anticipated by the Ministry of Culture or the Sandinista government. Expecting to find a widespread revolutionary political consciousness among the artisans he went to study, Field instead discovered that the majority of them "had neither fought for the FSLN during the insurrections . . . nor had they joined any revolutionary mass organizations" after the triumph. Most confided that, given the opportunity, they would vote for the PLI (*Partido Liberal Independiente*) rather than the FSLN. Nevertheless, the personnel, policies, and programs of the ministry, ENIARTE, and DA — elitist and unrepresentative as they were of the artisans' own preferences, and ineffective as they were in serving their interests — helped to stimulate the development of some organic intellectuals among the artisans who became leaders in UNAD and guided the challenge to the official agencies (Field 1987, 16).

Meanwhile, the government's hope that a renewed supply of native artisanry would function as a form of import substitution and thus have a substantial economic impact was for the most part not realized. Its "Vajilla Project," backed by funds from the International Development Bank, was designed to assist the San Juan de Oriente co-op in the production of daily tableware. Ministry planning reports (which Field found in some respects patronizing to members of the co-op) promised substantial returns on the investment, and some new machinery was purchased and installed. But the project failed, partly because the escalating contra war made it difficult (and even dangerous in some cases) to get needed raw materials (including propane to fire the kilns), partly because some materials were not well matched to the machinery purchased, and partly because some equipment malfunctioned. Artisans also complained about the long hours and boredom of the repetitive tasks involved in commercial production. More decisive, however, was the fact that the majority of Nicaraguan people had long since come to use (and prefer) imported glass and plastic dishes rather than locally made ceramic ones. Consequently, there was no substantial domestic market for what the co-op was making (Field 1987, 105–22).

However daunting, these problems — the Ministry of Culture versus ASTC, instrumentalist ideologues versus proponents of unhampered creativity, popular versus elite musicians, workshop versus non-workshop poets, the Dirección de Artesanía versus ENIARTE versus UNAD (and all of them versus the women potters of San Juan de Oriente) — were far more amenable to eventual resolution than was the ancient and profound political, economic, and cultural split between western Nicaragua where the vast majority of Nicaraguans (Sandinistas and non-Sandinistas alike) had grown up, and the Atlantic coastal area, about which most of them knew little or nothing.

THE ATLANTIC COAST: CULTURE AND CONTRADICTORY CONSCIOUSNESS

Because of its very magnitude and complexity, because of the Sandinista government's own political naiveté, cultural elitism, and administrative ineptitude, and because it came to be used opportunistically as a lever in the Reagan administration's struggle to depose the Sandinista government, the stubbornly intractable problem of the Atlantic coast took on a veritably gothic destructiveness.[25] As the Sandinistas were to learn slowly, painfully, and at great political cost, shaping effective policy for the Atlantic coast required that one know something of the historical-cultural process that had brought the *costeño* population to where they were in mid-1979. Unfortunately they knew next to nothing, and — as it turned out — were reluctant to admit their ignorance. For their part, Atlantic coast people had substantial experience in resisting those whose agendas they did not share.

A HISTORY OF RESISTANCE. At the deepest structural level, few *costeños* had been prepared by their historical experience to believe that help could be expected to come from the "Spanish" on Nicaragua's west coast. Rejecting union with Nicaragua in 1877, the King of Mosquitia — verbalizing what had been abundantly clear ever since the first seventeenth-century raids by Miskitos on the Spanish interior towns — said that "the religion, customs, manners, and laws of Nicaragua are in no way compatible" with those of Mosquitia. President Zelaya's manner of "incorporating" the coast into Nicaragua seventeen years later made matters worse: he militarily occupied the coast, deposed the king, forced the inhabitants to sign a declaration of allegiance, and made Spanish the official language.

Costeños understandably found such tactics difficult to distinguish from those of the Spanish *conquistadores*, whom hindsight assured them it had been wise to resist. Vehemently they protested to Queen Victoria that Zelaya's move had left them "in the hands of a government and a people which have not the slightest interest, sympathy or affection for the inhabitants of the Mosquito Reserve; and as our usages, customs, religion, laws, and language do not correspond, there never could be unity." Armed confrontations followed, and were quelled only after the Nicaraguan government called for assistance from U.S. troops waiting on a battleship offshore (Bourgois in Walker 1982, 308–9; Vilas 1989, 40–42).

Hence to the extent that *costeños* were waiting for anything in the late 1970s while the Sandinistas were conducting a valiant armed insurrection against the Somoza regime, it was not for deliverance from the west, but rather for the restoration of the Miskito Kingdom or the period of what they remembered as good times, good wages, and well-stocked commissaries.[26] With regard to the former, popular Miskito culture was rich in myths associated with the period, with schemes for restoration, with claims to royal lineage, and even with arguments over where the monarch's scepter and crown jewels might be hidden (Bourgois in Walker 1985, 207).

Whether or not royal lineage could in fact be established—or the scepter and crown jewels found—*costeños* had repeatedly proven that they could both adapt to enforced change and retain cherished and functional elements of their culture as a basis for continuity in their identity, both individually and collectively. That ability stood them in good stead through not only the Somoza years, but also through their confusing and turbulent encounter with the anti-Somoza Sandinistas.

CULTURAL CHANGE, SYNCRETISM, AND SURVIVAL. *Costeños* made their initial cultural compromises by trading local meat and fish for British-made fishing lines, cotton clothing, machetes, cooking pots, and guns in the seventeenth century, but the culture of the *costeño* groups showed a remarkably creative and syncretistic capacity to survive, adapt, and incorporate. As late as the 1930s, Conzemius compared coastal culture and society with previously published accounts and reported that much had survived—foods, work habits, songs, dances, stories, names, handicrafts, and fishing, hunting, and agricultural practices (Conzemius 1932).

Three decades later, anthropologist Mary Helms found many traditional lifeways, beliefs, and values thriving among the Río Coco Miskitos: techniques of hunting and fishing, the fashioning of gourds and calabashes into useful and beautiful objects, the making of bark cloth and baskets, the construction of rafts and houses, and a complex system of communal land use (Helms 1971, 188–97; Nietschmann 1973, 35; Dennis 1981, 276).

Indeed, as Helms argues, "until the latter part of the nineteenth century culture change [on the coast] was characterized more by the addition of new items than by large-scale replacement of indigenous customs and traditions." Thus long after the Moravians arrived, traditional beliefs in spirit beings (*lasas*) survived and were mixed with Christian beliefs in Satan. Beliefs and practices originally associated with shamans (*sukyas*) survived in those of contemporary "spirit healers." The traditional Creole *aobaia* continued to be danced in front of Moravian churches on Christian holidays. A patient in a Moravian hospital or tuberculosis sanatorium might be treated with a combination of prescription medicine, "bush remedies," and a prayer by a lay pastor (Helms 1971, 182–215; Vilas 1989, 56).

Similar borrowings, adaptations, and syncretisms were in evidence in social structure in Asang—a six-hundred-member village whose history reached not into the mists of antiquity but only to its founding in 1910. The village was organized through an elaborate kinship system, but it was not—Helms insisted—a "peasant society"; rather, it was a "purchase society" shaped partly by a system of wide-ranging trade and wage labor that allowed local people to maintain autonomy and a more or less stable social organization while buying tangible goods to relieve manifest daily needs and appropriating cultural features that made sense to them.

"Traditional" matrilocality, for example, had its relatively recent origin in the practical necessity (as local people saw it) for men to hunt, fish, and travel long distances to trading posts, and to allow women to stay with children and tend crops in their absence. Similarly, traditional agricultural, fishing, and hunting practices were modified to meet wage-labor and other changes introduced with the arrival of traders and corporate resource-extracting enterprises. Although many *costeños* learned to trade their labor for goods in the outside market economy, for example, food and other commodities continued to be shared reciprocally within the community, in a system that took no account of types and quantities, and in which, as Nietschmann observed, "the most productive food givers . . . [were] usually the smallest receivers" (Nietschmann 1973, 184–85). At a higher organizational level, the village functioned by blending traditional Miskito custom, the social mores and regulations of the Moravian church, and (more rarely) national statutes. As appropriate in individual instances, the array of codes was arbitrated by village headmen and Moravian lay pastors (Helms 1971, 6–10, 26, 45, 57, 60–65, 158–67; Nietschmann 1973, 43, 58).

Conzemius's visit to the coast coincided with the depression in the United States, the latter stages of the guerrilla war of Sandino to push the U.S. Marines out of Nicaragua, and the early days of Anastasio Somoza García's rise to power. Helms's visit occurred on the eve of the Somoza regime's drive to rationalize and appropriate all of the productive resources of the coast. All of these dynamics had profound effects upon the economic and social order on the Atlantic coast, and hence upon the social and cultural lives of its people.

Especially in the banana business, the depression came quickly (and coincided with banana-tree diseases as well). In forty-five years, the industry had grown enormously: Standard Fruit Company alone shipped four million bunches in 1929. But by 1940, shipments from El Bluff fell to only 637 bunches (Vilas 1989, 46–49). Companies scaled back their operations or closed; workers lost their jobs; commissaries disappeared; coveted imported consumer goods became scarce; families and communities accustomed to a cash economy were thrown entirely back upon subsistence agriculture, hunting, and fishing.

THE SOMOZA REGIME AND THE COAST. The depression of the 1930s was just beginning to wane when the first of the Somoza dynasty began to move into a central position of power in Nicaragua. Like Zelaya before him, Anastasio Somoza García came to power publicly committed to modernizing the coast and incorporating *costeños* more fully into national life and culture. And although the regime maintained a low public profile on the coast — embodied in a few "petty government officials and sleepy military outposts" — it began early and continued perennially to appropriate the region for its own economic and political purposes, couching those purposes in the lofty rhetoric of nationalism, economic development, and progress (Hale 1994, 58).

On the eve of a scheduled state visit to the United States in 1939, Somoza wrote to President Roosevelt that it was "of paramount importance to link together . . . the productive regions of the east coast with . . . the interior and the Pacific coast." He proposed canalization of the San Juan River and a "complementary waterway" from Lake Nicaragua to the Pacific. In a 1942 speech to the national assembly, Somoza spoke again of "the campaign of spiritual and real nationalization which will definitely incorporate into the heart of the nation our Nicaraguan brothers in that great and fruitful area." A projected new highway was to "strengthen the spiritual, social and commercial bonds between the Pacific and those wild and rich regions, bringing us into contact with the civilization of the Atlantic and its markets."[27] Lofty rhetoric notwithstanding, Somoza's real agenda was to "incorporate" the east coast as a source of revenue for himself and his family and friends.

By the end of the 1940s — having arranged lucrative links with U.S. and Canadian mining companies — Somoza was getting $3,000 per month in "considerations" as well as 15 percent of the total production of the Las Segovias gold mine. Mining companies were also paying off *Guardia Nacional* officers regularly (Vilas 1989, 47–49, 60). The Somoza sons followed their father's lead. In the mid-1960s, President Luis Somoza began a banana export enterprise before shifting to sugar cane. The family came to own saw mills and cattle ranches on the coast, and had a central role in the burgeoning shrimp and lobster fishing industry (Hale 1994, 120).

Larger developments from the 1960s onward continued to impel the regime's rationalization of resources, land, and people on the coast. From the end of World War II onward, developmentalist approaches were urged upon every Central American country by such entities as the International Bank for Reconstruction and Development (1945), the Central American Common Market (1960), and John F. Kennedy's Alliance for Progress (1961). Local elites, in Nicaragua as elsewhere, were easy marks for such a strategy, which reinforced their own sense of cultural (and moral) superiority. "It is time," opined one Nicaraguan bourgeois intellectual in 1961, "for the state to . . . integrate these rich lands, whose inhabitants have lived in total abandonment and in moral and material poverty, without any concept of family, religion or faith, in complete ignorance of the world and its civilization" (Vilas 1989, 81).

As Charles Hale has observed, the Somoza government saw the Atlantic coast as an "escape valve" for reducing demographic pressure and as "virgin territory for further economic expansion" (Hale 1994, 119). Between 1958 and 1967, a series of national laws aimed to rationalize the use of all of eastern Nicaragua's natural resources. Coupled with laws directed toward acculturation through education in general and Spanish-language instruction in particular, the strategy of economic development left no doubt about the cultural bases and implications of the regime's plan for the coast. The regime's Instituto Agrario Nicaragüense (IAN) wanted to convert what it considered "insufficiently cultivated" lands and to transform Indian villages into production cooperatives. One such plan—a million-acre project backed by the IDB—was scheduled to utilize four thousand families for export cattle production. In response to a similar plan for forest development that deprived them of a half-million acres of their traditional lands, the Indians (who were in fact cultivating the land and using the forests on the same sustainable basis as they had for centuries) retaliated by burning forests. For its part, the Somoza government vacillated, as Vilas has observed, "between accepting these experiments as part of a strategy of anticipated reform that would forestall greater conflicts and seeing them as a breeding ground for 'subversion'" (Vilas 1989, 82–85). What the regime in fact preferred was a more traditional arrangement: contracts and commissions with corporations from which kickbacks could be required—such as those granted for large-scale fishing from 1953 onward. The export-oriented fish industry expanded until uncontrolled harvesting began to destroy the supply. During the regime's last ten years, thirty-four oil concessions—more than 90 percent of them on the east coast—were granted to Texaco, Chevron, Union Oil, and other companies; and 72 percent of all concessions granted between 1950 and 1979 went to Somoza family members, friends, or *Guardia Nacional* officers (Vilas 1989, 63–80).

ECONOMIC DEVELOPMENT AND HUMAN NEEDS. Despite the idealistic "development" rhetoric, objective conditions for the majority of *costeños* were not encouraging. When anthropologist Mary Helms arrived on the coast in the mid-1960s, she observed a general "feeling of deprivation and isolation" among the Miskitos. The recent settlement of a long-running boundary dispute between Nicaragua and Honduras had closed off lands long used by Nicaraguan-based lumber and banana companies, thus adding to local economic distress. A single Alliance for Progress doctor was trying to serve all fifteen thousand people on the lower section of the river. Logging roads were falling into disrepair; to travel by the river to western Nicaragua required a dangerous journey of several weeks.[28]

Relations between local people and the government were mutually wary: Miskitos avoided contact with government agents, who for their part considered assignment to the coast—for such minimal functions as recording vital statistics—equivalent to banishment. Spanish-speaking Nicaraguan school teachers held themselves aloof from the community, and Miskito students reciprocated by dropping Spanish on the way out the schoolroom door. Asang villagers considered rice and beans—staple of the west coast diet—more fitting to trade for consumables at the trading posts than as food (Helms 1971, 128–29, 134, 139). Miskitos were not obligated to serve in the military or to pay taxes on land or personal property. "Neither labor, time, nor produce," Helms observed, "is channeled toward the state on any regular basis" (Helms 1971, 33, 41, 114–15, 174–79).

Anthropologist Bernard Nietschmann, who worked several years later in the coastal village of Tasbapauni (two hundred houses of rough-sawn wood perched on stilts), encountered similar circumstances and attitudes. Professional medical service was a day-long boat trip away in Bluefields; rice and beans were scorned as "Spanish food" and eaten only occasionally. "The company commissaries and supply boats are gone," Nietschmann reported, "money is scarce, and store-bought items are expensive." Understandably, there was a widespread "feeling of want and desperation" (Nietschmann 1973, 17–18, 44, 55).

Thus on the eve of the Sandinistas' triumph over Somoza, the eastern half of the war-torn country they were obliged to try to put back together was riddled with cultural-political contradictions. *Costeños* wanted to be left alone, but were suffering from economic and social abandonment. They had come to prefer wage labor and commerce to a traditional subsistence economy and many of its associated cultural patterns, but proletarianization had not come without cost, and they were suffering acutely from the vagaries of the commercial system that had brought them commissaries and packaged food.

The social, cultural, and political situation on the coast was further complicated by the fact that *costeños* were also divided (culturally, racially, linguistically, and by class) amongst themselves: Miskitos on the north coast, around Puerto Cabezas and inland; Creoles around Bluefields and to the south; and mestizos mostly inland on the agricultural frontier.[29] The historically developed race/class/cultural hierarchy placed Miskitos, Sumus, and Ramas at the bottom, doing the least desirable and most dangerous work in the mines. Mestizos (mostly immigrants from the Pacific coast) were one level above, mostly providing agricultural wage labor, and mired in alcoholism and illiteracy. Many Creoles were in skilled jobs and administrative positions in Bluefields, and there was a "minuscule layer" of North American and European whites as owners and managers of companies (Vilas 1989, 4–6; Bourgois in Walker 1982, 209).

"The root of the problem," Atlantic coast native Alta Hooker candidly affirmed, "is that people are divided by what I call class racism. We Creoles have always considered ourselves more intelligent than any of the indigenous peoples . . . who live out in the bush. But the Mestizos, who are descendants of the Spanish and come from the Pacific side of the country, think themselves superior to everyone." Hooker's testimony was corroborated from the lower end of the social hierarchy by Dionisia Frank López, a Sumu Indian woman: "For sure the Miskitos don't like us. . . . They say the Sumus are worthless. In the past they killed our men for their land, they pushed us out. . . . Now there are more Miskitos than us. We let them work beside us and we say nothing. They buy our produce, but only if they can get it cheap. . . . The Miskitos are different from us. . . . The Miskito men don't respect their women or children" (Angel and Macintosh 1987, 47–48, 32–34).[30]

CONTRADICTORY CONSCIOUSNESS: ANGLO AFFINITY AND ETHNIC IDENTITY. The pressing question that arises from these complexities is, how were residents of the Atlantic coast likely to respond to either developmental agendas or reform initiatives — of whatever ideological stripe — emanating from the west coast–based Nicaraguan state? Arguing from a Gramscian perspective, Charles Hale has observed that in general,

> subordinate ethnic group members' responses to oppression are multi-valent, combining rejection with partial acceptance, resisting through efforts to appropriate and subvert the cultural symbols of the dominant order. As a result, they create a cultural form, in part actively resistant, in part expressing the "commonsense" premises that come directly from dominant actors and institutions, and in part consisting of symbols whose meanings remain undefined, ambiguous. That cultural form is never static or completely resolved, always subject to renegotiation. (Hale 1994, 25)

As a result of being caught in a three-century-long historical process of resistance and accommodation to a series of powerful and aggressive antagonists (the Spanish, the British, U.S. corporations, the Nicaraguan state in its various incarnations), Hale concludes, by the late 1960s the majority of *costeños* had developed a "contradictory consciousness," characterized by strong ethnic identity on the one hand and a paradoxical affinity for Anglo values, social and cultural practices, and institutions on the other (Hale 1994, 83, 219). They "did not come to espouse Anglo affinity because it was coercively imposed upon them," Hale argues. Rather, it developed "out of their efforts to secure subsistence, resist oppression, and assert or defend a separate identity while living under multiple spheres of inequity." Since *costeños* were virtually always in conflict with the west coast–based Nicaraguan state, by drawing close to North American values, practices, and institutions during periods of heavy U.S. influence and involvement they were able paradoxically to *strengthen* their ethnic identity and to *increase* their ability to resist the state. Such an "Anglo affinity" thus "deepened the militancy with which they asserted their right to be different"; their contradictory consciousness then "became central to their identity and to the logic of their collective action" (Hale 1994, 57, 202).

At various points during the preceding three centuries, that collective action had taken the form of overt resistance—most consistently to the mestizo-dominated state apparatus of Nicaragua. Also immediately pertinent was the fact that by the late 1970s the name-giving hero of the FSLN—General Augusto C. Sandino—had at best an ambiguous status on the coast. By working through local leaders, Sandino and his forces had been able to operate extensively in northeastern Nicaragua, opening up an extensive liberated zone along the Río Coco and establishing a headquarters in the Indian town of Bocay. But following his death, the Moravian church had launched a highly successful "redemption campaign" to vilify him and expunge his memory (Hale 1994, 53–56). To *costeños*, Sandino's campaign was remembered not as a paradigm for national liberation and reconstruction, but (as the Moravian church and the U.S. Marines agreed) as "the time of the bandits" that put an end to a golden age of steady wages and a reliable supply of consumer goods (Helms 1971, 32; Dennis 1981, 284).[31] In any case, *costeños* had had no immediate experience before July 1979 because the anti-Somoza insurrections had not reached to the coast (Helms 1971, 112–13; Bourgois in Walker 1985, 202, 208). With few exceptions, as Hale observes, *costeños* "passed the Sandinista insurrection against the Somoza dictatorship as detached observers of a distant political drama" (Hale 1994, 14).

Thus to the *costeños*—who moreover had not participated in the west coast's post-1950s "social earthquake" (as Vilas calls it) of rapid proletarianization, urbanization, and National Guard repression—the post-Somoza Sandinistas were not *compañeros guerrilleros* welcoming them to participate in the exalted project of national liberation and reconstruction, but merely the latest incarnation of the historically distrusted "Spanish" (Vilas 1989, 97). Thus to the *costeño* population, the arrival of the Sandinistas after July 1979 did not necessarily imply either liberation or the triumph of popular democracy over a fascist regime. Instead it looked more like merely the most recent episode in the "deeply ingrained internal colonial relations between Mestizo Nicaraguans and Miskitu people" (Hale 1994, 15). And to make matters worse, the post–World War II anti-communism espoused by the Moravian church (to which one out of every two *costeños* belonged by 1960) provided another set of reasons to fear the Marxist (hence implicitly atheistic) Sandinistas.

The Sandinista encounter with the east coast of their own country was thus destined to be riddled with paradox, contradiction, and conflict. Unfortunately for both parties, the Sandinistas proved slow in grasping the reasons why that was so.

THE SANDINISTAS AND ATLANTIC COAST LIFE AND CULTURE. The Sandinistas' learning process was complicated in the first instance by their ignorance of the social and cultural history of the Atlantic coast (an ignorance they shared with virtually all western Nicaraguans, regardless of political orientation). Some central features of their ideology and revolutionary practice and (increasingly) the pressures of counterrevolution presented other difficulties.

When the first FSLN cadres arrived on the coast after July 1979, they faced not only a cultural situation they were ill-prepared to understand, but also a daunting array of pressing social problems: an environment ravaged by decades of exploitation; minimal and poor-quality infrastructure (few schools or roads, and those in poor condition; virtually no public medical facilities except those provided by the Moravians); no industries except extractive ones; and illiteracy rates of 75 to 95 percent even in urban areas (Bourgois in Walker 1982, 304; Vilas 1989, 8).

Initial Sandinista intentions toward the Atlantic coast and its manifold problems appear to have been honorable. In its 1969 program statement, the FSLN had referred to the coast as "the region of the country that has permanently suffered the most iniquitous Yankee exploitation," whose mines in particular "have been nothing more than true concentration camps belonging to the Yankees." Promising to develop mines, forests, fishing, agriculture, and cattle growing in a humane fashion, the FSLN committed itself to stimulating and reinforcing "local cultural values" and to eliminating the "ignominious discrimination" suffered by coastal ethnic and racial groups (Gilbert and Block 1990, 8–10).

So far, so good. But as potential liberators and rebuilders of the devastated Atlantic coast, it turned out, the Sandinistas carried the burdens not only of the area's pressing immediate infrastructural and social needs and the historically hostile relationship between Atlantic and Pacific Nicaragua, but also of some dysfunctional elements of their own ideology.

Despite the idealism of the Sandinistas, Hale observes trenchantly, "Indians occupied an ambiguous and marginal position in revolutionary theory." Of all the Sandinista leadership, Jaime Wheelock and Ernesto Cardenal had the most to say about Indians, and to both of them, Indianness was "a cultural attribute, surviving from a more illustrious past," while political identity had to do essentially with notions of class and nation. Thus Atlantic coast people could become acceptably Sandinista revolutionary subjects "by sharing in Mestizo-defined nationalism and class-consciousness" (Hale 1994, 92–93).

The corollary of such cultural-ideological constructions of the Atlantic coast problem for most Sandinistas was (again in Hale's insightful analysis) a "deeply ingrained association of Miskitu consciousness, identity and demands with cultural backwardness." The Sandinistas' depreciation of Atlantic coast culture and their condescending confidence that they knew what was best for their Atlantic coast countrymen were thus two sides of the same coin.[32] As a result they "tended to exclude Miskitu people from the category of 'historical subjects' and to constitute a national identity nourished by an Indian past but headed resolutely toward a unified Mestizo future." The upshot was that "Miskitu people and Sandinista cadres locked themselves into cultural forms that were mutually antagonistic" (Hale 1994, 12, 35, 164–65).

Ultimately, then, the Sandinistas responded to the challenge of the Atlantic coast in rather generic ideological terms, as both Vilas and Hale have argued, rather than specific cultural-historical ones—subsuming it "under the general problem of exploited and oppressed classes and social groups, notwithstanding its peoples' socioeconomic, cultural, and historical specificities and their marked internal differentiation." This "reductionist and incomplete" viewpoint, Vilas observes, led the Sandinistas "to privilege the Costeños' most obvious material traits: They were poor farmers and mine and lumber company workers, exploited by foreign capital and merchants. At the same time, certain cooperative productive practices based on reciprocity . . . and certain characteristics of village life were interpreted as survivals of primitive communism" (Vilas 1989, 96, 115; cf. Hale 1994, 87).

The FSLN had also inherited, as Vilas notes, "the general deficit in Latin American revolutionary thinking on the 'Indian question,'" which together with the Sandinistas' ignorance of the history and culture of the coast led them to assume that all "Indians" were alike. "In 1980," reported Atlantic coast Creole nurse Alta Hooker, "I went to Managua to study anesthetics. The course was in Spanish, and as I normally speak English I found it quite tough going. And the other students were very different from me. It really shocked me when they asked if they needed passports to visit the Atlantic Coast and if we wore native costumes. They even asked why we wanted to live there! They knew next to nothing about the Atlantic Coast." Hooker's pain illustrated intimately and personally what Interior Minister Tomás Borge admitted several years later: the Sandinistas "had difficulty grasping the ethnic character of the Miskito problem" (Angel and Macintosh 1987, 46; Marcus 1985, 348–51).

Such divisions and animosities were the residue of centuries of conflicted history of which the Sandinistas were woefully ignorant. They could not be expected to yield to an ideologically based globalizing approach to "revolutionary integration" of the Atlantic coast, particularly when — as Vilas has noted — *costeños* tended to read "integration" within an indigenist discourse of the inevitable and "necessary" subordination of indigenous groups within national projects (Vilas 1989, 105). Thus Sandinismo embodied what Hale has called "a debilitating contradiction: a promise of equality, fused with the premise of Indians' cultural backwardness; a discourse of radical inclusiveness, in which the nation continued to be defined and controlled by Mestizos" (Hale 1994, 209).

The result of these many levels of confusion was that the *costeños* were not only unsympathetic to revolutionary movements, as the Sandinistas expected, but were suspicious and hostile. Hence the early days of Sandinista involvement on the coast brought fundamental historical, cultural, class, and ethnic problems starkly to the fore: after years of suffering at the hands of the west coast "Spanish," *costeños* were not about to trust a government dominated by them. Conversely, the "Spanish" were too inured to their generalized feelings of superiority to engage with the gritty facts of life on the coast. Worse yet, as Bourgois has pointed out, the few local "Spanish" who had occupied privileged positions during the Somoza years immediately "took advantage of the initial cultural disorientation of the Sandinistas to befriend them and to defame the Amerindian majority, who had always been their implacable class and ethnic enemies" (Bourgois in Walker 1982, 306, 312).

Despite their initial befuddlement, the Sandinista government plunged into working on the coastal enigma. Four months after the triumph, Minister of Culture Cardenal promised to open a Coast University, "so the Miskitu and Sumu can relearn the culture of their elders" (Hale 1994, 94). Two months later the government established the Nicaraguan Institute for the Atlantic Coast (INNICA). Several months later Decree No. 388 guaranteed that teaching in the first four primary grades would be done in both English and Miskito, and the Ministries of Culture and Education agreed to cooperate with INNICA to "preserve, rescue, and promote" the culture of the Miskitos, Sumus, and Ramas. Shortly after the first anniversary of the revolution, the Ministry of Education agreed to develop a special literacy program in English and the native languages of the coast.[33]

In August 1981, two years after the triumph, the Sandinista government attempted to clarify its policies on the Atlantic coast by issuing a Declaration of Principles of the Popular Sandinista Revolution on the Indian Communities. Its eight points proclaimed the territorial and political unity of the nation and Spanish as its official language; declared equal rights for all and a struggle against racial and cultural discrimination; supported local communities' own forms of organization, efforts to preserve local culture and language, and participation in national affairs; guaranteed rights to land while establishing national claim to all natural resources; and promised to improve living conditions. A year later, the government divided the coast into two Special Zones—a northern one dominated by Miskitos and a southern one in which Creoles and mestizos were the majority (Vilas 1989, 107–11).[34]

Both were necessary strategic moves, but at a practical level problems not only persisted but grew. The government invited additional confusion by superimposing its new institutions over the old Somoza-era ones. The dogmatic opposition of mid-level FSLN administrators to the church alienated Moravians (a large majority of the population), and Sandinista health programs threatened the church's historical monopoly in that area. Sandinistas used undue force to get people to join FSLN mass organizations, assigned Pacific coast mestizo officials to the region instead of qualified (and available) local Creoles, and traded openly in the conventional stereotypes of coastal people: "palm trees, may poles, lazy men, sexy women—primitive and backward people who needed to be civilized." To the Sandinistas, *costeños* equaled Indians equaled Miskitos equaled cultural backwardness and political naiveté. "The revolution was better able to understand the mountains than the jungle," as Vilas notes perceptively. "The mountains . . . [as in Omar Cabezas's much praised *testimonio*] were 'an immense crucible where the best of the FSLN were forged.' The jungle, in contrast, was synonymous with primitiveness—a mystery, the unknown, not to be trusted" (Vilas 1989, 116–18, 136).[35]

Although *costeños* had neither organized to oppose Somoza nor flocked to join the post-Somoza mass Sandinista organizations (of workers, or *campesinos*, or artists, for example), they were not complete strangers to tactics of organized opposition. Miskito Sam Pitts had organized an armed opposition following the "incorporation" moves of the Zelaya government and was killed by government troops. Other *costeños* organized against Zelaya's transfer of their lands to political cronies (Hale 1994, 46–57). Coastal workers (including many mestizo workers) had risen in repeated strikes against banana companies in the 1920s, but suffered such massive repression that they remained quiescent until the 1960s, when renewed economic distress on the coast and the civil rights movement in the United States, coupled with "nativization" of the Moravian church, provided both new stimuli and a new focus for organization.[36]

By 1974, some *costeños* had organized the *Alianza para el Progreso de Miskitos y Sumus* (ALPROMISU) to address problems created by the Somoza government's forestry policies and get better prices for agricultural products. ALPROMISU was pressured from both right and left: the government tried to co-opt its leaders (especially after the organization began to form bonds with the international indigenist community), and left-leaning students of the *Movimiento Estudiantil Costeño* in Managua denounced it as ineffectual. In the half-dozen years between the founding of ALPROMISU and 1979, several other *costeño* organizations appeared, including the National Association of Sumu Villages (SUKAWALA) and Southern Indigenous and Creole Communities (SICC). In early 1979, scant months before the triumph, a conference to plan the development of the coast helped to coalesce *costeños'* resentment against the central government (Bourgois in Walker 1982, 312; Dennis 1981, 288; Vilas 1989, 89; Hale 1994, 116).

Several factors combined to predict increasing militancy among Miskitos and other *costeños* at this time: (1) young Miskito leaders had the required energy, organizational skills, and political ambition; (2) the Sandinista state's formal commitment to cultural democracy forced it to be somewhat permissive with regard to some coastal issues, and its drive for new national cohesion (especially with respect to U.S. imperialism) caused it to behave in provocative ways with regard to other coastal demands; and (3) as the months passed, U.S. intervention directed toward sustaining and exacerbating ethnic tensions rose markedly (Hale 1994, 201).

Organized challenge to Sandinista policy on the coast emerged only weeks after the triumph, when Miskitos in northern Zelaya demanded that the government create an ethnic-based mass organization. In November 1979, President Ortega arrived to supervise the dissolution of ALPROMISU and the formation of MISURASATA, whose goals included "recovering and promoting our culture," "reconstruction of our history," and (surprisingly) "learning Spanish." Granted a seat on the ruling National Council of State, MISURASATA was nevertheless in conflict with the FSLN from the beginning, and continually raised its demands as the months passed (e.g., for an entire set of mass organizations on the Atlantic coast to parallel the putatively national FSLN ones; for absolute control over a third of national territory despite the fact that MISURASATA represented only Miskitos, who constituted only about 25 percent of the coastal population) (Bourgois in Walker 1985, 202; Vilas 1989, 122–27; Rivera in Blakemore 1988, 102). By February 1980 tension was so high that when Sandinista soldiers broke into a literacy campaign closing ceremony to arrest MISURASATA leaders, gunfire ensued and eight people died. Later, SICC members objected to the presence of Cuban advisors, teachers, and doctors. Street demonstrations followed (Vilas 1989, 143ff.; Bourgois in Walker 1985, 203).

Almost simultaneously, Ronald Reagan was elected to the presidency after promising to remove the Sandinistas from power, and the Atlantic coast struggle shortly thereafter took on new complexity. Through a variety of

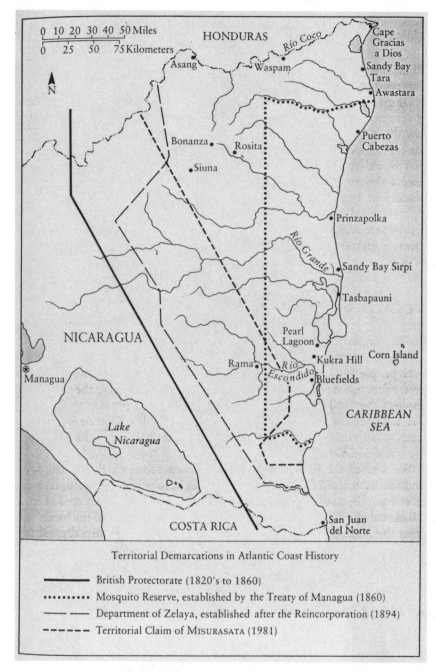

Territorial Demarcations in Atlantic Coast History

― British Protectorate (1820's to 1860)

•••••••• Mosquito Reserve, established by the Treaty of Managua (1860)

— — Department of Zelaya, established after the Reincorporation (1894)

- - - - - Territorial Claim of MISURASATA (1981)

Territorial Demarcations in Atlantic Coast History. (Reproduced from Hale, *Resistance and Contradiction*, 1994; used by permission of Stanford University Press) means ranging from domestic and international propaganda, to buying off MISURASATA leaders and paying their office expenses, to funding opposition military operations, the Reagan administration set about making life more difficult for the Sandinistas on the Atlantic coast by manipulating historic cultural, racial, and ethnic divisions.[37]

A critical turning point came in early 1981 when the Sandinistas arrested the MISURASATA leadership, all of whom were set free soon thereafter except for Steadman Fagoth, suspected of having been a Somoza informer. A succession of arrests, accusations, counteraccusations, and rumors followed. By late autumn, Fagoth had formed the rival organization MISURA, established military training camps in Honduras, and begun military raids on infrastructure, local institutions, and social service personnel. Tension rose still further as the United States initiated what became a months-long series of military maneuvers (Falcon View, Big Pine I and II) on the Honduran coast, and mounted a disinformation campaign that charged the Sandinistas with cultural genocide, torture, and massive human rights violations (Vilas 1989, 128–29, 145–48; Bourgois in Walker 1985, 204, 213–14; Hale 1994, 77–81, 116).[38]

In December 1981, nearly a year into the Reagan era, INNICA's William Ramírez, while condemning U.S. aggression, admitted the existence of a "strong ethnocentric tradition" on both coasts. But he reaffirmed that Nicaragua's ethnic groups had a right to organize and defend their interests, and said the Sandinista government considered it "fundamental" that every such group have the possibility to "develop its cultural and artistic expressions." The dream of imperialism, he said, was to separate the Atlantic coast from the rest of Nicaragua, but "that we will never permit" (*esto no lo permitiremos jamás*) (William Ramírez 1982b, 4).

In January 1982, the Sandinista government made what proved to be the politically and culturally fateful decision to evacuate the entire civilian population from what had by then become the Atlantic coast war zone in order (so the argument went) to remove them from the danger of military cross fire. Approximately half the population crossed into Honduras as refugees, and the rest were taken to a new settlement area called Tasba Pri—five villages located about forty miles west of Puerto Cabezas—and formed into agricultural production cooperatives. Unfortunately, the cooperatives failed when prices fell and people sought better paying wage work nearby.

The manifold cultural problems and contradictions of Tasba Pri also acted to exacerbate political and economic ones. Some Sandinista troops sent to defend the area engaged in what human rights investigators called "cultural disrespect"; houses were built *for* families to whom it was important that the man of the family built his own house; house lots were too small to accommodate the fruit trees that were symbolically important in the culture; material and economic scarcity prohibited the gift exchanges tradition required; conferring individual land titles upon Tasba Pri residents, one team of investigators observed, "implied distinctions among neighbors and a concept of ownership that were not part of traditional community life."[39]

The social and cultural losses associated with returning Tasba Pri residents to their home areas three years later were also high. The village of Waspan, which formerly had had substantial buildings, a bank, government offices, a clinic, schools, a Catholic church, and several Moravian churches, was now almost completely overgrown by the jungle. Wooden buildings were badly damaged or destroyed; the ball field was ringed by rusted metal bleachers; only the charred frame of the Catholic church remained.[40]

Whether the Sandinistas could have achieved a harmonious incorporation of a multicultural, multi-ethnic, historically alienated, and hostile Atlantic coast had they known and foreseen more (and had the United States not manipulated the situation as it did) cannot be known. Indeed, at the end of five costly and tortured years, not much *was* known, or clear. Nevertheless, it had become increasingly clear that the only culturally and politically workable solution was some form of autonomy for the coast.

Ever since the early stages of the conflict, the Sandinistas had feared both the fact of separatism itself and its political import as a symbol of the durability of U.S. imperialism in Nicaragua. What they therefore sought in the autonomy process that was finally forced upon them, as Hale has observed, was "an autonomy limited enough to safeguard state prerogatives but expansive enough to engender participation, a measure of legitimacy, a chance to rule by hegemony rather than coercion" (Hale 1994, 219).

Plans for autonomy began to be developed toward the end of 1984. In early December, the government named a national commission to plan for autonomy, and conceded publicly that "the ethnic groups of the Atlantic Coast must enjoy special rights of autonomy that guarantee their ethnic identity." Simultaneously, MISURASATA called for the government to recognize "the Miskito, Sumo, and Rama populations as sovereign indigenous peoples . . . with the natural right to freely determine their own political economic, social and cultural development in accord with their values and traditions."[41] Conciliatory policy guidelines issued six months later reaffirmed national unity, called for the creation of autonomous regions with their own governments, and reasserted the importance of the struggle against racism and ethnocentrism, but also made its own political point by linking those two universally condemned -isms to separatism.[42]

Even though an independent commission judged the plan to offer "more possibility to achieve more self-determination than the Atlantic Coast had ever had," the Miskito organizations repudiated it as autocratic, whereupon the national autonomy commission turned its work over to northern and southern regional commissions. Moreover, the very presence of the autonomy commissions called into existence other indigenous organizations with their own agendas and renewed activity within existing ones. Creoles in the south advocated disfranchisement of mestizos not born on the coast, and the Sumo organization SUKAWALA feared that the small number of Sumos would allow them to be overwhelmed by the larger ethnic groups. The similarly outnumbered Ramas, on the other hand, wanted only to be let alone. The numerically dominant mestizos (over 60 percent of the entire coastal population) had no organization at all.[43] Even as these discussions were under way, however, the United States Congress was approving $100 million more aid for the contra war against the Sandinista government—a move which guaranteed that none of the parties to the Atlantic coast negotiations would have the leisure to work out their differences among themselves (LeoGrande in Walker 1987, 202–27).

By the time of the 1989–90 electoral campaign between Daniel Ortega and Violeta Chamorro, the autonomy law had been passed. It recognized "the right of the Atlantic Coast communities to preserve their cultural identity, their languages, art and culture . . . [and] to live and organize themselves according to their legitimate cultural and historical traditions." It specified Spanish as the official language of the Nicaraguan state, and it recognized "the languages of the Communities of the Atlantic Coast" as official languages within the Autonomous Regions. It was the responsibility of the Autonomous Regions "to promote national culture, as well as the study, preservation, promotion, development, and dissemination of the different cultures and traditions of the Atlantic coast's communities."[44]

Significant as it might have become in time, the step was too little and (as it turned out) too late. The Atlantic coast was virtually a disaster area: infrastructure destroyed by years of the contra war, local markets fallen apart, increased dependency of rural areas upon the already overtaxed facilities and services of the small cities, rural population crowding into the cities, agricultural activities in outlying areas virtually at a halt, rivers contaminated and resources exhausted (Vilas 1989, 181). Moreover, the Chamorro government that came to power after the elections of 1990 was determined to roll back as many as possible of the economic, political, and cultural changes made by the Sandinistas, including the autonomous status of the Atlantic coast.

PHASING OUT THE MINISTRY OF CULTURE

Paradoxically, an additional casualty of the manifold pressures of the contra war was the Ministry of Culture itself. The ministry's ideological, organizational, and operational problems went hand-in-hand with the budgetary and other crises of the years beyond 1982.

During the Sandinista government's first several years, the ministry's budget had risen rapidly (although it never claimed more than about 0.5 percent of the national budget): from about ten million *córdobas* for the final six months of 1979 to more than fifty million for 1981 and to nearly eighty-four million in 1983. By 1987 it had risen to 1.6 billion, but hyperinflation more than eliminated any positive effect the increase might otherwise have had.[45] During most of those years, moreover, the ministry had allocated 40 to 50 percent of its entire budget to administration and its sports program, so that little remained for the cultural activities it otherwise claimed were so central to its overall project.[46]

By early 1988, the ninth year of the revolution and the last of the Reagan presidency, the costs of U.S. policy were visible on every hand in the daily life of Managua, where nearly a third of the country's population lived—much of it driven there by the pressures of the contra war.

On a hill above the city, in the middle-class neighborhood of Pancasán, $20,000 Toyota land cruisers were parked in front of some of the most comfortable houses set on lawns tended by gardeners. Below, the lone white tower of the Bank of America stood in the open fields of what before the earthquake of 1972 was the center of Managua. Early in the morning in Pancasán, one could hear on one side the traffic from the highway to Masaya; on the other, behind the rows of middle-class homes, roosters crowed from the backyards of rural people, displaced by the war, living in tiny wooden shacks with dirt or cement floors, watching Spanish-dubbed Disney cartoons, Mexican or Brazilian *telenovelas*, or news of the peace talks and new contra atrocities on the *Sistema Sandinista de Televisión*. A little further to the northwest, in the Huembes market—built before the contra war heated up and there was still money for such luxuries—women were beginning another day of cooking tortillas on wood-fired cement stoves while vendors in stalls and on the sidewalk spread out a grab bag of local traditional and imported commercial products: herb remedies and Tylenol, candles and Eveready batteries, *frijoles* and Corn Flakes.

The economic results and contradictions of the war stood out sharply at the Huembes market. For North Americans living in Nicaragua there were piles of fresh fruits and vegetables at low prices: a pineapple that cost two dollars in the United States could be bought for the equivalent of about forty cents. But for Nicaraguan people, the prices were very high; maids with their own children to support were working for 60,000–90,000 *córdobas* (equal to a dozen or so pineapples) a week; a librarian at the National Library with a salary of maybe two to three times that was paying 400,000 *córdobas* for blue jeans. And rationed basic necessities (rice, *frijoles*, sugar, soap, oil, coffee) sometimes were available only on the black market at prohibitive prices.

A few of the economic strains could be minimized or avoided by some, but others could be avoided by no one: most days Pancasán had water only between midnight and 6:00 A.M. (there was little money to buy repair parts for Managua's aging water system, installed by the U.S. Marines before they departed in 1933).[47] For many weeks electric power was cut off every day for two to five hours (because of a similar repair parts problem, complicated by the dynamiting of high-tension towers by contra troops on the Honduran border). Meanwhile, the black market exchange rate was rising relentlessly. Twenty- and fifty-*córdoba* bills (the latter carrying Sandinista founding hero Carlos Fonseca's picture) were being overprinted with three zeroes to keep up with inflation.

A year later, the economic news was even worse. National debt had risen 50 percent in four years, to nearly $8 billion, the gross domestic product stood at a negative 9 percent, and real incomes were below 1950 levels. In the space of four months or so, the official exchange rate (on the new *córdoba*) had moved up from 2,300 to 6,000 to the dollar. Officially the rate of inflation during 1988 was listed at 31,000 percent, but was estimated by some to approach 50,000 percent, so that state employees' salaries at the end of the year were worth only a little more than 6 percent of what they had been at the beginning. Fighting to turn the curves downward, the government cut the national budget by nearly half.[48]

Amid such circumstances, the cultural programs the Sandinista government had launched in 1979 were in serious difficulty. The National Library's book purchase budget was zero. New parks—named for heroes and martyrs of the revolution—stood empty and weed-grown. The cultural supplement to the Sandinista newspaper *Barricada* was cut from sixteen to eight pages and began to appear irregularly. At the tiny National Museum there was scarcely money for office supplies, and its skeleton of a staff had access only to one ancient jeep that stayed out of commission most of the time for lack of parts or gasoline.

Attending performances of traditional music or dance at night was complicated by the lack of public transportation, and those who managed to do so frequently sat for prolonged periods in a darkened theater waiting for the electricity to come back on. ENIGRAC's phonograph records of Nicaraguan music were still available in record shops, but few had money to buy them or machines to play them on. Consequently it was cheap radios rather than expensive phonograph records that were shaping popular musical tastes, and the radio stations one heard through the windows while walking through the neighborhoods were playing Latin American and North American popular music instead of Monimbó *marimba* player Elias Palacios or the Mejía Godoy brothers.[49]

The final blow to the Ministry of Culture came early in 1988: as a result of a general budget-cutting policy of *compactación*, the ministry disappeared, and its functions were parceled out to the Ministry of Education and the ASTC. As a face-saving gesture, Ernesto Cardenal was made head of a new National Cultural Council. Ministry of Culture officials were careful to explain the dismembering on budgetary grounds, and to deny that it had anything to do with the ministry's own ineffectiveness, but the conclusion that the ministry had slowly done itself in was almost inescapable.[50] Later in 1988, the ASTC itself was dissolved and replaced by a new Institute of Arts and Culture, whose state sponsorship made it in effect a new (if smaller) Ministry of Culture (Beverley and Zimmerman 1990, 103, 109).

. . . .

Out of the midst of the beautiful Lake Nicaragua spring two magnificent pyramids, clad in the softest
and richest green, all flecked with shadow and sunshine, whose summits pierce the billowy clouds.
They look so isolated from the world and its turmoil — so tranquil, so dreamy, so steeped in slumber
and eternal repose. What a home one might make among their shady forests, their sunny slopes, their
breezy dells, after he had grown weary of the toil, anxiety and unrest of the bustling, driving world.
— Mark Twain, upon seeing Ometepe Island in Lake Nicaragua, 1866

. . . .

The relations of power whereby one portion of humanity can select, value, and collect the pure
products of others need to be criticized and transformed. — James Clifford, *The Predicament of Culture*

. . . .

The origins of museums can be traced a long way back, and their
ideological roots run deep: to the fifth century B.C. treasury of
the Athenians at Adelphi, to the great collections of the Hellen-
istic period two centuries later, to the libraries of Rome such as
the one at Hadrian's villa, and thence to the monastic libraries and medieval
church collections, and the sumptuous Renaissance collections of the Medicis
and others. Eleven years before Columbus sailed for the New World, Pope
Sixtus IV created a museum of antiquities on the Capitoline Hill to house indigenous cultural artifacts Catholic missionaries were collecting even as they
destroyed the cultures themselves (Miller 1974, 21).

It was thus virtually inevitable that in the post-conquest colonization process Latin America would be relieved of its ancient cultural artifacts. The
conquistador Gaspar de Espinosa looted graves in Panama as early as 1519
(Lange and Stone 1984, 30). The splendid feathered headdress of Moctezuma

273

now exhibited in the Museum of Anthropology and History in Mexico City is a replica; the original was taken back to Spain by Cortez himself and ended up in a museum in Vienna, as both a spoil of war and a dramatic symbol of what James Clifford has called "the restless desire and power of the West to collect the world" (Clifford 1988, 196).

In the modern era, museums proliferated rapidly. The first special purpose museum buildings appeared at the end of the seventeenth century, on the eve of what became a great burst of museological activity (Crook 1972, 19–32). Museum building reached a crescendo in the late nineteenth century, when the development of national museum collections became one of the less visible but nevertheless important aspects of state formation and expansion. Especially in North America and western Europe, that development was characterized by a profound political-cultural irony: rich and powerful countries were assembling museum collections gathered from subject peoples whose cultures they viewed as inferior to their own and whose only value consisted in having made "contributions" to superior ones. As larger countries went about filling their cultural storehouses, small and vulnerable countries unfortunately had little power to protect themselves against losing the tangible record of their past.

Previous chapters have sketched some of the cultural transformations associated with conquest, colonization, elite-oriented modernization, and "benign" entrepreneurial intervention, and have tallied some of the consequent cultural costs for indigenous and other non-elite people. This chapter examines the process by which another set of actors — putatively objective and disinterested scientific investigators, government officials, museum curators, sharp-eyed dealers in antiquities, purely mercenary grave robbers, ordinary people who needed a day's work — scavenged among the relics of those decimated, dispersed, disorganized, and essentially defenseless people, shipping cartloads and boatloads of artifacts back to the highest bidder in a highly competitive market in which the legal tender could include cash, social and political status, or professional standing.

The story of the expropriation of Nicaragua's archaeological treasures through such processes illuminates some aspects of the cultural politics of great-power expansiveness, of arguments over human origins and cultural development, and of an emerging ideology of science. In turn, it raises larger political and ethical questions: Upon what grounds, if any, may a nation-state lay claim to artifacts that predate the state itself? Whose interests, defined how and by whom, are most likely to be served by the enterprise of cultural conservation and preservation? And what are the larger social, political, and cultural implications of those "contested encodings of past and future" that inform all such enterprises (Clifford 1988, 218)?

The mid-nineteenth century colonial adventures of European nations offered especially attractive opportunities (as well as political and cultural inducements) to expand the holdings of their fledgling museums. The will of Sir Hans Sloane, whose collections became a founding cornerstone of the British Museum, asserted that what he had collected over a lifetime "[tends] many ways to the manifestation of the glory of God, [and] the confutation of Atheism and its consequences." Such collections served as warrants of imperial power, as concrete evocations of the remote cultures being dominated, and as measures of the value of the "higher" home culture to which the dominated cultures had made "contributions." Far into the nineteenth century, the British Museum's director still insisted — with inexorable logic — that his staff wear top hats whenever they went into the galleries (Crook 1972, 47; Miller 1974, 259).

The intersection of culture and power was especially evident in the sacking of Kumasi, capital of the Ashanti region, by a punitive military expedition led by Britain's Sir Garnet Wolseley in 1867. In Jeanette Greenfield's recent account, "the capital and . . . palace were taken by Wolseley and ransacked of every valuable object: the king's sword, pure hammered gold masks . . . massive breastplates . . . caps mounted in solid gold . . . bags of gold dust and nuggets . . . calabashes worked in silver and gold, embroidered and woven silks. . . . The town of Kumasi and the palace were then destroyed by fire" (Greenfield 1989, 139).

Although perhaps an especially egregious example, Kumasi was only one among many such sites, relieved of their moveable antiquities in what Greenfield calls a "spirit of intense competition and rivalry" among the major European museums. Scores of expeditions fanned out to Chinese Turkestan and elsewhere in Asia, to Greece and Egypt, to Africa and Latin America, to the Pacific, to North America. Augmented by the efforts of wealthy private collectors, scientific investigators, missionaries, military adventurers, and grave robbers, those expeditions swelled the storerooms and exhibit rooms of the British Museum, the Louvre, the Vatican Ethnological Museum, the Smithsonian Institution, Harvard's Peabody Museum of Archaeology and Ethnology, and scores of others (Greenfield 1989, 106ff.).

Inevitably, intense competition developed among individual collectors, museums, and countries. The French and British fought it out in Greece, and news of the epic rivalry of Bernardino Drouetti and the British Museum's Giovanni Battista Belzoni in Egypt was followed avidly (Miller 1974, 198–201). In the process, magnificent cultural treasures were carted off: the Elgin marbles, the head of Ramses II, the Black Obelisk of Shalmaneser III, the

Reception of the Nineveh Sculptures at the British Museum. (Reproduced from Miller, *That Noble Cabinet*, 1974; used by permission of Ohio University Press)

Koh-i-noor diamond and the Benin bronzes to the British Museum; the frieze of the temple of Aegina in Greece to Bavaria; the bust of Queen Nefertiti to Berlin; Assyrian sculptures from Khorsabad to the Louvre.

Occupying a special niche in this intensely competitive cultural-political process were the specifically ethnological museums established in Europe after the 1830s. From the Renaissance onward, museums had focused principally upon Greek sculpture, but as geologists (such as Charles Lyell, who published the first volume of his epochal *Principles of Geology* in 1830) and archaeologists (such as Jacques Boucher de Perthes in the late 1830s) forced a reconsideration of accepted notions of human origins, museums came under pressure to shift some of their attention. By the time of Darwin's *Origin of Species* in 1859, ethnological collecting was a wave waiting to break.

Ethnological museums had opened as early as 1837 in Leiden and St. Petersburg, and 1841 in Copenhagen. The advent of the "museum age" in the 1870s saw the opening of new ones in Rome, Bremen, Leipzig, Hamburg, Berlin, Dresden, Amsterdam, Rotterdam, the Hague, Stockholm, and Oslo. Many were well funded by the state; some were backed by wealthy private collectors such as Alphonse Pinart in France. The new German empire committed major resources to the Prussian Museum für Völkerkunde. Guided by Adolf Bastian, the founding father of German ethnology, the museum opened in 1886 in Berlin in the world's first major museum building devoted

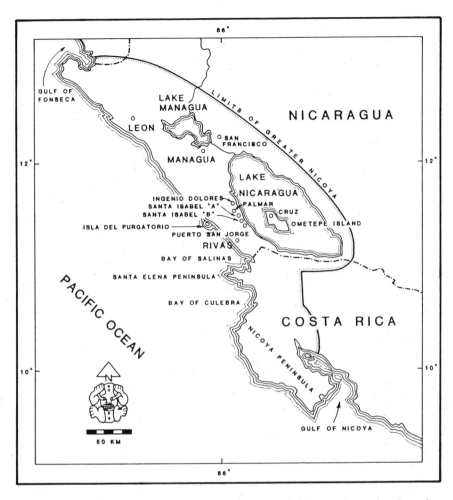

Archaeological sites in western Nicaragua. (From Lange and Stone, eds., *Archaeology of Lower Central America*, 1984; used by permission of School of American Research)

to anthropology and ethnography. By the end of the century it had assembled the largest ethnographic collection in the world (Cole 1985, 9–90).

The advent and growth of anthropological, ethnological, and archaeological investigations in Latin America during the second quarter of the nineteenth century provided yet another focus for the museums. The first Mayan discoveries were reported in 1822; the major explorations of John Lloyd Stephens and Frederick Catherwood took place between 1839 and 1842; and the Mexican expeditions of Henry Christy and Edward Burnett Tylor followed in 1856 (Kardiner and Preble 1961, 50–68; Stuart and Stuart 1983, 40).[1]

Such developments were a special threat to the cultures of small, poor countries such as Nicaragua, which usually lacked any museum at all, had few if any native archaeologists or ethnographers, and had enacted no protective legislation of any kind. Although located outside the pre-conquest "high culture" areas to the north and south that drew far more attention, Nicaragua nevertheless had abundant cultural treasures (Lange and Stone 1984, 165–94; Lange et al. 1992). Those treasures came to the world's attention at the fortuitous conjunction of Nicaragua's leap to strategic importance as an interoceanic route following the discovery of gold in California in 1848, the advent of the "museum age," and the emergence of ethnology and anthropology as scientific disciplines.

THE NICARAGUAN HARVEST

The British traveler John Cockburn returned from a voyage to Central America in the early 1730s with two pieces of bark cloth given to him by Nicaraguan Indians. From one he made himself a blanket, and from the other a jacket. "This serviceable Gift," he said, "was much diminished before I came to England, having given Part of it away to several Persons, to whom I had Obligations, and who desired to have Pieces of it to keep by them as a Curiosity." Also among Cockburn's Nicaraguan *collectanea* was the hair of an Indian woman whose head wound he had helped to dress. "She desired me to accept of her Head of Hair," he said, "which I had cut off, and which, in her Opinion, was no contemptible Present. Indeed, I was very well pleas'd with the Reward, and it being a Curiosity of the Kind, I was afterwards at a great deal of Pains to preserve it among other little Things . . . and have brought it with me to England. This Hair is very long and of great Strength, is of a Jet Black, and both to the Sight and to the Touch differs much from that of other Women." Cockburn's collection of Nicaraguan artifacts was swelled a bit more when, abandoned by his Indian guides and despondent, he found a string of tigers' teeth left by Indians on the beach. "These Teeth I have brought home with my other little Things," he reported (Cockburn 1735, 181, 187, 203).

One gathers that Cockburn's random collecting was complexly motivated: by curiosity, social obligation (snippets of bark cloth as boon from afar), practicality (bark cloth jacket), admiration for local people and culture (the woman's generosity and pride), embryonic scientific interest (tigers' teeth and the hair's tensile strength), and perhaps even sexual titillation (the hair's sensual appeal). Those motives, it turned out, were highly predictive of those that would inform the more systematic collecting of museums and others a century later.

Nicaraguan antiquities in fact caught the attention of Captain Edward

Belcher of the British Navy as early as 1838, the very year in which Nicaragua finally became an independent state following the collapse of the Central American Federation. Belcher wanted to go to Momotombito Island in Lake Managua, where he had heard there were "many objects worthy of attention, particularly the idols of the aborigines," but a too-small boat and bad weather forced him to abandon his plan (Belcher [1843] 1970, 1:165). About a year later, the Austrian explorer Emanuel von Friedrichsthal apparently became the first collector to actually ship a stone monolith from Nicaragua to a museum: a six-foot tall, half-ton statue from Chontales that he sent to the Museum für Völkerkunde in Vienna (Taylor and Meighan 1978, 395; Nowotny 1956, 1961).[2]

Later institutional collectors were less deterred by weather than Belcher and far less content with a single artifact than Friedrichsthal. Thus during the years between independence and the end of the nineteenth century, Nicaragua steadily lost its cultural treasures to collectors dispatched by major museums—especially the Smithsonian Institution, the British Museum, the Peabody Museum, and various Swedish state museums.[3]

With regard to the collection of cultural artifacts from Central America, the Smithsonian Institution was founded at a propitious moment. The Smithson bequest of 1829 came seven years after the initial Maya discoveries, and the Smithsonian's doors opened not many months before the rush of California-bound gold seekers brought intense attention to the region. Although the Smithsonian's first secretary, Princeton physicist Joseph Henry, was oriented primarily toward research and had little interest in forming permanent museum collections, the appointment of zoologist Spencer Baird as assistant secretary in 1850 altered the institution's focus. Baird was a born collector who adopted the strategy of building collections in order to force Congress to establish a national museum to replace the meager "National Cabinet of Curiosities" housed in the Patent Office. By 1863, Joseph Henry himself was soliciting the aid of government officers, travelers, and others in building the Smithsonian's collections of "facts and materials" on races inhabiting the continent of the Americas. Such volunteer efforts swelled the collections from fewer than a thousand specimens to more than thirteen thousand in 1873, and at the close of the 1876 centennial exposition Baird urged foreign governments to deposit more than four hundred tons of exhibits (some forty boxcar loads) in the Smithsonian's permanent collection (Cole 1985, 1–90).

Unfortunately, the close of the Philadelphia exposition also led to a severe reduction in federal funding for the Smithsonian rather than to the increased support Baird sought. It was a particularly unpropitious time for such austerity; New York's American Museum of Natural History (1869), backed by

Cornelius Vanderbilt (part of whose fortune was extracted from his Nicaraguan transit route concession) and others of the city's elite, offered serious competition in addition to that of the European museums.

Unable to match the other museums' funding or modern facilities, or to support trained collectors in the field, the Smithsonian relied heavily upon volunteer collaborators. An important early one was E. George Squier, the publication of whose *Ancient Monuments of the Mississippi Valley* (1848) had inaugurated the Smithsonian's "Contributions to Knowledge" series and established Squier as "the first authoritative voice in American archaeology" (Patterson and Stanton 1959). The appointment of Squier as U.S. chargé d'affaires in Central America in 1849 offered the Smithsonian a splendid opportunity to acquire Nicaraguan artifacts, since Squier's principal duty—to reconnoiter the strategically coveted Nicaraguan canal route—would necessarily carry him through areas of the country potentially rich in archaeological interest. When the *Correo del Istmo de Nicaragua* (León) reported on 1 June 1849 that Squier had been named to the post, its editor was already aware that he was "dedicated to the antiquities of the Indians." [4]

In addition to technical competence, Squier had an animating sense of nationalistic mission. A few months after he arrived in Nicaragua, he told Secretary Henry he hoped that a National Archaeological Museum "worthy of our age and country" would be formed in the United States. "It is a fact not at all creditable to us," he said, "that we have no public collection of this kind worthy to be mentioned . . . while some of the museums of Europe are really rich in relics of aboriginal American art." The Louvre's catalog of American antiquities, he noted, ran to 130 pages. [5] Accompanied by a competent illustrator, Squier was determined not only to document Nicaragua's ancient monuments, but also to retrieve some of them for the Smithsonian. [6]

Squier saw his first small prehistoric idol on a streetcorner in the Jalteva section of Granada—the so-called *piedra de la boca* (stone with a mouth). Elsewhere in the city several others stood on corners, including *El Chiflador* (the whistler). Although it was now much broken, local people recounted that "when it was perfect, its mouth was open, into which the blowing of the wind made a mournful, whistling sound, exciting suspicions that it was the incarnation of one of the ancient 'demonios' of the Indians. The pious padres demolished it in consequence" (Squier 1852, 1:203–4). [7] Some days later, Squier encountered another monument on the plaza in León. "The face was perfect," he noted, "with the exception of a part of the mouth. . . . The whole expression was grave and serene." He immediately "procured" the statue, sent it to the Smithsonian, and resolved to find more (Squier 1852, 1:301–2).

Responding to Squier's inquiries, an old priest told him there were many statues on the islands of Ometepe and Zapatero in Lake Nicaragua. [8] When

Piedra de la boca statue (From Squier, *Nicaragua: Its People, Scenery, Monuments, and the Proposed Canal*, 1852)

Monument taken from plaza in León by Squier and sent to Smithsonian. (From Squier, *Nicaragua: Its People, Scenery, Monuments, and the Proposed Canal*, 1852)

Squier confided his interest in such antiquities to community leaders of the Indian municipality of Subtiava (adjacent to León), they asked him—appropriately enough—about the condition of Indians in the United States ("I was ashamed to tell them the truth," he reported). Subtiava leader Simon Roqué told Squier about some idols his ancestors had buried, which he offered to give him if the location were kept secret. Within the next few days, four idols arrived at Squier's residence, and were forthwith dispatched to the Smithsonian (Squier 1852, 1:203–4, 280, 302, 318–19, 325).[9]

Presently Squier heard that a small group of other statues hidden in the forest between León and the coast were still visited by local natives "for the per-

Nineteenth-century illustration of Ometepe Island. (Reproduced from Rosengarten, *Freebooters Must Die!*, 1976)

formance of dances and other rites pertaining to their primitive religion."[10] Taken there by a local guide, Squier discovered the remains of what had apparently been a large (60'×200') platform scattered with fragments of stone statues—evidence, he judged, of "systematic violence, not only anciently, at the ... Conquest, but subsequently, and within a very few years."[11]

By late July, Squier had arranged an expedition to the island of Momotombito (which Belcher had wanted to visit earlier), whence came the idol he had seen in the plaza at León (Squier 1852, 1:301–2). In a forty-foot bongo (or bungo) he set out, accompanied by a native guide, the editor of *El Correo del Istmo*, and the American consul from León. After walking through fragments of pottery and stone vessels on the beach and cutting through tall grass and shrubs with machetes, they came to an open square surrounded by perhaps fifty fallen statues. "Amongst the few still entire," Squier said, "was one of large size, and which a party, sent by the English Consul, had a few years before endeavored to carry away for the British Museum, but after getting it part of the way to the lake, had abandoned it in despair" (Squier 1852, 1:303–

Monument taken from Zapatero by Squier for Smithsonian Institution. (From Squier, *Nicaragua: Its People, Scenery, Monuments, and the Proposed Canal*, 1852)

17). Clearing a road and cutting small trees to use as skids, the party moved one large statue and a "colossal head" to the boat. The former was sent to Realejo and shipped to the Smithsonian.[12]

Other expeditions followed—to the hills near Lake Nihapa, where rumor had it that there were rock paintings and an ancient Indian temple cut into the rocks; to Masaya to look for rock inscriptions; to the island of Pensacola, where they found several statues much better preserved than the ones from Momotombito; to the island of Zapatero, where they saw ancient mounds and fifteen nearly perfect statues. Pieces from these expeditions were also sent to the Smithsonian.[13] On Zapatero Island Squier was powerfully moved when he saw one of the ancient idols raised upright again. Digging a hole to receive the lower end of the nine-foot-high pedestal, he and his helpers passed ropes beneath it and heaved with all their strength. No sooner was it upright, he reported, than "our helpers gave a great shout, and forming a double ring around it, commenced an outrageous dance, in the pauses of which they made the old woods ring again with [their shouts]."[14]

The Pensacola statues were truly extraordinary, and Squier's sensitivity to the cultural politics of finding and raising some of them upright again is evident. Alternately scolding his native helpers and urging them on with

Monument being sketched by illustrator for Squier's expedition on Zapatero Island. (From Squier, *Nicaragua: Its People, Scenery, Monuments, and the Proposed Canal,* 1852)

offers of extra wages and homemade liquor, he succeeds in unearthing several statues buried during the conquest to protect them from "Catholic zealots." Later Squier stumbles across another massive monument, almost completely buried. Two hours' work by his men bring to view a specimen unlike any he has seen, with "an extraordinary and forbidding aspect." "As it stood in the pit," he said, "with its monstrous head rising above the ground, with its fixed stony gaze, it seemed like some gray monster just emerging from the depths of the earth, at the bidding of the wizard-priest of an unholy religion. My men stood back, and more than one crossed himself as he muttered to his neighbor, '*es el diablo!*' 'it is the devil!' I readily comprehended the awe with which it might be regarded by the devotees of the ancient religion, when the bloody priest daubed the lapping tongue with the yet palpitating hearts of his human victims!"

The multivalent and contradictory resonances of the statue itself (gray monster of the nether world versus the palpable present, "unholy religion" versus Christianity, religious belief versus scientific skepticism, contemporary Nicaraguan natives versus pre-conquest ancestors) extend to the small celebration once the statue is exhumed and upright. "With bleeding hands, and completely bedaubed with mud," Squier reported, "I had at last the satisfaction to lead off in a '*Viva por la niña antigua!* — Hurrah for the old baby!' I am not quite sure but I took a drop of the aguardiente myself, while the shower was passing. Pedro and his crew responded by a '*Vivan los Americanos del*

Monument from Island of Pensacola.
(From Squier, *Nicaragua: Its People,
Scenery, Monuments, and the Proposed
Canal*, 1852)

Norte!' which . . . meant that they 'wouldn't object to another drink.' This
was given of course, whereupon Pedro insinuated that '*Los Americanos son
diablos!*' — 'The Americans are devils'; which remark, however, Pedro meant
as a compliment" (Squier 1852, 2:34–39).

Reflecting on the fate of the antiquities as he wrote up his findings for the
U.S. government, Squier recalled his reading of the *cronista* Oviedo's account
of the forcible conversion of Nicaraguan Indians by Fray Bobadilla, who got
permission from the local *cacique* to destroy the idols of "the spacious and
sumptuous temple which the Indians, under the special direction of the devil,
had erected there," and to replace them with a cross. He battered the faces of
the idols and would have burned them all, but "during the night some did
take them away and [bury] them, so that they could not be found." It was
"not unlikely," Squier judged, "that those are the very idols exhumed for me
by the Indians of Subtiava, two of which, after doubling the Horn, now frown
down . . . from the west corridor of the Smithsonian Institution!"

Squier's book served in turn as a guide for later collectors, including Frederick Boyle, who arrived in 1866 to collect antiquities for the British Museum,
the history of whose ethnological endeavors throws light upon the intra-
institutional cultural politics of such enterprises.[15] The museum had grown

Monument taken from Subtiava by Squier
for Smithsonian Institution. (From Squier,
*Nicaragua: Its People, Scenery, Monuments,
and the Proposed Canal,* 1852)

out of the private collection of Sir Hans Sloane (1660–1753), an enterprising
collector who as an already prosperous young medical doctor had in 1687
accompanied the new British governor of Jamaica to his duties as a sugar
plantation overseer. Sloane thus pursued his scientific investigations in a
slave-holding colonial economy controlled by a motherland already wracked
by the class divisions that gave rise to the Luddite rebellions a few decades
later. The contradictions were manifold: The knowledge he gained of the
colonial slave economy of Jamaica later enabled him to enlarge his fortune
by trading in chocolate and sugar, even while continuing to build a lucrative
medical practice among the socially eminent, to gain a reputation as a public-
spirited physician who treated indigent patients for free, and to support James
Oglethorpe's Georgia colony for the poor and oppressed of England.

Although Sloane's collections were derided by some as his "knick knacka-
tory," he succeeded Sir Isaac Newton as president of the Royal Society (1727–
1751). His collections grew to include some fifty thousand books and more
than eighty thousand scientific specimens, including eleven hundred "things
relating to the customs of ancient times or antiquities, urns, instruments,
etc." and three hundred fifty "artificial curiosities" from primitive peoples.
Benjamin Franklin came to see them and sold Sloane an American "purse
made of the stone Asbestos" to add to his store (Alexander 1983, 32).

Near the end of his life, Sloane took steps to insure that the collections
would be properly cared for and used after his death. Parliament established

the British Museum — to be built around Sloane's and several other major collections — in 1753. Financed by a public lottery, the museum opened its doors in 1759.

Sloane had had some interest in ethnology (a German visitor who saw his collection in 1710 reported that it contained "many Indian and other foreign clothes and weapons") and in the early years after the museum's founding, its ethnographic collections received items from British explorers adventuring in every corner of the expanding British Empire, such as those Captain Cook dispatched from Polynesia (Crook 1972, 45; Miller 1974, 75–76). But for more than a century, ethnology remained a poor stepchild at the British Museum, whose directors, trustees, and staff peered loftily down from beneath their top hats at anything that was not Greek sculpture.

By 1807 the museum's Department of Antiquities — although devoted mostly to classical (i.e., Greek) antiquities — had a "South Sea Room" described by one visitor as containing "idols of the various islands . . . in their hideous rudeness, a singular contrast with the many works of art" (Miller 1974, 75). The challenges from geology and ethnology following the 1830s brought pressure upon the department (given custody of the ethnology collections in 1836) to shift some attention beyond Greek sculpture, however. In 1842 the trustees gave a small sum to make drawings and casts of newly discovered Mayan ruins, but on the whole their response to the new imperatives was grudging: in 1850 the ethnology room was described by a visitor as "a collection of articles illustrative of the manners and customs . . . of rude ancient races" in which "five paltry cases" were devoted to all the arts and culture of China and Japan. Department head Edward Hawkins — a powerful figure in the institution since the mid-1820s — wanted to get rid of the museum's Mexican artifacts, and Principal Librarian Antonio Panizzi opined in 1857 that "it does not seem right that such valuable space should be taken up by Esquimaux dresses, canoes and hideous feather idols, broken flints, and so on" (Miller 1974, 191–92, 221–22). But Hawkins retired in 1861, and the new curator, A. W. Franks, was more positively disposed toward ethnological collecting. In 1866 Franks sent Frederick Boyle to Nicaragua (Alexander 1983, 19–42; Crook 1972, 19–69; Miller 1974, 75–76, 191–200, 221–22, 299).

Boyle went about his mission straightforwardly and unapologetically. In Juigalpa a local priest claimed to know nothing about *piedras antiguas*, but the mayor told him about an idol in the garden of an old Indian outside town. Finding a three-foot-high statue, Boyle and his companions offered the man a dollar to dig in his garden, which he claimed was a burial ground. A bit of digging with Bowie knives turned up a large urn and bits of bone, gold, and pottery. The Indian claimed to know where "the whole treasury of a great Indian princess" was buried, but rejected Boyle's offer to pay for

Sepulchral statuary taken from Chontales and near Mombacho by Boyle for British Museum, 1866. (From Boyle, *A Ride across a Continent*, 1868)

anything they might find. Further efforts at persuasion and bribery at other sites yielded little, but the next day Boyle found a two-acre cairn strewn with overthrown statues — mostly pounded to pieces "by the zeal of converting padres" — and one giant monolith more than twelve feet high. In La Libertad in Chontales province, "graves were so plentiful we had only the embarrassment of choice," he reported. "Every hill round was topped with a vine-bound thicket, springing, we knew, from the cairn of rough stone reverently piled above some old-world chieftain. . . . The tombs are in thousands. . . . We determined to attack the very largest to be found." A large one about five miles from town yielded marble and earthenware objects in abundance, but proved too difficult to excavate (Boyle 1868, 1:143–204).

Site after site lay littered with treasures: seven statues in an abandoned indigo field near Granada, cairns at the foot of the volcano Mombacho littered with pottery and broken statues, vast numbers of stone celts and funerary urns (some as large as 20"×30") scattered through the countryside. Following Squier's lead, Boyle then headed for the islands of Ometepe and Zapatero, and from there to Lake Nihapa, where he found that the rock paintings Squier had seen had suffered greatly during the intervening fifteen years (Boyle 1868, 2:42–46, 66–160). But there were treasures in abundance, nevertheless, virtually free for the taking. Early in 1867 Boyle wound up his collecting, went to the port of Realejo, shipped his artifacts to London, and departed for Costa Rica (Boyle 1868, 1:79, 2:149–52), leaving the field to other collectors. "All portable antiquities mentioned in this book," Boyle reported, "are now in the British Museum" (Boyle 1868, 1:xxiv).[16]

Pottery taken from Ometepe and Zapatero by Boyle for British Museum, 1866. (From Boyle, *A Ride across a Continent*, 1868)

Although the Smithsonian lacked the resources of the British and other European museums, its modest but dogged volunteer-based efforts slowly paid off in Nicaragua. Following the Squier expedition, the Smithsonian apparently received little if anything until after both the William Walker filibuster war and the Civil War were over, but from the mid-1860s onward it collected steadily, working mainly with four collectors: the linguist Carl Hermann Berendt, long-time Nicaraguan resident Dr. Earl Flint, Dr. J. F. Bransford of the U.S. Navy, and Charles C. Nutting.

Berendt and Flint appear to have been friendly competitors in their collaboration with the Smithsonian. Berendt, who had travelled in Central America and done research on Mayan and other indigenous Mesoamerican languages at least since the early 1860s, began to send Nicaraguan antiquities to the museum by the mid-seventies (Berendt 1868, 420–26). In December 1874 he sent a stone statue; other "antiquarian specimens" went both to the Smithsonian and to a dealer in New York.[17]

Earl Flint, who by the mid-seventies had lived in Granada for more than twenty years, began sending antiquities to the Smithsonian at least as early as 1869.[18] In a March 1875 letter to Joseph Henry, Flint apologized for a delayed shipment, including among his reasons his "vying with the Dr. [Berendt, presumably] to get more than he did."[19] Toward the end of April 1876, the museum received a dozen more specimens (stone celts, spearheads, pottery statues), and a little more than a month later several dozen other objects arrived. Flint continued to send artifacts to the Smithsonian at least until the fall of 1877, even while seeking another patron to support his work.[20]

Pre-Columbian pottery vase, a typical effigy figure, taken by Earl Flint from Nindirí for Smithsonian Institution. (Reproduced by permission of Smithsonian Institution)

Although Flint said later that "what little I have done was out of love for the thing," he in fact both resented the financial sacrifices necessitated by his volunteer work for the Smithsonian and felt caught in the sordid politics of a burgeoning collecting system that included rubber tappers who collected a bit on the side, entrepreneurs under contract to museums or dealers,

Seated female effigy figure taken by Flint from La Finca Casa Blanca on Ometepe Island for Smithsonian Institution. (Reproduced by permission of Smithsonian Institution)

professional grave robbers (*huaceros*), and careerist scientific researchers.[21] A lucrative market was developing for things that "have cost me much time and trouble to collect and money besides," Flint wrote to Secretary Henry, alluding obliquely to "what I have been offered for these antiquities." "What I have sent [the museum] could have sold for a good price," he told Baird, adding later, "Many times was I tempted to sell my collections, as they pay good prices for them here — the French pay well & have [driven?] the price up. Within the last few days I had to pay double for some dishes from Nindirí."[22]

For Flint the personal costs continued to mount. A long trip in search of a rumored jadeite mine "cost me more than my duty to my family will justify," he wrote to Baird, "depriving me of things that cannot be replaced." Noting that local residents are digging into the best untouched sites "as fast as possible," he pleaded to be provided with "funds . . . to collect all I can, doing nothing else, for four or five years." Meanwhile the market continued to beckon; "I could get $200 from the Frenchman" for a single stone found on the trip, he told Baird.[23] In mid-summer Baird replied that the Smith-

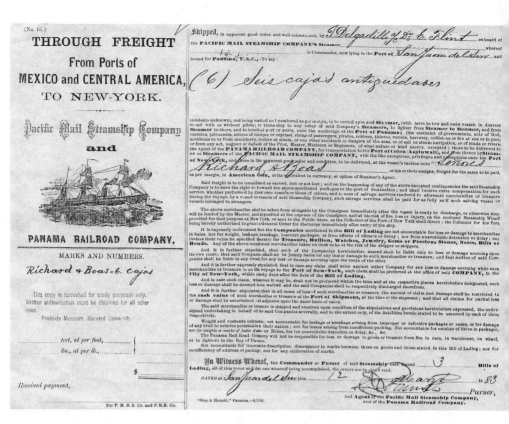

Shipping manifest for six boxes of antiquities sent by Earl Flint to Peabody Museum of Archaeology and Ethnology, Harvard University, March 1883. (Reproduced by permission of Peabody Museum)

sonian had no money to keep Flint employed as a collector, suggesting that Harvard University's Peabody Museum of Archaeology and Ethnology had more. Within weeks, Peabody director Frederic W. Putnam had offered to employ Flint, who quoted him a price of $200 per month ("as low a figure as possible").[24]

Flint collected assiduously for the Peabody Museum for nearly twenty years. "There is so much to do that I don't know where to begin," he told Putnam, adding later that "I am so absorbed in this work that I don't attend to my social obligations. Up as soon as I can see to work; keep it up till dark." Frustrated by having to "leave mounds unopened for lack of time," he continued to ship cases of artifacts, and promised Putnam that "if you want enough to fill your museum from floor to ceiling, all you have to do is to find the means." A year later he wrote to Putnam that he expected to get "a good haul" from Tola, where artifacts had been "less disturbed" than on Ometepe. Six more cases of artifacts followed early in 1883.[25]

Flint's "hauls" were not made wholly without impediment, but he repeatedly proved himself a skillful negotiator and manipulator. "[I] offered a very intelligent guide at Teustepe any price to find a vase entire and cure his wife in the bargain," he told Putnam. "He found one small one and so I cured his wife and gave him 40 cts—got off cheap. But the jar is unique."[26] More difficult to deal with were the local people for whom artifacts retained spiritual value; as Boyle had learned to his consternation, some of them were still resisting their discovery and expropriation. Toward the end of his first year's work for the Peabody Museum, Flint told Putnam that the "superstitious fears of . . . natives [determined to] preserve their relics" made it difficult to visit some of the sites found for him by local people. One cave visited seventeen years earlier by a priest who tried to "conjure away the evil spirits" was still "held in awe by the ignorant," he reported.[27]

In Flint's correspondence with the two museums, the contradictions, conflicts, and mixed motives that underlay the scramble for antiquities in the 1870s—even within the museums themselves—are plainly evident. Although Flint eventually shipped some twenty-seven hundred artifacts to the Peabody Museum, it appears that Putnam was not entirely pleased with his spending so much time (as he preferred to do) making copies of cave drawings that, however valuable scientifically, were relatively useless as exhibit material.[28] "As you say," Flint promised Putnam in August 1878, "I intend to lay myself out on idols and pottery. They are the only two things that can tell to the eye. Am determined this time, not to be led away by the *caves*—as you say it is expensive and don't *show* in the museum."[29]

Whatever the agendas of the museums, Flint preferred to see himself as working unselfishly and disinterestedly in the service of science and civilization. "For the benefit of mankind," he told Baird, "that is the reason that Dr. B[erendt] always urged me to have everything go—keep nothing back— all together would be valuable, separated of no value whatever—as I did not feel competent to do them that justice that history requires—I sent them to the centre of American civilization, thereby bringing them into view of the whole scientific world."[30] But the unsavory truth was, as Flint well knew, that the larger enterprise going on at the "centre of American civilization" was ridden with competitiveness, suspicion, personal jealousy, and nationalistic pride that were corroding the humane and scientific motives so many claimed. "The fact is," Flint himself admitted to Putnam in the early months of his collecting for the Peabody Museum, "[I] am afraid of competitors . . . [and] selfish in wishing to be the first one in. . . . [I] am also jealous of collections going to Europe."[31] "Dr. B[erendt] don't collect gratis," he complained to Baird, "and myself and [U.S.] Minister [to Guatemala] Williamson were vexed when we found out he was collecting for [Europe?]. When here, he wanted the field all to himself and seemed vexed when I got a rare article ahead of him." Indeed, a letter Berendt had written to him recently revealed that he was in fact doing archaeological work for the Prussian government as well as for the Smithsonian.[32] Arriving in Nandaime to "work a mound" in the late spring of 1878, Flint discovered that "the Frenchman had got the start of me and dug into it in all directions." The "Frenchman," he added later, "has been [excavating] for 3 years . . . [and] has gotten all the neighborhood around here . . . to take it to him and as he has orders from his father (a millionaire) to pay for it well, has got the monopoly—has a cartload on hand—keeps men digging all the time."[33]

U.S. Navy Captain John F. Bransford (1846–1911), who collected in Nicaragua for the Smithsonian in the mid-1870s, was on the whole less competitive and jealous than Berendt and Flint. Bransford's main interest was natural history, but chancing to see burial urns in a ditch on a *hacienda* near Moyogalpa on the island of Ometepe on his first trip, he turned much of his attention to antiquities (Bransford 1881, iii, 1).[34] For three months in early 1876, Bransford lived at a *hacienda* south of Moyogalpa on Ometepe, with "free permission," he reported later, "to dig wherever I chose." "Almost everywhere," he said, "may be found relics of the ancient inhabitants, and in the woods that clothe the foot hills are still to be seen the gods of their idolatry" (Bransford 1881, 7). Moving to the Hacienda de Baltaza two miles south, where "the Spanish proprietor . . . [had] for years collected antiquities and sold them in Rivas and Granada," he nevertheless still found the picking excellent. Seven miles to the north at Chilaite, where the specimens were "unusually abundant" and the soil "literally filled with shards and small images," he unearthed twenty burial jars (Bransford 1881, 46–47).

All through the summer, the treasures Bransford packed and shipped arrived steadily at the Smithsonian: earthenware vessels, burial urns, stone implements of various sorts, ceramic whistles, and gold, shell, and jadeite beads.[35] The following February Bransford returned to Ometepe, collecting mostly to the north of Moyogalpa around Santa Helena and Chilaite. The most beautiful pieces came from the *hacienda* Santa Helena, on the lake shore, where specimens even lay scattered among the roots of trees blown over by a recent hurricane. A few yards back from the shore, a line of burials only three feet down yielded vessels "of infinite variety in form and design of ornamentation"—the ubiquitous shoe-shaped burial urns, and others in the shape of human beings, dogs, alligators, or armadillos. One perfectly preserved tripod vase had doves for feet. Flat burial jars found over many skulls were as much as twenty-one inches in diameter and nine inches deep, and painting on some of the pottery was still in nearly perfect condition.[36] The large stone monoliths that had so animated Squier thirty years earlier were also still in evidence on Ometepe: on each side of the gateway to an old church enclosure at Los Angeles, lying near houses, in the woods, and on the shore of the lake where, Bransford speculated, "They were probably abandoned . . . after an unsuccessful attempt at embarkation" by earlier collectors. The best of them, however, had long since been hauled off. On hillsides on the south end of the island and here and there on basalt blocks strewn on the shore, there were rock carvings in abundance that Bransford sketched for his Smithsonian report (Bransford 1881, 62–66).

From Ometepe Bransford returned to the mainland and went south into Costa Rica. With Earl Flint he made an arduous overland trip in May to try to locate the source of the mine used for the jadeite objects found in so many of the excavations.[37] When he left for home in July he shipped thirty-five boxes packed with more than six hundred specimens; a few especially valuable ones he carried with him in a valise (Bransford 1881, 50–60).[38]

In the early 1880s the Smithsonian also commissioned Charles C. Nutting (1858–1927) to collect birds and antiquities in Costa Rica and Nicaragua.[39] Working in an open field under a brutal Central American sun and staying "right on the spot every moment" to keep his helpers from stealing the specimens, Nutting assembled nearly one hundred specimens from Ometepe Island, many of them from what he called a "mine" of pottery he encountered.[40] "I am convinced," he wrote to Baird late in March, "that there is no field more likely to yield a harvest to the collection of antiquities than the Island of Ometepe, notwithstanding the large drafts made upon it by Drs. Bransford and Flint." Nutting was particularly excited by a stone idol he had acquired, the only one still intact of the seven he encountered, he reported, that had not been described by earlier explorers. "It is on nobody's ground," he judged, "and no one will object to its removal." Equally important from a practical standpoint, it lay near both a good cart road, to which a few minutes' work with machetes would clear a path, and some unopened graves. "The fact is," Nutting said, "this island seems to be a perfect *mine* of antiquities and I have seen enough to give me a touch of . . . the 'mining fever.' Previous explorers have reaped a rich harvest, but I think other harvests, perhaps equally rich, remain." At the end of the expedition Nutting had five large crates of antiquities sitting on the dock at San Juan del Sur awaiting shipment to the Smithsonian: burial urns, small clay pots, a rudely carved stone head, and buckets full of pottery and stone fragments. The still uncrated stone idol proved to be "a great popular attraction."[41]

Collecting in Nicaragua at the same time as Nutting (although apparently unaware of his presence) was Swedish zoologist Carl Bovallius (1849–1907), who went to Central America in 1881.[42] Bovallius arrived on the island of Ometepe on New Year's Day 1883 and hastened to visit Earl Flint for advice.[43]

Pottery male figure and vase taken by Bovallius from Ometepe Island for Sweden's
Naturhistoriska Riksmuseet.

He focused first on the little town of Moyogalpa, which had also been Bransford's headquarters, but digging near one of Bransford's former sites yielded
nothing of consequence. He stayed on the island for more than a month,
however, "roving through it on horse-back and on foot in all directions,
ascending the volcano, rowing and sailing over the delightful lagoons and
bays that border its shores" (Bovallius [1887] 1977, 234, 265). After excavations at a half-dozen more sites yielded few of the splendid specimens found
by earlier collectors, Bovallius tried his luck on the mainland north of Rivas,
but again without much success.[44]

Passing through Granada to replenish his photographic supplies, Bovallius
went on to Zapatero, where he camped on the beach at Chiquero Bay while
making his investigations on the north end of the island (Bovallius [1887]
1977, 272).[45] He made his best discoveries at Punta del Sapote, where he found
pottery. At both Punta del Sapote and Punta de las Figuras there were free-
standing and caryatid-type stone monoliths Squier had missed, and the tiny
offshore island of Ceiba offered rock carvings as well as stone objects and
pottery (Bovallius 1886, 41; [1887] 1977, 291).[46]

To his dismay, Bovallius found that at least eight of the Punta del Sapote
statues described and sketched by Squier were no longer there, and that
others had suffered markedly in thirty years. The elaborately carved stone

Vase taken by Bovallius from Punta del Sapote on Zapatero Island for Sweden's Naturhistoriska Riksmuseet.

Free-standing monument documented by Bovallius at Punta del Sapote on Zapatero Island.

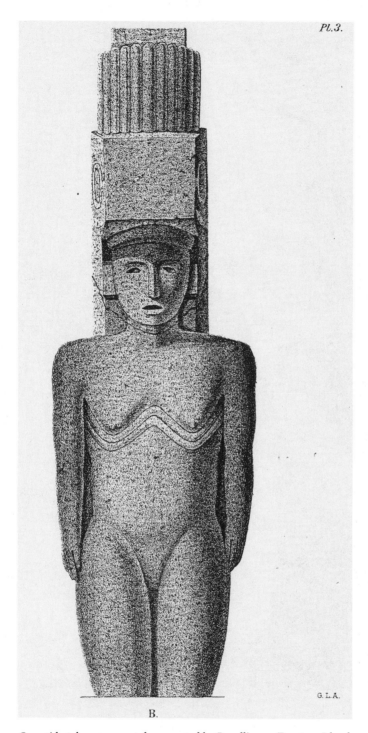

Pl. 3.

G. L. A.

B.

Caryatid-style monument documented by Bovallius on Zapatero Island.

pedestal that Squier and his helpers had so laboriously and joyously set upright again (Squier 1852, 1:58) no longer was surmounted by a carved figure; it lay "entirely crushed and moldered" in the undergrowth. Ceiba had no remaining statues at all, though local legend had it that some had been taken from there "long ago" to a nearby *hacienda* (Bovallius 1886, 43). Ceiba's rock carvings were relatively plentiful, however. One mountain ridge nearly one hundred meters long by fifteen meters wide Bovallius found "densely covered" with carvings—human figures, animals, and geometrical designs (Bovallius 1886, 42–47).[47] "I lamented bitterly," Bovallius wrote later, "that my limited resources did not permit me to take some of the statues to Sweden. They are still there awaiting destruction, partly by climate and vegetation and partly by the hand of man. It is very common . . . for them to be broken up and used as stones to cook on or steps to a house" (Bovallius [1887] 1977, 277). Bovallius finally shipped only three dozen "easily transportable" pottery and stone specimens, some of them scavenged in house-to-house searches through nearby neighborhoods by a young local woman. Compared with what others who had preceded him had already removed, it wasn't much (Bovallius 1886, 1; [1887] 1977, 282).[48]

Unfortunately, the objects Bovallius shipped home did not end up immediately in a well-appointed and stable scientific museum of the type idealized in the rationalizing narratives of the collectors, but rather were treated for decades like disregarded stepchildren within an unstable family of frequently antagonistic institutions wracked with their own internal disagreements and contradictions.[49] F. A. Smitt (1839–1904), who for nearly thirty-five years (1871–1904) headed the department of the Naturhistoriska Riksmuseet in which ethnographic materials were kept during the time of Bovallius's collecting in Nicaragua, was according to a contemporary analyst "solely and exclusively interested in fishes" and "did not care to register other incoming objects." To make matters worse, Professor Hjalmar Stolpe (1841–1905), who was responsible for the archaeological and anthropological collections, didn't get along with Smitt. "It was somewhere into this mess," Berggren reports, "that Bovallius sent his collections."[50] Stolpe was appointed head of a separate ethnographical department in 1900 (Etnografiska Afdelning), but in 1930 its collections were taken apart and packed away. Some were unpacked in 1935 when the collections were renamed the Statens Etnografiska Museum, but not all had been unpacked even a half-century later.

With the departure of Bovallius, the Nicaraguan field appears to have entered upon a prolonged period of quiescence—at least so far as major foreign museums were concerned. In less than forty years (from Squier to Bovallius), Nicaragua had seen vast quantities of irreplaceable archaeological artifacts shipped from its shores in a process that was awesome in its finality, but whose social, political, and cultural meanings and implications remain unsettled even yet.

THE SUBTEXTS OF COLLECTING

One of the more disquieting qualities of modernism, James Clifford has observed, is "its taste for appropriating or redeeming otherness," and its tendency to remain quite oblivious to the politics of the enterprise (Clifford 1988, 193). Collectors who worked the Nicaraguan field during the forty years of its most intense activity (as well as the curators to whom they shipped their booty) saw their work as disinterested and scientific—as simply in the service of a generic and apolitical "greater understanding," as benefitting an undifferentiated "humanity" in undifferentiated ways. But even the most scientific and disinterested of them worked within particular ideologies and in the service of particular centers of power. Hence considerations of class, gender, race, state, power, and (very frequently) empire were amply in evidence in their work (cf. Greenfield 1989, 232ff.).

Earl Flint, for example, had practiced medicine in Nicaragua for twenty years before he began his work as a contract supplier of antiquities to museums in the United States. His few later cryptic references to those years suggest that, whatever his commitment to relieving human suffering or advancing scientific knowledge about human origins, his life had in fact become entangled in the contradictions common to most of those who go from rich countries to seek their fortunes in poor ones.

As a resident of Granada from 1850 onward, Flint tried to carve out his own little private piece of Nicaragua at the same time that he was helping museums "save" other pieces of it. In 1872, he bought a large tract of land and attempted (as many others were doing at the time) to remove the *campesinos* who were living on it—in his view, as "squatters."[51] His efforts mired him in a series of expensive lawsuits, debilitating him and distracting him from his primary obligations: to raise his growing family, maintain his medical practice, ship antiquities northward, and seek recognition as a scientific archaeologist.[52]

Flint's efforts to possess and "clear" his land of the *campesinos* who were living on it were financially disastrous for him. He sued repeatedly; he appealed to the President; he asked the U.S. government for assistance; in desperation, he even tried to sell the land back to the Nicaraguan government.[53] Nothing availed, and his son's tuition at Cornell University added a new burden.

Thus Flint's repeated (and increasingly agitated and angry) appeals to the museums for money must be seen as arising both (perhaps equally) from a commitment to scientific archaeology and from the growing debt deriving from his land venture. Similarly, his demonstrable debilitation over the years must be understood as the result of both his aging and fatigue from his actual work on the one hand, and the enervating encounter with its contradictions on the other.

Shifting from the Smithsonian to the Peabody Museum also proved much less advantageous financially than he had hoped. "I would like some of your economizers to ride with me in the hot sun, on a mule, over the mountains, and live on tortillas & beans and fight mosquitos at night" to seek out antiquities, he wrote to Putnam, in one of his letters asking for more money. But the tightfisted Bostonian museum managers were intent on getting the maximum yield for minimum outlay; a decade later Flint was still complaining (now bitterly) of his "Peabody poverty." [54]

Meanwhile, Flint's medical patients were deserting him because of his frequent absences on collecting trips, more and more doctors were moving into the area, he was aging, and legal costs for the lawsuits mounted. By early 1880 his debts forced him to mortgage his house and rent it out. Buying a drugstore in Rivas from a government minister, he relocated his family there and concentrated on paying off his debts. [55] But the results were not encouraging in any sector, and the constant struggle fatigued him. "My only vacation will be the graveyard," he told Putnam. "[I] don't expect again to see my native land." To make matters worse, the supply of antiquities was drying up, he added later. "In 4 years [I] have not been offered six pieces for sale," he complained to Putnam, adding that he was becoming ("like my old friend Berendt") "disgusted with the world in general." "My life is embittered," Flint at length admitted. "I am getting old and rusty. Don't make any more [collecting] excursions." [56] His eyesight failing and his handwriting increasingly shaky, Flint shipped his last little batch of specimens to the Peabody Museum in late March 1899: a few pebbles from the beach, a ceremonial pendant, and a clay whistle from Ometepe. [57]

The cultural politics of British Museum collector Frederick Boyle's expedition were conflicted at best. Fortunately, Boyle was not insensitive to the impact of the various mid-century interventions upon Nicaragua and its people. If "eight hundred wild Californians, all nuggets and bowie knives, each one of whom is bound to have three meals a day, and liquor whenever he . . . pleases . . . descend upon a village of seven hundred inhabitants, and stay there ten days," he mused when he sailed into the "lotus dream" of Greytown's "green leaves and wavy palm trees," "the town . . . will be sacked as by an army of Huns." On up the river he lamented the fate of San Carlos, "sacked by buccaneers, battered by Nelson, burnt in civil wars, and blown up by filibusters" (Boyle 1868, 10–13, 61). Burdened with the usual set of mid-nineteenth century ethnocentric and racist views, however ("a rule of white men is eagerly desired by every influential person in the country," he said approvingly), he responded condescendingly to Nicaraguan people, and irascibly to their guarded and suspicious reactions to him (Boyle 1868, 1:63). The indigenous people were too suspicious to trust him, he said, and the acculturated mestizos were either too modern and profit-driven to care about what he was doing, or—if they did—too protective of what they knew to share it with him for nothing. Rebuffed by the old Indian in whose Juigalpa garden he encounters his first statue, Boyle rails against "the senseless distrust of the national character" (Boyle 1868, 1:152). As for the mestizo population, they "know nothing and care nothing about such things":

> their minds are so full of yards of cotton and manzanas of maize, that any most wonderful remains they may find in their jungle wanderings are forgotten within a month. . . . The Indians, on the other hand, full of exalted traditions of their forefathers, and deeply revering, if not worshipping, every stone which those forefathers reared, will rarely assist the explorer in his search, and will take every opportunity to dishearten him and turn him back. As a last resort, they will use violence to preserve the sacred relics; or they will destroy them with their own hands, and bury the fragments. (Boyle 1868, 2:46–47) [58]

Such obstinate refusal to cooperate with a scientific enterprise Boyle viewed as but further confirmation of a generally degraded national character. "There is not a road in Nicaragua; there is not a manufacture; . . . there are no exports, except hides and natural produce . . . there are no schools; there is not a bank. . . . What is there besides bigotry, and turbulence, and vice?" (Boyle 1868, 1:79). It would have been better, he judged, had the filibusters remained to bring their brand of progress, since the lazy, mixed-blood, degenerate Nicaraguans were so determined to loll away their lives in hammocks. "I really believe," he confided,

> it is the hammock which has pulled down the active old Spanish spirit to its present stagnation. The national ensign of Nicaragua should be a hammock waving over a graveyard. For the people are dead, and their ghosts loll all day in the murderous net. You enter a house—there is the owner swinging in his hammock, undressed, unwashed, not reading, not working, not thinking. There he lies, with his children beside him, backwards and forwards gently swaying in a half-doze. Between his lips is the paper cigarette, near his hand is the jug of lemonade, but in his head there is not an idea, whether of virtue or vice. . . . The doctor receives his patients, the lawyer his clients, the lady her lover, the deputy his constituents . . . all

Hammock in native hut, mid-nineteenth century. (From Boyle, *A Ride across a Continent*, 1868)

lying in the devoted hammock. To the hammock flies the lover in search of consolation, the disappointed candidate, the henpecked husband, the ruined storekeeper. . . . Fields are cultivated in it, battles are won, books are written, reforms are introduced, education is spread, everything is changed, and Nicaragua takes a foremost place in the world's civilizations. But when the well-meaning visionary leaps out to carry through these dreams, his back bends, his head swims, he sinks into his hammock and dreams again. (Boyle 1868, 2:99–104)

As Boyle left Granada (burned ten years earlier by William Walker) he expressed a nearly palpable contempt for the "ruin and dirt and stagnation" of the city, still in the historic grip of an elite mired in "turbulence, pride and jealousy," and whose "mental qualities . . . are the curse of the country." Passing through the "still loveliness" of Squier's beloved Nindirí by moonlight ("I had not conceived, in the whole world together, such fairy loveliness as she displays"), he found brief respite from the ugliness of Granada and Managua ("dirty little town" with "a reputation for turbulence, noise, and immorality, which it has justly earned"). From León ("a mass of brick mounds, empty spaces, tottering, fire-stained walls, and mud-built huts") Boyle could not get to Realejo quickly enough (Boyle 1868, 1:79, 2:182).

Racial and other cultural stereotypes cropped out with great frequency in the "scientific" communications of other collectors. Employing language common to the era in which he spoke, Smithsonian collector Earl Flint said some tombs he opened contained "the bones of . . . two races, with the beastly prolongation of the lower jaw and the distorted tibia of the inferior race, and the well formed skull of the superior race . . . still seen in its purity among the Jibarros on the frontier of Bolivia." To the Peabody Museum's director Putnam, Flint later described a tibiar bone he had found as "nearly equal to the best English." Some cave inscriptions he referred to as "*effeminate* off-shoots of a language of great antiquity." Discussing contemporary theories of human origins, Flint asserted, "When the American Nation gets out of its teens and asserts its manhood, Europe will dwindle away like the California Indians. Then they will carve out the American order, and probably make Venuses by machinery."[59] Similar language and assumptions were to be found in the writings of virtually all of those who collected in Nicaragua, and the paradigms they developed were in turn employed in teaching the public about culture. After he was appointed head of the Department of Ethnology and Archaeology for the 1893 Chicago World's Fair, for example, the Peabody Museum's Frederick Putnam asserted that the "great object lesson" of the fair's ethnological exhibits would be "to show in their natural conditions of life" examples of the "unsuspecting peoples" who were "forced . . . to give way before [the] mighty power" of the Europeans who followed Columbus (Karp 1991, 346–47).

TOWARD A MUSEUM FOR NICARAGUA

The logic of Nicaragua's experience with foreign museums and collectors suggested the need for its own museum, but it was to be years before Nicaragua had a national museum even in name, and decades before it had even a modest one in fact. As early as 1871, historian Pablo Levy lamented that in Nicaragua there were "no collections public or private, no astronomical observatory, no botanical garden. National antiquities [lie] buried, and there [is] no collection of them. There [are] no schools of art."[60] In truth, there was neither the money nor the necessary governmental or administrative structures to create and support such institutions. An early twentieth-century popular guide to the British Museum, discussing its ethnographic collections in terms of stark oppositions between civilized, western European, Christian nations on the one hand, and "untutored natives," "barbaric man," and "loathsome cannibals" on the other, asserted that "museums are possible only when a nation has reached a high state of civilization" (Shelley 1911, 7, 304–28). The elite bias of such an assertion notwithstanding, the politics, ethics, and logistics of establishing a museum (of whatever quality) in nineteenth-century Nicaragua were daunting.

When E. George Squier arrived in Nicaragua in 1849, ancient stone statues were to be found sitting on street corners in León, in Granada, in Managua—placed there when, by whom, and why no one any longer knew. Thirty years later, Earl Flint saw others standing beneath each pillar of the nave of a church on Zapatero, and reported that "for years past the smaller ones have been taken away [to be] used for bounds to landed property," steps to houses, or stones to cook on.[61] What the average Nicaraguan might have felt or thought upon passing such an object is also unknowable. Presumably, however, s/he would have been at least subliminally aware of the *presence* of some (even if imperfectly understood) past to which s/he was connected in some (even if ineffable) way.

To the extent that such a sense of connectedness (or relatedness), of one's existence in history, is a base of identity, hence of continuity, of *worthwhile-ness*, hence of felt power, leaving ancient stone idols to the weather on street corners might arguably be preferable to "protecting" them in museums. Protection is after all a value- and assumption-laden (hence political) metaphor as well as a fact: it is by definition protection *from* something or someone *for the benefit of* something or someone else. Consequently, moving a stone statue from Zapatero to a street corner in the ancient indigenous Jalteva section of Granada was a political act, but not the *same* political act as moving it to the Smithsonian Institution, the Peabody Museum, or the British Museum.

What would have happened if foreign museums, dealers, and grave robbers had left Nicaragua's aboriginal artifacts alone is impossible to say. At the very least, had the museums not called attention to them and thus helped to stimulate the market, the dealers and grave robbers would likely not have pursued their depredations so urgently, thus presumably leaving more undisturbed sites for future investigation.[62]

It would be too facile to assume, in any case, that had none of these parties intervened, Nicaragua would have cherished and protected its own antiquities in what came (especially during the late nineteenth century) to be the accepted scientific (i.e., museum-based) manner.[63] The records that remain suggest, in fact, that Nicaragua's antiquities were most often removed by simple and straightforward means: locating them serendipitously or with the help of local informants, digging them up with local labor, crating them up, hauling them to the port of Realejo, and shipping them home. Opposition from local people for whom the objects still had religious, cultural, or political significance appears to have been sporadic and largely ineffectual.

Official opposition was even rarer, apparently, and also of little effect. In February 1852 an official of the Nicaraguan government complained to the U.S. chargé d'affaires that the Atlantic Pacific Canal Company, operating under contract to the U.S. government, was destroying "the Old Castle" at San Juan del Norte and reusing materials from it "without even having the courtesy to advise the Supreme Government." Even after the U.S. promised to investigate, the depredations continued, and the Nicaraguan government complained to the chargé again about the "scandalous . . . violence which was committed under International Law without any motive whatever," and promised to "make proclamation of [our] rights in all the civilized nations of the world . . . notwithstanding [our] debility in opposition to the strength with which [we are] threatened and cannot resist." [64]

Meanwhile, the country's few protective laws were easily circumvented. "Father is trying to get out a couple of idols ere they are prohibited," Earl Flint's son wrote to Peabody Museum's Putnam in the spring of 1883, enclosing a letter from the Nicaraguan government informing Flint that President Chamorro's government could not at present give him a license (*licencia*) to remove the statues from the Solentiname islands, but would inform him should there be any change in policy.[65] But within a month, Flint had talked President Chamorro ("an old and intimate friend") into giving him permission to excavate and remove the statues.

Chamorro's object in refusing at first, Flint reported, "was to establish a museum here, and in the meantime prevent the indiscriminate excavations for mercenary purposes." In any case, he noted, "There is plenty to do on private lands, and years of work in Costa Rica where . . . they don't prevent export." [66] Meanwhile, Flint confided to Putnam, "The President hinted to me of his intention of [securing?] my work for commencing a new museum. Did not encourage him. He asked what I earned when working for you. I told him and he thought it cheap enough." [67] "I told President," Flint reported nearly a year later, "that to establish a museum required a building, money and curator and that the latter were scarce, even in the states." [68]

Nearly a decade later, President Zelaya—his interest in developing economic ties with other countries sensitizing him to the image Nicaragua presented to foreign visitors—began (possibly during a visit to the home of self-taught botanist-zoologist-anthropologist Diocleciano Cháves) to consider forming a national museum. Born in 1844 in Managua to a family of modest circumstances, Cháves was orphaned at eight and received no formal education. He ran away to Granada to study with a cabinetmaker, and later went to work on a cacao plantation owned by a French family who took him under wing, taught him French and some science, and encouraged his interest in collecting natural objects. Cháves stayed with them for fifteen years before returning to Managua. He continued to study botany, entomology, and archaeology on his own, published a few pamphlets on Nicaraguan botanical specimens, and eventually began to submit articles to the bulletin of the British Museum (Osorno Fonseca 1944; Cháves [1970s?]).[69]

Nicaragua's Industrial, Commercial, and Scientific Museum was established in August 1897 and opened in 1900 with Dr. David Guzmán as director. Like many museums of the time, its collection was a hodgepodge: photographs of indigenous people in the Congo, paintings of socially prominent Nicaraguan women, plaster of Paris models of fruits, a few musical instruments, pharmaceutical articles—even an artificial leg or two.[70] By the time the museum was renamed in 1902 (by one account it became the Mercantile Museum; by another the Museum of Natural and Scientific History) Diocleciano Cháves was serving as its director and had given it his own collections. The thirty-five hundred or so items in the museum's collection included minerals and mining machinery, medicinal plants and precious woods, agricultural and industrial products, live animals, and *bellas artes*, but apparently none of the pre-Columbian artifacts so avidly collected in Nicaragua by foreign museums.[71]

A final irony is that—notwithstanding the efforts of all the Putnams and Flints to the contrary—by the end of the museums' nineteenth-century frenzy of collecting and preserving, the battle had been lost to the private market of well-heeled entrepreneurial collectors. A "Taxidermist and Dealer in Naturalists' Supplies and Specimens" (his letterhead announced) wrote to the Peabody Museum's Putnam in 1892, offering to sell "a soap box full" of relics, "many of them perfect and many of them imperfect. The class of trade that I have here in the store, of course, calls for perfect showy specimens, and I have no especial use for this lot. I think, however, that it would make a very interesting collection for a museum, provided you are not already overstocked with that class of material." Putnam appears to have bought the lot, as well as subsequent offerings. The dealer, for his part, tracked his merchandise carefully and kept his categories straight. Writing to Putnam several years later, he described a previously shipped piece as being "suitable for a museum, but hardly suitable for a private collection."[72] The images are striking and unequivocal: "perfect showy specimens" for buyers with cash in hand versus soapboxes full of unmarketable detritus for museums. Even poor museums in rich countries could hardly hope to compete in such a market; poor countries with no museums had no hope at all of entering it, and little of stopping the flow of their own cultural treasures into it.

CHALLENGE OF RESTITUTION

As the foregoing analysis suggested, the market-driven redistribution of cultural artifacts from marginalized cultural and ethnic groups, poor colonies, and client states to centers of national wealth and power was a pervasive feature of the virtually worldwide politics of culture in the nineteenth century. That process generated a vast array of inequities, contradictions, and smoldering resentments.

In the twentieth century, an increasingly salient aspect of the cultural politics of that long-running process has been the efforts of small nation-states and marginalized cultural groups to recover expropriated cultural artifacts they consider to embody or represent their cultural identity. The character of the resulting national and international negotiations, law suits, and ongoing investigation suggests that the resolution of whatever claims Nicaragua may in the future wish to enter with regard to its own purloined antiquities will occur for the most part beyond its own borders. And in the meantime, those that remain continue to suffer from abuse and neglect, and to pass into private hands.

The intensity of international negotiations concerning cultural restitution has increased steadily since World War II. As early as 1930 the British government returned some objects removed from the kingdom of Kandy more than a century earlier (Greenfield 1989, 260). More recently, such efforts have extended and sharpened the debate over cultural property rights and the politics of cultural conservation and representation, and more specifically over the social, cultural, and political roles of museums (cf. Karp 1991).

Although it was but a small episode in a drama whose most active centers lay elsewhere, the Nicaraguan experience related in Chapter 7 offers some insights into these issues. In the first place, of the types of artifacts so avidly sought by E. George Squier and later collectors and dealers, those that have (however improbably) remained in Nicaragua did not fare particularly well, even after the major museums departed with their booty in search of more lucrative fields. Between 1924 and 1935, more than two dozen stone monoliths were moved from their original locations to the Jesuit Colegio Centroamericano de Granada, but when the institution later moved to Managua the statues were left behind. In 1969, they were put into a collection in the Instituto Nacional del Oriente in Granada, but they were badly cared for there, and when the institute moved, they were abandoned (Arellano 1977a, 43–65, 123–32). Some subsequently turned up in public buildings, the national airport, private homes, and elsewhere. Two 1971 listings of the country's historical-artistic patrimony (not entirely in agreement) reported that some twenty of the monoliths still standing in a patio of the abandoned Colegio de los Jesuitas (presumably the Colegio Centroamericano) in Granada were in "serious danger" of damage; another fifty were under better care in a museum in Juigalpa built by the Clan Intelectual de Chontales.[73] One stood in a public park in Boaco, and two others stood on a bridge in León; nearly twenty were in

U.S. Army personnel examine stone monoliths from Zapatero Island, 1932. Original *National Geographic* caption (May 1932) says, "These two, by consent of the Nicaraguan government, will eventually adorn the entrance to the barracks building at Fort Humphreys, Virginia." (Photograph by Newell F. Johnstone; © National Geographic Society)

schools; several were in Somoza's house and that of his daughter Liliam; more than forty were in the hands of some of the country's most prominent families (Cuadra, Carrión, Pataky, Zamora, Buitrago, and others); the National Museum had a total of six, and several were in the indigenous cultural center in Subtiava.[74] What is known definitely to remain in Nicaraguan public collections are a few much-damaged Zapatero and Ometepe Island statues, a few thousand examples of pre-Columbian pottery, and scattered objects of other types. What remains unexcavated that might yet be gathered into public collections is known only sketchily.[75]

Whether any Nicaraguan artifacts will ever be returned from either private collections or other governments to public collections inside the country will depend partly on the development of the international discourse concerning collection and restitution. From 1956 onward, UNESCO took the lead in formulating international conventions to curb the illegal traffic in antiquities, putting forth its Recommendation on International Principles Applicable to Archaeological Excavations (1956), a Convention on the Means of Prohibiting and Preventing the Illicit Import, Export and Transfer of Ownership of Cultural Property (1970), and the Convention Concerning the Protection of the World Cultural and Natural Heritage (1972). A series of regional UNESCO conferences on cultural policy culminated in a world conference in Mexico City in 1982; its recommendations included measures designed to curb the traffic. Unfortunately, UNESCO's recommendations, conventions, and model statutes have too frequently been off-puttingly verbose, ambiguous, and difficult to translate into enforceable sanctions, and UNESCO itself has no enforcement powers (Greenfield 1989, 241, 252–352).

Even though the new UNESCO conventions themselves have proved (in Greenfield's judgment) "largely ineffectual," a new climate of world opinion, new international and national laws, some vigorous lawsuits, and new self-regulating policies instituted by museums (some of them modeled on the UNESCO conventions) have led to the return of some illicitly traded artifacts, including Latin American ones. Within the United States in recent years, a few items of new legislation, several landmark legal cases, and one or two binational treaties have marked a shift in a progressive direction: the 1970 United States–Mexico treaty on the recovery and return of stolen archaeological, historical, and cultural properties, and a similar one signed with Peru in 1981; the United States versus Hollinshead case (1974) concerning a rare Mayan stela illegally removed from Guatemala; the National Stolen Property Act (1976); the McClain case (1977), which arose from a theft of pre-Columbian artifacts from Mexico; and the Cultural Property Law of 1982, designed to implement the 1970 UNESCO convention (Greenfield 1989, 187–208).[76] Two dramatic recent cases were Italy's return of twelve thousand pre-Columbian artifacts to Ecuador in 1983 and the Fine Arts Museum of San Francisco's return to Mexico of some murals from Teotihuacán in 1986 (Greenfield 1989, 223-24, 257-59; Seligman in Messenger 1989, 73-84). During the 1980s, UNESCO's efforts were further hampered by internal division and the withdrawal of support by the conservative Reagan and Thatcher governments in the United States and Great Britain.

Despite these advances, it would take decades of public education and innumerable separate legal actions to rectify the centuries-long flow of Latin American antiquities into the museums of wealthy industrialized countries. Moreover, beyond the competing claims of museums and local people — the elders of Subtiava against the Smithsonian, for example — lie different (and equally difficult) political questions: Whose artifacts are they, anyway, and within what definitions of *belonging to* does one decide who is their appropriate custodian? Upon what basis — historically or ethically — must one adjudicate the legitimacy of claims? Upon what grounds — for example within UNESCO guidelines — are contemporary nation-states to be accorded the "right" to all the archaeological artifacts fortuitously located within their borders (which in most cases bear little relation to ancient ones)? And who is ultimately served most by protecting or returning the cultural *patri*mony of a nation-state whose stability is guaranteed by a web of patriarchal institutions?

It is not even clear, one is finally forced to admit, that the best way to guarantee access to and an understanding of anyone's past through historical objects is to "conserve," "preserve," and "interpret" those objects in museums — even the more politically sophisticated contemporary ones. As Clifford and others have argued, even in the most respected museums, "historical relations of power in the work of acquisition are occulted. The making of meaning in museum classification and display is mystified as adequate representation. The time and order of the collection erase the concrete social labor of its making" (Clifford 1988, 220).

Even if one grants a contemporary nation-state's "right" to own artifacts located within its borders, to display them (or not) as it sees fit, and to convey them to whomever it chooses, one must ponder the political implications of thus linking ancient artifacts to either the concept or the fact of the modern nation-state, itself but a recent blip on any timeline long enough to include the creation of such artifacts. The most likely prospect, it seems, is that nation-states will use such artifacts principally as warrants for their own legitimacy, however different their values and modes of social organization may be from those of the peoples who created the artifacts, and whatever the internal inequalities (of race, religion, gender, class, and culture) within the nation-state itself.

However the decisions about restitution are to be made for large, powerful states with multiple bases for legitimacy, at least for small and weak states such as Nicaragua — perennially contending with and menaced by larger and more powerful ones — the ethics of the choice may be somewhat less problematic: to the extent that one is willing to grant the future utility of the very notion of a nation-state, certainly there are worse fates for stone statues, jade amulets, and clay pots than to move them from the storerooms and galleries of the imposing museums of North America and western Europe to the modest ones of Latin America, where at least they might play a role in encouraging threatened groups to hold onto some self-determination.

CHAPTER 8 A PRODIGIOUS CHILD OF NICARAGUA

RUBÉN DARÍO AND THE IDEOLOGICAL USES OF

CULTURAL CAPITAL

. . . .

The poet should have as his only object ascension to his immortal sublime paradise: Art.

—Nicaraguan president René Schick Gutiérrez, quoting Rubén Darío, 1966

. . . .

This [Sandinista] revolution was a dream of Darío . . . who was a revolutionary.

—Minister of Culture Ernesto Cardenal, 1982

. . . .

As foregoing chapters have shown, the Somozas and the Sandinistas took markedly different approaches to the issue of culture, evoking in turn remarkably disparate responses (both positive and negative) from Nicaraguan citizens. The Somozas treated traditional culture as expendable, while courting the United States and eagerly importing its popular, commercial culture; much of the Sandinistas' cultural program focused upon anti-imperialism and cultural independence. The Somozas neglected to build public cultural institutions; the Sandinistas made major efforts to do so. The last of the Somozas built one grand palace of culture in Managua and imported ballet and classical music for the elite who mingled in evening dress below its crystal chandelier; the Sandinistas called the building a gigantic white elephant and staged performances by folkloric and political performers before audiences who came in shorts and sandals. Each accused the other of erecting "rascally signs in sacred places."

Through it all, nevertheless, there were some paradoxical continuities and

313

similarities. Most pertinent to our purpose here is that both Somocistas and Sandinistas attempted to appropriate some (one might even argue all, but that is not my purpose here) of Nicaragua's national heroes as legitimizing warrants for their own ideology and political programs. The present chapter considers how every Nicaraguan government from the 1880s onward (but especially the Somozas and the Sandinistas) tried to appropriate and possess Nicaragua's premier national poet Rubén Darío as cultural icon and legitimizing political symbol—as poet laureate of its politics—thereby gaining ascendancy over internal rivals and legitimacy on the geopolitical stage.[1] The following chapter turns to General Augusto C. Sandino, whom the Somoza regime assassinated and whose memory it vilified and tried to erase, and whom the Sandinistas subsequently resurrected as their founding ideological, political, and cultural hero.

Most of the critical commentary on Darío has been called forth and shaped by his being a seminal pan–Latin American and international literary figure. That for more than a century he has also been the focus of a much contested discourse concerning national cultural identity and political ideology *within* Nicaragua itself (my focus here) is less well known (cf. Stansifer 1979). Such an analysis offers insight into the dialectical relationship between culture and ideology: on culture as a generative matrix for ideology; on the instrumental use of culture for overtly ideological purposes such as regime legitimation or the delegitimation of rivals; on the ideological control of cultural processes (such as censorship); on the institutionalization of ideologically skewed representations of cultural history through instruments like museums or school textbooks; and on the shaping of the cultural landscape through cultural preservation efforts, monuments, and public symbols.[2]

DARÍO AS CULTURAL CAPITAL

Regardless of their politics, Darío's fellow countrymen have venerated him virtually to the point of deification. Although they have done so because he was indisputably a writer of the first rank, justly acclaimed internationally, they had other reasons as well. Chief among them is that Darío embodies so much of the negotiable cultural capital of a country that is small and poor, that ever since the colonial period has been wracked by internecine conflict, and that by virtue of its geographical character and position became a pawn in great power struggles.[3]

At the national level, Nicaragua has never been unified or stable enough to develop a secure sense of its own political or cultural identity. As we have seen, factions have contended ceaselessly for the right to define it. On the geopolitical stage, the country has never been large, powerful, or rich enough to demand; all it can hope to do is negotiate cunningly. Thus the strength of the hand held by any faction or by the country in such contestations or negotiations depends inordinately upon two fragile cards: moral suasion and cultural legitimacy. One of the few potentially plausible visages for the latter card is that of Rubén Darío.[4]

Thus when the aging *vanguardista* Luis Alberto Cabrales wrote during the mid-1960s of Darío's birth nearly a century earlier, there was no mistaking his mythic paradigm. Cabrales invoked the Christmastime of 1866, when a "great peace" lay over Nicaragua—a peace like that reported in the gospels as a sign of an impending divine birth. Young Rosa Sarmiento de García Darío is on her way from cosmopolitan León to picturesque rural Metapa to await the arrival of her first-born. Along the way she dreams of Jerusalem (which in her musings she confuses with León) and of Bethlehem-Metapa. "What kind of child was this which was going to be born?" Cabrales asks rhetorically. "What destiny, what star was guiding her toward Metapa?" Perhaps, he says, Rosa guessed that the awaited one would be "a prodigious child" (Cabrales 1964, 1–2). Ultimately, however, one must understand the dialectical relationship between the self-transcending struggle of the prodigious child—Félix Rubén Sarmiento García—to make himself into Rubén Darío, and the later struggle of his admirers, imitators, and idolizers to define and claim what "Rubén Darío" *became* as historical construct.

Notwithstanding the virtual deification of Darío within Nicaragua, little consensus has emerged on the meaning of his work beyond his unquestioned position as the country's most eminent man of letters, its cultural trump card.[5] By all odds, the bitterest struggle among claimants was between the Somoza government and the emerging FSLN movement (later the Sandinista government). For each side, the possibility of claiming *el divino Rubén* as warrant for its own cultural legitimacy seemed a most desirable prize. But because Darío's politics were neither as simple nor as categorical as was required by the agendas of the antagonists, this prize could be won only by tailoring the complex data to specific ideological requirements. Rather than argue that Darío "properly" belongs at any specified point along any political spectrum (however defined), it proves more productive to try to comprehend the political-cultural dialectic that has emerged from his own countrymen's repeated insistence upon locating Darío's "correct" position on that spectrum.[6]

DARÍO AND NICARAGUA

Although Darío said that "I always have had, on land or sea, the idea of Fatherland," one does not have to read much of his work to realize that throughout his life Darío struggled over his relationship to Nicaragua (Darío 1917b, 17). In some respects, he was fighting to escape Nicaragua, especially its provincialism and rusticity, and the financial insecurity and social marginality suffered by its writers. Thus regardless of their political persuasion, Darío's countrymen have had to face the troublesome paradox that Nicaragua's best-known writer's self-identification with his land of birth was problematic at best. He both spent virtually all of his adult life living and writing elsewhere, and wrote considerably more about the elsewheres than he did about Nicaragua. Indeed after Darío left for El Salvador when he was fifteen, he never spent more than a few weeks or months at a time in Nicaragua until he returned there to die at the age of forty-nine. He lived for short periods in Guatemala and Costa Rica, and for months or years at a time in El Salvador, Chile, France, Spain, and Argentina.[7] The center of his cultural universe — *la patria universal* — was not Nicaragua, nor even Latin America, but France. Paris was the "capital of capitals" — "a paradise," and Darío wrote far more about it than he did about any other place.[8]

Trying to understand what Darío wrote about Nicaragua presents several major problems: most of it is found in occasional journalistic pieces rather than in the canonical belletristic works; and it is affectively ambivalent, laced with apparent ideological contradictions, and fragmented among Darío's triple agendas of separating himself from Nicaragua, affirming his Nicaraguanness, and complaining that his country was denying him the recognition and honor he deserved. Thus the search for substantial references to Nicaragua in Darío's writings turns out to resemble gleaning, rather than mining the rich lode one might hope to encounter in an author who has come to be worshipped by his countrymen for expressing so powerfully who and what they believe themselves to be.

Although Darío read Walt Whitman avidly and admired his lyrical celebrations of the United States — in fact aiming, as recent critics have asserted, "to be for Nicaragua and Latin America as a whole what Whitman had been for U.S. culture" — Darío offers few glimpses of his own life in Nicaragua.[9] Except for brief recapitulations of quotidian details of his early years and sketches of a few episodes, neither his *Autobiography* nor *Voyage to Nicaragua* is very revealing in this regard.[10] A substantial portion of the latter is drawn more or less undigested (in extensive quotations) from Thomas Gage, José Dolores Gámez, and other historians. Comments upon the indigenous or traditional culture of Nicaragua are brief and infrequent, despite Darío's oft-quoted assertion that "if there is poetry in America, it is in old things."[11]

Nor is Nicaragua very present as a subject in Darío's poetry. Within a corpus that offers the nine-hundred-line "Canto a la Argentina" (Song to Argentina) and shorter poems celebrating Chile, Brazil, Colombia, and even the Dominican Republic, one finds little on Nicaragua. Indeed all of Darío's poetry contains fewer than thirty references to the country of his birth, about the same number as to Argentina, and half as many as his invocations of ancient Greece (Darío 1954, 905–36, 1050–51, 1178; Harrison 1970). The most sustained treatment of *la patria* occurs in the four-dozen or so lines of "Tríptico de Nicaragua" and the two hundred of "La cegua" (The blind one), a poetic rendering of a Nicaraguan popular legend (Darío 1954, 1187–89 and 252–62, respectively). Otherwise, one must be content with gleaning scattered images like those found in "Canción 'Mosquita'" and the love poem "Allá lejos" (There in the distance).[12]

Thus the fact that Darío was a prodigiously creative writer from a small, poor, and backward country at a time when larger Latin American countries were set upon rapid, mostly European-style modernization necessarily enmeshed him in tortuous structural dilemmas. Prominent among them was the question of what was to be gained and lost by identifying oneself actively with such a country.[13] More specifically, both Darió's political development and his attempt to come to terms with being Nicaraguan were complicated by his determination to rise above his social origins — those defined for him within Nicaragua by his family circumstances and those defined within a wider orbit by his being Nicaraguan.

Arriving in El Salvador as a fifteen-year-old, Darío soon met President Rafael Zaldívar, who admired his precocious poetry and offered assistance and support. The young poet told the president that what he wanted most was "a good social position" (Darío 1912, 54, 65). In the years thereafter, such insistent social aspirations proved to be a major factor in alienating him from his homeland. Never flagging in his aspiration, Darío subsequently found himself obliged to compromise considerably in pursuit of it and to bear the consequent pain. In a striking image in his autobiography, he recalled the ominous dark cloud of volcanic ash hanging over the port of Corinto as he sailed for Chile at the age of twenty, carrying his little valise of shabby clothing. It was at once a cloud of sadness, regret, nostalgia, and self-doubt. But the image also suggests somewhat forebodingly that his quest carried with it the risk of betraying his own country and culture (Darío 1912, 61).

When Darío disembarked in Chile, he asked (despite his penury) to be shown to the best hotel, as he had done earlier in San Salvador. Standing dejectedly to the side of the teeming station clutching his poor little valise (symbolic of his miserable little personal store of only marginally marketable cultural capital), he was delighted to be met by an elegantly attired man in a splendidly appointed coach. In the critical gaze of this gentleman (already acquainted with the youngster's precocious poetry), Darío saw reflected all his own provincialism, his lack of style and sophistication: "That look took in my poor body of a skinny youth, my long hair, the bags under my eyes, my little Nicaraguan jacket, some tight pants that I had thought very elegant, my problematic shoes, and above all my valise" (Darío 1912, 66–67).

Like many a country boy come to the city—timid, self-conscious, provincial, without money, proper clothing, or social skills—Darío moved into a tiny room and began working assiduously to acculturate and polish himself. Through the good offices of his benefactor, he found a job as a journalist with *La Epoca*, which was housed in an opulent building adorned with paintings by Jean Antoine Watteau and copies of classical Greek statues. Two years later Darío emerged elegantly dressed, with a stylish moustache and a dignified bearing, a broad acquaintance with the latest French writers, and a book (*Azul*) that marked prodigious talent. Hence the Darío who returned home as a twenty-two-year-old was still technically Nicaraguan, but he had initiated a painful and confusing dance around the question of his nationality and cultural identity that would continue throughout his life (Watland 1965, 94–100).[14]

In later years, Darío was quite candid about his preference for upper-class manners and lifestyles, and more specifically for what he considered to be the sophisticated and cosmopolitan culture of Europe. In his autobiography he recalled living on herring and beer in Santiago as a young man "to be able to dress elegantly, as befitted my aristocratic friendships," and he repeatedly recited the names of the rich, powerful, and famous people he had socialized with. "It pleases me," he said, "to see diamonds on white necks. I like people with elegant manners and fine words and noble ideas." At another moment in *El viaje a Nicaragua*, Darío asserted that "aristocrats everywhere are the maintainers of tradition and sustainers of culture." "Today as always," he said in another extended lyrical moment, "money makes poetry, embellishes existence, brings culture and progress, makes villages beautiful, brings relative happiness to workers. Money well employed produces poems, makes imagination palpable, makes the stars dance" (Darío 1912, 71, 110; Watland 1965, 202; Darío 1917b, 99, 153).

At the end of his autobiography when he spoke of leaving Nicaragua to assume the post of minister to Spain in 1907, Darío expressed the belief that he would never have to return to his native land, where such an unfavorable situation had discouraged an anxious and talented youth. The elegant, gold-braided diplomatic uniform he was entitled to wear upon his arrival in Spain could hardly have been more metaphoricallly appropriate.[15] The bond between Darío and Nicaragua certainly was not strengthened by the fact that the response of successive Nicaraguan governments to his growing fame did little more than mirror his ambivalence, despite his repeated attempts to garner their support.[16] The earliest promise of such support—a special legislative

Darío in ambassadorial uniform, ca. 1907. (Columbus Memorial Library, Organization of American States; reproduced by permission)

resolution that would have sent young Darío to Europe to be educated at state expense — vanished when he chose to read at a presidential reception some verses he later described as "red with anti-religious radicalism." "My son," the president responded, "if you now write thus against the religion of your parents and your country, what will happen if you go to Europe to learn worse things?" (Darío 1912, 44–45).

Following his first youthful sojourn in El Salvador, Darío briefly held a sinecure in the office of the secretary to the president that allowed him leisure to write. Later, he was accorded rather grudging official recognition, serving variously as a Nicaraguan delegate to the Columbus centenary celebration in Spain, as Nicaraguan consul in Paris, as a delegate to the Pan American conference in Río de Janeiro, and as a member of the commission on the Nicaraguan-Honduran border dispute (Darío 1912, 59–60, 111, 244, 257, 261).

Yet such recognition was always more formal and sporadic than substantial or reliable. Although in 1885 the president of Nicaragua ordered a volume of the eighteen-year-old Darío's poems published at government expense, the poet was denied the governmental post he asked for several years later upon his return from Chile, having already published his epochal *Azul.*[17] In late

1892 he was still trying to get salary payments for services he had rendered to the government as much as six years earlier, and in 1898 he tried again unsuccessfully to secure a diplomatic post. "What has Nicaragua done for me?" he complained to a friend from Madrid the next year. To another he confided that he was "more in touch with Holland or Norway than with my *país natal*" (Darío 1912, 137; Jirón Terán [1915] 1981, 52–53).[18]

Nearly a decade later in 1907, when Darío returned briefly to Nicaragua, the government declared him the guest of honor of the nation. Welcoming throngs filled the port of Corinto and the stations through which his special train passed on its way to León, where the streets were decorated and banquets were held in his honor (Stansifer 1979, 61–62). Even after President Zelaya appointed Darío minister to Spain, the government delayed sending him any money for three months and never provided enough funds for him to live in customary ambassadorial style. The funds provided came more and more irregularly, and some of his plaintive letters to Zelaya went unanswered. After two years in such straits, Darío gave up and abandoned the post, selling books and furniture to pay his debts (Watland 1965, 219–21).[19]

Shabby official treatment of Darío continued throughout his life. In November 1915, while he lay in the throes of his final illness, his friend Dr. Luis Debayle was still trying to get his back salary from U.S.-installed president Adolfo Díaz. Díaz refused, but proffered a small monthly sum for medical treatment and arranged a train to take him to León. As his death approached, the government—in an egregiously self-serving gesture—published a decree in the newspaper outlining the honors to be accorded him upon his death. Upon reading it, Darío observed sardonically that he would have preferred to receive them earlier.

At Darío's death, the government declared a period of national mourning, mounted a lavish funeral, accorded him (somewhat inexplicably) honors as a war minister, and named an official commission to carry a message of condolence to his second wife. Through a rather bizarre chain of events, Darío's brain and other organs were removed for special preservation and study before being parceled out to his widow, Dr. Debayle, and the university. The rest of his mortal remains were solemnly interred in the cathedral in León (Torres 1966, 500–509).[20]

DARÍO'S POLITICAL FORMATION

As has often been noted, Darío spent his early years in León, the seat of Liberal politics in Nicaragua, and wrote some of his earliest poems to be read at local political meetings.[21] He had his first taste of anything approaching radical politics under the tutelage of Polish professor José Leonard

(1840–1908), who spent a brief turbulent interval teaching at León's Instituto de Occidente (Darío 1912, 45–46; Torres 1966, 38–40).[22] Leonard had taken part in a failed uprising of Poles against Russia (1863–64). His anti-Jesuit inaugural lecture at the institute provoked the Jesuit order to condemn him as "a dangerous radical and pernicious influence," but the support he enjoyed from President Zavala protected him for two years. Leonard's commitment to freedom of conscience, the free commerce of ideas, and social radicalism influenced fourteen-year-old Darío profoundly. Darío defended Leonard in León's *La Verdad*, wrote (as Urbanski notes) in support of subjugated people in Poland, Cuba, and elsewhere, and began to write poems against the Jesuits and even against the pope and to read nineteenth-century liberal French writers as well as the romantic, anticlerical Ecuadoran rebel Juan Montalvo (Urbanski 1967, 18–19, 25).[23]

During his young manhood, Darío also had a series of friends and associates with oppositionist political ideas and commitments. At *La Epoca* his coworker Manuel Rodríguez Mendoza was a political writer; and during the late 1880s in Valparaíso Darío met Francisco Galleguillos Lorca, who had risen above his humble origins and work as a laborer and miner to become the "underworld doctor" of the area. When Darío accompanied Galleguillos on one of his clandestine nocturnal missions of mercy, however, he found himself less attracted to than repulsed by the good doctor's underworld clients (Darío 1912, 82–83; Achugar, 1986, 870–71).

The most powerful revolutionary Darío encountered was Cuban José Martí, whom he met on a trip to New York in 1893. Darío had already written effusively of Martí years before he met him, observing that Martí wrote "more brilliantly than anyone in Spain or America. . . . [His] every phrase . . . [is] golden, or smells of roses . . . and his thought is a flash of lightning."[24] An essay Darío wrote upon Martí's death in 1895 called him a "superman" committed to alleviating "the miseries and grief of the wounded and lost human flock," a veritable martyr who gave his life not only for his "dream of a free Cuba" but also for "the true future triumph of America," and whose blood belonged to "a whole race" (Darío 1917b, 213–15).

Darío also became friends with the young Argentinian poet and socialist Leopoldo Lugones (1874–1938), whom he admiringly called "a completely conscious revolutionary" (Mapes 1938, 102–8).[25] A half-dozen years later in Paris Darío became friends ("immediately," he said) with the insistently anti-U.S. Colombian novelist José María Vargas Vila (1860–1933), who had had to flee his country after taking part in a revolutionary movement in 1885 (Darío 1912, 237, 261).[26]

Darío continued to express elements of the Liberal politics of his natal León through his lifelong championing of the reunification of the Central

American states in his poetry and in such activities as editing *La Unión* in San Salvador.[27] Some essays went considerably beyond genteel liberal politics. "El canal por Nicaragua," which he wrote at age nineteen, is incisively caustic in its denunciation of the selfishness, profiteering, wastefulness, and gaudy ostentatiousness of the principals of the Panama Canal project, as well as the sickness and death suffered by local construction workers. Another 1895 essay on the same subject unsparingly condemned the arrogance of U.S. machinations in the enterprise.[28] Filibuster William Walker, he said, brought Nicaragua "only the barbarity of blue eyes, cruelty and the rifle." Following Spain's defeat in 1898, Darío asked in "Los cisnes,"

> Will we be given over to the cruel barbarians,
> Will so many millions of us be speaking English?
> Are there no more noblemen or brave *caballeros*?
> Shall we be silent now to cry later?
>
> (Darío 1912, 63; 1954, 732)

In the Whitmanesque "Ode to Roosevelt" (1904), Darío contrasted "the future invader" Roosevelt's arrogant pride, brutal power, and overweening confidence with the more ancient and vital culture, the passion, the deep faith, and vibrant dreams of *la América española*.[29] Following the U.S.-managed deposition of President Zelaya, which Darío perceived as the latest installment of filibuster imperialism, he wrote "El fin de Nicaragua," excoriating his countrymen for giving in to "the masochism of the big stick" and reminding them that United Fruit's profits were guaranteed by a "bloody fiesta of death."[30] In "Panamericanismo" Darío assailed U.S. efforts to assert its dominion over Latin America, and in a poem later to become a favorite of his Sandinista partisans, "El triunfo de Calibán" (The triumph of Calibán), he fulminated against the barbarian Yankees who "eat, eat, calculate, drink whiskey and make millions."[31]

Viewed as a whole, however, the record of Darío's expressed political views is much less clear than these stark examples suggest. Standing in contrast to them is his "Salutación al águila" ("Salutation to the eagle"), which he wrote in 1906 while he was a member of the Nicaraguan delegation to the Pan American conference in Río de Janeiro (Torres 1966, 334–36). "Salutación" envisioned the northern eagle, bearing in its beak the olive branch of "a vast and fecund peace," joining in harmony with the Latin condor. Many commentators have suggested that the poem may have represented an evanescent feeling of Darío's, but it stands as a document in his political development nevertheless.[32] In essence the poem rationalizes and justifies as a "necessary war" precisely the brutality "Ode to Roosevelt" excoriated two years earlier. Whereas the earlier poem had counterposed the poets of the age of Netzahualcoyotl and the culture of the Incas to the "cult of Mammon" reigning in the North, "Salutación" reduced the cultural achievements of Mayan Palenque to no more than illustrious moments on the way to the "happy victory of the future" symbolized by the eagle. The poem ends expressing the hope that Latin America may receive the "magic influence" of the United States (Darío 1954, 804–7). As late as 1911, aboard a steamer headed for France, Darío listened approvingly as Panama's consul in Havana reflected that "what Panama lost in romantic sovereignty" from U.S. intervention, "it will gain in practical advantages and positive advances" (Barcía 1977, 1:175). His poem "God Save the Queen" praised the poets, beautiful women, and valiant warriors of "great and sovereign Britain" but made no mention of the social and political realities of the country's imperial past and present (Darío 1912, 168–71).

Hence the literary and political record Darío left is mixed — as ambivalent as his relationship with his native country during his turbulent life.[33] Such a record has thus invited the kind of controversy that has ensued over his "real" political views and his "proper" place in Nicaraguan cultural history, even before his vital organs had been distributed like sacred relics and the rest of his body laid to rest in the cathedral in León.

"NUESTRO RUBÉN" BEFORE SOMOZA

Only two months after Darío's death, Nicaraguan poet Salomón de la Selva (1893–1958) called him the "Hispanic Keats" and asserted that he was a "universal" poet whose work was for "all of humanity." Selva eulogized Darío as "a prophet, an inspiration . . . the anointed leader of the people. For us [Latin Americans?] he is the treasure of hope, the master of tomorrow . . . [who] united all the Latin American countries, awaking in them the sense of their true greatness."[34]

During the two-decade interim between Darío's death and the advent of the Somoza dynasty it fell principally to the *vanguardistas* to define Darío's significance within Nicaraguan culture. An essential part of the *vanguardista* agenda of defining and articulating an authentic and revitalized national cultural identity was to rediscover the authentic Darío who had been masked by his effete imitators and by the gratuitous historical process of deification mounted and sustained — albeit willy-nilly — by the state. Coronel Urtecho's "Oda a Rubén Darío," which announced the birth of the *vanguardia* movement, took the grand Darío marble-and-gold-leaf sarcophagus in the cathedral at León as its focal image, burlesquing its grandiose pomposity. The theme of Coronel Urtecho's ode (and a central feature of the *vanguardista* agenda) — as Ernesto Cardenal explained in the late 1940s — was "to divest

Rubén of his anachronistic vestments, the moth-eaten mask of a prince in which he was presented in great military parades, in the name of that other sincere Rubén, . . . this intimate Rubén, without artifice, the Rubén in his pajamas. . . . Beneath the fake gold leaf and phony stones existed the other true Darío . . . [he of] 'the inner torture' " (El Pez y la Serpiente 1978–79, 10–11, 21).

This Rubén, the *amado enemigo* (beloved enemy), provided vital inspiration and guidance. Pablo Antonio Cuadra still recalled clearly in an interview years later that

[We] owed [our] instinct to seek the universal to Rubén Darío. We wanted to see what was going on in the world, to assimilate it. . . . Deep down, we were followers of Rubén. We wanted to join the cosmopolitan with the national. . . . At the beginning, we attacked him a little, but that was very short-lived. We attacked the part of Rubén we considered evanescent and dangerous—things that were too precious and exotic. We wanted something more direct. . . . Later we realized that it was Rubén himself who was pushing us forward. (White 1986, 19)

The *vanguardistas'* efforts constituted the first conscious and formal attempt to reconstruct Darío as a cleansing and reorienting national hero. They sought to pierce the devitalizing public mantle thrown about him both by sycophantic politicians eager to post the cultural capital embodied in Darío to their philistine, nationalistic accounts, and by inferior writers capable of no more than imitating the more obvious features of a modish style. Their struggle, as Cardenal explained, "was not against Darío, but against the falsifiers of Darío" (El Pez y la Serpiente 1978–79, 14).

For some of the *vanguardistas*, admiration of Darío's literary brilliance and what they saw as his fearless temple-cleansing iconoclasm sharpened their critique of Nicaragua's political situation. Coronel Urtecho's ode appeared, after all, at the outset of General Sandino's guerrilla war against the U.S. Marines. Unfortunately, however, as noted earlier, the *vanguardistas'* subliminal anti-democratic elitism lapsed into an admiration for rising fascist movements in western Europe, and thence into the delusion that emerging strongman Anastasio Somoza García might be controllable and usable as an instrument for the construction of a tolerably progressive and stable nationalism in Nicaragua.[35] That delusion in turn seriously compromised their efforts to develop an adequate conception of Darío's place within a projected Nicaraguan cultural renaissance.

But whatever the *vanguardistas'* degree of clarity and level of effort might have been otherwise, they would have availed little once Anastasio Somoza García became president in December 1936. Somoza well understood the advantages of controlling the public image of venerated national cultural figures, and, as he subsequently made clear, his own preferred uses for indigenous culture were quite different from theirs.

THE SOMOCISTA DARÍO

During the early 1930s, before Anastasio Somoza García rose to the presidency, it was evident that even the most macabre elements of the Darío image clearly still had a hold on the public imagination. A special issue of *Revista Femenina Ilustrada* published in 1932 included a celebratory poem on Darío's brain. Illustrated by two photographs of the organ placed on pedastaled cake plates, Manuel Maldonado's poem rhapsodically evoked its furrows and folds, compared it to "the nut of some extraordinary oak grown on the heights . . . with the soul of a laurel," and called it a "perennial fountain of light" and a "prodigious dynamo" (Toledo de Aguerri 1932, 164–65).

Even before Anastasio Somoza García assumed the presidency, the Nicaraguan government was involved in reshaping Darío's image to state requirements. The preface to a 1935 Ministry of Public Instruction volume of Darío's writings piously called him "[our] great national poet" and "a noble son of this land." But the volume's editor cut and recast Darío's work in a high-handed manner, changing the import of the original texts (Ministerio de Instrucción Pública 1935, 19). Lines disappeared that could have caused offense to the United States, whose troops had only recently departed. Some three dozen lines were cut in which Darío commented caustically on New York City: on the "omnipotence of the multimillionaires" and the "mammonic madness [*locura mamónica*] of the vast capital of the check." A longer cut removed all of his criticism of the social and political distortions associated with building the canal.[36] Other excisions tidied up Nicaraguan history by denying the existence of certain political currents. For example, the editor struck Darío's observation that "although the conditions of life of [Nicaragua] are so different from those that give rise to so many protests by workers in European and [North] American nations, one or another wavering wind of the socialist spirit has not ceased to blow there" (Darío 1917b, 47, 68).

Especially in his *El viaje a Nicaragua* (1909), Darío had lamented the lack of conditions in Nicaragua to support creative endeavors. Virtually none of those laments survived the editor's pencil. A phrase that referred to the poverty of archival resources in Nicaragua (*los pobres archivos nicaragüenses*), which might logically have been taken to imply governmental irresponsibility, was rewritten as the paucity of archives in those times (*lo poco de aquellos pobres archivos*), suggesting that such lacks were a general characteristic of the era, for which no government should be held explicitly responsible (Ministerio de Instrucción Pública 1935, 59). Speaking of the difficulties Gámez and other historians had had in doing their work in Nicaragua, Darío had said, "No one there has been able to dedicate himself to pure letters. . . . Particularly in Nicaragua there is an abundance of primary material . . . but the environment is hostile, the conditions of existence are not propitious, and the best mental plant that sends up a triumph of shoots dries up quickly." He went on to assert that "freedom of thought did not exist," and to name a series of Nicaraguans of talent and promise who amid such conditions had failed to carry their work to completion, to publish, or to be recognized and honored in their homeland (Darío 1917b, 55, 68). None of this line of thought survived in the extracts chosen by the loyalist editor.

From the beginning, the Somoza government kept its guiding hand upon the image of Darío.[37] By 1940 the government had appointed Darío's son Dr. Rubén Darío Contreras as Nicaraguan ambassador in Buenos Aires.[38] The Ministry of Public Instruction published a forty-eight-page booklet, *Nicaragua: Land of Rubén Darío*, as the first in a series of readings intended for use in the public schools.[39] Another appeared in 1943, but there were apparently no others until the late 1950s, when the government began to produce Darío anniversary booklets and volumes.[40]

The Somoza regime's celebration of Darío proceeded alongside its manipulative and reactionary politics. In 1955 the Ministry of Foreign Relations published a Darío memorial issue of its public relations magazine, *Azul* (named after Darío's first major book), which reprinted Darío's poem to his friend Luis Debayle's daughter Salvadora, now Somoza's wife. The next issue of *Azul* featured the state visit of Vice President Richard Nixon, and a later one carried a full-page photograph of the brutal Guatemalan president, Colonel Carlos Castillo Armas, captioned as an "eminent and democratic statesman."[41]

In the 1960s the Somoza government responded to the centenary of Darío's birth as another opportunity to shape public understanding of the meaning of his life and work.[42] Especially revealing was president René Schick's address in 1966 upon being inducted into the *Academia Nicaragüense de la Lengua* (of which ex-*vanguardista* Pablo Antonio Cuadra was director).[43] Long a Somoza functionary, Schick had been Somoza García's personal secretary before being appointed minister of education in 1956. More recently he had been translating Luis Somoza Debayle's Cold War rhetoric into acceptable legal terminology. Over his younger brother's objections, Luis handed Schick the presidency in 1963 through a rigged election.[44]

Schick's address focused upon Darío's politics.[45] Following the requisite lyrical invocations of Darío as "maestro and modeler of our language, father of our culture and eponymous hero of our nationality" (10), Schick launched into his argument. Its core was that Darío had comprehended human misery and was committed to national dignity and sovereignty, yet because of his aristocratic commitment to Pure Art, he was essentially apolitical and opposed to all direct challenge to established authority or order.

Schick as president knew well that revising Darío's image had become all the more desirable now that the fledgling Sandinista opposition was beginning to make its presence known even as its first military operations were being defeated (Bermann 1986, 251–58). In developing his argument, however, Schick had to tread a thin line for two reasons: because contradictory evidence could easily be found in Darío, and because not much could be gained by holding Darío out to be a simpleminded partisan of the transparently reactionary and repressive politics of the Somoza regime.

Trying to play both ends against the middle, Schick admitted Darío's "ongoing concern for social and political problems" and even his condemnation of the exploitation of workers (21). Darío rejected "the ruling economic system, governed by merciless laws," Schick said, without specifying the system(s) to which he may have been referring. Rather surprisingly, Schick talked briefly of powerful German and Saxon nations that "launched themselves powerfully upon the world with their military, economic . . . [and] cultural might" (24). Copiously quoting Darío's strictures against the social and political repercussions of the Panama Canal project, he recalled Darío's advice to Latin American governments to be cautious and firm "in the defense of our dignity and our sovereignty" (27).

Had he stopped there, Schick's interpretation might have proved congenial even to the triumphant Sandinistas a dozen years later. But the most delicate and crucial part of the argument was yet to come. Cataloging the contending current images of Darío—bohemian, ivory-tower aristocrat, intellectual *caudillo* singing the ideal of Central American union, platonic philosopher, Jacobinic liberal exalting "breakers of chains" such as Máximo Jérez and Simón Bolívar (11)—Schick insisted that Darío intended to "distance himself from all partisanship," "daily political events," and especially "militant politics" and class struggle (*la lucha de clases*) in order to be a pure artist (14, 20). "The poet should have as his only object," he quoted Darío as saying in 1894, "ascension to his immortal sublime paradise: Art" (15). At length, the only social and political role Schick was willing to grant to the poet was to "open avenues of hope and enthusiasm to people" (11–15, 23).

Schick's mental agility was tested in confronting the historical fact of Darío's admiring relationships with such radicals as Martí, Lugones, and his old teacher José Leonard. Schick viewed the "belligerent influence" of Leonard not as a part of Darío's explicitly political formation but as a source of his "fundamental" platonism (18). Schick read Darío's relationship with

Lugones as clear evidence of his "invincible political skepticism" (16), despite the admiration Darío had expressed for Lugones. Having denominated Lugones as "his friend . . . of the red incandescences" (16), Schick interpreted the final image in Darío's *El Tiempo* essay on him—"red carnival dragons that remained in the streets from the last carnival . . . completely white"—in politically symbolic terms, although in context the image clearly refers more broadly to the mutability of all aspects of one's life in the world.[46]

More vexing for Schick was Darío's admiration for José Martí. Schick argued that Darío's reference to Martí as "giving his precious life for Humanity and for Art and for the true future triumph of America," and his assertion that "the blood of Martí did not belong to Cuba, it belonged to a whole race, to a whole continent," represented his categorical "condemnation for intervention by the artistic genius in political torment." "Not even to fight for the freedom of a country," Schick argued, "seemed to [Darío] a sufficiently powerful motive to abandon the battles—less bloody but no less transcendent—of the spirit and of Art" (16). It was, however, a tortuous reading. Evidence abounds in Darío's essay that he in no way intended to condemn Martí for intervening or to suggest that the only proper plane of action for Martí (and by extension for all artists) was the transcendent one of Pure Art. Darío was clearly seeking to place Martí's illuminating example on the broadest possible political and cultural ground.

In sum, then, Schick argued that when Darío came to the crossroads between "direct social action and artistic duty," he refused to compromise and proudly raised "the flag of pure art" (17). But because a completely depoliticized Darío would be as useless a legitimizing hero to the Somocistas as to the self-deluded bearers of red dragons/flags, Schick labored to show that Darío indeed possessed a "higher" politics that just happened to coincide with the politics of the Somoza government (17).

Arguing that Greek democracy "disgusted" Plato, Schick held that Darío's thought was "penetrated by a superior political concern" grounded in his "fundamental platonism" (18). Fortunately for Somoza's Liberal Nationalist Party, the "divine Rubén" was "primordially a [Platonic] liberal" who "pleaded for a liberal Christian humanism"—the "noble liberal tradition" that "one must construct men from inside" (21–25). Even more to Schick's purpose, Darío was unsympathetic to modern electoral democracies (19). Instead, he was committed to an "aristocratic ideal, made concrete in the eminent man, the only one who, by virtue of his spiritual energy, talent, and gift of rule is in a condition to assume the direction of the state" (22). According to Schick, Darío believed "that it should be those who are knowledgeable, experienced those who are morally superior and capable who govern in public matters. . . . He found that the masses are not always capable of choosing the one who really, in terms of his merits, ought to assume public power. . . . What he was looking for was a formula of selection which would permit those who were best prepared to take over the direction of collective matters — a system which would eliminate demagoguery, mendacity, charlatanry and ignoble calumny against the adversary" (19).

Standing upon that classic justification for autocracy, Schick reached both for the fascist and Cold War rhetorics and for the time-tested legitimizing code phrases of Latin America's liberal oligarchies. "Neither exploitation from above nor radicalism from below," he asserted, "find acceptance in [Darío]. The insensitivity of the powerful and the blind ire of the oppressed can only provoke a universal explosion which will destroy the bases of our civilization. . . . His doctrine . . . of unity and work, of peace and order still has force" (21, 35).

Hence for the Somoza government to hang the medal of the *Orden de Rubén Darío* around the neck of some favored personage was an act of both co-optation and self-legitimation.[47] In one such act in 1969, the government named its grandiose new national theater (a pet project of Anastasio Somoza Debayle's wife Hope Portocarrero de Somoza) El Teatro Nacional Rubén Darío. Indeed, such behavior was not unlike the mounting of a lavish state funeral for Darío a half-century earlier after thirty years of abusing and neglecting him. Naming the new theater for "a penniless boy born in this remote corner of the Hispanic world" seemed merely poignant to the reporter for the *New York Times*. But the political and social irony of the theater's lavish opening night struck Nicaragua's radical students as outrageous. Carrying signs alluding to Nicaragua's elevated illiteracy rate ("With what the theater cost, ninety schools could have been built") and chanting "¡Viva Che!" and "¡Viva Fidel!," the students gathered in front of the nearby cathedral as long lines of chauffeur-driven Mercedes automobiles delivered the opening-night audience. Using the cathedral as backdrop, the students presented their own play entitled "Oh, What a Wonderful Family," featuring an abusive landlord, his drunken brother-in-law, and his pregnant unwed daughter in search of an abortion.

DARÍO AND THE SANDINISTAS

From the mid-1960s onward, the Somoza regime's efforts to co-opt and domesticate Darío's image were increasingly at odds with the FSLN's attempt to rescue Darío from the regime's clutches and resituate him within Nicaraguan culture and politics. Early in the FSLN's history it became clear that rescuing and redefining Darío (along with other Nicaraguan cultural heroes such as the *cacique* Diriangén, Benjamín Zeledón, and Sandino) was to be a major item on the Sandinista political-cultural agenda (cf. Wheelock Román [1974] 1981). This effort was part of the FSLN's larger project of reinterpreting Nicaraguan history and culture and placing the resulting revisionist interpretations in the service of national transformation.

The Somoza government's conferring of the Order of Rubén Darío upon its cultural favorites was particularly galling to young anti-Somoza Nicaraguans. As early as March 1960, FSLN founder Carlos Fonseca Amador had declared that "the Somoza family has outraged the memory of our premier national poet" by bestowing medals carrying his name upon "the worst people of America," and in October anti-Somoza student magazine *Ventana* carried an article calling Darío "the first legitimate sign of independence, no longer [only] of Nicaragua, but of Hispanic America."[48] Returning to Darío a decade later, however, Fonseca argued that "ignorance of certain essential aspects" of Darío's work in Nicaragua was chargeable to the "reactionary tyranny" of the Somoza regime and to "North American cultural aggression."[49]

Inevitably, the approach of the Darío centenary of 1967—coming as it did after the Cuban revolution, the Bay of Pigs fiasco, and the U.S. invasion of the Dominican Republic—brought increased critical attention to social and political themes in Darío. The Universidad Nacional Autónoma de Nicaragua at León (UNAN) was a center of student activism, and many student leaders of the period went underground with the FSLN. Yet a two-volume centennial collection of essays on Darío issued by the university in 1967 was surprisingly cautious in reevaluating him. Edited by oppositionist poet Ernesto Gutiérrez and university rector Carlos Tünnermann Bernheim (later ambassador to the United States for the Sandinista government), the volumes nevertheless treated the issue of Darío's politics rather timidly and cursorily.[50] The most overtly political essay, written by Guillermo Rothschuh, proclaimed Darío "a poet of great national ardor" and recounted his imprecations against U.S. imperialism in Latin America.[51]

But not all of the centennial reevaluation of Darío was as favorable as that which derived from the fledgling FSLN, and by no means all of the unfavorable criticism came from Somocistas or other political reactionaries. Octavio Paz observed that Darío's poetry lacked substance ("earth, people") and that he "forgot or did not want to see the other half: the oligarchies, the oppression, this landscape of bones, broken crosses and soiled uniforms that is Latin American history. He had enthusiasm; he lacked indignation" (Paz [1965] 1972, 55). During the centennial year Jean Franco characterized Darío's life as "a stormy sea of marital adventures and passionate affairs interspersed with guilt-ridden remorse when he longed for the tranquil harbor of religion." She viewed Darío's interest in Indian legend and folklore as confined to Indians of the pre-Columbian era, and essentially aristocratic and alienated. Compared to Martí, Darío's resistance to entrenched authority was "ivory tower," Franco charged. Moreover, his poems about working-class people (such as "¡Al trabajo!" [To Work], which exhorted workers to imitate the industriousness of the bee and the beaver) were "devoid of political content." Like other *modernistas*, Franco observed, Darío "took the trappings of the literary and humanistic culture" of a cultivated minority and celebrated it as a "universal" tradition (Franco 1967, 22–34, 48).[52]

About the time of the Sandinista triumph in mid-1979, Darío began to be attacked even more severely by critics on the left. Françoise Perus charged that Darío conceived of the poet as a "profoundly elitist . . . cantor of the class in power" who looked no further than the possibility of "substituting some elites for others" who might treat their bards better (Perus 1980; Zimmerman 1982, 165–66; Beverley and Zimmerman 1990, 55).

Carlos Blanco Aguinaga's stringent criticism was grounded in dependency theory (Blanco Aguinaga 1980). Situating modernist writers such as Darío as intellectuals organic to the system of dependency in Latin America, Blanco Aguinaga focused on Darío's much-analyzed story "El rey burgués" (The bourgeois king), a brief fable about a poet who has abandoned the unhealthy city and gone to live in the forest in order to seek ideal poetry. Hungry and in rags, the poet is brought before a king, ensconced in his sumptuous palace and surrounded by courtesans and sycophants. Although the monarch prides himself on being an *aficionado* of the arts, as a "bourgeois king" rather than a "poet king" he fails to recognize this "rare species of man." Informed that the stranger is indeed a poet, the king commands "Speak, and you shall eat." The poet passionately declares that he wishes to write a poem that will serve as a "triumphal arch" to welcome a coming messiah "of all power and light" who will usher in "the time of great revolutions." Instead, the king sets him to grinding out silly and repetitive tunes on a music box. Eventually the "poor devil" of a poet dies in the freezing winter, his hand still on the crank, while inside a gaggle of professors of rhetoric recite bad verse at a lavish banquet.

For Blanco Aguinaga, the central point of the story is that the problem with the king is not that he *is* a king, but that he is instead a bourgeois imitation of a *real* king, who would provide the refuge and support the poet asks for and requires (Blanco Aguinaga 1980, 525–27). Thus in the story the organ-grinding poet is the archetype of the poet in the real world in which Darío found himself. Finding that reality so inhospitable, Blanco Aguinaga argued, Darío invented an ideal realm of poetry (reigned over by a "real" king) in which he could "cause to be born that which does not exist, making a rich metaphor of precious stones substitute for a vulgar reality" (Blanco Aguinaga 1980, 529–30).

In Blanco Aguinaga's view, the binary opposition between the real and the ideal was the primary contradiction that led Darío to seek a place "at the banquet of the dominant classes." Hence Blanco Aguinaga observed that the pieces Darío wrote for newspapers were especially rich in accounts of cultural expositions attended by the social elite, titillating cultural notices from European capitals, and tales of his own dealings with the nobility. Such rationalizing and justifying pieces reassured the Latin American oligarchy concerning their access to *la gran cultura* of Europe and thus "confirmed . . . [their] motivating ideology" (Blanco Aguinaga 1980, 535–41). Even more clearly, Darío's prose poem "God Save the Queen" openly celebrates British imperial domination and accepts its contradictions "because above the vigor of your workers, the drudgery of your sailors and the unknown labor of your miners, you have artists who dress in silks of love, in the golds of glory, in lyrical pearls."

In Darío then, "civilization and poetry come to be inseparable from prosperity and power" (Blanco Aguinaga 1980, 542–44). Hence Darío reacted to the rising demands of workers at the turn of the century essentially like a member of the ruling class. In an article titled "La obra del populacho" (The work of the mob), Blanco Aguinaga pointed out, Darío referred to a "wave of perversity" that had broken out amongst the "unconscious and rude masses" in Chile, who went "screaming through the streets, menacing, drunk, brutal, ferocious" until the government "had to employ arms" against them. And in 1898, during his first visit to Barcelona (historically a cauldron of working class–based radical politics), Darío worried over "the deaf agitation of the social movement, which later would break out in red explosions" (Darío 1955, 3:26–34; Darío 1912, 217).[53]

Thus when the Sandinistas turned their attention to Darío after the revolutionary triumph, they faced a double task: to reconstruct a Darío deformed by their predecessors in power, and to defend him against emerging left critics of the 1960s and 1970s.[54] Some steps were easy to take. The elite Teatro Nacional Rubén Darío was renamed Teatro Popular Rubén Darío, and performances of popular music and dance replaced those by touring symphony orchestras and ballet companies. But other steps in reconstructing Darío's image required a broad reinterpretation of his life, politics, and published writings.[55]

The earliest post-Somoza documents in the effort to assimilate Darío into the revolutionary project were Nicaraguan historian Jorge Arellano's *Nuestro Rubén Darío* and *Rubén Darío: textos sociopolíticos*, and Carlos Tünnerman Bernheim's *Rubén Darío y su tiempo*, all issued in 1980. *Nuestro Rubén Darío* (published by the National Library, headed by Arellano) was a collection of poems, politically tame except for the "Ode to Roosevelt." By omitting the pro-U.S. poem "Salutación a la águila," it signalled that some manipulation of the Darío canon would likely be necessary to resituate the poet politically. *Rubén Darío: textos sociopolíticos* drew mainly from Darío's essays and journalism, and included pieces that were to become favorites in the new discourse: "La insurrección en Cuba," "El triunfo de Calibán," "Las palabras y los actos de Mr. Roosevelt," and the story "D.Q.," a special favorite.[56]

"D.Q." depicts young Spanish troops in the Spanish-American War, hungry and desperate but "burning to fight" (*quemante de luchar*) Yankee troops and fantasizing about hoisting their flag over the capitol in Washington. Word comes, however, that the cause is lost. The conquering enemy presents himself in the form of "a great blond, limp-haired, bearded devil, an official of the United States, followed by an escort of blue-eyed hunters." All the Spaniards surrender their arms except for one nameless soldier known only as "D. Q.," the color-bearer. Older than most, solitary, and poetic, he is so confident of the "nobility of our race and the justice of our cause" that when it comes time to surrender the colors he walks calmly to the edge of a bottomless abyss and hurls himself into it. The story may be read as *modernista* fantasy celebrating *hispanidad* (D.Q. as Don Quixote), or — the preferred Sandinista reading — as anti-U.S. protest (the U.S. official as an unmistakable Uncle Sam) (cf. Palau de Nemes 1981).

More explicitly political yet was Tünnerman Bernheim's assertion in *Rubén Darío y su tiempo* (issued by the Ministry of Education in connection with its internationally heralded literacy campaign) that "to rediscover Rubén Darío will be one of our great cultural and pedagogical duties" (Tünnerman Bernheim 1980, 7). In his introduction to Tünnerman Bernheim's book, Darío biographer Edelberto Torres decried "the silence that ignorance tried to lay upon his name like a heavy slab without an epitaph." The rediscovered Darío, however, is "a man integrated with his epoch" enough to write

> Tremble, tremble, tyrants in your royal chairs
> Not one stone upon another of all the Bastilles
> Will remain tomorrow.

"To clear away *somocismo*" is the duty that will be realized," Torres asserted. Illiterate Nicaraguans previously unable to read a single "strophe of Rubén or a declaration of Sandino" will now read both in *Rubén Darío y su tiempo* and the pocket-sized *Ideario Político de Augusto C. Sandino*, also published by the Ministry of Education. "Rubén and Sandino have much to do in Nicaragua," Torres said, "the one, guide of its culture, and the other, captain of its liberties, are sufficient to make of Nicaragua . . . the great country that both loved. Rubén sang to it in verse, and Sandino defended it with arms that sounded like homeric hexameters" (Tünnerman Bernheim 1980, 10–11).

The revisionist effort gathered force at the mid-January 1982 opening of the national Rubén Darío celebration, when Minister of Culture Ernesto Cardenal proclaimed categorically that Darío was an anti-imperialist and "revolutionary" who "anticipated the [Sandinista] revolution in his song" (Ministerio de Cultura 1982a, 233–38).[57] Cardenal argued that Sandino, who was an intellectual despite his being a mere artisan, was influenced by Darío and became in turn the teacher of Fonseca.[58] Asserting direct political descent from Darío through Sandino to the contemporary FSLN, Cardenal proclaimed, "This revolution was a dream of Darío. And a decision of Sandino. And a strategy of Carlos Fonseca" (Ministerio de Cultura 1982a, 236). A week later, the Sandinista newspaper *Barricada* published "Twelve Propositions to Rescue Rubén Darío," which proposed that the task the Sandinistas faced was no less than to "debureaucratize, popularize, nationalize, re-edit, humanize [and] liberate" the poet (Rothschuh Tablada 1982, 2–3).

At the opening of a tiny Darío museum in León, Comandante Carlos Núñez said that in the rescue effort he and others had had to work hard to give Darío "the place he deserves, within a new vision and a new thought" (Ministerio de Cultura 1982a, 99–106). In Núñez's speech, the ragged poet's prediction in "El rey burgués" about the coming of a messiah is quoted as if it had issued directly from Darío himself instead of from a character in a work of fiction, and (more importantly) as if it had specifically prophesied the Sandinista revolution. "In this new revolutionary time, we are receiving," Núñez said, the poems Darío envisioned as "triumphal arches" of a new cultural and political order in which art will be understood as "an arm of the Revolution." Telescoping the few happy years Darío spent in León as a child and adolescent, and the few agonized months he passed there thirty years later, just before his death, Núñez referred to León as the city where the poet "always lived and developed" (*siempre vivió y se desarrolló*), where he "studied, lived, and died." Selecting phrases from a few pieces such as "Ode to Roosevelt," the commandante thus projected a visionary and revolutionary Darío who was "Nicaraguan to the marrow of his bones." Hence the government had declared Darío a "National Hero of Our Culture," and his birthday as the nation's *Día de Independencia Cultural*. The Sandinistas were placing him, Núñez said, "on the altar of the country, beside our General of Free Men Augusto César Sandino." At the close of the ceremony, the newly renamed Orden Independencia Cultural "Rubén Darío" was presented to Darío biographer Edelberto Torres, former *vanguardista* José Coronel Urtecho, musicians Salvador Cardenal and Luis Enrique Mejía Godoy, Minister of Culture Ernesto Cardenal, and posthumously to the young martyred poet Fernando Gordillo.[59]

Historian Jorge Arellano also played a leading role in the Sandinista effort to rescue and reconstruct Darío after 1979. By mid-July 1982, Arellano asserted, "The popular Sandinista revolution has recovered . . . [and] revealed the progressive, revolutionary Darío who was hidden, buried before July 19, 1979" (Arellano 1982b). Quoting from the portions of Darío's writings that

AÑO DEL CENTENARIO DE AZUL

EL MINISTERIO DE CULTURA

En el marco de la VII Jornada de la Independencia Cultural Rubén Darío, la celebración del Centenario de Azul y continuando con el rescate del arte popular, presenta:

Revista Nacional de Artistas Aficionados.

Selección de Danza y Música. Sábado 6 de Febrero, a las 7:30 de la noche.

Con la participación de la música, la danza, el canto y la pintura de todo el país.

PRECIOS

1er. Balcón	C$35,000.00
Platea	C$25,000.00
2do. Balcón	C$15,000.00
3er. Balcón	C$10,000.00

Boletos a la venta en la taquilla del Teatro Popular Rubén Darío, de 9:00 A.M. – 5:00 P.M.

MINISTERIO DE CULTURA DE NICARAGUA

Newspaper advertisement for music and dance performance in the Rubén Darío Popular Theater, Managua, 1988, in commemoration of the centenary of the publication of Darío's *Azul*.

had come to be favorites of those who preferred his putatively radical side (the "Ode to Roosevelt" and a few other poems, the essay "El triunfo de Calibán," and the newspaper articles he had written against Roosevelt), Arellano projected a Darío "open to the precursors of modern social thought, including the dialectical materialism of Marx and Engels" (Arellano 1982b, 104).[60] Simultaneously, the Ministry of Culture issued a new anthology of Darío's essays edited by Arellano, selected to emphasize favored themes such as anti-imperialism and nationalism (Arellano 1982d).

In constructing an anthology of brief extracts from Darío the following year, however, Arellano exercised less editorial restraint and responsibility (Arellano 1983b). Ranging in length from a half-dozen lines to a page, the extracts were drawn widely from Darío's poetry and prose works. The extracts (not identified as to source) were arranged under thematic titles supplied by the editor: "Pan y trabajo" (Bread and work), "Innumerables mendigos" (Innumerable beggars), "William Walker: conquistador nórdico" (William Walker: Nordic conqueror), "La amenaza del imperialismo yanqui" (The menace of Yankee imperialism), and the like. Favoring some of the portions of Darío's work excluded in the Somoza-era student anthologies, the anthology clearly was intended to bring the poet's politics into line with Sandinista ideology.

To a degree far beyond that unavoidable in any process of extracting, Arellano's editing of the excerpts misrepresented the original sources. The excerpts "Un tirano que hay que combatir" (A tyrant who has to be combatted), "La ira y odio al capitalista" (Wrath and hatred toward the capitalist), and "La nueva buena del socialismo" (The new good of socialism) can be traced to an article entitled "Dynamite," published in a Buenos Aires newspaper in 1893 (Mapes 1938, 24–28). Several years before Arellano's anthology appeared, Blanco Aguinaga had noted the author of the essay's extraordinary familiarity with *fin de siècle* political theorists, and raised the possibility that instead of writing the article himself, Darío may have been persuaded to sign an article written by some "ruling class ideologue" who wanted to use the rising young poet's fame to legitimize his own reactionary political views (Blanco Aguinaga 1980, 546).[61] Regardless of whether Darío wrote the piece or not, the essay is usually included in the Darío canon (cf. Darío 1955, 1:643), and in extracting and titling his selections from it, Arellano stood them on their head ideologically.

"All of Europe is mined with the socialist rot [*la caries socialista*]," the original essay begins, summoning the revolting image of a mouthful of rotting teeth and gums. "Anarchism shows its face everywhere. . . . The hungry of Europe bring us [in Latin America] their contagion of wrath stored up for centuries," it continues, unmistakably warning *against* rising militancy among the working class and satirizing the array of political ideologies that were fueling it, rather than celebrating either.

> The enemy . . . is the worker, who has some savings; the proprietor, who has houses . . . the noble woman, who has diamonds; the judge, who has authority; the king, who has a crown; the believer, who has God. God also is the enemy. The pseudo-anarchists imported to [Latin America] have written in their threatening papers . . . "neither God nor country." Engels said . . . "The time will come when there will be no other religion than socialism." [Such] philosophers . . . preach to the ignorant and closed masses the death of beliefs and of religious ideals. The *philosophy of appetites* broadcasts itself like a pestilent wind. (Mapes 1938, 25)

As the "rage of anarchy" has spread, the writer went on, workers have become discontented with their lot: "One has to be rich at all costs, and given that we cannot be, we will destroy the property of others, [and] level the heads of humanity with fire and blood. Let us seek to gorge ourselves and be happy in this life, for there is nothing beyond."

To the writer of the essay, conventional historical and ideological distinctions are unimportant: "Socialists, anarchists, communists—all are one. The use of more or less soap is all that distinguishes them. They are [all] sons of Cain" (*Cainitas*). In Arellano's anthology, however, the italicized portion of the following quotation—removed from its original rhetorical context and thus stripped of its ironic tone—appears as Darío's *apologia* for Marxism under the title "Un tirano que hay que combatir" (A tyrant who has to be combatted): "Country? They have none. *These days their country (that of the socialists, anarchists, communists) is the world. Karl Marx in founding the International erases frontiers, and wherever a bourgeois is seen, a proprietor, one recognizes a tyrant who has to be combatted*" (Arellano 1983b, 35).

The original essay becomes even more bitingly satirical in presenting the beliefs and actions of socialists and their ilk: For them, it says, "Morals don't exist, classes don't exist, property doesn't exist, justice doesn't exist, God doesn't exist. And if it exists, dynamite it!" (Mapes 1938, 26). Even the physiognomy of such misguided people is grotesque: "grim eyes, oversized jawbones," and "markedly zoological" features. According to the original essay, "the orators of the tavern are going to infect the good worker . . . by making him dream of an anarchist Shangri-La that will come with the absolute triumph of the Messiah named Democracy" (26). The author subsequently launches into lengthy satire of the blacksmith, the shoemaker, and the carpenter who sally forth deluded by such nonsense. Irony and satire build insistently as references to "shirtless crowds" [*turbas*] of "dynamiters and strikers" pile one upon the other (Mapes 1938, 27). Yet this caricature of deluded workers, decontextualized and set out under Arellano's title "Rage and hatred toward the capitalist" as one of Darío's "socio-political texts," appears to ratify and celebrate precisely that which was being satirized and rejected in the original essay.[62]

Another major contributor to the post-1979 effort to reconstruct Darío was Vice President Sergio Ramírez, himself a novelist.[63] Ramírez was scathing in his contempt for the ethereal, bohemian, depoliticized Darío who wrote verses on the fans of opulent women. In his view, this Darío was bequeathed to the nation by the Nicaraguan bourgeoisie who had dressed in swallow-tail coats both to bear the poet's casket through the streets and to sign the Chamorro-Bryan treaty granting the United States the right to build the canal through Nicaragua, the one that "Rubén had feared so much." Ramírez also complained that the Somoza regime had "abused" the figure of Darío by "lowering him to a provincial symbol celebrated in tacky literary contests and the crowning of muses in country clubs" (White 1986, 82; cf. Ramírez 1983a, 189–202). How could such a bourgeoisie not falsify Darío, teaching in the schools only "his sonorities and oriental tales"? Such a deception, Ramírez observed, resulted from "the perfidy, the absolute cultural incapacity of a backward and atrophied bourgeoisie" (especially that of the Somoza epoch) who presented "the real substance of [Darío's] poetry as the casual delirium of a dreamer."

For Ramírez, therefore, the task of the revolution was to rescue Darío from such fraud so that he may "speak for his people" (Ramírez 1984a, 99–100).[64] When the Sandinista government conferred the Orden de Independencia Cultural "Rubén Darío" upon novelist Julio Cortázar in 1984, Ramírez called Darío a "cultural hero [and] prophet in his [own] country . . . who felt and understood the struggle of his people" as had his spiritual and political brothers Bolívar, Martí, and Sandino. That was the Darío (born in the same year that Marx's *Das Kapital* appeared, Ramírez noted) who loved and had children by a "*campesina* concubine" (Francisca), the Darío who was honored at a banquet by stevedores in Valparaiso and whose carriage was pulled by the working people of León when he returned to Nicaragua in 1907 (Ramírez 1984a, 96 and 99).

Writing six months later, Nicaraguan poet Julio Valle-Castillo further elaborated this effort at political rehabilitation (Valle-Castillo 1984). Admitting Darío's moments of apolitical detachment, Valle-Castillo nevertheless argued that his aestheticism was not a sign of his co-optation (as Blanco Aguinaga had contended), but a calculated gesture of opposition to the crass vulgarity of the bourgeoisie. The ubiquitous swan, which for Blanco Aguinaga concentrated all of Darío's sycophancy and co-opted aestheticism into a single image, Valle-Castillo interpreted as an "anti-imperialist symbol."[65]

He characterized José Martí not as merely one of Darío's literary heroes, but as his political "father and teacher." Surveying the record of Darío's "personal political participation," Valle-Castillo went so far as to suggest that he was actually involved in some clandestine arms sales—an involvement, he asserted, that would help to account for Darío's whereabouts during what he said was a previously obscure period of his life (September 1882–July 1883, when Darío was just turning sixteen years old).[66]

Whatever their character or effect, the Sandinistas' efforts to rescue and reconstruct Nicaragua's national poet were brought to a forced close by their defeat in the elections of early 1990. Yet that turning point in Nicaraguan cultural and political history by no means terminated the struggle over Darío. As had occurred at previous junctures, the struggle was only reactivated.

During the final days of the electoral contest, Jorge Arellano—a major contributor to the effort to transform Darío into a proto-Sandinista partisan—leveled several charges on the front page of *La Prensa* against the Sandinista government and its efforts to "absorb, bureaucratize and control culture." The government had defaulted on its promise to honor Darío by issuing editions of his works; the Orden de Independencia Cultural "Rubén Darío" had been bestowed only on "foreigners in solidarity with official politics"; and former Minister of Culture Ernesto Cardenal's "standardizing" poetry workshops had prohibited the writing of "Darian" poetry, choosing instead to turn out a "series of little Cardenals" scribbling formulaic "exteriorist" poetry (Xavier Solís 1990). Another anti-Sandinista writer lamented the sorry state into which the government had allowed the El Teatro Nacional Rubén Darío to fall (physically and culturally) as a result of its revolutionary "popularization" of culture. Juxtaposing a photograph of the theater (a mini–Kennedy Center designed by U.S. architect Edward Durrell Stone) with that of Managua's grandiose 1930s Darío statue (Darío in toga, angel perched upon his right shoulder), the writer unconsciously echoed René Schick's insistence that Darío forswore all party politics in favor of Pure Art. The writer also took the Sandinistas to task for holding party meetings in the theater, allowing those who came to cultural performances to enter in short pants and sandals, and adorning the entrance with a gigantic likeness of Sandino instead of Darío. Predicting that the Sandinistas would be ousted in the elections, the writer foresaw the tantalizing possibility of finally making proper amends to the nation's premier poet, presumably by banishing in one stroke Sandino, sandals, short pants, and Sandinista culture.[67]

Fortunately for the Sandinista and Somocista partisans, Darío's life and work offered a tantalizing array of data for opposing exegetical agendas: sufficiently diverse and contradictory to admit of a variety of interpretations. Commenting upon Darío's "sovereign indifference to political coherence,"

Statue of Rubén Darío by Italian sculptor Mario Favilli, formally unveiled in Managua on 15 September 1933. (Columbus Memorial Library, Organization of American States; reproduced by permission)

Rubén Darío pictured on Sandinista-era 500-córdoba bill.

Octavio Paz suggested that Darío ultimately "was not a political thinker. [Neither] in his public nor in his private life was he a model of rigor" (Paz [1965] 1972, 53). Thus the same profusion of contradictory biographical and literary data that precludes neat political readings of his life and work also makes him available to any camp willing to edit him selectively, and whose ideology is untroubled by the reductionism that inevitably results. Hence have arisen Darío as Somocista liberal/nationalist/elitist and also Darío as Sandinista anti-imperialist/nationalist/proletarian.

In their feuding over Darío, Somocistas and Sandinistas alike extrapolated too facilely from the mere fact of his corporeal unity to an assumption of an intellectual-historical-political unity. Any assertion that Darío is or was this or that particular thing tacitly posits that there was one unified Rubén Darío who can be discovered and authenticated by appropriate reference to the documentable details of his life and the words he wrote and left to posterity. But the assumption that those two bodies of data are mutually corroborating proves to be problematic.

Salgado has recently argued, in fact, that Rubén Darío "was a fictional poetic being . . . who ended up displacing another personage—this one historical—named Félix Rubén García Sarmiento" (Salgado 1989, 339). Salgado distinguishes meticulously between the historical *personage* Félix Rubén García Sarmiento and the historical *construct* which is the poet Rubén Darío, and she details the process by which the former constructed the latter (especially in his autobiographical or autobiographically based writings). Her analysis thus suggests that the contested *re*constructions engaged in by the Somocistas and Sandinistas were in one sense merely extensions of a dissociative-*con*structive process begun by García Sarmiento/Darío himself. Examining texts "in which the poet establishes an autobiographical pact with the reader," Salgado explicates the dialectical process by which the mythical construct (the hero-poet Rubén Darío) was established and projected, and through which the reader's sympathy is engaged and her/his belief in the fiction elicited and sustained.

EPILOGUE

Within Nicaragua, the struggle over Darío has been but one constitutive episode within a long history of conflicted negotiation over national cultural identity. As earlier chapters of this book have suggested, this history stretches from ethnocidal conquest in the sixteenth century, through liberal modernization and emergent nationalism during the nineteenth century, to nationalist guerrilla insurgency in the opening decades of the twentieth, through a half-century dictatorship and thence to revolution and counterrevolution.

Other Nicaraguan cultural figures have been struggled over, but none of them as vigorously and perennially as the *niño prodigioso* (prodigious child) of Metapa. And in a tiny nation that since the days of *el divino Rubén* has thought of itself as—and dreamed of becoming—a nation of poets, perhaps the best metaphor for the protracted struggles by ideologically opposed partisans to possess him as ideological and cultural legitimizer is the pious and macabre parceling out of Rubén Darío's dead body.

The purpose of examining this contested discourse has not been to decide what Darío's politics actually were or were not. I have sought rather to explore the dialectical relationship between culture and ideology as it inheres in the struggles to possess him. The most dramatic episode of that struggle has highlighted some salient aspects of the dialectic: the instrumental (regime challenging or legitimizing) use of culture—and especially of concentrations of cultural capital such as that which aggregates around an internationally celebrated cultural figure; the ideological control of cultural processes (through editorial manipulation, for example); and the institutional privileging of selective versions of cultural history through public symbols and ceremonies.

Regardless of their ideological position, Darío's partisans seldom proved able either to tolerate or to process the complex nuances and contradictions of his thought and work.[68] When all is said and done, the political perspectives congenial to the Somocistas can in fact be located in Darío's works. But so can those favored by the Sandinistas. Moreover, each array can be demonstrated without employing the editorial manipulations of which both parties have been guilty.

Fortunately, polar readings are not entirely without merit. Each contributes in some ways to a fuller understanding of Darío. But the nuancing needed is unlikely to emerge from such (ultimately crude) readings, even when considered comparatively. What the ideologically opposed Darío partisans needed to comprehend was the reality of a non-unitary Darío, one of multiple motivations, multiple perspectives, multiple roles, and multiple voices — even, one might argue, multiple and sometimes contradictory identities.[69]

The critical point for our purpose here is that the cultural capital which was potentially usable by whatever political faction was attached to the idealized (thus inescapably dehistoricized and denationalized) *construct* known as Rubén Darío. But that capital could be mobilized only by assuming the internal coherence of the construct and its congruence with (indeed its indistinguishability from) the historical (and historically engaged) personage García Sarmiento, who was claimably Nicaraguan and who made his living mostly by being a journalist. While "Rubén Darío" was considerably more likely to express himself on the transcendent aesthetic glories of Paris than upon the dilemma of tiny Nicaragua caught in the gears of great power politics, García Sarmiento (writing under the *nom de plume* Rubén Darío) was about as likely to comment upon either subject.[70] In any case, it is finally the dialectical relationship between the two that must be understood, rather than the reductionist "reality" of one or the other. Comprehending that dialectic may at least prevent us from misunderstanding and misrepresenting the operation of historically situated cultural processes as they have been misunderstood and misrepresented by the partisans examined here.

CHAPTER 9 ANCESTRAL FEATS AND FUTURE DREAMS SANDINO AND THE POLITICS OF CULTURE

I am . . . proud that in my veins flows, more than any other, the blood of the American Indian, whose regeneration contains the secret of being a loyal and sincere patriot.

— Augusto C. Sandino, July 1927

Tell your people there may be bandits in Nicaragua, but they are not necessarily Nicaraguans.

— Sandino to Carleton Beals, February 1928

We are the descendants of Sandino. . . . Let us fight as he fought . . . so that his dream of a Free Homeland and a happy people may become reality.

— Carlos Fonseca Amador, 1960

Nicaraguan President Adolfo Díaz's struggle to regain Masaya from rebel General Mena in 1912 produced one of Nicaragua's revered indigenous cultural heroes: General Benjamín (*El Indio*) Zeledón. Zeledón was the leader of a popular resistance; his six hundred troops included mainly peasants and poor artisans whose struggle he explicitly likened to that of Andrés Castro and the heroes of San Jacinto who helped defeat William Walker. Like Sandino who followed him, Zeledón cast the struggle not only in political but also in cultural terms. "This unwonted outrage inflicted upon Nicaragua" by Díaz and his U.S. supporters, he said, "is not only an outrage against this disgraced country; it is . . . an outrage for a whole race worthy of the esteem of history of many centuries." In a letter to Admiral Southerland two weeks before his death, Zeledón accused the United States of violating both international law and Nicaraguan sovereignty and protested "in the name of my country, in the name of the army I

Benjamín Zeledón on Sandinista-era 5,000-córdoba bill.

command, and in the name of my race" (Instituto de Estudio del Sandinismo 1982d, 127, 133, 149).

One of those who saw General Zeledón's body paraded in public was seventeen-year-old Augusto C. Sandino, to whom he became a link to other indigenous heroes reaching all the way back to the rebel *cacique* Diriangén. The death of "the unbeaten and glorious General Zeledón," Sandino wrote later, "gave me the key to our national situation. . . ; for that reason, we consider the war in which we have been persisting to be a continuation of his" (Bermann 1986, 164; Ramírez 1984b, 2:305). Thus it was not only the spirit of resistance that continued, but also the effort to ground (and legitimize) that resistance in racial identity and cultural pride and continuity.

Toward the end of his book about General Sandino, Gregorio Selser writes, "Ancestral feats have ever blended into a harmony with future dreams." Thus Sandino's "epic of yesterday," he continues, "is today a legend and will tomorrow be a myth" (Selser [1978] 1981, 199, 201).[1] Although both Sandino's epic feats themselves and the legends and myths subsequently woven about them have been explained almost exclusively in political and military terms, both were profoundly cultural in their bases and implications.[2] This chapter explores a few salient cultural elements of the feats themselves, and of the epic, the legend, and the myth.

Like Rubén Darío, Sandino is a key element in a cultural-political dialectic that now stretches over a century and reaches across class, culture, ideology, and national boundaries. Sandino was born at the beginning of the Zelaya period. He and his "crazy little army" fought the U.S. Marine Corps during the period of the most overt and complete U.S. occupation of the country. He was assassinated by the first of the Somoza surrogates of U.S. political, economic, and cultural domination. During Sandino's life and the decades beyond, writers from throughout the Americas elaborated a Sandino myth

Departamento de Propaganda y Educación Política del FSLN

Sandino poster, 1988 ("Death to Imperialism. I will not surrender; I await you [U.S. Marines] here. I want a free country or death.")

that gained international currency. He was resurrected in the 1950s by Fidel Castro and Che Guevara as a model guerrilla strategist, and from the early 1960s onward by Carlos Fonseca and other early members of the FSLN as political mentor and cultural hero. For the Sandinista government, Sandino was the quintessential exemplar of eternally vigilant and uncompromising nationalistic resistance to an imperialism explicitly expressed politically, economically, and militarily, but which in the final analysis is profoundly and en-

Sandino and Sandino birthplace on Sandinista-era 1,000-córdoba bill.

compassingly cultural in its roots, rationales, and designs. In Sandinista Nicaragua Sandino's image was everywhere—on flags and currency, on murals and monuments, on posters and billboards, and in the ubiquitous graffiti reminders of the ongoing struggle—and his memory was constantly reinforced in song and poetry.

As with the analysis of Rubén Darío that precedes it, the point of this chapter is not to decide who has "told the truth" (politically or culturally) about Sandino.[3] It is rather to show that Sandino's most ardent partisans and detractors have situated their analyses and judgments—as well as their politically opportune projections of a popular image of Sandino—on a cultural ground. This chapter excavates and examines some of the cultural strata from which those "ancestral feats" arose, as well as the cultural contexts that lent them their initial meaning and the cultural processes through which the legend and the myth were at length constructed. Whatever Sandino was in life, the mythic constructs are as thoroughly embedded in the culture of Nicaragua as constructions of George Washington, Abraham Lincoln, or John F. Kennedy are in the culture of the United States.

Every culture constructs and reconstructs its civilizing heroes repeatedly. What is at issue here is not their right to do so, but rather the cultural-political import of such constructions and reconstructions—both within a small and poor country itself, and in such a country's relations with a much larger and more powerful one historically, culturally, and ideologically predisposed to distrust and devalue cultures different from its own.

THE (MORE OR LESS) HISTORICAL SANDINO

As is frequently the case with those whose lives have been turned into national myth, reliable details on Sandino's early years are not abundant.[4] Fortunately, the story falls into several fairly well defined periods: from his birth in 1895 until he armed his first band of twenty-nine men in late 1926; from then to his death in 1934; from his death to the birth of the FSLN in 1961; and the resurrection, revitalization, and canonization of Sandino after 1961 by the Sandinistas.

What is known with reasonable certainty is that Sandino was born on 18 May 1895 in Niquinohomo, a small town not far from Granada. His parents, neither of them yet eighteen, were Margarita Calderón, an Indian servant girl, and Don Gregorio Sandino, who—depending upon the source one credits—seems to have been either a "small farmer" or "the scion of a moderately wealthy landholding family." Sometime later, Don Gregorio married and brought his young illegitimate son to live with him, at which point Augusto Calderón became Augusto C. Sandino. He attended school first in Niquinohomo and later in Granada, and then returned to work with his father. He apparently did so until he was about twenty-one, when he went to the Costa Rican border and worked as a mechanic before returning to Niquinohomo to establish his own business selling grain. It seems generally agreed that at about the age of twenty-five, as the result of an altercation (characterized in numerous ways in a variety of accounts) Sandino shot and wounded a man in Niquinohomo and thus had to flee to Honduras, where perhaps following some intermittent work in gold mines and on plantations he found a job as a mechanic in a sugar mill outside the port of La Ceiba. He subsequently worked a short time for an American company in Guatemala before turning up in Tampico, in the oil fields of Mexico, in 1923. There he became an employee of Huasteca Petroleum Company (part of the Standard Oil of Indiana syndicate) and fathered a daughter (Macaulay [1967] 1985, 51, 279n.).[5] Three years later, having risen to be—again, depending upon which account one credits—either "a book-keeper" or "head of the Gasoline Sales Department" of Huasteca, he resigned and returned home to Nicaragua and soon began to form his army.[6]

Biographical details for the remaining eight years of Sandino's life, although in some respects not as full as one would like, are relatively plentiful and more or less agreed upon: he fought to expel the marines from Nicaragua, and when they left he laid down his arms and retired to the Río Coco region to establish an agricultural cooperative. A year later he returned to Managua, where he was assassinated. For purposes of cultural analysis, however, the documentable details are less important than the myth that has been woven around them, both during the few public years of Sandino's life and in the six decades since his death.

CREATING AND ELABORATING THE MYTH

In Sandino's own writings, references to his early life are scarce, but it is clear that he understood the necessary relationship between the mission he had chosen and the projection of a mythicized persona. Commenting elliptically about those years to journalist Froylán Turcios during the spring of 1928, he emphasized only that his parents were two eighteen-year-old "muchachos," that he had grown up amid "unpardonable privations" (presumably referring to the years before his father took him into his home), that he had been educated in one of the schools started by the Zelaya government, and that he had left home at twelve "looking for adventure," traveling through "the principal cities of Central and North America." Five years later he elaborated further to José Román that he had had to help his mother pick coffee from the time he could walk, that when she was ill he had to go out at night and steal so that she would not die of hunger, that at the age of nine he had to go with her when she was imprisoned for a small debt, and that while there he watched in horror as she had a miscarriage.[7]

Whether Sandino left home at twelve looking for adventure, as he himself asserted, or stayed in school until he was fifteen as later accounts suggest he probably did, it is clear that when he referred to his early life and his development as a public figure, he always emphasized a dialectic between his humble origins and Indo-hispanic blood on the one hand, and his pivotal role in a grand cause on the other. He saw himself as maintaining with high principles and firm resolve the vision of the latter and its indissoluble connection with the former.

Thus, discovering early in life that he shared first names with a Roman emperor, Sandino changed his middle name to correspond to it, and Augusto Calderón became Augusto César Sandino (Macaulay [1967] 1985, 49). Years later, he told Basque journalist Ramón de Belausteguigoitía that he began his crusade when he heard a voice (like the prophets and apostles of old) saying "traitor!" (¡Vendepatria!). At that moment, he said, "I decided to fight, understanding that I was 'the one called' [*el llamado*] to protest the betrayal of the country and of Nicaraguan ideals" (Belausteguigoitía [1934] 1985, 91). But the other pole of the dialectic was also ever present: when a couple of months before the attack on Ocotal he sent to Froylán Turcios (who as editor of the magazine *Ariel* was helping to publicize Sandino's cause) a photograph to be used for publicity purposes, he emphasized that the caption was to identify him as "not a professional politician, but a humble artisan." His office, he insisted, "is mechanic, and with my hammer in my hand I have earned my bread all my life." Five years later he reiterated the theme, saying he was "not even a soldier, [but] nothing more than a *campesino* fighting for the autonomy of our people" (Ramírez 1984b, 1:259, 2:331).

As a humble artisan called to purposes of transcendent importance (combining the roles of prophet, disciple, and savior so easily comprehended within a Catholic culture), Sandino emphasized repeatedly his firm resolve, incorruptibility, and willingness to sacrifice himself. "I will neither sell myself nor surrender," he told Turcios; "they will have to conquer me" (Ramírez 1984b, 1:111, 147). Thus when Rear Admiral Sellers wrote to demand that Sandino surrender, reminding him loftily of the United States' "solemn obligation to maintain order in Nicaragua," Sandino addressed his response to Sellers as "the representative of imperialism in Nicaragua" (Ramírez 1984b, 1:233).

However else such rhetoric and gestures are to be explained, they are the self-conscious productions of one who understood that the success of his crusade depended substantially on his own self-presentation — to both friend and foe. What assured both the success of that crusade and the continuity of such self-presentation beyond Sandino's own death, moreover, was precisely the integration of both crusade and constructed self-image into a powerful preexistent cultural system.[8] Christ-like, Sandino renounced property and political aspiration: "I will never have property," he told Belausteguigoitía. "I have nothing." People called him "San Digno," U.S. journalist Carleton Beals reported, or "Worthy Saint." His soldiers accepted him not only as military and political leader, but as father (*Father*), and stories circulated of mountain people following him in hopes of getting some object (relic) he had touched. There were accounts of double rainbows appearing around his head after a rainfall, and on the day when he began to disarm his troops he took them (Christ-like) to a nearby hill to tell them — because, he said, "the spirit of God comes more readily on the heights and in solitude." And as many have related, Sandino's father, upon hearing the machine guns of the National Guard announce his son's death, said, "Now they are killing him. Those who are redeemers always die crucified."[9]

Thus within an Indo-hispanic, Catholic culture, carrying within its soul and body—indeed preserving on its very landscape—the collective memory of the Spanish conquest, of filibuster William Walker's cultural arrogance and brutality, of the deposing of Zelaya and the ensuing political turmoil, and the pain and embarrassment of marine occupation, the image of a proletarian, anti-imperialistic Moses/Christ proud of his Indian blood was likely to be powerful. But it was also a heavy burden for one man or myth to carry: Caesar *redivivus*; indomitable *muchacho* David; redeeming Christ; heroic Indian *cacique*; liberating Bolívar; General of Free Men; mystic with a double rainbow around his head; and archetypal incorruptible patriot. As with any such myth, close comparison with the verifiable facts out of which it arose uncovers inconsistencies and contradictions that reveal as much about the engendering culture as does the myth itself.

Indeed even Sandino himself was of two minds (at least) about some aspects of the cultural heritage he claimed. Although his political and moral commitment was grounded in the traditional culture of the rural *campesinado*, for example, he was in some respects ambivalent about that culture. Characteristically for the period, he roughly equated culture with language and race (or "blood"). In his first manifesto of July 1927 (directed to "Nicaraguans, Central Americans, and the Indo-Hispanic Race"), he said, "I am a Nicaraguan, and I feel proud because in my veins circulates, more than anything else, Indian blood. . . . My highest honor is to have arisen from the bosom of the oppressed, who are the soul and nerve of the Race." The ties of blood/race (and implicitly here, of class) prove very strong. Sandino speaks repeatedly of "my racial brothers" (*mis hermanos de raza*), of "the pride of a race" (*el orgullo de una raza*), of "safeguarding the dignity of the race," of "the valor and mettle of my race" (*el valor y coraje de mi raza*), and (logically, then) of the Yankees who are "our legitimate enemies by race and language" (*nuestros legítimos enemigos, por raza e idioma*) (Ramírez 1984b, 1:117–19, 127, 363, 365, 204, 195).

To dramatize those cultural/racial qualities, Sandino told of a nine-year-old boy "of pure Indian race" who approached him in the mountains of Quilalí in November 1926, bringing food and asking to join the army. Like "so many children of Our America," Sandino said, his eyes shone with "the indomitable pride of our forebears" (*el orgullo indomable de nuestros ascendientes*). Unable to convince the child that he could not withstand the rigors of the campaign, Sandino allowed him to join, and he participated in thirty-six battles as a "child-man" (*niño hombre*) worthy of his racial/cultural heritage (Ramírez 1984b, 1:281).[10] Moving as it is, however, the anecdote (parable, really) is problematic because as Sandino well knew, the "racial America" with which he identified was not pure Indian but Indo-hispanic. Proud as he was of the Indian blood in his veins, he nevertheless knew that he was (as he said) *indolatino*.[11]

Moreover, if the "child-man" parable highlights the Indian component of Sandino's pride in his "Indo-latino" identity, how is one to understand the (implicitly white) Hispanic component, since logically one might expect him to have equated the Spanish with the hated Yankees (the white suprema-cist William Walker, for example, or the marines at Ocotal) as at least loose homologues of the *conquistadores*? Presenting his wife (paradoxically named Blanca) to Basque journalist Belausteguigoitía, however, Sandino tells him with what appears to be pride and satisfaction that she is "95 percent Span-ish" because "here the Spanish mixed little with the Indians." Later during his visit, Belausteguigoitía asks Sandino what he thinks of Spain, and Sandino replies, somewhat unaccountably, "Look: Earlier, sometime ago, I protested the colonizing work of Spain, but now I view it with profound admiration. . . . Spain gave us its language, its civilization, and its blood." Pushing him a bit, Belausteguigoitía goes on to ask him if he believes in the "moral influence of Spain on the future America," and Sandino answers "undoubtedly" (Ramí-rez 1984b, 2:297–300; Belausteguigoitía [1934] 1985, 192–200). Hence unless Sandino was merely saying what he thought Belausteguigoitía wanted him to say, his cultural self-image appears to be at least in this respect ambivalent: holding on to pure Indianness with one hand, and reaching out for at least a mestizo (perhaps even a white) cultural legitimacy with the other.

As though to make up for the relatively elliptical quality of—and perhaps in the process to modulate the ambivalences and contradictions within—Sandino's account of his own life, sympathetic commentators began quite early to elaborate a public version of both his personal character and his crusade. Honduran poet and journalist Froylán Turcios, editor of the widely read journal *Ariel*, first took up his pen in defense of Sandino during the fall of 1927.[12]

Turcios's championing of Sandino was in large measure explicitly cultural: "the symbol of our Race," Turcios called him.[13] Such a perspective figured strongly in Turcios's promotion of the Sandino cause. In mid-October 1927, he wrote to Sandino that he had "opened an active campaign" on his be-half in *Ariel*, to the end that Sandino's heroism would "resound throughout the Americas" and in "the hearts of the patriots of every country." Turcios proved a powerful spokesman, and his journal attracted Sandino partisans from throughout Latin America.[14] Sandino, Turcios wrote in February 1928, is "a formidable purity of virile perseverance and self-denying sacrifice for his country and his race . . . a fertile stimulus, a superhuman effort which

Islas Allende, "Sandino," from *El Repertorio Americano*, Chile, 1928. (Reproduced from Arellano, *Sandino en la Plástica de América*, 1981)

will open new routes to the spirit in its continual ascension toward eternal ideals."[15]

One of Sandino's more influential early champions was the Nicaraguan writer Salomón de la Selva, whose biographical sketch in the *Nation* early in 1928 both projected Sandino in explicitly cultural terms and introduced a cultural motif that was to prove irresistibly attractive to his more hagiographic biographers. Characterizing Sandino's natal Niquinohomo as an "ancient village founded by the Toltecs . . . a thousand years ago," Selva recounted how General Moncada had offered Sandino "an untouched maiden" as an inducement to become one of his lieutenants: "This beauty, this veritable pearl, this rival of the Graces, I had intended for my delight. But as we are forever friends, and as you shall represent my policies to your Department, I cheerfully give her to you. Take her." But seeing the girl ("a frightened child of thirteen") in tears, Sandino refuses to touch or defile her. "This girl," he tells Moncada, "is the embodiment of Nicaragua. She shall not be yours or any man's to violate or give away." And with that, Selva says, "he put the girl on his horse and rode off into the darkness." As Selva tells it, then, the story reads (as he himself says) "like a troubadour's tale." From that day forward,

Selva says, Sandino was "a man at whose name the politicians quaked." Embroidering an incident in which Sandino shot a man and fled Niquinohomo, he asserts that it occurred because politicians, unable to bribe him with offers of high office, hired assassins to kill him, and Sandino wounded one of them during the encounter (Selva 1984, 2–3).

In the *Nation* in early 1928, Carleton Beals published another widely circulated version of the Sandino story (Beals 1928).[16] The only journalist from the "colossus of the North" able to overcome the daunting logistical and security problems, Beals visited and interviewed Sandino in his camp at San Rafael. He found the guerrilla leader physically attractive (immaculately polished puttees, "Texas Stetson" hat, full forehead, firm jaw, "liquid black eyes . . . of remarkable mobility"), "utterly without vices," and possessed of "an unequivocal sense of personal justice and a keen eye for the welfare of the humblest soldier," which in turn stimulated "a fierce affection and a blind loyalty" in them. Sandino assured Beals that he was fighting only for "love of country" and to protect "our inalienable rights," and that he would never accept public office. "[When] the invader is vanquished," he vowed (summoning up as he always did the linked images of working-class and *campesino* culture), he would return to his trade as a mechanic, and his men would be "content with their plots of ground, their tools, their mules, and their families."[17]

Beals sharpened the cultural contrast between Sandino and his opponents, moreover, by graphic references to the insensitivity, brutality, and wanton destructiveness of the U.S. Marines: homes burned, crops destroyed, hospitals bombed, children wounded by shrapnel. Meanwhile Sandino and his army, supported by their own people, protected by an informal espionage system and an intimate knowledge of the forests and countryside, make the marines look "a bit ridiculous with all their machinery of war, their science, and their airplanes."

Others followed the lead of Turcios, Selva, and Beals: Max Grillo in Costa Rica's *Reportorio Americano* in June 1928; Emigdio Marabato in a pamphlet published in Veracruz in mid-1929; and Alberto Ghiraldo's *Yanquilandia bárbara* of the same year, which celebrated Sandino as the successor of such great liberators and cultural heroes as George Washington and Simón Bolívar.[18]

One of the early lyrical celebrations of Sandino was Basque journalist Ramón de Belausteguigoitía's *Con Sandino en Nicaragua* (1934). Belausteguigoitía spent several weeks with Sandino in the mountains, each day confirming his first impression of seeing a man "half saint, half thinker . . . with a tormented spirit, but precise and definitive in his convictions." The journalist came away impressed by what he judged to be Sandino's "extraordinary personality," nobility, serenity, high principle, "delicate and fine" spirit, and "great spiritual elevation." Marveling at the success Sandino's "army of pyg-

Sandino pictured in the *New York World Telegram*, 18 October 1935. (Reproduced from Arellano, *Sandino en la Plástica de América*, 1981)

mies" was having against the marines, he predicted that "tomorrow the whole world will count him among its great heroes."[19]

As it turned out, of course, the response was more mixed than that. To some it was imperative that Sandino be remembered with honor as a hero; to others it was just as imperative that he be either not remembered at all, or recalled in dishonor as a petty tyrant, a brutal criminal, a mere bandit. During

Sandino seal used on correspondence and documents, 1927–33.

the half-century following his death, the struggle to define who Sandino was and what he did had two principal sites: within Nicaragua itself, and between Nicaragua and the United States. On both grounds, the struggle was cast in terms that were as much cultural as they were political or military.

REMEMBERING AND FORGETTING: SANDINO DURING THE SOMOZA PERIOD

Immediately after Sandino's assassination in February 1934, National Guard troops were dispatched to Wiwilí to do away with his followers who were working to establish a cooperative agricultural settlement. Hodges asserts that following the forced disbanding of the last remnants of Sandino's troops in 1937, his movement "completely disappeared from the political scene. He was remembered as a bandit — little more" (Macaulay [1967] 1985, 256; Hodges 1986, 161). Although that may have been true in a limited political sense, the stringency of the Somoza regime's efforts to harass any remaining Sandino sympathizers and erase him from popular memory suggests that Somoza understood that Sandino was not only a formidable political opponent but also a cultural icon whose power would linger beyond Sandino's own death.

Soon after Sandino's death, Anastasio Somoza García wrote (or more likely caused to be written and published in his name) a book-length attack on him. Published in 1936, the book drew upon the most cherished elements of Latin American culture to discredit Sandino and cast him as a brutal and dishonorable person—indeed, to read him out of the culture, as one would be read out of a church or political party.[20]

Prefaced by a full-page picture of Somoza resplendent in medal-bedecked white military dress uniform, and concluded some 566 pages later with a presidential proclamation granting Somoza several more medals to hang on his jacket, *El verdadero Sandino o el calvario de las Segovias* (The true Sandino, or the Calvary of the Segovias) set out not only to argue against Sandino's political legitimacy and effectiveness, but also to destroy him as a cultural figure. "The writers who have elevated Sandino to the height of one of the most radiant figures of the American Continent," it said, "have done so on wings of fantasy, and as a deliberate attempt to forge a hero as a symbol. . . . [But] although they wanted that, they could not forge it with the legend, because in the light of truth he fell from his pedestal." The book scoffed at Froylán Turcios as Sandino's "mentor and glorifier" who credulously "placed upon the shoulders of the guerrilla the cloak of the immortals" (Somoza García 1936, 72, 109).

Somoza's Sandino is the obverse of Beals's, Selva's, and Belausteguigoitía's. Sandino's illegitimate birth becomes one of the book's central political and cultural metaphors. In school he is punished for being an obstreperous student, and he uses the language "of bad people" (*de gente maleante*). Personally he is characterized as selfish and self-centered, violent, brutal, tyrannical, despotic, an irreligious violator of graves, and finally demented (cf. Somoza García 1936, 2–9, 33, 89, 149, 169–70, 199–201, 227).

Sandino's army consists not of patriotic and self-sacrificing Nicaraguans, but a "ferocious band" (or alternatively, "horde") of men "from different countries of the world" interested only in "sacking, burning, and assassinating," causing thousands of innocent and pacific citizens to flee in terror before a "war of extermination."[21] Sandino's officers are especially sorry cultural specimens: Francisco Estrada is "a great lover heedless of his conjugal duties"; Carlos Salgado "knows how to read and write, but with great difficulty. His letters are a puzzle [*rompecabezas*]"; José León Díaz is "a drunk"; General Pablo Umanzor has "a poisoned soul and the heart of a panther"; General Pedro Altamirano ("black in color and of repugnant appearance") only knows how to sign his name, cannot read, and is "a robber and a drunk"; and Heriberto Reyes is "an ignorant and drunken *campesino*" (Somoza García 1936, 12–16, 38, 73, 126, 170). The summary effect is to locate Sandino and his men—from a culturally elitist (and at least in the case of Altamirano, racist) perspective—within an immoral, uneducated, illiterate, rural, uncultured lower class.

Counterposed with Somoza's culturally delegitimizing effort, however, were strong positive ones—a formal one on the part of the *vanguardia*, and an informal one consisting of stories and songs circulating within popular tradition.

Although the *vanguardia* movement was (as Beverley and Zimmerman phrase it, and as previous chapters have noted here) "ideologically incoherent and unstable," a number of the *vanguardistas* strongly supported Sandino, incurring considerable political risk in the process. In Beverley and Zimmerman's elegant précis, "Both Sandino and the *vanguardistas* were products of a failed Liberal project of national autonomy and development. Both were nationalist, anti-*yanqui*, and anti-bourgeois. Both accepted the need for armed struggle against U.S. intervention. Both placed great value on Nicaragua's indigenous past and the peasant base of the nation. Both had a sense of the transformative role of culture in the process of national liberation" (Beverley and Zimmerman 1990, 61, 179–80, 208n.; cf. Hodges 1986, 9).

The *vanguardistas* did not write voluminously in praise of Sandino, but what they wrote was important because it occurred early in the struggle to define the meaning of his campaign and to appropriate his memory. Alberto Ordóñez Argüello's brief lyric "A Sandino" presents an arresting image of Sandino high in his El Chipote encampment — an image that will "perpetuate in sculpture / the ancient spirit of the race." The repeated phrase "get out, Yankees" (*Váyanse, yankees*) of Joaquín Pasos's "Desocupación pronta, y si es necesario violenta" (Prompt, and if necessary violent, withdrawal) is unequivocal, and his "Canción de proveeduría" satirizes the souvenirs (chocolate soldiers, phonograph records of martial music) of a brutal war in which airplanes from a rich and powerful country bomb innocent civilians in a poor and weak one (Asís Fernández 1986, 71; El Pez y la Serpiente 1978–79, 115, 125).[22]

Reinforcing the writings of the *vanguardistas* in preserving and shaping the memory of Sandino were the stories and songs that circulated in oral tradition from the late 1920s onward, some composed by Sandino's soldiers themselves. Carleton Beals told of a Sandino soldier singing a song "with a simple, Whitmanesque flavor," and Belausteguigoitía recorded the texts of several (Beals 1928, 288; Belausteguigoitía [1934] 1985, 160–66).[23] Songs about Sandino continued to be collected from oral tradition on up into the 1960s. For the most part they cast the conflict in terms of polar oppositions: patriotism versus treason (Sandino versus Moncada), unwarranted aggression versus understandable self-defense (the marines versus Sandino's guerrillas); imperialism versus independence (the United States versus Nicaragua); a humane society versus *yanqui* bourgeois materialism; the weakness of power versus the paradoxical power of weakness.[24]

Poems about Sandino (or dedicated to his memory) were published from the 1930s onward; of the fifty collected by Jorge Arellano, ten come from 1930–

50, and nearly half from the 1960s. Mario Cajina Vega's "¡Sandino!" (1952), quoting from and challenging Somoza's published attack, salutes Sandino as "the nameless one" (*el Innominado*) who "resurrected history," "dignified courage," and "stained the immaculate shirt-fronts" of the political parties with "wholesome blood" (*sangre saludable*) (Asís Fernández 1986, 150–51). "May Sandino be born again amongst us," Ernesto Mejía Sánchez said in a brief poem addressed to Nicaraguan poets in exile (Asís Fernández 1986, 89–91). In two additional poems dating from 1956, the year of Somoza García's assassination, Mejía Sánchez quoted ironically President Eisenhower's comment upon his death ("He was a great friend of the United States, in public and in private") and described both Sandino and Somoza's assassin, the young poet Rigoberto López Pérez, as "exterminating angels."[25]

Probably the best known poetic treatment of Sandino dating from the 1950s is in Ernesto Cardenal's *Hora cero* of 1959. The poem's four sections evoke life under the Central American dictatorships, the economic imperialism of the United States and of U.S. corporations (especially the United Fruit Company), the Sandino campaign, and the later "April conspiracy" against Somoza in 1954 (Beverley and Zimmerman 1990, 68–70). In its treatment of the Sandino campaign, the poem recapitulates the major images and themes emphasized by Sandino himself and his early chroniclers: Moncada's treason, Sandino's solitary resistance and determination, the valor of his "crazy little army" (*pequeño ejército loco*), the numerical and technological superiority (and paradoxical ineptitude) of the marines, Sandino's agreement to disarm, and his martyrdom at the hands of Somoza (Asís Fernández 1986, 108–26).

Cardenal's *Hora cero* appeared in the year that Fidel Castro toppled the regime of Batista—an effort in which several former Sandino guerrillas had played an important role. During the following nearly three decades, Nicaragua's *Frente Sandinista de Liberación Nacional*—itself called into existence partly by the wave of revolutionary hope that followed in the wake of Castro's victory—became the principal shaper of the Sandino myth.

TOWARD THE SANDINISTA SANDINO

From the moment of Sandino's assassination in early 1934 until the early 1960s, keeping his memory—or more correctly, a certain memory of him— alive was a task that anti-Somoza poets, singers, journalists, and others in Nicaragua shared informally and (for the most part) without organization. The only even embryonic organization was among students.

Already by the early 1930s, Somoza and the National Guard considered the University at León a "hotbed of Sandinismo." Somoza's *El verdadero Sandino* (1936) reprinted Sandino's manifesto of 15 September 1931, which it said was being distributed by students there.[26] Organized student resistance to Somoza—emboldened by parallel moves in 1944 against military dictatorships in El Salvador, Guatemala, and Honduras—arose during Dr. Enoc Aguado's oppositional electoral campaign of 1946–47. As director of the student publication *Vanguardia juvenil*, young Tomás Borge (later Sandinista interior minister) described Somoza as "el Führer nicaragüense" and his Guardia Nacional as "la Gestapo Nica" (Blandón 1982, 187). "We are following the holy example and direction [*santo y seña*] of Augusto C. Sandino," affirmed a student leaflet: "We the young people of Nicaragua should, in his name, destroy the exploiters . . . who after spilling his blood killed the people so as to show the identity between the Nicaraguan people and Sandino himself. May his enemies know that he has not died, that Sandino is beginning again" (Fonseca 1981, 2:164).

Student resistance (hence the further elaboration of the Sandino myth for anti-Somoza purposes) abated markedly during World War II and the beginning of the Cold War. But the advent of the Eisenhower years in 1952 brought renewed agitation, including (most dramatically) the April 1954 coup attempt by Ernesto Cardenal and others. The key figure in the recovery, transformation, and transmission of Sandino to the young anti-Somoza resistance of the 1960s and 1970s was Carlos Fonseca, who was approaching adolescence as the student movement against Somoza emerged in the mid-1940s, and who arrived at the university in León in 1952.

The illegitimate son of one of Somoza's administrators in Matagalpa and a poor woman who worked as a domestic for a bourgeois family, Fonseca grew up in a house so poor it even lacked a door. To earn a little money he sold his mother's homemade candy and sold *Rumores* ("a squalid local weekly," as Tomás Borge recalled it) in the streets (Borge [1989] 1992, 73).

Fonseca may have heard of Sandino already by the time he was twelve, and was proud to discover that a relative (also named Carlos Fonseca) had been among his guerrilla troops (Borge [1989] 1992, 77). In 1950 he entered high school (the Instituto Nacional del Norte), proving himself a gifted and serious student. His excellent command of French gave him access to Marxist literature, much of which was available in French translations. Around 1953 he acquired a political mentor, Ramón Gutiérrez, familiar with revolutionary movements elsewhere in Central America. Gutiérrez found Fonseca "an authentic proletarian" with whose personal experience Marxism fell into easy and natural congruence (Borge [1989] 1992, 80).

Following the April 1954 coup attempt against Somoza, Fonseca founded a political magazine he named *Segovia* in honor of Sandino's struggle in that region (Borge [1989] 1992, 82). In 1955 he and Tomás Borge, along with Silvio Mayorga, began a serious study of Sandino's thought, using (ironically enough) Somoza's *El verdadero Sandino* as their first text and then moving on to the many biographies of Sandino published between his death and the mid-1950s (especially that of Gregorio Selser, one of the first books published in post-Batista Cuba).[27]

In May 1960, while still in his early twenties, Fonseca wrote of Somoza's "massacre" of the followers of "the glorious General Augusto César Sandino," who demonstrated that "our people can wage victorious battles against enemies who are very powerful materially." Nicaraguan young people in particular, he said, "ground their desires in the glorious theme" of Sandino: liberty or death. Two months later he called Sandino "the most brilliant personage" of Nicaraguan history. "We are . . . the descendants of Sandino . . . [who] were little children or had not been born when they vilely assassinated him," he said. "Now we have grown and are men. Let us fight as he fought . . . so that his dream of a free country and a happy people may become a reality" (Fonseca 1981, 1:100–114, 115–28).

To promulgate Sandino's legacy Fonseca founded the journal *Nueva Nicaragua*, a small publishing house, and the New Nicaragua youth movement. His selection of what he considered to be most important of Sandino's ideas he collected in the pamphlet *Ideario político del General Augusto César Sandino*, used as early as 1961 for training young Sandinista guerrillas. By 1963, Fonseca imposed Sandino's name firmly and irrevocably upon the resistance movement in Nicaragua, and for years he continued to bring his version of the Sandino story to bear upon unfolding events (Hodges 1986, 163–64). Thus to a considerable degree, the Sandino of the early FSLN—hence of the post-1960s resistance movement—was the Fonseca Sandino.

"The heart of the matter, from the late 1950s on," said some young Sandinista historians a quarter-century later, was "to recover the memory of Sandino's struggle [and] . . . to convert [that] historical memory into political consciousness" (Wallace 1985, 11, 14). The problem was that the historical personage upon whose objectively verifiable experience and popular memory the conversion was focused presented (as did the historical Rubén Darío before him) a very mixed array of ideas, values, and actions for interpretation (cf. Hodges 1986, 19–40; Hodges 1992). And because that was so, the necessary conversion occurred through a process both culturally determined and culturally revealing. The Sandino that issued from Fonseca's effort was in many respects the familiar (if not completely historical) Sandino of the popular songs and stories, but he was also a Sandino shaped to both the ideological requirements of the FSLN's particular historic moment as well as to more general and longstanding ones within the culture.[28]

Some of that shaping is especially evident in Fonseca's 1966 biography of Sandino, which selected, highlighted, and reconstructed those elements of

Sandino's life that would make him most attractive as a popular mythic figure useful in the renewed struggle (Fonseca 1981, 1:343–59). Although most earlier commentators had spoken of Sandino's rather substantial formal schooling, for example, Fonseca said that he had not had an opportunity to go to school, but had taught himself (*se cultivó*) to read and write. Passing quickly over his early life (which earlier commentators had treated in greater detail), Fonseca emphasized his proletarian origins, his representativeness as a victim of imperialism, his militancy, his courage and patriotism ("The sovereignty of a people is not discussed; it is defended with arms in hand"), his asceticism and sobriety ("The clear water of the mountains is the only thing I have drunk in recent years," Fonseca's Sandino responds when offered alcohol), the self-sacrificing dedication of his troops (dressed in rags and sleeping under banana leaves) compared with the subhuman savagery of the marines (who toss children into the air and impale them on bayonets, and literally tear them limb from limb), his paradigmatic political insights and strategies (the "determining role of armed struggle," the necessity for social transformation, the "decisive role of campesino workers in guerrilla combat," and the necessity for taking up arms in struggles for liberation in other countries).

In his account of the guerrilla war, Fonseca presented a version of what has come to be referred to as the Black Legend of (in Schroeder's précis) "technologically superior, racist, white male English-speaking marines putting down a peasant-based rebellion in a rural, non-modern, Spanish-speaking mestizo and Indian world." The drama was so stark that it would appear to have been a fabrication were it not that it is more than amply substantiated in the U.S. Marine Corps' own detailed archival records.[29] Marine Corps patrol reports show that rural *campesinos* were "routinely interrogated, their bodies and homes routinely searched, poked, prodded, scrutinized," that people (children included) were impressed as guides and porters, that property was "confiscated" (stolen), that prisoners were summarily shot (while "trying to flee," explained the reports), that hundreds of "suspicious" houses and fields were burned and thousands of tons of food destroyed by patrol commanders for whom (the records leave no doubt) "the slightest incriminating evidence" was a sufficient pretext. Any citizen seen with a firearm (or without, if he or she fled the approaching marines or National Guard troops) was fair game to be shot. "Folks were damned if they ran," concluded Schroeder from the record, "and damned if they remained aloof." People spotted digging in the fields were assumed to be hiding military supplies or weapons; a concentration of horses or cattle was "suspicious," as were people who stopped to look up at the unfamiliar war planes swooping overhead. One Marine Corps pilot, spotting a group of men with machetes clearing a road (a common local activity), attacked them with machine gun and bombs and reported coolly that they were working "in a manner that was [so] noticeably theatrical" that their labor was "obviously a sham."[30]

Singled out for special condemnation in survivors' recollections was one Lieutenant Lee of Massachusetts, second in command of Company M, commanded by "Chesty" Puller, who formed his early reputation as "the tiger of the mountains" in Nicaragua before going on to World War II fame. Company M was a small, independent group that roamed the mountains in search of Sandino, learning and testing the counterinsurgency tactics that came to be employed so ferociously in a later war — including especially the cultivation of a climate of fear and terror among local inhabitants. Lieutenant Lee was nearly universally recalled by survivors as "absolute evil in human form." Even if the rumors of his tossing children into the air and spearing them on his bayonet (reported by others besides Fonseca) were probably not true, their frequent repetition testified to the fear and horror he inspired. Schroeder's examination of the archival record led him to conclude that "the legend of Lieutenant Lee is solidly rooted in fact," and that other marine commanders probably did not behave very differently.[31]

Hence Fonseca's characterization of the nature of the military conflict between Sandino and the marines — however mythicized in some of its details — was essentially grounded on fact. Nevertheless, Fonseca's own ideology appears to have predisposed him to misread some key elements of both Sandino's politics and the culture of the period. One episode in the Fonseca biography highlights the intricate connections between culture and ideology in the construction of a popular myth for political purposes. Reading in Belausteguigoitía's earlier biography that the proletarian hymn the "Internationale" was sung in Sandino's camp in 1933, Fonseca concluded that it signified that Sandino's soldiers understood themselves to be part of the international Communist movement of the 1930s (Fonseca 1981, 1:353). Despite Somoza's strenuous attempts to link Sandino with Mexican "Bolshevism," however, Hodges and others make clear that Sandino himself repeatedly had at best a turbulent and ambivalent relationship with the Comintern as well as with the Mexican and other Latin American Communist parties, with which he broke decisively (Hodges 1986, 98–106; Hodges 1992, 68–83).[32]

How could it happen, then, that the "Internationale" formed part of the repertoire of songs sung wholeheartedly by Sandino's soldiers? The apparent answer is that it didn't, but instead that Fonseca's eagerness to appropriate Sandino as the founding hero of what at length became the FSLN led him to misread the incident Belausteguigoitía relates — that is, to reconstruct a complex cultural incident to conform to the emerging anti-Somoza political culture of the early 1960s.

As Belausteguigoitía actually relates the incident, one of Sandino's officers brings two singers before an assembled group of soldiers: the small (*minús-culo*), childishly restless (*inquieto; siempre de un lado para otro*) "Cabrerita," and an Indian with a square face and "absolutely Indian cheekbones" (Belausteguigoitía [1934] 1985, 161–67). "We were ready," Belausteguigoitía says, "to receive the popular muse of Sandino's fighters." As the guitars begin to sound, it turns out that Cabrerita wants urgently for the group to understand his syndicalist feelings (*tiene empeño en hacernos ver sus sentimientos sindicalistas*). So by himself he sings "one of his favorite songs, an *Internacional*": "Arise, loyal people / To the cry of Social Revolution. . . ." Fortunately, the singer has a charitable and patient group of listeners, for they are unmoved by the sentiments, which seem to them abrupt and out of context (*los exabruptos del cantor no les levantan los nervios*).

But then Cabrerita begins to sing with the Indian, and these new songs, coming from the heart of the mountains (*sacados de la médula de la montaña*), make a lively impression (*impresionan a todos vivamente*). "It is the popular soul" now, Belausteguigoitía observes, "saturated with patriotic feeling, the high idealism of Sandino which has impregnated these simple souls, making them sing of the beauty of their sacrifice." As he yields to the power of the music, Cabrerita himself is transformed (*ha cambiado ya su aire malicioso, y parece dejarse sumir en la emoción de . . . [la] música*). The Indian, for his part, undergoes a kind of transfiguration (*una especie de transfiguración*): "His eyes look like they are trying to hold back the weeping," Belausteguigoitía reports, "and his enormous mouth gives pathetic inflections to the song. There is a moment, however, in which irony shines in the songs, and Cabrerita seems to transmit something of his jovial air to his sad *compañero*." So at last we hear something of the popular muse, Belausteguigoitía says, a (culturally appropriate) *corrido*:

> I am going to sing to you, gentlemen,
> A verse about present events,
> Giving honor
> To a valiant general.
> > Then fill up the cups to overflowing;
> Let's drink more wine,
> And give toasts because
> The valiant Sandino lives.

The next song is to the tune of "Adelita," the (culturally comprehensible) theme song of the Mexican revolution. "And so darkness came," Belausteguigoitía says, and "we went to sleep in a serene night of blinking stars."

The serenity issues, one judges, partly from the resolution of a cultural conflict: the childish Cabrerita is merely tolerated for his initial culturally incongruent offering, but when he grounds himself in duo with the Indian he is reintegrated culturally with the group and becomes both freed and effective expressively. The duet itself is—as is suggested by Belausteguigoitía's description of its effect on the Indian—a metaphor for a kind of cultural syncretism that is central to Sandino's understanding of both himself and Nicaragua.

Thus the drama Belausteguigoitía narrates has to do precisely with cultural congruence and conflict, and it demonstrates that how assimilable political ideology proves to be is (at least in this case) a function of how culturally comprehensible it is. It was a lesson Sandino's successors themselves repeatedly stumbled awkwardly over, as I have previously suggested. Fonseca's misreading of the text (the written one and the cultural one) came, one may hazard to guess, out of a rather striking structural parallelism that led him to collapse himself, Cabrerita, and Sandino into something of a cultural monad: humble origins, illegitimate birth to an upper-class father and lower-class mother, partial alienation from a depreciated cultural system, consequent anxiety and ideological fervor, and a drive to reconnect with politically/culturally legitimate origins.

Although cultural elements were important in Fonseca's rendering of Sandino, they were generally overshadowed by more specifically ideological and strategic concerns. A longer, more elaborate and nuanced, less insistently ideological, and more explicitly cultural treatment was Sergio Ramírez's "El muchacho de Niquinohomo" of 1973.[33]

Against a deftly handled recapitulation of Nicaragua's four-century struggle against conquest, foreign domination, and collaboration by native elites, Ramírez presents Sandino explicitly (although not exclusively) in terms of cultural contrasts, conflicts, and contradictions. The David versus Goliath myth is not far in the background as he describes Sandino as "a young man abstemious, timid, and of small stature . . . from a little Nicaraguan village . . . [of] huts made of straw and mud" (25). The social and cultural distance between Sandino and his father is accentuated (Don Gregorio belongs here to "a group of rich *ladinos*"), while the proletarian link with his mother is tightened by repeating the incident of her miscarrying before the eyes of nine-year-old Augusto. Eventually Augusto is taken into his father's house (as in earlier accounts), but not as an equal of the legitimate children; together with the other illegitimate children, he has to work for his keep, eat in the kitchen, and wear hand-me-down clothes. When he finally flees Niquinohomo after the oft-related shooting, he goes to the plantations of Honduras, which Ramírez significantly describes as a spatially transposed example of the worst of U.S. culture: a tropical far west (*un* "far west" *tropical*) of lawlessness, bars, drunkenness, and duels (28).

In strong contrast with Somoza's culturally condescending portrayal of

Pen drawing of Sandino by unknown artist, 1974. (Reproduced from Arellano, *Sandino en la Plástica de América*, 1981)

Sandino and his men as illiterate peasants, Ramírez praises the elegant, scripturelike style and language of Sandino's writing: "neither rhetorical nor gratuitous, charged with passion but also charged with truth." It was, he said, a language of an artisan and *campesino*: "plain but lyrical, with the simple tone of a rural teacher." His letters to his commanders were "like lessons, like poems." Those soldiers who had never learned to read were doing so, so that (presaging the later Sandinistas' literacy campaign of 1980) the often sneered-at "crazy little army" was in fact "like a great school" (33).

When Ramírez turns to the confrontation between Sandino and the marines, the contrast is cultural as much as military, as it frequently was in Sandino's own account in his letters. Ramírez focused on Sandino's July 1927 attack on Ocotal—long since rendered into myth by earlier biographers. To the "well trained and elegantly uniformed" marines whose putatively superior size and strength translates paradoxically into clumsiness and immobility, Nicaragua is a nightmare of swamps, mosquitos, and fever, where poorly equipped little brown people, "ignorant" of modern military tactics and strategy, stage small-unit lightning ambushes before disappearing into the brush. David-like, they "knock down airplanes almost by throwing rocks" (*a pedradas*). To Sandino's troops, every stick in the road, every animal's cry, is a sign in "the Sandinista language of war" that informs and protects them, as do the orphaned campesino children (*el coro de los ángeles*) who were taught to shout and make noises as a signal of approaching marines (33–36).

Such a campaign—in which putative weakness becomes real strength (and vice versa), in which in effect the culturally last become first—is directed from, supported by, and provided refuge in the secret base at El Chipote, Sandino's fantastic, perhaps surrealistically mobile fortress (cf. Macaulay [1967] 1985, 83–104). "That mythical place" (*aquel lugar mítico*), Ramírez calls it, which the marines could not find on any map: "El Chipote, high prominence defended by passes and to which no known road goes, always covered by clouds. On the peaks, huts [*ranchos*] of palm have been built as dwellings, storehouses for food, corrals for horses, workshops to repair arms, for fabricating munitions, tailor and shoe shops, all within the poverty of the area. . . . From there . . . the elements of the Sandinista war go out to the world" (36–37).[34]

When the marines finally are vanquished after "six long years of solitary heroism by a handful of workers and *campesinos*," Ramírez relates, Sandino ("so small of stature and so simple") makes a nearly Christ-like triumphal entry into Managua and then goes to disarm his troops. Ramírez describes the scene in almost cinematically graphic terms:

From distant places [they] arrive . . . many of them old people, others still children, covered with mud, with sweat, with dust, without shoes, standing with their old rifles, a few mounted, their red and black flag flaming on whatever kind of stick from the mountains, entering town by the hundreds, under the strictest discipline, to put their arms in the designated places, to return without recompense, without having expected anything, to their villages, to their families, thousands of men whose toil was paid for only by that victory. (49)

Fittingly, Ramírez repeats Don Gregorio's comment upon hearing the assassins' machine guns: "He who puts himself forward as a redeemer dies crucified" (*él que se mete a redentor muere crucificado*) (51).[35]

The mythicized Sandino of Sandino's own letters and statements, of Turcios, Selva, Belausteguigoitía, Román, the *vanguardistas* and their successors, Fonseca, Ramírez, and so many others was in the first instance a Sandino in and *for* Nicaragua — but also more largely for Latin America in particular and later the emerging post-colonial states of the postwar era. And *that* Sandino, as I have emphasized, was in tension with a demonized Somoza Sandino, who served as a focus for reactionary politics not only within Nicaragua, but also between Nicaragua and the United States. Within that politics, culture was again a decisive factor.

SORRY COUNTRIES, SORRY PEOPLE: BANDITS, CULTURE, AND FOREIGN POLICY

The summer of 1927 in the United States was a time of high passions and sharp dichotomies focused on larger-than-life cultural heroes and villains. In May, twenty-five-year-old Charles Lindbergh had landed *The Spirit of St. Louis* in Paris and returned home to a tumultuous welcome; Babe Ruth was well on his way to a record sixty home runs; Al Capone had just topped $100 million a year from his Chicago rackets; Samuel Insull was busy interlocking his $3 billion utilities empire; H. L. Mencken's iconoclastic and elitist *American Mercury* was at the height of its popularity; and Sacco and Vanzetti were waiting for the governor of Massachusetts to decide whether they would die (Macaulay [1967] 1985, 84).

On 16 July 1927, Sandino and his *pequeño ejército loco* attacked the U.S. Marine Corps garrison at Ocotal (cf. Macaulay [1967] 1985, 62–82).[36] Although not the epic event it was transformed into by Sandino's more admiring biographers (in Marabato's account, Sandino and sixty sandal-shod Nicaraguans assaulting six hundred marines, the latter supported in Alemán Bolaños's account by "four hundred pirates and two hundred renegade Nicaraguans"),

Sandino image from Managua wall, 1988. (Photograph by author)

it was dramatic enough to focus substantial public opinion in the United States (Ramírez 1984b, 1:377–86; Alemán Bolaños 1932, 30).[37]

By the time of the Ocotal attack, the marines had been in Nicaragua for more than a dozen years. Implicit in U.S. policy in Nicaragua was a summary cultural judgment similar to that expressed the following summer by marine field commander Captain Bleasdale. Writing to corps commandant General Lejeune, Bleasdale was scathing in his contempt for Sandino's fellow countrymen:

> A people, the majority of whom have spent their lives in . . . dishonesty, deception, espionage, and general crookedness, are a little difficult to cope with. . . . If, as a people, the Nicaraguans had any sense of law, order, honesty, and common ordinary decency, there would be no occasion for the United States to lend its assistance to them to straighten out the pathetic mess they have made of their efforts to negotiate the complicated machinery of modern civilization. . . . This is a sorry country and a sorry people and the better Nicaraguan knows that when it becomes a better land, it will be because of the United States and your Marines. (Macaulay [1967] 1985, 126–27)

But congressional sentiment and public opinion about the enterprise were not nearly so clear and categorical as Bleasdale. The *New York Times* reported day after day on the "outburst of editorial attacks" on U.S. policy in the Latin American press, noting in particular that a group of Nicaraguan exiles in San Salvador had met with aviation hero Charles Lindbergh, who was making a good-will trip through Central and South America, and asked him to help stop U.S. hostilities in Nicaragua.[38] By the time the *Times* reported on 4 January 1928 that a thousand more marines were being sent to Nicaragua to assure "free and fair elections," there was vehement protest in Congress. Montana Senator Burton Wheeler (the Progressive Party's vice-presidential candidate in 1924) said the United States had a moral obligation to uphold the Nicaraguan constitution; Representatives Sol Bloom and George Huddleston charged that it was unconstitutional for the United States to be waging an undeclared war. Even Alabama Senator Thomas ("Cotton Tom") Heflin, usually a reactionary, introduced a resolution declaring that "the sending of armed forces by the United States into a neighboring republic for the purpose of overthrowing a Government resulting from the expressed will of the people is wrong, inexcusable and indefensible." A couple of weeks later, Washington Senator Clarence Dill protested the use of U.S. troops "to protect investments of Americans abroad." Even more expansively, Nebraska Senator George Norris denounced the "unauthorized and indefensible war" against Nicaragua, suggesting that the troops could be more usefully and legally employed in Philadelphia, Pittsburgh, New York, or Chicago, "where it is admitted they have not had an honest election in thirty years."[39] Other congressmen supported the policy proudly and unapologetically, however. Responding to Senator Dill's demand that U.S. troops be brought home, Maryland Senator William Bruce snarled that "the Senator would have our nationals scurry out of a country like frightened rats, leaving the spoils to the rebels. I thank God for the marines we sent!"[40]

The strategic political and cultural problem for the U.S. government—in view of the international sympathy for Sandino, the division among the U.S. public, and the scattered though powerful congressional opposition to U.S. policy—was how to deflate the Sandino bubble, how to convert the positive image to a negative one, how to diminish the international sympathy for Sandino that produced crowds shouting "Sandino!" in Buenos Aires during President Hoover's "good will tour" of Latin America (Selser [1978] 1981, 138). The problem of how to fight Sandino, it turned out, was inseparable from what to call him, and *that* problem was as much cultural as political. After toying briefly with the designation "guerrilla" in early 1928, the marines decided (as General Lejeune told the Senate Foreign Relations Committee, "for lack of a better term") to fall back on the culturally loaded (and revealing) designation that was already common in the popular press: "bandit" (Macaulay [1967] 1985, 111–12).

And so it was. As early as a few days after the attack at Ocotal, the *New York Times* had reported that Sandino "is said to have promised his followers that if they capture Ocotal they could loot at will. He is reported to have boasted that he would 'drink Yankee blood.'" U.S. Secretary of State Frank Kellogg was later quoted as calling Sandino's troops "nothing more than common outlaws" who were "resort[ing] to banditry, preying on the country and terrorizing the inhabitants." The next day the troops were characterized as "malcontents" and "a band of bandits and assassins" (as General Moncada labeled them), and Sandino was quoted as calling himself "the Wild Beast of the Mountains." The pattern continued on through the summer and fall and into the early weeks of 1928: Sandino was "a cruel desperado," a "chieftan of a band of marauders," a "fanatic," "the Pancho Villa of Nicaragua." His "desperately cold-blooded," "lawless gang" of men "[thought] no more of shooting a man than cracking a mule with a whip." Meanwhile, the marines were "engaged in the perilous work of running down elusive bandits and trying to make life and property safe."[41]

Such nomenclature was maintained consistently, both in the public press and in official government statements, throughout the Sandino period. In his 1927 book *American Policy in Nicaragua*, President Coolidge's special envoy Henry Stimson related (without questioning its appropriateness) General

Moncada's stigmatizing portrayal of Sandino. "I was told," Stimson wrote, "that Sandino had lived in Mexico for twenty-two years where he served under Pancho Villa, and only came back to Nicaragua on the outbreak of the revolution in order to enjoy the opportunities for violence and pillage which it offered." Four years later, having decided that perhaps the intervention hadn't been such a good idea, Stimson told the former president that the marines were "not adapted" to service in "the bandit provinces."[42]

The cultural arrogance of the Yankees was patent: "It seems impossible," Ocotal commander Captain Hatfield wired Sandino a few days before the attack,

> that you could remain deaf to our reasonable proposals. In spite of your insolent responses . . . I give you one more opportunity to surrender. . . .
>
> Moreover, if you are able to escape . . . I will put a price on your head, and you will never be able to return to your country, which you pretend to love so much, except as a bandit. . . . If you come to Ocotal with all of your troops and give up your arms, you and your soldiers will have guarantees which I will grant you as the representative of a great and powerful nation. . . .
>
> Otherwise, you will be an exile and outside the law like hogs (*puercos*), pursued and repudiated everywhere, waiting for a shameful death.[43]

Sandino's letters revealed that he was troubled by the "bandit" appellation — duly picked up by Coolidge's successor Herbert Hoover — and acutely aware of its cultural dimensions. Turning the cultural marker back upon those who used it so facilely, however, he set the bandit image in the context of the user's own history and culture: Washington is called the "father of his country" (like Bolívar and Hidalgo), Sandino noted, "only I am a bandit, according to the ruler with which the strong and weak are measured" (Ramírez 1984b, 1:124). Carleton Beals said Sandino told him that "we are no more bandits than was Washington. If the American public had not become calloused to justice and to the elemental rights of mankind, it would not so easily forget its own past when a handful of ragged soldiers marched through the snow leaving blood-tracks behind them to win liberty and independence." "Do you still think of us as bandits?" Beals said Sandino asked him just before he departed. "You are as much a bandit," Beals responded, "as Mr. Coolidge is a bolshevik." "Tell your people," Sandino suggested, "that there may be bandits in Nicaragua, but they are not necessarily Nicaraguans" (Beals 1928, 341, 204). Several years later Sandino insisted that "the real and legitimate bandits are in the caves of the White House in Washington, from which they direct the sacking and assassination of our Spanish America" (Ramírez 1984b, 2:116; cf. 2:167). Nor did Sandino's partisans let the opportunity pass. Selva categorically rejected the bandit designation and countered that Sandino was a liberator like Simón Bolívar and José Martí. "In the Hall of National Heroes at the Pan American Union in Washington," he said, "Nicaragua's pedestal is empty. She now has a candidate" (Selva 1984, 5).

In the view of Sandino and his partisans, the conflict was as deeply cultural as it was military, and the cultural contrast that lay always nearest at hand was that between Nicaragua (the rescued virgin of Selva's account) and the United States. As early as May 1927, a day after General Moncada signed the infamous Espino Negro agreement with Henry Stimson (providing for continued U.S. military occupation of Nicaragua and leading to—among other things—the formation of the National Guard that would keep the Somoza dynasty in power for more than forty years), Moncada summoned Sandino, then a general in his Constitutionalist army, to meet with him. To Sandino, Moncada's very physical aspect bespoke both his political betrayal of Nicaragua and his cultural capitulation to the Yankees. Moncada was reclining, Nicaraguan-style, in a hammock slung beneath a big shade tree, but hanging around his neck was a gold cross of the type worn by U.S. Marines. To Sandino's insistence that it was his duty to fight for liberty even though it might cost him his life, Moncada smiled sarcastically and said, "No, man, why are you sacrificing yourself for the people? They will not thank you. I tell you this from my own experience: life ends and the country remains. The duty of every human being is to enjoy and live well, without worrying too much." The image is elaborated when the two meet several days later in Boaco and Sandino finds Moncada again straddling the cultural divide: sitting in a Nicaraguan rocking chair but dressed in a Palm Beach suit, shoes shining brightly (Ramírez 1984b, 1:96–99; cf. Bermann 1986, 194–98).

Moncada's political-cultural vacillation was odious to Sandino not only because it depreciated Nicaragua's own political integrity and culture, but also because he found North American culture itself so contemptible. Phrases of scathing contempt pile one upon the other in his letters: the Yankees are "cowards and felons," "barbarians of the North," "loathsome reptiles," cynical hypocrites, "blonde beasts," and "invading pirates" who assassinate, rape, rob, and burn the homes of peaceful *campesinos*. President Hoover was a "furious impotent beast" (cf. Ramírez 1984b, 1:119, 127, 135, 215, 218, 221, 271, 274, 319, 323, 388; 2:46, 80, 179, 352). While the marines rain destruction from their cursed (*malditos*) airplanes on Ciudad Antigua and its church, which was its people's pride and joy, Wall Street bankers kneel before their strong boxes and worship their own God of Gold. This, Sandino says, "is Yankee civilization." Confirming his judgment, Beals reported that on his way to meet with Sandino early in 1928 he heard stories of American atrocities (such as the bombing of homes and a hospital in Chinandega) "that make German misdeeds seem tame" (Ramírez 1984b, 1:208, 326; Beals 1928, 233, 260, 289; Hodges 1986, 108–14).[44]

To Sandino, the most palpable (indeed almost comical) evidence of the corrupt and empty misdirection of dysfunctional Yankee civilization was the credulousness and lumbering ineptitude of its vaunted marines, arrogantly armed to the teeth, wandering lost in the forests and jungles, packing their sophisticated military hardware on outsized mules that had to be fed hay and oats shipped in from the States (while Sandino's little Nicaraguan ones foraged freely), outwitted and outmaneuvered by barefoot soldiers who knew the people, knew the land, and used long-"obsolete" but paradoxically appropriate military technology (Ramírez 1984b, 1:384; Macaulay [1967] 1985, 153; Beals 1928, 314–15).

In an anecdote repeated by many a later commentator, Sandino typified this marine credulousness and ineptitude. Threatened in the El Chipote fortress by a marine assault, he said, "We began to make dummies of straw, which we dressed in sombreros like the ones we wore, and put in the most visible locations. Meanwhile, in the night, we departed. For two more days the aviators bombarded the place . . . until they realized there was no enemy there. When they arrived and tried to pursue us, we were already far away." Whether the incident happened in just that way or not, Sandino's meaning is both double and clearly cultural: as in English, the Spanish word he used for "dummies" (*peleles*) means both a mannequin figure (such as a scarecrow) and a simple-minded person (*tonto, pobre diablo, infeliz*). Thus the "incompetent and ostentatious" marines had, Sandino said drily, "much to learn about our system" (Ramírez 1984b, 1:228, 322).[45] They had been both visually tricked and culturally outwitted by people they considered to be dummies (Captain Bleasdale's "sorry people"), but who at least knew enough to build dummies to trick dummies.

Even more pointed are Sandino's comments on the marines' way of celebrating July 4. "It seems incredible," he observed early in March 1929, that

at every step the pirates take in the Segovias, they leave opportunities to ridicule them and show themselves before the civilized world as incompetent and ostentatious soldiers. . . .

I am informed . . . [that they] are good about making sham celebrations [*simulacros*] of the 4th of July. . . . It could be that they do it in their eagerness to terrorize with [such] noises people who have fewer resources.

It is said that they put an orange on the head of a man, and shoot at it from a substantial distance. That they perforate the orange, but don't touch the man's head.

The serenity that they demonstrate in such cases would be difficult to retain in the Segovias.

I have no men here with oranges on their heads.[46]

One judges that in addition to ridiculing such culturally characteristic ostentatiousness and bravado, Sandino is making a comparative cultural judgment: his final phrase juxtaposes his own men (who don't have, he implies, oranges *for* heads) with those whose calm betrays their typically serene ignorance of the difference between their heads and an orange.

GENDER IDEALS AS CULTURAL NORMS: SANDINO AND WOMEN

The cultural aspects of the Sandino struggle and the myths it generated focused on a number of highly contested items that have drawn repeated commentary (physical violence, honor, and patriotism, for example). Similarly important—but never engaged analytically by any commentator—was gender, which proves to repay close attention, because of both the power of gender paradigms as cultural markers and norms, and their consequent centrality in the cultural-political discourse about Sandino. As insistently as Somoza and the United States used the bandit image to discredit Sandino, his partisans built aspects of the Sandino myth around an idealized account of his treatment of women. In the latter case as in the former, the ascertainable facts are at considerable variance with the myth, and the differences offer insight into the cultural politics of the construction.

In his political manifesto of 1 July 1927, two weeks before the attack on Ocotal, Sandino hinted at the centrality of a gender metaphor to his project by referring to his "young country" as "that tropical brown-skinned woman" (*esa morena tropical*) (Ramírez 1984b, 1: 119; Marcus 1985, 398). What was the nature of Sandino's own relationships with women, and what were the operative gender ethics of his "crazy little army"? And more broadly, how were culturally valued (or devalued) gender paradigms deployed to mythicize (or discredit) Sandino?

The incontrovertibly documentable details of Sandino's own relationships with women are not plentiful, but they are sufficient to suggest that the relationships themselves were at least more numerous—and perhaps of a somewhat different character—than his champions led their audiences to believe. Sandino recalled his first childhood infatuation as an occasion of acute pain, linking it with the birth of his desire to read and learn. As an eleven-year-old, he said, he was a very poor student and thus "famous in the whole school for [his] ignorance." A girl in his class, knowing of his interest in her, shamed and tormented him by challenging him to read a book. Unable to do so, he determined to become a good student, apparently fusing in the process two passions that remained more or less fused for the rest of his life.

His first real love some years later was also, as he said, "terrible." To his cousin Mercedes Sandino he wrote letter after passionate letter, in one of which he threatened to kill both himself and her if she refused him. But he never summoned the courage to send any of them, instead continuing to love her "platonically with a deep and secret love." Somehow the relationship must have flowered, however, for he told José Román that it was just before he was going to marry Mercedes that he had to flee Niquinohomo because of the shooting incident (Román 1983, 47–54; cf. Ramírez 1983b, 28). Indeed, he further confided that the incident occurred not over political differences as Selva suggested, and not in the town plaza, but rather in church during mass because the story (whether true or not he did not say) had gotten around town that he was involved in an amorous relationship with the widowed sister of the other party.

Two passionate and anguished letters Sandino wrote to his beloved after he left town survive ("You, my life, my angel, receive kisses without end and hugs from your Augusto"), but he himself passed on to other women (Ramírez 1984b, 1:71–72, 75–76). He worked for a while in La Ceiba, Honduras, as virtually all commentators mention, but left there (as no one but Román notes, although Sandino himself said so explicitly) to escape more troubles with women (*otra vez por asuntos de faldas*) (Román 1983, 55). By 1923 he was in Mexico, where (again as none of his partisans, either during his life or afterwards, ever mentioned) he seems to have acquired a wife and had a daughter, as Macaulay concluded from his 1925 application for employment with Huasteca Petroleum (Macaulay [1967] 1985, 51).

The point at which most biographers pick up the story of Sandino and his women companions is in early 1927, when at the age of thirty-two he married a nineteen-year-old telegrapher named Blanca Aráuz. Preserved in his papers are at least two of his own tender and romantic accounts of the ceremony: Sandino in uniform with high boots, Blanca in a white dress and veil with a crown of orange blossoms, the church brightly lit with candles and filled with flowers and smells that, he said, "reminded me of the days of my infancy." The public did not attend the ceremony, he explained, because "we wanted it to be an act of absolute intimacy," but when the couple emerged from the church his men fired salutes with pistols and machine guns (Ramírez 1984b, 1:102–3; 2:389, 404–5).

Certainly Blanca's several surviving letters to Sandino suggest that she was deeply committed to him, and he told José Román that he looked forward to the birth of their child because he wanted to give it "all of the paternal love" he had lacked in his own young life (Román 1983, 83; Ramírez 1984b, 2:339). Nevertheless, Blanca was not his only beloved during the six years of their marriage, as he himself confessed to Román. As early as August 1928 he already had a mistress, Salvadoran nurse Teresa Villatoro. In a letter to one of his officers early in 1931, he took considerable pains to explain his somewhat situationist view of conventional morality with regard to such relationships, and to affirm that it was Blanca who had his "unlimited affection." Eventually, he told Román, he resolutely sent Teresa away because of the deep temperamental differences between them, her difficult character (*un carácter la chingada*), and because his wife was coming (Ramírez 1984b, 2:161–62; Macaulay [1967] 1985, 103, 124, 157, 214, 293n.).[47]

No doubt aware of the force such a criticism would have in *marianista* culture, Somoza attacked Sandino with respect to his relationships with women — especially his mother and his wife. He is charged with mistreating his mother (shown old and haggard in a photograph) — an unpardonable transgression within the culture — and with cynically and ambitiously changing his name from Calderón to César, callously rejecting the last name of "the woman who had carried him in her belly" (Somoza García 1936, 8). Sandino deceived Blanca into marrying him, Somoza said, only because she was useful to him as a telegrapher. The sound of machine guns rather than wedding bells that followed the service — reported by others as implicit evidence of the political as well as emotional solidarity of the union — Somoza cast as a profanation of a sacred rite. When their child was about to be born, according to the Somoza account, Sandino crudely and insolently refused to let Blanca be seen by a doctor or midwife. During her hard labor he paced like an "infuriated tiger," and after her death from a hemorrhage he put her body in a room and refused to let anyone see her. Shamelessly indulging his own emotion, he reclined on her body, kissed her face, and pronounced that what was important was not that she had died, but that she had died being caressed. At the funeral he interrupted the priest and launched into a dramatic discourse of his own, full of foolishness (*disparates*). Three days later, Somoza reported, "the true Sandino" departed for Wiwilí, taking Blanca's cousin with him as a concubine (Somoza García 1936, 8–11).

Thus the Somoza account attempted to discredit Sandino partly by showing his relationships with and treatment of women to be reprehensible in comparison with an accepted cultural standard. Blanca herself, by the same standard, is described as a woman of "sweet character and a certain natural culture." In three of her letters to Sandino included in the book, she writes tenderly of crying because she misses him, of how their yet unborn child wants to see him, of a rainbow that promises his return, and of her dreams of being happily with him (Somoza García 1936, 411–12, 426–27, 433–34).[48]

Since the purpose of the Somoza book was to vilify Sandino, one cannot accept uncritically its account of his relationships with Blanca and other women. But one can piece together a first approximation account from a few surviving letters and some remarkably candid remarks about women that Sandino made during a protracted series of conversations with José Román early in 1933. The image that emerges, far from placing Sandino outside (or above) traditional *machista* male socialization, shows that he was both formed, and continued throughout his life to function, squarely within it ("I want to be frank about women," Sandino told Román. "I like them!" [¡*Claro que me gustan!*]).[49] One would not expect that he would have been formed in any other way; the point here is that evidence that he continued to function within that socialization is in direct conflict with the idealized Sandino presented by his more hagiographic biographers.

Some of the contradictions of Sandino's gender socialization emerged with regard to his efforts to prevent his men from engaging in the abusive sexual excesses that frequently characterize military personnel deprived of female companionship for long periods. Those efforts were a generalization of his own ascetic, ethically elevated, and politically correct ("this girl is Nicaragua") refusal to possess the nubile virgin offered to him by Moncada—a story repeated by many a biographer after Selva reported it. Numerous commentators assert that his soldiers were strictly forbidden to rape women, and summarily shot if they did. The implication is that Sandino's troops were exemplary in this regard, and that such behavior was in some measure indicative of their elevated political and social principles.[50]

But again, the reality seems to have been more complex than the myth. As early as February 1928, on his way to Sandino's camp, Carleton Beals took note of one of Sandino's officers "moving his family, his cattle, asses, concubines and household goods to safety" from the war. Evidence suggests that such extended households were not uncommon among Sandino's men. Indeed, having explained to Román his strictures against rape, Sandino went on to say (although no later commentator except Román notes that he did so) that it was really unnecessary for his men on the Río Coco to rape women, because there was such an abundance of available Indian and *campesina* women (*abundan las indias y campesinas*). Hence, he said, his men "have the freedom to love whoever they want," so long as the women give their consent (are *conseguidas por las buenas*).

To Román it appeared likely that the men would indeed "love whoever they want[ed]," and that *las buenas* might be interpreted rather liberally. After attending a riotous two-day harvest binge (*juerga*) of eating, drinking, dancing, and group sex (*sexo colectivo*) among the zambos with some of Sandino's men, Román concluded that sex among them was as natural as

Sandino silhouette from album *Canto épico al FSLN* (ENIGRAC LPP-031/032, ca. 1985)

Sandino image on fence. (Photograph by author)

"eating, defecating, being born, or dying." Young girls could be bought from their mothers for tobacco, and women changed partners for whatever reasons they wished (Román 1983, 86, 100–102, 113).

Notwithstanding such apparent ease of getting women, Román judged, some of Sandino's men continued in more time-honored patterns (*por las malas*). "I like all women," Captain Julio Castro told him. "You know, a woman on her back [*boca arriba*] has neither size nor color." Confiding that before the war his favorite sport was to "make love to and conquer a tender little Indian girl" (*enamorar y conquistar a una indita tierna*) every week, he appears not to have reformed. He doesn't consult them, he says; he rapes them, gives them a trinket of some sort, and admits his paternity of the children. "All the women around here adore me," he boasts; "The only argument I use is a stick and a pistol, because that is all the Indians understand." "It may seem strange to you," he tells Román, "but one has to fly them [like a bug] on a string, so that they serve well and are contented." Fortunately, he says, *el general* doesn't know his habits (Román 1983, 60–61).

When it came to reviving and refining the myth, however, the influential Carlos Fonseca biography passed over the entire matter of Sandino's women as if the evidence—whether positive or negative—were immaterial in the life of a totally committed, ascetic, single-minded general of free men. His wedding with Blanca is dispensed with in a phrase: "Once the ceremony was over,

A 50 AÑOS...SANDINO VIVE

Line silhouette of Sandino, 1984, with caption "After 50 Years, Sandino Lives."

he headed for the mountains." Women are referred to only when they aid the guerrilla effort by cooking, caring for the wounded, or serving as couriers (Fonseca 1981, 1:344–49; cf. Salvatierra 1934, 53).

In Sergio Ramírez's later account, however, Sandino's own romantic version of the wedding returns: candles and forest flowers reappear in "that humble church which was like that of his own village," and the sights and smells carry Sandino (as in his own account) back to his infancy. Metaphorically the wedding becomes both rebirth (he "felt like new" upon emerging from the church, Sandino had said) and virginal union. Appropriately, therefore, Mercedes Sandino, the woman or women of La Ceiba, the Mexican wife and child, and Teresa Villatoro are absent from Ramírez's narrative of the life of *el muchacho de Niquinohomo*.[51]

Sandino was indeed a transcendent figure in some respects, but he was also very much the product of his time and place, of his culture. My intent in exploring this aspect of the mythicization of Sandino has not been to judge him moralistically—against either the mores of the time or those of other times or places—but to elaborate a single example of how specific norms and values of the culture figured in the efforts of both partisans and detractors to turn his personality and work to their particular political and cultural purposes. I have also attempted to suggest—both in text and in a series of images of Sandino, ranging from the photographically detailed to the barely liminal—how the complexly human historical Sandino, like all human beings full of inconsistencies and contradictions, was abstracted and formed (and many times re-formed) into a coherent cultural-political icon. In Chapter 10, I elaborate upon the role of gender in this formation and reformation by offering a broader exploration of gender as a continuing site of conflict within Nicaraguan culture.

CHAPTER 10 NEW WOMEN AND (NOT SO) NEW MEN

CULTURAL RECALCITRANCE AND THE POLITICS OF

GENDER

. . . .

The educated woman will be truly one for the home: she will be the companion and collaborator of man in the formation of the family. You [women] are called upon to form souls, to sustain the soul of your husband; for this reason, we educate you . . . to continue the perpetual creation of the nation. Beloved little one [*Niña querida*], do not turn feminist in our midst.—Justo Sierra (1848–1912), Mexican minister of education under Porfirio Díaz, quoted in Miller 1991, 47

. . . .

For me the best woman to marry is one who works. . . . The woman wakes first to cook, then she goes with her man to the fields. When they return she does the housework and prepares the food for her husband; then she gathers up the dirty clothes to wash them in the river, returns home, cleans the house and prepares the food. . . . When [the man] comes in from the fields he just goes and rests in the hammock. She doesn't say anything, it's the man who gives the orders, and after he's eaten then he sleeps with his lady. If a man has money it's because his woman helps him. This is true all over Nicaragua. . . . My only pleasures have been women and work, and because of this I have lots of children—but then I also have five women and they all keep me . . . and help me.—Miskito Moravian minister Rafael Dixon, ca. 1985, quoted in Angel and Macintosh 1987, 35–36

. . . .

Some strands of the history of women in Nicaragua from the conquest onward have been woven through previous chapters of this book. This chapter examines more closely the history of gender relations in Nicaragua, women's quest for equity, and the nodes and structures of resistance to that quest. It concludes by focusing upon the decade between the Sandinista triumph of 1979 and the advent of the U.S.-backed Chamorro government, during which only modest progress was made in transforming gender relations, despite the Sandinistas' formal commitment to such a transformation.[1]

When a woman marries, wrote "Ariel" (no doubt a woman) in Managua's *Los Domingos* in early November 1921, "I feel like something comes loose inside me . . . like divine grace flees from my soul." Skillfully she sketched the archetypal marital scenario for Latin American women:

Idealized image of woman. (From *Los Domingos*, 16 June 1918)

From this day forth, they tell them, you will follow your husband. You will obey him, adapt yourself to his character, to his way of being, his vices, his virtues; you will lose your personality . . . your talent; you will lose the right . . . to adorn your own life. If you have . . . whatever emotion, of love, of sympathy, of talent, you must be sure that emotion passes. The husband . . . is your warden [*carcelero*]. The same thing happens as happens in jails: the warden . . . throws the latch on the door that guards the robber, vulgar and perverse, just like he throws it on the one that guards the rebellious spirit. . . . A woman who marries has stopped living.[2]

Nearly sixty years later, just after the fall of Somoza, some superficial changes were in evidence, but the underlying paradigm had not changed appreciably. "Anyone visiting Nicaragua in the past year cannot but be struck by the visible examples of women's changing status," a North American woman reported. But, she added, "*Machismo* is not dead in Nicaragua" (Flynn 1980, 30).

To explore the many paradoxes, ironies, and contradictions of gender relations in Nicaragua, both currently and historically, it is useful to focus on the tension between the essential durability and continuity of those relations on the one hand, and Nicaraguan women's persistent (even if many times hesitant and uneven) movement toward liberation on the other.[3] What is clear at every historical moment is that each effort to raise the social status of women has come into conflict with what Jill Matthews has called the established (hence resistant) "gender order" of the culture — the "historically constructed pattern of power relations between men and women and definitions of femininity and masculinity."[4]

My objects, then, are (1) to explore some basic aspects of these definitions and power relations, and to chronicle some dramatic moments of what I will call the continuous "cultural recalcitrance" deriving from the established gender order; (2) to show the relative inability of formal ideology, official policy, or women's organized opposition to modify or overcome that recalcitrance; and (3) to examine the cultural politics of resulting conflicts over the nature of social policy and the directions of social change with respect to gender.

CULTURAL RECALCITRANCE

"The very deep-rootedness of the oppression of [Nicaraguan] women, its tenacious and at times violent defense by men, and the often ingrained acquiescence in it by some women," Molyneux has observed, "make it something that cannot simply be abolished by decree" (Molyneux 1988, 129). For our purposes here, cultural recalcitrance will be defined as the synergistic operation of all culturally based or culture-linked forms of opposition (intentional or not, organized or not, from whatever quarter) to modifying an established order — in this case, the gender order.[5] Cultural recalcitrance manifests itself in the *durability* of assumptions, values, behaviors, social and cultural norms, and images of men and women; in the lack of *congruence* between emerging progressive ideology or policy, and established social or cultural practice; in passive or active *resistance* to new policy, new institutional forms, or initiatives for change; and in the conscious, programmatic *recovery, reinforcement,* and *reassertion* of old gender paradigms.

Foremost among the reasons for such recalcitrance are (1) that the gender order is constantly reproduced by the practices of everyday life; (2) that recalcitrance is legitimized and further reproduced by institutions (including especially the Catholic church); (3) that it is reinforced by a broader hegemonic order (of which *machismo* is a central feature) created in the service of men's interests; and (4) that for a variety of reasons having to do with their formation and incorporation into the overall gender order and its various institutional regimes, women frequently think, believe, and act ambivalently with respect to the project of liberation, and thus collaborate in their own victimization.[6]

CULTURAL REPRODUCTION. Visitors to Nicaragua have repeatedly reported two paradoxically counterposed patterns: the opportunistic quickness with which Nicaraguan people adopt new cultural behaviors and practices when it appears in their short- (or long-) term interest to do so, and the stubborn durability of other accustomed behaviors and practices. Cultural reproduction is a dialectically resistant-incorporative process, it turns out, that on the one hand tends to buffer already established cultural patterns against impulses to change, and on the other hand either incorporates inevitable accommodative adjustments into existing patterns, or converts them into new long-term ones. Two examples, both focused on gender, may illustrate.

The (mostly women) owners of inns along the mid-nineteenth century transit route, reported one traveler who was alert to short-term opportunistic accommodation along the eastern (San Juan river) end of the route, "send out their handsomest young women [to solicit business], because they know by experience that Californians have a keen eye to good looks. If a traveller passing near a door glances in, one of the damsels will remove the *cigarro* from her lips . . . and accost him somewhat as follows: 'How do you do, California? You hungry? Come in my house. I got plenty good things. . . .' And she looks at him out of her dark, long-lashed eyes as sweetly and bewitchingly as she can." The women merchants at the western (Virgin Bay) end of the route were equally enterprising, using "all the little stock of English that they were masters of . . . to entice the hungry and thirsty travellers to buy, eat and imbibe, and leave a little of their California gold in Nicaragua. . . . The prettiest señoritas received the most patronage."[7] These examples, deriving from a culturally turbulent era in Nicaraguan history, demonstrate both the stable features and the incorporative-accommodative capacities of the gender order: women behaving in the coquettish ways characteristic of *machista* culture, but also learning the rudiments of English in order to move across another traditional cultural barrier into entrepreneurial activity.[8]

Other gender-based patterns have demonstrated remarkable stability through many social and cultural transformations. Traveling in Nicaragua on the eve of the current century, Gustavo Niederlein, head of the scientific department of the Philadelphia Commercial Museum, took note of "the large number of naked children, mostly boys," playing in the street. "The girls," he observed, "generally wear chamises." During my own stay with a middle-class family in Nicaragua nearly a century later, the practice Niederlein observed was unchanged: the two-year-old son was regularly allowed to play and run through the house unencumbered by clothing, while his only slightly older sister was not.[9]

Cultural reproduction of established male-dominant gender paradigms was assisted substantially by advertising accompanying the increased influx of products from the United States from the 1920s onward. A newspaper advertisement of early 1920 warned the aristocratic woman—normally the "flower

LA FLOR DE LA VIDA SOCIAL

es la aristocrática dama que por su belleza, su elegancia y su discreto ingenio constituye el mejor adorno de los salones distinguidos. Desgraciadamente, las exigencias sociales afectan el delicado sistema nervioso de la mujer y alteran su salud, sobre todo durante la época en que sufre los efectos del proceso fisiológico que le es peculiar. Dolores de cabeza, cólicos, depresión mental, fatiga y malestar son los tormentos a que se ve sometida la mujer en tales ocasiones. La vida, entonces, se convierte para ella en un martirio. Sus gracias se marchitan, su ingenio se embota y su capacidad de agradar disminuye.

Todo eso, por fortuna, puede evitarse con las

TABLETAS BAYER DE ASPIRINA Y CAFEÍNA

(en tubos de etiqueta roja), las cuales no solo alivian los dolores del proceso periódico sino que combaten la nerviosidad y el cansancio que suelen venir después de las gratas horas pasadas en los salones, a la vez que aumentan el vigor físico y estimulan las facultades mentales. La acción de estas Tabletas es tan rápida que diez minutos después de tomarlas se experimentan sus benéficos efectos. Belleza e ingenio son el secreto de los mejores triunfos femeninos; pero belleza e ingenio requieren una base indispensable: buena salud. Por eso la mujer cuidadosa de sí misma y del puesto que ocupa en la sociedad usa siempre las Tabletas Bayer de Aspirina y Cafeína para evitarse así las dolencias que perjudican sus encantos y los trastornos que afectan su capacidad intelectual.

"The Flower of Social Life," advertisement for Bayer Aspirin. (From *Los Domingos*, 6[?] March 1920)

of social life"—to protect her "delicate nervous system" with Bayer's blend of aspirin and caffeine, lest she suffer headaches, mental depression, and fatigue (especially during "the time when she suffers the effects of the physiological process peculiar to her"). A Cardui y Hepalina "tonic for women" advertisement from early 1921 featured an idealized, seductively nude sculptured female figure menaced by a large mallet held in strong male hands. Two front covers of the Latin American edition of *Reader's Digest* in the

NEW WOMEN AND (NOT SO) NEW MEN   387

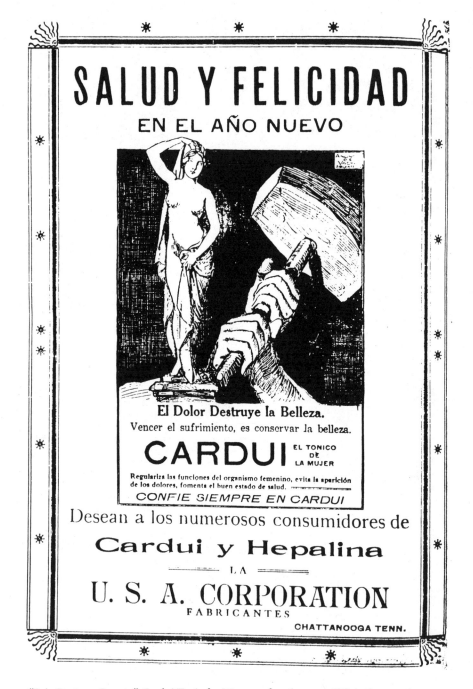

"Pain Destroys Beauty," Cardui Tonic for Women advertisement, U.S.A. Corporation, Chattanooga, Tennessee. (From *Los Domingos*, 16 February 1921)

Covers from *Reader's Digest*, Latin American edition, July 1945 and May 1949, featuring idealized Latin American woman and man. (Used by permission of Reader's Digest Association)

late 1940s presented idealized images of the Latin American Woman and the Latin American Man. The woman's upper body rises virginally from a white and red, provocatively off-the-shoulder gown, white flowers in her dark hair, silver cross upon her bosom, ambiguously votive/phallic lighted candle in her hand, eyes cut seductively to the side toward the viewer. Only the man's upper body is included in the image; it is rigid and erect, clad in a blue-dress military tunic, gold epaulets gleaming in the light emanating from the smiling sunshine figure over his left shoulder. His white-gloved left hand, at breast height, holds his sword in a suggestively phallic position. His eyes are narrowed to calculating slits; his jaw is tight and encircled by the gold chin strap of the dress helmet; he looks resolutely away.

Observers generally agree that a primary site of gender-construction is the family. The typical Argentinian family, Schmuckler concluded from an analysis of gender and authority, is no less than "a *factory* where gender meanings are . . . constructed" continuously through daily family discourse and interactions.[10] Although it is "unusual to find direct dialogues about the definitions of what is a woman or what is a man," Schmuckler argues, "all rules of family functioning have some meaning for gender." Synthesizing what they observe within the family and what they absorb outside it, children develop gendered behaviors through processes whose outcomes depend upon the relations of authority within particular families. In the more authoritarian families, "the voice of the father is assumed to express the social norms based on biological, supernatural or sacred beliefs." The father's authority—based upon "the pure facts of his masculine gender and his biological paternity"—is therefore uncontested, and dominant gender models are imprinted upon children as the natural ones. In less authoritarian families, Schmuckler observed, both discourse and practice tend to question and demystify dominant gender models as social constructs open to negotiation. The degree of the mother's authority, then, is obviously a function of the family's relative proximity to the authoritarian or negotiating pole. Whatever their position, Schmuckler emphasizes, mothers are "transmitters of the family order," and hence key agents in the larger process of cultural reproduction.

Nicaraguan women report experiences fully congruent with Schmuckler's model. Raised by mothers who themselves had been formed within the established gender order, women who came of age during the social, political, and cultural upheaval of the 1960s and 1970s experienced marked gender-based conflict with respect to both identity and social-cultural roles. Leticia Herrera (b. 1949), who became an FSLN guerrilla leader and later a high Sandinista official, characterized her "super-conservative" mother as "the traditional Latin American woman, busy with the domestic chores, the children. . . . [She] never left the circle of what was accepted for women of her time" and "never told me anything" about sexuality (Heyck 1990, 88, 95). Future FSLN guerrilla leader Doris María Tijerino (b. 1943) recalls that "in the Nicaraguan family, instructing children is the responsibility of the mother, so my mother was the one from whom I learned about the world." Psychology professor Verónica Cáceres, born to a "domineering Somocista father" in the mid-1950s in a small village on the Honduran border, remembers that her mother read a lot and "wanted to improve herself, but papa never let her. . . . My father never liked for her to go anywhere. And for us girls, hardly any boys ever dared to come over to the house because he was so strict." For a daughter to get a professional education was a constant struggle "because of the concept my papa had of what constituted a proper education for women" (Heyck 1990, 139–50).[11]

Such experiences suggest that, as Schmuckler repeatedly observed in the Argentinian families she studied, a major function of child-rearing practices was precisely to ratify and perpetuate the dominant ("natural") gender order. The widespread belief that "the child's sexual orientation is defined forever during his or her early years," for example, leads to the conclusion that "what is good for the daughter is bad for the son, and vice versa." The "mutual submission between mother and daughter and a unilateral submission of the mother to her son" encourages male children's (again "natural," according to

Bayer Tonic advertisement. (From *La Prensa*, 7 April 1938)

the gender paradigm) "capacity to dominate and be autonomous" (Schmuckler 1984, 117, 123). Such a gender-specific developmental agenda was more
than evident in a 1938 Managua newspaper advertisement for Bayer Tonic.
It featured two prepubescent girls delighted by a biceps-flexing prepubescent
male. "You will have strength, vigor, and happiness," it promised. "It will
enrich the blood, invigorate the muscles, strengthen the brain and nerves."

Among the families she studied, Schmuckler observed such formative patterns to inhere in the minutest details of daily life, encouraging boys to "ratify
the expected image of aggression, violence, dominance, and autonomy."
Hence male children were "prohibited from freely choosing to play indoors,
cooperating with [their] friends, playing with girls or being affectionate and
loving like [their] sisters." Female children had responsibilities in the house;
males did not. Boys could play unsupervised outdoors; girls could not. Boys

were served larger portions at meals. Other observers have corroborated such observations and added further examples: boys may urinate in public; girls may not. Young boys needn't wear swimsuits at public pools; girls (of whatever age) always do. In later adolescence, boys have no curfews or restrictions on their friends and associates; girls do.[12]

These socializing practices are fully in evidence in Nicaragua. Among families in Managua in the late 1980s, Lancaster observed that both male and female children were routinely provoked to rage, but that expressing rage was tolerated only in males; that profane language was acceptable from male children and adolescents, but not from females; that male children could ignore their mothers' orders, but females could not; and that teenage males could drink alcohol, a behavior absolutely proscribed for their sisters. In a particularly striking moment, Lancaster observed adults (one of them female) goading a young Nicaraguan male child into beating up a female child, urging him on with taunts about his masculinity. The intended lesson, Lancaster notes, is "show aggressiveness, dominate women, or be deprived of your masculinity" (Lancaster 1992, 41–42). In such a gender regime, the tyrannical behavior that routinely develops in sons is permitted because to do otherwise might make them homosexual.

Hence the paradigms of maleness and femaleness upon which the gender order rests, besides being self-reproducing, are virtually all-inclusive: they specify the bases for and structures of authority; they set the terms of personal, familial, and social relationships; they define body images and sexuality; they specify norms of personal growth and development; they govern modes of speaking and patterns of discourse; they control public and private behaviors, provide models for the public presentation of self, and regulate the use of both private and public space. And in Nicaragua as elsewhere, the paradigms guarantee a high degree of continuity in the shaping of men and women.

THE CHURCH. Rivaling the culturally reproductive processes of the family in their forcefulness are the formal structures, ritualized practices, explicitly (even dogmatically) articulated norms, and potentially painful and embarrassing sanctions of the Catholic church. Although the Catholic church has had to tack with the winds of political and cultural change in Nicaragua as it has elsewhere in Latin America, it has for the most part steered steadily against the winds of feminist demands to alter the established gender order.

Nicaragua's constitutions of 1838 and 1858 provided that "the Roman Catholic religion professed by the country is protected by the government" (Alvarez Lejarza 1958, 430, 532). A concordat between the Conservative government and the Holy See in 1862 recognized Catholicism as the official state religion and gave the church the right to supervise public education and to censor publications. Although the Liberal Zelaya administration (1894–1909) nullified the concordat, took over some church properties (including those of the *cofradías*), exiled some priests and nuns, and opened the country to other religious groups, the Conservatives' new constitution of 1911 reestablished Catholicism as the official religion, whereupon the church immediately embarked upon an effort to reconstruct its accustomed privileges and status. Two years later the Archdiocese of Managua was created, making Nicaragua independent of the church hierarchy in Guatemala for the first time in four hundred years (Foroohar 1989, 8–42).

By the early 1920s, as the movement for a change in the gender order began to gather force among Nicaraguan women (as I will demonstrate presently that it did), the church unequivocally declared in favor of the established paradigm. "The great woman," said a writer in Granada's *El Reflector* in 1926, is

the modest woman consecrated to the religious and social duties of the sphere of life in which she finds herself . . . the daughter who lives in obedience . . . the wife who guards in her heart the severe words pronounced by the minister of religion . . . living only for the being with whom she shares her fortune [*las dichas*] . . . [and] being . . . his guiding angel . . . the saintly widow who consecrates all her thoughts . . . to the Creator . . . the solitary nun who prays day and night and mortifies her body for the failings of humanity.[13]

Throughout the long years of U.S. occupation and the Somoza dictatorship that followed it, the Catholic church took an almost unrelievedly conservative position on most social and political issues. The Bishop of Granada blessed U.S. Marines as they left to fight the "bandit" Sandino in 1928, the church hierarchy urged Nicaraguans to surrender to occupying U.S. troops, and Archbishop Lezcano ordered church officials to collaborate with the National Guard and the marines. On the eve of World War II, Archbishop José Antonio Lezcano y Ortega admonished Nicaraguan Catholics that "Protestantism with . . . its spirit of rebellion against all teaching authority, has engendered rationalism, which in turn has produced materialism . . . which has produced Communism and the Bolshevik ideas of those who do not know God, nor any kind of moral, or law." In 1942, Archbishop Lezcano used the gold crown of the Virgin of Candelaria to crown Somoza's daughter Liliam Queen of the Army in Managua's cathedral. All authority, said a pastoral letter of 1950, "comes from God. God is the author of whatever exists. . . . When Catholics obey the government, they do not degrade themselves, but their act fundamentally constitutes compliance with God." Throughout the Cold War period, the church lent its full weight and blessing to the fanatical anti-communism of the Somoza regime. When the elder Somoza was assassinated in 1956, the Archbishop eulogized him as "a Prince of the Church," and Pope Pius XII sent official condolences. The summary result, as Foroohar notes, is that the majority of the Nicaraguan Catholic hierarchy remained isolated from and antagonistic to the radical wing of the church (which took a markedly different position on women's issues) until years after Vatican II and Medellín—as indeed it did virtually throughout Latin America (Foroohar 1989, 16, 21, 38–40, 67; Kirk 1992, 41).[14]

Thus the Catholic church was rarely found on the side of progressive social change in general, or supporting women's challenges to dominant gender paradigms in particular.[15] Catholic private schools in Nicaragua, as Foroohar observes, "were chiefly supported by the wealthy minority." As the chief definers and beneficiaries of those paradigms and the social structure that issued from them, the wealthy had a large stake in guarding the stability of the value system and its capacity to reproduce itself (Foroohar 1989, 42). At the outset of the Somoza government's second decade, the magazine *Criterio* set forth the gender paradigm of the Latin American Catholic church with remarkable clarity and force. "The woman," it said, "biologically and psychically, is destined for motherhood; this is the principal end of her life on earth. It is this maternal sentiment, so much flesh of her flesh and so spirit of her spirit, which should rule and have priority in a woman. . . . Without it a woman has little worth . . . [and from it radiates] the authentic personality of a woman" (Schmuckler 1984, 105).

This paradigm—variously modulated by class, region, and ethnicity—was a primary controlling and shaping influence in the daily lives of Nicaraguan women. Doris Tijerino recalls being taught by nuns that "marriage was a woman's cross; that life was a Calvary and that in a Calvary everybody bears her cross. Woman's cross was marriage and she had to bear it." Young women in her Catholic boarding school had to take baths in "a cotton garment reaching to our knees, slit up the sides to our waists so we could soap ourselves." They were admonished never to look at their bodies in order to avoid "bad thoughts," and the section on sexual reproduction was excised from the biology books (Tijerino 1978, 34, 50–51).[16]

HEGEMONY AND MEN'S INTERESTS. Men—inside the church or out—resist changes in the gender order primarily because they believe it is in their own interest to do so; they rationalize the resistance as being in women's interest as well. Forms may change, but patterns persist, and the legitimizing hegemonic ideas and reinforcing hegemonic structures prove remarkably stable. Since at least a decade or so after independence, Nicaraguan men have expressed their confidence that they know what a woman "naturally" is—

hence properly ought to be—and have shown no reluctance to inscribe those ideals on her very body. A writer in *El Correo del Istmo de Nicaragua* advised in 1850, "So that a woman may enjoy complete perfection in her beauty, she needs to have"

Three white things: complexion, teeth, and hands
Three black ones: eyes, eyebrows, and eyelashes
Three pink ones: lips, cheeks, and finger nails
Three long ones: figure, hands, and hair
Three short ones: teeth, ears, and feet
Three broad ones: bosom, forehead, and the space between the eyes
Three narrow ones: mouth, waist, and instep
Three thick ones: arms, calves, and thighs[17]
Three small ones: frown, head, and nose.[18]

A quarter-century later, the anonymous writer of the 1873 play *El Espíritu del Siglo* (examined in Chapter 2) took the legitimacy of the gender order as his central theme, equating the survival of Nicaraguan culture with women's submission to men's social and political imperatives, which women recognize as superior to their own silly and ephemeral desires. Still a half-century later, in early 1926, when Granada's *El Reflector* essayed to define "the integral woman," its terms were substantially those of *El Espíritu del Siglo*. "In the hour of failure, grief, and discouragement," the *El Reflector* writer promised,

man always has a refuge and loyal electuary for his troubled soul: woman! . . . There is no pain woman does not mitigate in her three supremely powerful guises of sweetheart, wife and mother! . . . We refer to the woman who is truly woman, the woman penetrated by her true and almost divine mission . . . and not the modern liberated woman [*mujercilla moderna*], mannish, disfigured and mutilated, unknowing victim of that great insubstantiality called *la moda*.

The woman of chastity, the woman of fidelity, the woman of love, select spirit of her three divine phases, that always was and eternally will be an inexhaustible fountain of tenderness, sovereign over man. . . . But this modern woman, daubed [*pintarrajeada*] and semi-nude, who divorces . . . who hastens to "cocktails" and smokes and plays cards and roulette . . . those, we say, neither inspire nor console, nor alleviate pain and disillusionment. On the contrary, they distress and torment all the more.

An intelligent woman, long-suffering and strong, with a solid religious and moral education, who is well possessed by her mission . . . can stand the most astute or perverse man on his head. . . .

La Mujer Nicaragüense, sintetizadora de los emblemas morales del perfecto hogar, se singulariza porque encarna la mejor armonía de las virtudes de la época patriarcal y de los principios de la cultura moderna en todo cuanto es superación intelectual y cultivo de la personalidad.

GUIA GENERAL ILUSTRADA, al exaltar los merecimientos de la Mujer Nicaragüense, rinde a Ella un cumplido homenaje en la figura de la **Primera Dama de la República, doña Salvadorita Debayle de Somoza**.

Official photograph of Salvadora Debayle de Somoza, ca. 1940. (From *Nicaragua. Guía general ilustrada*, 1940)

[We prefer] the woman of concern, she who as sweetheart always had the modesty to say "I adore you," who as wife always had the energy to say "I pardon you," she who as mother sang us to sleep with an "I bless you."[19]

By the eve of World War II, fifteen years later, the patriarchal ideal of the adoring, pardoning, blessing woman was still undimmed and essentially unchanged. The caption for a requisite photograph of President Somoza's wife in an illustrated guide to Nicaragua proclaimed her to be the veritable archetype of "The Nicaraguan Woman," "synthesizer of the moral emblems of the perfect home . . . [who] incarnates the best harmony between the virtues of the patriarchal epoch and the principles of modern culture."[20]

Evidence abounds that men were acutely aware of their own potential losses should the paradigm be seriously challenged or substantially altered. Bearing the names of two of Nicaragua's most venerable patriarchal families, Pedro Joaquín Cuadra Chamorro disingenuously assured the young ladies of the Colegio Profesional de María Auxiliadora in 1928 that "whoever has even a little knowledge of the world . . . can with profound sadness say *adiós* to the old patriarchal customs, almost all of which are now gone forever. [Time was] when the woman, that Heaven in miniature . . . was the major enchantment of the home, within whose compass, narrow if you wish, but sweetly tender, she passed her life of abnegation and sacrifice, without ever trying to pass beyond its threshold, except perhaps to carry bread to the poor or consolation to the home of another."[21] The specter of a radical transformation of the dominant gender order—the only one in which men could conceive of continuing to understand themselves, "their" women, and their relationships—was fearful indeed.

In its most characteristic *machista* configuration, the hegemonic gender order emphasizes *hetero*sexuality and a double standard of sexual conduct: male sexual superiority, liberty, aggressiveness, and dominance, and female purity, inferiority, passivity, and submission.[22] With relatively minor local variations, the code is pan–Latin American (indeed virtually pan-historical): an idealized, binary sexual ethics that sanctions men's compulsive philandering and demands women's absolute fidelity; elaborate, ritualized competition for sexual dominance; and passion and violence in the pursuit of position within the male hierarchy (Chasteen in Szuchman 1989, 123–40). The code is perhaps most forcefully dramatized in the Argentinian tango, which Archetti argues "reflects male concerns about women's behavior," and hence about the stability of the gender paradigm. "In tango," Archetti observes, "men are the judges and the women are judged." The bad woman (*la milonguita*)—self-indulging product of a complex of paradigm-threatening social, economic, political, and cultural changes (*la mujercilla moderna*, in *El Reflec-*

tor's phrase) — is contrasted with the idealized mother (Archetti 1988, 4–11). Arnold's observations of prostitutes in Peru in the early 1970s foreground the self-definitions forced upon women by men's *machista* behavior (Arnold in Lipshitz 1978, 57–69). Sexless, weak, and childlike wives and good women are to be shielded from sex, which by its nature is uncontrollable. Prostitutes therefore represent "the potential, dangerous sexual powers of the unsubdued woman," and the brothel is a place where "terrifying, sexual women" may be kept under some semblance of control.

The *machista* paradigm operates as forcefully in Nicaragua as elsewhere in Latin America. Almost simultaneously with Arnold's research among Peruvian prostitutes and their clients, Nicaraguan folklorist Enrique Peña Hernández presented what he took to be evidence that, in an uncorrupted state of nature, *macho* behavior is not only natural but in fact desired by women, whose apparent resistance to male sexual aggressiveness is but mere coquettish dissimulation. Writing of "free love among the Indians" of the indigenous barrio of Monimbó, Peña Hernández posited that

> love knocks at the door at a young age. . . . The little Indian women are of amazing fecundity. . . . One sees how used the Indian men are to making love. They are friends of brusqueness and violence.
>
> Many still get a sexual partner in a primitive, almost savage way. . . . Waiting for her with improbable skill, he drags away his dark one [*morena*] (many say that she allows him to drag her away) . . . and makes her his, tames and domesticates her, with the power and authority of the true *macho*. As to feeling conquered and dominated by the man, it seems that after all she is pleased. (Peña Hernández 1968, 49–50)

Peña Hernández's putatively objective ethnographic account conceals but poorly a voyeuristic longing reminiscent of that of many a nineteenth-century traveler passing through Arcadian Nindirí, many an *encomendero* eyeing his Indian labor force, many a *conquistador* gazing upon the unclad natives gathered innocently and inquisitively on the shore. That longing betrays in turn the folding of the "natural" female qualities and dispositions of "the little Indian women" (*las mujercitas indias*) into ideal models for non-indigenous Nicaraguan women, as in Rubén Darío's delicious musings about Nicaraguan women as he returned home after one of his many long absences. There was something special about the Nicaraguan woman, Darío opined, that distinguished her even from other Central American women: "It is . . . a type of Arabic languor, of creole *nonchalance*, combined with a natural elegance and fluency in her moving and walking." Quoting contemporary psychologist Havelock Ellis, Darío observed that the kinesic seductiveness of her walking "has within it something of the graceful condition of the feline animal, whose whole body is alive" (Darío 1917b, 95).

As Gould has observed, the public sexual conquests of Chinandega oligarch Edmundo ("Mundo") Deshon a half-century later dramatized the remarkably durable capacity of such gender paradigms to focus and organize social and political power in Nicaragua. Deshon, who was at the time engaged in a struggle with the *campesino* community over some of their lands he wanted to buy and develop, used his sexual conquest of Cándida Pastrán, daughter of the Chinandega mayor and widow of *campesino* community leader Regino Escobar, to "boastfully demonstrate the convergence of sexual and class oppression." Deshon's expensive gifts to Pastrán and his sexual domination of her threatened the masculinity of *campesino* men and wounded their pride; conversely, Pastrán's "sell-out" (as her own community interpreted it) suggested that the "[*campesino*] organization's bonds of solidarity [were] illusory . . . [and] that [her] loyalty to the martyred leader was secondary to her own material advancement." Simultaneously, the affair buttressed the elites' argument "about the illegitimacy, lack of leadership and weakness of the organization," showed the community to be "immoral and without honor," and revealed Regino Escobar to be "less than a man, a weak cuckold." In sum the episode revealed, concluded Gould, "how elite males operated in a discursive universe where sexual conquest symbolized class power and where the latter was experienced passionately" (Gould 1990a, 231–32).

Virtually simultaneously with Deshon's *macho* escapade, Doris María Tijerino was being imprisoned and tortured by the Nicaraguan National Guard. Twenty years later she recalled vividly how the gender paradigm shaped the process. It was, she said, "abuse by those who consider anyone who opposes them as subhuman and Communist. If you were also a woman, that, for them, made everything worse. It was a *vagancia*, something that made you totally useless to society and thoroughly despicable. For them, political participation for women and prostitution were one and the same thing. They regarded women prisoners from their *machista* perspective, and we were treated twice as bad; first because we were anti-Somocista, and second, because we were women" (Heyck 1990, 64).

An advertisement in *La Prensa* in the mid-1970s revealed the self-doubt that underlay and impelled such brutality. "Good news for MEN," proclaimed the advertisers:

OPOVITAM (with testicular extract) reinforces virile vigor. OPOVITAM . . . is a new product composed of testicular extract and other masculine sexual glandular substances that reestablish and reinforce the virile capacity of men prematurely declining [*decaídos*].

OPOVITAM is very effective in cases of SEXUAL WEAKNESS, STATES OF PHYSICAL AND EMOTIONAL DEPRESSION, LACK OF MEMORY, FATIGUE OR MENTAL WEARINESS, and other symptoms of premature declining in men.[23]

Thus Nicaraguan men characteristically construct a Nicaraguan woman who presents herself in three distinct guises, each (according to the polyvalent hegemonic construction) perpetually in the service of certain of his own interests: (1) the faithful and unthreatening submissive woman in her three "divine phases," as *El Reflector*'s writer phrased it: the self-abnegating and ever-blessing mother (*la mujer sufrida*); the virginal and ever-adoring sweetheart (*la mujer castidad*); the desexualized and ever-pardoning wife; (2) the liberated but masculinized and deformed feminist woman (the painted *mujer moderna*, the *mujercilla*, the dancing *milonguita*); (3) and the intensely sexual woman—the fecund and coquettish *mujercita india*, eager to be dominated and domesticated; the sexually unsubdued and terrifying but irresistibly tantalizing prostitute, ironically promising the needy child-man an all-assuaging union with his mother.[24]

Fearful of the losses they would suffer in any transformation of the gender order, men are careful to link the paradigm to power—in sanctioned rituals of social dominance (*gauchos* and the all-too-scarce women of the pampas, Peña's *machos verdaderos* and eagerly available *mujercitas indias*), in the brutalities of physical torture (the National Guard and women prisoners), in calculated political-cultural strategies ("Mundo" Deshon and Cándida Pastrán). But although power is the text, fear is the controlling subtext, and the ultimate fear is fear of one's own inherent lack (or loss) of power. The gender paradigm in general and *machismo* in particular thus function as the testicular extract, the structural *Opovitam* that promises permanent protection from fading, doubt, depression, weakness, and the waning of "virile vigor."

As Lancaster has shown, these dynamics of *machismo* operate with particular power and virulence among Nicaraguan males with regard to male homosexuality.[25] Even more specifically, male sexuality is defined within an active-honor (*hombre-hombre*, or manly man) and passive-shame (*cochón*) dichotomy that stigmatizes not the homosexual act itself but the act*or* who takes the passive role (Lancaster 1992, 270–71).[26] "Only the anal-passive *cochón* is stigmatized," Lancaster observes, and one "is either a *cochón* or one is not." If one is not a *cochón*, then "it scarcely matters that one sleeps with *cochones*. . . . What matters is the *manner* in which one is attracted to other males. . . . The one who initiates action, dominates, or enters is masculine; whoever is acted upon, dominated, or entered is feminine."

The pervasive cultural (and political) power of such a construction of male sexuality lies, Lancaster argues, in the fact that "the stigma threatens . . . all men . . . who fail to maintain a proper public face." Hence "everyone wishes to pass the stigma along; no one wishes to be left holding it." The ambiguity of the resulting public discourse about sexuality means that "the *hombre-hombre*'s exemption from stigma is never entirely secure." That fact in turn "conjures a terror that rules all men, all actions, all relationships." Paradoxically, then, "insecurity about one's masculinity or sexuality" can be exorcised (completely in contradistinction to the situation in the United States), "by mounting—thus sexually subordinating—a *cochón*."

Systemically considered, then, Lancaster argues, "*machismo* is not a set of erroneous ideas that somehow got lodged in people's heads. Rather, it is an organization of social relations that generates ideas . . . [which] has its own materiality, its own power to produce effects. . . . [It is] a real political economy of the body." The conquest of women, then, is a feat performed for two audiences: first, for "other men, to whom one must constantly prove one's masculinity and virility," and second, for oneself, "to whom one must also show all the signs of masculinity. . . . constantly asserting one's masculinity by way of practices that show the self to be 'active,' not 'passive.'" In such a system, women are not primary or final objects of desire, but rather "intermediaries . . . [within] an ongoing exchange system between men" (Lancaster 1992, 236–37).

WOMEN'S AMBIVALENCE AND LIBERATION. It would have been well had Nicaraguan women been unified in their historical task of liberation. But they have not been. Like women in other times and places (indeed like all human beings), they have frequently felt it necessary to place their own short-term interests (however conceived) against the broader, long-term interests of the group(s) to which they belong. Hence the larger project of liberation has been modulated (even deformed) by women's competing allegiances to race, class, region, and religious belief. Moreover, the feminist and anti-feminist elements of women's own traditional cultures interact in complex ways with both the repressive and the liberating elements of modernity, the benefits of familiar arrangements inevitably modulate the attractions of change, and the seductive possibility of easy collaboration highlights the arduousness of emancipatory struggle. In the late 1920s, Nicaraguan feminist Josefa Toledo de Aguerri (1866–1962) understood the dilemma.[27] The passivity of so many women in the face of their own oppression, she said, "comes from the fact that with regard to *ideas*, the woman lives within the ancient form of colonial life; with regard to *forms*, thrown fully into modern frivolity. These causes produce her accommodation and lull her action."[28]

Women's collaboration in their own victimization (however understandable contextually) goes beyond the passivity that worried Toledo de Aguerri, however, to include forms of active collaboration that substantially reinforce the recalcitrance of the gender order. The roots of such collaboration reach back through colonial Spanish America into pre-conquest indigenous culture. Before the Spanish arrived, as Miller has pointed out, lower-class indigenous women found liaisons with upper-class men an attractive path to social mobility and status. Queen Isabella dispatched thirty well-born Spanish women with Columbus on his third voyage, to assist in establishing Spanish culture in New Spain. So effectively did they serve that function, Miller suggests — not a few of them demonstrating drives for wealth fully equal to men's — that "the mantilla of the *doña* should be added to the cross and sword as icons of Spain in America" (Miller 1991, 20).[29]

Unfortunately, such collaborative values and behaviors have proved remarkably durable in Nicaragua, as elsewhere in Latin America. In her study of *marianismo*, Stevens reports, "It is common practice for a prudent middle-class mestizo mother of a pubescent boy to hire a young female servant for general housework 'and other duties,' the latter expression being a euphemism for initiating the boy into adult heterosexual experience" (Stevens in Pescatello 1973, 97). Similarly, a retired creole headmistress of a Moravian school on Nicaragua's east coast confessed her own collaboration in the exploitation of other women: "To make things easier at home," she said matter-of-factly, teachers "were always able to find a Miskito woman who would do the housework, wash our clothes and cook the food. All of us schoolteachers hired them as maids. The American wives also hired maids, but they were Creole women" (Angel and Macintosh 1987, 41).

Despite other pronounced cultural differences between the east and west coasts, such contradictions of gender and class relations were evident on both. Gould sketches the political fortunes of *Somocista* political leader Irma Guerrero, who "combined her father's important political contacts, *obrerista* rhetoric, and her own charismatic personality to ascend the staircase of *Somocista* success." Guerrero founded the *Somocista* women's political organization Frente Popular Femenino in 1956, and "denounced the plight of single mothers." *Somocista* males, Gould observes, "often viewed *La Irma* as a real *macho* (thus as a woman 'who did not threaten their own values')," and working women "admired her ability to manipulate the power structure" (Gould 1990a, 233). A full generation later in remote Quilalí, Collinson found, "men so habitually ditched their women . . . [that] it was something of a status symbol merely to have a man about the house"; consequently, women "put up with any manner of abuse . . . just to keep them in the house." Other women (through both family connections and political conviction) supported and even fought with the U.S.-backed contra forces; the widow of contra leader Jorge Salazar became a member of the contras' National Directorate (Collinson 1990, 10, 163). "When men gather," Lancaster reported from his research in Managua in the mid-1980s, "it is usually the women who send for liquor and prepare the chasers, and they usually do so without being asked." Those same women consider aggressive men more attractive as prospects for marriage than mild-mannered ones, while "solicit[ing] aggressive behavior in their sons" and forbidding it in their daughters (Lancaster 1992, 44).

Replicating themselves from one generation to the next, such collaborative behaviors appear to correlate less with political ideology than one might expect. A Nicaraguan grandmother recently recalled that the father of her two children "didn't help me. . . . It didn't matter to him if I ate or not. He filled up at his mother's while I was hungry at home and had to drag firewood from the hills so that we could eat" (Hart 1990, 34). More surprisingly, however, her otherwise assertive young feminist daughter Marta believed that "it's better for [a woman's] lover to have another woman than for her to have another man" (Hart 1990, 15).

Paradoxically, Marta is urged into collaboration not only by the *machista* culture, but also by elements of her putatively feminist ideology. Finding herself in a "liberated" relationship with a liminally feminist man, she talks with him about the possibility of their having other lovers. Later suspecting that he has one, she tries to elicit a confession. He is evasive, but she confirms it through her own inquiries to others. "I felt bad when I found out, really sad," Marta admits. "But I remembered that we had an agreement . . . [and] I said to him, 'Look, I understand you.' Suppose that I can't be with him for three months; I understand that he needs another woman." Marta later finds out who the other woman is and contrives to meet her while concealing her relationship to the man they share. "I went out of curiosity," she confides: "I momentarily felt jealous, but afterwards, I didn't. He doesn't see her constantly; certainly I wouldn't agree if it were a permanent relationship . . . but I began to think that it would have been worse if I had another man. . . . He wouldn't accept that I had someone else. . . . And also, I love him. To have one here and another there isn't correct for me. It wouldn't seem right."

Even when she articulates her own preferences, Marta betrays the extent of her socialization into collaborative attitudes and behaviors. "I like a man to tell me things about his life," she says. "But mostly I like sexual relations with him. [Mine is] a tolerant man who understands me, who isn't jealous; he knows my work is important and doesn't think I'll go with someone else. He has confidence in a woman, and I like that." In Marta's construction, however, lacking jealousy and having confidence emphatically do not mean that she may do as she wishes for her own purely personal reasons. On the contrary, it means that whatever her lover may be doing for *his* own purely personal reasons, he is confident that she will be faithful to him (Hart 1990, 251–56).

As Marta herself recognizes, moreover, collaborative behavior does not occur in a context of unconstrained choice between two equally feasible alternatives. "The majority of men in Nicaragua have what we call a *querida*, another woman," she says, but

> in general, here in Nicaragua, you don't find many married women who have lovers. Married women have told me that when they had lovers, they felt bad. To tell their husbands, or not tell them? There was this nervous tension, and it seemed he was going to find out, and then they'd lose their marriage. However, the . . . *querida* is usually a single woman. . . . It's not that the woman accepts [the man having another woman], but there's nothing else to do; you separate or stay in the situation. Sometimes the woman stays because they love each other, or she still loves him. . . . It isn't as if the wife is seeing the other woman with her own eyes; in some ways, it doesn't bother her. (Hart 1990, 256)

Hence in the case of *doña* María and her feminist daughter Marta, the gender paradigm is stronger and hence the gender order more recalcitrant than one might assume. Both are particular manifestations of some cultural continuities of great power and intricate organization, as I learned at the end of the 1980s when a bright woman doctor friend explained to me that she acquiesced to driving her husband ten miles to the bus stop in Managua in the evening so he could go to visit his young mistress (returning to pick him up in the wee hours) because she did not know of any Nicaraguan professional woman whose situation differed from hers, because she herself was considered an "old woman" (at thirty-five) with a daughter and thus no other man would want her, and because in practical terms life as a separated or divorced woman would be almost impossibly difficult.[30]

The presence of these factors—cultural recalcitrance, the cultural reproduction of the gender order, the gender regime of the Catholic church, the symbiotic linkage of men's interests and hegemonic ideology, and women's ambivalence and collaboration in their own victimization—guarantees that the process of liberation will be fraught with great difficulty, in Nicaragua as throughout Latin America.

TOWARD LIBERATION: LATIN AMERICA AND NICARAGUA

Even by the mid-1920s, when *El Reflector* essayed to define the ideal woman, Nicaraguan women were already moving to challenge the gender order and the paradigms upon which it was built. In so doing, they drew ideas, strength, and inspiration from the larger movement for change among Latin American women, the roots of which run deep in Latin American history.[31]

THE LATIN AMERICAN CONTEXT. Sor Juana Inés de la Cruz's spirited defense of a woman's right to develop her mind and live her own life made her the "icon of female intellectual independence" for Latin American women from the colonial period onward. But Sor Juana (1648–1695) was one of a tiny minority of colonial women who finagled any autonomy (Bergmann 1990, 151–72). Although the colonial legal system was in some respects aimed, as Lavrin has noted, "at protecting women from their own frailty or potential abuse by men," it also placed them "under their father's control before marriage and their husband's after it."[32] Women averaged nearly ten children each, and models of female behavior were "harsh and very demanding." Wife beating was not punishable unless it affected the wife's health. Rape was "not as severely punished as sodomy." Colonial authorities worked—through canon and civil law, preaching and confession, and learned treatises—to enforce Christian marriage, Iberian-style (that is to say, patriarchal) families, and Catholic sexual conduct upon indigenous and other colonial women, defining each in such a way as to place the bulk of the burden of sexual/moral honor upon women (Lavrin 1989, 4–10). Women were educated only for their accepted social roles as wives and mothers; most remained illiterate. Life in a convent—the surest avenue to protection and an education—was available only to a small percentage of women whose family wealth and influence were sufficient to get for them one of the relatively few places available. The few formal means of redress available to women could be invoked only after abuses from men (especially husbands) had reached extremes (Lavrin 1989, 21).

As the new Latin American nations struggled to establish themselves following independence, those of every political faction or persuasion sought to claim and manage the allegiance of the women whom they had depreciated, controlled, and abused during the previous three centuries (Miller 1991, 30).[33] Fortunately, Enlightenment discussions of the "rights of man" opened the rights of women to (tentative) discussion, clerical control of education declined somewhat, and newly established universities (while excluding women from attending) at least discussed the issue of women's education. Nisia Foresta Brasileira Augusta (b. 1810) translated Mary Wollstonecraft's *Vindication of the Rights of Women* (1792) into Portuguese in 1832. Private seminaries for women began to appear at mid-century, but not until 1881 did the first woman receive a university degree in Latin America (in Chile). Numerous women novelists, poets, and journalists emerged thereafter, as did women political activists, but most of the latter had their say in political journals rather than on a public podium. School teachers from the new women's seminaries, Miller notes, "formed the nucleus of the first women's groups to articulate . . . a feminist critique of society" at the end of the century (Miller 1991, 72).

Movement was more rapid after the turn of the twentieth century. Early twentieth-century civil code reforms in some Latin American countries gave women more rights (e.g., to education and to divorce), and resolutions designed to pressure specific national governments emanated from various international forums. Women were full participants in a series of scientific congresses (1898–1909), and in 1910 Argentinian university women convened the first Congreso Femenino Internacional in Buenos Aires, attended mainly by women from the southern cone countries. The exclusion of women from the Second Pan American Scientific conference in 1915–16 led to the first call for a Pan American union of women. The male governor of Yucatán organized two more radical feminist conferences in 1916; at one of them, one delegate demanded that a paper which advocated sex education and proclaimed that women were the full sexual and intellectual equals of men be burned. The wave of change was not to be held back, however; numerous Latin American women's conferences followed in the 1920s.[34]

What Miller judges to be "the first governmental organization in the world to be founded for the express purpose of working for the rights of women," the Inter-American Commission of Women (IACW), was founded in 1928. At its first meeting in 1930, women demonstrated against the United States' occupation of Nicaragua and generated a feminist and pacifist platform. In 1938 the commission proposed a Declaration in Favor of Women's Rights, and during World War II it led a move to insert the phrase "the equal rights of men and women" into the charter of the emerging United Nations. As the war got under way, however, the IACW's pacifism brought increasing pressure upon it from the United States, and it declined in status and influence (Miller in Bergmann 1990, 16).

In 1948 the Comisión Interamericana de Mujeres (CIM) was founded at a meeting of the Organization of American States, and that same year the first Inter-American Congress, called by the Women's International League for Peace and Freedom (WILPF), met in Guatemala City. The organizing committee for the Congress was "severely harassed and made the object of rumors" in the limited press coverage it received; the *New York Times* published a single brief notice in the women's section under "Food." The Congress nevertheless drew delegates from throughout the hemisphere and engaged with the issues of nuclear war, dictatorship, militarization, political prisoners, and forced exile.

Although some international political dynamics (the birth of UNESCO, the advent of USAID money and the Alliance for Progress) aided the emerging women's movement in Latin America, others (the death of some feminists of the first modern generation, the rise of dictatorships, Cold War anti-communism) subjected it to intense pressure. Left-wing women's groups and individuals (especially those active in the urban guerrilla movements of the late 1960s) were targeted for government repression as "Communist-inspired," while right-wing ones received money and other support from the dictatorships and the CIA.[35] The phenomenally repressive political situation in Uruguay in the 1970s held women's gains to a minimum; progress in Brazil, though uneven, was much greater. In Chile, where women had been in the vanguard of opposition to the post-Allende military dictatorship, Augusto Pinochet managed to co-opt much of the women's movement — naming his wife head of the National Secretariat for Women, and insisting that the family was a basic institution of the natural order and that women had to accept "the superior destiny of [the] maternal vocation" and the customary social quiescence and political disfranchisement that proceeded from the concept (Miller 1991, 211; Jaquette in Lowenthal 1986, A55). Thus the unsteadiness and unevenness of women's progress derived from the marked differences among Latin American countries (political regimes, economies, cultural histories, ethnic and racial mix), differences among women themselves, differing political ideology, and differing conceptions of appropriate strategy within any women's movement, of whatever character.[36]

Following the United Nations' declaration of 1975 as International Women's Year, in any case, feminist discourse flourished throughout Latin America, women's publications multiplied rapidly (more than 150 appeared between 1980 and 1988), and women's organizations gathered force. National, historical, and other differences notwithstanding, recent socially, culturally, and politically insurgent movements of Latin American women have consistently shared many features. Preeminent among them in recent years, as Jaquette observes, is the view "that women of all classes, ethnic groups, and ideologies can be politicized around the realities of daily life" (Jaquette in Lowenthal 1986, A57). The Nicaraguan women's movement, like the larger Latin American one of which it was very much a part, arose initially out of somewhat more general and idealized concerns, but eventually came to focus directly upon those realities.

THE NICARAGUAN WOMEN'S MOVEMENT. In the early 1880s, scholar Daniel Brinton noted that in the traditional Nicaraguan festival drama *El Güegüence*, all of the women performers (including the heroine) are mute (Brinton [1883] 1969, xliii). But outside the drama they have not remained so, and indeed they were not even at the time Brinton wrote. Although it has frequently been asserted (and almost universally assumed) that Nicaraguan women had never exerted or organized themselves on their own behalf until the mid-1970s, the issue had in fact been joined many decades earlier.[37] Thus the paradox was not that a full-fledged Nicaraguan women's movement emerged virtually out of a vacuum in the mid-1970s (indeed it had not), but that women who participated in that *phase* of the movement apparently knew little or nothing about the prior efforts of their mothers, grandmothers, and even great-grandmothers.

As Miller has argued, the advent of public "normal schools" for women during the last quarter of the nineteenth century had much to do with the rise of feminist ideas and women's organizations throughout Latin America, helping to produce a new group of educated middle-class women, aware of their precarious social, economic, and legal status. Organization around that awareness was spurred by women teachers in the normal schools, who kept regularly in touch with each other through national and international meetings (Miller 1991, 35–36, 355n.).

As early as 1852, at least one Nicaraguan woman successfully petitioned the legislature to allow her to enter the University of Granada, and by the 1870s, serious discussions of women's rights were being heard with some regularity, as they were elsewhere in Latin America.[38] In 1872, a writer in *Semanal Nicaragüense*, while parroting the conventional, patronizing wisdom that a woman's mission is "the sweetest, most poetic . . . most highly civilizing and glorious" of all, went on to assert that "degenerate and enervated people . . . denied woman a soul and viewed her as a man's vile instrument of pleasure. Christianity . . . rehabilitated her . . . as the *compañera* and friend of man, equal to him. Her character as mother and wife lend divinity . . . to his nature and purify the materialism of love, converting it into a celestial passion."[39] Framed as it was within the limits of conventional Christian piety, it was hardly an uncompromising statement, but it was a start.

Writing less than a year later in *Semanal Nicaragüense* (and less than two months after the play *El Espíritu del Siglo*, also in the same newspaper, had reaffirmed the dominant gender order), Máximo Lira asserted that while women are at a disadvantage in physical combat with men, intellectually they are "at least equal individuals of the other sex." Their failure to produce superior intellectual work, Lira judged, was chargeable solely to "the very simple reason that they have never been given an education that would enable them to produce such work." He buttressed his case by enumerating a list of distinguished women reaching from Minerva (the goddess of wisdom, invention, and the arts) through the Middle Ages (when mostly illiterate men preoccupied themselves with war, he said, while many women cultivated their minds and nuns studied the sciences) and on to the modern epoch. Although

Lira admitted that many contemporary women find themselves ensnared in "a web of ignorance and frivolity," he argued that "there is no other solution than liberty."[40]

Real gains for Nicaraguan women came slowly, but within a decade the Colegio de Señoritas had opened in Granada. Staffed primarily with North American women teachers, the Colegio began to break some of the old patterns of women's education, and to end the muteness of Nicaragua's women.[41]

One turn-of-the-century woman who spoke out powerfully was Chinandega poet Rosa Umaña Espinosa (1872–1924). Orphaned as a child, supporting herself as a seamstress, lacking formal education, and living as an unhappy wanderer (*infelice peregrina*), she was determined to write, and to write honestly about her own experience and that of other women (Cerutti 1984a). Her poetry centered on the pain and abuse of attachments to men (Umaña Espinosa 1916, 15, 19, 21, 23), and especially upon the dishonest pretense that a double sexual standard enforced upon women. Her poem "Alma negra" (Black Soul) speaks of a depraved mother who inscribes the conscience of a whore (*conciencia de ramera*) upon her daughters; in another, virgins sell their virtue at the foot of the altar; other poems dare to address abortion and infanticide (Umaña Espinosa 1909, 20, 24, 35, 37).

Umaña Espinosa's contemporary Josefa Toledo, an early student at the Colegio de Señoritas, chose more public forums for her advocacy of women's needs and rights. Born in Juigalpa in rural Chontales in 1866, Toledo finished primary school but had to return home at age eight to help her widowed mother.[42] At fifteen she convinced her mother to allow her to attend the new Colegio, where despite opposition from her family and taunting by city girls as a country bumpkin (*la chontaleña*) she showed great aptitude as a student and reveled in the Colegio, which she later called "a center of feminine light."[43] In 1887 she returned to teach at the Colegio, and four years later became its director. She went on to found similar institutions in Managua (1912) and elsewhere, as well as schools and social service clubs for mothers and working women. Proclaiming that "God created Eve so that Adam would have a suitable helper [*ayuda idónea*], which makes God the first feminist," she went on to a long and brilliant career as leader of the feminist movement in Nicaragua.[44]

In the autumn of 1918 Toledo de Aguerri founded *Revista Femenina Ilustrada*; her *Revista Mujer Nicaragüense* followed a few months later. In the first issue of *Revista Femenina Ilustrada*, she couched the goals of Nicaraguan feminists in an extended nautical figure, speaking of "the saving port where our boat will arrive laden with good faith in our purposes and hope for the realization of ideas advantageous for our countrywomen. She may navigate at

Cover of *Revista Femenina Ilustrada*, 1921.

times against contrary winds and in places where reefs impede her progress. But we are confident that sometime she will arrive, even if with sails ripped and keel destroyed, with the precious cargo intact."[45]

Toledo de Aguerri took a strong though politic feminist position in *Revista Femenina Ilustrada*, insisting upon blending "essentially feminine arts with a firmness essentially virile," and envisioning no less than a "national feminism" in Nicaragua.[46] Feminism, she explained to a reader, was a doctrine through which women could gain their rights within the juridical order and their legitimate place in society. Lamenting the "long period of lethargy" in which women had lived, the violent winds (*vendavales*) of reaction, and earlier attempts to "discredit feminist theory," she nevertheless proclaimed that "now feminism advances triumphant, firm, imposing" (*imponente*). Toledo de Aguerri reminded her readers that the League of Nations subscribed to the principle of equal pay for equal work, and that mothers should not be "either living machines or beasts of cargo" (Toledo de Aguerri 1935a, 22–28). Approaching the end of her first year as editor of *Revista Femenina Ilustrada*, she admitted that the feminist desire of Nicaraguan women was "in general asleep," but observed that when the "nervous awakening" comes, women move "with a new vigor in the blood which glimpses the previously unknown sensations that lie beyond." "We walk slowly," she said in the journal's first anniversary issue, "our work is quiet like the bee . . . [but it is] fortified by . . . our intense desire to mobilize a heroic feminine will for effective work" (Toledo de Aguerri 1935a, 34–39).

Revista Mujer Nicaragüense, which succeeded *Revista Femenina Ilustrada*, placed increased ·emphasis upon practical issues related to child-rearing, health, literacy, and the like, but retained its predecessor's forthright feminist orientation.[47] It carried an admiring portrait of militant British feminist Emmeline Pankhurst (1858–1928), continually compared Nicaragua's retrograde situation with feminist advances in other countries (including the United States, which to Toledo de Aguerri seemed a model), and vowed that women would press forward in the face of whatever ridicule and calumny.[48]

As her work in Nicaragua became more widely known, Toledo de Aguerri traveled throughout Latin America, visiting other feminist leaders, evaluating women's progress, and adding her voice and energy to the international feminist movement.[49] Modern feminism, Toledo de Aguerri declared in an expansive address she sent to the Auxiliary Congress of Women of the Americas (*Congreso Auxiliar de Señoras de las Américas*) in 1919, "requires transformations in the modern spirit, enabling the woman to provide for herself . . . to be the owner [mistress] of her own self, to apply her own criterion and direct her influence toward tasks which men possess as if by divine right" (Toledo de Aguerri 1935a, 3–8).[50]

Although Toledo de Aguerri was confident of "the inevitable development of a universal feminism," which comes "like an avalanche to inundate the last corner of the planet," she was capable of great diplomacy in her challenges to the gender order (Toledo de Aguerri 1935a, 14).[51] At the First Central American Feminine Congress on Education in 1938 she contrasted two types of feminism. At one extreme (as she saw it) was "social feminism" — "the crude, rude, activist feminist struggle between men and women" — which teaches women to dress like men and imitate "their vices and liberties." Through its distortions and exaggerations, she argued, such a radical "masculinized feminism" "destroys what it wishes to ennoble." Such a feminism was giving way, she judged, to a "constructive" and "opportunistic" feminism that was more "moderate, conservative and practical" — one in which, "without losing the prerogatives won in the socialist campaign," women may act "with the femininity that is inherent in them." The ideal, she insisted, was the "moral masculinization" of women and the "moral feminization" of men, which would at once strengthen women and make their love for men more intense (Toledo de Aguerri 1940, 6–12).

In the mid-1930s Nicaraguan feminists — no doubt inspired by women who had recently won the vote in the United States (1920), Ecuador (1929), Brazil and Uruguay (1932), and Cuba (1934) — turned much of their attention to women's suffrage. Indeed the issue had been joined in Nicaragua within a few months after the Nineteenth Amendment was added to the U.S. Constitution in 1920. Writing in the Managua weekly *Los Domingos* in October 1921, Aristides Duran disparaged the push for the vote among Central American women as "pure platonism" that would lead to a "freakish and ridiculous" (*estrambótico y ridículo*) result, and introduce a "current of corruption" into the "beloved home." Violating the time-honored expectation that they should leave the house only "to be baptized, married, and buried," women would go forth to participate in "meetings and political scandals" during the day, visit cabarets at night, and indulge in free love at opportune moments. The latter, Duran averred, should exist "only among we men," and among women whose situations allow them to indulge in it without bringing dishonor upon their families.[52]

By the time Nicaraguan women's drive to gain the vote emerged in the 1930s, they were organized into the Cruzada de Mujeres Nicaragüenses (Nicaraguan Women's Crusade), which in turn was affiliated with the Liga Internacional de Mujeres Ibéricas e Hispanoamericanas (International League of Iberic and Hispanoamerican Women, or LIDMI) and other international women's organizations.[53] Those affiliations kept them well aware that theirs was not an isolated struggle, and that its issues and outcomes were of vital interest to women everywhere.

Male members of Nicaragua's National Assembly at first turned what Toledo de Aguerri described as "a visage of atrocious irony" toward the women's suffrage project at the end of the decade of the 1930s. Theirs was a smile of depreciation, she said, toward the woman when she ceases to be a "graceful cardboard doll" (*graciosa muñeca de cartón*). But since the results of reserving the vote solely to men had been palpably disastrous, she observed, it was imperative that the new constitution then being considered address the issue of women's political rights.[54] "In the name of justice and reason we come," said the women's petition, and Toledo de Aguerri even reassured delegates that "the emancipation of women does not mean a distancing from men, but rather a spiritual coming together." Delegate Octavio Pasos Montiel spoke in favor of the change, noting wryly that 150 million women in the world were already voting. Many male members of the National Assembly were openly recalcitrant, however; former *vanguardista* José Coronel Urtecho, who twenty years earlier had spoken so passionately against the entrenched interests of older generations, voted against the change.

Taking great pains to rationalize and justify his own opposition, delegate Dr. Guillermo Sevilla Sacasa produced a brief text that was virtually a map of Nicaragua's *machista* culture and its most prominent nodes of recalcitrance (Sevilla Sacasa 1939). Invoking the spirit of his own noble and virtuous mother, he proclaimed his general admiration for all mothers, wives, sisters, and daughters, and intoned the canonical cultural tenet that the properly self-abnegating woman (*la mujer abnegada*) "stimulates a man with the thousand virtues she leaves in her path." In a gentlemanly moment of generosity, he admitted that now and then among the "general feminine mass" (*la masa general de la femenina*) there arises a woman ("gracious and proud of herself") who is worth more than a hundred men, and who might even exercise the vote better than they (Sevilla Sacasa 1939, 5). But such women were all too rare, he lamented; most characteristically, Nicaraguan women (to whom he referred possessively as "our Nicaraguan women") were "weak and ingenuous," lacking in "intellectual fortitude"—"unstable spirits who at times commit incomprehensible blunders." Worst of all, lacking "philosophical and religious independence" as well as the capacity for logical and clear thinking that characterizes men, "our Nicaraguan woman," Sevilla Sacasa warned, is "a weak feather rocked by the least wind of religious influence," a "dry leaf" to be blown about by whatever wind of emotion or illogic. Were she to be given the vote, he warned, the National Assembly would shortly be full of representatives chosen by unscrupulous priests willing to manipulate (*manosear*) them for political ends. Clearly, he concluded, women were not capable of exercising the vote properly and with the "propriety and independence" (*idoneidad e independencia*) that the State desires and requires—even, presumably, if that state was the flagrantly anti-democratic *Somocista* one.[55]

Palpably self-serving and unself-critical as were such arguments, the struggle dragged on for years before women's voices finally prevailed.[56] In the fall of 1950, more than seventy-five Nicaraguan women signed a petition to the National Assembly, calling continued opposition to women's suffrage "absurd and ridiculous" and a mockery of "international treaties, internal law, and the aspirations of Nicaraguan women." In the absence of moral respect that still did not exist, they insisted, the law would have to back (*respaldar*) women. "All over the world and throughout Latin America," they said, "the hour of the woman has sounded." Instead of the League of Nations charter cited by their feminist predecessors, they now cited that of the United Nations as a universal warrant for their demands, and pointed out that Nicaragua was one of only five Latin American countries in which women still lacked the vote. But in Nicaragua, recalcitrance was so great that they were not to receive it until 1955 (Comité Central Femenino 1950, 1–8; Miller 1991, 96).

Ultimately, however, it was not the first generation of feminist women who gained much practical advantage from their efforts, but the daughters of the second. Born after World War II, those daughters—as young women by the mid-1960s and early 1970s—were obliged to work out identities and seek social and political places for themselves during a phenomenally turbulent period of the country's history.

Statue in honor of mothers ("To the Mother. Complete Abnegation and Love"),
Jinotepe, 1988. (Photograph by author)

Doris María Tijerino, later a Sandinista guerrilla, *comandante*, and head of
the Sandinista police, was raised by a mother who herself was from a wealthy
family of English background in which "daughters . . . were relegated to the
house, to being a good mother, an obedient wife, and an accomplished hostess." Although Doris María's mother became wife, mother, and hostess, her
way of being a "good mother" consisted partly in helping her own daughter

imagine and construct new ways of being a woman. An avid reader, she saved her books for Doris María, to whom she gave them at age thirteen. Doris María was especially moved by Gorky's *Mother* (1907), about (as she described it) a woman of "a minimal cultural level" who had "only a woman's sentiments and a mother's heart to help her understand" the political events of her time (Heyck 1990, 53–72; Tijerino 1978).

At the same time, other women were on the move in overtly political ways. In the mid-1950s Subtiavan women joined *campesino* protests against the expropriation of lands traditionally belonging to the community, created their own organization to retake them, and—as Gould reports—used "their condition as mothers and wives to protect . . . protesters from serious harm" at the hands of Somoza's National Guard troops (Gould 1990a, 234). A half-dozen years later and a few miles to the northwest in Chinandega, rural agricultural workers became targets of brutal National Guard repression following a series of strikes and land takeovers led by Engracia Zapata, a militant seamstress from Tonalá. Women made up nearly half the protest movement, and were (Gould concludes) "willing to assume leadership roles in part to prove themselves to communities traditionally prone to devalue and denigrate single mothers." Having grown up and learned to survive within *machista* and patriarchal structures, they already were skillful in manipulating them (Gould 1991a, 225–41, 253).

Although men were glad enough for women to participate in times of crisis, even the most politically progressive of them had their limits. Gladys Báez, from a peasant background, first got involved in political activity with other wives and mothers of men imprisoned following the assassination of Somoza García in late 1956. Two years later she joined the workers and peasants union, gave her first public speech on May Day 1960, attended the Moscow Women's Conference in 1962, and returned to help found the Organization of Democratic Women. She left the Socialist Party in 1964, however, in disgust over its sexism. Unable to reach accord with her Socialist husband, who wanted her to confine her political work to being a union member and reserve the balance of her time and energy for being "a proper wife and mother," Báez ended her marriage and went on to help found the Patriotic Organization of Nicaraguan Women in the late 1960s. The organization, made up of peasant and working-class women, set up safe houses for young FSLN militants and worked to improve prison conditions (Randall 1981, 163–83).[57]

The time was still not ripe for a new national Nicaraguan women's movement, however. A national women's meeting (held—only coincidentally, it seems—in Toledo de Aguerri's hometown of Juigalpa) in 1969 drew only a handful of women, one of whom was Gladys Báez. Báez insisted that the meeting go on, even with so few in attendance, and later called the event "a very historic day for Nicaraguan women because for the first time in our lives we had called upon ourselves to meet as women to discuss our role in Nicaraguan society" (Enríquez in Marcus 1985, 257–58).

The United Nations' International Women's Year (1975) lent further stimulus to the newly reviving effort. In a commemorative anthology of women's writing published by the National University (UNAN), rector Mariano Fiallos Oyanguren lamented the "evident discrimination" against women, cautioned (as had Toledo de Aguerri) against imitating the "highly belligerent" and "antimasculinist" women's liberation movements in industrialized countries, and argued that in an underdeveloped country such as Nicaragua, the difference between the exploitation of women and of men was "only a question of degree."[58] The UNAN anthology was nevertheless promising in that it presented eleven women writers, most of them born after 1940, whose work was fresh and vigorous. Several (Vidaluz Meneses, Michele Najlis, Gioconda Belli, Rosario Murillo) were destined to have major careers as writers, and two (Meneses and Murillo) eventually were to occupy high positions in the Sandinista cultural apparatus. Curiously, the anthology failed to acknowledge the earlier women's movement in Nicaragua. The oldest poets it included (María Teresa Sánchez and Mariana Sansón) were born in 1918, the year Josefa Toledo de Aguerri—already more than fifty years old and a veteran feminist—began to edit the first of her two path-breaking journals.[59] Thus by failing to make the vital connection with the vigorous feminism of their mothers' and grandmothers' generations, young Nicaraguan feminists of the 1970s obliged themselves to build everything again from the ground up.

The reasons for this costly lack of awareness and connection are not obvious. Presumably it had something to do with the shared sense among post-1960 anti-Somoza militants that a full break with the past was essential, and that therefore the only useful political organizations and strategies would have to be newly invented. On the other hand, the FSLN itself made recovery and revitalization of the Sandino legacy the central feature of their emerging strategy. Young Sandinistas (both male and female) frequently reminded themselves and their audiences that women fought with and supported Sandino, but the incontrovertible historical fact is that the six-year Sandino campaign was a brief episode compared to the six decades or so of active, organized struggle that Nicaraguan women had maintained by the early 1960s. One might reasonably conclude from the comparison both that there was a cultural predisposition to search for and revere outstanding males, to comprehend essentially violent male paradigms of struggle, and to feel more comfortable with them than with female ones. In any case, the legacy of Sandino was recovered and mobilized, while that of Nicaraguan feminism was not. Magda Enríquez opened her essay "We Women Learned What We

Were Capable of Doing" (in Marcus 1985), for example, by referring to "the extraordinary history of the participation of women in all of Nicaragua's struggles," but having mentioned briefly the resistance of indigenous women to the conquest, women's participation in the wars of independence, and the "barefooted men and women" who fought with Sandino, she passed directly to the women who fought with the FSLN during the 1970s (p. 257). The 1984 booklet *Mujer en Nicaragua* opened with a brief section entitled *Nuestra memoria*, which asserted that "our history includes heroic pages on which women stood out for their intelligence and dignity." It mentioned (without elaboration) indigenous women who refused to bear children to become slaves to the Spanish, women who participated in the struggle against the filibuster William Walker and in the nationalist struggle of Benjamín Zeledón in 1912, women fighters in Sandino's guerrilla army, women who organized against the Somoza regime, and women strikers in the textile factories in the 1940s. No aspect or incident of the Nicaraguan women's movement I have just described was mentioned, however.[60]

In any case, the tentative moves made by Gladys Báez and others at the end of the 1960s finally bore fruit in April 1977 when FSLN commander Jaime Wheelock urged the formation of a women's movement. An organizational meeting at Managua's Las Palmas church the following September was packed, and the Asociación de Mujeres Ante la Problemática Nacional (AMPRONAC) was born (Randall 1981, 2; Ruchwarger 1987, 47; Enríquez in Marcus 1985, 258). Initially made up mostly of middle-class and bourgeois women, AMPRONAC was protected to some degree by the very *machista* culture it attacked in the guise of the Somoza regime, which — like the Sevilla Sacasas of the 1930s — viewed women as harmlessly insubstantial "dry leaves" not worth serious political attention.

AMPRONAC proved to be a formidable organization, nevertheless. AMPRONAC women marched, demonstrated, and investigated the regime's repression and atrocities, staged hunger strikes, picketed, occupied churches and the United Nations' Managua office, and in general made life difficult for Somoza's National Guard, even lobbing their tear-gas canisters back at them. Galvanized by the assassination of *La Prensa* editor Pedro Joaquín Chamorro in January 1978, AMPRONAC grew and began to attract large numbers of rural peasant women as well. By mid-year, an influx of radical FSLN women had pushed AMPRONAC further left; it became avowedly anti-imperialist, anti-capitalist, and anti-sexist as well as anti-Somoza. But the brutal repression that followed the September 1978 insurrection against Somoza brought great pressure upon AMPRONAC; the National Guard arrested and tortured AMPRONAC women and murdered some of their husbands. Virtually destroyed, the organization went underground, but women continued to use their by-then well-developed community networks to support anti-Somoza guerrilla activity (Ruchwarger 1987, 48–51; Enríquez in Marcus 1985, 258).

Shortly after the fall of the Somoza regime in July 1979, AMPRONAC became AMNLAE (Asociación de Mujeres Nicaragüenses Luisa Amanda Espinosa) and took on the formal task of "guaranteeing the accomplishments of the Revolution, and, in so doing, guaranteeing women's freedom." Chapters were formed throughout the country in both rural and urban areas, and by the end of its first year AMNLAE counted some seventeen thousand women; a year later there were about twenty-five thousand in eight hundred chapters. Granted official status by the government and given a seat on the Council of State, the organization produced a newspaper and radio and television programs, and worked on women's issues (education, health care, literacy) with various government ministries.

Despite its rapid growth and official legitimation, however, AMNLAE faced formidable structural and cultural barriers. A number of other Sandinista mass organizations competed for government funds as well as women's time, energy, and loyalty.[61] Class and rural-urban divisions complicated communication and coordination, women's "liberation" as a concept was still ill-defined, and many men were suspicious of, anxious about, and hostile to the changes women were demanding in the gender order (Ramírez-Horton in Walker 1982, 154–56). Within weeks after the Sandinista triumph, it was clear that the flagrantly reactionary policies and behavior of the Somoza regime toward both men and women had in some respects presented a more vulnerable target than the quietly stubborn recalcitrance of the gender order itself.

THE SANDINISTAS AND THE GENDER ORDER

The Sandinistas' formal commitment to women's liberation and gender equality predated the founding of the FSLN itself. Traveling in the USSR in the late 1950s, FSLN founder Carlos Fonseca marveled approvingly at women driving trucks and working in the same professions as men, for the same pay. "Women in this country play a supremely important role," he observed, noting that more than half of the university students and seven-eighths of the doctors were women (Fonseca 1981, 1:51–54). Section 7 of the FSLN's Historic Program of 1969 focused upon the emancipation of women, promising that "the Sandinista people's revolution will abolish the odious discrimination that women have been subjected to compared with men" and "will establish economic, political, and cultural equality between women and men" (Rosset and Vandermeer 1986, 181–89). There was little the FSLN could do to bring about such changes, however, until it grew from a tiny vanguard into a formidable guerrilla force in the early 1970s. Fragile at first, the FSLN guerrillas welcomed all who would join them, male and female alike. That welcome was to be, as it turned out, the most unequivocal and least problematic the Sandinistas ever extended to women (cf. Gorman and Walker in Walker 1985, 91–92; Booth 1985, 138–42).

WOMEN IN COMBAT. There were ample precedents for women's participation in the emerging FSLN military struggle against Somoza. Latin American women had fought valiantly beside men in every period since the conquest: Amazonian women in the 1540s, Haitian women in the 1790s, women in various countries during the struggles for independence, Bolivian women with the Movimiento Nacionalista Revolucionaria in the 1940s, and Cuban women in the 1950s (Miller 1991, 16, 30–34, 135–46; Cherpak in Lavrin 1978, 219–35). In the mid-1930s, Josefa Toledo de Aguerri, looking to Nicaraguan women's history for inspiration, recounted the "magnificent and sublime" heroism — "a poem of nobility, arrogance and valor," she called it — of eighteen-year-old Rafaela Herrera Mora, in a five-day battle in defense of the Castillo de la Concepción on the San Juan river against British attacks in 1762.[62]

The few women who fought with the fledgling 1960s FSLN were by no means immune to conventional treatment by their comrades in arms, but most were determined to stay the course. Gladys Báez, the first woman to go with the FSLN into the mountains, encountered direct pressure to leave, but reminded herself "that I'd come to stay and they had no right to intimidate me" (Randall 1981, 177; Morgan 1990, 42). Its formally feminist commitment boosted by the need to swell its ranks as the guerrilla war expanded, the FSLN soon admitted as many women to the fighting units as could be found, and celebrated their participation in song.[63]

Many of the troops, both men and women, saw their combat experience as a watershed that promised to permanently transform gender relations. "Sometimes when a *compañero* and a *compañera* got married on the mountain," one man recalled with evident pride, "we had a party in the camp. . . . It wasn't a valid marriage; it was just for the time we were on the mountain. We respected the women. Unless we married someone, we didn't sleep together. The women slept separately and the men separately. There was no disagreement, no weakening. We were all like brothers and sisters" (Hart 1990, 92).[64]

By the time of the triumph in 1979, many reports assert, a quarter to a third of all combat troops were women, and a few women had risen to high command positions.[65] Interviewed soon after the triumph, Sandinista army commander Humberto Ortega celebrated both the historical precedents for

Nicaraguan women's participation in combat and their valor during the anti-Somoza struggle (Harnecker in Marcus 1982, 83; cf. Randall 1981, 40–79, 129–49).

In any case, the participation of Nicaraguan women (at whatever percentages) in all phases and aspects of the struggle against the Somoza regime provided abundant evidence that they were more than capable of being full partners in the process of social, political, and cultural transformation that followed the triumph.[66] As it turned out, however, the period of armed struggle was the easier part. In the meantime, the Sandinistas moved quickly to articulate policies and create programs that would address the more glaring problems of the gender order.

POLICY VERSUS THE GENDER ORDER. From the beginning, Sandinista policies and programs gave evidence of formal and practical commitment to the cause of gender equality. High government officials spoke often and eloquently of the necessity to reconfigure the gender order, and practical steps to achieve gender equality followed. Decree Number 48 barred the media from exploiting women as sex objects (in advertising, for example).[67] Prostitution was criminalized, and procedures were established to investigate the paternity of illegitimate children. The Adoption Law of 1980 allowed single women to adopt children. A law promoting breast feeding outlawed the advertising of powdered milk substitutes. The Agrarian Reform and Cooperative Laws of 1981 equalized women's and men's rights with regard to wages and land tenure (Molyneux in Fagen et al. 1986, 288; Collinson 1990, 41, 111). Some women were named as heads of ministries; women's production cooperatives were organized; Child Development Centers (Centros de Desarrollo Infantil, CDIs) were established; job training programs were created. In September 1982 Interior Minister Tomás Borge proclaimed that the "new revolution . . . of women . . . will complete the process of national liberation." It would be, he said, "the most beautiful battle" of all (Borge in Marcus 1985, 47; Instituto Nicaragüense de la Mujer 1988, nos. 54, 55, 57, and 64). What was required, as a whole succession of Sandinista officials proclaimed, was no less than the creation of "the new man" — as solid in feminist practice as he was clear in political ideology.

But it was not to be, for the structures, values, and attitudes that had created and sustained the gender order proved profoundly recalcitrant.

As soon as the armed struggle ebbed into the background (and well before the contra war commenced), conventional gender paradigms reasserted themselves. Within a year after the Sandinistas rode triumphantly into Managua, women made up no more than 10 percent of the Sandinista army; only three remained among the seventy-four top commanders, and only thirteen among the entire officer corps of 231. Women and men who had previously been trained together in the army began to be trained in separate units (Ramírez-Horton in Walker 1982, 152–57; Randall 1981, 138). Some women reported that gender-based conflict was more prevalent both in the Sandinista army and in the FSLN than had been admitted. Monica Baltodano, who had joined the FSLN in 1972 and helped lead the final offensive on Managua at the age of twenty-three, was particularly outspoken about male chauvinism within the FSLN and the Sandinista army (Randall 1981, 65–66). By late 1984 Tomás Borge was admitting that "we haven't confronted the struggle for women's liberation with the same courage and decisiveness [as shown in the liberation struggle]. . . . [Women] remain fundamentally in the same conditions as in the past" (Fagen et al. 1986, 288–89).

Other indicators of gender-based conflict were equally discouraging. Although reported rapes had declined dramatically after 1979, they began to rise again in 1985, when AMNLAE's legal office reported that half the cases it handled involved spouse abuse, and more than 90 percent of those involved physical battering (Morgan 1990, 45–47). Sexist cartoons published in *Semana Cómica* (Comic Weekly) early in 1988 brought vociferous protests from women, but only a vacillating response from the government (Collinson 1990, 20–23, 69, 77–79, 118–19, 168–69; cf. Lancaster 1992, 92–105; Valdivia 1991). After much public complaint, a government (SSTV) television series on sex and youth, which addressed masturbation, homosexuality, birth control, and sexually transmitted diseases, was canceled.

Daily life for nonmilitary women in Nicaragua also continued to be very hard after the Sandinistas came to power—both for many of the same reasons it always had been, and for new ones related to the anti-Somoza war just ended and the contra war just begun. A 1985 study by the Women's Legal Office (OLM) and the Office on Family Orientation and Protection of the Ministry of Social Security (INSSBI) documented that nearly half of all women between the ages of twenty-five and forty-four were victims of beating, and in a separate study psychologist Damaris Enríquez found marital rape quite common. Other reports indicated that prostitution was still high in Managua.[68]

The burdens of daily life for women also continued to be reinforced by policy-resistant structural inertia. Pre-revolutionary wage differentials between men and women in industry were still mostly in place in the textile industry (where 70 percent of workers were women and 80 percent of the supervisors were men), and women had few opportunities for training in higher-paying jobs. An effort by one women-owned factory to train women mechanics brought only a lukewarm response from the Ministry of Labor.

Otilia Casco Cruz, wife of political worker and El Regadío agricultural co-operative president Tacho Olivas Cruz, put it bluntly a half-dozen years after the triumph:

> All this has made me think how much easier it was for Tacho to become [politically] involved. . . . He's had more opportunities to study since the triumph. It's the men, rarely the women, who are asked to attend courses. We're still stuck as housewives. I've told Tacho we women have been held back through all of history, and in these few years since the triumph not enough has been done to pull women up. Ah, there's plenty of blah, blah, about women's participation, but if a woman makes it, it's because she made sure not to bog herself down with a man and children. . . . [My] sister . . . used to be really involved in health work, but now that she's married her husband completely dominates her. He won't even let her out of the house without permission. . . . That man might be some big shot in the army but he's no saint when it comes to his family duties. (Angel and Macintosh 1987, 103)

Two more detailed examples illustrate the interaction of general cultural recalcitrance, policy ineptitude, and institutional resistance: a group of women potters and another group of women tobacco workers.

WOMEN POTTERS AND FARM WORKERS. Both the stubborn pertinaciousness of the conventional gender order and the collusion of government agencies in reinforcing and perpetuating it were evident to anthropologist Les Field, who spent more than a year studying the work of women ceramic artisans in San Juan de Oriente and Jinotega, and to Gary Ruchwarger, who spent fourteen months studying gender relations on the Oscar Turcios Chavarría state collective farm outside Estelí. Both studies were done in the late 1980s, eight to ten years after the Sandinistas came to power (Field 1987 and Ruchwarger 1989).

Early in the 1950s, nearly 94 percent of Nicaragua's more than forty-five thousand artisans were women (Field 1987, 93).[69] After a Banco Central–financed project established the pottery cooperative in San Juan de Oriente in 1978, however, thus raising the social status (and potentially increasing the economic rewards) of pottery making, men became more actively involved in the industry and a de facto sexual division of labor developed. Women were discouraged from using kick wheels or designing and painting vases, but were given the more repetitive and boring tasks and expected to help with the heavy work of using the clay-mixing mill, loading kilns, and feeding in wood during firing. One male designer's agreement to teach a woman produced a controversy that nearly destroyed the cooperative.

Unlike Banco Central's earlier San Juan de Oriente project, the *cerámica negra* industries in Jinotega and Matagalpa were owned, operated, and controlled solely by women who did all of the work themselves, from hauling the clay from the mountains to selling the final products. Burdened both by conventionally exploitative relationships with men (philandering husbands who beat them or abandoned them with children, or who denied them any independent social life) and by the economic and other pressures of the U.S.-financed contra war, the women (first in Matagalpa and later in Jinotega) turned to the Ministry of Culture's ENIARTE agency for help in obtaining raw materials and improving marketing.[70] Having been seeking active artistic traditions in order to demonstrate its commitment to indigenous and national culture, ENIARTE responded quickly.

The Matagalpa women's experience with ENIARTE proved both discouraging and insulting, however: the agency proposed a plan that the women considered inappropriate to the nature of the craft and required work arrangements that would not allow them to continue to take care of their families. Worse, ENIARTE refused to consider an alternative proposed by the women themselves. "They didn't really respect us," the women reported. "We are women and they think we are uneducated and ignorant—they don't take our ideas seriously." Field's interviews with both ENIARTE officials and the women ceramicists about the history of the pottery tradition confirmed that ENIARTE had promulgated the insupportable story that the *cerámica negra* was an indigenous tradition descended from pre-Columbian times. The women themselves proved quite knowledgeable about its actually quite recent origins and characterized ENIARTE's version of their history as "false and insulting" (Field 1987, 193, 201–12).[71]

The dilemma of women on the Oscar Turcios Chavarría tobacco farm was more serious because far more women were working on farms than were making pottery. The farm was one of the largest of a number of Sandinista state farms formed from confiscated *Somocista* lands. Until 1983 it had employed nearly six thousand workers at the height of the tobacco harvest season, but it was later subdivided and at the time of Ruchwarger's study employed between twelve hundred and nineteen hundred workers. The general "feminization" of the rural work force that was evident in Nicaragua after 1983 was strongly in evidence on the Oscar Turcios farm: 60 percent of the permanent workers and 75 percent of temporary ones were women. All but 25 of the 238 women Ruchwarger studied were mothers, and 70 percent of them were single mothers abandoned by the fathers of their children (Ruchwarger 1989, 4, 14, 23, 79).

Problems of gender inequality were dramatically in evidence on the farm. Forty out of sixty-five coordinator and managerial positions were held by men, and there were twenty men for every woman in technical jobs. Eighty-two percent of working-class women employees were in (usually low-paying) production jobs, and 98 percent of all women employees were concentrated in the bottom three wage-skill categories, while men were spread evenly across all categories. Moreover, men did not view such a distribution as inappropriate. Male union leaders interviewed by Ruchwarger viewed women workers as "soft, rapid in manual work, flexible, weak, obedient, submissive, fearful, and without leadership qualities," while describing men as "rough, tough, physically strong, capable of leadership, and knowledgeable" about all jobs (Ruchwarger 1989, 89).

Problems such as these at the Oscar Turcios farm and many others showed that the agricultural workers' union (the Asociación de Trabajadores del Campo [ATC]), which was formed in 1977 to agitate for better working and living conditions, had in general failed to address women workers' concerns effectively (Ruchwarger 1989, 18–22). A series of conferences between 1983 and 1987 had highlighted the problems, ventilated complaints, and generated a list of workers' demands, but for a variety of reasons (men's ingrained attitudes, lack of resources, the pressures of the war), relatively little was actually done. After 1985, the ATC mounted a drive to increase the number of women in leadership positions, and women workers' assemblies were formed, but neither proved very effective. "Women workers at Oscar Turcios," Ruchwarger concluded, "are engaged in an uphill battle against gender inequality" (Ruchwarger 1989, 80, 88–89, 93–96). It was evident, as one of the ATC's own reports concluded in 1985, that the Agrarian Reform Law was "in itself, an insufficient guarantee of equality between the sexes" (Collinson 1990, 42–51).

For years, that fact had been evident to women who attempted to take advantage of the ATC's training programs for women workers and union leaders. Alicia Andino, a single mother in her early twenties who worked in a tobacco factory and was an elected representative to the ATC, complained bitterly in the mid-1980s about "all the housework, children and husbands who stop us from getting involved in outside activities." What was needed, she said, was "to sit these men down so that their women can tell them that we're not just born to be slaves and bring up the kids alone. It's the men who have to change. Even the revolutionary men. . . . [Try] going to a party alone and not getting a beating from your husband when you get home!" (Angel and Macintosh 1987, 119–20).

Flor Ramírez, head of the tobacco workers' section of the Asociación, had seen the worst of both systems. One of eleven children, she had no schooling until age twelve, and then learned to read before marrying a cane cutter and going to work on a coffee plantation where men earned twice as much as women for the same work. "We'd work from five in the morning to five in the evening," she recalled, then make the kids' supper and Lord knows what else while the men sat back waiting for their coffee to be served. . . . Then, in 1973, the union sent me on an agricultural technical course. . . . That's when the problem started with my husband. He didn't like me going out, wearing trousers, using make-up, with my hair cut short, and mixing with other people. Though he eventually came round to understanding the Revolution, he was still very macho. He had to be the one in charge. He couldn't accept me coming in late from meetings or going off on some union work for a week. It came to the point where he said, "It's me or the union," so I told him it was the union. (Angel and Macintosh 1987, 125–26; Hart 1990, 117)[72]

CULTURE AND REPRODUCTIVE CHOICE. The recalcitrance of Nicaraguan culture during the Sandinista period, as well as the unwillingness of government agencies and programs to try to change it, emerged in particularly stark relief during post-1979 public debates over reproductive choice. Immediately after the Sandinista triumph, the Ministry of Health refused international offers to donate contraceptives, fearing that it would be charged with manipulating the birth rate (Wessel 1991, 539). Concerned about creating a labor shortage, the Sandinista leadership was also opposed to changing the unrevised Somoza-era criminal code, under which abortion was illegal. Instead of changing the law, the government opted to try to mitigate its worst effects through sex education, declining to prosecute, and making contraceptives available. But neither men nor the church approved of contraceptives (though for markedly different reasons), which in any case were expensive and hard to obtain (Molyneux 1988, 114–18).[73]

President Daniel Ortega himself incited a storm of protest at AMNLAE's tenth anniversary celebration by attacking reproductive choice, raising the specter of "depleting our youth," and charging that a woman who aborts "negates her own continuity" (Molyneux in Fagen et al. 1986, 288; Collinson 1990, 143; Molyneux 1988, 122).[74] It availed little that Health Minister Lea Guido declared abortion to be a woman's right, that Nicaragua's maternal death rate of three per thousand was six times that of most developed countries, and that studies showed that fully one-half the women admitted to the Bertha Calderón national women's hospital were there because of complications deriving from illegal abortions.

WOMEN'S COLLABORATION AND THE GENDER CONTRADICTIONS OF IDEOLOGY

As during earlier years, a substantial amount of the post-triumph opposition to changing the gender order came from women who judged it either morally correct, or politically expedient, or both, to collaborate. An early AMPRONAC statement on the many problems of post-Somoza reconstruction mentioned the historical marginalization of women and argued that the existence of *machismo* gave women a double burden in the reconstruction process. But the statement went on to rationalize men's behavior as the product of an oppressive economic system that "*makes* men play the role of oppressors and reduces women to the role of submissive slave" (my italics) (Maier 1980, 155).[75] As U.S. pressure on Nicaragua mounted through the contra war, AMPRONAC's successor AMNLAE reduced its identification with feminism and made "defense of the revolution" its first priority. President Daniel Ortega's wife, Rosario Murillo, head of the Sandinista Association of Cultural Workers, asserted in 1985 that "in a Revolution, a specific women's organization can't exist as it would be a way of perpetuating inequality" (Molyneux in Fagen et al. 1986, 288; Collinson 1990, 119). Such statements pointed directly to features of Sandinista ideology, present since the beginning, which made it probable that the Sandinista leadership would fail to understand some essential aspects of women's subordination, and that women themselves — to the extent that they adopted the ideology — would collaborate in continuing that subordination.[76]

Embedded in the progressive language of the 1969 Historic Program (and eventually throughout Sandinista ideology and practice) were at least three factors that promised these unhappy results: (1) a "revolutionary" gender paradigm still freighted with many values and assumptions drawn from the old gender order; (2) the critical but unresolved issue of whether women's needs and demands could or should be addressed in and for themselves, and if so in what relationship of priority to the larger revolution; and (3) a too-facile assumption about what results might be expected to emerge "naturally" for women through the process of socialist revolution.

The means specified for achieving the gender equality promised by the Historic Program of 1969 disguised but poorly the relatively conventional gender paradigm upon which that commitment rested: of the seven points relating to women, five focused specifically upon mothers and children (working mothers, rights of children born out of wedlock, maternity leave, day care centers, and the like). Another dealt with prostitution. Only the final one promised in general to "elevate the political, cultural and vocational level of women," and that one specified that the elevation was to occur not by addressing women's issues as such, but rather indirectly "through her participation in the revolutionary process." Whether that would in fact happen, or was as automatic as the leadership supposed, was another question.

During the early post-Somoza years, the official Sandinista position on women's issues was that (1) the problems of women derived principally from the contradictions of capitalism and foreign domination of Nicaraguan culture and life; (2) those problems would therefore disappear as an organic result of the transition to socialism and the recovery of national autonomy; and (3) because in any case the foregrounding of women's issues would be divisive and therefore retard the progress of the revolution, the first priority had to be not women's needs and rights but the "consolidation of the revolution." "The fundamental problem of women," insisted National Directorate member Carlos Núñez in 1981, "[is to] participate in the revolutionary transformation" (Centro de Documentación 1989, 25). Interior Minister Borge, who spoke frequently on the issue, insisted that "the definitive answer to the liberation of women can emerge only with the total resolution of the class contradictions." Gender relations will be transformed, he argued, "like relations between classes, in the process of transforming the means of production." Hence to abolish prostitution and other abuses that are logical and inevitable results of capitalism, there is therefore "no other alternative except to change the basic economic structure of society" (Borge in Marcus 1985, 47).

Even as Borge and other Sandinistas spoke, however, women in Latin America and elsewhere were raising serious questions about the marriage of Marxism and feminism in which the former seems always to become the dominant and subsuming partner, and about how confident women may justifiably be about finding their issues adequately addressed within a socialist paradigm. Feminist critics charged that Marxists had historically failed to address adequately the issue of sexual oppression, preferring to study "the relationship of women to the economic system, rather than that of women to men"; that they failed to comprehend "the differences between men's and women's experiences under capitalism," and "underestimated the patriarchal domination of wives in favor of emphasizing the . . . solidarity of the working class family"; and that women's hopes for change are frustrated as often in socialist systems as in capitalist ones (Hartmann in Sargent 1981, 1–42; Stolcke in León 1982, 11–31; MacKinnon 1982, 516–23; Schmuckler 1984, 3; Miller 1991, 101–3, 146).

Molyneux argues that "women's interests" have to be defined carefully in any such calculation, since "women's oppression . . . [is] multi-causal in origin and mediated through . . . different structures, mechanisms, and levels," and different groups of women (defined by race, class, or other factors) may both construe their interests differently and in fact be affected differently by the same legal or structural change (Molyneux in Fagen et al. 1986, 280ff.). She distinguishes usefully between *strategic* interests (those related to structural change) and nonstrategic *practical* interests that do not challenge "prevailing forms of gender subordination." Hence, Molyneux cautions, one can neither

Leoncio Sáenz, *Nacimiento*, 1983. (Reproduced from Unión Nacional de Artistas Plásticos (UNAP) y Asociación Sandinista de Trabajadores de la Cultura (ASTC), *Pintura contemporánea de Nicaragua* [n.d.])

assume "women's unity and cohesion on gender issues" nor evaluate completely unambiguously what the state does (or declines to do) with regard to the established gender order.

Whatever the capacity of socialist governments in general to implement their theoretical commitments to advancing women's interests in concrete and durable ways, the case of Nicaragua presented what Molyneux calls a "particularly severe constellation of negative circumstances" for women working to challenge traditional gender paradigms: severe economic problems that reduced resources for programs women demanded and needed; pervasive destabilizing efforts from the United States; a powerful, conservative mainstream Catholic church on record as favoring the traditional gender order; a large private economic sector able to avoid and frustrate much of the intended impact of corrective legislation; a "relatively small social base of support" for feminist ideas and programs; and a labor surplus that denied Nicaraguan women most of the power that might have derived from being able to withhold their labor in exchange for concessions on matters of gender (Molyneux in Fagen et al. 1986).

As it was, the inducements for women to put "consolidation of the Revolution" ahead of whatever agenda of their own they might develop were extraordinarily powerful, and their base and resources for doing otherwise scarce indeed. By the mid-1980s, it was clear that the revitalizing revolutionary struggle to topple Somoza had not been sufficient to bring to fruition even the modest and ambivalent feminist vision of Sandinismo. That incontrovertible fact tended to focus women's attention intensely upon the 1986–87 debate over the new constitution. Women could not expect substantial gains until further structural changes were made, which in turn would require substantial alterations in Nicaragua's entire legal apparatus.

THE NEW NICARAGUAN CONSTITUTION, WOMEN, AND THE OLD GENDER ORDER

Women had never fared well before the law in Nicaragua. The constitution of 1838 (Chapter 3, Article 17) conferred citizenship upon *todos los habitantes del Estado* who were over twenty years old (eighteen if married), owned property, or had an office or profession that provided a livelihood (Alvarez Lejarza 1958, 425). But since the Spanish language uses the masculine form of nouns and adjectives as the generic form, it was not clear at all that citizenship was in fact conferred on women as well. The constitutions of 1848 and 1854 cleared up the ambiguity by specifying (Chapter 3, Article 8, and Chapter 4, Article 12; Alvarez Lejarza 1958, 473, 507) that only *varones* (men) were eligible for citizenship.[77] The civil code of 1871 forced women into a condition of continual dependency on their husbands, denying them (according to Article 133) the right to sign a contract, enter into debt or receive payments on a debt, or receive an inheritance (Borge de Sotomayor 1953, 47). At the time the constitutional process began, Nicaragua's criminal code had not been revised since 1974; its civil code (a descendent of the 1804 Napoleonic code) dated from 1904 and was a veritable catalog of gender biases. It provided that a woman's home was that of her husband, and remained so even after his death. Divorce was possible by mutual consent, but according to a double standard: a man could divorce his wife for a single act of adultery, but a woman could divorce her husband for infidelity only if he lived with another woman in his own house, or "notoriously" with one elsewhere. Indeed a married man's dalliances might be classed as concubinage, but a woman's amounted to adultery pure and simple. Divorced men could remarry immediately, but divorced women had to wait three hundred days (nine times thirty, plus another month just to be sure, presumably, whose child was whose). Under no circumstances could an adulterous woman marry her lover, but an outraged husband who murdered him might expect lenient treatment under the law, and in any case was free to marry his own lover if (and whenever) he chose. The task, then, was not only to rewrite the constitution but also to maneuver a whole new civil code through the National Assembly, since Nicaragua's civil law system (like that of most Latin American countries) did not recognize judicial power to make law.

Opposition to a few of the gender-linked issues addressed during the process (day care for children, for example) was small and based mostly upon the scarcity of resources. But others (rape, spouse abuse, equality in the work place, and especially abortion and reproductive freedom) sparked intense controversy throughout the process, which began in April 1985 with the naming of a Special Constitutional Commission to prepare a draft. Only two of the commission's twenty-one members were women, and women constituted fewer than 15 percent of the members of the National Assembly that would eventually have to receive, debate, and enact the new constitution. And by no means all of the women members considered themselves feminists; the first woman vice president of the National Assembly went so far as to declare that feminism "leads not to the liberation but to the libertinage of the woman" (Morgan 1990, 13).[78]

Women asserted themselves most coherently and forcefully in more than seventy *cabildos abiertos* (open councils) held throughout the country to discuss the first draft prepared by the commission. Seven of the *cabildos* were specifically for women, and hundreds of women participated in all of the others as well. Over eight hundred women crowded into the women's *cabildo* in Managua, and the seventy-five who signed up to speak carried the meeting far into the night. The *cabildos*, many of them televised, produced a number of substantial alterations in the document. Article 27 specifically prohibited gender-based discrimination; Article 48 called for "absolute equality between men and women . . . in the enjoyment of political rights." As *de facto* heads of half of all Nicaraguan families, women insisted successfully that Articles 72 and 100 be modified to recognize such families. Many women attacked the double standard for divorce, and argued successfully that the traditional con-

International Women's Day ceremony in front of National Palace, Managua, 1988. Platform flanked by paintings of Augusto C. Sandino and Carlos Fonseca Amador. (Photograph by author)

cept of *patria potestad*, which Michele Najlis called "one of the most shameful institutions that has existed in the course of humanity," must be removed from the draft.

The commission's second (September 1986) draft was debated heatedly for ten weeks. The cultural recalcitrance that would stubbornly impede the transformation of the larger gender order was most evident in the debate

AMNLAE member María, at International Women's Day, Managua, 1988. (Photograph by author)

over reproductive freedom. As Morgan observes, "There was nothing in Nica-raguan culture . . . to soften the blow when women began to talk about reproductive freedom" (Morgan 1990, 52).

In the first draft, neither abortion nor "motherhood freely chosen" (the euphemistic code phrase for reproductive freedom) had been mentioned. AMNLAE's presentation to the commission had requested the right for women "to responsibly and freely decide the children they want and the moment in their lives in which they want to have them," and many (both women and men) spoke in favor of changing the law against abortion. But opposition was passionate. The church vehemently opposed the change, and letters to the editors of Managua's dailies called abortion "a policy of death," "unnatural and criminal," and "death in the mother's womb." The Sandinista president of the National Assembly, Carlos Núñez, argued that the constitution "should not address the issue of abortion directly," and most women legislators agreed (Morgan 1990, 62). At length, the new constitution was silent on abortion.

EPILOGUE: RETURN TO THE OLD GENDER ORDER

The final months of the Sandinista government were not good ones for women. The new constitution was better for them than any previous one had been, but still stopped far short of what women had argued for. Economic problems worsened, and many of the resulting pressures fell particularly heavily upon women. Nevertheless, men's opposition—both formal and informal—to reforming the gender order remained strong, as indeed did that of many women. A year before the election that was to end Sandinista rule, Ana Lucia Silva, director of the Office of Family Protection, reported sadly that "eight years of the Revolution have not been sufficient to be able to say that in Nicaragua, women have reached a great degree of development and consciousness." [79]

Gender was by no means the only sector of culture in Nicaragua that proved recalcitrant, but it was more recalcitrant—for more reasons, in more ways—than any other. In every period from the conquest onward, the gender order had rooted itself more deeply and firmly in Nicaraguan life and institutions; in every period, new features grew within its increasingly elaborate structure. No doubt the Sandinistas' intentions were sincere from the 1969 FSLN platform onward, but by then the obstacles to change were almost impossibly great: legally, socially, politically, ecclesiastically, culturally, and psychologically. At length the gender order proved to be perhaps the most tightly tied of the many Gordian knots binding the country against the thoroughgoing reconstruction it so badly needed. Small victories were won, small legal concessions wrung from the process, but like Porfirio Díaz's minister of education a century earlier, a substantial majority of the population was dead set against seeing the *niñas queridas* of Nicaragua turn feminist in its midst.

CONCLUSION

Culture is such a complex and dynamic field that drawing even the most tentative conclusions about any particular cultural system is hazardous — especially if the cultural system in question is, like Nicaragua's, relatively poorly mapped, little studied, and in an unremitting state of turbulent change. What one sees above all in Nicaragua is the perennial dialectical construction, deconstruction, and reconstruction of culture and its meanings by partisans who passionately believe that the outcome matters greatly with regard to their own political or social agenda. Consequently there is almost literally never a moment of even apparent stasis — either in the system itself or in the discourse — about which one might in reasonable confidence render more than the most tentative and conditional judgment. And yet the need for closure here at the end of my analysis imposes an obligation to reflect in a summary way upon what I have said, to draw some threads together, and to think about possible future lines of development in the politics of culture in Nicaragua, especially in relation to the dramatic cultural shifts currently manifesting themselves globally. To begin, I recapitulate briefly.

BEFORE INDEPENDENCE

Although the conquest and the colonial period were time-limited, their cultural-political effects have proven very durable over a period of now nearly five hundred years. The conquest itself set some of the most basic determinants of the country's subsequent cultural history: the introduction of new biota (desirable plants and animals, less desirable weeds, undesirable pathogens) permanently transformed the ecosystem. The decimation of the original indigenous population through epidemic, overwork, and slavery insured that the genetic, social, and cultural heritage of the country's pre-conquest inhabitants (syncretistic as it in fact already was) was permanently replaced by essentially alien and hostile ones. Native religion and language changed; dress and diet changed; houses and ways of living in them changed; the structures of human relationships (marital, parental, filial, social) changed. Catholicism — as theology and ideology, as church form and polity, as value system, as social and cultural code — achieved a relatively quick and permanent dominance over the vast majority of the population. Under the Spanish colonial institutions of the *encomienda*, the *repartimiento*, and the tribute system, ownership and use of land and other resources changed forever, as did notions of their proper use and stewardship both for survival and as a base for maintaining and elaborating social, economic, ethical, and cultural systems. A capitalist agroexport economy replaced an essentially communal, subsistence one. The country was divided between the increasingly mestizo, Catholic, Spanish-speaking west and the increasingly black, Protestant, heavily English-speaking east, as well as between the north-south poles of the two principal urban centers of León and Granada, both of them dominated by commercially and politically hostile but in many ways ideologically and ecclesiastically collaborative elites.

THE NINETEENTH CENTURY

One of the most salient facts about Nicaraguan cultural history, emphasized throughout this book, is that the country has always been a cultural bridge. From the dawn of its history until the conquest, Nicaragua was a bridge north to south, with the predominant movement of indigenous peoples north to south along the west coast and from south to north along the east coast. After the conquest, routes of movement rotated ninety degrees due to Nicaragua's strategic position on a narrow isthmus between two oceans controlled by more powerful geopolitical and economic actors (Spain and Great Britain initially, and the United States later on). In the nineteenth century, major-power intervention surged after the discovery of gold in California, and the early phases of economic, political, and cultural intervention by the United States became most dramatically evident in the transit route turmoil. Much of the mid-section of Nicaragua became an inter-ocean transit route for passage for North Americans either rushing to seek their fortunes in gold or returning dejectedly from having failed in the quest. Tens of thousands of travelers transformed small Nicaraguan coastal towns with unfamiliar street grids and buildings, filled the markets with new consumer products, seeded people's language with new words (and inevitably the alien perspectives and values they carried), and laced the landscape with new roads, littered in due course with empty sardine tins, cracker boxes, and liniment bottles. Intervention from the United States reached new heights with the William Walker filibuster war of the late 1850s, conceived as both a military and a cultural-political crusade.

Meanwhile, the convergence of León and Granada's elites around a liberal-Positivist developmental agenda — in evidence long before independence — spelled disaster for Indian people, who faced increased expropriation of land, discriminatory taxation, repressive labor law, and forced acculturation through education. Prominent among the many forms that non-elite opposition to that agenda took were sporadic armed resistance by indigenous groups, and a continuous contestational cultural discourse embodied in popular literature, music, dance, and drama. Such opposition proved relatively ineffective, however. During the Zelaya administration at the end of the century (1893–1909), consolidation of elite dominance was paralleled by a national drive for greater cultural (as well as economic and political) independence. The separate development of the Atlantic coast, for centuries a fact of Nicaraguan national life, was exacerbated by the reactivation of British colonialism until 1860 and the permanent presence of aggressively evangelical Moravian missionaries after 1849. Paradoxically, Zelaya's moves to free Nicaragua from foreign economic control were accompanied by the arrival of major North American corporations eager to exploit the commercial potential of bananas, lumber, and other commodities on the Atlantic coast.

CULTURAL POLICY AND CULTURAL INSTITUTIONS:
SOMOCISTAS AND SANDINISTAS

Turning from the more or less durable structural features and continuous historical processes of the politics of culture in Nicaragua to the more specific and definable features of cultural policy and institutions, one is urged to the conclusion that for most of its history, Nicaragua has been without either official cultural policy or consequential public cultural institutions. It has of course had policy in other sectors (education, church-state relations, media) that have cultural foundations, dimensions, and impacts, but policy that speaks directly to issues of culture has for the most part been lacking. Across all periods and regimes, the lack of cultural policy and institutions has allowed the majority of the country's irreplaceable archival records to disappear, its traditions to remain but poorly documented, its creative artists and writers to languish frequently in benign neglect if not actual repression, and its surviving sectors of traditional and vernacular culture to struggle vainly against the increasing dominance of modernizing, centralizing, rationalizing paradigms and values. This was especially the case during the more than forty-five years of the Somoza regime.

CULTURE AND THE SOMOZAS. During the Somoza years, the lack of policy left the country even more vulnerable than it might otherwise have been to the hegemony of U.S. popular media and consumer culture. To the extent that the regime had a cultural agenda at all, it was characterized by cultural sycophancy toward the United States, especially with regard to film and print and broadcast media; outright neglect of public cultural institutions; overt censorship and repression of cultural activity; aggressive agroexport development that had devastating impacts upon the accustomed cultural practices of rural people; and cynical mobilization of selected symbolically valuable elements of traditional culture for political purposes.

Fortunately, the Somoza regime's reactionary cultural politics and policies were the focus of fairly continuous opposition from a variety of sectors. The roots of some of the opposition reached back to the *vanguardia* movement of the late 1920s and early 1930s, some of whose most prominent members placed themselves in open opposition to the bourgeois culture of their elitist parents, committed themselves to the rediscovery and revalorization of the more indigenous and traditional aspects of the country's culture, openly opposed U.S. cultural intervention, and supported General Sandino's campaign against Somoza and the U.S. Marines. Such opposition found fresh expression later among the Generation of 1940, whose most prominent and prolific member was Ernesto Cardenal, who later became the Sandinista government's minister of culture. A generation later in the 1960s, students at León's Autonomous National University of Nicaragua (UNAN) took up the challenge under the inspired leadership of Rector Mariano Fiallos Gil. A host of talented young writers, musicians, actors, and others set themselves in implacable opposition to the regime, declaring that politics and culture were inseparable—that culture was and had to be a major instrument of opposition. Another pivotal sector of opposition was the indigenous barrios of Subtiava and Monimbó, where a variety of elements of traditional culture (music, religious forms and observances, artisanry and technical skill) were mobilized to harass, confuse, and immobilize the military and political machinery of the regime. Among the rural inhabitants of the Solentiname archipelago, Father Ernesto Cardenal employed liberation theology, experimental poetry workshops, and primitivist painting as focal activities for an oppositional community that was later to provide models for cultural policy initiatives of the Sandinista government.

CULTURE AND THE SANDINISTAS. Culturally speaking, the Somoza regime was a relatively easy act for the post-1960 Sandinistas to follow; it presented such a clear and well-defined target, and the field was virtually completely open to thoughtful intitiatives in every potential sector of activity. Both Sandino himself and FSLN founder Carlos Fonseca Amador had been intensely interested in the role of culture in national political and social life, and many of the early FSLN leadership were themselves writers and musicians. The Sandinista attempt to formulate official cultural policy and create a broad array of public cultural institutions—whatever its merits and demerits, successes and failures, clarities and confusions—was therefore highly conscious, dramatic, and effectively unique in Nicaraguan history.

Initial optimism concerning revolutionary possibilities in the cultural sector was understandably high, and there was a great flurry of activity in the early years. People who had never read before were taught to read in a highly publicized literacy campaign. Museums and libraries were established, albeit on a modest scale. Books were published by the hundreds, and phonograph records were produced by the scores. Films were made. Culture was seriously, broadly, and explicitly discussed as a central structural feature of national life and as a relevant consideration within other policy sectors.

Unfortunately, the Sandinistas' idealistic cultural enterprise soon ran aground upon fiscal constraints imposed by the widening contra war, the ultimately class-bound cultural politics of much of the leadership, administrative ineptitude, and conflicts both within the Sandinista cultural establishment itself and between the Sandinistas and broad sectors of the public over issues of artistic freedom and the political instrumentalization of culture. A further irony was that even the Sandinistas' best conceived cultural policies, best designed institutions, and most flourishing programs were in some cases no match for certain doggedly recalcitrant features of the culture such as church dogma and gender paradigms.

Particularly problematic was the stubborn historical reality of the separation between the east and west coasts, which presented the Sandinista government with a bewildering array of cultural, political, economic, racial, and class challenges. A backlog of social and economic needs left over from the Somoza period made effective response urgent after the Sandinista triumph in 1979. Unfortunately, the Sandinistas' own west coast-linked ignorance, arrogance, and elitism, compounded by ideological narrowness and rigidity, predisposed them to repeated errors of analysis and judgment. And each error or misjudgment was quickly seized upon, magnified, and turned to political advantage by both local oppositionist organizations and the Reagan administration in the United States, which were eager to exploit every sector of discord. A belated but major effort to fashion a mutually palatable form of autonomy for the east coast was aborted by the Sandinistas' defeat in the elections of 1990.

MUSEUMS AND MONOLITHS, DARÍO AND SANDINO, MEN AND WOMEN: SOME CASE STUDIES

In a series of case studies following the chapters on the cultural ideas and practices of the Somoza and Sandinista governments, and on the organized opposition to them, I looked closely at two pivotal cultural figures in Nicaragua (poet Rubén Darío and rebel general Augusto C. Sandino) and at two revealing processes in the politics of culture (the unregulated removal of antiquities in the late nineteenth century, and the growth of the women's movement).

MUSEUMS AND MONOLITHS. Quite fortuitously, Nicaragua experienced renewed post-independence intervention by major powers just at the time when recently established ethnological museums in Europe and the United States were beginning to engage in highly competitive collecting. The activities of five particular collectors who came to Nicaragua from that juncture until the end of the century—E. George Squier and J. F. Bransford for the Smithsonian Institution, Frederick Boyle for the British Museum, Earl Flint for the Smithsonian and the Peabody Museum of Archaeology and Ethnology, and Carl Bovallius for Sweden's national museum—foregrounded key features of the cultural politics associated with the collecting enterprise. Squier and Bransford were especially motivated by the potential of major ethnographic collections to boost national prestige. The objects Boyle shipped back to the British Museum bolstered newly legitimized ethnological collections that were competing for status against classical statuary and the newly acquired treasures of Greece, Mesopotamia, and colonial Africa. Earl Flint, like most of his fellow collectors, saw his collecting as disinterested, scientific, and of equal benefit to an undifferentiated "mankind." In fact, however, his activities as well as his personal and professional self-understanding were deeply enmeshed in issues of race, class, gender, power, and empire.

However motivated and whatever the overt and subliminal agendas, the result of the competitive collecting for small and poor countries such as Nicaragua was that boatloads of irreplacable archaeological artifacts found their way into the exhibit cases of major museums and onto the private antiquities market. By the turn of the century, Nicaragua's half-hearted attempts to control the expropriation of its antiquities had proven almost completely unavailing, and its even more tentative gestures toward building a national museum had come to almost nothing.

Recent efforts by UNESCO and others to achieve international accord concerning the ethics of collecting antiquities and the politics of repatriating items removed illegally by large and powerful countries from smaller and weaker ones such as Nicaragua have foregrounded a number of intensely contested issues: To whom do such objects most properly "belong," and in what sense of belonging should one most properly pose such a question? Upon what do the claims of contemporary nation-states rest, given that their physical boundaries, worldviews, and values generally correspond poorly if at all to aboriginal ones? What are the most humane and equitable uses of such objects, and how likely are modern museums to serve those ends? And what are the ideological and political dimensions of museum display and interpretation?

DARÍO AND SANDINO AS FOCAL CULTURAL FIGURES. Much of the politics of culture in Nicaragua has been organized by and through an ongoing national discourse concerning a number of what I have here called focal cultural figures. From among those who come most immediately to mind (feminist writer and editor Josefa Toledo de Aguerri, rebel general Benjamín Zeledón; writers Pablo Antonio Cuadra, José Coronel Urtecho, and Ernesto Cardenal; FSLN founder Carlos Fonseca Amador; university rector Mariano Fiallos Gil; martyred *La Prensa* editor Pedro Joaquín Chamorro), I have paid close attention to two upon whom national attention seems more or less permanently riveted: poet Rubén Darío and "General of Free Men" Augusto César Sandino. My argument has been that the lives and writings of these two, and especially the highly contested national discourse about them, offer a window into some of the most persistent features of the politics of culture in Nicaragua.

RUBÉN DARÍO. Darío in particular, because he never cast himself as an easily definable partisan figure, has been singled out as the repository of much of the country's most domestically and internationally negotiable cultural capital. He has perennially been the subject of intense argument concerning the "correct" interpretation of his own politics and cultural views, which — fortunately for partisans of all political persuasions — were varied and ambiguous enough to admit of a wide variety of plausible interpretations. For Somocistas, Darío was thus an idealized "art for art's sake" artist who never deigned to sully his art with explicitly political concerns. Insofar as Somoza partisans were able to view him in political terms, he was a classic liberal for whom the established political and social order was the obviously legitimate one, for whom avowedly oppositionist or revolutionary politics were anathema, for whom the key to progress was the gradual, nonprogrammatic and noncoercive elevation of individual minds and hearts.

For the Sandinistas, on the other hand, Darío was first and foremost Nicaragua's *national* poet. As such, his preeminent concern was to define, celebrate, and defend its cultural identity; to proclaim its integrity; to articulate what amounted to an overt political program for its emancipation (particularly with regard to the aggressive depredations of the blond and blue-eyed barbarians of the Colossus of the North). Thus the Sandinista Darío was in effect the harbinger of the Sandinista revolution itself — at least a socialist, and in fact (if the underlying truth be known) a proto-Marxist revolutionary.

Darío partisans of all persuasions edited (usually selectively, in order to reinforce some particular political perspective) and published his works, argued endlessly about him in public orations and learned journals, erected monuments to him, honored him in public ceremonies, and invoked his words and his memory as warrants for their own opinions and ideology, and as benedictions upon their own political acts. So protracted and convoluted has this process become that "Rubén Darío" may now more usefully be understood as a political-cultural construct than as an identifiable historical personage.

AUGUSTO CÉSAR SANDINO. A similar though more circumscribed process has unfolded with regard to General Augusto C. Sandino. Although Sandino has more usually been thought of as a military-political figure, he both understood and projected himself in terms that were as fully cultural as they were military and political. Throughout his life and the six decades since his death, Sandino was the subject of a political-cultural mythicization process conducted by his own troops, his many biographers, and generations of political partisans and opponents.

To his own troops and his contemporary partisans, Sandino was the David-like General of Free Men, drawing his fighting strength from the poor peasants who swelled his ranks and his tactical superiority from their native cunning and ingenuity, standing off the brutal, airborne, and highly mechanized Goliath of the U.S. Marine Corps with homemade weapons, in defense of the cultural integrity and political sovereignty of Nicaragua. His death at the hands of Somocista assassins was rendered by many supporters as appropriately Christ-like. The Somoza regime, on the other hand (in collaboration with the government of the United States), portrayed Sandino as a pathetic ne'er-do-well, a machete-wielding slaughterer of innocent people, a politically and militarily inept leader, a pawn of international Communism, and a self-deluded and politically insignificant "bandit." Sandino's latter-day partisans represent him as the archetypal national hero—the founding father of anti-imperialistic Nicaraguan nationalism, the designer of brilliant guerrilla tactics and strategy, the codifier of correct and efficacious ideology, the Adam-like progenitor of the FSLN itself, the embodiment of the essence of Nicaraguanness and the custodian of its cultural identity and values.

This latter attributed quality of cultural custodianship is especially revealing with regard to traditional gender paradigms. Because the gender order is such a central feature of Nicaragua's cultural system (as it is of any country's), and because it is such a primary site of conflict within the larger politics of culture, Sandino's champions and detractors repeatedly used gender issues and categories in their characterizations of him and in the myths (both positive and negative) they wove about him. The Somoza regime portrayed him as an irresponsible ingrate of a son who abused his own mother, a user and defiler of sacred womanhood, an unfaithful and worthless husband of a pure and good-hearted woman. The Sandinistas countered that he was the essence of noble manhood, that he revered and protected women, and that he punished severely those of his men who neglected to do likewise.

Taken together, the Darío and Sandino case studies, besides illuminating the specific cases of Darío and Sandino, offer a window into the role of focal Latin American cultural figures in the negotiation of national cultural identity, especially during periods of dramatic political transformation, crisis, and reconstruction, and shed light on the dialectical relationship between culture and ideology: on culture as a generative matrix for ideology; on the instrumental use of culture for overtly ideological purposes; on the ideological control of cultural processes (such as censorship); on the institutionalization of ideologically skewed representations of cultural history through instruments like museums or school textbooks; and on the shaping of the cultural landscape through cultural preservation efforts, monuments, and public symbols.

NEW WOMEN AND (NOT SO) NEW MEN. My final case study explored the history of gender constructs and gender relations in Nicaragua as a primary arena of the politics of culture, focusing on women's quest for social, economic, political, and cultural equity, and the nodes and structures of resistance to that quest. I explored the cultural recalcitrance that issues from the socially reproductive practices of everyday life (primarily, but not exclusively, those of the family), from institutions (especially the Catholic church), from the symbiotic linkage between the hegemonic order (especially *machismo*) and men's interests, and from women's own sometimes ambivalent and collaborative behavior.

The existing literature on women in Nicaragua is virtually unanimous in maintaining that there was no organized women's movement for equity prior to 1975. Careful investigation reveals, however, that the growth of such a movement paralleled the larger movement of women throughout Latin America from the late nineteenth century onward. Particularly through the life and organizing activities of the indefatigable Josefa Toledo de Aguerri, one can document the existence of an organized and systematic drive for women's rights in Nicaragua at least back to the years of World War I, and one finds its first stirrings much earlier than that.

The attitudes, policy pronouncements, accomplishments, and failures of the Sandinista government with regard to equity for women offer substantial insight into the operation of the politics of culture in the arena of gender, and especially into the forms and processes of cultural recalcitrance. From early in its history, the FSLN had proclaimed the rights of women as a central policy concern, but had paradoxically conceived of those rights as falling mostly within conventional gender paradigms; it was principally the rights of *mothers* that were singled out for special attention in the FSLN's 1969 platform. Thus the FSLN's conception of women's rights was *ab initio* infused with conventional gender assumptions. The necessity to swell the ranks of the Sandinista guerrilla army, together with the desire to give socially and politically marketable substance to the abstract commitment to women's rights, filled the army with many women combatants, including some high officers. But following the Sandinista triumph in 1979, the conventional prerogatives were reallocated to men. By many reports, gender relations had not gotten better, but on the whole worse. The reversals were especially evident in some of the Ministry of Culture's *artesanía* initiatives, as well as within many of the agricultural cooperatives. Cultural recalcitrance with regard to women's rights and their social and economic status emerged quite virulently in the post-triumph struggles for reproductive choice, and in the process of writing and ratifying a new constitution. The coming of the Violeta Chamorro government following the defeat of the Sandinistas in the elections of 1990 resulted in the policy-directed rollback of most of the modest gains women had been able to make during the Sandinista period.

CYCLIC REPETITION: THE ONGOING CULTURAL DISCOURSE

In his book *Condemned to Repetition: The United States and Nicaragua* (1987), Robert Pastor argues that in its relationship to Nicaragua (as to most of Latin America), the United States has compulsively repeated the same mistakes again and again (Pastor 1987, 3–15). As one views the politics of culture within Nicaragua itself, similar compulsions and repetitions are painfully evident.

In the first place, Nicaragua has been a site for perennial ideological and value conflicts that frequently involved intense argument about what culture is and ought to be, and what if anything the state ought to do about culture. Such conflicts cropped up again and again between Spanish and indigenous systems in the post-conquest period, between European liberal-positivist and Latin American ones from at least independence onward, between León Liberals and Granada Conservatives, between the Somozas and their opponents from the mid-1930s through the end of the 1970s (as well as between various factions among the Somoza opposition), between orthodox Catholicism and liberation theology after the early 1960s, and between more and less orthodox Marxists during the Sandinista period.

Since Nicaragua has never had an extended period of cultural tranquillity or unity, many of the perennial internal conflicts have occurred not between long-established and well-defined cultural sectors or groups, but between those that were themselves in flux, struggling to define themselves, to bring themselves into being, to establish themselves in relation to others. In some respects, then, with regard to Nicaragua one might usefully think in terms of a protocultural system or a system in process of formation rather than a cultural system in the usual sense. However problematic such a notion, it at least highlights the fact that efforts to define, claim, or establish boundaries for a national culture have been a consistent feature of the politics of culture in Nicaragua at least since the Zelaya period a century ago.[1]

The poignancy of this emergent rather than fully resolved situation in

Nicaragua is underscored by the fact that—in view of its small size, economic and political marginality, and continual susceptibility to economic and political interventions—Nicaragua has been especially *needful* of having a reasonably integrated national culture, however pluralistic in its local details. The transit-route intervention of the nineteenth century, for example, would presumably have been less disturbing and destructive (culturally and otherwise) had it not occurred within the framework of the historical León-Granada and east-west opposition that kept the country perennially at war with itself, culturally as well as politically.

Bearing these factors in mind helps one to understand, in fact, why the repeated economic and political interventions have had such powerful cultural impacts—from the conquest through the British domination of the Atlantic coast, the brief boom along the transit route, the William Walker period, the U.S. intervention against Zelaya, the garrisoning of the country by the U.S. Marine Corps for twenty-five years thereafter, broad-scale U.S. intervention through more than forty years of Somoza client regimes, the contra war of the Reagan years, and U.S. backing of the coalition that defeated the Sandinistas in the 1990 elections.

It was in the first place easier to intervene in a divided country than in a united one. Beyond that, most of the interventions were read in contradictory ways by local factions, and the contradictoriness of the readings tended to set the factions even more stringently in opposition to each other. A further paradoxical effect has been that intervention—either actual or threatened—from outside has served *internally* in many instances as an analytical short-circuit and scapegoat, preventing more candid admission of internal problems and more forthright confrontation of the internal contradictions of the culture.

There appears to be little reason to doubt that the contentious discourse concerning culture will remain a permanent feature of Nicaraguan national life. Immediately after the Sandinista government was defeated in the 1990 elections, for example, intense debate over Rubén Darío and Augusto C. Sandino surfaced with renewed vigor. Shortly after the post-Sandinista Chamorro government came to power, historian Jorge Arellano was inducted into the *Academia Nicaragüense de la Lengua*. Choosing Darío as the subject of his inaugural address—as had Pablo Antonio Cuadra almost a half-century and René Schick Gutiérrez a quarter-century earlier—Arellano undertook to explicate Darío's lifelong "cultural project."[2] Absent from Arellano's address were the concerns that had so preoccupied him in his pro-Sandinista interpretation of Darío less than a decade before. Darío's "cultural project," Arellano now advised his fellows in the Academia, was "essentially *Europeista*," deriving essentially from his "titanic and limitless desire to appropriate the totality of European culture," particularly the French (and even more particularly the Parisian) sector of it. Paris—"grand and marvelous Paris, so dangerous and so good"—Arellano urged, was Darío's "intellectual home" for much of his adult life, and so it remained until the end-of-the-century social crises attendant upon industrialism caused him to turn toward *la España paternal y eterna* and toward "our America." Abandoning his own 1982 argument that Darío himself was open to "the dialectical materialism of Marx and Engels," Arellano characterized as *ignorantes* and "literary sociologists of sacred Marxism" (*sociologistas literarios del sacromarxismo*) those critics who wished to limit the universalist cultural project of Darío to a narrow ideology and to singing "the mythology of the [local] household gods."[3]

As with Rubén Darío, the struggle over the meaning of Sandino's life and the right to the cultural and political capital he embodied did not end with the Sandinistas' defeat in 1990. The first issue (April 1992) of the post-Sandinista cultural journal *Revista Nicaragüense*, edited by none other than Jorge Arellano (so lately a Sandinista partisan and more lately a Sandinista opponent), contained two calls to arms for the next phase of the revisionist cultural battle. Napoleón Chow's eyewitness account of a 1969 meeting between Nicaragua's venerable writer José Coronel Urtecho and the FSLN's founder-martyr Carlos Fonseca recalled that Fonseca—"his voice intense and authoritarian with convinced intransigence"—accused Coronel of being second only to Somoza in being responsible for Nicaragua's tragic situation. In the context of post-Sandinista cultural politics, Coronel's reported characterization of the outrageously confrontational Fonseca as "demon-possessed" (*en energúmeno*) could hardly be read as other than an implicit judgment of the entire Sandinista political-cultural project. Héctor Vargas's brief article on Sandino complained angrily of the FSLN's Orwellian, totalitarian Marxist "confiscation of our national hero."[4] Clearly the stakes were thought to be still too high to let the matter rest.

The resuscitated cultural-political arguments also extended beyond revered cultural figures to embrace the much broader issue of the gender order. During the final days of the Sandinista government, anti-feminist Nicaraguan women continued their adamant opposition to even such modest gains as women had made since the overthrow of Somoza. Writing in *La Prensa* in May 1988, Ana María Ch[amorro?] de Holmann charged that "to destroy the family is the goal of Revolutionary States, communists, totalitarians and materialists. . . . The family is the major obstacle to the revolution, since in it one finds the nucleus of unity, authority and respect."[5] Warning of "ideologies foreign to our traditions and contrary to our creed" that had led the country into a "dance of libertinage," and a "crisis of authority . . . which has overturned the modern world," Ch. de Holmann lamented the husband's "lack of authority . . . as head of the family." Meanwhile the woman, she said, "has abandoned her role as wife and mother, adopting postures and manners, tasks, work, and positions that deny her condition as woman, diminishing the femininity and delicacy that characterize her. . . . Social Revolution! Sexual liberation! Filial Revolt! Conjugal independence! That is the current cry, and in the wake of that cry follows an echo of pain: abandoned children, rebellious young people, drug addicts, alcoholics . . . pregnant teenagers." Meanwhile, the Nicaraguan man, Ch. de Holmann insisted (in about as clear an example of conscious and willful recalcitrance as one might imagine), "has to recover his authority and grasp his functions as head of the family. . . . The woman has to go back to the role that belongs to her, returning to her originality."

Such sentiments, which were widespread in Nicaragua, made reproductive freedom a key issue in the election. The FSLN failed to take a clear position on abortion, but Violeta Chamorro's UNO platform pledged to protect children "from their conception." Dressed in white for the campaign and carefully projected by UNO as loyal wife and widow, reconciling mother, Virgin Mary and Queen, *doña* Violeta proclaimed, "I am not a feminist nor do I want to be one. I am dedicated to my home as Pedro taught me" (Morgan 1992, 140; Kampwirth 1992a).

Soon after it came to power, the Chamorro government renewed emphasis upon "Christian family values" and moved to bring policy on abortion and contraception into agreement with the Catholic church's position. Bolstered by the turn in attitudes and policy, the Catholic church reinforced its accustomed opposition to birth control, premarital sex, and abortion. Humberto Belli, the new minister of education, halted sex education in the schools and installed a new series of textbooks (financed with USAID money) based upon conventional gender paradigms (including *patria potestad*) and explicitly Christian values.[6] The new (male) minister of health ordered that Sandinista-era billboards saying "Prevent Aids: Use a Condom" be replaced by ones reading "Prevent Using Condoms: Be Faithful to Your Partner," highlighting with unintentional irony the history of the pervasive double standard of sexual conduct in Nicaragua. The new government also mounted an anti-abortion campaign supported by the U.S. right-to-life movement, aired the anti-abortion film *The Silent Scream* on television, and returned drug commercials (many of them built around conventional gender paradigms) to television (Wessel 1991, 544–47; Kampwirth 1992b, 38). The two men and one woman appointed to a new committee on therapeutic abortion at the Bertha Calderón women's hospital were all charismatic Catholics disposed to interpret the guidelines extremely narrowly. Hospitals in general stopped giving contraception information to women who had just given birth, television reproductive health care programs for adolescents were eliminated, and access to reproductive health care was dramatically curtailed (Morgan 1990, 146; Kampwirth 1992b, 23, 35–38).[7]

Women lost ground in other sectors as well. The problems of women workers on farms, already serious under the Sandinistas, grew much worse; the number of women workers on private farms fell from seven thousand in late 1990 to two thousand in mid-1991 as managers fired them to keep from having to deal with pregnancy leaves and child-care arrangements and expenses. Not surprisingly, reported cases of household violence increased sharply (Kampwirth 1992b, 24, 30).

One result of the reactionary swing in policy was that women's organizations — newspapers, radio programs, research organizations, women's houses, and the like — increased in number as women's own efforts had to replace state programs that had developed under the Sandinistas. But again, a large, doggedly recalcitrant sector of the public resisted. The Sandinista newspaper's Friday women's supplement *Gente*, Kampwirth notes, received "a steady stream of angry, anti-feminist letters" (Kampwirth 1992b, 41–43).

In retrospect, Molyneux's cautionary observations about structural tensions and contradictions within the feminist project are apt. Women themselves had been seriously divided throughout the constitutional process, and they remained so during the election. AMNLAE hesitated and wavered repeatedly at critical moments. During the 1990 electoral campaign, some women wore "Daniel is my gamecock" T-shirts, and UNO women who unexpectedly supported abortion rights clashed from time to time with Sandinista women who opposed them (Morgan 1990, 105n.; 1992, 140–44).[8]

The double irony after those elections was that, having made as much progress as they had, against great odds, during the century between Josefa Toledo de Aguerri's first fledgling efforts and the 1990 elections, Nicaraguan women had to renew the struggle against a new conservative government — headed by a woman and as fiercely committed to the old gender order as the Somozas had ever been; and that in that struggle the opposition from among women themselves to restructuring the gender order would be even stronger (and far better organized) than it had ever been even during the feminist struggles of their mothers and grandmothers, of which they still apparently knew but little.

EPILOGUE: MIAMI COMES TO MANAGUA

On the last Sunday morning of January 1993, Cable News Network carried a report on the return of wealthy Nicaraguans from Miami to Managua after the fall of the Sandinista government. The report focused on the teenage and young adult offspring of wealthy anti-Sandinista Nicaraguan parents who had spent the past twelve years living well in Miami, the effective cultural metropole of Nicaragua since the early days of the Somoza regime. Determined efforts by the "Miami boys" (as they are called) and their parents to recreate their cherished Miami social and cultural "scene" have transformed the Managua night: neon-lit bars and exclusive clubs, designer clothing, Nicaragua's first surf shop, one-hour photo processing, expensive cars cruising the scene, and pervasive preening, posturing, and dalliance shaped by the old gender roles and rules. For the younger set, wealthy parents built a private school more modern and sumptuous than any other school in the country, naming it—in an ironic symbolic twist reminiscent of President Reagan's "Founding Fathers" characterization of the contras—Escuela Lincoln, with a picture of Abe over the door. Meanwhile, the report continued, masses of Managua residents were living in poverty, prostitutes were plying the streets hoping to divert a bit of the wealth, and enterprising and desperate children were staying up later hoping to wash the more numerous windshields at stoplights.

It was as if the revolution had never been, as if the 1972 earthquake had unhappened and the Avenida Roosevelt had reassembled itself from the rubble, as if the gaudy movie of the cotton-rich days of the 1960s were rolling again, as if the ghost of old Somoza García walked again, charming the *norteamericanos* with his colloquial English—as if indeed the Miami boys were not (as they fancied) gyrating to Madonna under the neon, but swaying to "Managua, Nicaragua" by Kay Kyser and His Orchestra ("With Vocal Chorus by The Campus Kids featuring Gloria Wood," as the Columbia red label promised).[9]

A peculiar feature of Nicaraguan cultural and political geography is that buildings and houses carry no street numbers, but instead are identified by their relationship to other known features of the landscape—"a block above the Hotel Colón," for example. Once a house or building becomes designated in relation to such a feature, however, it continues to be so designated, even if the anchoring feature disappears. Thus it is not unusual for an address to locate the desired house or building as being "a block and a half to the south of where the statue *was*." At one level, the pervasive use of such address bears witness to the consensual admission that, whatever the superficial character of the landscape, it is the landscape of the mind that matters most—not things as they are, but things as they have been.

The metaphor is instructive. It is as if the Somozan Temples of Music (gaudy derivative Victorian gazebos that they were) still stand in the parks at the end of the Avenida Roosevelt, which, buried though it is beneath the earthquake rubble, is no less a promenade for the ghosts of Commodore Vanderbilt and William Walker, the transit route hopefuls, Rubén Darío's *ex-*

celente gorila Teddy Roosevelt, the U.S. Marine *comandantes* and Charles A. Lindbergh, ardent Phillies fan Anastasio Somoza García, Ronald Reagan and Ollie North's contras, and now the Miami boys. As sure of their footing as if they were following a map only they themselves can see, they still walk the streets that once formed and still do form some of the most durable and ineradicable grids of Nicaraguan political and cultural life.

NOTES

INTRODUCTION

1. Oddly enough, such questions or criticisms are rarer if one claims to be writing history or writing about science ("What do you *mean* by 'history'?" "What *is* 'science'?") unless the books themselves directly address such questions. This despite the fact that the terms *history* and *science* are at least as problematic as *culture*.

2. I borrow the term *gender order* from Connell 1987, who uses it (following Jill Matthews) to refer to the "historically constructed pattern of power relations between men and women and definitions of femininity and masculinity" (p. 98).

CHAPTER ONE

1. In this chapter I use the term Nicaragua to refer to the area encompassed by the contemporary nation-state, although unification of the east and west coastal areas was not achieved even formally until the late nineteenth century, and effectively until much later. Nicaragua's most recent boundary dispute was settled in 1960.

2. This final factor is reserved for discussion principally in Chapter 7.

3. My brief sketch here follows Willey's summary in Lange and Stone 1984, 341–80.

4. The extent of pre-conquest maize-based agriculture in Pacific Nicaragua is still not completely clear (Lange et al. 1992, 273).

5. All subsequent quotations from Oviedo are taken from his *Historia General y Natural de las Indias*. Abel-Vidor (in Lange et al. 1992) observes that although several years in Italy (1499–1502) left him acutely aware of the corruption of the Catholic church, Oviedo nevertheless arrived in Dominica in 1514 as a "solid idealist of Christian imperialism." Abel-Vidor judges (perhaps overgenerously) that Oviedo's acceptance of Christian imperialism "has no negative bearing" on the quality of his observations in America, and that there is "no indication that his ideology ever impaired his powers of observation" (pp. 269–72). Rodríguez 1984 emphasizes Oviedo's posture of general opposition to the attitudes and behaviors of the *conquistadores* (p. 114). On the *cronistas'* limits as reporters of phenomena and experience in post-conquest Nicaragua (e.g., geographical disorientation, preference for quantitative description, insufficient attention to native peoples, conceptual confusion, terminological imprecision, exaggeration), see Rodríguez 1984, 15–31, and Delgado-Gómez in Williams and Lewis 1993, 3–20.

6. See Myers in Williams and Lewis 1993, 183–213, on the visual representation of New World phenomena in Oviedo. Myers is especially sensitive to the paradox that within Oviedo's narrative, "American phenomena are simultaneously placed within the European conventions for the representation of known objects and practices and also described as something completely new" (p. 189).

7. A mostly untestable (but I think generally reliable) assumption here is that cultural patterns reported so soon after the conquest as being identifiably "Indian" probably were, and that they predated the conquest.

8. My discussion here is drawn from Crosby 1986, 145–216. I use "weeds" (an admit-

tedly nonscientific term) as Crosby does: to refer in a limited sense to "whatever plants spring up where human beings do not want them" (p. 28), but also more generally to unwanted organisms of whatever variety that multiply rapidly.

9. Skeletal remains in Nicaragua's Greater Nicoya region show that either fat/protein diseases or chronic intestinal diseases afflicted a large percentage of the population in the pre-conquest period (Lange and Stone 1984, 190).

10. Newson notes that groups living near resource-rich areas were also much more likely to come into contact with Europeans, and thus to suffer greater population loss. She also points out that one must distinguish between the biological and cultural survival of native people, since some groups have a greater range of adaptive strategies and therefore demonstrate a greater capacity to survive biologically through cultural adaptation (which paradoxically may entail specifically *cultural* loss and disappearance) (Newson 1987, 9–14).

11. Epidemics continued into the eighteenth century. A measles and smallpox epidemic in 1693–94 enveloped the entire province; others followed in Subtiava (1701–11) and in Realejo, Managua, and Boaco in 1715. Subtiava, Rivas, and Boaco suffered plagues in 1725. The 1740s witnessed plagues in Las Segovias, Matagalpa, and Subtiava, and another measles epidemic struck Subtiava, Masaya, and much of the rest of the province in 1769–70. Measles and smallpox returned to Realejo and Subtiava in 1781 (Romero Vargas 1988, 60).

12. On the theme of cannibalism in *cronista* and other documents of the conquest, see Palencia-Roth in Williams and Lewis 1993, 21–64. I consider both the *encomienda* and tribute payments subsequently. Never as important in Nicaragua as they were elsewhere in Latin America, mineral and metal mining declined markedly by the end of the sixteenth century and did not revive until gold was discovered in Nueva Segovia in 1699 (Newson 1987, 91, 102, 146).

13. Sherman cites Lockhart's tabulation of documents on slaves in Peru, which showed that between 1531 and 1543, "over two-thirds of the Indians were from Nicaragua."

14. For a comparative discussion of Governors Pedrarias Dávila, Francisco de Castañeda, and Rodrigo de Contreras in relation to the slave trade, see Sherman 1979, 53–60.

15. Newson believes that 200,000 is a "conservative estimate" and 500,000 a "reasonable" one that agrees with many contemporary estimates. Sherman 1979, 78–79, questions (1) whether estimates based upon the size of ships are fully reliable in view of the necessity to carry other cargo, the relative profitability of slaves and horses, and the like, and (2) whether if losses during shipment were as high as others report, traders would have been willing to continue to accept them.

16. Details on Las Casas's activities in Nicaragua are available in Wagner and Parish 1967, 79–84; Mejía Sánchez 1986; and Rodríguez 1984, 143–49. While granting the ethical force and sincerity of Las Casas's efforts, Rodríguez 1984 faults him for his confidence in the possibility of constructing a "good colonialism" that would result in Christianizing the Indians and organizing their labor more humanely (pp. 144–45). Arias in Williams and Lewis 1993, 163–79, offers an excellent brief analysis of the major elements of Las Casas's narrative. Merrim, in Williams and Lewis 1993, faults Las Casas's "counter-discourse" for reducing "all spaces and events to a single paradigm of Indian innocence and generosity abused by Spanish brutality and greed" (p. 152).

17. On the intertextual relationship of Las Casas's *Brevísima relación* to the discourse on native peoples, see Merrim in Williams and Lewis 1993, 149–62. Merrim is especially attentive to the essentializing dialectic in Las Casas's text.

18. Sherman 1979 cites the chronicler Herrera's report that "for two years [Nicaraguan

Indians] did not sleep with their women, so that no slaves would be born for the Castilians" (p. 56).

19. As early as 1512, the Laws of Burgos promulgated regulations and established institutions (including public markets and the *fieles ejecutores*, who were responsible for maintaining accurate weights and measures, good hygiene, and acceptable food quality) to assure the continuation of Spanish food culture in Spanish America. Super's exploration of post-conquest changes in food production and distribution and consequent changes in diet for the indigenous population in Mexico and the central Andes is suggestive. Granting that newly introduced bananas and plantains produced more calories per unit of land than any other staple of what became the sixteenth-century diet, Super argues that Spanish colonial food policy and institutions were "designed to provision [Spanish America] with Spanish foods," and that seeds, animals, and tools were sent from Spain to "produce the staples essential to the [heavily meat- and wheat bread–dependent] Spanish diet" and the other two elements of the "Mediterranean trilogy," oil and wine. Although not well adapted to growing conditions in much of Latin American, wheat was established by the 1530s, and its production became "a cultural imperative [for the Spanish], a driving force that shaped the social and physical landscape." The case was virtually the same for cattle, although the abundance of range land made them even easier to grow than they had been in Europe. Increases in cattle/meat production reduced the land available for growing maize, the primordial staple of the Indian diet. Diminution in maize-growing lands, plus demands on Indian labor and associated changes in social organization, reduced caloric intake among Indians. Super also notes that changes in the uses of traditional food and drink (alcohol, for example) caused serious dietary and health problems (Super 1988, 15, 32–34, 41–42, 55–67; Super and Wright 1985, 2–7).

20. The subordination, though pervasive, was not total. Indigenous names for objects, communities, and the like continued to be used in some cases (cf. Incer 1985), while some indigenous terms survived in hispanicized forms. But the languages as functioning whole systems of communication disappeared fairly quickly.

21. Stanislawski (1983, 50, 69) notes that in the sixteenth century, sixty tributary Indians were considered the minimum required to support one *encomendero*, and in 1528 a royal decree set three hundred as the maximum number in any one *encomienda*.

22. Nicaraguan Governor Contreras relieved the exploitation of *tamemes* somewhat by encouraging the building of ox-carts (Sherman 1979, 119).

23. The following discussion of *encomenderos* is drawn mainly from Stanislawski 1983, 72–125.

24. The biographical list in Himmerich y Valencia 1991, 113–266, includes numerous *encomenderas* (e.g., nos. 381, 385, 386, 388, 395, 401, 413).

25. Newson 1987 notes that in fact the *encomienda* survived in Nicaragua until 1721 (p. 277).

26. Newson 1987 notes that women were also drawn into the *repartimiento* by being forced to provide food for men working on the *haciendas* and in public works projects (p. 162).

27. Weiss 1993, 45–73, provides a useful historical discussion of the roots of popular theater in Latin America. For a historical survey of the scholarship on *El Güegüence* itself, see Arellano 1977c, 54–60. *El Güegüence* was first published by Brinton in 1883 from a conflation of two texts obtained in Nicaragua by Carl H. Berendt in 1874 (Pérez Estrada 1984, 2–3; Arellano 1991b, 280). Brinton believed (cf. [1883] 1969, p. xlii) that the play was

composed no later than the early eighteenth century, and perhaps much earlier. Arellano 1982a says at one point (p. 150) that it derives from the mid-sixteenth century, and at another (p. 22) from the mid-seventeenth. In *Ventana: Barricada Cultural*, 31 March 1984, pp. 4–5, he again places it in the period 1520–50. *El Pez y la Serpiente* 10 (Winter 1968–69) is devoted entirely to *El Güegüence*. My reading here (based upon Brinton [1883] 1969, which includes the bilingual text of the play) benefits from the observations of Arellano 1977c and 1991b; Peña Hernández 1968, 180ff.; and Burns 1991, 110–14.

28. The name Güegüence may come from a combination of the Nahuatl word (*hue*) meaning "man" with the "reverential" *tzin*, traceable back at least to colonial times, during which the term *huehue* was (according to Oviedo) used to refer to revered old men who were responsible for seeing to the defense of the community (Brinton [1883] 1969, xlv).

29. My synopsis here follows Brinton [1883] 1969.

30. The continued popularity of the play in Nicaragua is evidenced by the fact that shortly after it came to power in 1990, the post-Sandinista Chamorro government sponsored a national symposium on *El Güegüence* (see Instituto Nacional de Cultura 1992).

31. On the mythic dimensions of the Chamorros' place in Nicaraguan history, see Zepeda Hernríquez 1987, who denominates the Chamorros and the Sacasas Nicaragua's "two charismatic families" (pp. 95–105).

32. On the persistent imaginative importance of the original city of León, see Zepeda Henríquez 1987, 83–93.

33. This rebellion was part of the larger conflict surrounding early movements toward independence.

34. Scholars do not agree on arrival dates, numbers of priests, dates for the establishment of convents, and the like; dates and numbers used here should therefore be considered approximate rather than exact. Molina Argüello 1970 notes the general difficulty of investigating the history of the church in Nicaragua, owing to (among many other factors) the burning of church records in the 1685 pirate attack on León (p. 35). I am grateful to Susan Ryan for her excellent assistance with my research on the church in Nicaragua.

35. Newson 1987 cites a document of 1531 which said that Indians near Imabite "managed to hide two hundred idols for ten days, but when the Spaniards discovered them, they broke them into pieces" (p. 115).

36. For an extensive analysis of those methods, see Tormo 1962, 129–60. Prien 1985, 198–203, discusses the differences between peaceful and armed mission efforts.

37. Gruzinski in Lavrin 1989, 96–117. All quotations in this section are from Gruzinski, who focuses specifically upon the Nahuas in Mexico. Unfortunately I know of no analogous study that focuses upon Nicaragua itself, but Gruzinski's evidence is drawn from sources (confession manuals, church regulations concerning the sacrament of marriage, influential theological treatises of the era) applicable more broadly within the Catholic evangelical enterprise in the New World, and thus presumably within Nicaragua.

38. These local events in Nicaragua were part of the larger mid-sixteenth-century debate within the Catholic church—focused by the Las Casas-Sepúlveda debates at Valladolid (1550–51) and the Council of Trent (1545–63)—over theological orthodoxy, the necessity for "law, regimen and good order" in church polity, and ethical-theological questions related to the colonial enterprise (Hanke in Greenleaf 1971, 47–52; Dussel in Richard 1980, 404–10). The Council of Trent's insistence upon the Latin liturgy, resistance to translating the Bible into Indian languages, reluctance to evaluate local mission stations individually, and commitment to a dark, Augustinian estimate of human nature in general and the

depravity of Indians in particular ran counter to Las Casas's defense of the Indians, but others of its reformist impulses reinforced it (Prien 1985, 247–48; Poole in Ramírez 1989, 11–19; Dussel 1981, 56–57).

39. In the following discussion, all quotations otherwise unattributed are from Oviedo (page numbers in parentheses). Cf. Incer 1990, 98. Even though Bobadilla was accompanied by a scribe, it is of course impossible to judge the accuracy of the reports of the conversations.

40. A later respondent replied that both were male (320), and another (325–26) that Çipattoval was female. Another also spoke of the female deity Omeyateçigoat (328), and upon being asked whether a male or female deity was superior (*Quál teneys por mayor señor, al padre ó á la madre ó al hijo?*), assured Bobadilla that all were equal (*Todos son iguales*) (329). Other responses suggested that a question Bobadilla posed to ascertain gender may have been taken to refer only to whether or not the gods were like human beings (e.g., *son hombres, como los indios* [323]). For a discussion of Tamagastat and Çipattoval in Nicaraguan mythology, see Zepeda Henríquez 1987, 13–23.

41. Barnadas points out in "Catholic Church" (in Bethell 1984, 1:533) that Jesuit *reducciones* were considerably more humane and respectful of Indian culture than those created by other orders. But the Jesuits arrived late in Nicaragua (1616), long after the most devastating missionary transformations of Indian life and culture. In *Nicaragua: viajes*, his extensive discussion of the missionary *reducciones*, Incer mentions only those of the Mercedarians and Franciscans (pp. 247–84).

42. Some allowance must be made for Cockburn's Anglocentric point of view, and the struggle between the British and Spanish for control of Nicaragua under way at the time, but corroborating reports of Indian hostilities against Catholic missionaries throughout the colonial period are abundant (for example in Incer 1990, 247–84).

43. Being relatively distant from the most important colonial administrative centers, Nicaraguan Indians escaped the worst of forced Christianization — such as the seventeenth-century Andean religious "wars to the death," as Barnadas characterized them — in which the church used "Inquisitorial methods" to force a "schizophrenic duplicity" upon Indians. Unfortunately, the folk-Catholic syncretistic process in Nicaragua during the post-conquest period has hardly been investigated at all. This lack obliges me to extrapolate from more detailed investigations that focus on other areas in Mesoamerica and Central America. The similarities between present-day folk Catholicism in Nicaragua and that in those other areas makes it seem reasonable to conclude that the earlier processes were also similar.

44. Romero Vargas notes that of the twenty-one censuses taken in Nicaragua between 1662 and 1817, that of 1778 is most reliable. Its racial categories included *indios, españoles, mestizos, mulatos,* and *ladinos* (Romero Vargas 1988, 45).

45. Those whose families had arrived in the first waves of conquest designated themselves as "honored person[s] of the first [or most ancient] *conquistadores*"; those who came somewhat later were *pobladores*. Others with less ancient claims to status had to settle for honored person (*persona honrada*), honored and noble person (*persona honrada y hidalgo*), or noble gentleman and person of quality (*caballero hijodalgo y persona de calidad*). Still other coveted honorifics emphasized cleanliness (*limpieza*) or nobility (*nobleza*) of blood (Himmerich y Valencia 1991, 6–9).

46. The term *sambenitados* [*sanbenitados*] resonated strongly with the history of the Spanish Inquisition and of the social and cultural freight carried by all who had been touched by it. The *sanbenito* (from *saco bendito*) was the yellow sackcloth "garment of

shame" worn as a sign of sin. Its decoration (crosses, pitchforks, flames) varied depending upon the severity of the sin, and being condemned to wear it might also carry a sentence of flogging at the church door, imprisonment, torture, or burning at the stake (Romero Vargas 1988, 269–74; Plaidy 1978, 158–61).

47. Romero Vargas's population figures are not always consistent with each other, but these percentages seem roughly accurate. The mestizo/mulatto/negro population continued to grow in relation to Spanish. Nandaime went from 78 percent mulatto and 22 percent Indian in 1771 to 89 percent and 5 percent in 1816; children baptized in Nagarote went from 30 percent mulatto, 50 percent Indian in 1778 to 70 percent and 18 percent in 1821 (Romero Vargas 1988, 470–73 [tables]).

48. Until the discovery of indigo, Spanish textile makers had imported woad as a dyestuff from France and Portugal. Informed that the Indians used *xiquilite* for the purpose, Philip II ordered experiments done on it; favorable reports led to efforts to develop production.

49. My brief discussion here is based upon Romero Vargas 1988, 92–105. Known at least from the 1630s, the *cajas de comunidad* were required by the Spanish for all indigenous communities after 1766. Ejidal lands were also granted to *ladino* villages, but I am not concerned with those here. Another important category included the *terrenos de la comunidad indígena*. I am grateful to Jeffrey Gould for clarifying these differences.

50. Romero Vargas's tabulation (1988, 238) of workers for thirteen *haciendas* in the mid-eighteenth century showed that Indians constituted 37 percent of the workers (in addition to 15 percent mestizo, 20 percent mulatto, and 23 percent slave).

51. I take the term and concept "gender order" from Connell 1987, 119–42. Connell uses the term to refer to "the macro-politics of gender"—the dynamic interplay of gender definitions and categories with the gender rules and practices of the whole range of social, political, and cultural institutions.

52. Unfortunately, data on pre-conquest gender arrangements in Nicaragua are not plentiful, and those that are available (for example, in immediate post-conquest accounts written by the *cronistas*) are not of high quality. Presumably, an indigenous woman from a polyandrous, female-dominant society would have experienced the conquest as more calamitous than would a woman from a monogamous, male-dominant one. Neither of the two most recent (and otherwise detailed) studies in which one might hope to encounter such data (Lange and Stone 1984 and Lange et al. 1992) even includes "women" as an index entry. As late as 1869, British captain Bedford Pim reported that women on the Mosquito coast of Nicaragua still enjoyed superiority to men (Pim 1869, 306–7).

53. My discussion here is based almost entirely upon Sherman (1979), from whom all quotations not otherwise attributed are taken.

54. Sherman notes that most such cases that found their way into colonial court records involved men of relatively high social standing; presumably there were many more offenses committed by others of lower social rank, of which we have no record (Sherman 1979, 312).

55. Unfortunately, Vargas 1988 does not discuss the special circumstances of women in the eighteenth century. For extended discussions of gender conflict during the colonial period see Lavrin 1989 (especially the article by Boyer, pp. 252–86), which explores the historical roots of colonial patriarchalism.

56. The precise import of Cockburn's observation is rendered unclear by his general tendency to compare the brutal Spanish unfavorably with the humane English.

1. Burns 1991, 41, notes that at one time (1823-24), four different governments located in León, Granada, Managua, and El Viejo claimed to rule the country. Other regional and factional stresses complicated the conflict between León and Granada: between Atlantic and Pacific regions, between the majority of Atlantic residents and the coast's privileged foreign enclaves, and between the rest of the country and its southwestern Guanacaste area, which seceded to join Costa Rica in 1824 (Burns 1991, 16-17).

2. For a good brief summary of the core tenets of Positivism—prevalent throughout Latin America—see Woodward 1971, ix-xiii. Here as elsewhere except in the previous chapter, I necessarily use "indigenous" loosely—to mean those people still more genetically and culturally Indian than not—rather than strictly, as one may use it with reference to areas (such as Guatemala or the Andes) where, despite the conquest, substantial aggregations of relatively unmixed indigenous populations remain.

3. There were also some real differences between the two elites: Conservatives wanted to preserve the elite in their traditional roles in a two-class society while giving peasants a degree (in practice, very small indeed) of protection; Liberals were willing to forge an alliance with the bourgeois modernizers without regard to its impact upon Indian heritage and peasant culture, of which they were essentially contemptuous. Conservatives opposed granting land and resources to foreign capitalists (equated with Protestantism, democracy, and modernization); Liberals encouraged foreign trade, investment, and immigration (Woodward 1984).

4. *Nicaragua indígena* 1 (April-December 1947): 3.

5. In his otherwise excellent analysis, Burns employs the term "folk" in an insufficiently problematized way, but such a usage is not detrimental to my purposes here.

6. Doolittle, "Statement of a Journey from New York to San Francisco, Cal[ifornia], in 1849," manuscript, 1878 (C-D 68), Bancroft Library, University of California, Berkeley, pp. 1-5. Used with permission.

7. Hulbert and Walker, "Land of Gold: An Ill-Fated Journey to California via Nicaragua . . . in 1852" (C-B 586), Bancroft Library, University of California, Berkeley, pp. 23-25. Used with permission.

8. For fuller discussion of historical interest in a canal across Nicaragua, see Burns 1991, 160-61; Bermann 1986, 103-22; and Woodward [1976] 1985, 121-23.

9. The account that follows is based upon Squier 1852.

10. This image has proven perennially attractive and turns up in contemporary Nicaraguan poetry. See Cardenal, "Squier en Nicaragua," in Cardenal 1983b, 48.

11. Squier 1852, 1:108, 151, 192, 353. Pianos were reported in Nicaragua at least as early as 1856 (Cardenal Argüello 1962, 37).

12. Leed 1991, 111-29, 217-23, presents a broader analysis of the "gendered activity" of travel, and especially of its function as a sexual metaphor.

13. Letters of 18 and 24 March 1849, 27 November 1849, and 9 and 17 May 1851, Samuel Smith Wood Papers, Manuscripts and Archives, Yale University Library.

14. Letters of 18 December 1851; 4 and 20 March and 2 December 1852; ledger entry 3 February 1853. Wood's store and stock were destroyed in the mid-1854 U.S. bombardment of San Juan del Norte, but he was advertising again in the bilingual *Central American* as late as 29 September 1855.

15. *Central American* (San Juan del Norte), 29 September and 13 October 1855.

16. On the eve of the canal boom Realejo was in no condition to absorb the burdens of the transit traffic. Passing through a few years before Stillman, Captain Edward Belcher described the town as "a collection of hovels" along "one main street about two hundred yards in length" (Belcher 1843 [1970], 1:29).

17. Stillman's high standing as a scientist and careful observer was later attested to by his being chosen to write the text for Eadweard Muybridge's famous *The Horse in Motion* (1880). His observations on Nicaragua in the nineteenth century are some of the most incisive I encountered.

18. Cleveland, "Across the Nicaraguan Transit" (M-M 65), Bancroft Library, University of California, Berkeley, pp. 4, 11. Subsequent page references in parentheses.

19. In Scott's formulation, "weapons of the weak" refers to such stratagems as "foot dragging, dissimulation, desertion, false compliance, pilfering, feigned ignorance, slander, arson, sabotage," and similar means (Scott 1985, xv–xvi, 28–47).

20. An excellent short treatment of the often analyzed political and military aspects of the Walker war may be found in Bermann 1986, 51–73.

21. My brief sketch of Walker's early life is based primarily on Bermann 1986, 51–55, and May 1973, 78–80.

22. Andrés Castro became one of the cultural heroes of the Sandinistas of the 1970s. See *Ventana: Barricada Cultural*, 12 September 1981.

23. *New York Times*, 5 November 1855, p. 3. For research assistance with these matters I am grateful to my former student Gita Dhir.

24. *DeBow's Review* 24 (February 1858): 146–51.

25. Walker's agenda for political and cultural change was not merely idiosyncratic. Squier had already put his fellow countrymen on notice about the cultural inferiority of Nicaraguan people, and the popular media had taken up the theme. One contemporary writer characterized Nicaraguans as "semi-barbarians" and "timid natives." But "they are capable of high improvement," he said, "and will form . . . an excellent free population . . . when Nicaragua shall have been recolonized from the United States" (Wheldley 1852, 263). The *United States Democratic Review* ("The Nicaraguan Question," 41 [January 1858]: 115–19) agreed: Central American people in general were "a rabble of ignorant Indians and mulattoes . . . negroes . . . and renegades of all colors" whose "ignorance of our civilization is profound and hopeless," who had "no aspirations, no wish for progress or improvement," and whose happiness consisted "in the placid enjoyment of the sensual luxuries afforded . . . [by] the tropics." Their governments, not surprisingly, were "abominable bastard democracies" and "sluggish anarchies, liable at any moment to despotism, their natural end, or to barbarism, their natural and real condition." The British journal *Blackwood's*, reflecting widespread sentiment of the time, admitted that Nicaraguan people had "a great deal of natural grace, and are extremely polite and formal in their manners," but lamented that they were "contented" to live in a state of "poverty and listless indolence," lying in hammocks, gambling ("the prevailing vice") and going to cockfights ("the national sport"). By keeping themselves in a "constant state of revolution . . . cutting each other's throats, battering down each other's cities, [and] spending their money in gunpowder," Nicaraguan people "have managed to reduce themselves and their country to such a wretched state of misery that it really [appears] to be the duty of some civilised nation to step in and keep them all in order" (*Blackwood's*, undated tear-sheets [probably 1856], pp. 316–24).

26. *El Nicaragüense*, 25 January 1856, p. 1; *Frank Leslie's Illustrated Newspaper*, 6 June 1957.

27. *El Nicaragüense*, 20 September 1856, pp. 2–3. Reprinted in *Frank Leslie's Illustrated Newspaper*, 1 November 1856. Quoted from Fondo de Promoción Cultural 1976, 146–47.

28. *Telégrafo Setentrional* (Granada), 28 February 1857, p. 1; 7 March 1857, p. 8 (original article in English); 13 June 1857; *New York Times*, 16 October 1858, p. 2, and 23 November 1858, p. 4. Within the United States there was much opposition to Walker's escapades, especially in anti-slavery publications. See for example the anti-slavery *National Era*, 23 October 1856, p. 171; 30 October 1856, p. 174; 5 February 1857, p. 22; 9 April 1857, p. 59; 4 June 1857, p. 90; 24 December 1857, p. 205; 7 January 1858, p. 2.

29. For a discussion of resistance movements elsewhere in Latin America, see Burns 1980, 53–67, 86–131. The movements embraced intellectuals, *costumbrista* writers who drew materials and themes from folk culture, and more concrete efforts such as the six-decade "native alternative" in Paraguay—brutally terminated by the War of the Triple Alliance (1864–70).

30. Wheelock [1974] 1981, 98, mentions (but provides no details on) what he terms "luddite demonstrations" (*manifestaciones "luddistas"*) against landlords and sugar-processing machinery between 1845 and 1851. It is important to bear in mind that not all Indian uprisings were directed against the elite; Indians frequently fought against each other as well.

31. Gould 1989, 4–6, estimates that only approximately 20 percent of the western Nicaraguan population remained Indian in 1900.

32. Burns 1991, 110–20, has an excellent synopsis of these forms of resistance in nineteenth-century Nicaragua. Such expressions are nearly universal in traditional culture (cf. Levine's interpretation of black culture in North America [Levine 1977]).

33. *Semanal Nicaragüense*, 20 and 27 March, 3, 17, and 24 April 1873; Beinecke Library, Yale University. All subsequent references are to this source.

34. Scene 6; subsequent scenes indicated in parentheses in the text.

35. The word *hidalguía*, which Pancracio uses to characterize his own nobleness, resonates pointedly with the legitimizing rhetoric characteristically used by the *conquistadores* and first settlers (*primeros pobladores*) to jockey for social and cultural position following the conquest. This anonymous play articulates this cultural opposition fifteen years before the appearance of Darío's *Azul* (1888), more than a quarter-century before it was given its archetypal expression in José Enrique Rodó's *Ariel* (1900), and on the very eve of the birth of other major *modernista* writers and social critics to whom the theme eventually appealed. Only the precocious José Martí (1853–95) was addressing related themes, and his writings were only just beginning to appear.

36. Burns 1991 has an extended discussion of the development of the patriarchy in nineteenth-century Nicaragua (pp. 66–109).

37. The process of acculturation was of course not simple or linear, but rather complex and in some respects contradictory. It operated in different sectors of individual, social, and cultural life to different degrees, proceeded at different rates, and evoked different forms of resistance, syncretism, and capitulation.

38. Major musicians in León were composers Concepción Valladares (1837–1912) and Pablo Vega y Raudes (1850–1919), who Vega Miranda called "the greatest composer Nicaragua has had," and who organized the first school of music in the city; brass player Marcelo Soto (1866–1934); singer and vocal teacher Gregorio Vargas (1867–1917); composer and conductor Macario Carillo (1881–1937); instrumentalist Juan Noguera (1884–1919), and—the greatest of them—José de la Cruz Mena (1874–1907). In Granada and nearby Masaya were composer, teacher, and conductor J[uan?] del Carmen Vega (1845–1919), who formed

a celebrated string quartet and had his own school ("El Progreso"); violinist Alejandro Ramírez (1845–1911), who formed a "conjunto filarmónico" in the year of Zelaya's inauguration; violinist Dolores Gutiérrez Pérez (1850–1918), a student of Carmen Vega; violist and church musician Francisco Vega (1863–1936); and Alejandro Vega Matus (1875–1937), a prolific composer in a variety of popular and classical forms. Managua, not yet an important cultural center, boasted only Granada-born violinist, composer, and conductor Vicente Barberena (1850–1923) and composer of popular songs Luis Felipe Urroz (1857–1915), who came from one of Nicaragua's several musical families (the Vegas, Zúñigas, Zapatas, and Menas). Vega Miranda's article appears to have been written in the 1940s.

39. It is important to note that not all ejidal lands were held by indigenous groups. Many non-indigenous towns and cities had them.

40. Legislative decrees relating to ejidal lands and the status of indigenous communities appeared regularly from the mid-nineteenth century on into the 1930s. See *Nicaragua indígena* 1 (April 1947): 3–140.

41. Stansifer 1977, 477–79, argues that Zelaya granted concessions no more liberally than his predecessors, and monitored them carefully.

42. This factor was brought into focus for me by Salvatore 1991, which details "the mapping of South America into the North American imagination" through travel narratives written by reform-oriented Yankee merchants. Such narratives identified with the local ruling class. Pervaded with issues of gender, race, social discipline and social order, work habits, and the like, they generally avoided raising issues of working-class resentment, and thus transmitted "visions of order" congenial to the ruling class of their own countries.

43. There can be no doubt that Squier's views were sought out and respected. Just before going to Central America, he had published *Ancient Monuments of the Mississippi Valley* (1848), a pioneering work in archaeology and the first volume in the newly created Smithsonian Institution's scientific publications series. His speeches, articles, and books were widely distributed and often reprinted throughout the remainder of the nineteenth century—in the United States, Latin America, and Europe. His two-volume *Nicaragua: Its People, Scenery, Monuments and the Proposed Interoceanic Canal* (1851) was reprinted in London in 1852 and in New York in 1853 and 1856. A one-volume German translation appeared in Leipzig in 1854. There were one-volume editions in New York in 1860 and again in 1892. His *Notes on Central America* (New York: Harper, 1855) was published in England the following year, and an extract that appeared in *Bulletin de la Societé de géographie* was published separately in Paris the same year, as was the entire work (in Spanish). His *States of Central America* (New York: 1858) appeared in a briefer German edition in Leipzig in 1865 (reissued in 1874). His later work *Peru: Incidents of Travel and Exploration in the Land of the Incas* (a small portion of which had appeared in Paris as early as 1868) was published simultaneously in two New York (Harper and Bros.; Hurst and Holt) editions and in London in 1877. A German edition followed in 1883. As late as 1927, it was translated into Spanish and published in two (abbreviated) editions in Peru by Editorial Rozas. A Spanish translation of Squier's *Honduras: Descriptive, Historical and Statistical* (London: 1870) was published in Honduras in 1908 (Tegucigalpa: Tipografía Nacional). His article "The Spanish American Republics and the Reasons of Their Failure," published in the *American Whig Review* in late 1850, was translated into Spanish and appeared (in Spanish) in Paris in a small volume entitled *Compendio de la historia política de Centro-America* in 1856. In 1855, under the pseudonym Samuel A. Bard, Squier published the novel *Waikna, or Adventures on the Mosquito Shore* (New York: Harper), brought out the next year in London and in a Swedish translation nearly thirty years later (Landskrovna: J. L. Törnqvist,

1883). Squier was also a regular speaker before learned societies (geography, archaeology, ethnology, history) and a contributor to popular and scholarly journals.

44. Ms. Journal of Squier's travels in Central America, 1849–50; E. George Squier Papers, Manuscripts Division, Library of Congress.

45. Readers interested in further detail on this period may refer to Walter 1993, 10–65; Bermann 1986, 151–79; and Booth 1985, 27–35.

CHAPTER THREE

1. *El Diarito*, 17 April 1926, p. 1, 15 May 1926, p. 1.

2. For a brief moment, it had appeared that the quake's destruction of Managua would allow the ancient León-Granada antagonism to flare into open conflict again: both cities began raising armies to fight each other for the right to be proclaimed the capital once again. They were kept apart by the U.S. Marines (Pezzullo and Pezzullo 1993, 25).

3. Even before the earthquake, Managua had boasted a "Yankee style" orchestra as well as a panoply of U.S. consumer products. Detailed information on these entities is scarce. The 1940 edition of *Guía ilustrada de Nicaragua*, section 3, p. 16, presents a photograph of one of the temples of music: an octagonal stone or masonry pagoda constructed in a vaguely imperial idiom.

4. Words and music for almost all the pieces were by Nicaragua's most famous composer of the period, Luis A. Delgadillo. Delgadillo's version of "Los palomitas blancas" (used by Sandino's troops and later revived by the Sandinistas [for example on the phonograph record *Nicaragua Vencerá* produced by the Sandinista government's ENIGRAC in 1979]) omitted the usual derogatory reference to General Moncada, who signed the infamous Espino Negro agreement with the United States at Tipitapa in 1927.

5. Arellano 1982a, 77; *La Prensa*, 12 February 1957. *La Prensa*'s notice of the symphony's performance postdates Somoza García's death by a few months, but implies that the orchestra had been functioning for quite some time.

6. The following discussion is based upon Cháves [1970s?]; Fonseca 1944; and interviews with museum director Leonor Martínez de la Rocha, January-May 1988.

7. The few sources I have located which refer to Cháves's work indicate that he was involved in these activities, but I have encountered no corroborating data. His publications include *Apuntes de historia natural* (Managua: Tipografía Nacional, 1901) and *Lista preliminar de las plantas de Nicaragua* (Managua: Imprenta Nacional, 1931).

8. Cháves to Erwin P. Dieseldorff, 18 June and 19 September 1939; Dieseldorff Collection, Box 152, Folder 3; Manuscripts Section, Howard-Tilton Memorial Library, Tulane University. The 1940 edition of the *Guía ilustrada de Nicaragua*, section 12, p. 21, mentions a museum "rich in ceramics" in the Colegio de Señoritas in Managua, but offers no details. "Inventario del Museo Nacional de Nicaragua (diciembre 1972)," *Boletín Nicaragüense de Bibliografía y Documentación* 8 (November-December 1975): 19–22, appears to offer (in only four pages) a complete listing of the collection.

9. The formal U.S.-Nicaraguan treaty establishing the Guard was finally signed after long negotiations on 22 December 1928. Somoza assumed the presidency in 1936, after a rigged election in which the National Guard counted the votes. He retained the directorship of the National Guard following his election (Bermann 1986, 223; Millett 1977, 61, 70, 181–82; Walter 1987, 108).

10. Representative radio schedules in *La Prensa*, 19 January 1938, p. 4, and 29 April 1938, p. 6.

11. Emanuel Celler to Roosevelt, 16 November 1937, Official File 3093, Franklin D. Roosevelt Library. From the early 1930s through the opening of World War II, a series of regional and worldwide radio conferences were held to moderate the increasing tension over the allocation of shortwave and broadcast radio frequencies. Nicaragua participated in the 1933 North and Central American Regional Radio Conference in Mexico City. One of the most important conferences for the Americas was the 1937 Inter-American Radio Conference in Havana, which produced the Inter-American Radio Convention, signed in December. Nicaragua was a signatory (Secretary of State Cordell Hull to Roosevelt, 1 May 1934; Roosevelt to Congress, 3 August 1937; State Department memorandum to Roosevelt, 23 April 1938; all in Official File 2973, Franklin D. Roosevelt Library).

12. Unfortunately I have discovered no published record of the programming of these stations.

13. *El Diario Nicaragüense*, 24 November 1926, p. 1; State Department Decimal File 817.42/33 12 June 1933, National Archives and Records Service; *La Noticia*, 22 September 1934, p. 2, and 16 July 1937, p. 4; *Nicaragua. Guía general ilustrada*, sec. XIII, p. 7. Unfortunately, the schedules contain no further details on the pro-fascist broadcasts.

14. Radio Corporation of America, *Report to Stockholders*, 24 February 1934; Official File 1314, Franklin D. Roosevelt Library.

15. Unfortunately, neither Nordenstreng and Varis nor Wells singled out Nicaragua for study.

16. Additional data compiled from *Television Factbook* and *Television Digest*, 1961–79.

17. Also prominent (as throughout Latin America) were the *telenovelas*, produced mostly in Mexico and Brazil.

18. *La Prensa* had been bought in 1933 by Pedro Joaquín Chamorro Zelaya. His son took over the editorship two decades later and became an implacable enemy of the last of the Somoza line before being assassinated in January 1978 (Diederich 1981, 39, 154). Diederich notes (p. 71) that Anastasio Somoza Debayle (younger son of Somoza García) was less concerned about controlling newspapers than radio, because the majority of Nicaraguans were illiterate. Although I draw corroborative evidence from print media, I have chosen to focus on nonprint media instead. A systematic study of culture in the print media during the Somoza and Sandinista periods would require a book in itself. For an excellent analysis of direct political repression during the 1940s, see Walter 1993, 129–63.

19. Walter 1987, 293–96, observes that although government income quadrupled in the decade 1946–56, the percentage used for almost everything but the National Guard declined. Education remained at about 10 percent, but public works declined from 30 to 19 percent.

20. It is important to bear in mind that the evidence concerning censorship and repression is mixed, since the regime used them selectively. During the early 1940s, for example, *Nuevos Horizontes* published some of Cuadra's work and sponsored a daily radio program that broadcast Pablo Neruda's "Nuevo canto de amor a Stalingrad" (*Nuevos Horizontes* 1 [August 1943]: 12, 20).

21. As Holbek 1981 argues, such an opportunistic political-cultural agenda was common among late nineteenth-century European elites who preferred to romanticize and mobilize aspects of picturesque rural culture for nationalistic purposes, rather than to deal with the complexities of working-class culture, likely to be antagonistic to their political project.

22. *Nicaragua indígena* 1 (July-September 1946): 46.

23. Ibid., 1 (January-March 1947): 2.

24. Ibid., 1, no. 1 (December 1941): 4–6; 1, no. 3 (January 1947); Segunda época, nos. 11–12 (1956) and nos. 13–14 (1957): 3. The journal was erratically numbered and dated; I have reproduced publication data as given. My characterization of the institute here is based upon an almost complete run of the journal for the years 1941–62 in the Hemeroteca Nacional in Managua. Editorials in *Nicaragua indígena* 18 (January 1958): 3–4, and 23 (November 1958): 3–4, proposed a museum of indigenous culture (Museo Indigenista de Nicaragua), but it was apparently never built.

25. Walter (1987, 158; 1993, 184–86) notes that government jobs actually began to expand early during the regime's history: from 5,321 in 1936–37 to 9,500 in 1944–45 to nearly 16,000 in 1955–56. Because all government employees were required to contribute 5 percent of their salaries to the PLN (*Partido Liberal Nacionalista*, controlled by Somoza) and to support the regime, the party's income doubled within a few years in the late 1940s (p. 347).

26. *La Prensa*, 12 May 1955.

27. Williams 1986 documents essentially the same story for export beef production during this period.

28. Cf. *La Prensa*, 8 and 22 July, 5 and 12 August, 2 September 1956; 10 November and 15 December 1957; 2 and 16 February, 29 June, 26 October, 1958 (all section 2, p. 1).

29. *El Diario Nicaragüense*, 1927–29; ibid., 10, 20, 27 January, 11 February, 19 March 1931; *El Centroamericano*, July-August 1937; *La Prensa*, 7 March 1935. Since files of newspapers from this period available to me are somewhat spotty, I have had to draw upon some from outside Managua. Comparisons with available Managua newspapers suggest, however, that differences were not substantial in this respect. In *Three Gringos in Venezuela and Central America*, 187, Richard Harding Davis reported the presence of two American phonograph salesmen in Corinto in the mid-1890s.

30. A confidential memorandum for the Chairman of the [U.S.] Maritime Commission (ca. 1936) details the means Pan American employed to gain an exclusive concession for air passenger service from the U.S. to Latin America: intense lobbying of Congress, the masking of accident rates, highly profitable subsidies on a monopoly contract for airmail service, and an adroit public relations campaign managed by the Madison Avenue firm of Batten, Barton, Durstine & Osborn (Official File 2875, Franklin D. Roosevelt Library).

31. Black 1981, 62–68; *La Prensa*, 13 March and 4 May 1948.

32. *Los Domingos*, 31 December 1922, p. 20; 25 February 1923, p. 20; 10 April 1920, p. 20; 22 May 1920, p. 20.

33. Advertisements in Managua's *El Diarito*, 16 April 1926, p. 2, indicate that all three (Teatro Margot, Cine el Otro, and the Capitol) were showing U.S. films.

34. *La Prensa*, 3 March 1935; 19 March 1935. The situation was by no means unique to Nicaragua; it was endemic in Latin America (cf. Dorfman and Mattelart [1971] 1984, 12, 114).

35. Robinson to Roosevelt's secretary Louis Howe, 24 June 1933; Official File 73, Franklin D. Roosevelt Library.

36. H. Bartlett Wells, "Nicaraguan Measures to Facilitate Introduction of Motion Pictures," 20 December 1938; Record Group 59, 817.4061 Motion Pictures/7, National Archives and Records Service.

37. *La Prensa*, 13 April 1940, p. 4; 2 November 1941, p. 6. Three films were from Mexico, two were from Argentina, and one was Cuban.

38. The convergence of state policy and the dissemination of ideology through popular culture is particularly evident here. In connection with his state visit to the United States in 1939, Somoza importuned President Roosevelt repeatedly for assistance with reopening the National Guard training academy, which he wanted a U.S. military officer to head. Roosevelt agreed to provide the assistance, naming West Point graduate Major Charles L. Mullins Jr. as the academy's commandant. By the spring of 1941, the U.S. had indeed constructed a "Little West Point" for Somoza's National Guard (Somoza to Roosevelt, 22 May 1939; President's Secretary's File, Box 45; 1 April 1941 memo to Roosevelt, Official File 432; Franklin D. Roosevelt Library).

39. *La Prensa*, 27 December 1933, p. 1; 9 February 1934, p. 4; 17 January 1935, p. 6; 27 January 1940, p. 4; 13 April 1940, p. 4; 29 August 1941, p. 4; 2 November 1941, p. 6; 11 September 1949, p. 2. Foreign Service of the United States to Department of State, 30 September 1950; Confidential U.S. State Department Central Files: Nicaragua, 1950–54: Internal Affairs, Reel 9. A Nicaraguan government report enclosed with the memo listed a total of fifty-seven theaters in fifteen towns and cities in Nicaragua. Tunstall 1977, 142, cites 1948 UNESCO figures that included Nicaragua among the countries in which U.S. films claimed 70 percent or more of the market.

40. *Annual Report of Prencinradio, Inc.*, 30 June 1943; Official File 4512, Franklin D. Roosevelt Library (Rockefeller letters appear as appendices to the report).

41. Foreign Service to Department of State, 30 December 1950; Confidential U.S. State Department Central Files: Nicaragua, 1950–54: Internal Affairs, Reel 9. Subsequent quotations from this document.

42. *Commonweal* 51 (14 October 1949): 15; *Newsweek* 34 (10 October 1949): 89–90.

43. Foreign Service to Department of State, 28 April 1950; Confidential U.S. State Department Central Files: Nicaragua, 1950–54: Internal Affairs, Reel 9. Subsequent quotations from this source.

44. *La Prensa*, early 1935 through mid-1950s.

45. I make no claim about U.S. "domination" of the media in Nicaragua, but rather hope to convey some sense of the ubiquity of U.S. cultural forms in the media, and of the highly politicized content of those forms. Buckman 1990, 193, argues that of some seven thousand cultural articles in two dozen or so "elite" Latin American newspapers and magazines from the years 1949 and 1982 (none of them from Nicaragua, unfortunately), only 10–20 percent originated in the United States. In taking U.S. *origin* as the sole indicator of potential influence, however—hence omitting articles on "local" cultural events patterned on U.S. models (beauty pageants, baseball, Kiwanis or Lion's Club meetings, and the like) and others that although locally written, reflected U.S. cultural values or assumptions—Buckman substantially underestimates the problem.

46. While Disney was in Latin America, his animators—key members of what Mosley has called "the most brilliant and the most overworked and underpaid [staff] in Hollywood"—won their strike (Mosley 1985, 188, 195–97; Eliot 1993, 150).

47. Burton in Parker et al. 1992 presents a detailed analysis of the cultural politics of *The Three Caballeros* in the context both of the Office of the Coordinator of Inter-American Affairs and of Disney's own personal politics and cultural views (pp. 21–41). Burton focuses on "ten perverse propositions of desire" that are the organizing subtexts of the film: Latin America as a war-time Toontown, the packaging of Latin America as pure spectacle, narratives of colonial conquest, hierarchies of willing-and-waiting-to-be-conquered subjects, the reassuring politics of Donald Duck's sexual inadequacy and his ambiguous sexual identity, the sexual dominance promised to Latin American men as a reward for

submission to colonial power, the ostensible humaneness of the conquerors, the illusory reciprocities of the exchange, and the hidden agendas of "intercultural understanding."

48. As with most areas of ideology and policy, Somoza attempted to play both ends against the middle with regard to labor and the left. As Gould has pointed out, by intervening periodically on the behalf of striking workers, Somoza portrayed himself as a defender of the working class and strove to unify the labor movement in order to use it against his Conservative opponents. The *obrerista* leadership consequently supported him until the early 1940s. Somoza approved the progressive Labor Code of April 1945, and actually permitted the founding of the Socialist-dominated Confederación de Trabajadores Nicaragüenses (CTN) in early 1946. From its own perspective, the left responded favorably, Gould argues, because the labor movement was "young and potentially expansive . . . [but] weakened by internal division, constantly harassed by management, and seriously threatened by the possibility of a right-wing takeover." Ultimately, however, Somocista unionism was "an integral component of Somoza's strategy to foment labor-capital harmony, politically debilitate the landed oligarchy, and establish *somocista* hegemony over the Nicaraguan bourgeoisie." At length Somoza turned to avid anti-Communist rhetoric, however, in order to curry favor with the United States, and began to "portray the Left as a foreign-dominated version of what the national labor movement could do more efficiently and authentically under the guidance of the *jefe obrero*." Emerging labor-student opposition forced Somoza to cancel his candidacy for the presidency twice in the late 1940s, and Somoza jailed most leaders of the labor movement in January 1948 (Gould in Bethell and Roxborough 1992, 243–48, 261, 274).

49. President's Secretary's File, Box 45; Franklin D. Roosevelt Library.

50. That the display had in fact served also as a dress rehearsal for the much more important upcoming visit of the king and queen of England did not diminish its importance to Somoza (Diederich 1981, 21). For a revisionist perspective on the oft-repeated assertion that the Roosevelt administration was cynically cozy with the Somoza regime, see Clark 1992, 39–82.

51. Somoza to Roosevelt, 24 December 1942, Official File 432, Franklin D. Roosevelt Library; Bermann 1986, 228; Black 1981, 70–72; Walter 1987, 169.

52. Somoza to Franklin Roosevelt, 17 July 1940; President's Personal File 5913, Franklin D. Roosevelt Library.

53. Unsigned memo, 30 January 1942; telegram from Somoza to Roosevelt, 17 September 1942; Somoza to Roosevelt, 24 December 1942; State Department to Roosevelt, 31 May and 28 August 1943; Official File 432, Franklin D. Roosevelt Library.

54. G. W. Johnstone to Major General E. M. Watson of Roosevelt's staff, 5 May 1941; Official File 813b, Franklin D. Roosevelt Library.

55. Roosevelt's secretary M. H. McIntyre to Director of the Budget, 31 July 1941; Official File 4512, Franklin D. Roosevelt Library; Scott 1959, 200. Apparently none of the structure or duties of the office were changed; the renaming occurred to mark the moving of the office to the Office of Emergency Management. Rockefeller continued to head the Office until 19 December 1944. In early 1945, the office was again renamed as the Office of Inter-American Affairs, headed by Wallace K. Harrison, who had been one of Rockefeller's deputies (Executive Order of 23 March 1945; Official File 4512, Franklin D. Roosevelt Library).

56. Scott 1959, 309–20, notes that some musical programs coordinated by the Library of Congress and the Pan American Union featured a better balance of U.S. and Latin American classical, popular, and traditional music.

57. Executive Order of 16 August 1940, Official File 813b, Franklin D. Roosevelt Library.

58. Roosevelt to Attorney General, 3 February 1941; Official File 813b, Franklin D. Roosevelt Library.

59. William P. Cochran Jr. to Secretary of State, March 12 and 27 May 1942; Record Group 59, Box 3698, 811.42717/17, National Archives and Records Service. Total annual appropriations for all such institutes between the end of World War II and the Korean war averaged only a half million dollars (Scott 1959, 324–28). A 30 June 1943 cash statement for the various institutes of inter-American affairs sponsored by the U.S. government showed only $99,000 in the cash account for Nicaragua, out of a $9 million overall budget, over 80 percent of which was allocated to the main office in Washington (Official File 4512, Franklin D. Roosevelt Library).

60. Stewart to the Secretary of State, 21 September 1942. Record Group 59, Box 3698, 811.42717/28, National Archives and Record Service (NARS). Nicaragua's institute was a bit late coming. By 1939 ten institutes (all named the North American Cultural Institute of [name of country]) had been set up, and the funds for some of them were being funneled from "private" support committees through New York banks (Scott 1959, 324–43).

61. "Discurso de Rodolfo Rivera," attached to letter of James B. Stewart cited above.

62. Report on North American Cultural Institute of Nicaragua, April 6, 1943; Record Group 59, Box 3698, 811.42717/37, National Archives and Records Service. Clipping from *El Centroamericano*, 26 January 1943, included in this file.

63. "Report on Cultural Relations Program in Nicaragua During 1942," Record Group 59, Box 3698, 811.42717/35, National Archives and Records Service. Unfortunately the report does not always distinguish adequately between the work of the institute itself and other "cultural relations" activities of the embassy.

64. The embassy appears not to have tried to determine what people's motives were for bringing their art work. Any of the most probable ones (a wish to communicate valued aspects of their culture to people in the United States, a hope for monetary gain or fame, a need for cultural validation) would have repaid careful exploration.

65. Mendieta had only recently become rector of the university, a post in which it turned out he served only one year (*New York Times*, 2 September 1941, p. 15, and 12 September 1942, p. 3; Mory 1971, 29).

66. Quarterly Report of the North American Cultural Institute of Nicaragua, 20 September 1943; Record Group 59, Box 3698, 811.42717/48, National Archives and Records Service.

67. Lowry and Hooker, "Role of the Arts and Humanities," in American Assembly 1968, 50–59.

68. *La Flecha*, 16, 18, 20 September and 23 October 1947, p. 1.

69. Memorandum to the President, 1 May 1952, quoted in Leiken and Rubin 1987, 97; *La Prensa*, 20 February 1955, p. 1. Paradoxically, former U.S. Ambassador to Brazil Adolf Berle reported to President Eisenhower after a 1953 trip to Managua that "nobody in the American Embassy speaks Spanish; they rely on their Nicaraguan clerks" (Berle and Jacobs 1973, 615).

70. *Presupuesto General de Egresos e Ingresos de la República, 1950–51*, pp. ix, 127ff. U.S. dollar figures assume an exchange rate of approximately 7:1. The few available government statistics on library use during the 1950s and 1960s are so erratic as to be questionable. The *Boletín de Estadística* III época, no. 11 (October 1966): 119, reports 263,000 readers in 1951, half as many the following year, an average of around 65,000 for the 1955–59 period, and around 90,000–100,000 during the early 1960s. No libraries were named in the report.

71. For the first time in 1966, the official *Boletín de Estadística* (III época, no. 11 [October 1966]: 125–26) reported on museum visitors during the past two decades. The figures (which I suspect are not trustworthy) showed a rise in attendance from 20,000–25,000 in the late 1940s to double that number in the mid-1950s and 75,000 in the early 1960s (the overwhelming majority in Managua).

72. *Presupuesto General de Ingresos y Egresos de la República* (1968), pp. 151–52, 345–571. All dollar amounts assume an exchange rate of 7:1.

73. *Presupuesto General de Ingresos y Egresos de la República por Programas 1969*, pp. 47, 162–63, 446–47. By 1975, with the regime under growing pressure from the *Frente Sandinista de Liberación Nacional* (FSLN), the allocation for all cultural programs had dropped to 0.12 percent of the budget. *Presupuesto General de Ingresos y Egresos de la República por Programas 1975*, pp. 39, 103, 477–78.

74. The cultural contradictions that followed the quake cut both ways. Former U.S. Ambassador Lawrence Pezzullo reported (Pezzullo and Pezzullo 1993, 55) that when many homeless embassy staff members were forced to camp out on the grounds of the embassy, the wife of then-Ambassador Turner Shelton refused to let them use the bathrooms in the embassy and showed far more concern for her rose beds than for the staff's comfort or safety.

75. *El Pez y la Serpiente*, no. 13 (Summer 1974), pp. 33–61.

76. Ibid., no. 1 (January 1961), pp. 6–7.

77. Ibid., nos. 1–13 (1961–74).

78. *La Prensa Literaria*, April 1976–August 1978. During the first years of the Chamorro family's ownership (1933–49), *La Prensa* published little serious coverage of cultural matters.

79. Arellano 1971 criticized the Bank of America publications program as a product of *un afán snobista e infructuoso* (a snobbish and fruitless anxiety) that was of little cultural benefit to the country since the collection of books the bank was acquiring was not available to the public, all but a few copies of its publications were given to its biggest depositors, and the money spent publishing such esoteric volumes could have been better spent publishing books of interest to a wider readership. Whether his criticism led (or was related) to his own later work with the Banco Central series I do not know. Banco Central published Arellano's *Pintura y escultura en Nicaragua* in 1978.

80. *New York Times*, 4 February 1973.

81. Interview with Luis Mejía Godoy (brother of Carlos), 11 March 1988. I return to the *nueva canción* movement and its Nicaraguan analogue *volcanto* in a subsequent chapter.

82. Booth 1985, 83, notes that the middle sector expanded by about one-third between 1960 and 1975 (from 11 percent to 15 percent) as the growth of commerce and industry boosted managerial, clerical, and sales jobs, and as employment continued to rise in the public sector.

83. *Taller*, no. 10 (October 1975): 63–64; my translation.

84. *La Prensa*, 1, 8, 10 July 1979.

CHAPTER FOUR

1. Two important additional generative centers were the Nicaraguan women's movement (early forms of which dated from long before the advent of the Somoza regime itself), and General Augusto C. Sandino's guerrilla war of 1927–33. Both are reserved for

separate discussion in subsequent chapters. Another important sector, much related to the other forms of cultural opposition I discuss here, was the post–Vatican II politicized wing of the Catholic church. Since extended discussions are easily available in Randall 1983a, Lancaster 1988, 84–99, Foroohar 1989, 67–158, Dodson and O'Shaughnessy 1990, 71–235, and Kirk 1992, 58–99, I omit it here, except as particular aspects of it illuminate the sectors upon which I focus.

2. Nicaragua's *vanguardia* movement was similar in many respects to larger contemporary movements among Latin American intellectuals and artists. From the 1920s on, as Jean Franco has pointed out, a number of Latin American writers turned away from the elitist subjects, forms, and themes that had been prominent since the mid-nineteenth century, and toward others related to indigenous cultural identity and survival, the loss of religious belief, the social and other implications of the industrial revolution, and the necessity for progressive political change. Many such writers also tried both to reflect the experience of working people, and to write in a way that would be attractive and accessible to them. Especially prominent were Peruvian César Vallejo (1892–1938), Chilean poet Pablo Neruda (1904–73), and Cuban Nicolás Guillén (b. 1904). All focused much of their work on both the problems of the masses and the necessity to communicate with them. Guillén drew materials from popular sources (as in his *Gypsy Ballad Book* of 1928) and sometimes tried to "give the masses a voice" by writing in a stylized lower-class dialect. Vallejo wrote a series of poems on the Spanish Civil War. The best known of the three, Pablo Neruda, sought to reflect mass experience and to speak to an illiterate or semi-literate audience. Novels of class struggle also began to appear in the 1930s and 1940s, as they did at the same time in the United States: Ecuadoran Enrique Gil Gilbert's novel about rice workers (*Nuestro pan*, 1942), Juan María's about Chilean miners (*Viento negro*, 1944), and other novels focused on the nightmarish world of the Latin American dictatorship. The masterpiece of the genre was Miguel Angel Asturias's *El señor presidente* of 1946 (Franco 1967, 147–72).

3. By highlighting these ideological strains, I do not mean to impute unanimity to the *vanguardistas*. As I will later emphasize, members of the group took quite different positions on these issues.

4. Besides Coronel Urtecho and Cabrales, the early *vanguardistas* were writers Pablo Antonio Cuadra, Joaquín Pasos, Luis Downing, Manolo Cuadra, José Román, Alberto Ordóñez Argüello, Octavio Rocha, and the caricaturist Joaquín Zavala Urtecho. It is difficult to establish a definitive roster for the somewhat loosely constituted group. This one is a composite from several sources (cf. Beverley and Zimmerman 1990, 60; Arellano 1982a, 57, lists only five members). Arellano 1969, 67, notes that except for two or three, all members of the movement "belonged to the intellectual and social elite . . . of Granada."

5. Cuadra 1938, 122, says this phrase came from Ernesto Psichari (1883–1914), a French writer who rejected the skepticism of his liberal intellectual family in favor of a life of disciplined action and made a long pilgrimage to Catholicism before being killed in combat in World War I.

6. Commentators do not agree on the founding date for the *Vanguardia* group. Cardenal says it was founded in 1930; Arellano says it was "fully constituted" by April 1931.

7. See for example Joaquín Pasos's poems in celebration of Indian life (Pasos 1986, 106–22), Pablo Antonio Cuadra's "Lamento Nahuatl" (White 1982b, 126), and José Coronel Urtecho's "Discurso sobre Azorín para ser traducido en lengua Nahual" (Discourse on Azorín to be translated into Nahuatl) (Cardenal 1986b, 77–80).

8. See for example Pablo Antonio Cuadra's "Por los caminos van los campesinos" (Coronel Urtecho et al. 1979, 129).

9. Following his editorship of the relatively short-lived *La Reacción* (1934-35), Cuadra joined Joaquín Pasos and Manolo Cuadra for a time on *Los Lunes de la Nueva Prensa* (as director) before going on to edit the influential *Cuadernos del Taller San Lucas* (Notebooks of the San Lucas Workshop) (1942-45). Later he became editor of *La Prensa Literaria*, producing a series of columns that were later collected into the best-selling *El Nicaragüense* (1967). As editor he responded ambivalently to Nicaragua's young radical anti-Somoza writers of the 1960s and 1970s—a dynamic to which I return below.

10. Tünnermann Bernheim 1973 cites these as preeminent concerns in *Poemas nicaragüenses*. Certainly they are present, but do not seem to me as prominent as Tünnermann suggests.

11. Williams 1977, 121-26, speaks of the emergent as "new meanings and values, new practices, new relationships and kinds of relationships . . . substantially alternative or oppositional" to the dominant culture, and that are in dialectical tension with "the residue—cultural as well as social—of some previous social and cultural institution or formation . . . effectively formed in the past, but . . . still active in the cultural process."

12. Arellano 1969, 70, argues that the *indigenismo* of the *vanguardia* amounted to little more than a superficial aestheticism. The *pueblo* of the *vanguardia*, he asserts, "was neither a marginalized and economically exploited *campesina* class nor the worker[s] who [were] beginning to exist as a social reality . . . but rather a more or less literary abstraction."

13. José Coronel Urtecho in *La Reacción*: "La democracia, guerra intelectual," 6 April 1934, p. 2; "Autoridad y democracia," 11 April 1934, p. 2; and "Autoridad libre y corporaciones libres," 21 April 1934, p. 2. The 24 April 1934 issue contained an article by Benito Mussolini about "The Yellow Peril."

14. As late as 1939, the U.S. embassy in Managua was concerned about the fascist tendencies of the *vanguardistas* and of *La Prensa*, although not solely for ethical or humanitarian reasons. In a 12 May 1939 dispatch to the State Department, the Ambassador complained of *La Prensa*'s "casual digs" at the United States, its printing of "a list of the American state laws against miscegenation" ("may have been from a German source," the dispatch noted), and its tendency to encourage "writings of a Fascist tendency, particularly when they oppose the expansion of American capital" (Meredith Nicholson to Department of State, Confidential U.S. Diplomatic Post Records: Central America, Nicaragua, 1930-45, Reel 19).

15. *La Flecha*, 22 August 1955, p. 1; reprinted Cuadra 1982, 143-45. Cuadra died of cancer in 1957. The entire July-August 1981 issue of *Boletín nicaragüense de bibliografía y documentación* (no. 42) was devoted to him.

16. By the early 1950s Cuadra's politics had shifted enough to allow him to accept the editorship of anti-Somoza *La Prensa*'s literary supplement.

17. Gutiérrez 1983, 92-93. In this volume, the poem is dated 1960, but it was first published clandestinely—whether before 1960, I do not know. When I interviewed him (2 March 1988) shortly before his death, Gutiérrez spoke of having participated in a student strike in Granada in the 1940s.

18. My discussion of Cardenal's development draws substantially upon Arellano 1979, Borgeson 1977, and Beverley and Zimmerman 1990, 66-72.

19. Cardenal's poetry from the Gethsemane years was published as *Gethsemani, Ky.* (1960).

20. From *El corno emplumado*, no. 19 (July 1966): 179–80; quoted in Borgeson 1977, 206.

21. Cardenal's reflections on Cuban life—especially its cultural aspects—were published as *En Cuba* (In Cuba) in 1972; *Poesía nicaragüense* (published in Buenos Aires and not available in a Nicaraguan edition until 1981) included poems by both older and younger anti-Somoza poets. In the mid-1960s, Cardenal also put his cultural politics into practice by establishing a small experimental community on Mancarrón island in the Solentiname archipelago—an effort to which I return presently. On *Oráculo sobre Managua*, see Beverley and Zimmerman 1990, 76–77, 83–84.

22. Most sources give 1957 as the date of autonomy, but Ramírez 1971, 104, says it did not occur until March 1958.

23. The Somoza regime's response may be found in Somoza García 1936, 261–62.

24. My discussion of Fiallos draws mainly upon Ramírez 1971.

25. Ramírez 1971, 67, says that Fiallos went so far as to ask President Arévalo for help in staging an invasion of Nicaragua.

26. For a broader historical discussion of resistance to the Somoza regime, see Booth 1985, 97–156; Ramírez in Ministerio de Cultura 1982a, 159–66; and White 1986, 78–81.

27. Poems by Roberto Cuadra, Yllescas, Uriarte, and Morales may be found in Cardenal 1986b, 431–59, 485–91, and 507–15. Beverley and Zimmerman 1990, 74, point out that the political positions of the *Generación Traicionada* writers later underwent considerable evolution, with Roberto Cuadra moving further to the right and Morales and Uriarte to the left.

28. *Ventana* no. 8 (n.d. [early 1961]), 2.

29. "El humanismo en Fernando Gordillo," *Ventana: Barricada Cultural*, 25 July 1987, p. 13.

30. *Ventana* no. 1 (June 1960): 1–12. The first issue also contained poems by Fernando Gordillo and Peruvian combatant César Vallejo, a story by Sergio Ramírez, and a brief essay on the problems of the university. *Ventana: Barricada Cultural*, the cultural supplement to the Sandinista party newspaper *Barricada*, preserved the name and spirit of the *Ventana* group's efforts in the 1960s. Ramírez quotation is from *Ventana: Barricada Cultural*, 30 January 1982, p. 3.

31. *Ventana* no. 2 (July 1960): 1, 10–14.

32. Ibid., no. 5 (October 1960): 2.

33. Ibid., no. 9 (n.d. [ca. August 1961]), 8–11; no. 10 (n.d. [ca. October 1961]), 1.

34. Ibid., no. 8 (n.d. [early 1961]), 2.

35. Ibid., no. 10 (n.d. [ca. October 1961]), 6.

36. Unión Nacional de Artistas Plásticos (UNAP) and Asociación Sandinista de Trabajadores de Cultura (ASTC) [1984?], 7–10; *Praxis*, August 1971 and May 1972. The *Praxis* group continued to function until dispersed by the earthquake of 1972.

37. Interview with Ernesto Gutiérrez, Managua, 2 March 1988.

38. *Taller*, no. 1 (November 1968), library of Jorge Eduardo Arellano, Managua; interview with Ernesto Gutiérrez, 2 March 1988, Managua. I am grateful to Señor Arellano for allowing me access to his library.

39. *Taller*, no. 10 (October 1975): 7.

40. Ibid., no. 11 (May 1976).

41. The following resume of literary expressions of opposition draws substantially from Beverley and Zimmerman 1990, 74–92, 180–89. The availability of Beverley and Zimmerman's excellent discussion of anti-Somoza writing in this period obviates the necessity of treating it at length here.

42. A thousand copies of the slim volume (seventy-eight pages) were printed at the Universidad de San Carlos in Guatemala. Randall 1984, 109–17, presents Najlis's brief reflections on her development as a poet and Sandinista militant.

43. "Te veo como un temblor," reprinted in Belli 1984, 52–53; my translation.

44. So prolific were those Nicaraguan writers committed to the revolutionary project that by the time Francisco de Asís Fernández put together a large anthology of Nicaraguan political poetry in 1979 (Asís Fernández [1979] 1986), approximately half the selections were by poets born after Anastasio Somoza García came to power in 1936.

45. Interview with Pablo Buitrago, Director, National School of Music, 10 March 1988. Delgadillo quotation from *La Prensa*, 18 May 1958, p. B-1.

46. López 1982; Pring-Mill 1987; interview with Vilma de la Rocha and Luis Enrique Mejía Godoy, Managua, 11 March 1988.

47. *Gaceta Sandinista* 2, no. 5 (May-June 1977): 9.

48. "El sonido de la lucha: Talleres de sonido popular," *Ventana: Barricada Cultural*, 4 July 1981, p. 16. *Taller* musicians reconvened after the triumph in 1979 and integrated themselves into the Centers for Popular Culture under the Ministry of Culture. The rebirth was complicated by heavy performance demands in the difficult days immediately following the triumph. As of mid-1981, the *Talleres* included the groups Igni Tawanka, Libertad, Grupo Pueblo, Grupo Trova (named for *nueva trova*, the Cuban version of *nueva canción*), Atahualpa, Ocho de Noviembre, and a number of solo performers.

49. Luis Enrique Mejía Godoy interview, 11 March 1988, Managua.

50. For taped copies of several now-rare records, as well as for copies of jackets, notes, and song texts, I am grateful to Cecilia Montenegro Teague.

51. Another militant album was Luis Mejía Godoy's *Amando en tiempo de guerra* (Love in Time of War), which celebrated women's participation in the insurrection. I return to it in my final chapter.

52. The paradigms that had been developed in the process were to reemerge, however, in the Sandinista government's ENIGRAC (Empresa Nicaragüense de Grabaciones Culturales; Nicaraguan Cultural Recording Company) after July 1979. I return to ENIGRAC in a subsequent chapter.

53. *Guitarra armada*, produced by Indica in Costa Rica (MC-1147), was reissued in 1980 by ENIGRAC (MC-015) (Pring-Mill 1987, 188n.).

54. Miranda de Peña 1979, 192ff.; Gould 1990b, 99. Lejarza 1943, 6–7, reported similar evidence. Adams 1957, 244, noted that residents of Masaya thought of Monimbó residents as "Indians" and hence as inferior to themselves. The term *jincho* was still current when I was in Nicaragua in 1988.

55. As noted earlier, I use the term *indigenous* loosely. The relevant consideration here is that although the percentage of culturally unmixed indigenous people in Nicaragua was small, the percentage of the population *characterized* (and stigmatized) by their social superiors as *indios* was much larger. I explore the Atlantic-Pacific coast aspect of the dialectic in a subsequent chapter on opposition to Sandinista cultural policy.

56. Adams 1957, 153–250. Adams appears to have been in Nicaragua for only about three weeks and to have gotten some of his information from informants of questionable reliability. Nevertheless, his study remains virtually the only one available from the period.

57. Incer 1977, 67, echoes Adams's judgment that virtually no distinctive cultural features differentiated the approximately six thousand Subtiavans from their neighbors in León.

58. Such themes have been prominent in recent Latin American testimonial literature

(Beverley and Zimmerman 1990, 172–211). Outstanding examples are Domitila Barrios de Chungara's *Si me permiten hablar* (1977) and Rigoberta Menchú's *Me llamo Rigoberta Menchú* (1984). I have analyzed the function of traditional culture in relation to political resistance in the latter in Whisnant 1989. Both Levine 1977 and Scott 1985 explore these oppositional practices among other cultural groups in other periods.

59. This brief account is drawn primarily from an extensive chronology in Instituto de Estudio del Sandinismo 1982a, 239–70. The uprisings in Masaya and Monimbó were front-page news in *La Prensa* for more than a year (see for example 6–8 and 20–28 February, 2 March, 22 April, 30 July, 8–12 September, 1978, and 27 February 1979).

60. On the artisans of Monimbó see for example *Ventana: Barricada Cultural*, 26 September 1981, p. 10.

61. Paradoxically, one of the aspects of their culture most beloved by the citizens of Monimbó, the *marimba* and its eminently danceable music, apparently did not become part of the culture of resistance. The marimba players (*marimberos*) fell quiet after the insurrection of February 1978. The most skillful of them, Elías Palacios, was working in a shoe shop, waiting for better days (Miranda de Peña 1979, 127).

62. English has no satisfactory equivalent for *concientización*, which suggests both coming to and transformation of political-social-cultural consciousness.

63. Translations of some of the political-theological discussions were published in Cardenal 1976.

64. Jiménez's work with poetry on Solentiname continued until repression by the National Guard against the community forced her to leave in early 1977. The workshops operated in Costa Rica until the Sandinista victory of July 1979, immediately after which Cardenal urged Jiménez to return to Nicaragua to establish them on a broader basis.

65. Some accounts of the destruction claim that Cardenal had managed to build a substantial library, museum, and collection of pre-Columbian artifacts on Solentiname, and that all were destroyed by the National Guard raid. In an interview on 2 March 1988, historian Jorge Arellano asserted that there never was a museum or library of any consequence on the island, and that Cardenal — warned in advance — had taken his own books and personal possessions to Costa Rica four months before the National Guard raid. Cardenal's own recollections in White 1986, 72, seem to confirm this interpretation.

CHAPTER FIVE

1. For a detailed and graphic account of the final destructive days of the Somoza regime, see Pezzullo and Pezzullo 1993.

2. Peña Hernández' *Folklore de Nicaragua* (1968) for example, was quite unsystematic and amateurish, as was Pérez Estrada's *Estudios del folklore nicaragüense* of approximately the same period. Even Pablo Antonio Cuadra's influential and frequently cited *El Nicaragüense*, already in its eighth edition by 1978, was rather insubstantial and romantic, as was his *Muestrario del folklore nicaragüense*. Pérez Estrada's earlier *Teatro folklórico nicaragüense* (1946) was more substantial. The work of Jorge Eduardo Arellano, the most prolific historian still resident in the country, was uneven at best (cf. Arellano 1969, 1977a, 1977b, 1977c, 1978, [1980?], 1982). More sophisticated analytically — and more pertinent to the conceptualization and formation of cultural policy — were Jaime Wheelock Román's studies of the indigenous roots of anti-colonial struggle and of the relationship between the dictatorship and imperialism (Wheelock Román 1974 and 1975). A fortunate excep-

tion to the general paucity of materials and the superficiality of those that existed was the case of the Atlantic Coast, of which there were several substantial studies (Helms 1971; Nietschmann 1973).

3. Incer's thorough and scholarly *Toponimias indígenas de Nicaragua* did not appear until 1985, and his *Nicaragua: viajes, rutas y encuentros, 1502–1838* not until five years later. Carl Hermann Berendt's *Palabras y modismos de la lengua castellana según se habla en Nicaragua*, the first sophisticated analysis of Nicaraguan language, had appeared in 1873.

4. Of the approximately sixty doctoral dissertations on Nicaragua published through 1979 (beginning with a thirteen-page dissertation from Columbia University in 1890), only six dealt with culture, and three of those focused exclusively on the Pacific coast: Lothrop, "The Ceramics of Northern Costa Rica and Western Nicaragua" (Harvard, 1921), Healy, "Archaeological Survey of the Rivas Region, Nicaragua" (Harvard, 1975), and Radell, "An Historical Geography of Western Nicaragua: The Spheres of Influence of León, Granada, and Managua" (Berkeley, 1969). Two great exceptions to the rule were of course the extensive scholarly and interpretative literatures on Rubén Darío and Augusto César Sandino (to some of which I return in subsequent chapters).

5. From versions published in 1981 and 1984 by the FSLN's Department of Propaganda and Political Education and translation by Reissner in Marcus 1982, 16–17.

6. *Serie Biografías Populares*; numbers in parentheses refer to pamphlets in the series.

7. Stone 1990, 40; Randall 1983a, 129, 140–41; Randall 1981, 8, 118; Randall 1984, 41–49, 155; Belli in *Ventana: Barricada Cultural*, 2 July 1983, pp. 11–12.

8. Randall 1981, 41–43, 96–98, 105, 118; Belli interview with Margaret Randall, *Ventana: Barricada Cultural*, 2 July 1983, pp. 11–12.

9. Interview with Margaret Randall, *Ventana: Barricada Cultural*, 2 July 1983, pp. 11–12.

10. *Proyecto de desarrollo educativo y cultural de Nicaragua* (Paris: UNESCO, 1983), pp. 71–72. A somewhat less ideologically oriented statement appears in Ministerio de Cultura 1982a, 277–78.

11. *Resumen del presupuesto del Gobierno Nacional* (1981), pp. 13–14. Expenditures for health care and education — still, in the heady days prior to the contra war, above those for defense — were more than twenty times greater.

12. Ministerio de Cultura 1982b, 277–84. A somewhat more elaborate scheme appears in *Resumen del presupuesto del Gobierno Nicaragüense* (PL 23–03), published at approximately the same time.

13. I return to the objections and controversy in the following chapter; my discussion here focuses on the creation and operation of programs.

14. Torres 1982, 5–8. The director of León's CPC recalled an earlier plan (apparently never implemented) related to the task of democratization: to have a Secretary of Culture in each of the mass organizations (see *Ventana: Barricada Cultural*, 19 July 1983). On the mass organizations, see Ruchwarger 1987.

15. *Ventana: Barricada Cultural*, 19 July 1983, p. 14.

16. Torres 1982; *Ventana: Barricada Cultural*, 3 April 1982, unpaged clipping; *La Chacalaca*, no. 1 (April-June 1982): 1. A year later, the number of *casas de cultura* had grown to fourteen. See interview with Emilia Torres by Margaret Randall in *Ventana: Barricada Cultural*, 2 July 1983, pp. 13–14. The journal *La Chacalaca: Re-vista Trimestral de Los Centros Populares de Cultura*, featuring the work of the CPCs, appeared irregularly from April 1982 at least until December 1985.

17. *La Chacalaca*, no. 2 (July 1982).

18. *Ventana: Barricada Cultural*, 2 July 1983, pp. 13–14.

19. "El trabajo de los Centros Populares de Cultura," *Ventana: Barricada Cultural*, 10 August 1985, p. 10. Statement by the General Directorate of the CPCs.

20. *Ventana: Barricada Cultural*, 12 December 1981, p. 11. Jiménez 1985 lists twenty-seven workshops in the armed forces.

21. *Poesía libre*, no. 1 (July 1981). At the Hemeroteca Nacional in Managua I was able to examine nos. 1–6, 8–11, and 16–18. The observations that follow are based upon these issues.

22. *Poesía libre*, no. 2 (August 1981).

23. Ibid., no. 3 (December 1981): 15–18 [Whitman]; no. 4 (March 1982): 15–30 [Sandburg]. With José Coronel Urtecho, Ernesto Cardenal had earlier published an anthology (Coronel Urtecho and Cardenal 1963) of translations of North American poetry that included these poets and others.

24. Stansifer 1977, 473, says that Zelaya established the country's first lending library in Managua (at some point between 1872 and 1884).

25. Stansifer also notes that the National Archives, founded in 1896, "occupied a small room . . . atop the National Palace, but it was doomed to a spartan budget and ignorant political appointees."

26. Interview with René Salgado, 7 June 1990.

27. Ministerio de Cultura 1982a, 169–75; *Barricada*, 4 October 1981, p. 4.

28. Exchange rate from Spalding 1987, 222.

29. Personal observation, July 1987–May 1988; interview with Director Ileana Rodríguez, 20 January 1988. Rodríguez was making efforts to acquire books and equipment (including computers for cataloging) through international support groups, but progress was slow. The substantially larger collection of the Central Bank (also open to the public), fully cataloged and housed in an air-conditioned building, was considerably better than the National Library.

30. *Nicaragua indígena*, no. 18 (January 1958), no. 21 (July 1958), and no. 23 (November 1958). The situation for archives was equally distressing. Dana Munro, a North American student in Nicaragua just after World War I, reported that he had "met a man who said that one of his relatives had worked in the national archives and could sell me many interesting papers which he had stolen" (Munro 1983, 22). More than a half-century later, Charles Stansifer found the National Archives to consist of "a pile of . . . unorganized papers on the top floor of the National Palace" (personal communication, 22 March 1993).

31. *La Prensa*, 19 August 1959, sec. 2, p. 1.

32. *Ventana: Barricada Cultural*, 6 March 1982, p. 13; *La Chacalaca*, no. 1 (April-June, 1982): 6 and no. 2 (July 1982): 71; Ministerio de Cultura 1982a, 151, 239–44. A year or so later, Juan Chow reported that there were twenty-three museums in Nicaragua, some not functioning or open to the public (*Ventana: Barricada Cultural*, [23 May 1983], p. 15). Since Chow did not name the museums, it is impossible to know how elaborate they were or what their relationship was (if any) to the museums being projected by the ministry.

33. Notice in *Barricada*, 24 October 1981, p. 6. The brief description of the exhibits that follows is based upon my visit to the museum in mid-April 1988.

34. Congruence with the political project was not necessarily a guarantee of access to resources, however. The Sandino Museum—the restored house of his father Don Gregorio Sandino—in Niquinohomo was quite modest. It consisted of three or four fairly well-kept rooms (a total of approximately one thousand square feet) containing a few period furnishings, arranged around a small garden featuring a single small statue of the general (personal observation, 27 April 1988).

35. While the Museum of the Revolution was a national showcase linked closely to official ideology, the drive to create museums arose from a more diffuse social necessity as well as from the central ideological project. The desires of families of young people killed during the Sandinista insurrection to honor their children's sacrifices by arranging displays of photographs and artifacts led to the creation of small local *galerías* of heroes and martyrs. See *Ventana: Barricada Cultural*, 4 June 1983, p. 7.

36. Personal observations, July 1987–May 1988; "Devolviendo al Pueblo su Verdadera Historia," *Ventana: Barricada Cultural*, 4 June 1983, p. 7.

37. Personal observation, July 1987–May 1988. Located in a superior building and with more professionally prepared exhibits was the Museo Nicaráo de Antropología in Rivas, near the southern border with Costa Rica. Opened in 1984 and supported by the ministry's Cultural Patrimony section, the museum was housed in a small (ca. two thousand square foot) building. It displayed varied anthropological exhibits mostly donated by private collectors. I was unable to visit the older and more established museum at Juigalpa.

38. See Bermann 1986, 256–60. The hostages taken by the thirteen Sandinista guerrillas who held the group for three and a half days included Somoza's brother-in-law. In exchange for their release, the Sandinistas obtained $1 million, the release of fourteen of their own (including Daniel Ortega), and guaranteed safe conduct for the entire group to Cuba. Details of the "historical corner" are in *Ventana: Barricada Cultural*, 16 February 1988, p. 6.

39. Burton (1986 and 1990) discusses analogous efforts elsewhere in Latin America.

40. *Ventana: Barricada Cultural*, 8 October 1979, p. 10.

41. Ibid., 21 September 1979, p. 5.

42. Ministerio de Cultura 1982a, 281; *Ventana: Barricada Cultural*, 28 March 1981, pp. 2–5.

43. Quoted from a roundtable interview, *Ventana: Barricada Cultural*, 28 March 1981, pp. 2–5. English has an adjectival form of Belli's term *mística* (mystical), but no nominal form; I have therefore rendered it as *mythos*, which seems closer to her meaning than *mystique* would be.

44. *Ventana: Barricada Cultural*, 25 September 1981, p. 8; 14 October 1981, p. 9.

45. Ibid., 7 February 1981, pp. 8–9.

46. Herrera died during the filming; his work was completed by Chilean director Miguel Littín. On Littín and Herrera, cf. Burton 1990.

47. *Ventana: Barricada Cultural*, 16 April 1983, p. 2.

48. Interview with Ibarra, 15 March 1988; Goepfert 1987.

49. Television schedules published in *Ventana: Barricada Cultural*, 28 September and 1 October 1981.

50. Interview with García, *Ventana: Barricada Cultural*, 30 July 1983, pp. 2–3 and undated clipping (ca. 1981); interview with Carlos Vicente Ibarra, ibid., 14 August 1982, p. 6; ibid., 6 August 1983, pp. 12–13.

51. Halleck in Mattelart 1986, 113–19; *El Nuevo Diario*, 7 January 1988, p. 7.

52. Arrólija Urbina 1983, 10; interview with Sra. Chaverría, Director of the National School of Dance, 3 March 1988.

53. Interview with Bayardo Ortiz, 3 March 1988.

54. Promoted as Nicaragua's most aboriginal instrument by the Ministry of Culture after 1979, the marimba was actually preceded historically (by a great deal) by drums and ceramic, bone, and wooden whistles. Nevertheless, marimbas had been known in Nicaragua for more than a century.

Most prevalent in Bantu-speaking Africa, the marimba was documented in Guatemala as early as 1680. It appears to have been brought into South America by African slaves in the nineteenth century (Sadie 1980, 7:776, 10:406, 11:682). As early as 1851, an American traveler in San Juan del Sur on Nicaragua's Pacific coast reported a performance ("liberally rewarded with silver . . . by an admiring crowd of Americans") by a native musician on a three-octave wooden marimba with gourd resonators (letter of 18 November 1851, Carpenter Family Papers [C-B 892], Box 2, 2:73–75, Bancroft Library, University of California, Berkeley). Apparently not widely popular in Nicaragua before 1900, however, the marimba (in its wooden form as the *marimba de arco*) slowly became more widespread from the 1920s onward, and even more so from the 1950s. Its heightened popularity after the 1950s may in fact have derived principally from Irene López's use of it in her city-based presentations of traditional dance (interview with Bayardo Ortiz, National School of Dance, 23 April 1988).

55. Ironically, prior to their popularity among the elite, the waltz, polka, and mazurka had developed from earlier peasant dances: the polka from seventeenth-century Scandinavian and early nineteenth-century Czechoslovakian country dances, the waltz from the south German *ländler*, and the mazurka from eighteenth-century Polish peasant dance (Clarke and Vaughan 1977, 314, 390, 532).

56. Approximately seventy students remained in the school as of March 1988. Interview with Sra. Chavarría, 3 March 1988. In a very critical review of a folk-based dance performance a few months earlier, Elving Vanegas highlighted other problems not necessarily deriving from lack of funds: slipshod rehearsals, the incorporation of folkloric elements not native to Nicaragua, and lack of psychological credibility in recreations of traditional program dances such as *El Güegüense* (Vanegas 1988).

57. *Ventana: Barricada Cultural*, 9 March 1988, p. 9.

58. *La Prensa*, 20 October 1957, p. B-5; Arellano 1982a, 149.

59. Interviews with Carlos Vicente Ibarra (15 March 1988) and Ernesto Gutiérrez (2 March 1988) (cf. Luzuriaga 1978). Demonstrating the continuing appeal of such highly charged symbols across political lines, a general staff officer of the anti-Sandinista contra forces chose *El Venado* as his *nom de guerre* in 1986 (Rosset and Vandermeer 1986, 252). The Ministry of Culture mounted its own production of *El torovenado* in Managua in 1988 to celebrate the 121st birthday of Rubén Darío (*El Nuevo Diario*, 15 January 1988, p. 3). *El torovenado* is also performed on the Protestant, primarily English-speaking Atlantic Coast of Nicaragua (Acuña 1981).

60. *Ventana: Barricada Cultural*, 28 September 1981, pp. 4, 27; October 1981, p. 9; Cardenal 1981b, 41; Murillo and Cardenal in Zwerling and Martin 1985, 41.

61. Ministerio de Cultura 1982a, 172; *Ventana: Barricada Cultural*, 8 October 1981, p. 10; 11 October 1981, p. 7; 20 October 1981, p. 10. Cf. Cardenal 1986a, 80. Occasional programs of classical music and dance continued to be presented in the Rubén Darío Theater.

62. Wedel 1983, 10–11; *Ventana: Barricada Cultural*, 18 August 1984, pp. 14–15; cf. Dore in Walker 1985, 419–20; Doyle 1984, 56–57; Martin 1987, 86–91.

63. Interview with Luis Enrique Mejía Godoy, 11 March 1988. Mejía Godoy also recalled DISCOSA, a private Nicaraguan firm, from the Somoza period, but I have discovered no information about it. SONORAMA and DISCOTECA ANDINO may also have been producing records in Nicaragua, but I also lack information on those firms. Some albums released by the Ministry of Culture after 1979 were manufactured by a company listed as SISA, but I have no information on the continuity (if any) between the entities.

64. *La Prensa*, 26 August 1956, sec. 2, p. 1; 20 October 1957, B-1; 6 November 1958, B-1. When I interviewed him early in 1988, Cardenal Argüello was extremely ill and unable

to recall crucial details of his efforts in the 1950s. Twenty years later, Cardenal produced several records in the Banco Central series of publications. His grandchildren Salvador and Katia Cardenal formed the performing group Guardabarranco in the 1980s. See Guardabarranco, *Si buscabas* (If you were looking) (Oakland: Redwood Records, 1985).

65. From typescript "Catálogo general: Música nicaragüense [de] ENIGRAC" (ca. January, 1988). See a brief article on ENIGRAC in *Ventana: Barricada Cultural*, 3 August 1987, p. 12; and "Enigrac: Una empresa de discos del pueblo," *La Chacalaca*, November 1985, pp. 54–56. The following analysis is based upon approximately forty ENIGRAC albums in the author's personal collection. On the first Ministry of Culture album (issued in early 1980, before the formation of ENIGRAC), *Vamos haciendo la historia!* (We are making history!), which I have not seen, see Pring-Mill 1987, 180.

66. ENIGRAC also issued LP albums of the poetry of Ernesto Cardenal (MC-003) and Leonel Rugama (MC-013), the songs of Chilean *nueva canción* martyr Victor Jara (MC-014), political songs of El Salvador (MC-019 and 027), and a two-album set from the 1983 Festival of Latin American *Nueva Canción* (MC-024 1, 2). Although these albums undoubtedly were explicitly political in content, I have omitted them from my discussion because I have not been able to locate copies. Only one album, *Valses de Mena* (Waltzes of [José de la Cruz] Mena, MC-034), was devoted to the music of a Nicaraguan classical composer. The album *Cantos a la Purísima y sones de Pascuas* (MC-035)—which I have not been able to examine—may have been a reissue of some of Salvador Cardenal Argüello's traditional recordings from the 1950s.

67. "Jorge Paladino, antes y después del triunfo," *Ventana: Barricada Cultural*, 20 July 1985, p. 4. In the absence of detailed studies of other performers of the period, one cannot know how typical Paladino's case was. The general cultural situation during the Somoza period makes it seem likely that it was not atypical, however.

68. *Románticos nicaragüenses* (CE-6020 [1987]) presented similar materials and arrangements.

69. Ministerio de Cultura, *Convirtiendo la oscurana en claridad* (Managua: Ocarina, 1980). The album carries the number Ocarina m.c. 002. Performers included Los de Palacaqüina, Grupo Xitlaly, Pancasán, Los Soñadores de Sarawaska, and a dozen or so other individuals.

70. ENIGRAC's "Catálogo general: música nicaragüense" lists other albums, but having been unable to obtain copies I can neither evaluate them nor be certain of issue dates.

71. My copy of the album was released by New Society Products, Inc. in New York; I assume that it is identical to ENIGRAC's MC-021.

72. Quoted from the (undated) Nicaragua Network edition of the *Canto épico* issued subsequently. My copy of the original ENIGRAC issue does not contain this language.

CHAPTER SIX

1. In some respects the issue of gender relations was even more pervasive and intractable than that of the Atlantic coast. I address that conflict separately in my final chapter. The Sandinistas' censorship of the press was also partly a cultural issue, but since it was not primarily that, nor motivated primarily by cultural considerations, I omit treating it here. For a compendium of complaints by the Sandinistas' opponents over this issue, see Chamorro Cardenal 1988.

2. On the Sandinista mass organizations see Ruchwarger 1987.

3. In Spanish, *unión* can mean "union" in several senses (as in a political union of states, for example), while *sindicato* most often means a union of workers. It is not clear to me why the Sandinistas used both terms here, since they tended to refer to all creative artists as "cultural workers."

4. ASTC did not, for example, take the trouble to send a representative (as did both the ministry and the Centers for Popular Culture) to the first Youth Festival of Amateur Artists organized by the Sandinista Youth (*Juventud Sandinista*; JS), which drew several thousand young people.

5. Belli 1981b, 2–3. MECATE was functionally related in turn to the Association of Rural Workers (ATC) and the Agrarian Education and Promotion Center (CEPA), the latter created in the late 1960s by the Jesuits to train peasant leaders. By September 1982, the ministry reported that MECATE had fifty functioning groups of artists and actors — a total of perhaps two thousand members (Ministerio de Cultura 1982a, 288). For accounts of popular theater during ensuing months, see *Ventana: Barricada Cultural*, 27 March 1982, p. 12; 9 October 1982, p. 7; 20 November 1982, p. 15; 19 March 1983, pp. 4–5; 16 April 1983, pp. 10–11; 14 April 1984, pp. 2–3; 1 May 1984, p. 14; 29 September 1984, p. 5; 17 November 1984, pp. 12–13; 2 February 1985, pp. 12–13.

6. *Ventana: Barricada Cultural*, 11 September 1982, p. 3.

7. *Presupuesto general de ingresos y gastos del Gobierno Central*, PL 23–01 (Biblioteca de la Asamblea Nacional, Managua).

8. *Ventana: Barricada Cultural*, 19 July 1983, p. 5.

9. Ibid., 9 July 1983, pp. 3–8; Guerrero 1982, 19–23.

10. ASTC, "Declaración de principios," in Ministerio de Cultura 1982a, 323–28. Whether the qualifying phrase represented the actual position of most ASTC members, or was added as a political necessity (because of the international politics of the moment, or in exchange for continued central government support) is impossible to judge from this distance.

11. Interview of July 1982 in White 1986, 29. Cuadra later objected to what he called "the dramatic struggle in Nicaragua of an ideology against a culture" — a totalitarian Marxist ideology that has imposed itself through "a dance of masks" which can produce "slogans but not poems, propaganda but not life," and which has marginalized those independent writers and artists who refuse to submit to the ideology (Bolaños Geyer 1985, 237–56).

12. *Ventana: Barricada Cultural*, 11 June 1983, p. 7.

13. Ibid., 19 July 1983, p. 26.

14. "Debate sobre nueva canción en Nicaragua," ibid., 28 August 1982, pp. 2–10; the debate continued in issues dated 18 September 1982, p. 6; 27 November 1982, p. 10; and 23 April 1983, pp. 1–9.

15. See also ibid., 13 August 1983, p. 6.

16. My observations here are based upon an interview with Pablo Buitrago, Director of the National School of Music, 10 March 1988.

17. The term *libre* in the title was inescapably polyreferential. While the word itself could be rendered as "free" in English (as in "free verse," which refers primarily to poetic form and technique and only secondarily to the implicit politics of aesthetics), in the specifically Nicaraguan revolutionary context it carried the principal association of "liberated" (i.e., politically free), as in the Sandinista code phrase *Patria libre o morir* (free country or death). But the more specifically aesthetic reading (free verse) also had a political edge, since eschewing established poetic forms and practices connoted rejecting the bourgeois and culturally sycophantic poetry of the Somoza era.

18. "Entre la libertad y el miedo," *Ventana: Barricada Cultural*, 7 March 1981, pp. 2–5, 12–13. For a good brief discussion of *exteriorismo* and the controversy over the workshops, see Beverley and Zimmerman 1990, 70–71, 98–100.

19. "Los talleres de poesía responden," *Ventana: Barricada Cultural*, 14 March 1981, p. 7.

20. Ibid., 21 March 1981, p. 9. In an interview I taped with him on 2 March 1988, shortly before his death, Nicaraguan poet Ernesto Gutiérrez recalled vividly the controversy surrounding Mayra Jiménez's attitudes and approaches to workshop students.

21. Near the end of the ministry's own life, Stephen Kinzer reported that "for several years, the [Solentiname] artists . . . were required to sell their works to local government officials, who in turn passed them on to foreign distributors. After the artists protested, the government relented. But not all artists feel they are treated fairly. 'They let us sell a few on our own, but most of them go to the Sandinista delegation at San Carlos,' said Eylin Guadamúz Pineda. 'What they pay us is barely enough to buy a cheap pair of blue jeans, and in foreign countries even the small paintings sell for $500 or more'" (Kinzer 1988).

22. Here I consider only one of the two groups of potters Field studied (the San Juan de Oriente cooperative); the other (the *cerámica negra* women potters of Jinotega and Matagalpa) I return to briefly in my final chapter. Both discussions depend heavily upon Field 1987, from which come all details not otherwise attributed.

23. The Banco Central study (*La situación de la artesanía nicaragüense*), published in 1976, noted that at least eight materials were still being worked by traditional artisans: plant fibers, leather, wood, metals, textiles, stone, and miscellaneous ones such as tree bark and gourds.

24. Field 1987, 104. The government extracted the maximum publicity out of those traditional artists still active. Articles on the pottery tradition appeared soon after the triumph (cf. Pérez Estrada 1982, 16, and Avendaño 1982). On 22 July 1987, the Sandinista daily *Barricada* reported on the Ministry of Culture's efforts to revitalize among the women of El Chile a weaving tradition which Minister of Culture Cardenal called "a thousand-year-old art transmitted from generation to generation." Another article on the El Chile women weavers appeared in *Barricada Internacional* on 24 September 1987, p. 19 (in which the tradition was said to be fifteen hundred years old), and in *Ventana: Barricada Cultural*, 11 January 1988, p. 11.

25. The scholarly literature on both the Coast itself and more particularly on the Sandinistas' political and cultural dealings with the Atlantic Coast is vast. My treatment of the issues here is synoptic only. For a detailed examination of the cultural politics of the Atlantic Coast from 1894 onward, see Hale 1994.

26. Helms has recently argued (1989, 1–5) that historical experience had in effect mapped the cosmos along an east-west axis according to which emissaries from the east (that is, the coastal side) were good and civilized (the British who brought trade goods; English-speaking Moravians who gave indigenous men positions as lay pastors, taught them "good" manners, and dressed them in white shirts and ties for church; and — later — wage-paying U.S. corporations). Those from the west on the other hand — the Spanish, Catholics, and their successors the western Nicaraguan "Spanish" functionaries — were culturally alien, savage and uncivilized. Hence, Helms argues, the "intrusion of heretofore distant Hispanic Nicaraguan culture . . . into Miskitu social and cosmographical space" after the triumph implied not rescue and deliverance but social and cultural chaos.

27. Although the State Department reported a few days later that the project would not be worth the cost, Roosevelt asked Congress for $200,000 to undertake the necessary engineering surveys for a highway and a barge canal (22 May 1939 Somoza to Roosevelt,

22 May 1939 Roosevelt to Somoza, 3 April 1939 State Department to Roosevelt in Official File 432; 24 July 1939 Roosevelt memo to Congress in Official File 1305; Franklin D. Roosevelt Library).

28. Dennis 1981, 272, reported that in the late 1970s the only way for *costeños* to get to western Nicaragua if they couldn't afford the expensive daily LANICA flight to Managua was up the Río Escondido from Bluefields to Rama, and then overland.

29. Vilas 1989, 4, gives the total 1981 coastal population as approximately 272,000: 172,000 mestizo (63.5 percent); 67,000 Miskito (24.6 percent); 26,000 Creole (9.5 percent); 5,500 Sumu and Rama (2 percent); and a remnant of 1,500 Garifuna (0.5 percent). Bourgois (Walker 1982, 317) presents slightly different figures.

30. Such paradoxical divisions had a long history. During the early nineteenth century, as Hale has noted, it was Creoles rather than Miskitos who dominated as intermediaries between *costeños* and European entrepreneurs. After the 1830s the Miskito kings rarely resided with the Miskito population; most sent their children to Belize or England to be educated, and the new Mosquito Reserve excluded most of the traditional Miskito areas and was in any case governed by a Creole elite. After the Zelaya government's takeover of the coast in 1894, it was the mestizos who gained ascendancy (Hale in CIDCA/Development Study Unit 1987, 39–44).

31. Charles Hale's nuanced examination of the complexities of Sandino's activities on the Atlantic Coast shows that Sandino understood and respected local culture, operated extensively on the Coast, and in fact had considerable support among *costeños* (Hale 1994, 52–56).

32. For some revealing examples of the attitudes of individual Sandinista soldiers to coastal people, see Hale 1994, 104–8.

33. Vilas 1989, 108, 123; "Ley sobre educación en lenguas en la Costa Atlántica," 2 May 1980 (Decreto No. 388), in *América indígena* 42 (April-June 1982): 359–61. Hale notes that English and native languages were offered only after the ministry had been confronted by militant coastal groups opposed to its initial plan to do literacy training in Spanish only (Hale 1994, 134).

34. The Spanish text of the Declaration may be found in *Nicaráuac*, año 3, num. 8 (October 1982): 19–20.

35. Cabezas's *La montaña es algo más que una inmensa estepa verde* (Fire from the mountain) recounts the political initiation and formation of a young FSLN guerrilla fighter in the mountains, and his struggle with cultural habits (e.g., *machismo*) that impede the emergence of the New Man of the Sandinista era. Within the narrative the mountain is a polyvalent symbol: Sisyphean challenge, abstract power, historical memory, all-knowing Mother, and benevolent-malevolent Nature.

36. Vilas 1989, 83–86. Vilas points to the formation of the Social Action Committee of the Moravian church (*Comité de Acción Social de la Iglesia Morava*), and notes that Creole officials of the nativized church were in touch with the U.S. civil rights movement.

37. This aspect of the history alone has generated a great deal of analysis; I merely outline a few of its salient cultural dimensions here. Readers interested in further detail might begin by consulting Norsworthy and Robinson 1987 and Walker 1987 (in the latter, see especially Diskin, pp. 80–93). For the evolution of, and interrelationships between, armed organizations among the Miskitos, see Hale 1994, 240–41.

38. For an interpretation of these events congruent with U.S. policy of the period, see Nietschmann 1989.

39. Vilas 1989, 149ff.; Bourgois in Walker 1985, 204; *LASA Forum* 17 (Spring 1986): 14; Hale 1994, 98–99.

40. *LASA Forum* 17 (Summer 1986): 10. For details on the economic costs of the contra war, see Fitzgerald in Spalding, 1987, 195–213.

41. *LASA Forum* 17 (Spring 1986): 15–16.

42. Ibid., 17; Vilas 1989, 171.

43. *LASA Forum* 17 (Spring 1986): 17, and 17 (Summer 1986): 1–3.

44. For the full text of the law on autonomy, see Hale 1994, 231–39.

45. *Resumen del Presupuesto del Gobierno Nacional* (1981), pp. 13–14; *Presupuesto del Gobierno Central* (1983), 1:470; *Presupuesto General del la República por Programas* (1987), 1:5–7.

46. For a synoptic analysis of the early years of the sports program, see Wagner in Walker 1982, 291–302.

47. Managua's water system "has been purified by adding so much chlorine that it tastes like ipecac," Carleton Beals reported in the early 1930s (Beals 1933, 205).

48. *Nicaragua, Costa Rica, Panama Country Report*, No. 2 (London: The Economist Intelligence Unit, 1989) [dated April 14].

49. Personal observations, January-May 1988.

50. Interviews with Leonor Martínez de Rocha, Museo Nacional (9 March 1988), Jorge Eduardo Arellano (9 March 1988), Luis Enrique Mejía Godoy, ENIGRAC (11 March 1988), and Carlos Vicente Ibarra, División de Fomento de Arte (15 March 1988).

CHAPTER SEVEN

1. Sir Edward Tylor's *Anahuac* (on his Mexican expedition) appeared in 1861, and his *Researches in the Early History of Mankind* followed four years later.

2. The monolith remains in the museum (item number 12592).

3. French collectors also appear to have been active in Nicaragua during this period, but I have located only a few anecdotal references to their activities.

4. *Correo del Istmo*, 1 June 1849, p. 12.

5. Letter to Joseph Henry, 2 December 1850. Published in *Smithsonian Institution 5th Annual Report* (Washington, D.C., 1851), Appendix no. 2, pp. 79–80. The catalog to which Squier referred may be the 130-page *Notice des Monuments Exposés dans la Salle des Antiquités Américaines (Mexique et Pérou)* (Paris: Vichon, Imprimeur des Musées Nationaux, 1850). Since the volume was octavo size, however, it was less impressive evidence of strong competition than Squier implied.

6. The illustrator was John William Orr (1815–87), who had recently contributed wood engravings for *Pictorial Guide to the Falls of Niagara* (Buffalo: Buffalo Press of Salisbury and Clapp, 1842) and *The Traveler's Illustrated Pocket Guide and Hotel Directory* (New York: Trow and Co., 1848).

7. A year later, another idol on a Managua street corner caught the attention of Jacob D. B. Stillman (Stillman 1967, 47).

8. The name of the island is given in various sources as either Zapatera or Zapatero; for the sake of consistency, I have used the latter throughout.

9. Arellano 1977a, 20, says that Squier shipped only two statues to the Smithsonian. Squier refers to more pieces than that, however (e.g., 1:302, 317, 325; 2:62, 92–93). In his

letter to Joseph Henry of 2 December 1850 (published in the Smithsonian's fifth annual report), Squier says, "The ship *Brewster* has just arrived from the Pacific, bringing six monuments in addition to those which I shipped via San Juan de Nicaragua for the Institution." Current Smithsonian records list seven pieces (catalog numbers 92848–54) as being in the collection, noted as corresponding to Squier's illustrations as follows: 92848 (1:302), 92849 (1:312), 92850 (1:318), 92851 (1:318 [*sic*; probably 319]), 92852 (not indicated), 92853 (2:64), and 92854 (2:64). Only 92850 and 92851 are listed in Smithsonian records as being from Subtiava. For unknown reasons, the pieces were not formally accessioned until 1862, and not fully cataloged until 1882. Six of them appear in the Smithsonian's manuscript Museum Catalog: Anthropology, vol. 1, as nos. 953–58, placing them among the museum's very earliest acquisitions. I am grateful to Hope Connors for helping me to locate these records, and to Molly Coxson for her assistance in interpreting them.

10. Evidence is mixed concerning how much religious significance the statues may still have had for Nicaraguan Indians, but a number of reports suggest that it was not insignificant. "The descendents of the sculptors, fervent Christians though they be," reported British Museum collector Frederick Boyle more than a decade later, "can still find room in their hearts for other worship besides the Virgin and the very ugly saints provided for them — and the old gods come in for a share more than equal in times of trouble. A gentleman in Granada, whose house is near a broken idol with a wide mouth, called 'La Boca,' which stands at the corner of a street, told me that when a revolution is imminent, and during its progress, the gaping mouth of this statue is every morning crammed with flowers, which the watchful priests remove at night" (Boyle 1868, 2:47).

11. Letter to Joseph Henry, 2 December 1850; *Smithsonian Institution 5th Annual Report* (Washington, D.C., 1850), p. 78; Squier 1852, 1:310–23.

12. The mss. Museum Catalog: Anthropology, vol. 1 in the National Museum of American History, shows the original six Squier items (nos. 953–58) as coming from "Momotombita Is[land]," but the corresponding archaeological catalog card file (prepared in 1884) lists only two (92848 [old 953] and 92849 [old 954]) as from the island.

13. Squier 1852, 1:402; 2:11, 34, 52, 62. Smithsonian records list numbers 92852–54 as being from Zapatero Island. Some drawings of the "painted rocks of Managua" appear in the 1860 revised edition of Squier's book, p. 393.

14. Squier 1852, 1:54. Squier's descriptions of his expeditions in search of antiquities (especially stone statues) are far more elaborate than those of any other collector. He recorded not only the practical details of the enterprise, but also his own (frequently quite mixed) reactions, and those of his local helpers. His lengthy narratives are worth attentive reading. One can only speculate about the native helpers' reasons for dancing around the raised statue: no doubt it was partly to celebrate their own accomplishment, but perhaps they also felt some momentary primordial bond with the extinguished culture.

15. Squier notes that by the time he arrived in Nicaragua in 1849, collectors for the British Museum had already been at work at several sites, but I encountered no corroborating evidence of such activities. Boyle refers repeatedly to another apparently experienced collector who accompanied him on his forays ("Mr. Jebb"), but gives no indication that he is connected with the museum (Boyle 1868, 2:97, 101, 119, 141–44, 164, 174).

16. Boyle implied repeatedly that he had collected large numbers of artifacts. The museum currently reports, however, that it holds only ninety Nicaraguan items collected by Boyle (British Museum *Report MAGUS.RG*, 14 March 1991, nos. Am1866,0713.1.a through 0713.87; letter to author from Sarah Posey of British Museum, 15 March 1991).

Illustrations of a few of the British Museum pieces are in Newson 1987, following p. 206 (plates 3, 4, 8–10, 17).

17. Berendt to Spencer Baird, 17 December 1874; Berendt to Joseph Henry, 27 July 1875; U.S. National Museum Accession Records, Office of the Registrar, 1834–June 1899, Reel 38, Accession 4016. The stone statue appears as no. 17282 in the mss. Museum Catalog: Anthropology, vol. 4. The New York dealer (referred to in the correspondence as "B. Westermann") may have been B. Westermann and Company, a book dealer whose 1873 catalog included "maps, atlases, globes and other educational material." Museum accession records for this period are quite fragmentary; extant letters refer to other correspondence no longer in the file. Flint later suspected that Berendt may also have been sending pieces to Berlin (letter to Joseph Henry of March 1876; Smithsonian Institution Archives, Record Unit 305, Registrar, 1834–1958 [accretions to 1976], Accession Records [U.S. National Museum], Reel 43, Accession 5157), a suspicion confirmed by Berendt's own reference (*Journal of the American Geographical Society* 8 [1876]: 143) to "large collections of antiquities, made lately in Nicaragua for the Berlin museum by myself." Berendt traveled to Cuba as early as 1860. His research into Nicaraguan culture was not confined to material culture remains; he obtained the first text of *El Güegüence*, discussed in a previous chapter.

18. Nos. 7838–41, 17283–304, 17321; mss. Museum Catalog: Anthropology, vol. 4; Smithsonian Institution Archives, Record Unit 305, Registrar, 1834–1958 (accretions to 1976), Accession Records [U.S. National Museum], Reel 38. A letter from Flint to Spencer Baird of 19 January 1876 notes that Berendt visits him every month; ibid., Accession 5213, Reel 43. Flint's letter of 19 August 1876 (ibid.) refers to his "quarter century of residence" in Nicaragua, and in an undated letter (missing its first page) of approximately April 1877 (ibid.) he mentions having arrived "in this country in 1850."

19. Flint to Joseph Henry, 18 March 1875; Smithsonian Institution Archives, Record Unit 305, Registrar, 1834–1958 (accretions to 1976), Accession Records [U.S. National Museum], Accession 4016, Reel 38.

20. U.S. National Museum Accessions Record, Office of the Registrar 1834–June 1899, Reel 43, accessions 5157 and 5213, nos. 22076–87, 23266–95, 23276, 23293, 29001–13. Flint 1882, 289–302, refers to other travels and archaeological studies in Colombia, Argentina, Paraguay, Bolivia, and Peru.

21. Flint to Baird, 12 January 1878, U.S. National Museum Accessions Record, Office of the Registrar 1834–June 1899, Reel 43. *The American Antiquarian* 11 (1889): 388 warned its readers about "the great difference between a dealer in relics ('mere traffickers') and an intelligent collector."

22. Flint to Henry, 17 April 1875; Flint to Baird, 8 May and 19 March 1876. U.S. National Museum Accessions Record, Office of the Registrar 1834–June 1899, Reel 43.

23. Flint to Baird, 10 May 1877; U.S. National Museum Accession Record, Office of the Registrar 1834–June 1899, Reel 48, Accession file 6017. The identity of "the Frenchman"—mentioned several times by Flint—is never specified. The foreword to the Louvre's 1850 catalog of Mexican and Peruvian antiquities (*Notice des Monuments*, mentioned by Squier and cited above) mentions—but does not further identify—a number of French citizens who were collecting and writing about Latin American antiquities (which it called "the debris of the transatlantic civilization"), including the French consul in Lima. The Louvre was careful to point out that such objects "do not offer the strong interest that the monuments of Egypt owe to their intimate connection with our sacred history."

24. Baird to Flint, 14 June 1877, quoted in Flint to Putnam, 19 September 1877, Peabody Museum of Archaeology and Ethnology Accession File 78–42 (hereinafter cited as PMAE Accession File); Flint to Putnam, 17 January 1878, ibid.; Flint to Putnam, 19 November 1877, ibid. Flint noted that Dr. Bransford was currently charging $300 per month. From 1879 until at least 1891, Flint worked as "Assistant in the Field" for the Peabody Museum (*Twenty Third Report* [1891] of the museum, p. 66). The museum's 1895–96 report noted (pp. 6–7) that Flint "several years ago" sent to the museum two of the "large sculptures" from Zapatero earlier described by Squier. The Peabody Museum continued to collect Nicaraguan archaeological artifacts as late as 1959, when Gordon R. Willey and Albert H. Norweb led an expedition (officially sanctioned by the Nicaraguan government) that brought back sixty-four thousand specimens (mostly potsherds) (Healy 1980, xxv–xxvi). One splendid Nicaraguan piece from the Peabody collection appears in Newson 1982, following p. 206 (plate 4).

25. Flint to Putnam, 18 February, 18 June, 16 July, and 23 November, 1878; PMAE Accession File 78–42; Flint to Putnam, 20 May 1879, Peabody Museum Correspondence, Harvard University Archives (hereinafter cited as PMC-HUA), Box 2, Folder 1879 F-J; Flint to Putnam, 20 July 1879, PMAE Accession File 78–42; Flint to Putnam, 30 February 1883; PMAE Accession File 83–72.

26. Flint to Putnam, 18 June 1878, PMAE Accession File 78–42.

27. Flint to Putnam, 17 September 79, PMAE Accession File 78–42.

28. Total complied from Peabody Museum manuscript accession catalogs and card files (accession numbers 78–42, 79–72, 80–27, 81–27, 83–72, 84–14, 86–2, 87–5, and 99–43).

29. Flint to Putnam, 20 August 1878, PMAE Accession File 78–42. Unfortunately, no copies of Putnam's letters to Flint appear to have survived.

30. Flint to Baird, 16 April 1877; Smithsonian Institution Archives, Record Unit 305, Registrar, 1834–1958 (accretions to 1976), Accession Records [U.S. National Museum], Reel 43, Accession 5157.

31. Flint to Putnam, 18 February 1878; PMAE Accession File 78–42.

32. Flint to Baird, 19 March 1877, Smithsonian Institution Archives, Record Unit 305, Registrar, 1834–1958 (accretions to 1976), Accession Records [U.S. National Museum], Reel 43, Accession 5157. Berendt apparently "spent the last few months of his life" packing and sending some Guatemalan archaeological specimens to Berlin's ethnological museum (Luce 1895, 73).

33. Flint to Putnam, 31 May 1878; PMAE Accession File 78–42.

34. For a technical discussion of the urns, see Steward 1948, 4:124–25. Bransford first went to Nicaragua as a member of an expedition to survey the canal route.

35. Accession nos. 5266–67; catalog nos. 22303–411, 23756–841, 24255–61; card file at Natural History Museum. Smithsonian Institution Archives, Record Unit 305, Registrar, 1834–1958 (accretions to 1976), Accession Records [U.S. National Museum], Reel 44, Accessions 5266–67. Bransford 1881, 91, also lists nos. 31389, 32762–64, 32766–71, and 32773. The gold items were especially significant, since gold work was rare in the Pacific region of Nicaragua. Strong (in Steward 1948, 4:128, 137) says that much of what was dug up by treasure hunters was subsequently melted down.

36. For a concise but detailed technical description of the ceramic types found in the Pacific region of Nicaragua, see Strong in Steward 1948, 4:126–28. Stone, in Lange and Stone 1984, says that Bransford first recognized and named Luna Ware and Palmar Ware—the latter "one of the oldest Central American bichromes" (p. 25).

37. Flint to Baird, 10 May 1877; Smithsonian Institution Archives, Record Unit 305, Reg-

istrar, 1834–1958 (accretions to 1976), Accession Records [U.S. National Museum], Reel 48, Accession 6017. A brief notice of the trip appears in *Harper's Weekly*, 21 July 1877.

38. Acquisition 6017, catalog nos. 28426–997. Smithsonian Institution Archives, Record Unit 305, Registrar, 1834–1958 (accretions to 1976), Accession Records [U.S. National Museum], Reel 48, Accession 6017. Bransford to Baird, 31 August 1877; Flint to Henry, 7 August 1877, ibid.

39. It was the first serious collecting for Nutting, who seems to have made two collecting trips to Nicaragua in 1882–83. Shortly after collecting in Nicaragua, Nutting became a professor of zoology and curator of the museum at the State University of Iowa. He developed into a passionate collector, who later led or participated in scientific expeditions in the Caribbean and the South Pacific (cf. his *Barbados-Antigua Expedition: Narrative and Preliminary Report* [1919] and *Fiji-New Zealand Expedition* [1924]).

40. Nutting to Baird, 24 June 1882; Smithsonian Institution Archives, Record Unit 305, Registrar, 1834–1958 (accretions to 1976), Accession Records [U.S. National Museum], Reel 77, Accession 13208. The trip lasted from early February to late May 1882.

41. Mss. Museum Catalog: Anthropology, vol 13; nos. 61691–753 and 62091. Nutting to Baird, 16 and 24 March 1883; Smithsonian Institution Archives, Record Unit 305, Registrar, 1834–1958 (accretions to 1976), Accession Records [U.S. National Museum], Reel 77, Accessions 13208 and 13258. The stone idol (no. 13258) is something of a puzzle in Smithsonian records. In his 24 March letter (filed with accession 13258), Nutting refers to it as "life size," and says it weighs between one thousand and two thousand pounds. The original accession card, dated 20 June 1883, notes that the idol was received on 3 June in "3 pkgs." A later card for no. 13258 (dated 28 February 1884) gives the height of the statue as only 14½". The Smithsonian received another "small stone idol" (no size indicated) from Ometepe as late as 1909 (accession no. 50453).

42. Bovallius 1886, 1–12, indicates that he had read Squier's account of his work in Nicaragua, as well as the more recent ones of Berendt, Flint, and Bransford (but not that of Boyle, it seems). Whether he had read them before going is not clear, however. The principal motive for Bovallius's trip was to collect zoological specimens rather than antiquities.

43. Flint to F. W. Putnam, 5 February 1883, PMAE Accession File 83–72.

44. Some of the items Bovallius sent to the Museum of Natural History in Stockholm from Ometepe appear in the Museum's typescript catalog 1885.11, nos. 101–6. I am grateful to Staffan Brunius of Folkens Museum Etnografiska for supplying these records.

45. Apparently alone among those who collected antiquities in Nicaragua in the late nineteenth century, Bovallius took photographs, but they cannot now be found. He reported (Bovallius [1887] 1977, 273) that he discovered near the beach "a high conical edifice 30–40 meters high" made of "enormous blocks of uncut stone" and with a base forty meters in diameter. Since no previous collector had reported such a structure, Bovallius's report is puzzling.

46. Bovallius also reported ([1887] 1977, 282) that even before Squier's collecting in 1849, some statues had been moved to Granada. In the Folkens Museum Etnografiska typescript catalog 1885.11, the Punta del Sapote specimens appear as nos. 107–38, those from Punta de las Figuras as nos. 139–49, and those from Ceiba as nos. 151–59 and 164. Additional items (mostly fragments) from unspecified locations are in catalog 1893.3, nos. 1–27. Castillo-Barquero 1989 examines in detail the idols of Punta del Sapote (Mound 1).

47. The ridge may have been the Cerro del Panteón mentioned in Bovallius [1887] 1977, 267.

48. A letter to me of 16 December 1991 from Ivar A. Berggren of the Latin American Institute in Stockholm notes that on a subsequent trip to Nicaragua from Trinidad in 1900 to buy land "for the establishment of rubber and cocoa [sic] plantations," Bovallius bought some other statues.

49. Sweden got its first museum (the Statens Historiska Museet) in the seventeenth century, followed by the Kungliga Vetenskapsakademien [KVA] in 1739 (Royal Academy of Science; opened to the public in 1784 and renamed Naturhistoriska Riksmuseet in 1841). The Kungliga Vitterhets Historie och Antikvitetsakademien [VHAA] (Royal Academy of Letters and Antiquities) was established in 1753. The Royal Museum (now the national fine arts museum), founded in 1792, opened to the public in 1794.

50. Ivar A. Berggren to author, 16 December 1991.

51. Flint to Putnam, 12 May 1890; PMAE Accession File 99–43.

52. At length a few of those contributions came to be recognized by the scientific community. Stone credits Flint with having identified the Tola pottery style, and presenting "the first scientific report on the human footprints of Acahualinca" near Managua (Lange and Stone 1984, 25–26). Flint also supplied data to linguist Daniel G. Brinton, then engaged in the study of aboriginal American literature (Brinton [1883] 1969, x, xxxix, xli).

53. Flint to Putnam, 17 December 1885, PMAE Accession File 86–2; 18 March 1887, Frederic W. Putnam Papers, Harvard University Archives, Box 6 (hereafter cited as FWPP-HUA).

54. Flint to Putnam, 17 January 1878, PMAE Accession File 78–42 and 27 March 1889, PMAE Accession File 84–14.

55. Flint to Putnam, 23 November 1878, PMAE Accession File 78–42; 23 May 1880, PMAE Accession File 80–27; 9 March 1881, PMAE Accession File 81–27; 21 February 1882, PMAE Accession File 83–72; 17 December 1885, PMAE Accession File 86–2.

56. Flint to Putnam, 17 December 1885; PMAE Accession File 86–2; Flint to Putnam, 9 September 1886, PMAE Accession File 86–2; Flint to Putnam, 12 May and 18 August 1890, PMAE Accession File 99–43.

57. Flint to Putnam, 28 March 1899, PMAE Accession File 99–43.

58. The issue here is how Boyle *interpreted* the reasons for the Indians' resistance to revealing the locations of antiquities, not whether the interpretation in and of itself was warranted.

59. Flint, "Antiquities," p. 295; Flint to Putnam, 30 June 1878, PMAE Accession File 78–42; Flint to Putnam, 18 July 1878, PMAE Accession File 78–42; Flint to Putnam, 21 April 82; PMAE Accession File 83–72.

60. Quoted in Fiallos Gil 1965 from Levy 1873. Arellano 1982a mentions that when the Colegio de Granada opened in 1874 it had a "cabinet of physics, [and] a museum of natural history" (p. 29), but I have encountered no additional or corroborating information on that museum.

61. Flint to Putnam, 15 September 1878 and 30 June 1878, respectively; PMAE Accession File 78–42. Edward Belcher [1843] 1970, 1:172, had reported seeing the Managua statues as early as 1838, already "much worn, defaced by time."

62. Doris Stone (Lange and Stone 1984, 30) has recently pointed out that reports on archaeological finds in the 1860s stimulated looting. She also notes that a traveler's 1895 report of gold-filled graves at Chiriqui in southern Costa Rica resulted in the looting of four thousand graves in the area and "stimulated expeditions by foreign institutions."

63. Several commentators have noted that Lord Elgin was eager to remove classical

statuary from Greece partly because so much of it had already been ground up by local builders to make new cement.

64. Jesus de la Rocha to U.S. chargé d'affaires, 8 May 1852; Franco Castellón to U.S. chargé d'affaires, 12 July 1852. Dispatches from United States Ministers to Central America, 1824-1906, Reel 9, National Archives and Records Service (NARS) RG 59. The record does not reveal how the matter was ultimately resolved.

65. Rufus Flint to Putnam, 24 May 1883, PMAE Accession File 83-72. Whether the government had a normal policy of requiring and granting licenses is not clear; I encountered no other references to such a practice.

66. Flint to Putnam, 18 June, 9 July, and 22 August 1883, PMAE Accession File 83-72. Flint's reference to "private lands" suggests that the government's restrictions—whatever they were—may have applied only to public lands. Early the next year, Flint spoke of being "afraid the permission will not continue" (24 January 1884 to Putnam, PMAE Accession File 84-14).

67. Flint to Putnam, 24 January 1884, PMAE Accession File 84-14.

68. Flint to Putnam, 24 December 1884, PMAE Accession File 84-14. Even Spencer Baird of the Smithsonian was aware of such a danger within the United States itself. "I wish there was some law," Baird wrote to the institution's northwest territories collector James G. Swan, that would prohibit foreigners from "coming in and carrying off all our treasures" (Cole 1985, 37).

69. Zelaya's move came too late to prevent the transfer of another large collection of Nicaraguan antiquities to the Smithsonian. Assembled by the Nicaraguan government for exhibit at the Columbian Exposition in Madrid (1892-93), the collection included wood, gold, stone, and ceramic pieces from the archaeological "mines" of Ometepe and Zapatero, the Solentiname islands, Rivas, and elsewhere (Smithsonian accession 29404; nos. 171890-2310, 172701-9, received June 1895). Since no accession correspondence related to this collection appears to have been preserved, how it came to be assigned to the Smithsonian is not known. A full listing is available in *Catálogo de los objetos que envía la República de Nicaragua a la Exposición Histórico-Americana de Madrid* (n.p., n.p., n.d.). Luce 1895 and Hough 1895 contain further information on U.S. participation in the Exposition and on the Nicaraguan exhibit. Luce reported that the Nicaraguan collection had been assembled "with great care from comparatively recent excavations" (p. 35). Item nos. 740-1201 were from the private collections of Julio Arellano, Spanish Minister to Central America, and Julio Gavinet (not further identified). Presumably those portions of the exhibit were returned to their owners, since the portion shipped to the Smithsonian included only about 440 items.

The Smithsonian continued to receive archaeological specimens from Ometepe at least up into the 1930s, when Marine Corps Corporal Emil M. Krieger, stationed in Nicaragua in the U.S. campaign against rebel General Augusto C. Sandino, sent a collection of 26 earthenware and stone objects taken from La Finca Casa Blanca (accession 123959, catalog nos. 364926-945; cf. ms. Museum Catalog: Anthropology, vol. 75).

70. Cháves [1970s?], 4. The decree establishing the museum was published in *Diario Oficial*, Tercer época no. 319, 26 August 1897.

71. Guzmán 1902, 290-91. I am indebted to Charles L. Stansifer for supplying extracts from this article.

72. M. Abbott Frazar to Putnam, 20 and 28 February, 13 and 18 May 1892, FWPP-HUA Box 12, Folder 1892 D-F; 17 January 1895, Box 16, Folder 1896 E-G.

73. Cf. photographs of five of the Colegio Centroamericano statues in Baudez 1970 (nos. 79–83).

74. La Orden Miracle 1971, 61, 65; photographs 1–4 on pp. 111–12. A photograph of the Granada group shows twenty pedestals, but monoliths were missing from three. Thieck 1971 lists nearly fifty stone monoliths in nineteen private collections. Pieces from one of the more impressive private collections of ceramics (that of Eduardo Montiel Argüello) appear in a series of photographs on the back page of *La Prensa Literaria*, March 1976– January 1977. I have been unable to identify Montiel Argüello, or to locate the collection. His brother may have been a functionary of the Somoza government. Ferletti and Matilló Vila's lavishly printed *Piedras Vivas* (1977) confirmed the holdings of private families. Baudez 1970 also presents photographs of pieces in the private Managua collections of Enrique Neret (nos. 4, 5, 7, 11, 13, 16, 17, 77, 98) and Mario Belli (nos. 65, 66, 68–70, 76), as well as of a few of those at the Chontales museum in Juigalpa (nos. 84–89).

75. As late as 1948, the entire east coast of Nicaragua was still virtually unknown archaeologically (Strong in Steward 1948, 4:142). A 1959–61 expedition by Harvard's Peabody Museum retrieved mostly sherds. In the early 1970s the Smithsonian received 450 specimens (mostly fragments) from recent excavations near Monkey Point (accession no. 309560; catalog nos. 467511–44).

76. On the McClain case, which arose over objects removed from Mexico, see Hingston and Ewing in Messenger 1989, 129–47 and 177–83, respectively.

CHAPTER EIGHT

1. This chapter appeared initially as Whisnant 1992.

2. My intention here is limited to comprehending Darío in relation to a few aspects of the politics of culture within Nicaragua itself. I hope that scholars familiar with analogous cultural figures in other national histories will pursue the implications of my rather closely bounded observations. Similarly, it is not my aim to discuss Darío in relation to the still larger history of *modernismo*. Readers interested in either or both of these larger issues might well begin by consulting Beverley and Zimmerman 1990, 54–59.

3. I take the term "cultural capital" from Bourdieu (Richardson 1986, 241–48). In Bourdieu's construction, cultural capital may include not only valued cultural artifacts such as paintings, writings, and the like, but also nonmaterial certifications of worth or competence (e.g., academic credentials or literary recognition) and hereditarily transmitted, consensually recognized (hence marketable) "culture" or "cultivation."

4. At various times, Pablo Antonio Cuadra, José Coronel Urtecho, and Ernesto Cardenal have also been highly venerated. Another contender promoted vigorously by the Sandinistas is Carlos Fonseca Amador (cf. Del Río 1987).

5. Beverley and Zimmerman 1990 employ the partly analogous term "ideological signifier" with reference to Darío (p. 5).

6. Readers interested in mapping and comprehending Darío's politics, especially in relation to *modernismo*, should consult Schulman 1968 and forthcoming, Achugar 1986, and Zavala 1987.

7. The details of Darío's sometimes frenetic travels are most readily available in Torres 1966, 511–34. Interestingly, one result of Darío's traveling and living mostly outside Nicaragua has been that the bulk of the critical scholarship on him treats his nationality

as essentially inconsequential, preferring to interpret him as a pan- or generic "Latin American" figure. My intention here is to reverse that emphasis momentarily.

8. Darío 1909, 13, and 1912, 147, 156. Nearly half the articles included in Barcía 1977, for example, are about Paris.

9. Darío 1954, 603, 825; Beverley and Zimmerman 1990, 57. On Darío and Whitman see Peña 1984. While the analogy is suggestive, important differences between the careers and perspectives of the two writers — as well as the bodies of work each produced — render it problematic.

10. As Salgado 1989 argues, Darío alternately reported and withheld autobiographical details, depending upon their usefulness in the construction of his public persona. I return to this aspect of the story at the end of my analysis.

11. Darío 1917b, 35–40, 131, 149–51. The volume is in fact quite slight and relatively un-revealing of Darío's personal sense of his own country. Of the 162 pages of the 1917 *Obras completas* edition, 42 are blank and approximately 20 are given to direct quotations from Gámez and others. Darío notes without elaboration in *La vida*, p. 17, that a mulatto maid and Indian manservant told him traditional ghost stories (*cuentos de ánimas en pena*) during his childhood. To my knowledge, Darío's most substantial commentaries on Nica-raguan traditional culture consist of two brief articles (Darío 1892 and Mapes 1938, 114–17). The latter, a brief commentary on the Nicaraguan government's exhibit at the Exposición Histórico-Americana of 1892, at least shows that Darío had read the comments of Squier (Squier 1852) and other late nineteenth-century investigators of Nicaraguan antiquities. The larger *modernista* versus *costumbrista* debate concerning national/regional culture is discussed in Beverley and Zimmerman 1990, 42–43.

12. Darío 1954, 778, 316, respectively; cf. 65, 100–101, 226, 802. Assembling scattered ref-erences to *los indios* in Darío's poetry, Pablo Antonio Cuadra argues, however, that more than any other poet of his time, Darío claimed his origins by proclaiming "the pride of being mestizo" (Cuadra 1983, 315). Similarly, Schulman 1968 interprets the pervasive "nos-talgia for the tropics" in Darío as a "nostalgia of origins," which is in effect an identification with his country of birth.

13. As many critics have pointed out (cf. Beverley and Zimmerman, 1990, 42–43), this dilemma was a part of a larger one central to *modernismo*: the relationship between nationalism and cosmopolitanism.

14. As a Nicaraguan, Darío was of course as free as anyone to dress elegantly or read modish French writers. The problem was his *perception* of his Nicaraguanness as lia-bility, and his use of the change in style and cultural allegiance to mark his progress in transcending it.

15. Darío 1912, 265; Watland 1965, 217.

16. On the public lionization of Darío within Nicaragua, see Torres 1966, 350–52.

17. Of the approximately 450 items of Darío's writings listed in *Nicaraguan National Bibliography* through 1986, fewer than forty were published in Nicaragua, and almost half of those belonged to a series of sixteen thirty-page pamphlets issued in 1943 for use in the public schools.

18. Stansifer 1979 emphasizes that President Zelaya's awareness of Darío's well-known "questionable reputation" made him reluctant to appoint him to a diplomatic post (p. 60).

19. One must however bear in mind that Nicaragua was a very poor country, that most Central American countries during the period had very limited ambassadorial rep-resentation, and that in any case the Nicaraguan government could legitimately have been

ambivalent about Darío in view of his well-known propensity for bohemian excess in his personal life. I am indebted to Charles Stansifer for these insights.

20. Official photographs of Darío on his deathbed, of his splendid casket, his brain, his tomb, and of the grandiose romantic statue of him (in flowing robes, with winged angel perched on his shoulder) erected to him in Managua are in Torres 1966 following pp. 481 and 496.

21. "A los liberales" in Darío 1954, 30–31, refers to the Liberals as "soldiers of an idea."

22. A more extended discussion of this period may be found in Watland 1965, 44–52, 76, 98, 123, 130, 166, 200–201, 236.

23. For examples of his anti-clerical poems, see "El Jesuita" and "Al Papa" in Darío 1954, 25, 33. The latter refers to the pope as "Santo Tirano." Darío's reading of Montalvo may in turn have led him to Victor Hugo, universally known and celebrated at the time for his championing of the oppressed. Hugo's poem "Les raisons de Momotombo" had brought him some fame in Nicaragua, and he came to be cited far more often than any other writer in Darío's early poems. See Darío's "Un recuerdo de Victor Hugo" in Mapes 1938, 13, and his poems "A Victor Hugo" and "Victor Hugo y la tumba" in Darío 1954, 208–12 and 435–44.

24. Silva Castro 1934, 201. Originally published in *Revista de Artes y Letras* (1888) when Darío was barely twenty-one years old. For a more extensive comparative discussion of Darío and Martí, especially in relation to the issue of political commitment, see Schulman 1968, 205. Schulman argues that Darío's "capacity to identify himself with [the] problems, disgraces, and victories" of Central America is undeniable.

25. The essay quotes one of Lugones's long revolutionary poems, but focuses principally upon its literary qualities rather than its politics. See also Lugones's poem in honor of Darío in Darío 1954, xxxv–xxxvi, and Kirkpatrick 1989.

26. Darío called Vargas Vila "a singular and unmistakable poet, perhaps against his own will." Later, when Vargas Vila was Nicaragua's consul general in Madrid, the two served together on the Nicaraguan commission to mediate the border dispute with Honduras.

27. See his early poems to Máximo Jerez, Nicaraguan minister to the United States (d. 1881), who was a lifelong champion of union, in Darío 1954, 26, 67, 70, 75, as well as others on Central American union (ibid., pp. 65, 67, 68, 76, 87, 1003). On his work with *La Unión* see Torres 1966, 144–61.

28. "El canal por Nicaragua," in Silva Castro 1934, 19–29 (originally published in *La Epoca* [Santiago], 6 August 1886). Darío returned to the theme of "the Yankee canal builders of Nicaragua" in his very angry essay "El triunfo de Calibán" of 1898 (Mapes 1938, 160–62).

29. Darío 1954, 720–21. More extended is Darío's essay "El arte de ser presidente de la república: Roosevelt" (Barcía 1977, 2: 214–17), which characterizes Roosevelt as a "representative yankee," a "director of imperialistic appetites."

30. Barcía 1977, 1:261–64. Originally published in *La Nación* (Buenos Aires), 28 September 1912.

31. "Panamericanismo," in Ministerio de Educación Pública 1964, 111–17; and "El triunfo de Calibán" (*El Tiempo*, Buenos Aires, 20 May 1889) as reprinted in Mapes 1938, 160–64.

32. Paz [1965] 1972, 53, cautions that it would be "unjust" to characterize Darío's politics on the basis of a poem that arose from his "explainable and spontaneous enthusiasm" on the occasion of the Panamerican conference at which he read the poem.

33. Appropriately enough, Beverley and Zimmerman 1990, 58–60, read this dialectic as

part of Darío's attempt to find a path for Latin American cultural development between U.S. hegemony and "oligarchic immobilism." My interest here, however, is in highlighting the (only apparent, if Beverley and Zimmerman are correct) contradictions that provided proof-texts for later ideological struggles over Darío.

34. Selva 1916, 200–204. Quoted by Mejía Sánchez, 1968, 175, from the Mexican journal *Romance* 15 (February 1941). With Thomas Walsh, Selva also translated and published the bilingual *Eleven Poems of Rubén Darío*. For brief sketches of Selva, see White 1982b, 23, and Beverley and Zimmerman 1990, 58–59.

35. See White 1986, 9; Beverley and Zimmerman 1990, 61. Eventually sensing the unlikelihood of such a development, the *vanguardistas* one after another dropped their support for Somoza, although Coronel Urtecho continued to work in the government into the 1950s. In *Mea maxima culpa* (1975), Coronel Urtecho recanted his error in supporting Somoza. It should not be supposed that the *vanguardistas* were ideologically of one persuasion; as noted by many commentators (e.g., Beverley and Zimmerman 1990, 61) some supported the guerrilla war led by General Augusto C. Sandino. See for example the sections "Contra la intervención y el imperialismo" and "Poesía de protesta," in *El Pez y la Serpiente* 22/23 (1978–79): 113–30.

36. Ministerio de Instrucción Pública 1935, 11–13. Omitted lines quoted from Darío 1917b, 2.

37. Somoza García himself had personal as well as political reasons to take an interest in Darío's image: his wife, Salvadora Debayle Sacasa, was the daughter of Darío's oldest and most intimate friend, Dr. Luis Debayle. Darío and Debayle had played together as children, and Darío wrote poems to various members of the family. Debayle helped him repeatedly in his various relations with the government, and they remained close until Darío's death, after which Debayle conducted the autopsy. This link was first pointed out to me in an interview with Nicaraguan poet Ernesto Gutiérrez (Managua, 3 March 1988). As early as 1937, Somoza began to appoint his Debayle brothers-in-law to official positions in the government. Dr. Luis Manuel Debayle became special agent of the government and Somoza's personal representative; his brother Henri was appointed chargé d'affaires in Washington; another brother, Dr. León Debayle, was appointed Envoy Extraordinary and Minister Plenipotentiary (letters of 7 August, 11 November, 16 November 1937; Offical File 432, Franklin D. Roosevelt Library). For brief commentary on the services provided by the Debayle brothers to Somoza in Washington, see Clark 1992, 26, 29, 46–47, 54–55, 59.

For poems by Darío about Debayle and his family, see Darío 1954, 1144–48. Darío 1917b, 70, calls Debayle "one of the finest, noblest and purest souls I have ever known in my life." See also Watland 1965, 39, 216, 249–52. A photo of Darío with Dr. Debayle appears in Torres Bodet 1966 facing p. 128.

38. See *Nicaragua. Guía general ilustrada* (Managua: Talleres Gráficos Pérez, 1940), sec. 13, p. 20. The ambassador's name is given as Rubén Darío C. Darío's first son, Rubén Darío Contreras, was born in 1891. Another son, born to him and his common-law wife Francisca in 1907, carried the matronymic Sánchez (Watland 1965, 145, 204).

39. Ministerio de Instrucción Pública 1935. The booklet appears to have been a smaller version of a sixty-eight page booklet published earlier by the Sacasa administration. During the same period, Gustavo Alemán Bolaños produced a more ambitious series of sixteen twenty-five-to-thirty-page booklets for the Universidad Central de Nicaragua: *Cuadernos de divulgación de la obra de Darío para la instrucción pública*. Available bibliographic data do not make clear whether the project was in any way sponsored by the Somoza government, but Alemán Bolaños edited other government publications on Darío from the 1940s

until his death in 1958 (for example, Ministerio del Distrito Nacional, *Primeras notas de Rubén Darío*, and Ministerio de Educación Pública 1958).

40. Ministerio del Distrito Nacional, *Primeras notas de Rubén Darío* (1943); Ministerio de Educación Pública, *Rubén, treinta poemas* (1957); *Rubén Darío, crítica* (1964); and Comisión Nacional, *Rubén Darío, antología poética* (1967). Bibliographic data in the *Nicaraguan National Bibliography* do not make completely clear whether the Comisión Nacional was a governmental entity. It seems reasonable to suppose that it was.

41. *Revista Nicaragua* 3:4. See also *Azul* no. 36 (January 1955): 2–9; no. 37 (February 1955); and no. 41 (September 1955): 5. On Castillo Armas see LaFeber 1983, 120–27, and Schlesinger and Kinzer 1984, 113–14.

42. A sign of the slight liberalization of Nicaraguan politics that followed the assassination of Somoza García in 1956 was the Ministry of Education's publication of a collection of his journalistic pieces in 1964, which included the two anti-U.S. essays "El canal" and "Panamericanismo" as well as the anti-British "John Bull Forever" (Ministerio de Educación 1964, 89–109, 111–18).

43. Upon his own induction into the Academy in July 1945, Cuadra—in a speech that also focused upon Darío—had excoriated the English piracy and racist filibusterism that had so distorted Nicaraguan life, and the Yankee imperialism that had intervened "openly, with fixed bayonets and with cynical will to dominate." Cuadra linked Darío with "the other Nicaraguan hero, the . . . mythological Augusto César Sandino" (Cuadra 1985, 125–43).

44. Upon the assassination of his father in late 1956, Luis Somoza Debayle became president. Even the arch-conservative commentator Shirley Christian (1986, 28) remarked that Schick was Luis's "handpicked candidate" for president in 1963 (cf. Woodward [1976] 1985, 222; Bermann 1986, 247; Millett 1977, 226–27). To his credit, Schick tried to moderate some abuses by the National Guard, and managed to protect FSLN founder Carlos Fonseca Amador.

45. Schick Gutiérrez 1966, 9. Subsequent page references in parentheses are to this text.

46. Schick Gutiérrez 1966, 18; Mapes 1938, 108 (from *El Tiempo* [Buenos Aires], 12 May 1896).

47. Exactly when the Somoza government created the Order of Rubén Darío is uncertain. José Sansón-Terán, minister of education in 1966, said that Schick created it when he himself was minister of education (Cabrales 1966, 4). Gould 1990a, 136, says the regime awarded it as early as 1961 to Doña Tesla de Alvarado, a member of Chinandega's landed elite, in recognition of her "donation" of a large tract of formerly communal land (to which her title was obscure at best) to local peasants who had been struggling to regain control of it. Cerutti (1984c, 23) says it was given to Nicaraguan feminist leader Josefa Toledo de Aguerri as early as 1953, at least one instance that contradicts the Sandinista claim that the Somoza regime never conferred it upon those who truly deserved it. On Toledo de Aguerri see Chapter 10.

48. Fonseca 1981, 1:100; *Ventana* no. 5 (October 1960): pp. 1–2. How extensively Fonseca (a voracious reader) was reading in Darío during the formative years of the FSLN is unclear. Beverley and Zimmerman (1990, 30) say that he studied Darío's poetry intensively from 1965 until mid-1966 under the tutelage of Darío biographer Edelberto Torres. His detailed "Chronology of Sandinista Resistance," however (apparently completed about 1966), carries only two references to Darío, and fails to include his death among other important events cited for 1916 (Fonseca 1981, 2:91).

49. Fonseca 1981, 1:422–23. No date of composition is given for the brief essay, originally published in *Casa de las Américas* no. 117 (November 1979): 179–80. Internal evidence makes clear that it was written in, or later than, 1974. Fonseca was killed in 1976.

50. By choosing to represent Darío's writings only by his poetry, the editors were bound to omit most of the more overtly political items. The "Ode to Roosevelt" was, however, included (1:130–31). In defense of the editors, one must note that although UNAN had been technically autonomous for ten years, it was still subject to intense surveillance and periodic repression by the Somoza regime. Although Gómez Espinosa (1966, 320–24) had a year earlier published for the first time Darío's very political essay "Las palabras y los actos de Mr. Roosevelt" (from the *Paris Journal* [27 May 1910]), her overall treatment of Darío is romantic and uncritical.

51. Universidad Nacional Autónoma de Nicaragua, *Cuadernos universitarios* 1:83–88, 90–95. Former *vanguardista* Pablo Antonio Cuadra was represented by an essay on Darío reprinted from his earlier book *El Nicaragüense*, linking the poet to contemporary radical politics in Nicaragua by calling Sandino "the son of 'Ode to Roosevelt.'" A puzzling inclusion (1:53–60) in view of the presumed need to snatch Darío from the smothering embrace of the anti-Communist Somocistas was Stefan Baciu's belligerently anti-Marxist response to the treatment of Darío in Francisc Pacurariu's *Introduction to Latin American Literature* (Bucharest, 1965). Baciu found the book politically objectionable because it judged Darío through the Marxist-Leninist method ("one of the most reactionary that exists in the world").

52. Franco might have cited other pieces by Darío besides "To the Worker" that romanticized working-class life (e.g., "Epístola a un labriego" [Letter to a Peasant], or the paternalistic "El fardo" from *Azul*). Franco's evaluation appears to be based solely upon Darío's poetry rather than upon his journalistic writing, where other critics have found the bulk of evidence of his political insight and commitment.

53. More recently, feminist arguments against Darío and his contemporary *modernistas* have been elaborated in Sternbach 1988 and Davies 1989. Concentrating on *modernista* novels, Sternbach adduces substantial evidence that the patriarchal and essentially misogynist *modernistas* excluded women as writers and admitted them as fictional characters only in the guise of "prostitutes, fallen women, femmes fatales . . . [or] young statuesque beauties," while holding themselves to be "emblem[s] of civilization and culture." Davies concludes that Darío's *Prosas profanas* "establishes an analogy between sexual and literary creation where man's sexual prowess is a metaphor for artistic endeavor and achievement." She argues that "the virgin and the beast are contained within one female figure which is exalted or debased, idolized or sacrificed by the poet at will," and that Darío follows (as in "Coloquio de los centauros") the "common misogynist beliefs of the day regarding women" (Davies 1989, 283–86).

54. Like the Somoza regime, the Sandinistas had familial ties to Darío. President Daniel Ortega's wife Rosario Murillo was a grandniece of Darío and a friend of the family of his childhood friend Dr. Luis H. Debayle (Stone 1990, 40).

55. The Historic Program of the FSLN of 1969 had declared that the Sandinista people's revolution "will rescue the progressive intellectuals, and their works that have arisen throughout our history, from the neglect in which they have been maintained by the anti-people's regimes" (Rosset and Vandermeer 1986, 184).

56. Of *Nuestro Rubén Darío* I have seen only the fourth edition of 1984. "D.Q.," originally published in Buenos Aires in *Almanaque Peuser para el año 1899*, was reprinted in Ibañez 1970, 142–45.

57. The Instituto de Estudio del Sandinismo's 1982 anthology *Pensamiento antimperialista* also included ten pages of extracts from Darío.

58. It may be that Sandino was much influenced by Darío, but Sergio Ramírez's two-volume edition of Sandino's writings contains only two minor references to him (Ramírez 1984b, 1:87 and 2:198).

59. The Order of Rubén Darío was renamed by Decree #927 of 21 January 1982. See *Nicaráuac*, June 1982, p. 99.

60. Arellano (1982b) refers to (but does not quote from or cite a source for) "a dialogue" Darío wrote in 1892 in which, he says, Darío "announced the socialist future of humanity" (p. 104). I have so far been unable to find such a piece; no such title appears either in the *Obras completas*, Silva Castro's *Obras desconocidas*, or Mapes' *Escritos inéditos*. Presumably the dialogue is in prose rather than poetry, for no such piece appeared among Arellano's own selections in *Nuestro Rubén Darío* (1980).

61. O'Keeffe 1984 says that the article originally appeared in Buenos Aires's *La Tribuna* not under Darío's own name, but under the pseudonym "Des Esseintes." Although it probably would be impossible to prove conclusively that Darío either did or did not write the piece, at least the prose style seems uncharacteristic of him: too tight, too single-cadenced, too angry. It also has the strident tone of narrowly sectarian political propaganda and displays a wide-ranging familiarity with nineteenth-century political theorists (Bebel, Becker, Büchner, Cabet, Darwin, DeAmicés, Engels, Feuerbach, Hauptmann, Kelmich, Kobold, LaSalle, Marx, "Pourier" [Fourier, presumably], Schlenter, St. Simon, and De Waldow) — not evident elsewhere in Darío's writings. In any case it runs counter in its arguments to much that he demonstrably did write.

62. Arellano's decontextualizing of the extract he titles "the new good of socialism" is similarly misleading, and for the same reasons. Additionally, the essayist's original reference to "the accommodating logic of Engels" (*la lógica acomodaticia*) becomes merely "Engels' logic" (Arellano 1983b, 37). Unfortunately, space does not permit me to trace and compare all of Arellano's some five dozen quotations with their sources, none of which are given.

63. In 1981 Ramírez reissued a collection of Nicaraguan short stories he had edited in 1976, which included Darío's "The Bourgeois King" (Ramírez [1976] 1981, 39–60). The anthology also included Darío's stories "El fardo" and "Betún y sangre." Ramírez's decision to retain "El rey burgués" in the 1981 and 1986 editions suggests that he was either unaware of or unpersuaded by Aguinaga's reading of it.

64. Ramírez is particularly skillful in presenting the political contradictions within Darío's writing as an inevitable result of the historical circumstances within which he and other *modernistas* lived and worked — necessarily withdrawing into an ivory tower in order "to defend . . . their position as creator[s] in that epoch of capital accumulation . . . of crude and brutal colonialism, rude conquests and hungry masses" (Ramírez 1984a, 98).

65. Rama 1967, 34, had made essentially the same argument.

66. The "little known letter" Valle-Castillo quotes a portion of as evidence appears to stop short of proving any such involvement. It merely refers vaguely to a "promise" Darío had made to the letter's recipient, and shows that he knew some of the details of a voyage by one Colindres to New York to buy arms. Valle-Castillo presumably encountered the letter in Jirón Terán [1915] 1981. The letter in question is from Darío (in Puntarenas) to Vicente Navas in Managua, dated 2 October 1882 (when Darío was fifteen years old). An editorial note says the published copy was made from an original in the possession of one of Navas's descendants. Torres's discussion of this period of Darío's life (Torres 1966,

60–77) does not refer to any such incident. During this period Darío was under strict supervision in a boarding school in San Salvador as a result of some of his bohemian excesses.

67. *La Prensa*, 18 January 1990, p. 13. It is worth noting that since the only short pants to be seen in Nicaragua during this period were being worn by foreigners, the criticism may also have had a xenophobic edge.

68. In a forthcoming paper, Ivan A. Schulman examines the movement of recent criticism toward a comprehension of *modernismo* as "a heterogeneous art with dialogic voices instead of the monolithic expression." Schulman, "El modernismo de Rubén Darío," ms. p. 1. Quoted with permission of the author.

69. With somewhat different analytical aims, Beverley and Zimmerman 1990 have recently referred to Darío's "multivalent cosmopolitanism" (p. 57).

70. The point here is to note the differing degrees of probability; it is *not* to argue that there is no conscious oppositional politics in Darío's poetry. Examining his lyrical poems, for example, Zavala 1987 finds ample evidence — not only in overt theme or statement but also in the resonance of images and the tenor of metaphors — that Darío is anti-imperialist, anti-militarist, and pacifist (see esp. pp. 181, 190). I am grateful to Ivan A. Schulman for this reference. Schulman himself, in "El modernismo de Rubén Darío" (forthcoming), notes that Darío's direct criticism of the regnant social order is more abundant in his prose than in the poetry.

CHAPTER NINE

1. My work on Sandino was aided in its early stages by the meticulous research assistance of my student Gita Dhir.

2. An early scholarly study is Macaulay [1967] 1985. Hodges 1986 and Palmer 1988 are more recent studies that attend more closely to the connections between politics and culture. Hodges 1992 probes in much greater detail than can be encompassed here the issue of Sandino's politics, especially in relation to Joaquín Trincado's Magnetic Spiritual School of the Universal Commune. Schroeder [forthcoming] promises to be the definitive study of the social and cultural dimensions of the topic; I am deeply grateful to Schroeder for making completed chapters available to me, and for allowing me to cite and quote from them.

3. Schroeder [forthcoming] undertakes this task, basing his analysis upon Marine Corps records in the National Archives and upon recorded interviews with survivors of the rebellion conducted by the Instituto de Estudio del Sandinismo in the 1980s.

4. The following biographical details are drawn mainly from Macaulay [1967] 1985, 48–54, and Selser [1978] 1981, 62–64.

5. I have encountered no other assertion that Sandino fathered a child at this point in his life, but Macaulay's apparent source is Sandino's official record of employment at Huasteca. I return subsequently to the larger issue of Sandino's relationships with women.

6. For a detailed discussion of the political influences upon Sandino during this period, and of the consequent development of his thought, see Hodges 1986, 3–8, and passim.

7. Ramírez 1984b, 1:69, 79; Román 1983, 44–46. Several commentators mention Sandino's claim to have traveled in the United States, but there seems to be no documentary evidence that he did or did not. Ramírez 1984b contains only three of his letters dating from before 1926. In one to his father (perhaps from Honduras) written in 1922 when he

was twenty-seven years old, Sandino speaks plaintively of harboring "the illusion of going to other more civilized countries, where I could . . . at least look at the broad and clear light of civilization" (1:73).

8. Here I am concerned principally with the image of himself that Sandino projected beyond the Segovias. An important related matter was the persona he projected to his soldiers and other followers *within* the rebellion itself. As Schroeder demonstrates, whatever large cultural myths were invoked, the latter also depended considerably upon the contemporary climate of political repression and violence suffered by the mine workers among whom he first began to organize. "The raw materials necessary for the propagation of a language of nationalism among the laboring poor of the El Jícaro region existed," Schroeder demonstrates, long before either Sandino or the marines arrived (Schroeder [forthcoming], Chapter 4).

9. Beals 1928 (29 February): 232; Selva 1928, 7; Belausteguigoitía [1934] 1985, 144–45, 185. Cardenal [1972] 1974, 322, recounts similar reports (e.g., the spirit of God appearing as a dove) concerning Fidel Castro on the occasion of his first speech in Havana.

10. Schroeder [forthcoming], List 6.3 in Chapter 6, confirms the presence of three twelve-year-old boys among Sandino's original recruits.

11. Sandino spoke numerous other times of "Indo-latino peoples" and of the "spiritual vibration of the Indo-hispanic race." See Ramírez 1984b, 1:272, 301; 2:46, 252, 271, 349.

12. The following discussion of Turcios's role in elaborating the Sandino myth draws heavily upon Hodges 1986, 85–90.

13. Turcios to Sandino, 17 December 1928, in Ramírez 1984b, 1:306. *Ariel* took its inspiration from Uruguayan writer José Enrique Rodó's book of the same name, addressed to "the youth of America." For Rodó, Shakespeare's Ariel (Latin America) symbolized "the noble, soaring aspect of the human spirit," the antithesis of "brutal sensuality" of Caliban (the United States, which, although it believed itself to be "forger of a type of civilization that will endure forever," was in fact merely in "fervent pursuit of well-being that has no object beyond itself") (Rodó [1900] 1988, 31, 71, 79, 86). Rodó's central theme, Hodges notes, was the superiority of Latin America's "traditional humanistic and spiritual values to the crass utilitarianism, positivism, materialism, and social egalitarianism [*sic*] of the Yankees." Even more to the point here, Hodges observes that Rodó "proposed . . . [a] front of the Latin American republics against U.S. cultural imperialism." As Rodó himself put it, "the genius of our race must play [a formative role] in the recasting of tomorrow" (Hodges 1986, 85; Rodó [1900] 1988, 73).

14. Quotations from and specific citations for *Ariel* articles may be found in Instituto de Estudio del Sandinismo 1983, 211–31. See also Beals 1932, 189–90, and Ghiraldo 1929, 176–82.

15. Quotations are from Turcios letter to Sandino of 11 October 1929, quoted in Ghiraldo 1929, 161–62. Other letters from Turcios to Sandino appear in Somoza García 1936, 112–15. Letters from Sandino to Turcios appear in Ramírez 1984b, 1:146, 153, 206, 229, 252, 259, 270, and 305. At least a dozen pro-Sandino articles appeared in *Ariel* during the early months of 1928. Support for Sandino in *Ariel* continued until Sandino and Turcios parted company in January 1929, by which time Turcios had come to believe that Sandino had transformed "what had been a purely patriotic war against U.S. imperialism into a fratricidal civil war" (Hodges 1986, 85–89).

16. An expanded account appears in Beals 1932, 195–301. Britton 1987, 68–86, discusses Beals's difficulties with the U.S. State Department (which compiled a file on him and harassed him) as a result of his favorable reporting on Sandino.

17. Within the Sandino rebellion, the motive of patriotism was far more tentative and problematic than either contemporary or later biographers implied. "For most soldiers," as Schroeder demonstrates in a meticulous analysis of survivors' recollections, "love of the homeland [was] less important" than the far less transcendent aim of putting an end to the local violence and repression they had suffered at the hands of the Conservative *Chamorristas*. What Sandino did, Schroeder argues, was to graft his project (and the violence that *it* necessarily produced) "onto a radically different vocabulary and project of national honor, patriotism, and social justice" (Schroeder [forthcoming], Chapter 4, p. 42; Chapter 5, p. 45).

18. Grillo, "Augusto C. Sandino: héroe de Hispanoamérica," *Reportorio americano*, 2 June 1928 (reproduced in Ramírez 1984b, 1:368), and Ghiraldo 1929, 65.

19. Belausteguigoitía [1934] 1985, 76–78, 95, 129, 134–36, 140–43, 169. Portions of the book are reprinted in Ramírez 1984b, 2:288–92. Some improbably remote portions of the world began to count Sandino among their heroes from the earliest months of his campaign. Kuomintang troops marching victoriously into Peking as early as 1928 carried a huge portrait of him (Macaulay [1967] 1985, 113, 149; Hodges 1986, 105).

20. Selser [1978] 1981, 182, says the book was probably written by Camilo González, general staff chief of the National Guard and "former counterfeiting comrade" of Somoza (cf. Bermann 1986, 219–20).

21. Significantly, the Somoza attack made no mention of the prior *Chamorrista* violence in the Segovias (examined by Schroeder [forthcoming], Chapters 4–5), thereby heightening the impression that Sandino was violating cultural norms universally recognized and respected by others.

22. The normal meaning of *desocupación* is unemployment, but I render it as withdrawal here because it is the *desocupación* of the marines that is envisioned.

23. Arellano 1980c presents ten *corridos* and ten poems dating from the period of the conflict. About two dozen poems and *corridos* about Sandino, most dating from 1927–34, are collected in Instituto de Estudio del Sandinismo 1983, 135–64. The text of at least one anti-Moncada song, celebrating *los Segovianos* and presumably dating to the Sandino period, was collected from oral tradition in 1944 (Asís Fernández 1986, 140–41).

24. Cf. Schroeder [forthcoming], Chapter 6.

25. "La muerte de Somoza" (The death of Somoza) and "Los Somoza" (The Somozas) in Asís Fernández 1986, 91.

26. Somoza 1936, 262–64; Macaulay [1967] 1985, 226, citing National Guard documents of 1932. Ramírez 1971, 28, notes that a movement in 1931 to establish a federation of Nicaraguan university students was inspired partly by their sympathy with Sandino's struggle. Alemán Bolaños 1932, 77, reports related student activity.

27. Links between the students of the 1960s and Sandino and his struggle in the 1920s and 1930s are too numerous to pursue here. Tomás Borge, for example, reported proudly (Borge [1989] 1992, 57–59) that his father had met and supported Sandino, his mother had sold cigars from her factory to his soldiers, and that his uncle Sofonías Salvatierra had published a biography of him (Salvatierra 1934).

28. The specifically ideological dimensions of that reshaping have already received due attention: Hodges has traced the multiple and often conflicted sources and influences of Sandino's eclectic "rational communism," and both Hodges and Palmer have located him within the historical process that reached from the orthodox Marxism of the 1920s (with which Sandino broke decisively) to the later and much transformed Marxism of the FSLN (Hodges 1986, 3–107, 161–93; Palmer 1988). Hodges 1992 takes great pains to demonstrate

that the FSLN engaged in substantial censorship and manipulation of the available historical record (especially Sandino's letters, including those published in Sergio Ramírez's supposedly definitive and complete edition) in order to present a Sandino shaped to their particular ideological purposes (Hodges 1992, 156–57, 175–76, 181–82, 186).

29. Schroeder [forthcoming], Chapter 9. Schroeder's synopsis of these aspects of the rebellion, from which all my subsequent quotations come, is based upon his own meticulously detailed examination of Marine Corps records in the National Archives.

30. Ibid. Schroeder's data make clear that hundreds of such reports remain in Marine Corps archives, corroborated repeatedly by scores of survivor interviews gathered independently of each other.

31. Ibid. Schroeder also encountered a few records of torture, and other suggestions that it was employed more often than it was reported.

32. Somoza was not the first to try to link Sandino with Bolshevism. Only three months after the Ocotal attack, the *New York Times* reported (22 October 1927, p. 3) that local people formerly friendly to the United States had been converted to "radicalism and Bolshevism" by Sandino. For an excellent analysis of Sandino's relationship to Communist ideology and organization, see Hodges 1992.

33. Ramírez 1983b, 11–55; subsequent references in parentheses in the text. The biographical sketch was originally written as a prologue to the German translation of Ramírez's edition of Sandino's works.

34. Here, as in the case of Fonseca's treatment of the Black Legend, "the mythical place of El Chipote" was quite real, and not significantly different from Ramírez's description. U.S. Marine Corps charged with destroying the facility after its capture reported that there were various wooden buildings including a hospital and a barracks for two hundred men, as well as sufficient supplies of food and other stores to sustain three hundred men for six months (Schroeder [forthcoming], Chapter 6).

35. This is by no means the only biblical parallel in the myth. "What a pity the pirates are so large," Sandino said after killing some marines in one battle (implicitly calling up the David versus Goliath image), "because their uniforms don't fit our people" (Ramírez 1984b, 1:378). The David-Goliath analogy turned up frequently in the U.S. press. See for example "Sandino Calls Off His Gadfly War," *Literary Digest* 115 (18 February 1933): 8.

36. *New York Times*, 22 July 1927, p. 3.

37. Such myths downplayed Sandino's losses and emphasized his troops' boldness and marine cowardice. Schroeder [forthcoming], Chapter 6, establishes (on the basis of archival records) that in fact a combination of about sixty Sandinista soldiers, supported by perhaps eight hundred local people, attacked thirty-nine marines. In the bombing and strafing by planes that followed, probably half of Sandino's eight hundred supporters were killed.

38. *New York Times*, 4 January 1928, p. 3. As early as 22 July 1927, p. 3, the *New York Times* reported that the Pan American Federation of Labor had unanimously urged the immediate withdrawal of U.S. troops. On Lindbergh's tour, see Bermann 1986, 202. Halftemeyer (1946, 102) offers a brief account of Lindbergh's landing in Managua later in the summer, when thousands lined his route to the Palacio Nacional.

39. *New York Times*, 4 January 1928, p. 3; 5 January 1928, pp. 1–2; 21 January 1928, p. 3. Norris to J. Nevin Sayre, 4 February 1928, quoted in *Radical History Review* 33 (1985): 31. For a more detailed treatment of this opposition, see García 1973.

40. *New York Times*, 21 January 1928, p. 3.

41. Ibid., 19 July 1927, p. 10; 20 July 1927, p. 1; 4 August 1927, p. 10; 12 September 1927,

p. 25; 25 October 1927, p. 4; 26 October 1927, p. 8; 18 November 1927, p. 24; 26 November 1927, p. 5; 2, 3 and 28 January 1928, p. 1.

42. Stimson, *American Policy*, 85. Stimson letter to Coolidge of 29 April 1931, quoted in Macaulay [1967] 1985, 199-200. As Macaulay notes, Pancho Villa died the year Sandino first arrived in Mexico (1923), but had ceased his own military operations several years earlier. According to Stimson's arithmetic, Sandino would have had to have joined Pancho Villa at the age of about three. The Pancho Villa connection was often referred to in the U.S. press. See for example "Sandino of Nicaragua: Bandit or Patriot," *Literary Digest* 96 (4 February 1928): 44; "What Lies Behind the Nicaraguan Crisis," *World Review* 4 (13 February 1928): 30 (where Sandino is "the former lieutenant of Francisco Villa"); and Hackett 1934.

This cultural-political discourse of banditry is widespread not only in Latin America but also throughout the world, as Hobsbawm argued in *Bandits* and in *Primitive Rebels*, but that larger discourse and the historiographical issues it raises lie beyond my purpose here. For an excellent and extensive recent discussion, see Joseph 1990 and, in response, Slatta 1991.

43. Retranslated from Spanish text in Ramírez 1984b, 1:127-28. Macaulay ([1967] 1985, 75-76) characterizes the letter but does not provide a full text. In "To Let Nicaraguans Clean Up Nicaragua," *Literary Digest* 109 (2 May 1931): 9, Hoover is quoted as placing "Sandino and his fellow bandits . . . outside the civilized pale." The *Literary Digest* writer said Sandino and his men went "on the rampage . . . much as the Indians did in our old days of frontier fighting."

44. Macaulay ([1967] 1985, 229) expresses skepticism about some of the atrocity stories, but Schroeder's [forthcoming] more recent and thorough research confirms the majority of them.

45. The incident of the *peleles* appealed to Sandino biographers (cf. Alemán Bolaños 1932, 30; Ramírez 1983b, 39).

46. Ramírez 1984b, 1:322. In translation, some of Sandino's playful ambiguity is lost: His phrase *naranjas en la cabeza* can mean either "oranges *on*" or "oranges *in*."

47. Implicitly questioning Sandino's emotional clarity and resolution, Macaulay asserts that when Teresa was hit in the head by shrapnel, Sandino preserved a small piece of her skull that was removed when the wound was cleaned, and had it mounted in a gold ring he continued to wear as a token of the relationship. In his recent introduction to a new edition of Joaquín Pasos's *Poemas de un joven* (Pasos 1986), Ernesto Cardenal mentions (without elaboration) Carmen Sobalvarro, "a woman poet enamored of Sandino" (*una poetisa enamorado de Sandino*), apparently around 1929 (p. 10). Pérez Valle (1986, 27) also mentions the testimony of Francisco Gurdian (not otherwise identified) to the effect that at the end of his life Sandino was in love with President Sacasa's daughter Maruca. In an unpublished paper, based upon interviews conducted by the Sandinista Instituto de Estudio del Sandinismo with surviving members of the Aráuz family and Sandino's general staff, as well as official U.S. Marine Corps archival records, Schroeder has advanced the hypothesis that Sandino's "decision to marry was primarily intended to ritually integrate his cause into the social fabric" of the San Rafael region, which was the "geographic-spiritual center of the movement," and in which the Aráuz family was prominently represented by an extensive kin network. The hastily arranged marriage, Schroeder suggests, "consummated at the precise moment at which [Sandino's] column had reached its lowest ebb . . . and there was a pressing need to . . . breathe new life into an . . . almost moribund cause" (Schroeder [forthcoming], Chapter 7, pp. 10-23).

48. Ramírez 1984b contains no letters from Sandino to Blanca from this period (January 1933).

49. The following account, unless otherwise indicated, is based upon Román, *Maldito país*. I judge his account to be reliable partly because he comments on his conscientious habit of taking notes during the conversations, and of reconstructing draft versions of them immediately thereafter. Quotation is from p. 86. Román's biography, written in 1934, was not published until 1983.

50. For two versions of the virgin story in addition to those cited earlier, see "Sandino of Nicaragua," 42, and Vakil 1928, 35. On the prohibition as extended to Sandino's troops, see for example Grillo, "Augusto C. Sandino, héroe de Hispanoamérica," in Ramírez 1984b, 1:268. Schroeder [forthcoming], Chapter 4, points out that before Sandino, *Chamorrista* violence had made rape a serious social issue in the areas in which Sandino first recruited troops and formed his army. A number of surviving members of Sandino's army recalled the harsh, swift penalties that Sandino meted out for such infractions (Schroeder [forthcoming], Chapter 6).

51. Ramírez 1983b, 32–33. It is worth noting that the romantic account of the wedding was not repeated by all early biographers. Alemán Bolaños's otherwise hagiographic biography (1932, 16) says only that "the wedding was very simple" and that Sandino ordered machine guns to be fired at the conclusion of the ceremony; Salvatierra 1934, 53, passes over the wedding in a single phrase. On the fiftieth anniversary of Blanca's death in childbirth, the Sandinista newspaper *El nuevo diario* returned to the idealized account of Sandino's relationship with Blanca, printing a version of his remarks at her bier sharply different from those recorded by Somoza. Briefly but with dignity and eloquence, the account said, Sandino praised her "great spirit of love and kindness," and called her "a martyr of Nicaragua." A similarly idealized account of the relationship appeared in *Ventana: Barricada Cultural*, 26 September 1981, pp. 19–20.

CHAPTER TEN

1. The larger matter of assessing the costs and benefits to women of putatively progressive social upheaval and change is open to debate. Kelly-Gadol (Harding 1987, 16) argues, for example, that historically there has been "a fairly regular pattern of relative loss of status for women precisely in those periods of so-called progressive change."

2. "Las mujeres que se casan," *Los Domingos*, 6 November 1921, p. 13.

3. Virtually all prior commentators on the Nicaraguan women's movement have either said or implied that there was none before the mid-1970s. As I will show later, that was by no means the case.

4. The characterization of gender order I use here is from Connell 1987, 98–99, which comes in turn from Matthews 1984.

5. Some elements of the established gender order inhere in legal and institutional structures. One might characterize those aspects of resistance as *rigidity*. But since so much of the resistance is also active, thoughtful, and purposeful, the term *recalcitrance* seems to me more evocative and useful. Connerton (1989, 12, 34) uses the term "social habit memory" to discuss the role of "historical residue[s]" in resistance to change. While both terms imply processes more passive than the ones I am most interested in here, Connerton's analysis is especially useful in linking individual with social memory as a basis for socially sanctioned performance (of gender, for example).

Analyzing other forms of cultural recalcitrance would also be appropriate to my purpose here, but I have chosen gender because it is both of paramount importance in itself and because it underlies so many of the other forms, provides a site for their actualization, and heightens their virulence. On another pervasive form of cultural recalcitrance in Nicaraguan society—racism—see Lancaster 1992, 211–34.

6. The term *gender regime* is also from Connell (1987, 99), who uses it to refer to the operation of the gender order within any particular institution (such as the church).

7. Cleveland, "Across the Nicaraguan Transit" (M-M 65), Bancroft Library, University of California, Berkeley, pp. 37, 98.

8. The line is, however, not so sharply drawn as might appear, since Nicaraguan women have traditionally dominated the central markets in villages, towns, and cities.

9. When these norms emerged in Nicaragua is not clear. Traveling up the San Juan river around 1860, Daniel Cleveland repeatedly noted that children (presumably both male and female, since he did not report otherwise) ran naked until the age of ten or even later (Cleveland, "Across the Nicaraguan Transit" [M-M 65], Bancroft Library, University of California, Berkeley, pp. 21, 42). Such patterns—and the messages they communicate about male and female bodies and identities—are both widespread and consistently reproduced in Latin America. Kottak observed them in an Atlantic coastal town in Brazil in the 1960s and 1970s: girls wore dresses from the age of three months, while boys went naked until "near adolescence." "During a baby boy's first year," Kottak reported, "mothers commented on, fondled, and kissed his genitals. Fathers publicly grabbed the penises of older boys, stimulating them to erection, laughing at the child's reaction. Boys were encouraged to masturbate, to engage in homosexual play, and to have sexual relations with willing girls and women" (Niederlein 1898, 86; Kottak 1992, 73).

10. Schmuckler 1984, 76–123. Much of my discussion here is based on Schmuckler, from whom all quotations not otherwise attributed are taken.

11. Cáceres's account is worth reading in its entirety for the light it sheds on these issues.

12. Schmuckler 1984, 123. Kottak (1992, 68) also reports some of these practices. For some of my latter examples I am indebted to María Elena Valenzuela (personal communication, 10 March 1989).

13. "La grandeza de la mujer," *El Reflector*, 13 April 1926, p. 1.

14. After Vatican II in 1962 and the Medellín conference of Latin American bishops in 1968, the dissident liberation theology sector of Nicaraguan Catholics grew steadily and contributed greatly to the downfall of the Somoza regime. But since here I am attempting to account for recalcitrant cultural continuities, I do not explore that strand of church history, which in any case has not proved to be the dominant one. Interested readers will find good accounts in Randall 1983a, Lancaster 1988, 84–99, Foroohar 1989, 67–158, Dodson and O'Shaughnessy 1990, 71–235, and Kirk 1992, 58–99.

15. For an analysis of the church's historical positions on matters of sexuality and domestic life (hence on gender differences) in Latin America, see Lavrin in Lavrin 1989, 47–95, who points out that while the church's arbitrary and repressive managerial approach to sexuality imposed heavy burdens on both men and women, certain of them (for example, restrictions on contraception) fell especially heavily upon women.

16. Even liberal Catholic theologians are not always sanguine about the prospects for changing the Catholic church's historical role in legitimizing and reinforcing the dominant gender order in Nicaragua. "Reading the Bible from the perspective of the poor," Jesuit liberation theologian Juan Luis Segundo has observed, "is easier than reading it from

a women's perspective." His colleague Julio de Santa Ana admits bluntly that Catholic theologians "are trained to be macho bourgeois intellectuals." Brazilian Franciscan priest Leonardo Boff charges that the Catholic church as a whole is burdened by "the historical sin of marginalizing women," and Chilean church historian Pablo Richard has gone even further to assert that Christendom itself "is a macho structure . . . [which] has been continuously dominated by men." Interviews in Tamez 1987, 8, 15, 99, 109 respectively.

17. The Spanish words here are *brazos*, *bantorrillas* (*sic*; *pantorrillas*, presumably), and *piernas*. The latter usually means leg (in its entirety), but since *bantorrillas* specifies the lower leg in this case, I assume that *piernas* refers to the upper leg, the normal term for which would be *muslos*.

18. *El Correo del Istmo de Nicaragua*, 29 March 1850, p. 110.

19. *El Reflector*, 12 February 1926, p. 1.

20. *Nicaragua. Guía general ilustrada*, sec. 3, p. 27.

21. *El Diario Nicaragüense*, 10 March 1928, p. 1.

22. Synoptic treatments of *machismo* may be found in Giraldo 1972 and Guy 1991, 141–56. Although *machismo* carries a Spanish name, in its many cultural variants it is in fact a worldwide phenomenon.

23. *La Prensa*, 25 March 1974, p. 6 (cf. Dealy 1977, 65).

24. Stevens, "Marianismo" (in Pescatello 1973, 96), refers to the submissive component of this ideal as "prenuptial chastity" and "postnuptial frigidity." The partitioning is similar to the "Jezebel" and "Mammy" split that Deborah White observes in U.S. slavemasters' characterizations of slave women (1985, especially 27–61). I am indebted to Anne V. Mitchell for calling White's study to my attention.

25. My discussion here is drawn entirely from Lancaster 1992, 237–48, from which all quotations are taken. Lancaster argues that, unlike the situation in the United States, in which public concern and hostility are focused on *any* deviation by *either* sex from the heterosexual norm, in Nicaragua the issue is solely one of *male* sexuality, so that *machismo* is "not exclusively or even primarily a means of structuring power relations between men and women. It is a means of structuring power between and among *men*." But Randall's more recent interviews with Nicaraguan lesbians (Randall 1994) present evidence to the contrary.

26. In the United States, Lancaster points out, "the object is to label without being labeled, but not to use without being used, for it is the homosexual act itself that is prohibited and not any particular role within the act" (p. 249).

27. I return subsequently to Toledo de Aguerri, a central figure in the early feminist movement in Nicaragua. Readers will shortly become aware that by "feminist" I do not necessarily mean feminism of the post-1960s variety, to which the term has come to be most usually applied (unjustifiably narrowly, it seems to me).

28. Toledo de Aguerri 1935a, 69. Reprinted from *Revista Mujer Nicaragüense* no. 35 (undated; probably late 1920s).

29. Lavrin points out, however, that the number of Spanish women emigrating to the New World was never large, amounting in the first two decades of the sixteenth century to perhaps 5–17 percent. It rose to about 28.5 percent during the latter decades of the century before undergoing a "sharp decline." Lavrin also reports that "women slaveholders freed fewer slaves than men," perhaps because of the "greater economic dependence of some female slaveowners, such as single and widowed women, on the income produced by their slaves" and because of the reluctance of women slave owners to sell slaves who were part of their dowries (Lavrin in Bethell 1984, 2:322–23, 352).

30. It also seemed to me that deeper psychodynamics of co-dependency and collusion might be discovered beneath her "reasons," but their precise configuration lay beyond the information available to me.

31. Although I will here be dealing principally with the modern period, the roots of women's resistance to male domination in Latin America run deep. Behar's analysis of some intersections of gender, power, and religion during the Mexican inquisition (in Lavrin 1989, 186) focuses upon women's employment of "rich symbolic language of beliefs and acts for resisting, punishing, and even controlling the men who dominated them."

32. Lavrin in Bethell 1984, 2:327–28. Among the contradictions Lavrin notes is that in some respects the "legal and economic personality of the woman was not absorbed by the marriage." A woman's husband had to notarize a receipt for her dowry, for example, and promise to repay it from his estate prior to any other distributions. A man's promise of marriage (*palabra de casamiento*) was binding, so that "a man who promised to marry a woman and subsequently deflowered her was accountable for her honour before civil and ecclesiastical authorities." Women could and did sue (Lavrin in Bethell 1984, 2:329–33).

33. My sketch of the movement of Latin American women toward liberation draws heavily upon Miller 1991. Analyses of the history of women in Latin America have multiplied greatly in recent years (cf. Hahner 1976, Chaney 1979, Pescatello 1979, Agosín 1988, Jaquette 1989, and Jelin 1990).

34. For a more extended discussion of these conferences, see Miller 1991 and Miller in Bergmann 1990, 10–26. Not everyone was pleased by these developments, of course. When the Mexican *Congreso de Mujeres de la Raza* (Congress of Women of the Race) met in 1925, the Mexico City daily *El Universal* called it "a scandalous caricature of the National Congress . . . run by women trying to behave like men" (Miller 1991, 94). By the end of the decade, Miller points out, most Latin American women still attended all-female schools, and although women in Ecuador got the vote by 1929, Paraguay (the last holdout) gave it only in 1961.

35. Miller 1991, 182, points out that Chile's right-wing women's group *Poder Femenino* played an important role in toppling the government of Salvador Allende in 1973.

36. Feminist scholars have correctly paid much attention to differences between Latin American *women's* groups (which in general shy away from paradigm-challenging analyses and activities) and *feminist* organizations (which do not). As Jaquette and others have pointed out, nonfeminist organizations tend to emphasize that "women's demands are made legitimate by women's roles as mothers and wives," and hence reject "the more radical elements of the feminist agenda" (Jaquette in Lowenthal 1986, A45–52).

37. Molyneux has asserted, for example (Fagen et al. 1986, 294), that "there was no history of a popular and militant feminism in Nicaragua" before the Sandinistas appeared upon the scene. Molyneux (in Walker 1985, 145–62) and Ramírez-Horton (in Walker 1982, 147–60) take up the story with the advent of the FSLN, as do Randall 1981 and Angel and Macintosh 1987. Kampwirth (1992b, 7–8) also asserts that "under the Somoza dictatorship, there was almost no women's movement," and that "the origins of today's women's movement . . . [date] from the [armed] movement against the dictatorship." Although not concerned with activities that would qualify as militantly feminist by post-1960s standards, Cerutti's 1984 series of articles in *La Nación Internacional* (Costa Rica) (Cerutti 1984a–f) went further than any other commentator of the period to recognize the social, cultural, and political activism of early Nicaraguan women.

38. Noguera Carazo (1974, 4) refers briefly to Josefa Vega's 1852 petition to the legislature. She provides no source for her information.

39. "La mujer," *Semanal Nicaragüense*, 8 August 1872, p. 87. The recently founded (30 May 1872) *Semanal Nicaragüense* was to publish several proto-feminist pieces in ensuing months (Charno 1968, 486).

40. Máximo R. Lira, "La mujer: Sus derechos políticos y sociales," *Semanal Nicaragüense*, 12 June 1873, pp. 362–63 and 28 June 1873, pp. 370–71. I have seen nothing else written by Lira, and have been unable to identify him further.

41. Toledo de Aguerri 1935a, 3–7. Noguera Carazo (1974, 5–7; cf. Cerutti 1984b) says a Normal de Señoritas was founded in León in 1880, and uses the name Normal de Institutoras de Señoritas Americanas for the Granada *colegio* attended by Toledo de Aguerri. She also refers to an Instituto Nacional de Señoritas established by the Zelaya government in 1907. Shortly after the turn of the century, two Nicaraguan students wrote doctoral theses on the legal status of women (Cuadra 1905, Armijo Lozano 1912). Armijo Lozano's thesis was published by Tipografía Progreso Sofonías Salvatierra, a publisher presumably linked to the labor reform efforts of Sofonías Salvatierra, who founded a school for workers in Managua just after the turn of the century (Walter 1987, 51). This connection suggests a possible linkage between the nascent labor and feminist movements in Nicaragua. I have been unable to discover who the North American teachers were who staffed the Colegio, or to locate accessible copies of the Cuadra and Armijo Lozano theses.

42. Biographical details on Toledo are drawn from Portocarrero de Chamorro 1962, 16–19, and Cerutti 1984c.

43. Toledo de Aguerri's reference to the school as "a center of feminine light" (*ese centro de luz femenina*) is from her speech of 1912, "Un prospecto y un discurso," in Toledo de Aguerri 1940, 65. Noguera Carazo 1974, 5, says the school was founded in 1882 as the Normal de Institutoras de Señoritas Americanas. It had been preceded by the Normal de Señoritas in León, founded two years earlier.

44. Toledo de Aguerri also served as Nicaragua's Inspector General of Public Instruction (1923–25). Among the organizations she founded or helped to found were the Junta Femenina de Beneficencia, Club de Señoras de la Capital, la Liga Feminista de Nicaragua, Escuela de Prensa para Obreras, Escuela Nocturna de Obreras, la Mesa Redonda Panamericana, Unión de Mujeres Americanas, la Gota de Leche and Sala Cuna (Portocarrero de Chamorro 1962, 18, 66; Toledo de Aguerri 1932, 276–77; R. de Mendoza 1933). Toledo de Aguerri's brief accounts of founding the Escuela de Prensa and the Club de Señoras may be found in Toledo de Aguerri 1935a, 14–17. The best assembly of essential biographical details on Toledo de Aguerri is in Cerutti 1984c. Since after her marriage Toledo wrote principally under the name Josefa T. de Aguerri, I will henceforth refer to her as Toledo de Aguerri.

45. Reprinted in Toledo de Aguerri 1935a, 9. The pioneering importance of *Revista Femenina Ilustrada* thus far appears to have gone unrecognized. Greenberg (in Bergmann 1990, 182–231) lists only fifteen Latin American women's periodicals for the period 1900–1920, and her list includes none from Central America. This would make *Revista Femenina Ilustrada* the only Central American feminist periodical of the period. On early Latin American women printers, journalists, and periodicals, see Bergmann 1990, 173–81, and Hahner in Lavrin 1978, 254–85.

46. Quoted from *Revista Femenina Ilustrada* of June 1919; reprinted in Toledo de Aguerri 1935a, 11, 19.

47. Whether the former journal ceased publication at the appearance of the latter or overlapped it slightly is not clear. Toledo de Aguerri referred to the latter as both *Revista Mujer Nicaragüense* and *Mujer Nicaragüense*.

48. Toledo de Aguerri 1935a, 41, 50–52, 53–54, 60, 68–70. The earliest of the pieces was reprinted from *Revista Mujer Nicaragüense* no. 4 (October 1919).

49. In the early 1950s, at the age of 84, Toledo de Aguerri was honored as *Mujer de las Américas* (Woman of the Americas) (Portocarrero de Chamorro 1962, 19). For an account of the visit with Cuban feminist leader Maiben de Ostolaza, and Toledo de Aguerri's sanguine evaluation of *feminismo yankee*, see Toledo de Aguerri 1926, 66–68 and 215–18, respectively.

50. Toledo de Aguerri buttressed her theoretical claim with a long list of contemporary Nicaraguan women teachers, poets, editors, and other professionals. Since the names of early Nicaraguan women who openly challenged the gender order are difficult to come by, I append her list (together with the brief descriptive phrases she supplied for a few of the women) for possible use by future researchers: Aura Rostand (María de la Selva de Ibarra; sister of poet Salomón de la Selva) [poet, *escritora de pensamiento y acción*], Nila Jiménez de Orozco [*escritora y poetisa, dirige revistas literarias*], Sara Barquero, Justina Huezo de Espinosa, Blanca Vega, Carmen de Talavera, Yolanda Caligaris, Carmen de Mantilla, Carmen Sobalvarro, Blanca del Valle (María Fugle) [poet], Blanca Victoria Mejía [poet], Adriana de Calderón, Rosa Ch. Praslin de Buitrago, Sara P. de Rodríguez, Alicia Rostrán [humorist], Olga Núñez Abaunza, Sara Solís de Rivas [journalist], Angélica de Argüello [*luchando por la intromisión de la mujer en el voto político*], María Gámez, and María Cristina Zapata.

51. For evidence of her diplomacy, see her 1937 statement in honor of President Anastasio Somoza García's wife Salvadora in Toledo de Aguerri 1940, 29ff.

52. Duran, "Algo sobre el voto femenino," *Los Domingos*, 9 October 1921, p. 2.

53. I have encountered no firm evidence on what may have transpired with respect to the suffrage campaign between the 1921 article of Aristides Duran and the early 1930s. I have also been unable to discover an exact founding date for the Cruzada, or dates for its formal alliances with other Latin American women's organizations. Miller (1991, 93) notes that the Liga Internacional was in existence at least by the mid-1920s, but gives no date for its founding. Walter (1987, 52) says that a Liberal Party platform in the 1930s embraced "extension of political rights to women," but he gives no details. Sra. Juanita Molina de Fromen was a Nicaraguan delegate to the 1934 meeting of the Inter-American Commission of Women (13 June 1934 Inter-American Commission of Women to Marvin McIntyre [secretary to President Roosevelt], Official File 567, Franklin D. Roosevelt Library).

54. Toledo de Aguerri 1940, 21–25. The petition was issued by la Liga Internacional de Mujeres Ibéricas e Hispanoamericanas y Cruzada de Mujeres Nicaragüenses [LIDMI], Delegación Nicaragüense de la Liga Internacional Pro-Paz y Libertad, la Primera Liga Panamericana Femenina de Educación, "*el profesorado de la República*," el Comité Interamericano de Mujeres, and el Centro Femenino de Cultura Obrera. Title 2, Article 27 of Nicaragua's current constitution reserved the vote to males over twenty-one years of age; women were demanding that it be open to everyone over eighteen who could read and write (*La Prensa*, 24 February 1939, p. 1). That would have constituted something of a gain, but in view of the very high rates of illiteracy in Nicaragua at the time, the gain would have been limited to a relatively small number of middle- and upper-class women.

55. Some of the roots of his opposition, Sevilla Sacasa explained, were traceable to a painful experience he had as a very young judge in León. After convicting a priest of criminal wrongdoing, he found himself publicly attacked by the press and a group of women who came to the priest's defense. Narrating the episode in fulsome detail (pp. 11–14), Sevilla Sacasa presents himself as a model of (typically masculine) courage, dispassionate

judgment, high principle, and unswerving devotion to duty. Sevilla Sacasa, who was married to Somoza's only daughter Liliam, handled Somoza's legal affairs and later served as Nicaraguan ambassador to the United States. In 1974 he was taken prisoner in the FSLN's famous "Christmas party" raid on the home of José María Castillo Quant (Informational document on Sacasa attached to 28 May 1943 Roosevelt letter to Somoza, Official File 432, Franklin D. Roosevelt Library; Booth 1985, 142; Walter 1987, 236).

56. *La Prensa*, 24 February 1939, p. 1; Toledo de Aguerri 1940, 21–22. By the mid-1940s Nicaraguan women were well represented in the country's few small graduate and professional schools, and a number of them were writing their theses on women's social situation and legal status (Núñez Abaunza 1945; Huezo de Espinosa 1946; Borge de Sotomayor 1953; Luna Silva 1956). Núñez Abaunza later served as cultural attache in the Nicaraguan embassy in Washington and Vice Minister of Public Education (1950–56), and was the first woman deputy to serve in the national legislature (1957–71) (Noguera Carazo 1974, 11). Other evidence (*Corona Funebre* 1977) suggests that Núñez integrated herself thoroughly with the Somoza regime and its Liberal National Party.

57. I have encountered no further information on either the Organization of Democratic Women or the Patriotic Organization of Nicaraguan Women. It is not clear what happened to the earlier Nicaraguan women's movement of Toledo de Aguerri's generation, but it seems likely that it lost energy and focus after women were granted the vote in the mid-1950s. Toledo de Aguerri died on 28 March 1962, a few days short of her ninety-sixth birthday (Cerutti 1984c, 23).

58. Universidad Nacional Autónoma de Nicaragua 1975, 12–15. Fiallos noted that the percentage of women students at UNAN had risen from 23 percent to 37.5 percent in fifteen years. Fiallos, the son of former rector Mariano Fiallos Gil, had completed his doctorate in political science at the University of Kansas in 1968, a critical year of student activism.

59. Unrepresented, for example, was poet Rosa Umaña Espinosa (1872–1924). Sánchez's *Sombras*, published during her late teens, contained conventional lyric poetry except for the openly erotic "Extasis" (Ecstasy). The earliest anthology of Nicaraguan poetry I have seen (Ortiz [1912?]) presented no women poets, although Umaña Espinosa had at least two collections in print at the time. María Teresa Sánchez's own anthology of Nicaraguan poetry, published twenty-five years earlier than the UNAN anthology (*Poesía nicaragüense: (antología)* [1948]) included sixteen women poets born between 1835 and 1926, including Carmen Díaz (b. 1835), who fought in the one of the country's civil wars and wrote a militant poem of national liberation; Cándida Rosa Matuz (b. 1850); Dolores García Robleto (b. ca. 1870); Josefa María Vega (b. 1880); Berta Buitrago (b. 1886); Aura Rostand (b. 1905); Amada Aragón (b. 1907); Carmen Sobalvarro (b. 1908); Olga Solari and Annie Vallardes Sáenz (both b. 1916); Alicia Prado (b. 1918); Ruth Zúñiga (b. 1926); and others. Daisy Zamora's more recent *La mujer nicaragüense en la poesía* (1992) summarily dismisses all of the pre-1960s women poets as "lacking in merit" (Zamora 1992, 23).

60. The 1984 booklet was published by the Sandinista women's organization AMNLAE, discussed below.

61. On Sandinista mass organizations, see Ruchwarger 1987.

62. Toledo de Aguerri 1935a, 118–23; Palma 1988, 21–22. Palma also adds the name of Josefa Chamorro, who fought in the defense of Granada during Nicaragua's struggle for independence from Spain (p. 25). For a comparative discussion of women's participation in various Latin American guerrilla movements, see Lobao 1990.

63. Particularly noteworthy was the Mejía Godoy brothers' *Amando en tiempo de guerra*, released on the Discotec del Arte Popular label in Costa Rica in January 1979, six

months before the fall of Somoza. It offered several songs eulogizing heroic women: "Juana," a *nom de guerre* standing for the thousands of female combatants involved in the struggle; the teenage Sandinista martyr Arlén Siu; the war widow María Soledad; and white-haired Rosa Hernández, an illiterate *campesina* mother who had given six sons to the struggle. Two other examples are "El Zenzontle," on the Mejía Godoy brothers' 1979 album *Guitarra Armada* (Ocarina MC-015), and "Luisa Amanda Espinosa" on their *Canto épico al FSLN* (Pentagrama LPP-031/032) of 1984.

64. All of the young enlisted women Randall interviewed (1981, 129–49) insisted that the few minor gender-related problems they encountered were resolved easily, and that the troops frequently used filial and familial metaphors to characterize their relationships with male comrades in arms. The language of this particular example suggests, however, that the gender issues may have been more problematic than the participants in (and observers of) such temporary unions supposed.

65. Vilas 1986, 108–9, contests this figure. Using Nicaraguan Institute for Social Security and Welfare (INSSBI) data, he arrives at a total of 6.6 percent. "More than in direct combat," Vilas concludes, "women's participation seems to have taken place fundamentally in support tasks."

66. Readers interested in more detail than can be accommodated in my brief synopsis of women's participation in the armed struggle will find it in abundance in Tijerino 1978, Randall 1981, Deighton 1983, and Sola and Trayner 1988.

67. Such advertising was ubiquitous in every period following the introduction of major North American commercial advertising in the early years of the century. AMNLAE's 1984 booklet *Mujer en Nicaragua*, p. 48, includes one of the more outrageous examples (unfortunately not of sufficient quality to reproduce here): a photograph taken in a billiard parlor in Chontales shows an Alka-Seltzer advertising poster in the background, bearing the image of a bikini-clad woman pushing a package of the product into the front of the bikini panty. The caption says *Diga buenas noches con Alka-Seltzer y verá que buenas noches!* (Say good night with Alka-Seltzer, and you will see how good the night will be!).

68. For an extended analysis of wife beating in late 1980s Nicaragua, see Lancaster 1992, 34–47. Collinson 1990 (pp. 17, 20, 69) notes that the Sandinistas typically blamed capitalism for the existence of prostitution. Cultural anthropologist Milagros Palma 1988, 177, reports, however, that "the idea of the necessity for prostitution" has "always existed" in Nicaragua, noting that the ancient Nicaraguan folk drama *El torovenado* includes a prostitute among its *dramatis personae*. Fragmentary statistics for earlier decades suggest that rape and associated crimes were probably much underreported in Nicaragua. The *Boletín Mensual de Estadística* for 1937 lists only forty-two cases of rape in the entire country.

69. My synopsis is drawn from Field, to whose excellent study my brief account cannot do justice.

70. On the *artesanía* section of the Ministry of Culture, see Dirección de Artesanías del Ministerio de Cultura, "Reseña del sector artesanal," *Ventana: Barricada Cultural*, 17 August 1985, pp. 10–11. The Dirección de Artesanías was created in 1980. ENIARTE was the marketing entity within the Dirección.

71. Bransford (1881, 71) reported that women potters (some of them young girls) were actively practicing their craft in San Juan del Sur, some ninety-five kilometers to the south of San Juan del Oriente, a hundred years earlier.

72. Ramírez's date of 1973 for her training is puzzling, since the ATC was not formed until 1977.

73. More broadly, Molyneux (in Fagen et al. 1986, 290) notes that the *Ley de Alimen-*

tos (Family Law) of 1982, intended to democratize the family, "was not taken up by the executive and public discussion of the issues it raised all but ceased in 1983." For a more detailed discussion of the problems of distributing contraceptives and making legal abortion available through the therapeutic abortion committees, see Wessel 1991, 541–44.

74. Molyneux 1988, 125, notes that experience in other developing countries proves that pro-natalist policies "can coincide with extending reproductive rights to women." It is important to bear in mind that, as Kampwirth (1992b, 15) has observed, "public debate over abortion in the 1980s was initiated, not by AMNLAE, but by health professionals. . . . AMNLAE, which remained silent during the debate, supported decriminalization, but not legalization."

75. The AMPRONAC statement is undated, but obviously predates the publication of Maier's book in 1980.

76. In fairness one must note that the Sandinistas had only limited power to change (at least in the short run) the stubbornly deep-rooted cultural values, forms, and practices upon which the gender order had rested for so long. But the contradictions within official ideology were fully within their power to alter.

77. The ambiguity returned in the constitutions of 1858, 1893, and 1905 (Chapter 5, Article 8; Title 5, Article 20; Title 4, Article 14; Alvarez Lejarza 1958, 533, 561, 627). All constitutions after 1858 also specified that only those who could read and write were eligible for citizenship. The paucity of educational opportunities for women thus made it highly unlikely that women would qualify.

78. The discussion of the constitutional process that follows is based almost entirely upon Morgan 1990 and 1992 (the latter her brief consideration of women's issues in the transition back to conservative rule under Violeta Chamorro).

79. *El Nuevo Diario*, 20 January 1988, p. 1.

CONCLUSION

1. Lest one too facilely assume that such a dynamic is characteristic of most cultures in most times and places, one has only to think of the currently turbulent cultural conflict in Eastern Europe or the Middle East, which is occurring between long-established and fully defined cultures whose boundaries are not congruent with national ones.

2. Arellano 1991a. All subsequent quotations are from this source. The exact date of Arellano's induction is not given; it occurred prior to April 1991.

3. See Arellano 1982b, 104, and 1983b, 35. One of the early publications of the post-Sandinista Instituto Nicaragüense de Cultura (successor to the Sandinista Ministerio de Cultura) was the small volume of essays *Ciclo Dariano 1991*, edited by Jorge Eduardo Arellano. Among its contributors were several former partisans of a Sandinista reading of Darío: poet Julio Valle-Castillo, *testimonio* writer Lizandro Chávez Alfaro, Carlos Tünnerman Bernheim, and Guillermo Rothschuh Tablada (author of the "12 proposiciones para rescatar a Darío" cited earlier [Rothschuh Tablada 1982]), whose essay "Darío: poesía y política" signals that the argument explored here continues. An analysis of the specific ideological shifts evident in the publication (for a copy of which—sent to me after an earlier version of this chapter was published in *Latin American Research Review* [Whisnant 1992]—I am grateful to Jorge Arellano) is beyond both my purpose and the space available here.

4. *Revista Nicaragüense* 1 (April 1992): 87–92 and 136–38, respectively.

5. *La Prensa*, 6 May 1988. Subsequent quotations from this source.

6. Kampwirth 1992a, 11–12, 1992b, 20. Josefa Toledo de Aguerri was arguing for sex education in Nicaraguan schools as early as 1935 (Toledo de Aguerri 1935b, 45–53). Humberto Belli, member of the small charismatic religious sect City of God, headed the right-wing Puebla Institute in Washington, D.C., before returning to become Chamorro's Minister of Education (cf. Hockstader 1990).

7. Wessel (1991, 546) reports that by mid-1991 the committee had been disbanded, and the duty to decide about abortions given to the (male) director of the hospital. Abortions dropped immediately from approximately thirty per month to almost none.

8. Kampwirth (1992b, 19) characterizes the Sandinistas' 1990 electoral campaign as "long on *machista* images and short on content," and notes that prior to the election, the Sandinista Youth organization had begun to stage beauty contests. She observes further (pp. 5, 22, 26) that in post-Sandinista Nicaragua the women's movement "has splintered off into a variety of groups" to both the left and right of AMNLAE, and that in the absence of adequate social services, the movement has become in effect an "alternative state" in providing those services.

9. Columbia record 37214 (ca. 1947).

SOURCES CITED

MANUSCRIPT MATERIALS

Cambridge, Massachusetts
Harvard University Archives
    Peabody Museum Correspondence, 1851–1899
    Frederick Ward Putnam Papers, 1877–1899
Peabody Museum, Harvard University
    Earl Flint Papers

Durham, North Carolina
Duke University Library
    Jabez Lamar Monroe Curry Papers

Hyde Park, New York
Franklin D. Roosevelt Library

New Haven, Connecticut
Yale University Library
    Arthur Bliss Lane Papers
    Samuel Smith Wood Papers

New Orleans, Louisiana
Howard-Tilton Memorial Library, Tulane University
    Dieseldorff Collection

San Francisco, California
Bancroft Library, University of California, Berkeley
    Flavel Belcher Letters (C-B 524)
    Carpenter Family Papers
    Daniel Cleveland Papers (M-M 65)
    William G. Doolittle Papers
    Eri B. Hulbert and William W. Walker Papers (C-B 586)

PUBLISHED MATERIALS

Nicaraguan Newspapers

Granada:
El Centroamericano	*El Nicaragüense*
Diario de Granada	*La Reacción*
El Diario Nicaragüense	*El Reflector*
El Independiente	*Telégrafo Setentrional*

León:

Boletin de Noticias	*Correo del Istmo*
Boletin del Pueblo	*La Patria*
El Centroamericano	

Managua:

Barricada	*La Noticia*
El Debate	*Novedades*
Diario de la Capital	*El Nuevo Diario*
Diario Latino	*Los Nuevos Horizontes*
El Diarito	*Opera bufa*
Flecha	*La Prensa*
El Imparcial	*Semanal Nicaragüense*
La Mañana	*Ventana: Barricada Cultural*

Masaya:

Los Anales	*La Hora: Diario al Servicio de la Cultura*
El Defensor del Orden	*Los Nuevos Tiempos*

Articles and Books

Abelleira, Jorge. 1981. "Entrevista paralela con el cine y la TV Nicaragüense." *Ventana: Barricada Cultural*, 12 December, pp. 2–4.

Achugar, Hugo. 1986. " 'El Fardo' de Rubén Darío: receptor armonioso y receptor heterogéneo." *Revista Iberoamericana* 52 (October-December): 857–74.

Acuña, Gustavo. 1981. "El toro-venado de Rama." *Ventana: Barricada Cultural*, 27 June, p. 17.

Adams, Richard N. 1957. *Cultural Surveys of Panama, Nicaragua, Guatemala, El Salvador, Honduras*. Washington, D.C.: Pan American Union.

———. 1981. "The Sandinistas and the Indians: The Problem of the Indians in Nicaragua." *Caribbean Review* 10 (Winter): 23–25, 55–56.

Agosín, Marjorie. 1988. *Women of Smoke*. Pittsburgh: University of Pittsburgh Press.

Alegría, Claribel, and D. J. Flakoll. 1982. "La danza en la Revolución." *Ventana: Barricada Cultural*, 1 May, p. 7.

Alemán Bolaños, Gustav. 1932. *¡Sandino! Estudio completo del Héroe de las Segovias*. Managua: Imprenta de la República.

Alemán Ocampo, Carlos. 1981. "El torovenado y la resistencia cultural." *Ventana: Barricada Cultural*, 31 October, pp. 2–3.

Alerón, Salomón. 1983. "Un canto de piedra-cantera entre el humo de la lucha: entrevista a Pablo Martínez Téllez." *Ventana: Barricada Cultural*, 19 July, pp. 22–23.

Alexander, Edward P. 1983. *Museum Masters: Their Museums and Their Influence*. Nashville: American Association for State and Local History.

Alvarez Lejarza, Emilio. 1943. *El problema del Indio en Nicaragua*. Managua: Editorial Nuevos Horizontes.

———. 1958. *Las constituciones de Nicaragua*. Madrid: Ediciones Cultura Hispánica.

American Assembly. 1968. *Cultural Affairs and Foreign Relations*. Washington, D.C.: Columbia Books.

Angel, Adriana, and Fiona Macintosh. 1987. *The Tiger's Milk: Women of Nicaragua.* London: Virago.

Arce Castaño, Bayardo. 1982. "Por un arte nutrido de nuestras dificultades." *Nicaráuac* 2 (June): 65–72.

———. 1983. "Tanto arte . . . tanta actividad cultural." *Ventana: Barricada Cultural,* 19 July, pp. 2–4.

Archetti, Eduardo. 1988. "Argentinian Tango: Male Sexual Ideology and Morality." Unpublished manuscript, Department of Social Anthropology, University of Oslo.

Arellano, Jorge Eduardo. 1969. *El movimiento de vanguardia de Nicaragua: Gémenes, desarrollo, significado, 1927–1932.* Managua: Impr. Novedades.

———. 1971. "¿Cultura y empresa privada?" *Praxis,* no. 1 (August).

———. 1977a. *La colección Squier-Zapatera: estudio de estatuaria prehispánica.* Managua: n.p.

———. 1977b. *25 poemas indígenas de Nicaragua.* Managua: Universidad Centroamericana.

———. 1977c. *El Güegüence: Comedia-Bailete de la época colonial.* Managua: Ediciones Distribuidora Cultural.

———. 1978. *Pintura y escultura en Nicaragua.* Managua: Banco Central de Nicaragua.

———. 1979. "Ernesto Cardenal: de Granada a Gethsemany (1925–57)." *Boletín nicaragüense de bibliografía y documentación,* no. 31 (September-October): 25–43.

———. [1980?]. *Breve historia de la Iglesia en Nicaragua 1523–1979.* Managua: n.p.

———. 1980a. *Rubén Darío: textos sociopolíticos.* Managua: Biblioteca Nacional.

———. 1980b. *Nuestro Rubén Darío.* Managua: Ministerio de Cultura.

———. 1980c. *Corridos y poemas del Ejército Defensor de la Soberanía Nacional de Nicaragua.* Managua: Imprenta Nacional.

———. 1981a. "Historia de la pintura en Nicaragua: desarrollo contemporáneo." *Ventana: Barricada Cultural,* 14 November, pp. 13–14; 12 December, p. 5.

———. 1981b. *Sandino en la Plástica de América.* León: Editorial Universitaria.

———. 1982a. *Panorama de la literatura nicaragüense.* 4th ed. Managua: Editorial Nueva Nicaragua.

———. 1982b. "Rubén Darío, Antimperialista." *Casa de las Americas* 23, no. 133 (July-August): 104–8.

———. 1982c. "Breve bibliografía de la música nicaragüense." *Boletín nicaragüense de bibliografía y documentación* 49 (September-October): 1–7.

———. 1982d. *Rubén Darío: prosas políticas.* Managua: Ministerio de Cultura.

———. 1983e. *Lecciones de Sandino.* 2d ed. Managua: Ediciones Distribuidora Cultural.

———. 1983f. *Rubén Darío: tantos vigores dispersos (ideas sociales y políticas).* Managua: n.p.

———. 1991a. "El proyecto cultural de Darío." *Revista del Pensamiento Centroamericano* 46, no. 211 (April): 49–60.

———. 1991b. "El Güegüence: obra de teatro representativa del la Nicaragua colonial." *Mesoamérica* 22 (December): 277–309.

Armijo Lozano, Modesto. 1912. *Derechos políticos de la mujer.* León: Tipografía Progreso de Sofonías Salvatierra.

Arnove, Robert F. 1986. *Education and Revolution in Nicaragua.* New York: Praeger.

Arrólija Urbina, Alicia. 1983. "Los diez y ocho años de Irene López." *Ventana: Barricada Cultural,* 21 May, p. 10.

Asís Fernández, Francisco de (ed.). 1986. *Poesía política nicaragüense*. Managua: Ministerio de Cultura.

Avendaño, Gerardo. 1982. "Nuestros artesanos en la Revolución." *La Chacalaca* 1, vuelo 3 (December): 23, 26-28.

Ayón, Tomás. 1882. *Historia de Nicaragua desde los tiempos más remotos hasta el año de 1852*. 3 vols. Granada: Tipografía de "El Centro-Americano."

Azrael, Jeremy R. 1978. *Soviet Nationality Policies and Practices*. New York: Praeger.

Banberger, Ellen Lee. 1984. "Rubén Darío: el hombre y su época." Ph.D. diss., University of California, San Diego.

Barcía, Pedro Luis. 1977. *Escritos dispersos de Rubén Darío (recogidos de periódicos de Buenos Aires)*. 2 vols. La Plata: Facultad de Humanidades y Ciencias de la Educación, Universidad de La Plata.

Barillas Beltrán, Jovita. 1963. "Derechos civiles y políticos de la mujer." LLD diss., Universidad Nacional Autónoma de Nicaragua, León.

Baudez, Claude F. 1970. *Central America*. Translated by James Hogarth. London: Barrie and Jenkins.

Beals, Carleton. 1928. "With Sandino in Nicaragua." *Nation*, 22 February, pp. 204-5; 29 February, pp. 232-33; 7 March, pp. 260-61; 14 March, pp. 288-89; 21 March, pp. 304-15; 28 March, pp. 340-41.

———. 1932. *Banana Gold*. Philadelphia: J. B. Lippincott.

———. 1933. "Sandino Keeps His Word." *Nation*, 22 February, pp. 204-5.

———. 1938. *The Coming Struggle for Latin America*. New York: J. B. Lippincott.

Belausteguigoitía, Ramón. [1934] 1985. *Con Sandino en Nicaragua*. 2d ed. Managua: Editorial Nueva Nicaragua.

Belcher, Captain Edward. [1843] 1970. *Narrative of a Voyage Around the World Performed in Her Majesty's Ship Sulphur, During the Years 1836-1842*. 2 vols. Reprint. Folkestone and London: Dawsons of Pall Mall.

Belli, Gioconda. 1980. "Marco político para el desarrollo cultural nicaragüense." *Casa de las Américas* 200 (May): 61-63.

———. 1981a. "El tren de las seis visto por nuestra *Ventana*." *Ventana: Barricada Cultural*, 31 October, pp. 4-5.

———. 1981b. "MECATE: expresión destacada del arte popular." *Ventana: Barricada Cultural*, 14 November, pp. 2-3.

———. 1982. *Truenos y arco iris*. Managua: Editorial Nueva Nicaragua.

———. 1984. *Amor insurrecto*. Managua: Editorial Nueva Nicaragua.

———. 1986. *De la costilla de Eva*. Managua: Editorial Nueva Nicaragua.

Belt, Thomas. [1874] 1985. *The Naturalist in Nicaragua*. London: J. Murray. Reprint. Chicago: University of Chicago Press.

Berendt, Carl Hermann. 1868. "Report of Explorations in Central America." In *Annual Report of the Board of Regents of the Smithsonian Institution Showing the Operations, Expenditures and Condition of the Institution for the Year 1867*. Washington, D.C.: Smithsonian Institution.

Bergmann, Emilie, et al., eds. 1990. *Women, Culture, and Politics in Latin America: Seminar on Feminism and Culture in Latin America*. Berkeley: University of California Press.

Berle, Beatrice Bishop, and Travis Beal Jacobs (eds.). 1973. *Navigating the Rapids, 1918-1971: From the Papers of Adolf A. Berle*. New York: Harcourt Brace Jovanovich.

Bermann, Karl. 1986. *Under the Big Stick: Nicaragua and the United States Since 1848.* Boston: South End Press.

Bethell, Leslie (ed.). 1984. *Colonial Latin America.* Vols. 1–2 of *The Cambridge History of Latin America.* New York: Cambridge University Press.

Bethell, Leslie, and Ian Roxborough (eds.). 1992. *Latin America Between the Second World War and the Cold War, 1944–1948.* New York: Cambridge University Press.

Beverley, John, and Marc Zimmerman. 1990. *Literature and Politics in the Central American Revolutions.* Austin: University of Texas Press.

Black, George. 1981. *Triumph of the People: The Sandinista Revolution in Nicaragua.* London: Zed Press.

Blakemore, Steven (ed.). 1988. *Voices Against the State: Nicaraguan Opposition to the FSLN.* Coral Gables, Fla.: Institute of Interamerican Studies, Graduate School of International Studies, University of Miami.

Blanco Aguinaga, Carlos. 1980. "La ideología de la clase dominante en la obra de Rubén Darío." *Nueva revista de filología hispánica* 29 (2): 520–55.

Blandón, Jesús M. 1982. *Entre Sandino y Fonseca.* Managua: Departamento de Propaganda y Educación del FSLN.

Blasier, Cole. 1983. *The Giant's Rival: The USSR and Latin America.* Pittsburgh: University of Pittsburgh Press.

Boggs, Carl. 1976. *Gramsci's Marxism.* London: Pluto Press.

Bolaños Geyer, Enríque (ed.). 1985. *1984 Nicaragua.* San José: Libro Libre.

Bolaños Vega, Andres. 1954. *Colección Somoza.* 17 vols. Madrid: n.p.

Booth, John. 1985. *The End and the Beginning: The Nicaraguan Revolution.* 2d ed. Boulder, Colo.: Westview Press.

Borge, Tomás. 1981a. "El arte homo herejía." *Nicaráuac* 2 (January): 111–19.

———. 1981b. "Poesía y revolución: sueños posibles." *Plural* 10 (2a época), no. 115 (April): 29–31.

———. 1981c. *Los primeros pasos: La Revolución Sandinista.* Mexico, D.F.: Siglo XXI Editores.

———. 1984. "La poesia está en el poder." *Conjunto,* no. 59 (January-March): 19–25.

———. [1989] 1992. *The Patient Impatience: From Boyhood to Guerrilla: A Personal Narrative of Nicaragua's Struggle for Liberation.* Translated by Russell Bartley, Darwin Flakoll, and Sylvia Yoneda. Willimantic, Conn.: Curbstone Press.

Borge de Sotomayor, Amelia. 1953. *La mujer y el derecho.* León: Universidad Nacional de Nicaragua.

Borges Morán, Pedro. 1960. *Métodos misionales en la cristianización de América.* Madrid: Departamento de Misionología Española.

———. 1977. *El envío de misioneros a América durante la época española.* Universidad Pontífica.

Borgeson, Paul W., Jr. 1977. "The Poetry of Ernesto Cardenal." Ph.D. diss., Vanderbilt University.

Bourgois, Philippe. 1981. "Class, Ethnicity, and State among the Miskitu Amerindians of Northeastern Nicaragua." *Latin American Perspectives* 8 (Spring): 22–39.

Bovallius, Carl. [1886] 1970. *Nicaraguan Antiquities.* Reprint. Managua: Fondo de Promoción Cultural, Banco de América.

———. 1887. *Resa I Central-Amerika, 1881–1883.* Uppsala: R. Almqvist and J. Wiksell's Boktryckeri.

———. [1887] 1977. *Viaje por Centroamérica 1881–1883*. Translated by Camilo Vijil Tardon. Managua: Fondo de Promocion Cultural, Banco de América.

Boyle, Frederick. 1868. *A Ride across a Continent: A Personal Narrative of Wanderings Through Nicaragua and Costa Rica*. 2 vols. London: R. Bentley.

Bransford, J. F. 1881. *Archeological Researches in Nicaragua*. Washington, D.C.: Smithsonian Institution.

Bravo, Alejandro. 1983. "Cultura popular en León: CPC Antenor Sandino." *Ventana: Barricada Cultural*, 19 July.

Brinton, Daniel G. [1883] 1969. *The Güegüence; A Comedy Ballet in the Nahuatl-Spanish Dialect of Nicaragua*. Reprint. New York: AMS Press.

———. 1892. "Report upon the Collections Exhibited at the Columbian Historical Exposition." In *Report of the U. S. Commission to the Columbian Historical Exposition at Madrid*. Washington, D.C.: n.p.

Britton, John A. 1987. *Carleton Beals: A Radical Journalist in Latin America*. Albuquerque: University of New Mexico Press.

Buckman, Robert. 1990. "Cultural Agenda of Latin American Newspapers and Magazines: Is U.S. Domination a Myth?" *Latin American Research Review* 25 (2): 134–55.

Burgos, Elizabeth (ed.). 1985. *Me llamo Rigoberta Menchú*. Mexico, D. F.: Siglo Veintiuno Editores.

Burns, E. Bradford. 1975. *Latin American Cinema: Film and History*. Los Angeles: UCLA Latin American Center.

———. 1979. *Elites, Masses, and Modernization in Latin America, 1850–1930*. Austin: University of Texas Press.

———. 1980. *The Poverty of Progress: Latin America in the Nineteenth Century*. Berkeley: University of California Press.

———. 1991. *Patriarch and Folk: The Emergence of Nicaragua 1798–1858*. Cambridge: Harvard University Press.

Burton, Julianne. 1983a. "Latin American Film Cultures: The Continuing Quest for the National and the Popular." *Studies in Latin American Popular Culture* 2:256–61.

———. 1983b. *The New Latin American Cinema, 1960–1980*. New York: Smyrna Press.

———, (ed.). 1986. *Cinema and Social Change in Latin America*. Austin: University of Texas Press.

———, (ed.). 1990. *The Social Documentary in Latin America*. Pittsburgh: University of Pittsburgh Press.

Byam, George. 1849. *Wild Life in the Interior of Central America*. London: Parker.

Cabezas, Omar. [1982] 1985. *Fire From the Mountain: The Making of a Sandinista*. Translated by Kathleen Weaver. New York: New American Library.

Cabrales, Luis Alberto. 1964. *Rubén Darío, breve biografía*. Managua: Publicaciones de la Secretaria de la Presidencia de la República.

———. 1966. *El provincialismo contra Darío*. Managua: Ministerio de Educacíon Pública, Extension Cultural.

Calatayud Bernabeu, José. 1968. *Manolo Cuadra: El yo y las circunstancias*. Managua: Editorial Hospicio.

Cardenal, Ernesto. 1960. *Gethsemani, Ky.* Mexico, D.F.: n.p.

———. [1969] 1973. *Homenaje a los indios americanos*. Translated by Monique and Carlos Altschul. Baltimore: Johns Hopkins University Press.

———. [1972] 1974. *In Cuba*. Translated by Donald D. Walsh. New York: New Directions.

———. 1973. *Poesía nicaragüense*. Havana: Casa de las Américas.

———. 1976. *El evangelio en Solentiname*. 2 vols. Caracas: Editorial Signo Contemporáneo.

———. 1979. *Poesía y revolución: antología poética*. Mexico, D.F.: Editorial Edicol.

———. 1980a. "Cultura revolucionaria, popular, nacional, antimperialista." *Nicaráuac* 1 (May): 163–68.

———. 1980b. "Del afiche a la Revolución." *Nicaráuac* 1 (July): 128–29.

———. 1981a. "Revolution and Peace: The Nicaraguan Road." *Journal of Peace Research* 18:201–7.

———. 1981b. "La cultura de la nueva Nicaragua." *América Latina* (USSR), no. 1-2, pp. 39–51.

———. 1981c. "La unidad contra el imperialismo." *Nicaráuac* 2 (December): 103–7.

———. 1982a. "Defendiendo la cultura, el hombre, y el planeta." *Nicaráuac* 3 (January): 149–52.

———. 1982b. "Aprender la revolución." *Ventana: Barricada Cultural*, 10 October, pp. 3–5.

———. 1982c. "La democratización de la cultura." In *Colección popular de literatura nicaragüense*, no 2. Managua: Ministerio de Cultura.

———. 1982d. "Como un sol recién nacido: talleres de poesía, socialización de los medios de producción poéticos." *Ventana: Barricada Cultural*, 9 January, pp. 12–13.

———. 1982e. *Los campesinos de Solentiname pintan el evangelio*. Managua: Ediciones Monimbó.

———. [1982] 1984. *Nostalgia del futuro: pintura y buena noticia en Solentiname*. Managua: Editorial Nueva Nicaragua.

———. 1983a. *Nueva antología poética*. 4th ed. Mexico, D.F.: Siglo Veintiuno Editores.

———. 1983b. *Ernesto Cardenal Antología*. Managua: Editorial Nueva Nicaragua / Ediciones Monimbó.

———. 1986a. "La literatura de la reconstrucción." *América Latina* 4 (April): 75–82.

———. 1986b. *Poesía nicaragüense*. Managua: Editorial Nueva Nicaragua.

Cardenal, Ernesto, and José Coronel Urtecho. 1963. *Antología de la poesía norte americana*. Madrid: Aguilar.

Cardenal Argüello, Salvador. 1962. "Breves apuntes sobre la música en Nicaragua." *Revista conservadora* 3 (May): 35–41.

Cartas sobre la educación del bello sexo por una señora americana: reimpresas del orden de S.E. el señor presidente de la República don Fernando Guzmán, para el uso del bello sexo nicaragüense. Managua: Impr. del Gobierno, 1869.

Castellón, H. A. 1940. *Historia patria elemental para las escuelas de Nicaragua*. Managua: Talleres Gráficos Pérez.

Castillo-Barquero, Magdiel. 1989. "The Context and Meaning of the Zapatera Sculptures: Punta del Sapote: Mound 1." Master's thesis, University of Texas.

Catálogo de los objetos que envía la República de Nicaragua a la Exposición Histórico-Americana de Madrid. [1893?]. n.p., n.p.

Cedeño, Francisco. 1982. "Tepenáhualt [*sic*; Tepenáhuatl?], pilar del pueblo." *Ventana: Barricada Cultural*, 4 September, p. 6.

Centro de Documentación. 1989. *La mujer en la revolución nicaragüense: bibliografía*. Managua: Centro de Publicaciones del INIES.

Centro de Investigaciones y Documentación sobre la Costa Atlántica. 1974. "Trabil nani—muchos problemas: ¿Qué pasa con los Miskitos?" *Nueva sociedad* 74 (September): 103–14.

Cerutti, Franco. 1983. *El Güegüence y otros ensayos de literatura nicaragüense*. Roma: Bulzoni.

———. 1984a. "Una olvidada poetisa nicaragüense a sesenta años de su muerte: Rosa Umaña Espinosa." *Temas de Nuestra América* 2 (October): 7–15

———. 1984b. "Evolución cultural." *La Nación Internacional* [Costa Rica], 6 September, p. 23.

———. 1984c. "Luchadoras de la cultura." *La Nación Internacional* [Costa Rica], 13 September, p. 23.

———. 1984d. "Contribución feminina a las artes nicaragüenses." *La Nación Internacional* [Costa Rica], 20 September, p. 22.

———. 1984e. "Poesía con voz de mujer." *La Nación Internacional* [Costa Rica], 27 September, 22.

———. 1984f. "Las olvidadas de la poesía nicaragüense." *La Nación Internacional* [Costa Rica], 11 October, 18.

Chamorro Cardenal, Roberto. 1988. *Lo que se quiso ocultar: 8 años de censura sandinista*. San José: Libro Libre.

Chaney, Elsa. 1979. *Supermadre: Women in Politics in Latin America*. Austin: University of Texas Press.

Charno, Steven M. (comp.). 1968. *Latin American Newspapers in U.S. Libraries: A Union List*. Austin: University of Texas Press.

Cháves, Crisanta. [1970s?]. "Historia del Museo Nacional." Unpublished typescript in office files of the Director of the Museo Nacional, Managua.

Chavez Alfaro, Lizandro. 1980. "Nación y narrativa nicaragüense." *Casa de las Américas*, no. 120 (May): 69–73.

Christian, Shirley. 1986. *Nicaragua: Revolution in the Family*. New York: Vintage Books.

Churchill, Awnsham [1704] 1744–46. *A Collection of voyages and travels, some now first printed from original manuscripts, others now first published in English*. 6 vols. London: H. Lintot.

CIDCA/Development Study Unit. 1987. *Ethnic Groups and the Nation State: The Case of the Atlantic Coast in Nicaragua*. Stockholm: Development Study Unit, Department of Social Anthropology, University of Stockholm.

Clark, Paul Coe, Jr. 1992. *The United States and Somoza, 1933–1956: A Revisionist Look*. Westport, Conn.: Praeger.

Clarke, Mary, and David Vaughan. 1977. *Encyclopedia of Dance and Ballet*. New York: Putnam.

Clifford, James. 1988. *The Predicament of Culture: Twentieth Century Ethnography, Literature and Art*. Cambridge: Harvard University Press.

Cockburn, John. 1735. *A Journey over Land, from the Gulf of Honduras to the Great South-Sea*. London: C. Rivington.

Cole, Douglas. 1985. *Captured Heritage: The Scramble for Northwest Coast Artifacts*. Seattle: University of Washington Press.

Collinson, Helen, et al. (eds.). 1990. *Women and Revolution in Nicaragua*. London: Zed Books.

Comisión de Estudios de Historia de la Iglesia en América Latina [CEHILA]. 1985.

América Central. Vol. 6 of *Historia general de la iglesia en América Latina*. Salamanca: Ediciones Sígueme.

Comisión Nacional para la Celebración del Centenario del Nacimiento de Rubén Darío. 1967. *Rubén Darío, antología poética*. Managua: Comisión Nacional para la Celebración del Centenario del Nacimiento de Rubén Darío.

Comité Central Femenino Pro-voto de la Mujer de Nicaragua. 1950. *Exposición del Comité Central Femenino Pro-voto de la Mujer de Nicaragua (Adscrito a la Federación de Mujeres de América) a la Asamblea Nacional Constituyente*. Managua: Comité Central Femenino.

Connell, R. W. 1987. *Gender and Power: Society, the Person and Sexual Politics*. Stanford: Stanford University Press.

Connerton, Paul. 1989. *How Societies Remember*. New York: Cambridge University Press.

Conzemius, Eduard. 1932. *Ethnographical Survey of the Miskito and Sumu Indians of Honduras and Nicaragua*. Bureau of American Ethnology Bulletin 106. Washington, D.C.: Government Printing Office, 1932.

Corona Funebre en Recuerdo de la Doctora Olga Núñez de Saballos: Primer Aniversario de su muerte. 1977. Managua: n.p.

Coronel Urtecho, José. 1982. "Anotaciones y Exageraciones Sobre *La Montaña es Algo Más*." *Nicaráuac* 3 (June): 39–42

———. 1983. "Habla José Coronel." *La Chacalaca* 1 (April): 5–10.

———. 1985a. *Rápido tránsito (al ritmo de Norteamérica)*. Managua: Editorial Nueva Nicaragua.

———. 1985b. *Prosa reunida*. Managua: Editorial Nueva Nicaragua.

Coronel Urtecho, José, Ernesto Cardenal, Fernando Silva and Ernesto Gutiérrez (eds.). 1979. *50 años del Movimiento de Vanguardia de Nicaragua, 1928-29—1978-79*. Número Extraordinario de *El Pez y la Serpiente* 22/23 (Winter-Summer).

Cortázar, Julio. 1983a. "Esta revolución es cultura." *Areíto* 9 (34): 17–20.

———. 1983b. "Decir la palabra 'cultura' en Nicaragua." *Araucaria de Chile*, no. 22 (1983): 47–53.

———. 1985. *Nicaragua tan violentemente dulce*. 2d ed. Managua: Editorial Nueva Nicaragua.

Crabtree, Beth G., and James W. Patterson. 1979. *Journal of a Secesh Lady: The Diary of Catherine Ann Devereux Edmondston, 1860–1866*. Raleigh: North Carolina Department of Cultural Resources.

Craven, David. 1989. *The New Concept of Art and Popular Culture in Nicaragua since the Revolution in 1979: An Analytical Essay and Compendium of Illustrations*. Lewiston, N.Y., and Queenston, Ont.: Edwin Mellen Press.

Criado de Val, Manuel. 1981. *Cervantes: su obra y su mundo. Actas del I Congreso internacional sobre Cervantes*. Madrid: EDI-6.

Crook, J. Mordaunt. 1972. *The British Museum*. New York: Praeger.

Crosby, Alfred W. 1986. *Ecological Imperialism: The Biological Expansion of Europe, 900–1900*. Cambridge: Cambridge University Press.

Cuadra, Benjamín. 1905. *Situación jurídica de la mujer nicaragüense*. Granada: n.p.

Cuadra, Manolo. 1982. *Sólo en la compañía*. Managua: Editorial Nueva Nicaragua.

Cuadra, Pablo Antonio. 1934. *Poemas nicaragüenses, 1930–33*. Santiago, Chile: Nascimiento.

———. [1937] 1981. *Por los caminos van los campesinos*. Managua: Ediciones El Pez y La Serpiente.

———. 1938. *Hacia la cruz del sur*. Buenos Aires: Comisión Argentina de Publicaciones e Intercambio.

———. 1964. *Poesía: selección 1929–1962*. Madrid: Ediciones Cultura Hispánica.

———. 1977. *Tierra que habla: antología de cantos nicaragüenses*. 2d ed. San José: Editorial Universitaria.

———. [1969] 1981. *El nicaragüense*. 10th ed. Managua: Editorial El Pez y La Serpiente.

———. 1979. "La intervención extranjera y el proceso de autodeterminación en Nicaragua: aspecto cultural." *Encuentro*, no. 15:74–80.

———. 1980. *Siete arboles contra el atardecer*. Caracas: Ediciones de la Presidensia de la Republica.

———. 1983. "Rubén Darío y la aventura literaria del mestizaje." *Cuadernos Hispanoamericanos* 133 (August): 307–21.

———. 1985. *Torres de Dios: ensayos literarios y memorias del movimiento de vanguardia*. Managua: La Prensa Literaria.

Cuadra, Pablo Antonio, and Francisco Pérez Estrada. 1978. *Muestrario del folklore nicaragüense*. Managua: Banco de América.

Darío, Rubén. 1892. "Estética de los primitivos nicaragüenses." *Revista "Centenario"* 3, pp. 197ff. Reprinted in *Revista de Ideas Estéticas* 25 (October 1967): 291–98.

———. 1909. *El viaje a Nicaragua e Intermezzo tropical*. Madrid: Biblioteca "Ateneo."

———. 1912. *La vida de Rubén Darío escrita por él mismo*. Barcelona: Casa Editorial Maucci.

———. 1917a. *Prosa política*. Vol. 13 of *Obras completas*. Madrid: "Mundo Latino."

———. 1917b. *El Viaje a Nicaragua e Historia de mis libros*. Vol. 17 of *Obras completas*. Madrid: "Mundo Latino."

———. 1921. *Páginas olvidadas*. Buenos Aires: Ediciones Selectas América.

———. 1954. *Rubén Darío: Poesías completas*. Madrid: Aguilar.

———. 1955. *Obras completas de Rubén Darío*. 5 vols. Madrid: Afrodisio Aguado.

———. 1973. *El mundo de los sueños*. Edición de Angel Rama. San José: Universidad de Puerto Rico.

———. 1979. *Páginas escogidas*. Edición de Ricardo Gullón. Madrid: Ediciones Cátedra.

Davies, Catherine. 1989. "Woman as Image in Darío's *Prosas Profanas*." *Romance Quarterly* 36 (August): 281–88.

Davis, Richard Harding. 1896. *Three Gringos in Central America*. New York: Harper and Brothers.

Dealy, Glen Caudill. 1977. *The Public Man: An Interpretation of Latin American and Other Catholic Countries*. Amherst: University of Massachusetts Press.

Deighton, Jane, et al. (eds.). 1983. *Sweet Ramparts: Women in Revolutionary Nicaragua*. [London]: War on Want and the Nicaraguan Solidarity Campaign.

Del Río, Eduardo. 1987. *Carlos para todos*. Managua: Editorial Vanguardia.

Deneven, William (ed.). 1976. *The Native Population of the Americas in 1492*. Madison: University of Wisconsin Press.

Dennis, Phillip A. 1981. "The Costeños and the Revolution in Nicaragua." *Journal of Interamerican Studies and World Affairs* 23 (August): 271–96.

Deutsch, Sandra McGee. 1991. "Gender and Sociopolitical Change in Twentieth-Century Latin America." *Hispanic American Historical Review* 71 (May): 259–306.

"Devolviendo al pueblo su verdadera historia: los museos en la revolución." 1983. *Ventana: Barricada Cultural*, 4 June, p. 7.

Diederich, Bernard. 1981. *Somoza and the Legacy of U.S. Involvement in Central America.* New York: E. P. Dutton.

Dodson, Michael, and Laura Nuzzi O'Shaughnessy. 1990. *Nicaragua's Other Revolution: Religious Faith and Political Struggle.* Chapel Hill: University of North Carolina Press.

Dorfman, Ariel, and Armand Mattelart. [1971] 1984. *How to Read Donald Duck: Imperialist Ideology in the Disney Comic.* Translated by David Kunzle. 2d ed. New York: International General.

———. 1983. *The Empire's Old Clothes: What the Lone Ranger, Babar and Other Innocent Heroes Do to Our Minds.* New York: Pantheon.

Doyle, Judith. 1984. "Theatre of Extraordinary Reality: Interview with Alan Bolt." *Impulse* 11 (Summer): 56–57.

Dozier, Craig. 1985. *Nicaragua's Mosquito Shore: The Years of British and American Presence.* Tuscaloosa: University of Alabama Press.

Dratch, Howard, and Barbara Margolis. 1987. "Film and Revolution in Nicaragua." *Cineaste* 15, no. 3:27–29.

Dussel, Enrique. 1981. *A History of the Church in Latin America: Colonialism to Liberation, 1492–1979.* Translated by Alan Neely. Grand Rapids, Mich.: William B. Eerdmans.

Eliot, Marc. 1993. *Walt Disney: Hollywood's Dark Prince.* New York: Birch Lane.

Fagen, Richard R., Carmen Diana Deere, and José Luis Coraggio (eds.). 1986. *Transition and Development.* New York: Monthly Review Press.

Fay, Eliot G. 1942. "Rubén Darío in New York." *Modern Language Notes* 58 (December): 641–48. Reprinted in Mejía Sánchez 1968, pp. 424–31.

Ferletti, René, and Joaquín Matilló Vila. 1977. *Piedras Vivas.* Managua: Gurdian, División Editorial.

Fernández Morales, Enrique. 1961. "Doña Asilia, pintora primitivista." *El Pez y la Serpiente* 2 (August): 89–95.

Ferro, Marc (ed.). 1972. *Social Historians in Contemporary France: Essays from Annales.* New York: Harper and Row.

Fiallos Gil, Mariano. 1964. "Introduction al estudio del proceso cultural centroamericano." *Ventana*, no. 1 (second trimester): 3–63.

———. 1965. "Los primeros pasos de la reforma universitaria en Nicaragua." *Ventana*, no. 2 (July): 59.

Field, Les. 1987. " 'I am content with my art': Two Groups of Artisans in Revolutionary Nicaragua." Ph.D. diss., Duke University.

Flint, Earl. 1882. "Antiquities in Nicaragua." *American Antiquarian* 4:289–302.

Floyd, Troy S. 1967. *The Anglo-Spanish Struggle for Mosquitia.* Albuquerque: University of New Mexico Press.

Flynn, Patricia. 1980. "Women Challenge the Myth." *NACLA Report on the Americas* 14 (September): 20–35.

Folkman, David I. 1972. *The Nicaragua Route.* Salt Lake City: University of Utah Press.

Fondo de Promoción Cultural, Banco de América. 1976. *La Guerra en Nicaragua según Frank Leslie's Illustrated Weekly.* Managua: Fondo de Promoción Cultural, Banco de América.

Fonseca Amador, Carlos. 1981. *Obras.* 2 vols. Managua: Editorial Nueva Nicaragua.

Foroohar, Manzar. 1989. *The Catholic Church and Social Change in Nicaragua.* Albany: State University of New York Press.

Franco, Jean. 1967. *The Modern Culture of Latin America: Society and the Artist.* New York: Praeger.

Frank Leslie's Illustrated Newspaper. 1976. *The War in Nicaragua as Reported by Frank Leslie's Illustrated Newspaper, 1857–1860.* Managua: Fondo de Promoción.

Frappier, Jon. 1969. "U.S. Media Empire/Latin America." *NACLA Newsletter* 2 (January): 1–11.

Frente Sandinista de Liberación Nacional. 1981. *Las reglas del juego las dicta el pueblo.* Managua: Departamento de Propaganda y Educación.

Froebel, Julius. 1859. *Seven Years' Travel in Central America.* London: Richard Bentley.

Fuentes, Napoleon. 1982. "La praxis de Leonel Vanegas." *Nicaráuac* 3 (June): 163–67.

Gabuardi, Gloria. 1986. *Defensa del amor.* Managua: Editorial Nueva Nicaragua.

Gage, Thomas. [1648] 1958. *Thomas Gage's Travels in the New World.* Edited by J. Eric S. Thompson. Norman: University of Oklahoma Press.

Galarza, Pedro. 1985. "Seis años de Escuela en la Danza Nicaragüense." *Ventana: Barricada Cultural,* 10 August, pp. 14–15.

Galeano, Eduardo. 1981. "La revolución como revelación." *Nicaráuac* 2 (December): 109–14.

Gámez, José Dolores. 1889. *Historia de Nicaragua. Desde los tiempos prehistóricos hasta 1860, en sus relaciones con España, México y Centroamérica.* Managua: Tipografía El País.

García, Rogelio. 1973. "Opposition Within the Senate to the American Military Intervention in Nicaragua, 1926–1933." Ph.D. diss., Columbia University.

García Marquez, Gabriel. 1983. *El asalto: El operativo con que el FSLN se lanzó al mundo. Un relato cinematográfico.* 2d ed. Managua: Editorial Nueva Nicaragua.

Gasparini, Bill. 1983. "El Festival de la Nueva Canción, 1983: Artists of New Song Meet in Managua." *Nicaraguan Perspectives* 7 (Winter): 23–24.

Génie, Virginia T. L. 1980. "Cultura de ayer y de mañana: entrevista a Lizandro Chávez Alfaro." *Plural* 9, 2a época (July): 14–15.

Gentile, William Frank. 1989. *Nicaragua: Photographs by William Frank Gentile.* New York: W. W. Norton.

Ghiraldo, Alberto. 1929. *Yanquilandia bárbara.* Madrid: Editorial Historia Nueva.

Gilbert, Dennis, and David Block (eds.). 1990. *Sandinistas: Key Documents / Documentos Claves.* Ithaca: Cornell University Latin American Studies Program.

Giraldo, Octavio. 1972. "El machismo como fenómeno psicocultural." *Revista Latinoamericana de psicología* 4 (3): 295–309.

Girard, Augustin. 1970. *Cultural Development: Experience and Politics.* Paris: UNESCO.

Goepfert, Paul. 1987. "*Walker*: The Ugly American in Nicaragua." *Baltimore Sun,* 24 May, p. 3N.

Gómez Espinosa, Margarita. 1966. *Rubén Darío, Patriota.* Madrid: Ediciones Triana.

Gould, Jeffrey L. 1989. " 'At the Cost of a Thousand Sacrifices': The Demise and Survival of the Nicaraguan Indians, 1880–1924." Paper presented at the meeting of the Southern Historical Association, Louisville, Kentucky.

———. 1990a. *To Lead as Equals: Rural Protest and Political Consciousness in Chinandega, Nicaragua, 1912–1979.* Chapel Hill: University of North Carolina Press.

———. 1990b. " 'La Raza Rebelde': Las luchas de la comunidad indígena de Subtiava, Nicaragua (1900–1960)." *Revista de Historia (Costa Rica),* no. 21–22 (January–December): 69–117.

Grafton, Anthony. 1992. *New Worlds, Ancient Texts: The Power of Tradition and the Shock of Discovery.* Cambridge: Harvard University Press, Belknap Press.

Greenfield, Jeanette. 1989. *The Return of Cultural Treasures*. New York: Cambridge University Press.

Greenleaf, Richard E. (ed.). 1971. *The Roman Catholic Church in Colonial Latin America*. New York: Knopf.

Guamán Poma de Ayala, Felipe. 1987. *Nueva crónica y buen gobierno*. Edición de John V. Murra, Rolena Adorno y Jorge L. Uriaste. Madrid: Historia 16.

Guerrero, Douglas. 1982. "El movimiento cultural Leonel Rugama." *La Chacalaca* 1 (December): 19–23.

Gumicio Dagrón, Alfonso. 1979. "El cine militante en América Latina desde 1969." *Plural*, 2a época, 9 (November): 52–55.

———. 1981a. "Cine y revolución en Nicaragua." *Plural*, 2a época, 11 (December): 62–67.

———. 1981b. *Workers' Cinema: Theoretical and Practical Support for the Generation of Super 8 Workshops*. Managua: Taller de Cine Super 8, Central Sandinista de Trabajadores.

———. 1982. "Cine obrero sandinista." *Plural*, 2a época, 11 (July): 35–40.

Gutiérrez, Ernesto. 1976. "Tengo mis poemas que no puedo publicar." *Taller*, no. 12 (October).

———. 1980. "Poesía nicaragüense actual." *Casa de las Américas*, no. 120 (May): 64–68.

———. 1983. *En mi y no estando: antología poética*. Managua: Editorial Nueva Nicaragua.

Gutiérrez, J. Ramón. 1981. "La guerra de los indios de Matagalpa 1881." *Ventana: Barricada Cultural*, 5 September, pp. 2–3.

Gutiérrez Mayorga, Gustavo. 1978. "El reformismo artesano en el movimiento obrero nicaragüense, 1931–1960." *Revista del pensamiento centroamericano* 33 (April): 2–21.

Guy, Donna J. 1991. *Sex and Danger: Prostitution, Family and Nation in Argentina*. Lincoln: University of Nebraska Press.

Guzmán, David J. 1902. "Museo Nacional de Nicaragua." *La Patria* (León) 4:10 (January): 290–91.

Hackett, Charles W. 1934. "The Death of Sandino." *Current History* 40 (April): 78–80.

Hahner, June E. 1976. *Women in Latin American History: Their Lives and Views*. Los Angeles: UCLA Latin American Center.

Hale, Charles R. 1994. *Resistance and Contradiction: Miskitu Indians and the Nicaraguan State, 1894–1987*. Stanford: Stanford University Press.

Hale, John. 1826. *Six Months' Residence and Travels in Central America through the Free States of Nicaragua and Particularly Costa Rica*. New York: n.p.

Halftermeyer, Gratus. [1946?]. *Managua a través de la Historia: 1846–1946*. Managua: Editorial Hospicio S. J. de Dios.

Ham, Clifford D. 1916. "Americanizing Nicaragua: How Yankee Marines, Financial Oversight and Baseball Are Stabilizing Central America." *American Review of Reviews* 53 (February): 185–90.

Harding, Sandra (ed.). 1987. *Feminism and Methodology: Social Science Issues*. Bloomington: Indiana University Press.

Harnacker, Marta. "El gran desafío: entrevista a Jaime Wheelock." *Aréito* 9 (34): 12–16.

Harper's Weekly. 1976. *The War in Nicaragua as Reported by Harper's Weekly, a Journal of Civilization, 1857–1860*. Managua: Fondo de Promoción.

Harrison, Helene Westbrook. 1970. *An Analytical Index of the Complete Poetical Works of Rubén Darío*. Washington, D.C.: Microcard Editions.

Hart, Dianne Walta. 1990. *Thanks to God and the Revolution: The Oral History of a Nicaraguan Family*. Madison: University of Wisconsin Press.

Hartman, Betsy. 1987. *Reproductive Rights and Wrongs: The Global Politics of Population Control and Contraceptive Choice.* New York: Harper and Row.

Healy, Paul F. 1980. *Archaeology of the Rivas Region, Nicaragua.* Ontario: Wilfrid Laurier University Press.

Helms, Mary. 1971. *Asang: Adaptations to Culture Contact in the Miskito Community.* Gainesville: University of Florida Press.

———. 1975. *Middle America: A Culture History of Heartlands and Frontiers.* Englewood Cliffs: Prentice-Hall.

———. 1989. "Symbols of Ethnicity: Geo-Politics and Cosmography among the Miskitu of Eastern Central America." Paper presented to the XV International Congress of the Latin American Studies Association, San Juan, Puerto Rico.

Hernández, José R. 1969. *Historia: Radio Nacional de Nicaragua.* Managua: Tipografía Pereira.

Heyck, Denis Lynn Daly. 1990. *Life Stories of the Nicaraguan Revolution.* New York: Routledge.

Himmerich y Valencia, Robert. 1991. *The Encomenderos of New Spain: 1521–1555.* Austin: University of Texas Press.

Hirshon, Sheryl, and Judy Butler. 1983. *And Also Teach Them to Read.* Westport, Conn.: Lawrence Hill.

Hobsbawm, Eric. [1969] 1981. *Bandits.* New York: Pantheon.

———. 1969. *Primitive Rebels: Studies in Archaic Forms of Social Movement in the Nineteenth and Twentieth Centuries.* New York: W. W. Norton.

Hobsbawm, Eric, and Terence Ranger (eds.). 1983. *The Invention of Tradition.* London and New York: Cambridge University Press.

Hockstader, Lee. 1990. "Nicaragua's Latest War Is Over Children's Education." *Philadelphia Enquirer,* 2 August, p. 7a.

Hodges, Donald C. 1986. *Intellectual Foundations of the Nicaraguan Revolution.* Austin: University of Texas Press.

———. 1992. *Sandino's Communism: Spiritual Politics for the Twenty-First Century.* Austin: University of Texas Press.

Holbek, Bengt. 1981. "Tacit Assumptions." *Folklore Forum* 14 (Fall): 121–40.

Hough, Walter. 1895. "The Ancient Central and South American Pottery in the Columbian Historical Exposition at Madrid in 1892." *Report of the U.S. Commission to the Columbian Historical Exposition at Madrid.* Executive Documents of the U.S. House of Representatives: Document 100: Columbian Historical Exposition. Washington, D.C.: Government Printing Office, 339–65.

Huezo de Espinosa. 1946. *La mujer antigua y la mujer moderna.* Managua: Editorial la Nueva Prensa.

Huszá, Tibor, Kálmar Kulcár, and Sándor Szalai (eds.). 1979. *Hungarian Society and Marxist Sociology in the Nineteen-Seventies.* Budapest: Corvina.

Ibañez, Roberto. 1970. *Escritos desconocidos de Rubén Darío.* Montevideo: Biblioteca de Marcha.

Ibarra, Carlos Vicente. 1983. "¿Qué nos vino de Macondo?" *Ventana: Barricada Cultural,* 2 June, p. 7.

Incer Barquero, Jaime. 1977. *Imágenes del occidente.* Managua: Banco Central.

———. 1985. *Toponimias indígenas de Nicaragua.* San José: Libro Libre.

———. 1990. *Nicaragua: viajes, rutas y encuentros, 1502–1838.* San José: Libro Libre.

Instituto de Estudio del Sandinismo. 1982a. *Porque viven siempre entre nosotros: héroes y mártires de la insurrección popular sandinista en Masaya*. Managua: Editorial Nueva Nicaragua.

———. 1982b. *¡Y se armó la runga! testimonios de la insurrección popular sandinista en Masaya*. Managua: Editorial Nueva Nicaragua.

———. 1982c. *La insurrección popular sandinista en Masaya*. Managua: Editorial Nueva Nicaragua.

———. 1982d. *Pensamiento antimperialista en Nicaragua*. Managua: Editorial Nueva Nicaragua.

———. 1983. *El sandinismo: documentos básicos*. Managua: Editorial Nueva Nicaragua.

Instituto Nacional de Cultura. 1992. *Coloquio Nacional sobre El Güegüense*. Managua: Instituto Nacional de Cultura.

Instituto Nicaragüense de la Mujer. 1988. *Bibliografía nacional anotada sobre la mujer en Nicaragua*. Managua: Instituto Nicaragüense de la Mujer.

Jaquette, Jane S. 1989. *The Women's Movement in Latin America: Feminism and the Transition to Democracy*. Boston: Unwin Hyman.

Jara, René, and Hernan Vidal (eds.). 1986. *Testimonio y literatura*. Minneapolis: Institute for the Study of Ideologies and Literature.

Jelin, Elizabeth. 1990. *Women and Social Change in Latin America*. London: Zed Books.

Jiménez, Mayra. 1979. "Poesía de Solentiname." *Casa de las Américas* 20 (January): 110–26.

——— (ed.). 1980. *Poesía campesina de Solentiname*. Managua: Ministerio de Cultura.

——— (ed.). 1983. *Poesía de la nueva Nicaragua: talleres populares de poesía*. Mexico, D.F.: Siglo Veintiuno Editores.

——— (ed.). 1985. *Poesía de las fuerzas armadas: talleres de poesía*. Managua: Ministerio de Cultura.

Jirón, Manuel. 1986. *Quien es quien en Nicaragua*. San José: Editorial Radio Amor.

Jirón Terán, José. [1915] 1981. "Diez cartas desconocidas de Rubén Darío." *Darío de Centro-América* 35 (7 June): 1, 4. Reprinted in *Cuadernos de bibliografía nicaragüense* 2 (July): 41–57.

Johnson, Kent. 1985. *Nation of Poets: Writings From the Poetry Workshops of Nicaragua*. Los Angeles: West End Press.

Joseph, Gilbert M. 1990. "On the Trail of Latin American Bandits: A Reexamination of Peasant Resistance." *Latin American Research Review* 25 (November): 7–52.

Junta de Gobierno de Reconstrucción Nacional de Nicaragua. 1979. "Programa de la Junta de Gobierno de Reconstrucción Nacional de Nicaragua." *Estudios Centroamericanos* 34 (September): 835–42

Kampwirth, Karen. 1992a. "The Mother of the Nicaraguans: Doña Violeta and the UNO's Gender Agenda." Paper presented at the meeting of the Latin American Studies Association, Los Angeles, California.

———. 1992b. "The Revolution Continues: Women's Organizations under the UNO." Paper presented at the meeting of the American Political Science Association, Chicago, Illinois.

Kardiner, Abram, and Edward Preble. 1961. *They Studied Man*. New York: New American Library.

Karp, Ivan (ed.). 1991. *Exhibiting Cultures: The Poetics and Politics of Museum Display*. Washington, D.C.: Smithsonian Institution Press.

Kemble, Stephen. 1884–85. *The Kemble Papers*. 2 vols. New York: New-York Historical Society.

Kidd, Ross. 1983. "A Testimony from Nicaragua: An Interview with Nidia Bustos, the coordinator of MECATE, the Nicaraguan Farm Workers' Theatre Movement." *Studies in Latin American Popular Culture* 2:190–201.

Kinzer, Stephen. 1988. "Solentiname Journal: Font of Art, Inspired by Rebel Priest." *New York Times* [international edition], 18 May, p. 4.

Kirk, John M. 1992. *Politics and the Catholic Church in Nicaragua*. Gainesville: University Press of Florida.

Kirkpatrick, Gwen. 1989. *The Dissonant Legacy of Modernismo: Lugones, Herrera y Reissig, and Other Voices of Modern Spanish American Poetry*. Berkeley: University of California Press.

Klaist, Christian. 1981. "El largo aliento de los Sandinistas." *Nicaráuac* 2 (January-March): 169–74

Kottak, Conrad P. 1992. *Assault on Paradise: Social Change in a Brazilian Village*. New York: McGraw-Hill.

Kunzle, David. 1982. "Tres culturas revolucionarias." *Plural* 2a época, 11 (July): 41–47.

———. 1983. "Nationalist, Internationalist, and Anti-Imperialist Themes in the Public Revolutionary Art of Cuba, Chile, and Nicaragua." *Studies in Latin American Popular Culture* 2:141–57.

Lacayo, Francisco. 1982. "Los colectivos de educación popular." *La Chacalaca* 1 (July): 30–37.

LaDuke, Betty. 1982. "The National Fine Arts School." *Nicaraguan Perspectives*, no. 4 (Summer): 28–30.

———. 1985. *Compañeras: Women, Art and Social Change in Latin America*. San Francisco: City Lights Books.

LaFeber, Walter. 1983. *Inevitable Revolutions: The United States in Central America*. New York: W. W. Norton.

Lake, Anthony. 1989. *Somoza Falling*. Boston: Houghton-Mifflin.

Lancaster, Roger N. 1988. *Thanks to God and the Revolution: Popular Religion and Class Consciousness in Nicaragua*. New York: Columbia University Press.

———. 1992. *Life Is Hard: Machismo, Danger, and the Intimacy of Power in Nicaragua*. Berkeley: University of California Press.

Lange, Frederick (ed.). 1988. *Costa Rican Art and Archaeology: Essays in Honor of Frederick R. Mayer*. Boulder, Colo.: University of Colorado Press.

Lange, Frederick, and Doris Z. Stone (eds.). 1984. *The Archaeology of Lower Central America*. Albuquerque: University of New Mexico Press.

Lange, Frederick, Frederick D. Sheets, Anibal Martinez, and Suzanne Abel-Vidor (eds.). 1992. *The Archaeology of Pacific Nicaragua*. Albuquerque: University of New Mexico Press.

La Orden Miracle, Ernesto. 1971. *Catálogo provisional del patrimonio histórico-artístico de Nicaragua*. Managua: Comisión Nacional del Sesquicentenario de la Independencia de Centroamérica.

Las Casas, Bartolomé de. [1552] 1987. *Brevísima relación de la destrucción de las Indias*. Mexico, D.F.: Editorial Fontamara.

Lavrin, Asunción (ed.). 1978. *Latin American Women: Historical Perspectives*. Westport, Conn.: Greenwood Press.

——— (ed.). 1989. *Sexuality and Marriage in Colonial Latin America*. Lincoln: University of Nebraska Press.

Leed, Eric J. 1991. *The Mind of the Traveler: From Gilgamesh to Global Tourism*. New York: Basic Books.

Leiken, Robert S., and Barry Rubin (eds.). 1987. *Central American Crisis Reader*. New York: Summit Books.

León, Magdalena (ed.). 1982. *Debate sobre la mujer en América Latina y el Caribe*. Bogotá: Asociación Colombina para el Estudio de la Población.

Levine, Lawrence. 1977. *Black Culture and Black Consciousness: Afro-American Folk Thought From Slavery to Freedom*. New York: Oxford University Press.

Levy, Pablo. 1873. *Notas geográficas y económicas sobre la republica de Nicaragua*. Paris: Librería Española de E. Denné Schmitz.

Lilienthal, Peter. 1981. "Después de Nicaragua seré otro." *Nicaráuac* 2 (January): 165–68.

Lipshitz, Susan. 1978. *Tearing the Veil: Essays on Femininity*. London: Routledge and Kegan Paul.

Lira, Maximo R. 1873. "La mujer: Sus derechos políticos i sociales." *Semanal Nicaragüense*, 12 June, pp. 362–63, and 28 June, pp. 370–71.

Liss, Sheldon B. 1984. *Marxist Thought in Latin America*. Berkeley: University of California Press.

Lobao, Linda M. 1990. "Women in Revolutionary Movements: Changing Patterns of Latin American Guerrilla Struggle." *Dialectical Anthropology* 15 (2–3): 211–32.

Longpérier, Henri Adrien Prevost. 1850. *Notice des Monuments Exposés dans la Salle des Antiquités Américaines (Mexique et Pérou)*. Paris: Vichon, Imprimeur des Musées Nationaux.

López, Wilmor. 1982. *Reseña de la nueva canción en Nicaragua: antecedentes, desarrollo, y actualidad*. Mexico, D.F.: Ministerio de Cultura.

López Pérez, Manuel. 1960. "El baile de 'Las inditas' de Masaya." *Nicaragua indígena*, no. 30 (April): 5–8.

Lothrop, Samuel Kirkland. 1921. "The Stone Statues of Nicaragua." *American Anthropologist* 23 (September): 311–19.

————. 1926. *Pottery of Costa Rica and Nicaragua*. 2 vols. New York: Museum of the American Indian.

Lowenthal, Abraham (ed.). 1986. *Latin America and Caribbean Contemporary Record*. New York: Holmes and Meier.

Luce, Stephen B. 1895. "History of the Participation of the United States in the Columbian Historical Exposition at Madrid." In *Report of the U.S. Commission to the Columbian Historical Exposition at Madrid*. Executive Documents of the U.S. House of Representatives: Document 100: Columbian Historical Exposition. Washington, D.C.: Government Printing Office, pp. 7–278.

Lucero Trujillo, Marcela. 1978. "The Terminology of Machismo." *De Colores* 4 (3): 34–42.

Luna Silva, Armando. 1956. *La mujer en la diplomacia*. Managua: n.p.

Luzuriaga, Gerardo. 1978. *Popular Theater for Social Change in Latin America*. Los Angeles: UCLA Latin American Center Publications.

Macaulay, Neill. [1967] 1985. *The Sandino Affair*. Reprint. Durham: Duke University Press.

McCreery, David. 1993. "Wireless Empire: The United States and Radio Communications in Central America and the Caribbean: 1904–1926." *Southeastern Latin Americanist* 37 (Summer): 23–41.

Machón Vilanova, Francisco. 1923. *Educación de la mujer centroamericana: conferencia dictada en la Escuela Normal de Institutoras*. Managua: Tipografía Pérez.

MacKinnon, Catherine A. 1982. "Feminism, Marxism, Method, and the State: An Agenda for Theory." *Signs* 7:3 (Spring): 515–44.

McPhail, Thomas L. 1981. *Electronic Colonialism: The Future of International Broadcasting and Communications.* Beverly Hills: Sage Publications.

Maier, Elizabeth. 1980. *Nicaragua: la mujer en la revolución.* Mexico, D.F.: Ediciones de Cultura Popular.

Mántica, Carlos. 1973. *El habla nicaragüense: estudio morfológico y semántico.* San José: Editorial Universitaria Centroamericana.

Mapes, E. K. (ed.). 1938. *Escritos inéditos de Rubén Darío.* New York: Instituto de las Españas en los Estados Unidos.

Marcus, Bruce (ed.). 1982. *Sandinistas Speak: Speeches, Writings, and Interviews with Leaders of Nicaragua's Revolution.* New York: Pathfinder Press.

———. 1985. *Nicaragua: The Sandinista People's Revolution.* New York: Pathfinder Press.

Martin, Randy. 1987. "Nicaragua: Theater and State without Walls." *Social Text* 18 (Winter): 83–94.

Martínez Rivas, Carlos. [1953] 1982. *La insurrección solitaria.* Reprint. Managua: Editorial Nueva Nicaragua.

Mathews, Jane DeHart. 1975. "Arts and the People: The New Deal Quest for Cultural Democracy." *Journal of American History* 62 (September): 316–39.

Mattelart, Armand (ed.). 1986. *Communicating in Popular Nicaragua.* New York: International General.

Matthews, J. J. 1984. *Good and Mad Women: The Historical Construction of Femininity in Twentieth-Century Australia.* Sydney: George Allen and Unwin.

May, Robert E. 1973. *The Southern Dream of a Caribbean Empire, 1854–1861.* Baton Rouge: Louisiana State University Press.

Mejía Godoy, Carlos, Enríque Mejía Godoy, and Julio Valle Castillo. 1989. *The Nicaraguan Epic.* Translated by Dinah Livingstone. London: Katabasis.

Mejía Godoy, Carlos, Enríque Mejía Godoy, and Pablo Martinez. 1981. *La Misa Campesina Nicaragüense.* Managua: Ministerio de Cultura.

Mejía Sánchez, Ernesto. 1946. *Romances y corridos nicaragüenses.* Mexico, D.F.: Imprenta Universitaria.

———. 1968. *Estudios sobre Rubén Darío.* Mexico, D.F.: Fondo de Cultura Económica.

———. 1970. *Cuestiones rubendarianas.* Madrid: Editorial Revista de Occidente.

———. 1985. *Recolección a mediodía.* Managua: Editorial Nueva Nicaragua.

———. 1986. "Las Casas en Nicaragua." *Nicaráuac,* no. 12 (April): 151–60.

Meneses, Vidaluz. 1985. "El reto del trabajo cultural." *Ventana: Barricada Cultural,* 10 August, pp. 12–13.

Messenger, Phyllis. 1989. *The Ethics of Collecting Cultural Property.* Albuquerque: University of New Mexico Press.

Miller, Edward. 1974. *That Noble Cabinet: A History of the British Museum.* Athens: Ohio University Press.

Miller, Francesca. 1991. *Latin American Women and the Search for Social Justice.* Hanover, N.H.: University Press of New England.

Miller, Valerie. 1985. *Between Struggle and Hope: The Nicaraguan Literacy Crusade.* Boulder, Colo.: Westview Press.

Millett, Richard. 1977. *Guardians of the Dynasty.* Maryknoll, N.Y.: Orbis Books.

Ministerio de Cultura. 1982a. *Hacia una política cultural de la Revolución Popular Sandinista.* Managua: Ministerio de Cultura.

———. 1982b. *Colección popular de literatura nicaragüense: No. 2 Documentos.* Managua: Ministerio de Cultura.

Ministerio del Distrito Nacional. 1943. *Primeras notas de Rubén Darío: selecciones de la obra inicial del poeta y opiniones de grandes críticos.* Managua: Ministerio del Distrito Nacional.

Ministerio de Educación Pública. 1957. *Rubén, treinta poemas: homenaje del Gobierno de Nicaragua en el XLI aniversario de la muerte de Rubén Darío.* Managua: Ediciones del Ministerio de Educación Pública.

———. 1958. *Divulgaciones de Rubén Darío: texto para la "Cátedra Rubén Darío."* Managua: Ministerio de Educación Pública.

———. 1959. *Rubén Darío, crítica: homenaje del Gobierno de Nicaragua en el XLIII aniversario de su muerte.* Managua: Ministerio de Educación Pública Extensión Cultural.

———. 1964. *Rubén Darío periodista: homenaje del Gobierno de Nicaragua en el XLVIII aniversario de la muerte de Rubén Darío.* Managua: Ministerio de Educación Pública, Extensión Cultural.

Ministerio de Instrucción Pública. 1935. *Nicaragua, patria de Rubén Darío: arreglo para libro de lectura escolar.* Managua: Ministerio de Instrucción Pública.

———. 1940. *Nicaragua: Patria de Rubén Darío: Arreglo para libro de lectura escolar.* Managua: Ministerio de Instrucción Pública.

Ministerio de Interior de Nicaragua. 1982. "Projecto de ley de Medios." *Revista del Pensamiento Centroamericano* 37 (January-March): 114–23.

Miranda-Casij, Enrique. 1972. "La guerra olvidada." *Revista del Pensamiento Centroamericano* 144 (September): 75–82.

Miranda de Peña, Mayra Ines. 1979. "Reivindicación revolucionaria y cultural de Monimbó (grupo étnico) a la luz de su cronología histórica y su interpretación crítica." Ph.D. diss., Universidad Centroamericana.

Mitgang, Herbert. 1993. "Disney Link to the F.B.I. and Hoover Disclosed." *New York Times*, 6 May, pp. B1, B4.

Molina Argüello, Carlos. 1970. "Un obispo que nunca existió: Fray Pedro de Zúñiga y el obispado de Nicaragua." *Revista conservadora del pensamiento Centroamericano* 23 (February): 33–41.

Molyneux, Maxine. 1988. "The Politics of Abortion in Nicaragua: Revolutionary Pragmatism — or Feminism in the Realm of Necessity?" *Feminist Review*, no. 29 (Spring): 114–32.

Morales, Beltran. 1970. "Fernando Gordillo." *Taller*, no. 5 (October): 35–37.

Morales Alonso, Luís. 1983. "Ofrecemos nuestra cultura en viva ya a todo color." *Ventana: Barricada Cultural*, 22 January, pp. 8–9.

Morales Avilés, Ricardo. 1983. *Obras: no pararemos de andar jamás.* Managua: Editorial Nueva Nicaragua.

Morgan, Martha I. 1990. "Founding Mothers: Women's Voices and Stories in the 1987 Nicaraguan Constitution." *Boston University Law Review* 70 (January): 1–107.

———. 1992. "The Mother Law: Nicaraguan Women and Democratization in the 1990s." *Journal of the Southeastern Council of Latin American Studies* 23 (March): 138–51

Mörner, Magnus. 1967. *Race Mixture in the History of Latin America.* Boston: Little, Brown.

Morris, Nancy. 1986. "Canto porque es necesario cantar: The New Song Movement in Chile, 1973–1983." *Latin American Research Review* 21:117–36.

Mory, Warren M., Jr. 1971. *Salvador Mendieta: Escritor y apostol de la unión centroamericana.* N.p., n.p.

Mosley, Leonard. 1985. *Disney's World: A Biography.* New York: Stein and Day.

Munro, Dana G. 1964. *Intervention and Dollar Diplomacy, 1900–1921.* Princeton: Princeton University Press.

———. 1983. *A Student in Central America, 1914–1916.* New Orleans: Tulane University Middle American Research Institute.

Murillo, Rosario. 1981. "Praxis: llegó el jazz a la juventud sandinista." *Ventana: Barricada Cultural,* 12 December, pp. 8.

———. 1982. "La cultura es siempre un arma de combate." *Ventana: Barricada Cultural,* 7 February, p. 12.

Najlis, Michele. 1969. *El viento armado.* Guatemala: Universidad de San Carlos.

Narváez López, Carlos. 1959. *Célebres mujeres de la historia.* Managua: Talleres Nacionales.

Naylor, Robert A. 1989. *Penny Ante Imperialism: The Mosquito Shore and the Bay of Honduras, 1600–1914: A Case Study in British Informal Empire.* Rutherford, N.J.: Fairleigh Dickinson University Press.

Newson, Linda A. 1982. "The Depopulation of Nicaragua in the Sixteenth Century." *Journal of Latin American Studies* 14 (November): 253–86.

———. 1987. *Indian Survival in Colonial Nicaragua.* Norman: University of Oklahoma Press.

Newton, Norman. 1969. *Thomas Gage in Spanish America, 1603–56.* New York: Barnes and Noble.

"Nicaragua and the Filibusters." 1856. *Blackwood's Magazine* 79:314.

Nicaragua. Guía general ilustrada. 1940. Managua: Talleres Gráficos Perez.

Niederlein, Gustavo. 1898. *The State of Nicaragua of the Greater Republic of Central America.* Philadelphia: Philadelphia Commercial Museum.

Nietschmann, Bernard. 1973. *Between Land and Water: The Subsistence Ecology of the Miskito Indians, Eastern Nicaragua.* New York: Seminar Press.

———. 1989. *The Unknown War: The Miskito Nation, Nicaragua and the United States.* New York: Freedom House.

Nilsson, Nils G. 1980. *Swedish Cultural Policy in the Twentieth Century.* Copenhagen: Swedish Institute.

Ninkovich, Frank. 1981. *The Diplomacy of Ideas: U.S. Foreign Policy and Cultural Relations, 1938–1950.* New York: Cambridge University Press.

Noguera Carazo, Lucrecia. 1974. *Evolución cultural y política de la mujer nicaragüense.* Managua: AMNPE.

Nolan, David. 1984. *The Ideology of the Sandinistas.* Coral Gables: Institute of Interamerican Studies, Graduate School of International Studies, University of Miami.

Nómez, Naín. 1983. "On Culture as Democratic Culture in Latin America." *Studies in Latin American Popular Culture* 2:171–81.

Nordenstreng, Kaarle, and Tapio Varis. [1974] 1985. *Television Traffic—A One-Way Street? A Survey and Analysis of the International Flow of Television Programme Material.* Ann Arbor: UNIPUB.

Norsworthy, Kent, and William I. Robinson. 1987. *David and Goliath: The U.S. War Against Nicaragua.* New York: Monthly Review Press.

Nowotny, Karl Anton. 1956, 1961. "Ein Zentralamerikanischer Monolith aus dem Besitz von Emanuel von Friedrichsthal." *Archiv für Völkerkunde* 11:104–15, 16:135–39.

Núñez Abaunza, Olga. 1945. *Derechos de la mujer en la Constitución y legislación penal de Nicaragua.* Managua: Editorial "Novedades."

Núñez, Orlando. 1982. "Tres años de revolución y cultura en Nicaragua." *La Chacalaca* 2 (July): 41–43.

O'Keeffe, Richard, Sr. 1984. " 'Dinamita' by Rubén Darío: The Relevance of Anarchism." *Faith and Reason* 10 (Spring): 25–35.

Ortega Aranciába, Francisco. [1911] 1975. *Cuarenta años (1838–1878) de historia de Nicaragua.* Reprint. Managua: Colección Cultural Banco de América.

Ortega Saavedra, Humberto. 1979. *50 años de lucha sandinista.* Managua: Ministerio del Interior.

Ortiz, Alberto. [1912?]. *Cosas del mar.* Managua: n.p.

Ortiz, Roxanne D. 1984. *Indians of the Americas: Human Rights and Self-Determination.* New York: Praeger.

Osorno Fonseca, Humberto. 1944. *Diacleciano Chávez [sic].* Managua: Editorial Atlántida.

Overmyer, Grace. 1939. *Government and the Arts.* New York: W. W. Norton.

Oviedo y Valdés, Gonzalo Fernández de. [1547] 1855. *Historia General y Natural de las Indias.* Madrid: Imprenta de la Real Academía de Historia.

Palau de Nemes, Graciela. 1981. " 'D. Q.': un cuento fantástico de Rubén Darío." In Criado de Val 1981, pp. 943–47.

Pallais, Azarías H. 1986. *Antología.* Managua: Editorial Nueva Nicaragua.

Palma, Milagros. 1984. *Por los senderos míticos de Nicaragua.* Managua: Editorial Nueva Nicaragua.

———. 1988. *Nicaragua: Once mil vírgenes: Imaginario mítico-religioso del pensamiento mestizo nicaragüense.* Bogotá: Tercer Mundo Editores.

Palmer, Steven. 1988. "Carlos Fonseca and the Construction of Sandinismo in Nicaragua." *Latin American Research Review* 23 (1): 91–109.

Parker, Andrew, Mary Russo, Doris Sommer, and Patrick Yaeger. 1992. *Nationalisms and Sexualities.* New York: Routledge.

Pasos, Joaquín. 1986. *Poemas de un joven.* Managua: Editorial Nueva Nicaragua.

Pastor, Robert A. 1987. *Condemned to Repetition: The United States and Nicaragua.* Princeton: Princeton University Press.

Pataky, Laszlo. 1957. "Las Islas Solentiname." *Nicaragua indígena.* Segunda época (September-October): 35–36.

Patterson, Jerry E., and William R. Stanton. 1959. "The Ephraim George Squier Manuscripts in the Library of Congress: A Checklist." *Papers of the Bibliographical Society of America* 53 (first quarter): 309–26.

Paz, Octavio. [1965] 1972. *Cuadrivio: Darío, López Velarda, Pessua, Cernuda.* 3d ed. Mexico, D.F.: Editorial J. Mortiz.

Pearce, Jenny. 1982. *Under the Eagle: U.S. Intervention in Central America and the Caribbean.* Boston: South End Press.

Pellicer, Carlos. 1984. "En el centenario de Rubén Darío." *Casa de las Americas* 24 (January-February): 32–33.

Peña, Horacio. 1973. "Las casas de la cultura en Francia y el problema cultural en Nicaragua." *Encuentro* (September-October): 3–7.

———. 1984. "Approaches to Rubén Darío and Walt Whitman." Ph.D. diss., University of Texas.

Peña Hernández, Enrique. 1968. *Folklore de Nicaragua.* Masaya: Editorial Union.

Pendergast, William R. 1973. "The Political Uses of Cultural Relations." *Il Politico: rivista italiana di scienze politiche* 38 (December): 682–96.

Pérez Estrada, Francisco. n.d. *Estudios del folklore nicaragüense*. Managua: Tipografía Brenes.

———. 1946. *Teatro folklórico nicaragüense*. Managua: Editorial Nuevos Horizontes.

———. 1982. "Artesanía nicaragüense: Somos hombres de barro: artesanía nicaragüense." *Ventana: Barricada Cultural*, 16 January, p. 16.

———. 1983. "Artesanía nicaragüense." *Ventana: Barricada Cultural*, 30 January, p. 13.

———. 1984. "Sobre la cronología y el autor de 'El Güegüence.'" *Ventana: Barricada Cultural*, 31 March, pp. 2–3.

Pérez Valle, Eduardo. 1986. *El asesinato de Sandino: documentos testimoniales*. Managua: Ministerio de Cultura.

Pérez Estrada, Francisco. 1976. *Ensayos nicaragüenses*. Managua: Fondo de Promoción Cultural, Banco de América.

———. 1982. *Panorama de la Nicaragua pre-colonial: sector del Pacifico*. Managua: Ministerio de Educación.

———. 1983. "Artesanía nicaragüense." *Ventana: Barricada Cultural*, 30 January, p. 13.

Perus, Francoise. 1980. *Literatura y sociedad en América Latina: el modernismo*. Mexico, D.F.: Siglo Veintiuno.

Pescatello, Ann (ed.). 1973. *Female and Male in Latin America: Essays*. Pittsburgh: University of Pittsburgh Press.

Pezzullo, Lawrence, and Ralph Pezzullo. 1993. *At the Fall of Somoza*. Pittsburgh: University of Pittsburgh Press.

Picón-Salas, Mariano. [1944] 1962. *A Cultural History of Spanish America: From Conquest to Independence*. Translated by Irving A. Leonard. Berkeley: University of California Press.

Pim, Bedford. 1869. *Dottings on the Roadside in Panama, Nicaragua, and Mosquito*. London: Chapman and Hall.

Plaidy, Jean. 1978. *The Spanish Inquisition*. London: Robert Hale.

Porter, William Sydney [O. Henry]. 1919. Cabbages and Kings. New York: Doubleday, Page.

Portocarrero de Chamorro, Bertilda. 1962. *Influencia de la mujer educadora en la humanidad: Doña Josefa Toledo de Aguerri*. Managua: n.p.

Prego, Pepe. 1981. "Un taller para el nuevo teatro." *Ventana: Barricada Cultural*, 31 October, p. 14.

Prien, Hans-Jürgen. 1985. *La historia del cristianismo en América Latina*. 2d ed. Translated by Josep Barnadas. Salamanca: Ediciones Sígueme.

Pring-Mill, Robert. 1987. "The Roles of Revolutionary Song—A Nicaraguan Assessment." *Popular Music* 6 (May): 179–89.

"Programa de la junta de Gobierno de Reconstrucción Nacional de Nicaragua." 1979. *Estudios Centroamericanos* 34 (September): 835–42.

"¡Que esto no se detenga nunca!: con el taller de títeres del Sistema Sandinista de Televisión." 1983. *Ventana: Barricada Cultural*, 19 June, pp. 20–21.

R. de Mendoza, Margarita. 1933. *Decálogo del feminismo, o sea, Ideales y program de trabajo que tiende a realizar la "Liga Feminista de Nicaragua"*. Managua: n.p.

Radell, David Richard. 1969. "An Historical Geography of Western Nicaragua: The Spheres of Influence of León, Granada, and Managua, 1519–1965." Ph.D. diss., University of California, Berkeley.

Radell, David Richard, and James J. Parsons. 1971. "Realejo: A Forgotten Colonial Port and Shipbuilding Center in Nicaragua." *Hispanic American Historical Review* 51 (May): 295–312.

Rama, Angel. 1967. "Las opciones de Rubén Darío." *Casa de las Américas* 7 (May-June): 29–35.

Ramírez, John. 1984. "Introduction to the Sandinista Documentary Cinema." *Areito* 10 (37): 18–21.

Ramírez, Sergio. 1971. *Mariano Fiallos: Biografía*. León: Editorial Universitaria de la UNAN.

———. 1974. *El pensamiento vivo de Sandino*. Costa Rica: Editorial Universitaria Centroamericana.

———. [1976] 1981. *Cuento nicaragüense*. 2d ed. Managua: Editorial Nueva Nicaragua.

———. [1976] 1982. *Charles Atlas también muere*. 2d ed. Managua: Editorial Nueva Nicaragua.

———. 1982. "La Revolución: el hecho cultural más grande de nuestra historia." *Ventana: Barricada Cultural*, 30 January, pp. 15–16.

———. 1983a. *Balcanes y volcanes*. Managua: Editorial Nueva Nicaragua.

———. 1983b. *El alba de oro: la historia viva de Nicaragua*. Mexico, D.F.: Siglo Veintiuno Editores.

———. 1984a. "Darío y Cortázar." *Casa de las Américas* 25 (July-October): 96–101.

———. 1984b. *Augusto C. Sandino: el pensamiento vivo*. Revised ed. 2 vols. Managua: Editorial Nueva Nicaragua.

———. 1985a. "Así nació *Ventana*." *Ventana: Barricada Cultural*, 15 June, pp. 2–3.

———. 1985b. *Estás en Nicaragua*. Barcelona: Muchnik Editores.

Ramírez, Susan E. (ed.). 1989. *Indian-Religious Relations in Colonial South America*. Syracuse: Maxwell School of Citizenship and Public Affairs.

Ramírez, William. 1982a. "El problema indígena y la amenaza imperialista en Nicaragua." *Ventana: Barricada Cultural*, 16 January, pp. 13–14.

———. 1982b. "La amenaza imperialista y el problema Indígena en Nicaragua." *Nicaráuac* 3 (October): 3–10.

Ramos Escandón, Carmen, et al. 1987. *Presencia y transparencia: la mujer en la historia de México*. Mexico, D.F.: El Colegio de México.

Randall, Margaret. 1980. *Todas estamos despiertas: testimonios de la mujer nicaragüense de hoy*. Mexico, D.F.: Siglo XXI Editores.

———. 1981. *Sandino's Daughters: Testimonies of Nicaraguan Women in Struggle*. Vancouver: New Star Books.

———. 1983a. *Christians in the Nicaraguan Revolution*. Translated by Mariana Valverde. Vancouver: New Star Books.

———. 1983b. *—Y también digo mujer: testimonio de la mujer nicaragüense hoy*. Santo Domingo, República Dominica: Ediciones Populares.

———. 1983c. "Conversando con Sergio Ramírez: 'Hay aquí una fuerza centrífuga.'" *Ventana: Barricada Cultural*, 19 July, pp. 7–12.

———. 1984. *Risking a Somersault in the Air: Conversations With Nicaraguan Writers*. San Francisco: Solidarity Publications.

———. 1994. *Sandino's Daughters Revisited: Feminism in Nicaragua*. New Brunswick, N.J.: Rutgers University Press.

Randolph, James D. (ed). 1982. *Nicaragua: A Country Study*. Washington, D.C.: Department of the Army.

Richard, Pablo (ed.). 1980. *Materiales para una historia de teología en América Latina. Proceedings of VIII Encuentro Latinoamericano de CEHILA, Lima (1980).* San José: Departamento Ecuménico de Investigaciones.

Richardson, John G. (ed.). 1986. *Handbook of Theory and Research for the Sociology of Education.* Westport, Conn.: Greenwood Press.

Rizo, José. 1971. *Manual del guía de turistas.* Managua: Secretaria de Integración Turística Centroamericana.

Roberts, Orlando W. 1827. *Narratives of Voyages and Excursions on the East Coast and in the Interior of Central America, Describing a Journey up the San Juan River and Passage Across the Lake of Nicaragua to the City of León.* Edinburgh: Constable.

Rodó, José Enrique. [1900] 1988. *Ariel.* Translated by Margaret Sayers Peden. Austin: University of Texas Press.

Rodríguez, Ileana. 1984. *Primer inventario del invasor.* Managua: Editorial Nueva Nicaragua.

Román, José. 1983. *Maldito país.* Managua: El Pez y la Serpiente.

Romero Vargas, Germán. 1988. *Las estructuras sociales de Nicaragua en el siglo XVIII.* Managua: Editorial Vanguardia.

Rosengarten, Frederic. 1976. *Freebooters Must Die! The Life and Times of William Walker.* Wayne, Penn.: Haverford House.

Rosset, Peter, and John Vandermeer (eds.). 1986. *Nicaragua: Unfinished Revolution. The New Nicaraguan Reader.* New York: Grove Press.

Rothschuh, Jorge Eliécer. 1981. "Artesanas de Camoapa: tejedoras de pita y cabuya." *Ventana: Barricada Cultural,* 26 September, p. 11.

Rothschuh Tablada, Guiellermo. 1982. "12 proposiciones para rescatar a Rubén Darío." *Ventana: Barricada Cultural,* 23 January, pp. 2–3.

Ruchwarger, Gary. 1987. *People in Power: Forging a Grassroots Democracy in Nicaragua.* South Hadley, Mass.: Bergin and Garvey.

———. 1989. *Struggling for Survival: Workers, Women, and Class on a Nicaraguan State Farm.* Boulder, Colo.: Westview Press.

Rugama, Leonel. [1978] 1985. *The Earth Is a Satellite of the Moon.* Translated by Sara Miles, Richard Schaaf, and Nancy Weisberg. Willimantic, Conn.: Curbstone Press.

Ryan, Tony. 1983. "On Cultural Resistance: An Interview with Mancotal's Greg Landau." *Nicaraguan Perspectives,* no. 7 (Winter): 25–28.

Sadie, Stanley (ed.). 1980. *The New Grove's Dictionary of Music and Musicians.* 20 vols. London: Macmillan.

Salazar Solorzano, Joaquín. 1946. *Reivindicación de los derechos políticos de la mujer.* León: Tipografía Los Hechos.

Salgado, María A. 1989. "Felix Rubén García Sarmiento, Rubén Darío y otros entes de ficción." *Revista Iberoamericana* 55 (January): 339–62.

Salvador, Gabriel. 1964. "Nuestra música popular, albores de los cantos vernácular." *Revista del Pensamiento centroamericano* 9 (June): 45–56.

Salvatierra, Sofonías. 1934. *Sandino, o la tragedia de un pueblo.* Madrid: Talleres Tipográficos Europa.

Salvatore, Ricardo. 1991. "Yankee Merchants in South America: Narratives, Identity, and Social Order, 1810–1870." Unpublished manuscript, Southern Methodist University.

Sánchez, María Teresa. 193-. *Sombras.* Managua: Talleres Nacionales.

———. 1948. *Poesía nicaragüense: (antología).* Managua: Editorial Nuevos Horizontes.

"Sandino of Nicaragua: Bandit or Patriot?" 1928. *Literary Digest* 96 (4 February): 42.

Sargent, Lydia (ed.). 1981. *Women and Revolution*. Boston: South End Press.

Scherzer, Carl. 1857. *Travel in the Free States of Central America: Nicaragua, Honduras, and San Salvador*. 2 vols. London: Longman, Brown, Green, Longmans, and Roberts.

Schick Gutiérrez, René. 1966. *Rubén Darío y la política*. Managua: Editorial Nicaragüense.

Schickel, Richard. [1968] 1986. *The Disney Version: The Life, Times, Art and Commerce of Walt Disney*. Rev. ed. London: Pavilion Books.

Schiller, Herbert. 1969. *Mass Communications and American Empire*. New York: A. M. Kelley.

————. 1976. *Communication and Cultural Domination*. White Plains, N.Y.: International Arts and Sciences Press.

Schlesinger, Stephen, and Stephen Kinzer. 1984. *Bitter Fruit: The Untold Story of the American Coup in Guatemala*. New York: Anchor Books.

Schmidt, Herbert. 1978. *Roots of Lo Mexicano: Self and Society in Mexican Thought*. College Station: Texas A&M University Press.

Schmuckler, Beatrice. 1984. "Patriarchy and the Family: Interrelated Changes During Capitalist Development in Europe and Latin America." East Lansing: Michigan State University Office on Women in International Development, Working Paper No. 62.

————. 1985. "Gender and Authority in Working Class Families in Buenos Aires." Ph.D. diss., Yale University.

Schoonover, Thomas D. 1992. *The United States in Central America, 1860–1911*. Durham: Duke University Press.

Schroeder, Michael J. [forthcoming]. "The Sandino Rebellion in Nicaragua, 1927–1934: Toward a Social and Cultural History." Ph.D. diss., University of Michigan.

Schulman, Ivan A. 1968. "Martí y Darío frente a Centroamérica: perspectivas de realidad y ensueño." *Revista Iberoamericana* 34 (July-December): 201–36.

————. [forthcoming]. "El modernismo de Rubén Darío: la otra dimensión." To appear in the *Actas* of the Cien Años de *Azul* Symposium, University of Granada, Spain.

Schulman, Ivan A., and Manuel Pedro González. 1969. *Martí, Darío y modernismo*. Madrid: Editorial Gredos.

Scott, Donald H. 1959. "The Cultural Institute in Mexico City as an Example of United States Policy in Cultural Relations." Ph.D. diss., University of Southern California.

Scott, James C. 1985. *Weapons of the Weak: Everyday Forms of Peasant Resistance*. New Haven: Yale University Press.

Selser, Gregorio. [1978] 1981. *Sandino: General of the Free*. Translated by Cedric Belfrage. New York: Monthly Review Press.

Selva, Salomón de la. 1916. "Rubén Darío." *Poetry: A Magazine of Verse* 8 (April): 200–204.

————. [1922] 1982. *El soldado desconocido*. 4th ed. Managua: Editorial Nueva Nicaragua.

————. 1928. "Sandino." *Nation*, 18 January, pp. 63–64.

————. 1984. *Sandino: Free Country or Death*. Compiled by Jorge Eduardo Arellano. Managua: Biblioteca Nacional de Nicaragua.

————. 1985. *La guerra de Sandino o pueblo desnudo*. Managua: Editorial Nueva Nicaragua.

Selva, Salomón de la, and Thomas Walsh. 1916. *Eleven Poems of Rubén Darío*. New York: G. P. Putnam's Sons.

Sevilla Sacasa, Guillermo. 1939. *La mujer nicaragüense ante el derecho de sufragar; por qúe me opuse a que se le concediera: la verdad sobre mi actitud en la Constituyente*. Managua: Taller Gráfico Pérez.

Shatunovskaya, Irina. 1981. "El nacimiento del cine nacional." *América Latina* (USSR), no. 7:92–96.

Shelley, Henry C. 1911. *The British Museum: Its History and Treasures.* Boston: L. C. Page.

Sherman, William L. 1979. *Forced Native Labor in Sixteenth-Century Central America.* Lincoln: University of Nebraska Press.

Silva Castro, Rau (ed.). 1934. *Obras desconocidas de Rubén Darío escritas en Chile y no recopiladas en ninguno de sus libros.* Santiago: Prensas de la Universidad de Chile.

Simpson, Lesley Byrd (trans.). [1960] 1978. *The Laws of Burgos of 1512–1513: Royal Ordinances for the Good Government and Treatment of the Indians.* Reprint. Westport, Conn.: Greenwood Press.

Skármeta, Antonio. 1981. "La insurrección: gambito nicaragüense de film y novela." *Texto crítico* 7 (July): 90–95.

Slatta, Richard W. 1991. "Bandits and Social Rural History." *Latin American Research Review* 26 (1): 145–74.

Smith, Janet L. 1979. *An Annotated Bibliography of and about Ernesto Cardenal.* Tempe: Arizona State University Press.

Smith, Raymond T. (ed.). 1984. *Kinship Ideology and Practice in Latin America.* Chapel Hill: University of North Carolina Press.

Solá, Roser, and María Pau Trayner. 1988. *Ser madre en Nicaragua: testimonios de una historia no escrita.* Managua: Editorial Nueva Nicaragua.

Somoza García, Anastasio. 1936. *El verdadero Sandino o el calvario de las Segovias.* Managua: Tipografía Robelo.

Spalding, Rose J. (ed.). 1987. *The Political Economy of Revolutionary Nicaragua.* Boston: Allen and Unwin.

Squier, E. George. 1852. *Nicaragua: Its People, Scenery, Monuments, and the Proposed Canal.* 2 vols. New York: D. Appleton.

———. 1858. *The States of Central America.* New York: Harper and Brothers.

Stanislawski, Dan I. 1983. *The Transformation of Nicaragua, 1519–1548.* Berkeley: University of California Press.

Stansifer, Charles. 1977. "José Santos Zelaya: A New Look at Nicaragua's 'Liberal' Dictator." *Revista/Review Interamericana* 7:3 (Fall): 468–85.

———. 1979. "Rubén Darío and His Relationship to the Dictator Zelaya." *SECOLAS Annals* 10 (March): 57–65.

———. 1981a. *Cultural Policy in the Old and the New Nicaragua.* Hanover, N.H.: American Universities Field Staff.

———. 1981b. *The Nicaraguan National Literacy Crusade.* Hanover, N.H.: American Universities Field Staff.

Stephens, John L. [1841] 1949. *Incidents of Travel in Central America, Chiapas, and Yucatan.* 2 vols. Reprint. New Brunswick, N.J.: Rutgers University Press.

Sternbach, Nancy S. 1988. "The Death of a Beautiful Woman: Modernismo, the Woman Writer and the Pornographic Imagination." *Ideologies and Literature* 3 (Spring): 35–60.

Steward, Julian H. (ed.). 1948. *Handbook of South American Indians.* Washington, D.C.: Government Printing Office.

Stillman, Jacob D. B. 1967. *An 1850 Voyage: San Francisco to Baltimore by Sea and by Land.* Palo Alto, Calif.: Lewis Osborne.

Stone, Samuel Z. 1990. *The Heritage of the Conquistadors: Ruling Classes in Central America from the Conquest to the Sandinistas.* Lincoln: University of Nebraska Press.

Stout, Peter F. 1859. *Nicaragua: Past, Present and Future.* Philadelphia: J. E. Potter.

Stuart, George E., and Gene S. Stuart. 1983. *The Mysterious Maya*. Washington, D.C.: National Geographic.

Super, John C. 1988. *Food, Conquest, and Colonization in Sixteenth-Century Spanish America*. Albuquerque: University of New Mexico Press.

Super, John C., and Thomas C. Wright. 1985. *Food, Politics and Society in Latin America*. Lincoln: University of Nebraska Press.

Szuchman, Mark D. (ed.). 1989. *The Middle Period in Latin America: Values and Attitudes in the Seventeenth through Nineteenth Centuries*. Boulder, Colo.: Lynne Rienner.

Tamez, Elsa. 1987. *Against Machismo*. Translated by John Eagleson. New York: Meyer-Stone Books.

Taylor, R. E., and C. W. Meighan. 1978. *Chronologies of New World Archaeology*. New York: Academic Press.

"Teatro tercera muestra nacional." *La Chacalaca* 1 (December 1982): 36–37.

Television Factbook. Radnor, Pa.: Television Digest, [annual].

Teplitz, Benjamin. 1973. "The Political and Economic Foundations of Modernization in Nicaragua: The Administration of José Santos Zelaya, 1893–1909." Ph.D. diss., Howard University.

"III muestra nacional de teatro: la definición del teatro revolucionario Retro alimentado." *La Chacalaca* 1 (April 1983): 31–34.

Tercero de Debayle. 1966. *Valores femeninos de Nicaragua: (rasgos históricos sobre la mujer nicaragüense)*. Managua: Impr. Nacional.

Thieck, Frédéric. 1971. *Idolos de Nicaragua*. León: Departamento de Arqueología y Antropología de la Universidad Nacional Autónoma de Nicaragua.

Tijerino, Doris. 1978. *Inside the New Nicaragua*. Vancouver: New Star Books.

Tirado, Manlio. 1983. *Conversando con José Coronel Urtecho*. Managua: Editorial Nueva Nicaragua.

Toledo de Aguerri, Josefa. 1926. *Al Correr de la Pluma: Crónicas de viaje, escritas para "Revista Femenina Ilustrada" (De Agosto a Diciembre de 1920) Desde Costa Rica y Estados Unidos de América, Pasando por Panamá y la Habana*. Managua: Tipografía y Encuadernación Nacional.

———. 1932. *Enciclopedia Nicaragüense. Suplemento de Revista Femenina Ilustrada a la Edición Extraordinaria del Centenario de la Independencia Nacional*. Vol. 2. *Cultura Literaria y Científica*. Managua: Imprenta Nacional.

———. 1935a. *Anhelos y esfuerzos*. Managua: Imprenta Nacional.

———. 1935b. *Reproducciones. Temas pedagógicos*. Managua: Imprenta Nacional.

———. 1940. *Educación y Feminismo Sobre Enseñanza: Artículos Varios*. Managua: Talleres Nacionales.

Tormo, Leandro. 1962. *La evangelización de la América latina*. Vol. 1 of *Historia de la iglesia en américa latina*. Madrid: Centro de información y sociología de la Obra de Cooperación Sacerdotal Hispanoamericana.

Torres, Edelberto. 1966. *La dramática vida de Rubén Darío*. 4th ed. Barcelona: Ediciones Grijalbo.

Torres, Emilia. 1982. "Lineas de trabajo para los CPC — 1983." *La Chacalaca*, no. 3 (December): 5–8.

Torres, Hugo. 1983. "Conversando con el Comandante Hugo Torres: El arte como arma del pueblo." *Ventana: Barricada Cultural*, 19 July, pp. 16–17.

Torres Bodet, Jaime. 1966. *Rubén Darío: Abismo y cima*. Mexico, D.F.: Universidad Nacional Autónoma de México.

Tünnerman Bernheim, Carlos. 1973. *Pablo Antonio Cuadra y la cultura nacional.* León: Editorial Universitaria, UNAN.

———. 1980. *Rubén Darío y su tiempo.* Managua: Ministerio de Educación.

Tunstall, Jeremy. 1977. *The Media Are American.* New York: Columbia University Press.

Umaña Espinosa, Rosa. 1906. *Recuerdos y esperanzas.* Managua: Tipografía Moderna.

———. 1909. *Ayes del alma.* León: Tipografía Justo Hernández.

———. 1916. *Luz del ocaso.* León: Tipografía Justo Hernández.

UNESCO. 1940. *Intergovernmental Conference on Cultural Policies in Latin America and the Caribbean.* Paris: UNESCO.

Unión Nacional de Artistas Plásticos (UNAP) y Asociación Sandinista de Trabajadores de la Cultura (ASTC). [n.d.; ca. 1985]. *Pintura contemporánea de Nicaragua.* Managua: Editorial Nueva Nicaragua.

Union of Writers. 1982. "Relaciones entre la ASTC y el Ministerio de Cultura." *Ventana: Barricada Cultural,* 7 February, pp. 10–11.

Universidad Central de Nicaragua. 1943–44. *Cuadernos de divulgación de la obra de Darío para la instrucción pública.* Managua: Editorial Atlántida.

Universidad Nacional Autónoma de Nicaragua. 1967. *Cuadernos Universitarios, Segunda Serie, No. 2, Año 1. Enero de 1967. Número extraordinario en dos volúmenes para conmemorar el Primer Centenario 1867–1967 del nacimiento de Rubén Darío.* León: Universidad Nacional Autónoma de Nicaragua.

———. 1975. *Homenaje a la mujer nicaragüense en el Año Internacional de la Mujer. Cuadernos Universitarios,* second series, no. 15. León: Universidad Nacional Autónoma de Nicaragua.

Urban, Greg, and Joel Scherzer. 1991. *Nation States and Indians in Latin America.* Austin: University of Texas Press.

Urbanski, Edmund Stephen. 1967. "Rubén Darío's Teacher, Dr. José Leonard, and His Franco-Spanish-Latin American Cultural Activities." In Modern Language Association, *Papers on French-Spanish-Luso Brazilian-Spanish American Relations.* Chicago: Modern Language Association Conference, pp. 16–28.

Vakil, Jehangir J. 1928. "American Imperialism and Nicaragua." *The Modern Review* (July): 32–36.

Valdivia, Angharad N. 1991. "Gender, Press and Revolution: A Textual Analysis of Three Newspapers in Nicaragua's Sandinista Period, 1979–1988." Ph.D. diss., University of Illinois.

Valle-Castillo, Julio. n.d. *El inventario del paraíso: los primitivistas de Nicaragua.* Managua: Ministerio de Cultura.

———. 1981. "Zeledón: precursor del anti-imperialismo y Héroe Nacional." *Ventana: Barricada Cultural,* 3 October, pp. 2–3.

———. 1984. "Rubén Darío, Poeta y Ciudadano de su tiempo." *Casa de las Américas* 24 (January-February): 155–166.

Vanden, Harry E. 1982. "Ideology of the Nicaraguan Revolution." *Monthly Review* 34 (June): 25–41.

Vanegas, Elving. 1988. "Estrenos o desestrenos." *Ventana: Barricada Cultural,* 11 January, p. 7.

Vega Miranda, Gilberto. 1982. "Músicos nicaragüenses de ayer." *Boletín nicaragüense de bibliografía y documentación* 48 (July): 51–72.

Vicente Ibarra, Carlos. 1982. "Cine, revolución y cultura nacional." *La Chacalaca,* no. 2 (July): 38–40.

Vidal, Hernan, and René Furletti. 1986. *Testimonio y literatura*. Minneapolis: Institute for the Study of Ideologies and Literature.

Vilas, Carlos M. 1986. *The Sandinista Revolution: National Liberation and Social Transformation in Central America*. New York: Monthly Review Press.

———. 1989. *State, Class, and Ethnicity in Nicaragua: Capitalist Modernization and Revolutionary Change on the Atlantic Coast*. Translated by Susan Norwood. Boulder, Colo.: Lynne Rienner.

Wagner, Henry Raup, and Helen Rand Parish. 1967. *The Life and Writings of Bartolomé de las Casas*. Albuquerque: University of New Mexico Press.

Walker, Franklin, and G. Ezra Dane (eds.). 1940. *Mark Twain's Travels with Mr. Brown*. New York: Alfred A. Knopf.

Walker, Thomas W. (ed.). 1982. *Nicaragua in Revolution*. New York: Praeger.

——— (ed.). 1985. *Nicaragua: The First Five Years*. New York: Praeger.

——— (ed.). 1987. *Reagan versus the Sandinistas: The Undeclared War on Nicaragua*. Boulder, Colo.: Westview Press.

Walker, William. [1860] 1985. *The War in Nicaragua*. Reprint. Tucson: University of Arizona Press.

Wallace, Mike. 1985. "Interview With Nicaraguan Historians." *Radical History Review* 33 (September): 7–20.

Walter, Knut. 1987. "The Regime of Anastasio Somoza García and State Formation in Nicaragua, 1936–1956." Ph.D. diss., University of North Carolina, Chapel Hill.

———. 1993. *The Regime of Anastasio Somoza, 1936–1956*. Chapel Hill: University of North Carolina Press.

Watland, Charles D. 1965. *Poet-Errant: A Biography of Rubén Darío*. New York: Philosophical Library.

Wedel, Rudolf. 1983. "El teatro en la Revolución." *Ventana: Barricada Cultural*, 16 April, pp. 10–11.

Weiss, Judith. 1993. *Latin American Popular Theatre: The First Five Centuries*. Albuquerque: University of New Mexico Press.

Wells, Alan. 1972. *Picture Tube Imperialism? The Impact of U.S. Television in Latin America*. Maryknoll, N.Y.: Orbis Books.

Wessel, Lois. 1991. "Reproductive Rights in Nicaragua: From the Sandinistas to the Government of Violeta Chamorro." *Feminist Studies* 17 (Fall): 537–49.

Wheelock Román, Jaime. [1974] 1981. *Raíces indígenas de la lucha anti-colonialista en Nicaragua*. Managua: Editorial Nueva Nicaragua.

———. [1975] 1980. *Imperialismo y dictadura: crisis de una formación social*. 5th ed. Mexico, D.F.: Siglo Veintiuno Editores.

Wheldley, J. L. 1852. "Customs, Manners and Religion in Nicaragua, in Central America." *Christian Review* 17 (April): 263.

Whisnant, David E. 1983. *All That Is Native and Fine: The Politics of Culture in an American Region*. Chapel Hill: University of North Carolina Press.

———. 1989. "La vida nos ha enseñado: Rigoberta Menchú y la dialéctica de la cultura tradicional." *Ideologies and Literature* 4 (Spring 1989): 317–43.

———. 1992. "Rubén Darío as a Focal Cultural Figure in Nicaragua: The Ideological Uses of Cultural Capital." *Latin American Research Review* 27 (3): 3–49.

White, Deborah G. 1985. *Ar'n't I a Woman? Female Slaves in the Plantation South*. New York: W. W. Norton.

White, Steven F. 1982a. "Toward Cultural Dialogue with Nicaragua." *Third Rail* 5:45–64.

————— (ed.). 1982b. *Poets of Nicaragua: A Bilingual Anthology 1918–1979*. Greensboro, N.C.: Unicorn Press.

—————. 1986. *Culture and Politics in Nicaragua: Testimonies of Poets and Writers*. New York: Lumen Books.

Williams, Jerry M., and Robert E. Lewis. 1993. *Early Images of the Americas*. Tucson: University of Arizona Press.

Williams, Raymond. 1977. *Marxism and Literature*. New York: Oxford University Press.

—————. 1979. *Politics and Letters: Interviews with the New Left Review*. New York: Schocken Books.

Williams, Robert G. 1986. *Export Agriculture and the Crisis in Central America*. Chapel Hill: University of North Carolina Press.

Woodward, R. Lee, Jr. 1971. *Positivism in Latin America 1850–1900: Are Order and Progress Reconcilable?* Lexington, Mass.: D. C. Heath.

—————. [1976] 1985. *Central America: A Nation Divided*. 2d ed. New York: Oxford University Press.

—————. 1984. "The Rise and Decline of Liberalism in Central America." *Journal of Interamerican Studies and World Affairs* 26 (August): 291–312.

—————. 1986. "Conservatism, Liberalism, and Marxism in Central America." *Athenaeum Society Review* 3 (Spring): 5–21.

————— (ed.). 1988. *Central America: Historical Perspectives on the Contemporary Crises*. Westport, Conn.: Greenwood Press.

Xavier Solís, Pedro. 1990. "Darío olvidado en el aniversario de su nacimiento." *La Prensa*, 18 January, p. 1.

Zamora, Daisy. 1981. "Las artesanas y su lucha de siglos contra la penetración cultural." *Ventana: Barricada Cultural*, 26 September, p. 10.

—————. 1992. *La mujer nicaragüense en la poesía: antología*. Managua: Nueva Nicaragua.

Zavala, Iris M. 1987. "Lírica y fin de siglo: Rubén Darío bajo el signo del cisne." *Eutopias* 3 (Winter-Spring): 179–96.

—————. 1989. *Rubén Darío bajo el signo del cisne*. Río Pedras: Editorial de la Universidad de Puerto Rico.

Zepeda Henriquez, Eduardo. 1987. *Mitología Nicaragüense*. Managua: Editorial Manolo Morales.

Zimmerman, Marc. 1982. "Françoise Perus and Latin American Modernism: The Interventions of Althusser." *Praxis: A Journal of Culture and Criticism*, no. 6, pp. 157–75.

Zúñiga, Edgar. 1981. *Historia eclesiástica de Nicaragua*. Managua: Editorial Unión.

Zwerling, Philip, and Connie Martin. 1985. *Nicaragua: A New Kind of Revolution*. Westport, Conn.: Lawrence Hill.

INDEX

Page numbers in italic refer to illustrations.

Cape Gracias a Dios, 49, 112

Capitalism, 79, 183, 336, 338, 417, 427, 435; and prostitution, 507 (n. 68)

Capitalists, 60, 91, 94, 457 (n. 3)

Capone, Al, 368

Cara al pueblo (television show), 218

Cardenal, Ernesto, 6, 117, 145–46, 160–61, 168–69, 175, 177, 185, 190, 195, 199, 203–5, 210, 232, 244, 247, 259, 270, 313, 323, 333–34, 339, 359–60, 437, 440, 474 (n. 23); anti-Somoza poetry, 161; and April rebellion, 162, 360; Cuba visit, 211; early life, 161; and *exteriorismo*, 244, 246; *Hora cero*, 162, 175, 359; Indians, 259; and indigenous culture, 163; as Minister of Culture, 190, 199, 215, 247, 261, 333, 334, 339; and National Cultural Council, 270; poetry workshops, 244–45; and Rubén Darío, 323. *See also* Ministry of Culture; Solentiname

Cardenal, Salvador, 334

Cardenal Argüello, Salvador, 147, 228–29, 477 (n. 66); and CENTAURO records, 228

Carillo, Macario, 459 (n. 38)

Carnegie Endowment for International Peace, 137

Carrasco, Bishop, 36

Carrión, Gloria, 197–98

Carrión, Luis, 198

Casas, Bartolomé de las, 19, 20, 36, 156, 172, 452 (nn. 16–17), 454–55 (n. 38); and "good colonialism," 452 (n. 16)

Casco Cruz, Otilia, 422

Castillo Armas, Carlos (Col.), 326

Castillo Quant, José María: and FSLN Christmas party raid, 505 (n. 55)

Castillo Viejo, 67

Castro, Andrés, 76, 77, 344

Castro, Fidel, 117, 165, 211, 329, 346, 359, 496 (n. 9)

Cathedrals: León, 32, 42, 67, 320, 323; Managua, 109, 192, 393

Catherwood, Frederick, 277

Catholic church, 14, 19, 30, 33, 40, 191, 226, 266, 385, 392–94, 404, 429, 442, 446, 451 (n. 5), 454 (n. 34), 455 (n. 43), 467–68 (n. 1), 501 (n. 14); anti-Communism, 393; clergy, 19–21, 25, 28, 33–40, 51, 96, 197, 199, 280, 284, 287, 293, 377, 393, 413, and *cofradías*, 45, 110, 181, 393; and colonial oppression, 40; on condoms, 446; confession, 27, 35, 38, 403, 405; and contraception, 501 (n. 15); convents, 33, 38, 67, 405; and cultural recalcitrance, 385, 392; gender order in, 393, 501 (n. 16); liberation theol-

ogy, 501 (n. 14); monasteries, 41; and sexuality, 405, 501 (n. 15); and Somoza dictatorship, 393–94; Vatican II, 232, 394, 467–68 (n. 1); and women, 501 (n. 16)

Catholicism, 17, 34, 40–41, 156, 392–93, 434, 443, 467–68 (n. 1); folk, 40, 455 (n. 43); as state religion, 392

Cattle, 17, 25, 31, 44–46, 98, 254–55, 259, 378; and *cofradías*, 45; export production cooperative, 255

Cave drawings, 293

CDI. *See* Centros de Desarrollo Infantil

Ceiba Island, 296, 299, 348, 376, 382, 485 (n. 46); Carl Bovallius collecting on, 296; rock carvings on, 299

Celler, Emanuel (U.S. Representative), 113

Censorship, 6, 111, 116, 121, 143, 147–49, 161, 314, 393, 436, 442, 462 (n. 20); Catholic church and, 393. *See also* Repression

CENTAURO (phonograph records), 228

Centers for Popular Culture, 201–3, 238, 478; antecedents of, 202; first national meeting, 203; Granada, 202; León, 202, 473 (n. 14); mission of, 202–3; museums in, 210

Central American Common Market: development agenda of, 254

Central American Defense Council (CONDECA), 143

Central American Feminine Congress on Education, First, 411

Central American Festival of Popular Theater, 238–39

Central American Regional Radio Conference (Mexico), 462 (n. 11)

Central Intelligence Agency, U.S. (CIA), 1, 143, 215, 219, 407

Centro Femenino de Cultura Obrera, 505 (n. 54)

Centros de Desarrollo Infantil (CDI), 420

Ceramics, 14, 52, 147, 246, 248–50, 294, 422, 487 (n. 69); collections of, 208

Ceremonies: community control of, 181; suppression by Spanish, 22; survival of traditional, 180

Cerna, Lenin, 172

Cerro del Panteón, 485 (n. 47)

Cerutti, Franco: and women's activism, 503 (n. 37)

Chamorro, Don Diego, 31

Chamorro, Josefa, 506 (n. 62)

Chamorro, Pedro Joaquín (editor), 176, 440; assassination of, 184, 417

Chamorro, Pedro Joaquín (President), 59

Chamorro, Violeta, 267, 443, 446

Columbian Exposition (Madrid): Nicaraguan exhibit in, 487 (n. 69)

Comic strips, 6, 129, 133–36, 149, 215; politics of, 134, 136

Comité Interamericano de Mujeres, 505 (n. 54)

Comité Revolucionario Nicaragüense, 151

Commissaries, 94–95, 251, 253, 256; departure of on Atlantic coast, 256

Communism, 156, 186, 259–60, 393–94, 407, 441; Christian, 186; primitive, 260; rational, 497 (n. 28)

Communists, 117, 132, 136–37, 142–43, 158, 195, 337, 363, 399, 407, 445, 465 (n. 48); and blacklisting in film industry, 136–37

Communities, 1, 4, 6, 15, 24, 36, 43, 45–46, 59–61, 81–83, 90, 92, 121, 173, 179, 182, 183–84, 202, 210, 212, 219, 237, 246–47, 253, 261, 263, 267, 415; traditional, 4, 179

Concubinage, 36, 47, 338, 377, 430; among clergy, 47

Condega, 42

Confederación de Trabajadores Nicaragüenses (CTN), 465 (n. 48)

Confession, 27, 35, 38, 403, 405, 454 (n. 37)

Congreso de Mujeres de la Raza (Mexico), 503 (n. 34)

Congreso Femenino Internacional, 406

Congress of Nicaraguan Intellectuals, 110

Conquest, 4–5, 11, 13–18, 23–27, 30–56, 60, 62, 81–82, 98, 100, 102, 108, 147, 156, 158, 162–63, 189, 225, 273–74, 278, 282, 284, 342, 351, 365, 383, 399, 401–2, 417, 419, 433–35, 443–44; durable effects of, 434; impact of, 47, 61

Conquistadores, 5, 13, 17, 27, 62, 145, 156, 185, 223, 251, 352, 451 (n. 5), 459 (n. 35); mockery of, 223

Conservatives, 57, 92, 151, 154, 182, 393, 443; "Legitimists," 74–76

Constitutional Commission, 430

Constitutional convention: women and, 430

Constitutions of Nicaragua, 41, 59, 62, 116, 224, 370, 392, 393, 412, 429–30, 433, 443; and Catholic church, 392; and women, 429–30, 508 (n. 77)

Consumer culture, 3, 108, 121, 134, 436

Consumer products, 6, 121, 122–23, 148–49, 268, 435; and cultural reproduction, 386; rising demand for, 119–20

Contraception, 421; and Catholic church, 446; and Violeta Chamorro government, 446

Contra war, 208, 213, 217, 222, 235, 249–50,

267–69, 420–21, 423–26, 438, 444, 473 (n. 11); and Atlantic coast, 267

Contreras, Eduardo, 213

Contreras, Rubén Darío, 326

Convents, 33, 38, 67, 405

Coolidge, Calvin (President), 371

Cooperatives, 239; Agrarian Reform and Cooperative Laws (1981), 420; agricultural, 218, 422, 443; men and women in, 422; pottery, 246–48, 422; production (Atlantic coast), 255, 265; Sandino and, 349, 356; women's, 420

Coordinator of Inter-American Affairs, 131; and FBI, 140; Motion Picture Division, 132; and Walt Disney, 136. See also Nelson Rockefeller

Córdoba, Hernández de, 16

Corea, Chick, 242

Corinto, 94, 317, 320, 463 (n. 29)

Corn, 20, 31, 60, 117, 158–59, 173, 181, 231–32, 268

Coronel Urtecho, José, 145, 153, 155, 161, 187, 203, 224, 246, 334, 412, 440, 445; anti-democratic ideas, 156–57; and Carlos Fonseca, 445; and Rubén Darío, 323; in San Francisco, 153; and women's suffrage, 412

Corporations: Accessory Transit Company, 73–75; Atlantic Chemical Company, 94; Atlantic coast monopolies, 94; Emery Company, 93; Huasteca Petroleum, 348, 376; Nicaraguan Long Leaf Pine Company, 94; Pan American Airways, 123–24; Prencinradio, Inc., 131; Radio Corporation of America (RCA), 112, 114; Standard Fruit Company, 253; United Fruit Company, 112, 359; U.S., 93–94, 112, 114, 116, 121, 130, 162, 255, 257, 322, 348, 359, 436

Cortázar, Julio, 146, 189, 190, 338

Costa Rica, 49, 75, 147–48, 151, 161, 175, 177, 216, 218, 288, 295, 306, 316, 354; antiquities in, 295; Chiriqui graves, 486 (n. 62); ISTMO-Film, 216; music festivals, 175; television broadcasts from, 218

Costeños, 251–63, 480 (n. 28); adaptability, 252; Anglo affinity of, 257–58; divisions among, 256; and east-west axis, 479 (n. 26); hostility to Sandinista revolution, 261; militancy among, 263; and Moravian church, 259; and organized opposition, 262; proletarianization of, 256, 258; and resistance, 257–58; and Sandinistas, 258, 262; and Sandino, 480 (n. 31); trade with British, 252

Cotton, 3, 119, 182; agroexport production impacts, 121; growers, 3, 119; oligarchy, 119;

Dance, 16, 29, 38, 40, 45, 52, 63, 83, 109, 122, 144, 148, 155, 159, 185, 194–95, 201–2, 219–26, 239–40, 269, 283, 318, 332, 335, 378, 400, 436, 445, 476 (n. 54); dance-dramas, 83; European forms, 220–21; Experimental Workshop of Classical Dance, 222; traditional, 185, 221, 226

Darío, Rubén, 5, 7, 109, 112, 121, 144–45, 194, 199, 207, 221, 224–25, 230, 235, 241, 313–43, *319*, *347*, 361, 398, 438, 440, 444, 445, 448, 490 (n. 33); and aristocrats, 318; in Chile, 316–18; as construct, 341–43; in Costa Rica, 316; as cultural capital, 314–15; "divine" birth, 315; as focal cultural figure, 440; death of, 320; in El Salvador, 316–17, 494 (n. 66); feminist arguments against, 493 (n. 53); in France, 316; governmental positions, 319–20; in Guatemala, 316; idealization of, 440; and José Martí, 321; in León, 320, 334; and Leopoldo Lugones, 321; and Luis Debayle, 320; and Marxism, 337; museum, 334; and national identity, 342; and Nicaragua, 315–20; and Nicaraguan women, 398–99; oppositional politics in poetry, 495 (n. 70); Orden de Rubén Darío, 144, 329; and Panama Canal, 322, 338; and Paris, 316, 321, 343, 445; as political-cultural construct, 440; political formation, 320–23; political reconstructions of, 342; post-Sandinista representations, 508 (n. 3); Sandinistas and, 313, 329–43, 493 (n. 50); and Sandino, 333, 345; social aspirations, 317–18; and socialism, 494 (n. 61); in Spain, 316, 318; statue of, 230, 339, *340*; and traditional culture, 489 (n. 11); and upper class, 218; and Victor Hugo, 490; and Walt Whitman, 316; and Zelaya administration, 320

Davis, Richard Harding, 108, 463 (n. 29)

Debayle, Luis: and Anastasio Somoza García, 491 (n. 37); and Rubén Darío, 320, 326

Debayle, Salvadora, 326

Debayle de Somoza, Salvadora, *396*

Declaration of Principles of the Popular Sandinista Revolution, 261–62

Delgadillo, Luis, 174, 461 (n. 4)

Del Valle, Blanca (María Fugle), 505 (n. 50)

Deshon, Edmundo, 399

Díaz, Adolfo (President), 95, 111, 320, 344

Díaz, Benito, 25

Díaz, Carmen, 506 (n. 59)

Díaz, Porfirio, 433

Dictatorship, 11, 107, 134, 141, 143, 151, 157–60, 163, 168–69, 172, 187, 189, 203, 214, 227, 235, 258, 342, 393, 406–7, 503 (n. 37). *See also*

Debayle, Luis Somoza; Somoza Debayle, Anastasio; Somoza García, Anastasio; Somoza regime; Ubico, Jorge

Diet, 17, 21, 24, 120, 256, 434; pre-conquest, 17; Spanish, in New World, 453 (n. 19)

Dietrick Company, 94

Dill, Clarence (U.S. Senator), 370

Dimensión Costeña (musical group), 231

Dirección de Artesanía (DA), 248–50

Diriamba, 113

Diriangén, 27, 113, 248, 329, 345

Diseases, 17, 18, 20, 39, 47, 63, 93; banana-tree, 253; European, 18; fat/protein, 452 (n. 9); intestinal, 452 (n. 9); malaria, 17, 51; pre-conquest, 17, 452 (n. 9); sexually transmitted, 17, 47, 421

Disney, Walt, 129–37, 142; cartoons, 268; comic strips, 134, 136; company, and U.S. government, 134, 136; and FBI, 136; and House Un-American Activities Committee, 136; and Latin America, 136, 137; political ideas, 136; propaganda films, 134

Divorce, 62, 84, 88, 137, 404, 406, 429–30; double standard for, 430; women and, 404, 430

Dixon, Rafael, 383

Dominicans (religious order), 32–33, 36, 317, 330

Doolittle, William G., 62

Dorfman, Ariel, 146, 215

Downing, Luis, 153, 468 (n. 4)

Dowry, 502 (n. 29). *See also* Marriage; Women

Drama, 37, 96, 100, 102, 108, 223, 225, 258, 308, 362, 365, 407, 436, 507 (n. 68)

Drinking, 36, 60, 63, 145, 162, 365, 378

Drums, 16, 52, 182, 183, 185, 226, 231, 475 (n. 54)

Dulles, John Foster (Secretary of State), 143

Duran, Aristides, 412

Earthquakes, 2, 109–11, 130, 145, 147–48, 163, 191, *192–93*, 194, 205, 258, 268, 448; and cultural institutions, 147, 194

Ecology, 22, 218; agricultural impacts upon, 120

Economic development, 3, 94, 108, 120–21, 249, 254–55

Ecuador, 311, 411, 503 (n. 34)

Education, 59, 90, 144, 158, 164, 197, 217–18, 255, 261, 270, 303, 306, 311, 326, 333, 383, 390, 392, 395, 405–9, 411, 418, 425, 433–36, 446; public, 58–59, 91, 110, 153, 186, 191, 196, 220, 259, 266, 302, 304, 310, 326, 329, 338, 349, 394, 408–9, 446, 506 (n. 56); public law, 59;

Fascism, 113, 152, 155–57, 258, 324, 329, 462, 469 (n. 14); European, 155
Fathers, 19, 54, 73–74, 78, 86–88, 107, 110, 115, 117, 143, 153, 164, 196–99, 254, 276, 294, 306, 326, 339, 348–50, 365, 372, 390, 402, 403, 405, 423, 437, 441, 448; authority of, 390. *See also* Mothers
Faulkner, William, 168
Federation of Nicaraguan Students, 163
Femininity, 29, 385, 400, 409–13, 446
Feminism, 383, 392, 400, 401, 403–4, 406–20, 426–27, 429–30, 433, 440, 445–47, 493 (n. 53), 502 (n. 27), 503 (n. 36), 504 (n. 39), 505 (n. 49); British, 411; and Catholic church, 392; contradictions within, 447; definition of, 502 (n. 27); and Marxism, 427; masculinized, 411; opportunistic, 411; opposition to, 447; and socialism, 411
Feminist: God as, 409; movement in Nicaragua, 409; organizations vs. women's groups, 503 (n. 36)
Festival, 1, 28, 38, 40, 46, 52, 83, 175–76, 195, 202, 215, 219–27, 230–31, 234, 239–42, 407; corn, 231; of electronic music, 242; Indian, 38; *nueva canción*, 477 (n. 66); *palo de mayo*, 231, 234; patron saints', 28, 38, 40, 83, 175, 202, 219, 221, 223, 225, 231, 240; of romantic song, 230; Youth Festival of Amateur Artists, 478 (n. 4)
Fiallos Gil, Mariano, 143, 163, 164, 208, 224, 437, 440; exile of, 164; as rector of UNAN, 164–65, 208, 224
Fiallos Oyanguren, Mariano, 415
Field, Les, 422–23
Fiesta de San Jerónimo, 219
Filibustering: as cultural crusade, 78; songs about, 232
Film, 1, 6, 113–15, 128–33, 142, 201–2, 214–19, 225–27, 436, 446; documentaries, 214–15; European, 216; Hollywood, 6, 113, 120, 128, 130, 133–34, 142, 149, 174, 214; production facilities for, 216; and revolution, 214; Somoza regime and, 214; theaters in Nicaragua, 464 (n. 39); and U.S. government, 132. *See also* Instituto Nicaragüense del Cine; PRODUCINE
Final offensive (FSLN), 184, 421
Finca Casa Blanca, La, 291, 487 (n. 69)
Fine Arts Museum (San Francisco), 311
Fishing: export industry, 254–55, 259
Flint, Earl, 289–306, 439; and Acahualinca footprints, 486 (n. 52); arrival in Nicaragua, 483 (n. 18); and Carl Bovallius, 295; collecting for Peabody Museum, 292–93;

collecting for Smithsonian Institution, 289–92; contradictions of collecting, 293–94; as landowner, 300; and Tola pottery style, 486 (n. 52)
Folklore, 1, 144, 147, 180, 196, 204, 219, 221–22, 313, 330, 472 (n. 2), 476 (n. 76); school of, 144; trickster tales, 82
Fonda, Jane, 215
Fonseca, José, 169
Fonseca Amador, Carlos, 165, 195, 208–12, 225, 234, 269, 330, 334, 344–46, 360–61, 380, 418, 431, 437, 440, 445, 488 (n. 4), 492 (n. 44); culture and national life, 437; early life, 360; and José Coronel Urtecho, 445; and museums, 208–9; and Rubén Darío, 330, 492; and Sandino, 344, 360–68, 380; and theater, 225; in USSR, 195, 208–9, 225, 418
Fontaine, Joan, 130
Food, 14–15, 18, 21, 62, 66–67, 180–82, 240, 252–56, 351, 362, 383, 402, 406, 453 (n. 19)
Forced labor, 5, 20, 23, 32, 42, 59, 81, 91
Foreign policy, 3, 115, 368; and cultural policy, 137–38
Forests, 17, 20, 45, 60, 67, 69, 82, 93, 95, 102, 120, 255, 259, 273, 281, 331, 354, 374, 382
France (and French in Nicaragua), 46, 54, 153, 200, 202, 218, 276, 291, 306, 316, 318, 321, 323, 360, 456 (n. 48), 489 (n. 14)
Franciscans (religious order), 33, 39, 455 (n. 41)
Frank Leslie's Illustrated Newspaper, 74, 78
Franklin, Benjamin, 286
Frederic, George Augustus (Mosquito king), 100
Frente Estudiantil Revolucionario (FER), 165
Frente Popular Femenino, 402
Frente Sandinista de Liberación Nacional (FSLN), 152, 162–63, 175–79, 183–84, 188, 195–99, 212, 215–16, 224–25, 232, 234, 248, 250, 258–60, 262–63, 315, 329–30, 334, 346, 348, 361, 363, 379, 390, 415–19, 421, 433, 437, 440–42, 445–46; cultural alienation of leadership, 184; gender conflict within, 421; Historic Program (1969), 195–96, 418, 426; sources of cultural ideas, 195; in Subtiava, 183; and theater, 225; women combatants in, 419; working-class base, 196
Friedrichsthal, Emanuel von, 279
Frost, Robert, 153, 243
FSLN. *See* Frente Sandinista de Liberación Nacional
Funerals, 40, 142, 320, 329, 377; Indian customs, 40

Gage, Thomas, 32, 52, 316
Galeano, Eduardo, 146, 190, 244
Galleguillos Lorca, Francisco, 321
Gámez, José Dolores, 316
Gámez, María, 505 (n. 50)
García, Ivan, 217
García Sarmiento, Félix Rubén, 342–43
Gender, 2, 4, 7–8, 14, 30, 46–47, 83–84, 88, 126, 191, 300, 311, 375, 378, 383–433, 438–48, 451 (n. 2); conflict, 191; conquest and, 456 (n. 52); politics of, 4. *See also* Gender order; Gender paradigms; Gender relations
Gender order, 8, 46–47, 87, 385–86, 390–97, 400, 402, 404, 408, 411, 418, 420, 422, 425–26, 428–29, 431, 433, 441, 445, 447, 455 (n. 40), 500 (n. 5), 503 (nn. 24, 25, 26), 507 (n. 64), 508 (n. 76); and Catholic church, 501 (n. 16); colonial period, 46–47; and cultural recalcitrance, 431; definition of, 451 (n. 2); hegemonic, 397; and *patria potestad*, 431, 446; and power, 400; pre-conquest, 456 (n. 52); recalcitrance of, 404, 418, 420; Sandinistas and, 418–27. *See also* Gender; Gender paradigms
Gender paradigms, 7, 375, 385–86, 391, 394, 397, 399–400, 404, 420, 426, 429, 438, 441–42, 446; in advertisements, 125–28; feminine, 385, 411, 446; masculine, 88, 385, 392, 399, 401; post-triumph reassertion of, 420; revolutionary, 426; Sandino and, 375–79; social reproduction of, 392; in tango, 397. *See also* Gender; Gender order
Gender relations, 7, 14, 383, 384, 419, 422, 427, 442, 477 (n. 1); and class, 427; durability of, 384; women in combat and, 419
Generation of 1940, 6, 152, 160, 163, 195, 437
Genocide, 4, 265
Germany: films from, 130
Ginsberg, Allen, 204
Gold, 20; in California, 435; Chontales, 60, *61*; discovery in Nueva Segovia, 452 (n. 12); export of, 93–94; gold rush, 278; Las Segovias mine, 254
González, Armando Monge (Lieutenant Colonel), 114
González Dávila, Gil, 27, 33
Good Neighbor Policy, 137, 156
Gordillo, Fernando, 166, 168–69, 334, 470 (n. 30)
Gota de Leche, La, 504 (n. 44)
Gould, Jeffrey L., 399, 402, 415
Governors, 13, 18–19, 24–25, 28–29, 36, 38, 43, 48, 50, 286, 368, 406, 452 (n. 14); British-appointed Miskito, 50; Francisco de Cas-

tañeda, 18–19, 24; Pedrarias Dávila, 19; Rodrigo de Contreras, 19, 24, 453 (n. 22); and slave trade, 452
Gramsci, Antonio, 195, 257
Granada, 5, 14, 16, 21, 25, 30–31, 33, 42–44, 49–50, 54–57, *58*, 63–65, 67, 74–75, *76*, 77–81, 90, 96, 108, 110, 113, 138, 153–54, 160–63, 180, 192, 197, 202, 220, 246, 280, 288–89, 294, 296, 300, 303, 305–6, 308, 348, 393, 395, 408–9, 435, 443–44, 461 (n. 2), 468 (n. 4), 469 (n. 17), 486 (n. 60); burning by fili-buster troops, 77, 303; Christmas festival, 220; Colegio de Señoritas, 409; merchants, 31; musicians, 459 (n. 38)
Greenfield, Jeanette, 275
Greytown, 60, 69, 301
Grupo Gradas, 225
Grupo Pacaya, 176
Grupo Pancasán, 175–76
Grupo Praxis, 168, 225
Grupo Pueblo, 471 (n. 48)
Grupo Trova, 471 (n. 48)
Grupo Xitlaly, 477 (n. 69)
Guadamuz, Carlos José, 172
Guanacaste, 457 (n. 1)
Guardabarranco (musical group), 476 (n. 64)
Guatemala, 1, 18, 51, 75, 91, 124, 141, 143, 164, 198, 310, 316, 326, 348, 360, 393, 406, 485 (n. 32); church hierarchy in, 393; Quiché culture, 1; Sandino in, 348
Guerrero, Irma, 402
Guerrillas, 4–5, 154, 158, 160, 170, 174, 177, 184, 187–88, 197–99, 214, 216, 217, 224–25, 234, 253, 324, 342, 346, 354, 357–62, 371, 382, 390, 407, 414, 417–19, 441–42, 480 (n. 35)
Guevara, Che, 117, 329, 346`
Guido, Lea, 197, 425
Guillén, Asilia: and primitivist painting, 246
Guillén, Nicolás, 468 (n. 2)
Gutiérrez, Ernesto, 145–46, 148, 160, 168, 187, 330, 479 (n. 20), 491 (n. 37)
Gutiérrez, Ramón, 360
Gutiérrez Pérez, Dolores, 459 (n. 38)
Guzmán, David, 307

Haciendas, 25, 41, 44, 46, 120, 183, 226, 294, 299
Hale, Charles, 255, 257–60, 266
Hale, John, 54
Halftermeyer, Gratus, 110, 122
Hammock, 27, 52, 61, 63–64, 67, 69–70, *303*, 373, 383, 458 (n. 25); as national ensign, 302
Happy Land (musical group), 231
Havilland, Olivia de, 130

Industry, 20, 33, 49, 86, 111, 114–15, 120, 130–32, 137, 142, 253–55, 421–22, 467 (n. 82); destroyed by revolution, 191
Infanticide, 47
Inflation, 119, 268–69
Inquisition, 503 (n. 31)
Insecticide poisoning, 120
Institute of Arts and Culture, 270
Institutions, 1, 3–7, 13, 17, 23, 41, 45, 116, 118, 121, 132, 142, 144–47, 159, 179, 182, 191–92, 194, 200–202, 207, 215–19, 236, 241, 255, 257–58, 262, 265, 299, 304, 308, 311, 313, 321, 360, 385, 409, 431, 433, 434, 436–38, 442. *See also* Cultural institutions
Instituto Agrario Nicaragüense (IAN), 255
Instituto de Estudio del Sandinismo, 499 (n. 47)
Instituto de Occidente, 321
Instituto Indigenista Interamericano, 118
Instituto Indigenista Nacional, 118, 179, 246
Instituto Nacional del Norte, 360
Instituto Nacional del Oriente, 308
Instituto Nicaragüense de Cine (INCINE), 215–19, 225; international collaboration, 216; mobile cinema program, 216
Instituto Nacional de Señoritas, 504 (n. 41)
Insurrections, 81, 171, 176–77, 179–86, 187, 190–91, 193–94, 201, 203, 210, 212, 216–17, 225, 229, 232, 234, 241, 247, 250–51, 258; documentary films on, 215; Matagalpan (1881), 91. *See also* Opposition; Rebellion; Resistance
Intellectuals, 90, 110, 117, 141, 147, 155, 170, 179, 195, 247, 250, 331, 334, 459 (n. 29), 493 (n. 55), 501 (n. 16); Clan Intelectual de Chontales, 308; Congress of Nicaraguan, 110; Latin American, 468 (n. 2); organic, 250; women as, 408
Inter-American Commission of Women, 406
Inter-American Conference for the Maintenance of Peace, 138
Inter-American Radio Convention, 462 (n. 11)
International Bank for Reconstruction and Development (IDB), 254
Intervention, 55, 95; cultural, 6, 62, 66, 108, 121, 137, 154–55, 435, 437; as scapegoat, 444; by U.S., 5, 55, 84, 152, 212, 263, 323, 358
Italy: films from, 217

Jalteva, 21, 30, 280, 305
Jelapa, 42
Jerónimos (religious order), 33

Jesuits (religious order), 33, 41, 82, 153, 308, 321, 455 (n. 41), 501 (n. 16)
Jiménez, Mayra, 187, 203, 244–45; and *exteriorismo*, 244–45; and poetry workshops, 472 (n. 64)
Jiménez de Orozco, Nila, 505 (n. 50)
Jinotega, 60, 175, 422, 423, 479 (n. 22); *cerámic negra* industry, 423; women artisans, 422
Jinotepe, 202, 414
Journalists: women, 405
Juigalpa, 61, 202, 287, 302, 308, 409, 415; national women's meeting, 415
Junta Femenina de Beneficencia, 504 (n. 44)
Juventud Sandinista, 221, 242, 478; and beauty contests, 509 (n. 8)

Kazan, Elia, 132
Kellogg, Frank (Secretary of State), 371
Kennedy, John F. (President), 146, 254, 339, 347
Kyser, Kay, 448

La Aviación (prison), 117, 159
Labor: agricultural, 120; forced, 5, 20, 23, 42, 81, 91; sexual division of, 422; slave, 31, 50
La Ceiba Island, 348, 376, 382; rock carvings on, 299
Ladinos, 42–43, 53, 91, 365
Lake Managua, 15, 279; Momotombito Island, 279
Lake Nicaragua, 15, 31, 49, 54, 60, 62, 79, 186, 230, 246, 254, 273, 280; Solentiname archipelago, 186. *See also* Ometepe Island; Zapatero Island
Lake Nihapa, 283, 288
La Libertad, 288
Lancaster, Roger N., 392, 400, 401, 403
Language, 16–17, 76, 93, 97, 107, 118, 123, 133, 136, 145, 153, 161, 168, 170, 180–81, 192, 204, 223, 232, 234, 241–42, 244–45, 251, 255, 261–62, 267, 304, 326, 351–52, 357, 367, 392, 426, 429, 434–35; OtoMangue, 14; Spanish, in colonial period, 22; Uto-Azteca, 14
La Prensa (newspaper), 116, 118–19, 121, 134, 142, 149, 166, 170, 173, 176, 184, 208, 223, 339, 399, 417, 440, 445
Las Perlas, 94
Las Segovias, 374–75
Latin American Cultural Collective of Utrecht (KKLA), 232
La Veintiuno (prison), 117
Law for the Defense of Democracy, 116
Law of Freedom of Broadcast and Diffusion of Thought (1944), 116

Laws of Burgos, 23, 34, 36, 48, 453 (n. 19); and Catholic missionary enterprise, 34
League of Nations: and women's rights, 410, 413
Legends, 7, 118, 159, 180, 220, 245, 299, 317, 330, 363; of Sandino, 345, 347, 350, 357, 362
León, 5, 14, 16, 18–19, 25, 28, 30–34, 38, 42–45, 55–56, 57, 58, 63, 67, 74, 78, 81, 90, 96, 108–10, 113, 117, 121, 138, 161, 163–64, 167, 173–74, 179–83, 191–93, 202, 205–8, 216, 219, 224, 280–82, 303, 305, 308, 315, 320–21, 323, 330, 334, 338, 357–60, 427, 435, 437, 443, 444; musicians in, 459 (n. 38); pirate attack on, 454 (n. 34); Purísima, 219; in seventeenth century, 32
Leonard, José, 320–21, 327
León-Granada axis, 14, 30–33
Levy, Pablo, 304
Lezcano y Ortega, José Antonio (Archbishop), 393
Liberals, 41, 55–58, 74, 90, 92, 97, 110, 120, 137, 143, 151, 154, 156–57, 159, 163, 181–82, 205, 226, 250, 320–22, 327–29, 341–42, 358, 393, 435, 440, 443
Liberation: culture of, 190; and libertinage, 445; national, 195, 362; sexual, 446; women's, 7, 384–85, 401–5, 418; women's ambivalence and, 401
Liberation theology, 232, 437, 443, 501 (n. 14)
Libraries, 31, 54, 98, 110, 138, 140–41, 144, 146–48, 188, 196, 201, 205, 207, 208, 210–11, 226, 332, 437
Liga Feminista de Nicaragua, 504 (n. 44)
Liga Internacional de Mujeres Ibéricas e Hispanoamericanas, 505 (n. 54)
Liga Internacional Pro-Paz y Libertad, La, 505 (n. 54)
Lilienthal, Peter, 216
Limón, José, 142
Lincoln, Abraham (President), 347; school named for, 448
Lindbergh, Charles, 368, 449; Latin American goodwill trip, 370
Linder, Benjamin, 219
Lindsay, Vachel, 153
Lira, Máximo, 408
Literacy campaign, 205, 206, 220, 240, 263, 333, 367, 437; on Atlantic coast, 263; museum of, 210; songs of, 231
Little Corn Island, 117, 158–59, 173
Lombard, Carole, 130
López, Dionisia Frank, 257
López, Irene, 219–20

López, Wilmor, 227
López Pérez, Rigoberto, 164, 219, 359
Los de Palacagüina (musical group), 175, 177
Los Girasoles (musical group), 230
Los Soñadores de Sarawaska (musical group), 175
Louvre, 275–76, 280
Lower Central America, 5, 14–16
Lugones, Leopoldo, 321, 327–28
Lumber: mahogany, 50, 93; Nicaraguan Long Leaf Pine Co., 94; pine, 61, 67, 93–95, 183, 265

Machismo, 29, 84, 147, 378, 384–86, 397–403, 412, 415, 417, 425–26, 442, 480 (n. 35); Sandino and, 378
Madriz, José (President), 95
Maize, 14–15, 25, 47, 49, 60, 453 (n. 19)
Malaria, 17, 51
Managua, 1–2, 15, 21, 31, 35, 46, 58, 81, 83, 90, 108–10, 112–13, 115, 117, 119, 121–22, 129–30, 132, 138, 140–43, 145–49, 154, 159, 161–66, 174, 176, 180, 191–94, 197, 199, 202–3, 205, 207, 211–14, 219–21, 223, 225, 227, 229–30, 234, 238, 243, 249, 260, 263, 268–69, 279, 303, 305–6, 308, 313, 335, 339–40, 367, 369, 383, 391–93, 403–4, 409, 412, 417, 420, 421, 430–33, 448; Archdiocese of, 393; Avenida Roosevelt, 448; colonial period, 108; country clubs, 148; cultural development of, 109; earthquakes, 109, 110; Eastern Market, 197; El Teatro Castaño, 109; El Teatro Variedades, 109; emergence as capital, 108; Fiesta de Santo Domingo, 219, 223, 227; movie theaters, 130, 214; musicians in, 459 (n. 38); in nineteenth century, 108–9; as stage for Somoza regime, 108–9
Mancotal (musical group), 232
Manioc, 14–15
Mansfield, J. Carrol, 134
Mántica, Carlos, 192
Mantilla, Carmen de, 505 (n. 50)
Mariachi, 230
Marianismo, 402, 502 (n. 24)
Maribio, 14
Marimba, 175, 221, 226, 227, 228, 229, 270, 472 (n. 61); history of, 475 (n. 54)
Marine Corps, U.S., 2, 4–5, 95, 111–12, 121, 133, 137, 155, 163, 209, 212, 224, 253, 258, 269, 324, 345, 349, 352, 354–55, 358–59, 362–63, 367–68, 370–74, 393, 437, 441, 444, 461 (n. 2); brutality of, 354, 362, 373–74; Company M, 363; and radio, 112; and Sandino, 345, 354, 362, 367–68, 370–71; satire of, 224

Marquez, Gabriel García, 146, 190, 216
Marriage, 35–36, 46–47, 84, 93, 197, 330, 377, 383, 394, 403–5, 415, 419, 421, 427, 434, 503 (n. 32); customs, 22, 23; among FSLN combatants, 419; monogamy, 36, 47, 93; polyandry, 47; polygamy, 22, 47. *See also* Husbands; Wives
Martí, José, 321, 327–28, 331, 338–39, 373
Martínez, Tomás (President), 59–60
Martínez de la Rocha, Leonor, 461 (n. 6)
Martyrs, 40, 167–68, 175, 196, 210, 219, 234, 269, 321, 418, 445, 475 (n. 35); galleries of, 210
Marxism, 2, 114, 156, 195, 259, 336–38, 360, 427, 440, 445, 478 (n. 11), 493 (n. 51), 497 (n. 28); feminist critics of, 427
Masatepe, 198
Masaya, 31, 41–42, 58, 63, 65, 67, *70*, 76, 81, 95, 110, 113, 144, 147, 180–81, 184, 191, 202–3, 208–10, 219–21, 224, 229, 234, 249, 268, 283, 344, 452 (n. 11), 471 (n. 54), 472 (n. 59); Dramatic Company of Aficionados, 224; Fiesta de San Jerónimo, *221*; musicians in, 459 (n. 38)
Masculinity, 88, 385, 392, 399, 400–401; and aggression, 392
Masks: use in insurrection, 212
Mass organizations, 237, 245, 250, 262–63, 418, 506 (n. 57); ALPROMISU, 262; AMNLAE, 418, 421, 425–26, 432, 447; AMPRONAC, 417, 418, 426; and artisans, 250; ATC, 424; on Atlantic coast, 262; MISURASATA, 263, 265–66
Masters, Edgar Lee, 153, 204, 243
Masturbation, 421, 501 (n. 9)
Matagalpa, 42, 50, 76, 81, 98, 101, 113, 184, 202, 234, 360, 423; *cerámica negra* industry, 423
Mattelart, Armand, 215
Matthews, Jill, 385
Mature, Victor, 130
Matuz, Cándida Rose, 506 (n. 59)
Mayorga, Salvador, 198
Mayorga, Silvio, 360
MECATE. *See* Movimiento de Expresión Campesina Artística y Teatral
Media, 111, 114–16, 121, 130–31, 149, 174, 200–201, 214, 420, 436; film, 1, 6, 113, 115, 128, 130, 132–33, 142, 201–2, 214–19, 225–27, 436, 446, 464 (n. 45); radio, 111–14, 131–33, 139–41, 147, 158, 174, 219–20, 229–30, 269, 418, 447, 464 (n. 45); television, 111, 114–15, 149, 199, 201, 214–19, 226, 268, 418, 421, 446; video, 214, 216, 218–19
Medina, Felix, 224

Mejía, Blanca Victoria, 505 (n. 50)
Mejía Godoy, Carlos, 148, 175, 176–77, 230–31, 234, 270
Mejía Godoy, Luis Enrique, 151, 175, 176–77, 231–32, 234, 270, 334, 471 (n. 51); and *nueva canción*, 175
Melchior, Lauritz, 139
Men, 2, 19, 24, 27, 37, 47, 58, 60, 79–80, 93, 112, 120, 136, 147, 158, 175, 224, 232, 249, 253, 257, 262, 284, 294, 302, 328, 334, 348, 351, 354, 357, 361–62, 367–68, 371, 375–85 passim, *389*, 392–95, 397–406, 408–9, 411–13, 415, 417–30 passim, 433, 438, 440–42, 446; in advertising, 125–27; and gender order, 394–95; moral feminization of, 411; new, 4, 175, 239, 420
Menchú, Rigoberta, 1, 472
Mencken, H. L., 368
Mendieta, Salvador, 54, 141
Meneses, Vidaluz, 170–71, 198, 238, 244, 415–16
Menuhin, Yehudi, 139
Mercedarians (religious order), 33, 455 (n. 41)
Merton, Thomas, 162
Mesa Redonda Panamericana, La, 504 (n. 44)
Mesoamerica, 14, 16, 18, 289
Mestizaje, 14, 21, 30, 41–42, 195
Metapa, 42, 235, 315, 342
Mexican Revolution, 112
Mexico, 17, 33, 74, 114, 130–32, 140, 145, 151, 165, 200, 205, 209, 216, 218, 222, 230, 234, 274, 310–11, 348, 376; films from, 130–32, 217; Mexico City, 124; motion picture industry, 131–32; Pancho Villa, 372, 499 (n. 42)
Miami, 3, 124, 145, 195; as cultural metropole of Nicaragua, 448; Miami boys, 447–49
Midence, Fernando, 91
Miller, Francesca, 406, 408
Miners, 20, 67, 166, 332
Mines, 8, 18–20, 23, 25, 27, 60, *61*, 94, 254, 256, 259, 260, 291, 295; Atlantic coast, 259; Javali, 60
Mining, 20, 44, 49, 60, 67, 94–95, 98, 112, 166, 197, 254, 307, 316, 332
Ministry of Culture, 6–7, 186, 197–210, 213–20, 225–26, 228, 231, 236–39, 243–50, 267, 270, 336, 423, 443; and Atlantic coast, 261; budget, 200, 268; conflict with ASTC, 237–38, 241; Dirección de Artesanía, 248; divisions of, 201, 238; early strategy of, 200; elitism of, 241; ENIARTE, 248–50, 423; ENIGRAC, 228–32, 269; phasing out of, 267–70; sports program, 268

in, 475 (n. 54); Nahuatl, 14; Nahuat-Pipil, 14; Nicarao, 14–15, 18, 46–47

Pregnancy, 48; leave, 447

Prencinradio, Inc., 131

Presidency, 59, 90, 94, 103, 111, 143, 157, 263, 268, 325–26, 465 (n. 48). *See also* Presidents

Presidents, 1, 41, 59–60, 63, 69, 75–76, 79, 82–83, 90, 94–95, 111, 113, 116, 133, 136–38, 140–44, 160–61, 164–65, 182, 194, 197, 203, 212, 217, 225, 240–41, 249, 251, 254, 263, 286, 300, 306, 313, 317, 319–22, 324, 326–27, 338, 344, 359, 371–73, 397, 422, 425–26, 430, 433, 448, 492 (n. 44); Chamorro, 59, 306; Díaz, 344; Martínez, 59; Sacasa, 59, 90; Schick Gutiérrez, 144, 327–29, 444; Zavala, 321

Priests, 19–20, 25, 28, 33–35, 37–40, 51, 197, 199, 280, 284, 287, 293, 377, 393, 413; arrival of, 454 (n. 34). *See also* Catholic church

Primera Liga Panamericana Femenina de Educación, La, 505 (n. 54)

Primitivist painting. *See* Painting

Prisons, 56, 111, 117, 148, 159, 172, 209, 212–13, 415; La Aviación, 117, 159; La Veintiuno, 117; Little Corn Island, 117, 158–59, 173; women in, 400

PRODUCINE, 4, 6, 138–39, 142, 144, 163, 197, 269. *See also* Film; Instituto Nicaragüense de Cine; Somoza regime

Propaganda, 114, 116, 117, 129, 134, 139, 142, 168, 214, 265, 478 (n. 11)

Prostitution, 1, 46–47, 120, 398–400, 420–21, 426–27, 448, 506 (n. 68)

Prussian Museum für Völkerkunde, 276–77

Psichari, Ernesto, 468 (n. 5)

PTL (Praise the Lord) Club, 115

Puerto Cabezas, 256, 265

Puerto Rico, 123

Punta de las Figuras: Carl Bovallius collecting at, 296

Punta del Sapote: Carl Bovallius collecting at, 296–97

Punta Gorda, 49

Putnam, Frederick W., 292–93, 301, 304, 306–7

Quilalí, 159, 351, 402

Quinn, Anthony, 215

Race, 14, 30, 41–42, 54–57, 76–79, 83, 96, 98, 144, 182, 256–57, 262, 267, 300, 304, 311, 321, 328, 333, 344–45, 351–52, 358, 401, 427, 439, 460 (n. 42), 496 (n. 13), 503 (n. 34); as census category, 455 (n. 44); Garifuna, 480 (n. 29); Indo-Hispanic, 351–52; *mestizaje*,

14, 21, 30, 41–42, 195; Miskito, 50–51, 93, 231, 236, 251–53, 255–57, 260–63, 266–67, 383, 402; mulatto, 39, 43, 456 (n. 47); Negroes, 42, 114, 219; purity, 78; Rama, 49, 92, 112, 266, 480 (n. 29); Sandino and, 351; Sumu, 49, 257, 261, 263. *See also* Race-class system; Racism

Race-class system, 14, 30, 41–43, 56, 71, 256–57; Creoles and, 56, 83, 256–57, 262, 267; mulattoes and, 32, 39, 42–43, 456 (n. 47); pigmentocracy, 42; terminology of, 455 (n. 45). *See also* Race; Racism

Racism, 98, 132, 168, 257, 266; on Atlantic coast, 257; Sandino and, 357; in United States, 132. *See also* Race; Race-class system

Radio, 111–14, 132–33, 139–41, 147, 158, 174, 219–20, 229–30, 269, 418, 447; development of in Nicaragua, 111–12; international conferences, 462 (n. 11); Nicaraguan music on, 220; *Radio GN y Nacional*, 112; U.S. programs on, 113; YNDX, 113; YNOP, 112; YNRC, 113; BAYER, 112; *Radio Güegüense*, 113; *Radio Mundial*, 219; *Radio Rubén Darío*, 112

Radio Corporation of America (RCA), 112, 114

Radio GN y Nacional, 112

Radio Güegüense, 113

Radio Mundial, 219

Radio Rubén Darío, 112

Rama: city, 112; Indians, 49, 92, 112, 266, 480 (n. 30)

Ramírez, Alejandro, 459 (n. 38)

Ramírez, Flor, 424–25

Ramírez, Sergio, 146, 148, 165–66, 170, 194, 197, 203, 217, 225, 338; and Rubén Darío, 338; Sandino biography, 365–68, 382; study in Europe, 197

Ramírez, William, 265

Rape, 47, 373, 378, 405, 421, 430; marital, 421; and Sandino troops, 500 (n. 50); under-reporting of, 507 (n. 68)

Rats, 17, 205, 371

Reagan administration, 232, 241, 251, 263, 265, 268, 311, 438, 444, 448–49; and Atlantic coast, 251, 263, 265; and contra war, 267; and Sandinistas, 438

Realejo, 14, 19, 32–33, 42–44, 64, 67, 283, 288, 303, 305; decline of, 458 (n. 16); plagues and epidemics in, 452 (n. 11)

Rebellion, 18, 28, 33, 136, 162, 181, 184, 224, 242, 362, 393; of April 1954, 117, 360; by native groups, 28; Sandino, 495 (n. 3), 496 (n. 8), 497 (n. 17); by young people, 446. *See also* Insurrections; Opposition; Resistance

colonial period, 46–47; combatants, 172, 175, 390, 394, 399, 414–17, 419, 506 (nn. 62, 63, 65); divorced, 404; dowries of, 502 (n. 29); and economic power, 47; editors, 505 (n. 50); education of, 390, 405, 408, 411; images of, 127–29, *384, 387, 389,* 395; Indian, 65, 102, 378; industrial wages of, 421; intellectual ability of, 408; Inter-American Commission of, 406; Inter-American Congress of, 406; international conferences of, 406, 408, 411, 415, 503 (n. 34); and the law, 405–6, 413, 420, 429; and League of Nations, 410; and markets, 268; and mass organizations, 418; middle-class, 417, 505 (n. 54); Miskito, 257; mission of, 408; normal schools, 504 (n. 41); organizations of, 412, 415, 447, 504 (n. 44), 505 (n. 54); patriarchal ideal of, 395, 397; and patriarchal structures, 415; poets, 409, 505 (n. 50), 506 (n. 59); in pre-conquest Nicaragua, 46–47; production cooperatives, 420; professional, 505 (n. 50); and "progressive" change, 500 (n. 1); pro-Somoza, 184, 402; and revolution, 427; rights of, 405–6, 408, 412; Sandino and, 353, 375–82; self-abnegating, 400, 413, *414;* Spanish immigrants, 502 (n. 29); strategic vs. practical interests, 427; Subtiavan, 183, 415; suffrage movement, 59, 411–13; torture of, 417; and transit route, 64, 386; upper-class, 505 (n. 54); working-class, 415, 424; writers, 146, 160, 170–71, 188, 191, 197–99, 215, 227, 236, 238–40, 244, 415–16, 426. *See also* Feminism; Feminists; Mothers; Women's movement
Women's Legal Office (OLM), 421
Women's movement, 8, 103, 405, 407–8, 415–17, 438, 442; AMNLAE, 418, 421, 425–26, 432, 447, 508 (n. 74), 509 (n. 8); AMPRONAC, 417–18, 426, 508 (n. 8); and labor movement, 504 (n. 41); Latin American, 404–8, 411; Nicaraguan, 407–11, 417, 442; normal schools and, 408; post-Sandinista splintering of, 509 (n. 8); pre-Sandinista, 503 (n. 37); publications, 407; and realities of daily life, 407; right wing of, 407; right-wing repression of, 407. *See also* Feminism; Feminists; Women
Women's suffrage, 411–13
Wood, Samuel Smith, 65
Working class, 110–11, 117–18, 121, 196–97, 202, 232, 234, 247, 331–32, 337, 354, 415, 424, 427, 460 (n. 42), 462 (n. 21), 465 (n. 48), 493 (n. 52); culture, 121; culture, and development, 117

Worldvision (ABC), 115
World War I, 100, 109, 112, 442, 468 (n. 5), 474 (n. 30)
World War II, 6, 111, 116, 119, 134, 139, 141, 209, 219, 254, 259, 308, 360, 363, 393, 397, 406, 413; post-war economic boom, 119
World Youth Festival, 176
Writers, 6, 79, 95, 100, 111, 113, 116–17, 132, 140–41, 145–48, 152–55, 157–61, 166, 168–77, 179, 185, 187, 190–91, 195, 199–200, 203–5, 210, 224, 226, 232, 237, 240–41, 244, 246–47, 259, 270, 313–18, 321, 323–24, 326, 330–31, 333–34, 337, 339, 345, 353, 357–60, 393, 395, 400, 408, 412, 415, 431, 436–37, 440, 444–45; *costumbrista, 224;* dramatists, 222, 224; Generation of 1940, 6, 152, 160, 163, 195, 437; modernist, 224; and revolutionary project, 471 (n. 44); women, 146, 160, 170–71, 188, 191, 197–99, 215, 227, 236, 238–40, 244, 415–16, 426. *See also* Poets

Yankees, 75, 79, 84, 86, 100–102, 109, 154, 224, 259, 322, 333, 336, 351–52, 358, 371–74, 460 (n. 42), 461 (n. 3), 490 (n. 28), 492 (n. 43); Sandino and, 351, 372–73
Yllescas, Edwin, 166, 470 (n. 27)
YNDX, 113
YNOP, 112
YNRC, 113
YNSA-TV, 115
YNTCN, 115

Zaldívar, Rafael, 317
Zamora, Daisy, 170, 188, 198–99, 506 (n. 59); class origin, 198
Zamora, Marta, 248–49
Zapata, Engracia, 415
Zapata, María Cristina, 505 (n. 50)
Zapatero Island, 34, 280, 283–84, 288–89, 296–98, 305, 309–10; Carl Bovallius collecting on, 296; E. George Squier collecting on, 283; Frederick Boyle collecting on, 288; pottery from, *289*
Zarzuela, 58, 109
Zavala, Joaquín (President), 321
Zavala Urtecho, Joaquín, 145, 154, 468 (n. 4)
Zelaya, Department of, 94
Zelaya, José Santos (President), 90, 94; deposing of by United States, 95, 137, 182; and Rubén Darío, 320. *See also* Zelaya administration
Zelaya administration, 5, 55–56, 90–91, 102, 111, 120, 192, 262, 349, 393, 436, 480 (n. 30), 489 (n. 18), 504 (n. 41); Catholic church,

393; concessions to U.S. capitalists, 94; corruption during, 224; elite culture, 92; fall
of, 95, 102, 137, 182; first fruits levy, 91; foreign investment, 92; incorporation of
Atlantic coast, 251, 262; indigenous communities, 182; indigenous resistance to,
91–92; Instituto Nacional de Señoritas, 504
(n. 41); libraries, 474 (n. 24); national independence, 56, 436; National Museum, 111,
306; Nicaraguan canal, 94; occupation of
Bluefields, 94; promotion of culture, 91;
sale of common lands, 91; schools, 91, 349;
transfer of Atlantic coast lands, 262. *See
also* Zelaya, José Santos

Zeledón, Benjamin (General), 184, 232, 329,
344, *345*, 417, 440; and Sandino, 345

Zimmerman, Mark, 358

Zúñiga, Ruth, 506 (n. 59)

H. EUGENE AND LILLIAN YOUNGS LEHMAN SERIES

Lamar Cecil, *Wilhelm II: Prince and Emperor, 1859–1900* (1989)

Carolyn Merchant, *Ecological Revolutions: Nature, Gender, and Science in New England* (1989)

Gladys Engel Lang and Kurt Lang, *Etched in Memory: The Building and Survival of Artistic Reputation* (1990)

Howard Jones, *Union in Peril: The Crisis over British Intervention in the Civil War* (1992)

Robert L. Dorman, *Revolt of the Provinces: The Regionalist Movement in America* (1993)

Peter N. Stearns, *Meaning Over Memory: Recasting the Teaching of Culture and History* (1993)

Thomas Wolfe, *The Good Child's River*, edited with an introduction by Suzanne Stutman (1994)

Warren A. Nord, *Religion and American Education: Rethinking a National Dilemma* (1995)

David E. Whisnant, *Rascally Signs in Sacred Places: The Politics of Culture in Nicaragua* (1995)